PROBLEM SOLVING WITH C++

SECOND EDITION

JACQUELINE A. JONES and KEITH HARROW

Excerpts taken from:

Problem Solving with C
by Jacqueline A. Jones & Keith Harrow

Custom Publishing

New York   Boston   San Francisco
London   Toronto   Sydney   Tokyo   Singapore   Madrid
Mexico City   Munich   Paris   Cape Town   Hong Kong   Montreal

Pearson
Custom Publishing
is a division of

www.pearsonhighered.com

ISBN 10: 0-558-20651-4
ISBN 13: 978-0-558-20651-2

CONTENTS

PREFACE

TO THE STUDENT

The text leads you through the solution of the problem step by step, instead of just presenting a polished, one-step solution to the problem. You should be an active participant in developing the program, not a passive reader or memorizer.

There are some questions that we ask you in the body of the text, and many more questions appear in the Self-Checks which occur at the end of each section of text. Here is a very important piece of advice: Whenever you see a question in the text, stop reading for a moment and try to answer the question. If you can't think of the answer immediately, try reading ahead a little; then come back to the question. If necessary, read the entire chapter a second time. At this point, you should be able to answer almost all of the questions.

In addition to the Self-Check questions, there is a more complete set of exercises at the end of each chapter. You are also urged to do as many of these exercises as possible, including all of the simple ones at the beginning of each group of exercises.

Throughout the book, you are encouraged to write complete programs in a clear, consistent style. We try to set a good example by writing our own programs in this way, especially by including comments. We hope that if you always see programs which are written in a clear, consistent way, with comments, you will strive to follow this same pattern.

In glancing through the text, you have probably noticed many different special features which are included. The first occurs at the beginning of each chapter:

CHAPTER OVERVIEW   At the beginning of each chapter, there is a list of the items which will be covered in that chapter. The list includes the following:

♦   **Problem**—the problem to be solved in that chapter

♦   **Syntax Concepts**—the new features of the C++ language to be introduced

♦   **Programming Concepts**—the programming ideas which are somewhat independent of the choice of language

♦   **Control Structures**—the features of C++ which allow a programmer to control the way in which a program is built up from smaller pieces

♦   **Problem Solving Techniques**—the general concepts of how to go about writing a program to solve a problem

♦   **Statement of the Problem**—the detailed statement of the problem to be solved

In addition, throughout the text, there are sections set off in boxes. These boxes contain different types of material, depending on their headings. Here is an explanation of each of the types of boxes:

♦ **STYLE WORKSHOP**—This contains advice to a beginning programmer on what is considered to be the better way to write a section of code. As you write more and more programs in C++, you will become sensitive to issues of style.

♦ **HIGHLIGHTS**—This indicates a summary of the material that has been discussed so far or a list of the most important features relating to a topic. Be sure that you understand each Highlights section before you go on in the text.

♦ **CAUTION**—This indicates that you should be especially careful when using the particular feature of the language described in the box. This section often lists traps and pitfalls to avoid.

♦ **PROGRAM TRACE**—This indicates a step-by-step analysis of how a program works. It is most important that you understand this process. You must be able to follow the trace in the text and be able to do one on your own. In addition, your instructor might want a program trace that consists of a list of variables with their values.

♦ **EXAMPLE**—This is an example designed to illustrate some feature of the language just described in the text. Some of the examples are quite basic, but others introduce useful applications of the new feature.

♦ **SELF-CHECK**—This is a series of questions at the end of each section of text. Some of the questions are simple and can be answered in a word or two, while others require more thought.

Finally, each chapter contains two sections of intensive review material:

♦ **SUMMARY**—This is an overview, at the end of each chapter, of the material presented in that chapter. Be sure that you are comfortable with all of the points covered in the chapter summary.

♦ **EXERCISES**—This is a set of problems designed to test your mastery of the material presented in the chapter.

TO THE INSTRUCTOR

This text is intended to be used in a one or two-semester course covering introductory programming using C++. No previous knowledge of mathematics or computer science is assumed, other than a familiarity with the mathematical notation used in a high school algebra course.

Because the text represents something of a departure from standard treatments, it might be helpful to outline the format of the book. Each chapter starts with a statement of a real problem. The major portion of the chapter is then devoted to using problem solving techniques to develop a C++ program that will solve the problem. The problems are simple at first, but they reach quite a complicated level rather quickly. The first few problems involve numerical calculations, since this gives the student an easy way to check some of the results by hand. We have found that non-numerical examples used early in a text tend to be either trivial (e.g., printing patterns of asterisks or a message saying "Hello") or else so concerned with analyzing details of the problem that the point of the problem is lost. However, we do give a complete C++ program, with a brief explanation, in the Introduction. The Introduction also contains material on both the hardware and the software associated with a computer system.

In most cases, it is simpler to work with numbers in C++, especially at the beginning of the text. However, if an instructor desires to, it should be relatively easy to modify one or two of these numerical problems somewhat so that a subject area of relevance to the students is introduced. A number of the later examples are non-numerical, including a large text processing problem and a problem to construct and manipulate a database.

In the same way, an instructor could easily make the problems more oriented to scientific applications, business applications, and so on. For example, instead of sorting test scores, the students could be asked to sort readings from laboratory experiments or a company's sales data. We encourage instructors to modify the problems in this way. We have purposely tried to avoid emphasizing any one particular subject area, leaving it up to the individual instructor to decide on the exact orientation that a class should take. The text has been used successfully in this way for a variety of introductory programming courses, both at Brooklyn College and elsewhere.

The text leads the student through the solution of the problem step by step, instead of just presenting a polished, one-step solution to the problem. The student is an active participant in developing the program, not a passive reader or memorizer. To do this, there are some questions that we ask in the body of the text, and many more questions appear in the Self-Checks which occur at the end of each section of text.

Students are encouraged to write complete programs in a clear, consistent style. We try to set a good example by writing our own programs in this way, especially by including comments. We have found that students are incredibly imitative. Our experience shows that if students always see programs which are written in a clear, consistent way, with comments, they will strive to follow this same pattern.

As the student learns increasingly more sophisticated C++ constructs (**for** loops, **while** loops, **if** statements, functions, etc.), the programs become more and more complex.

Problem solving techniques, including pseudocode and the concept of an algorithm, are introduced at the beginning of the text. Other problem solving methods, including stepwise refinement and modular programming, are introduced a little later and then used consistently throughout the entire text. Most programs are written using a top-down approach, although the bottom-up method is also discussed.

The basic approach of the text is this: Present a real problem; interact with the student in writing a program to solve the problem; ask the student to solve a similar problem as a homework assignment.

Each chapter has a summary to review the newly introduced C++ statements and programming concepts. In addition to the numerous Self-Check questions, each chapter is followed by an exercise set, containing a minimum of 20 exercises per chapter, with many of the chapters containing 30 or more. Some of the exercises review the concepts just introduced; others further develop the ideas presented in the basic program; still others introduce entirely new problems suitable for homework assignments that are more challenging than simply modifying an existing program. An instructor can easily add to, or remove details from, any of these problems to arrive at a set of assignments that will be geared to the level and interests (scientific, business, or social sciences, for example) of a particular class. You should encourage your students to do as many of the exercises as possible in every chapter, including all of the simple ones at the beginning of each group of exercises, plus the Self-Checks.

The authors of any book on C++ are faced with a key question: when do they introduce objects? Some books introduce objects and classes from the start, exposing the student to object-oriented programming (OOP) very early in the course, often to the exclusion of the procedural approach. We prefer to cover almost all non-object-oriented features of C++ before giving a very brief introduction to simple classes (that is, classes with data but without behavior) in the last chapter. In particular, this means that we do not cover the ideas of OOP, the use of member functions, constructors, inheritance, operator overloading, etc.

Those instructors who want to put a little more stress on principles of OOP can supplement our material with one or two of their own favorite examples. On the other hand, we do feel that a first course should not include too much of this material.

The order of topics can be rearranged to some degree. The first six chapters develop a basic understanding of programming, including the concepts of loops, reading a set of data, stepwise refinement, functions, control structures, and so on. Chapter 7 then introduces arrays. These chapters form a core that can be followed by any of the remaining chapters (strings, sorting, or simple classes). With a few modifications to certain sections, an instructor can use essentially any permutation of these topics.

A typical course that meets for four hours per week should be able to cover essentially all of the book. We have used the text in this way for a number of years at Brooklyn College.

The book is not meant to be an encyclopedia on C++. In particular, there is nothing on recursion, pointers, side-effects, the use of global variables, dynamic memory allocation, and so on. The book is not designed to teach features of Unix or Windows or some other operating system; it is not intended as a broad introduction to the field of data structures. We feel that it is impossible to cover all of these things in a single text. We have given the students a solid introduction to programming, covering almost all of the basic features of C++; we have touched on how a C++ programmer interacts with the operating system; and we have given just the briefest introduction to the use of more complex data structures in C++. All of these topics can be pursued in greater depth, but we leave that for other books. After completing the book, a student will be ready for a course in assembly language programming, program design and analysis, or data structures.

The text has been designed for use with any C++ compiler, and the programs have been written to minimize the special features of any one compiler. Almost all programs will run (possibly with a few minor changes) using any compiler based on ANSI C++. A student using the text should be able to translate the programs into the appropriate C++ dialect quite easily.

We've tried hard to find all the mistakes in this book, but we're sure we've missed some. If you find a mistake, email and tell one of us, please!

Jacqueline Jones: jones@sci.brooklyn.cuny.edu

Keith Harrow: harrow@sci.brooklyn.cuny.edu

ACKNOWLEDGMENTS

It is always nice to acknowledge the assistance received in writing a book, and we have the pleasure of mentioning a large number of people. First, the faculty and staff at Brooklyn College deserve our gratitude. Aaron Tenenbaum, the chair of our department, has been extremely supportive over the many years we have worked on this and other texts. Many of our colleagues at Brooklyn College have shared their expertise with us. In particular, David Arnow and Gerald Weiss served as our resident experts on C++. Even though they did not always agree (with each other or with us), they have given us the benefit of their years of experience in writing real-world C++ code, and they helped us adjust this experience to an academic environment. Yedidyah Langsam was also very helpful in clarifying a number of issues, both language-related and pedagogic. A number of people have taught using an earlier version of this manuscript, and they have shared their experiences with us. For this, we are grateful to Paul Charosh and the late Chaya Gurwitz. Eva Cogan and Shalva Landy read chapters and suggested corrections. Both caught many errors that would have embarrassed us had they appeared without correction. Eva in particular was tireless; she read and made comments on every chapter, and her comments were invaluable.

While they were students at Brooklyn College, a number of people assisted in preparation of earlier versions of the manuscript. These include: Ari Bleicher, Alex Bloch, Dmitry Dukat, Hong Gao, Yuriy Grager, Yevgeny Kolyakov, Henry Mok, Boris Naronov, Malky Nissenbaum, Ezhar Paz, Vitaly Shub, Yukie Tanaka, Ailian Tsui, Alex Tsymbal, and Wen Eng Yang.

We owe a continuing debt to Dr. Barry Jacobs, a senior scientist at NASA's Goddard Space Flight Center. The problem-solving approach to programming that forms the theme of the text is based directly on his teaching method, which was inspired by the late Jack Wolfe of Brooklyn College. Nan Borreson, Richard Jones, and many other people helped enormously in revising earlier versions of the book, and their contributions are still reflected in the current text. Of course, our new friends at Pearson Custom Publishing deserve our thanks as well. Kimberly Yuster, the Acquisitions Editor, has been tireless in her efforts to help us produce a finished textbook. In addition, Don Golini, the Senior Managing Editor, Francesca Mullany, the Publisher's Representative, and Melissa Philbrook, the Development Editor, were all most helpful.

Naturally, we derive the greatest pleasure in thanking our families. Keith would like to thank his wife, Madeline, for accepting the countless hours spent in preparation of this and other books. Most of all, he would like to thank her for putting up with the boxes all over the den. Jackie would like to thank Mike Printz and her extended family and friends for all their encouragement.

KEY TO READING THIS TEXT

To make the text more readable, we have used several different fonts in the text. Here is a key to what they mean.

1. **BODY** The body of the text is in Times New Roman.

2. **PROGRAMS** The program code, input values, and program results are in Courier New, as shown below:

```
#include <iostream>
using namespace std;
int main {
    ...
    return 0;
}
```

3. **KEYWORDS** Certain words in C++ are called **keywords** or **reserved words**. When these words appear in the text, they are in bold Times New Roman. Some examples are **int, for, return, if, double, float, while, do, else, class**.

4. **OTHER IDENTIFIERS** Other names used in a program are underlined when used in the text. Examples of this are pre-declared identifiers like cin, cout, main(), sqrt(), and programmer-defined variable names and function names like number, square, gpa, result, classify(), and add1().

5. **PSEUDOCODE** *Pseudocode is shown in italics.*

6. **DEFINITIONS** The first use of a word or phrase that is being defined is in **bold**.

7. **QUOTED LINES** Lines quoted from a program that would require several different fonts in the text, or that would require many symbols to be underlined, are instead shown in bold italic; for example, *#include<iostream>*, or *cout << num << endl;* or *x = y + z − 3;*

INTRODUCTION

This book will try to teach you two things, one directly and one indirectly. Directly, it will try to teach you how to write computer programs in a language called C++. Indirectly, it will try to teach you quite a bit about problem solving. The indirect effect, which will probably be more beneficial to you than the direct one, will become clear as you proceed through the text. Let's start by talking about computer languages and C++.

COMPUTER LANGUAGES

Computers have had a considerable impact on our lives in the past 50 or so years, and their impact will be even greater in the future. Therefore, it will be more and more important for a person to be able to interact with these machines. Even though computers seem to be all-knowing, the only language that a computer "understands" is its own machine language. This machine language varies greatly from one computer family to another (e.g., mainframes or personal computers or workstations), and to a smaller degree from one computer model to another within the same family. However, from a human point of view, the most striking feature about all machine languages is that they are composed solely of long strings of 0's and 1's. For example, 0010101111000011 is one of the simpler subtract instructions in the machine language for the PC.

This strange format, as well as many other features of machine language that we need not discuss, makes it quite hard for a person to learn how to use such a language. On the other hand, it is even harder for a computer to use English, French, Chinese, or some other natural language that human beings are comfortable with. Why is it so hard? Natural languages, especially English, are notoriously ambiguous and imprecise. (How would a computer interpret this sentence: "The lady made the robot fast"?)

Thus, a computer would prefer to use its own machine language, while a person would prefer to use a natural language. As a compromise, high-level computer languages have been developed to bridge this communications gap. A typical high-level computer language is not as easy for an English-speaking person to use as English would be. Nevertheless, it is relatively simple for a person to learn one of these high-level languages. From the computer's point of view, the high-level language is not ambiguous and imprecise the way that natural languages are. However, the high-level language must still be translated into machine language. This translation is done by a computer program called a compiler. At the beginning of your first course in computer programming, the compiler (the program that translates what you wrote into machine language) and the computer (the physical machine) will seem almost identical to you. Gradually, you should learn how to distinguish something done by the compiler from something done by the computer itself. But right now you don't have to worry too much about the difference.

There are a large number of high-level computer languages. Two of the very first that were developed in the 1950s, Fortran and COBOL, are still used today. Some other common languages include C, Java, and Visual Basic.

THE C++ PROGRAMMING LANGUAGE

The particular language that we will use in this book is C++, which was based on an earlier language called C. C was designed to be a simple, portable language that would give the programmer access to all functions of the machine. C++ was an attempt to correct some of the problems of C and to add features of object-oriented programming. Over the past 20 or so years, C++ has become an extremely popular language for commercial and scientific applications. C++, and the other languages that are based more or less on C and C++, are today among the most popular languages used to teach computer programming at colleges and universities.

C++ was not designed for teaching purposes. As you read this book, you will see that there are a number of powerful features in the C++ language. Unfortunately, these features can also allow a naive programmer to go astray. As these features are introduced, we will explain the right way to use them and how to avoid the potential pitfalls.

Despite these pitfalls, C++ is relatively easy to use and widely available on a variety of personal computers, mainframe computers, and workstations. Once you know C++, you will find that it is very easy to learn another language.

In addition to being much easier to learn, a high-level language like C++ has another advantage over machine language. As we noted above, a machine language program that runs on a personal computer will not work on a SUN Workstation or an Apple Macintosh, and vice versa. But a C++ program can be used (by translating it into the appropriate machine language) on any computer for which there is a C++ compiler. A few minor changes may have to be made in the program, but a high-level language is relatively "machine independent," while a machine-language program is "machine dependent."

There are several different versions of C++. The versions differ very slightly from each other, as do dialects of a natural language like Chinese or Spanish. The version which we will use, called ANSI C++, is a version that has been approved by a committee of the American National Standards Institute set up to create a standard for the language. ANSI C++ has been implemented on a variety of computers, including PCs, Macs, and many other platforms.

There are a few important differences in how to use C++ on these machines, especially in the details of how the programmer interacts with the editor used to construct the program, and how the programmer interacts with the compiler. When we refer to C++ without specifying a particular version of C, we will be discussing features that are common to all implementations of ANSI C++. However, most of our programs, with a few exceptions that we will note later, will run with almost no change in just about any version of C++.

HIGHLIGHTS

To summarize our discussion: The computer programs that we write will be in a high-level language called C++. A high-level language is a compromise between a natural language and a machine language. A C++ program can be used on any computer that has a C++ compiler. The C++ compiler will translate the C++ program into the computer's own machine language.

SELF-CHECK INTRO-1

1. What do we call a set of instructions telling a computer how to solve a problem?

2. What is an example of a high-level language? What is an example of a natural language?

3. What language will we use to write our programs? Where is this language used?

THE PARTS OF THE COMPUTER: HARDWARE

Before we start our discussion of programming, we will talk a little bit about the physical parts of a computer system. These parts are sometimes called the <u>hardware</u>, and the programs are called the <u>software</u>. No matter whether your computer is a desktop or a laptop, old or new, it will have the following essential parts:

♦ the CPU, or <u>central processing unit</u>, is the brain of the computer, where all the actual computation and calculation takes place

♦ some sort of <u>input device</u>, most commonly a keyboard, where you type your commands and information into the computer

♦ some sort of <u>output device</u>, most commonly a monitor or computer screen, on which the computer displays the results of its computation

♦ some sort of <u>memory</u>, which is short term storage

♦ some sort of <u>long term storage</u>—most commonly a hard disk or flash drive.

COMPUTER PROGRAMS: SOFTWARE

Now that we have discussed hardware, let's talk about software. Software is not really tangible or something that you can touch (although it does sometimes come stored on CDs). A piece of software is a program.

A <u>computer program</u> is a series of instructions telling the computer what to do. Computers can be programmed to do many kinds of tasks. Almost surely, you already have worked with some computer programs. For example, you may have played computer games, and a computer game is a program. Someone wrote the instructions to tell the computer how to make the sound and graphics that are part of the game. You may also have worked with a word processing program like OpenOffice Writer or Microsoft Word; or a spreadsheet program, like Excel or Quattro Pro; or a database program like mySQL or Access. If you have used a computer to search the Internet, then you have used a program called a browser. In fact, if you have worked on a computer in any way, you have been using an operating system program. Programs like these constitute the <u>software</u> used with a computer system.

The topic of this book is programming. We are going to show you how to write programs. Unfortunately, a beginning course in programming will not be able to teach you everything you need to know to write a best-selling video game program, with graphics, animation, sound, and color. That kind of program is usually written by a team of expert programmers who have years of experience and training. However, each of these experts had to begin learning programming from the very beginning, as you are about to do. Don't be disappointed that the programs you learn to write are "too simple." The skills that you are building are the foundation for everything that can be done on the computer. It's like learning the alphabet and a few simple rules of grammar before trying to read *Hamlet,* learning scales before trying to play "Moonlight Sonata" on the piano, or learning how to throw a ball before you can play for a major league baseball team.

Many textbooks start with an extraordinarily simple program, just so you have a chance to see what a program looks like. We will do the same thing, but then we will shift to a different approach—one which asks you to write the programs. In the process, we are going to introduce you not only to programming in C++, but also to problem solving.

FIRST C++ PROGRAM

Let's look at a very simple C++ program, just so that you know what a program looks like in this language. The program will perform a simple task: it will tell the computer to display the message "Welcome to computer programming!" on the monitor of the computer. Here is the complete program to perform this task:

```
#include <iostream>
using namespace std;
int main()
{
    cout << "Welcome to computer programming!";
    return 0;
}
```

That's it! If you type this program in, save it, and run it, the computer will display this message on the screen:

Welcome to computer programming!

Each time you run the program, that message will appear on a new line. That's all this program does.

EXPLANATION OF THE PROGRAM

We will give a very quick explanation of what each line of this program does.

♦ The first line allows the compiler to perform standard input and output functions which let the program communicate with the outside world (e.g., to type messages on the screen or to read data from the keyboard).

♦ The second line allows using some shortcut names, for example to shorten the name of the header file from iostream.h to the simpler iostream.

♦ The third line is called the main program header. It tells the C++ compiler that we are starting to work on the main function of this program.

♦ The next line contains a left brace which introduces the action portion of the program.

♦ The line which starts with the word cout is used to print the line of output on the screen.

♦ The line which contains return 0 says that we ending our program in the normal way.

♦ The last line contains a right brace. This matches the left brace used earlier. It marks the end of the entire C++ program.

♦ Finally, note that some lines in the program are indented to the right, and some lines align one under another. We will talk much more about these issues of aligning and indenting later in the text.

That is the entire program. Most of the material that was shown here will appear in every program that you write. The first two lines, the line containing the left brace, and the line containing the right brace will always be the same from one program to the next. Obviously, real-world programs are much longer, which means that they contain more statements between the left and right braces. But the basic format of every program will look like this.

SELF-CHECK INTRO-3

1. What is the purpose of the main program header?
2. Which punctuation marks surround the action portion of a program?
3. Which line in the program is used to print something on the screen?
4. What does this first program do if you run it?

FIRST C++ PROGRAM

PROBLEM: The Squares of the Numbers from 4 to 9

SYNTAX CONCEPTS: comment, compiler directive, program header, variables and declaration statement, **int** data type, assignment statement, **for** loop, arithmetic operations, identifiers and keywords, <u>cout</u>, <u>endl</u>, increment and decrement operators

PROGRAMMING CONCEPTS: assignment, printing, incrementing, looping, saving a program, compiling a program, running a program

CONTROL STRUCTURES: for loop, compound statement

PROBLEM-SOLVING TECHNIQUES: pseudocode, algorithms, program tracing, software development cycle

HOW TO READ CHAPTER 1

The following outline shows the order in which sections can be covered. An oval indicates an enrichment section. The last section is followed by a summary, which lists the most important points in the chapter. The chapter closes with an extensive set of exercises.

OUTLINE:

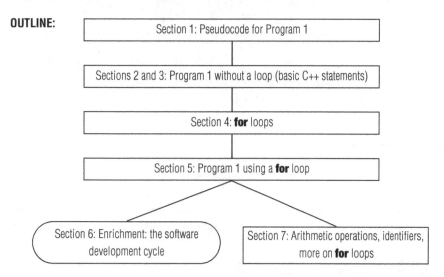

INTRODUCTION AND STATEMENT OF THE PROBLEM

In this chapter, we will write a complete C++ program to solve the problem posed below. In writing this program, we will introduce a number of C++ statements. Most of these statements will be used in all the programs in this book and almost all programs in the real world. We will also introduce several problem-solving techniques, including pseudocode and program tracing.

PROBLEM 1   Write a complete C++ program to do the following: Display a list of the numbers from 4 to 9. Next to each number, display its square—that is, the number multiplied by itself.

Let us analyze some points about this problem.

♦ First, *you* are asked to write a program. We will not present you with a finished program. Rather, we will try to lead you through the process of writing one. At first, it may be hard for you to write the program on your own. But by the second or third program (in Chapters 2 and 3), you should be able to supply many of the pieces. As we progress through the book, you should be able to write larger chunks of programs.

♦ Second, we are asking you to write a *program*. A **program** is a set of instructions telling a computer what to do to solve a problem.

♦ Third, we want a *complete* program, not little pieces. It is necessary to get into the habit of writing complete programs because the computer insists on them.

♦ Fourth, you will write a C++ program. There are many computer languages. We will use C++, a language widely found in the academic, scientific, and commercial worlds.

♦ Fifth, the *output* from our first program (i.e., what is printed) should look something like this:

```
4 16
5 25
6 36
7 49
8 64
9 81
```

You should realize that in the commercial or scientific world, a computer would never be used for such a problem since a person could easily do the calculations by hand. But this is a good first problem since it illustrates many important points.

SECTION 1   PSEUDOCODE FOR PROGRAM 1

In this section, we will start to write a program that solves Problem 1. We will call it Program 1. (Similarly, the program we write to solve Problem 2 will be called Program 2, and so on.) This section introduces pseudocode, which is often the first step in writing a program. Pseudocode is used by most programmers to help translate an English-language description of a problem to a program written in C++.

PSEUDOCODE AS A PROBLEM-SOLVING TOOL

In our first few programs, it will be relatively easy to go directly from the English-language description of the problem to the C++ program. However, most actual programming problems are too long and/or complex to be translated directly. A typical problem may take one or two pages (or more) of English to describe. Most programmers find it difficult to translate directly from English to C++ (or to any computer language).

As a problem-solving tool, programmers usually introduce at least one intermediate step between English and C++. The one that we will use is called **pseudocode**. Pseudocode is a restatement of the problem as a list of steps that describe the solution. Using the pseudocode, a programmer then writes the actual program. While there are other intermediate steps between the statement of a problem and the program, pseudocode is the most commonly accepted one. Although the main use of pseudocode is to help us to translate from English to C++, it is also an outline of the basic structure or logic of the program and a key part of what we will later call the documentation.

Let's give a definition: **pseudocode** consists of statements which are a combination of English and C++; pseudocode is not quite C++ code but can easily be translated. As we shall see, pseudocode can be refined and made more precise gradually. In fact, the pseudocode for one stage of the development process will often be used as a comment at the next stage.

ALGORITHM AND PSEUDOCODE FOR PROGRAM 1

To start writing the program to solve Problem 1, look at the problem statement again. Read it through carefully to make sure you understand what is being requested. Concentrate on what it asks you to compute or produce and what it asks you to do with the things you compute. Try to answer the following questions:

◆ What exactly is the program expected to do?

◆ What answers will have to be printed?

◆ How can the problem be translated from English into C++?

◆ If it is too hard to translate directly, is it possible to break the problem down into simpler steps which can be translated more easily?

Let's try to develop an **algorithm** for solving Problem 1. An **algorithm** is the collection of thought processes which give a precise method of solving a problem. The algorithm is then expressed in pseudocode.

The problem statement says to display a list of numbers, together with their squares, starting with the number 4. *Display* means print on the screen or just print. In the algorithm, we can say, "*Print the number and its square.*" The problem says the numbers will go from 4 to 9. That means we will get each of these numbers, compute its square, and then print.

Here is the method we will use to solve this problem:

Start with the first number and compute its square. Print the number and its square. Then do the same for each of the other numbers.

In English, it is common to write a description like this in a paragraph; sometimes algorithms and pseudocode take this form as well. But it is usually more helpful to write pseudocode as a series of sequential steps. Here is the pseudocode for Program 1:

start with the number 4
compute its square
print the number and its square
do the same for each of the other numbers from 5 to 9

Using this pseudocode, we will write the actual C++ code for Program 1 in the next few sections.

SELF-CHECK 1-1

1. What is the purpose of pseudocode? What does pseudocode consist of?
2. Why don't we translate directly from the statement of the problem to C++?
3. What is an algorithm?

SECTION 2 BASIC CONCEPTS OF A C++ PROGRAM

This section will introduce a number of features of the C++ language which must be included in every program, even though they do not appear in the pseudocode. In particular, we will discuss comments, the main program header, and the general outline of a C++ program. In the sections to follow, we will flesh out this outline and produce a complete C++ program to solve Problem 1.

COMMENTS AND PROGRAMMING STYLE

We will start Program 1, and every program we write, with a line that is not in the pseudocode. At the beginning of each program is a **comment**; the comment provides a short description of the problem to be solved. Later we will use comments in other places as well, but for now we will simply use a single comment at the top to describe the basic purpose of the program. The comment is not strictly necessary because a program without it is technically correct. But comments are considered the single most important part of **good programming style**. (We will have much more to say about style, both in this chapter and later.) In addition, in Section 7, we will talk about a second type of comment in C++.

A possible comment for this program might be this:

```
// Program prog1a.cpp:
//  print the numbers from 4 to 9
//  and their squares
```

Note that each line of the comment begins with //. Once the symbols // are seen by the C++ compiler, everything to the right is ignored. If the comment is too long to fit on a single line, we break it into several smaller comments. Note that we start the comment with the name of the program: prog1a.cpp.

STYLE WORKSHOP We will put the main program's comment at the very top, above everything else. Notice that we are talking about comments first, which shows how important they are. Every program that you write should include a comment.

THE PROGRAM HEADER

After the comment, we can start writing the program. The next three lines of our C++ program look like this:

```
#include <iostream>
using namespace std;
int main()
```

Any line in a program that starts with # is an instruction to the compiler, not an actual statement in the C++ language. The line containing #include tells the compiler to allow our program to perform standard input and output operations. Because these operations are so basic, this line of code will appear in all the programs we write.

The #include directive tells the compiler that we will be using parts of the standard function library. A **function** is a building block of a program; typically each function performs one particular task. Information about these functions is contained in a series of **header files**. In our case, we want the header file called iostream.h to be included in our program; iostream is short for input/output stream; putting the name inside the pointed brackets < and > tells the compiler the exact location of this header file. The line *using namespace std;* allows us to use certain shortcuts when specifying the names of items from C++ libraries.

The third line after the comment, *int main()*, is called the **main program header**. It tells the C++ compiler that we are starting to work on the **main function** of this program. Every program must have a main function since this is where the computer begins to execute the program. The word **int** says that this program will return an integer (more about this below), and the empty set of parentheses indicates that the main function will not be sent any information from the outside.

This is what we have so far:

```
// Program prog1a.cpp:
//  print the numbers from 4 to 9
//  and their squares
#include <iostream>
using namespace std;
int main()
```

Every C++ program we write will start with a comment followed by these three lines.

THE BODY OR ACTION PORTION OF THE PROGRAM

Now we are ready to get to the **body** or **action portion** of the program. Just as an English-language paragraph is composed of sentences, a C++ program is made up of C++ statements. Inside every C++ main program, after the header or top line, is a set of braces ({ and }) containing a series of C++ statements which comprise the body; this is called the action portion of the program. In most cases, we will show only the opening brace ({), leaving the closing brace (}) for later. However, to emphasize the structure, we have included the opening and closing braces here, using ... to indicate the missing statements. Ultimately, the body of the main program will consist of C++ statements derived from the pseudocode in Section 1.

THE STRUCTURE OF A C++ PROGRAM

Here is an outline of the structure of our C++ program. Note that some lines in the program are indented to the right, and some lines align under one another. We will talk more about these issues later in the text.

```
// ...
#include <iostream>
using namespace std;
int main()
{
    // action portion of the program goes here
    ...
}
```

SELF-CHECK 1-2

1.   What is the purpose of a comment? How does a comment begin?

2.   Which line in the program is an instruction to the compiler to use standard input/output operations?

3.   Which three lines will be used in all our programs?

SECTION 3 **DECLARATION, ASSIGNMENT, AND PRINT STATEMENTS**

In this section, we will introduce several of the most important C++ statements—those that allow us to declare variables, to store values in these variables, and to print information. Using these statements, we will be able to translate the pseudocode from Section 1 into C++. This will produce a first solution to Problem 1.

VARIABLES AND DECLARATION STATEMENTS; DATA TYPE int

The first C++ statement we will introduce is called a **declaration statement.** Although it is not shown in the pseudocode, it is a crucial part of every program. The declaration tells the computer which storage locations or variables to use in the program. A **variable** is a name for a physical location within the computer that can hold one value at a time. As the name implies, a variable can change its value (e.g., from 4 to 5) as the program is running. In order to decide which variables are needed to hold information, the program must be analyzed carefully. As a rule, each variable will have a single purpose in a program. You must know what that purpose is. As you start to write a program, you will have to decide which variables you need and what tasks will be performed using these variables. (If you decide later that you need other variables, you can always go back and add them.)

We begin by determining what variables we need. A fairly obvious one is a variable to hold the numbers from 4 to 9. Remember that the value of a variable can change, so the same one can hold each of the numbers from 4 to 9. We can choose almost any name for a variable. Probably numbersfrom4to9 is the most descriptive name, but we will use number, which is slightly shorter and almost as good. Now we need another variable to hold the value of the square of each number, and sqnumber is a good name.

STYLE WORKSHOP We could just as well call the variables x and y, bob and charlie, or rate and time. As long as we are consistent, this is no problem for the computer. But as one of our rules for good style, we recommend meaningful names that suggest how the variables are being used; these are called **mnemonic names**. That's why we have chosen number and sqnumber. Section 7 discusses the rules for valid variable names.

In addition to the names of the variables, we have to declare to the computer what type of data to expect in these storage locations. There are several different data types in C++. For now, we will distinguish between numbers with decimal points (for example, 3.1415 or −4.5) and integers (or whole numbers) such as 493 or −7. Since the variable number will always hold an integer, we will declare its data type to be **int**, which is the simplest integer data type in C++. Since sqnumber will always hold an integer, we will give it the same data type. The complete declaration in C++ looks like this:

```
int number,sqnumber;
```

STYLE WORKSHOP We could declare each variable by itself in a separate statement:

```
int number,sqnumber;        is equivalent to        int number;
                                                    int sqnumber;
```

In a simple program like Program 1, we prefer to combine two variables with the same data type in a single declaration, although we will use the other form in many of our later programs.

Notice the punctuation (;) at the end of the declaration. A **semicolon** terminates every complete statement in C++. Remember our analogy to a paragraph in English. In English, with a few exceptions, every sentence ends with a period (.). We don't use a period in C++ because it can be part of a number—for example, 4.50 or 3.1415. To avoid any possible confusion, a semicolon is used in C++ to terminate statements. Other pieces of punctuation (e.g., commas or colons) have other meanings.

The declaration statement is the second time we have needed a semicolon (we used one after **using namespace std**). A comment does not need a semicolon since it is not a C++ statement. The line containing #include does not need one since it is a compiler directive, not a C++ statement. Finally, the main program header does not need one because it is not a complete C++ statement.

Also note that there is a blank space between the words **int** and number. You cannot put a blank space in the middle of a word (e.g., num ber), but between words, you need one or more spaces or some other separator such as a parenthesis, comma, or brace. Once a separator is used, any number of extra spaces can be inserted for readability.

SELF-CHECK 1-3

1. What is the purpose of a variable?

2. Why is number a better name for a variable than numbersfrom4to9? Why is number a better name than n?

3. In addition to a name, what other piece of information is associated with each variable in the declaration?

REWRITING THE PSEUDOCODE

Now that we have names for the variables, we can rewrite the pseudocode using them. Rewriting and refining pseudocode as the solution to a problem is being developed is a common programming practice called **stepwise refinement**. (This concept will be discussed in much more detail in Chapter 4.) Typically, a programmer starts with a rough solution to the problem, then makes it more precise until everything is specified. Here is the pseudocode from Section 1, modified by the names number and sqnumber:

> *start with* number = 4
> *compute* sqnumber
> *print* number, sqnumber
> *do the same for* number = 5, 6, 7, 8, 9

STYLE WORKSHOP To improve readability, we will write a pseudocode statement, which is a mixture of English and C++, in two typefaces. The parts of the statement which make sense in C++ will appear in the same typeface as the program code. However, English words and phrases which are not part of the C++ language will appear in italics to emphasize the difference. Any pseudocode statement which has been translated entirely into C++ will end in a semicolon.

ASSIGNMENT STATEMENTS

It is important to remember that a simple declaration only sets aside space for the variables. It does not give them values. (Another form of the declaration statement does give a value to a variable and will be discussed in Chapter 3.) Now let us start the actual processing by giving values to the variables. Since the pseudocode says to start with <u>number</u> equal to 4, we must give the value 4 to the variable <u>number</u>. In later programs, we will learn a number of ways to give a value to a variable. One simple way is through an **assignment statement**, which computes a value and places it in a given storage location.

Since we want <u>number</u> to have the value 4, we write the following:

```
number = 4;
```

This particular assignment statement puts 4 into the storage location associated with the variable <u>number</u>. In an assignment statement, we use the symbol =, which is the **assignment operator** in C++. It is imperative that you realize the difference between an assignment statement in C++ and an equation in mathematics. The assignment statement is to be read aloud as "<u>number</u> is set to 4" or "<u>number</u> is assigned the value 4" or "<u>number</u> takes the value 4." A sloppy way to read it is "<u>number</u> equals 4" because that confuses the assignment operator with the English word "equals."

In general, a simple assignment statement in C++ is interpreted as follows: Evaluate the expression on the right-hand side of the assignment operator; then put this value into the variable on the left-hand side of the assignment operator, replacing what used to be stored there.

Here is the general form of an assignment statement giving the value of the expression <u>expr</u> to the variable named <u>varname</u>:

General Form of an Assignment Statement

> varname = expr;
>   ↑   ↑
> **name of variable**   **value of expression**

The expression <u>expr</u> on the right-hand side of the assignment statement is evaluated, and the computed value is stored in the variable <u>varname</u> on the left-hand side.

ARITHMETIC OPERATIONS IN ASSIGNMENT STATEMENTS

The right-hand side of an assignment statement must be a valid C++ expression. There are explicit rules for valid expressions. An **arithmetic expression** is one of the following: a constant (e.g., 3), a variable (e.g., <u>cost</u>), or a larger formula built from simpler expressions by arithmetic operations (e.g., <u>cost</u> + 3).

EXAMPLE 1-1

Here is a specific example of an assignment statement which gives the value of the expression <u>cost</u> + 3 to the variable <u>price</u>:

```
price = cost + 3;
```

Assume that initially <u>price</u> holds the value 7 and <u>cost</u> holds 5. Execution of any assignment statement begins on the right-hand side. First, the expression <u>cost</u> + 3 is evaluated; in this case, the expression has the value 5 + 3, which is 8. Then this value is stored in the variable <u>price</u> on the left-hand side, replacing whatever value <u>price</u> had previously. In this example, the assignment statement gives the value 8 to <u>price</u> (erasing the 7), and <u>cost</u> remains 5.

Let's get back to the assignment statement in Program 1. Remember that we have just written this:

```
number = 4;
```

Easy question: What is stored in <u>number</u> after we execute the assignment statement? Answer: 4.

Harder and more important question: What is in <u>sqnumber</u>? The natural inclination is to say 4 times 4 or 16. But the correct answer is nothing, or more precisely that <u>sqnumber</u> has not yet been given a value. When <u>number</u> becomes 4, <u>sqnumber</u> is not automatically set to 16, the square of <u>number</u>. The computer does not know the relationship between <u>number</u> and <u>sqnumber</u>; the computer "knows" nothing. We said that the names of the variables could have been <u>bob</u> and <u>charlie</u>. The computer wouldn't know that <u>charlie</u> is the square of <u>bob</u>. The computer didn't read the comment or the problem description to see what we wanted to do. Remember that the purpose of the comment is to help a person, not the computer, read the program. The program, not the problem description, is our way of telling the computer what to do.

The computer does *precisely* what you tell it to do—no more, no less. This is good news because once you learn to be perfectly precise and meticulous in spelling out your instructions, you can depend on the machine to execute them faithfully. But it is bad news because until you learn to be precise, the computer will follow your incomplete instructions to the letter without filling in the gaps. Your program may be missing a crucial step that you omitted because it was so "obvious" to you. Nothing is obvious to the computer.

The paragraph above is in some ways the most important one in the entire book. Please read it again. Continue to read it once a week until you believe it. As you run your programs, you will begin to appreciate what it means.

HIGHLIGHTS

The variable <u>sqnumber</u> does not yet have a value; obviously, it needs one since <u>sqnumber</u> must hold the square of <u>number</u>. Another assignment statement will do the trick:

```
sqnumber = 16;
```

This is perfectly valid in C++ and will place 16 into <u>sqnumber</u>, but it ignores a basic purpose for using a computer—to eliminate the need for a person to do boring and repetitious work. We have to remember that <u>number</u> currently holds 4, we have to multiply 4 by 4, and we have to know the answer is 16. We might as well do everything by hand. A slight improvement is to remember that <u>sqnumber</u> stands for the square of <u>number</u>. We can write the assignment statement like this: <u>sqnumber</u> = 4 * 4. (The * indicates multiplication.) Even here we must keep track of the current value (4) of <u>number</u>. A better way is to let the computer keep track by writing the assignment statement like this:

```
sqnumber = number * number;
```

Let's review what this means. The assignment statement says to take the value of <u>number</u> (which is 4) and multiply it by the value of <u>number</u> (still 4). This results in 16, and 16 is put into <u>sqnumber</u>. So <u>number</u> remains 4, and <u>sqnumber</u> becomes 16.

TRACING A PROGRAM

A useful way of visualizing the execution of a program is to think of each variable as a box. The box holds the current value of the variable (remember that it can change). At the beginning of the program, immediately after the declaration, a picture would show <u>number</u> and <u>sqnumber</u> with nothing in either box, as in Figure 1-1a. Actually, something is stored there (whatever was left by the last program to use these physical storage locations), but it is garbage that is no use to our program. After the first assignment statement, we find the picture shown in Figure 1-1b. At our current point in the program, we have the picture shown in Figure 1-1c.

Keeping track of the value stored in each variable is called **tracing** a program. It is one of the most important skills for a programmer to acquire because tracing shows exactly what the computer does at each step. At the end of Section 5, we show another way to trace a program.

DISPLAYING OUTPUT USING cout

Let's look back at the pseudocode. It says to print the number and its square. In general, whenever you have the computer calculate some value, it will be necessary to print the value if you want to see it. Everything described so far has gone on inside the machine. Even if you could see inside, things would happen much too fast for you to follow. Unless the computer gives you some external report of what it has done, you have no way of knowing whether the program is working. It is not necessary to print every calculation, just the ones that you want to know about. The printed or displayed results of running a program are called the **output**.

The pseudocode says, "*print* number, sqnumber." We can now revise it to the following, which is not quite C++ but close:

```
output number and sqnumber
```

The simplest way to print in C++ is using the standard output stream <u>cout</u>, as follows:

```
cout << "Welcome to computer programming!" << endl;
```

We can also use <u>cout</u> to print the value of a variable or an expression, as follows:

```
cout << number;
```

This evaluates the expression <u>number</u> and sends the value to the output stream; in other words, it prints the value of <u>number</u>.

In Program 1, we will use the following statement:

```
cout << number << " " << sqnumber << endl;
```

We'll clear this up a bit before we go on. First, let's describe exactly what this does; it displays the values of <u>number</u> and <u>sqnumber</u>, with one space between them (because of the blank within the quotation marks), then goes to a new line. In our example, <u>number</u> is 4 and <u>sqnumber</u> is 16, so the computer displays the following line of output:

```
4 16
```

FIGURE 1-1 Successive values stored in <u>number</u> and <u>sqnumber</u>

		4		4	16
number	sqnumber	number	sqnumber	number	sqnumber
(a) After the declaration		(b) After <u>number</u> = 4		(c) After computing <u>sqnumber</u>	

Now that we have seen its effect, let's be a bit more formal in describing the statement shown above. The simplest way to output information from a program in C++ is to send it to the **output stream** cout. The identifier cout (whose declaration appears in the header file iostream) is an object associated with a stream of characters that go to the screen. The **insertion operator** << is used to send information to this stream.

General Form of a Statement Using the Output Stream cout

```
cout << ... << ... << ... ;
          ↑      ↑      ↑
       list of literals or
       expressions to be printed
```

This form requires a bit of explanation, which is contained in the following set of guidelines.

GUIDELINES FOR USING cout

◆ The statement starts with the name of the output stream cout.

◆ The output stream cout is followed by the **insertion** operator << and then by the first item whose value we want printed.

◆ This can be followed by additional items to be printed, each one preceded by the **insertion** operator.

◆ A literal string consisting of a single blank within quotation marks (" ") means that a single blank will be printed. This blank serves to separate other values being printed.

◆ The stream manipulator endl tells the machine to skip to a new line. The **cursor** (the _ which blinks on the screen) marks the current print position on the screen or the printer. Sending endl to the output stream cout moves the cursor to the beginning of a new line.

◆ If endl is not printed, the next item to be printed will start on the same line—we will discuss this in more detail in Chapter 2.

◆ With just a few other exceptions to be covered later, other symbols in a literal string (e.g., letters or punctuation marks) will print exactly as they appear.

◆ The entire statement ends in a semicolon.

EXAMPLE 1-2

See if you can predict what will be printed by these statements:

```
number = 4;
cout << number+1 << endl;
```

First, number is assigned the value 4. In the next statement, the machine evaluates the expression number + 1 as 5; then this value is sent to cout, and the cursor moves to a new line. Note that the expression number + 1 is evaluated and printed, but the value of number remains 4. Because it is being used as part of an expression, the value of number does not change. Except in a few special circumstances, the value of number can change only if it is used on the left-hand side of an assignment statement.

The output from a program will be displayed on the monitor. Sending output to the screen is the simplest way to print your results; this is the **default** output method. (**Default** means that this is what the compiler assumes you want to do if you do not instruct it otherwise.) Often it is convenient to have a **hard copy** (a printout on paper) of your results to show your output to someone else. Your instructor will show you how to print your output in whatever program you are using.

SELF-CHECK 1-4

1. At any one time, how many values can be stored in a single variable? Can that value change? What happens to the old value?

2. What is <u>cout</u>? What is it used for in a program?

3. Where are the two most common places to send the output from a program? Which of these is the default method?

CHANGING THE VALUE OF A VARIABLE

After we finish printing the values of the variables, the pseudocode suggests that we should go on to 5 and 25, 6 and 36, and so on. We do not need a new variable to hold 5 (and one for 25), then another for 6, etc. As we emphasized before, a variable can have its value changed. We can reuse <u>number</u> and <u>sqnumber</u>. Earlier, we said that a variable should serve one purpose in a program. Reusing <u>number</u> and <u>sqnumber</u> does not violate that rule because <u>number</u> continues to stand for a number from 4 to 9, and <u>sqnumber</u> continues to stand for its square.

A simple assignment statement, <u>number</u> = 5, seems to do what we want. Then we can use <u>sqnumber</u> = <u>number</u> * <u>number</u> and sent the output to <u>cout</u>. Here are the next three statements:

```
number = 5;
sqnumber = number * number;
cout << number << " " << sqnumber << endl;
```

Finally, we can repeat the process with the same three steps for <u>number</u> = 6, 7, 8, and 9.

THE LAST LINE OF THE PROGRAM

After we have repeated the process for <u>number</u> = 9, there is nothing else to do in the program since the only action is to print these numbers and their squares. However, we must formally end the program. First we include a <u>return</u> statement; this statement is the *logical* end of the program; its execution terminates the program. Returning 0 is the traditional signal for normal termination (usually, returning 1 signals an error). After the <u>return</u> statement, we mark the *physical* end of the program with a closing brace to match the opening brace that appeared immediately after the main program header.

```
    return 0;
}
```

PROGRAM 1 (FIRST VERSION)

Here is what the entire program looks like using the ideas discussed above:

PROGRAM LISTING

```
// Program prog1a.cpp
//    print the numbers from 4 to 9
//    and their squares
#include <iostream>
using namespace std;
int main()
```

```
{
    int number,sqnumber;

    number = 4;                                    //inefficient method
    sqnumber = number * number;
    cout << number << " " << sqnumber << endl;
    number = 5;
    sqnumber = number * number;
    cout << number << " " << sqnumber << endl;
    number = 6;
    sqnumber = number * number;
    cout << number << " " << sqnumber << endl;
    number = 7;
    sqnumber = number * number;
    cout << number << " " << sqnumber << endl;
    number = 8;
    sqnumber = number * number;
    cout << number << " " << sqnumber << endl;
    number = 9;
    sqnumber = number * number;
    cout << number << " " << sqnumber << endl;
    return 0;
}
```

INCREMENTING THE VALUE OF A VARIABLE

There is a problem with this version of the program: the programmer is doing a lot of work that the computer could be doing. It is the programmer who computes the next value of <u>number</u>. If the programmer forgets which numbers have been processed, there could be an error.

There is a more subtle way to change the value of <u>number</u>, one that illustrates the difference between assignment and equality. When we go from 4 to 5, 5 to 6, or 6 to 7, we simply add 1 to the old value of <u>number</u> to get the new value. This is called **incrementing** the value of <u>number</u>. We can tell the computer to increment or add 1 for us.

To tell the computer to add 1 to the previous value, we use an assignment statement. To the left of the assignment operator is the variable <u>number</u>, which is to receive a new value. To the right of the assignment operator is the old value of <u>number</u> plus 1. So in C++ we write the following:

```
number = number + 1;
```

Remember how to read this. It does not say that <u>number</u> is equal to <u>number</u> plus 1, which is certainly ridiculous. Rather, it says that the new value assigned to <u>number</u> is the old value plus 1. The evaluation of an assignment statement starts with the expression on the right-hand side.

◆ In this case, the expression ***number + 1*** tells the computer to go to the storage location <u>number</u>, retrieve the value stored there, and add 1 to that value.

◆ Then the assignment statement says to store the new value in the variable specified on the left-hand side. In this case, the assignment statement says to put the computed value into storage location <u>number</u>.

◆ The fact that the same storage location <u>number</u> is used twice is purely coincidental from the computer's point of view, although to us it is the whole point of the statement since it has the effect of adding 1 to the value stored in <u>number</u>.

If <u>number</u> held 4, then after executing this statement, it will hold 5. The 4 is erased; 5 is stored in place of it. If 4 is erased, that is not tragic because we have already used the 4 to obtain a value for <u>sqnumber</u>, and we have printed both values.

Here are the C++ statements that we have been talking about. Can you predict what they will print?

```
number = 4;
sqnumber = number * number;
cout << number << " " << sqnumber << endl;
number = number + 1;                    // number is incremented
sqnumber = number * number;
cout << number << " " << sqnumber << endl;
```

These statements will print the following two lines of output:

```
4 16
5 25
```

We can continue to increment <u>number</u> in this way, going from 5 to 6, and so on, and that will give us our second version of the program, shown below.

PROGRAM 1 (SECOND VERSION)

Here is what the entire program looks like using the ideas discussed above:

🖥️ **PROGRAM LISTING**

```
// Program prog1b.cpp
//    print the numbers from 4 to 9
//    and their squares using an increment
#include <iostream>
using namespace std;
int main()
{
    int number,sqnumber;

    number = 4;                                    //inefficient method
    sqnumber = number * number;
    cout << number << " " << sqnumber << endl;
    number = number + 1;
    sqnumber = number * number;
    cout << number << " " << sqnumber << endl;
    number = number + 1;
    sqnumber = number * number;
    cout << number << " " << sqnumber << endl;
    number = number + 1;
    sqnumber = number * number;
    cout << number << " " << sqnumber << endl;
    number = number + 1;
    sqnumber = number * number;
    cout << number << " " << sqnumber << endl;
    number = number + 1;
    sqnumber = number * number;
```

```
        cout << number << " " << sqnumber << endl;
        return 0;
}
```

We will not deal further with this version of the program; instead, we will introduce the concept of a loop, then use a loop to write the C++ program.

STYLE WORKSHOP Observe that the pseudocode in Section 1 turned out to be similar but not identical to our final C++ program. In addition, comments and declarations are usually not included in pseudocode. In pseudocode, you can use any familiar mathematical symbols—for example, exponents or the square-root symbol. Most nonprogrammers find it easier to understand the pseudocode than the C++ program. This means that the pseudocode can guide someone who is attempting to follow the logic of the program. Often a copy of the pseudocode is included as part of the documentation of the final program.

SELF-CHECK 1-5

1. What is the last line of every program?
2. Does the last line need a semicolon?
3. In the output, each pair of values prints on a new line because of the use of _endl_. What would happen if we omitted the _endl_?

SECTION 4   THE **for** LOOP

In this section, we will introduce a powerful C++ feature called a **for loop**, that will allow us to derive a much better solution to Problem 1.

PROBLEMS WITH THE FIRST VERSIONS OF PROGRAM 1

The program at the end of Section 3 will work, but it is an inefficient way to solve the problem. We are doing a large amount of repetitious work. In this particular problem (the squares of the numbers from 4 to 9), the work is not too bad. But if the problem had asked for the squares of the numbers from 4 to 79, or even worse, from 4 to 179, the size of our program would increase tremendously, even though the problem descriptions are almost identical. We need to get the computer to do this boring, repetitious work. Computers don't hate repetition. In a sense, they like nothing better than to do the same thing over and over.

REPEATING A SERIES OF INSTRUCTIONS; USING A LOOP

There is a much better way of doing repetition. This new method incorporates the idea of incrementing as part of a larger structure. Look back at these three lines of our program for a moment:

```
number = number + 1;
sqnumber = number * number;
out << number << " " << sqnumber << endl;
```

If you think about it, these lines work for all the values in the program except for the first. If _number_ were 11, then line one would change it to 12, and lines two and three would set _sqnumber_ to 12 times 12 = 144 and print 12 144. If _number_ were 14, line one would would make it 15, then 15 and 225 (its square) would print. More to the point, if <u>number</u> were 4, these lines would change it to 5 and then compute and print 5 25, which is just what we want printed next. In fact, this is the main reason why we wrote the second line as <u>sqnumber</u> = <u>number</u> * <u>number</u>, rather than simply using <u>sqnumber</u> = 4 * 4.

To get the computer to keep coming back to lines two and three, each time with a new value for <u>number</u>, we will use a **loop**, one of the most powerful features of any programming language. A loop gives us the ability to write a statement once but have the computer execute it over and over. In this program, we want to increase <u>number</u> to 5, then go back and execute lines two and three again. As we noted above, one way to get <u>number</u> to 5 is to write this:

```
number = number + 1;
```

But that by itself will not help to get <u>number</u> to be 6, 7, 8, and 9.

A better method is available, one that illustrates the power of a language like C++. Instead of our writing the statements to add 1 and keeping track of how many times to repeat the calculations, we can let the computer do it. C++ has a special kind of statement, called a **for loop**, that increments the value of a variable and repeats a group of instructions which can use the value of that variable. Looking ahead a bit, we will include the lines that compute <u>sqnumber</u> and then print in a **for** loop; the **for** loop will increment the value of <u>number</u> to get a new value, use that value to compute a value for <u>sqnumber</u>, and then repeat the process. This will ensure that these two lines are executed for several different values of <u>number</u>. Among other things, the **for** loop will automatically do the incrementing and repeating for us.

REFINING THE PSEUDOCODE

Now let's return to the pseudocode we developed in Section 1. In that pseudocode, we treated the number 4 separately, then said to repeat the same thing for the other numbers from 5 to 9. We can rewrite the pseudocode, as shown below, so that it treats all the numbers the same way. This method is exceptionally useful because it leads us into a **for** loop structure.

for each number from 4 to 9, do the following:
   compute the square of that number
   print the number and its square

Recall that pseudocode can be refined so that it becomes closer to actual C++ code. Now that we have names for the variables, and we know a bit more about C++, we can refine this pseudocode. From Section 3, we know how to translate the second and third lines into C++. In the display below, the top line is still pseudocode, but the second and third lines are the C++ statements we want to repeat for different values of <u>number</u>:

for each value of number from 4 to 9, do the following:
```
   sqnumber = number * number;
   cout << number << " " << sqnumber << endl;
```

This pseudocode will ultimately become the **for** loop we use in Program 1.

SELF-CHECK 1-6

1.   What does incrementing a variable mean? What statement can we use to add 1 to the value of a variable named <u>x</u>?

2.   What arithmetic operations are represented in C++ by the the symbols + and * ?

3.   What do we call a series of statements that are written once but executed several times?

A SIMPLE EXAMPLE OF A for LOOP

Before we include a loop in Program 1, let's look at a few simple examples of the way to use a **for** loop in C++.

EXAMPLE 1-3

Here is an example of a simple **for** loop that will print the numbers from 1 to 5 (the comments on the right are to you; you should not put them in your programs):

```
int i;
for (i = 1; i <= 5; i = i + 1)          // header of the loop
    cout << i << endl;                  // body of the loop
```

The top line is sometimes called the **header** of the **for** loop. Note that the header does not end in a semicolon because by itself it is not a complete C++ statement, just as the header of a main program is not one. The header is always followed by something called the **body of the loop**. The header together with the body is a complete C++ statement.

This simple **for** loop starts by giving an initial value to a variable (in our example, i̱), which we will call the **index** or **control variable**. The process of giving a variable an initial value is called **initialization**, and we say that i̱ is initialized to 1. The **for** loop tells the computer to repeat the body of the loop, which in our example contains the single <u>cout</u> instruction, for several values of i̱. In this case, it will output the value i̱ for i̱ = 1, 2, 3, 4, and 5.

Let's go through this in a little more detail. The **for** loop header specifies three things, separated by semicolons: what initial value to use, what test determines whether or not the loop should continue, and how the loop control variable should change (in this case, increment) each time through the body of the loop. Here is a diagram of these features in our example:

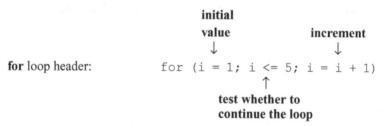

In this example, the initial value for i̱ is 1. The test to determine whether to continue is to see if i̱ is less than or equal to 5. The statement $i = i + 1$ means that at the end of each pass through the body of the loop, the control variable i̱ will increase by 1; when the i̱ value reaches 6, it causes the test controlling the loop to become false. Note that all of this information is contained in the header of the **for** loop.

The **for** loop header is followed by the body of the loop. We are allowed to specify one statement that will be executed each time through the loop. In this case, that one statement is <u>cout</u>. Each time through the body of the loop, the current value of i̱ is sent to <u>cout</u>. Then the new value of i̱, which is obtained by adding 1 to the previous value of i̱, is used to test the condition controlling the loop.

CAUTION Even though the increment step ($i = i + 1$) is contained in the header, it is executed *after* the body of the loop on each pass.

TRACING THE for LOOP

Now let's go step by step through the **for** loop. Going step by step is called **tracing** or **hand simulating** a program and is an extremely important programming tool.

PROGRAM TRACE

◆ The variable i starts at 1, which is compared to the final value of 5. Since 1 is less than or equal to 5, the program enters the body of the loop and sends the value of i to cout, printing 1. This completes the first pass through the **for** loop.

◆ Then we increment i by 1 to 2 and compare this new value to 5. Since 2 is less than or equal to 5, we execute the body of the loop. This time the program prints 2 on a new line. This completes the second pass.

◆ Then i increases to 3, which is less than or equal to the limiting value of the control variable (5), so we print 3.

◆ Similarly, i increases to 4, and we print 4.

◆ Then i increases to 5, which is also allowed since we test whether the current value is less than *or equal to* the final value. The program prints 5.

◆ Then i increases to 6. At this point, the condition i <= 5 is no longer true. Therefore, we do not enter the body of the loop when i has the value 6. Instead, the **for** loop is completed, and we continue with the next statement following the loop. In our example, since the body of the loop consists of a statement to print the value of i, the entire **for** loop prints the values 1, 2, 3, 4, and 5, each on a separate line.

A for LOOP USING A COMPOUND STATEMENT

Let's look at a slightly more complicated example, which is very close to what we want to do in Problem 1. In this example, we will do two things inside the body of the **for** loop.

After the header in a **for** loop, we are allowed to execute only a single statement. However, a pair of braces is used in C++ whenever we want to execute a series of statements where normally just one is allowed. This entire series, called a **compound statement**, can then be treated as a single statement.

EXAMPLE 1-4   Let's write a loop to compute the expression i * i, store it in a variable called sq, then print both i and sq.

```
int i,sq;
for (i = 1; i <= 5; i = i + 1) {
     sq = i * i;
     cout << i << " " << sq << endl;
}
```

We will not trace this **for** loop in detail because it is so close to the loop that will be used in Program 1. However, note the pair of braces around the body of the loop. Note also that while there is a semicolon before the closing brace, the closing brace should not be followed by a semicolon.

STYLE WORKSHOP The opening brace is on the same line as the **for** loop header, and the closing brace is directly underneath the word **for**. The statements inside the body of the loop are indented 5 spaces. Aligning and indenting like this is not technically necessary, but it makes a program much more readable. In Section 6, we will talk more about what you can do to make programs readable.

CAUTION If the header of a **for** loop is followed by a semicolon, then the **for** loop has no body, and the program continues with the next statement.

EXAMPLE 1-5 Consider the following loop, which has a semicolon after the header:

```
int i;
for (i = 1; i <= 5; i = i + 1);               // note the semicolon
    cout << "hello" << endl;
```

Because of the semicolon, the body of the loop is considered to be a null (empty) statement and does nothing. The loop increments and tests i five times, then prints the word *hello* once. This is probably not what the programmer had in mind.

SELF-CHECK 1-7

1. How many components does a **for** loop header contain? What is the purpose of each component?

2. How many statements can appear in the body of a **for** loop? Is there a way to get around this restriction?

3. In Example 1-5, what does the compiler consider to be the body of the **for** loop? What does the compiler consider to be the statement following the **for** loop? Does the compiler care that this statement has been indented?

SECTION 5 A BETTER VERSION OF PROGRAM 1

In this section, we will use the **for** loop from Section 4 to provide a better version of Program 1. We will rewrite the entire program with a **for** loop and then trace it to make sure it works.

USING A for LOOP IN PROGRAM 1

Now that we have seen how a **for** loop can repeat a series of steps, let's return to number and sqnumber. In Program 1, we want to repeat a series of statements (computing sqnumber, then printing number and sqnumber) for several values of number. We can write this in C++ with a **for** loop using the values of number from 4 to 9, going up by 1 each time. The **for** loop used in Program 1 will look like this:

```
for (number = 4; number <= 9; number = number + 1) {
    sqnumber = number * number;
    cout << number << " " << sqnumber << endl;
}
```

Even before we trace how it works, you should be able to guess what the loop does. It repeats the statements inside the body of the loop for number = 4, 5, 6, 7, 8, and 9, which is exactly what we want.

PROGRAM 1 (THIRD VERSION)

We will repeat the entire program here in exactly the form that you would use to type it into the computer. If you printed the program, it would look just like this. Such a printout is called a **program list-ing**. In addition, we have shown the **output**—that is, the results of the program displayed on the screen or printed. If you compiled and then ran the program (once again, see the appendix), the output would look just like this. Be sure that you understand the difference between the program listing and the output. In most cases, you will need a copy of both if you are giving the program to someone else (e.g., to an instructor to be graded).

💻 PROGRAM LISTING

```cpp
// Program prog1c.cpp:
//   print the numbers from 4 to 9
//   and their squares
#include <iostream>
using namespace std;
int main()
{
    int number,sqnumber;
    for (number = 4; number <= 9; number = number + 1) {
        sqnumber = number * number;
        cout << number << " " << sqnumber << endl;
    }
    return 0;
}
```

OUTPUT

```
4 16
5 25
6 36
7 49
8 64
9 81
```

PROGRAM TRACE Now let's trace exactly what happens as this program is executed.

♦ The variables number and sqnumber are declared.

♦ When the **for** loop statement is executed, number starts off with the value 4 (what is in sqnumber at this point?).

♦ Since this value is less than or equal to the limiting or final value of number (in this case, 9), we can execute the body of the loop.

♦ Inside the body of the loop, sqnumber is set to number * number, which in this case is 4 * 4 = 16. The values of number and sqnumber are sent to cout which prints the values 4 and 16.

So far, this is exactly what we had before we introduced the **for** loop, but now the computer will increment the value of number each time through the loop.

♦ When we reach the closing brace, the program automatically goes back to the loop header, where number increases by 1, making it equal to 5.

♦ Since 5 is less than or equal to the limiting value of 9, we execute the body of the loop.

♦ This time, sqnumber is set to 5 * 5 = 25, and cout prints 5 and 25 on a new line.

♦ Then number increases by 1 again, so that it now has a value of 6.

♦ The body of the loop is executed, sqnumber is set to 6 * 6 = 36, and 6 and 36 are printed.

♦ Similarly, when number is 7 and 8, we print 7 49 and 8 64.

♦ After printing, we go back to the header, where number increases to 9.

♦ Since 9 is less than or equal to 9, we execute the body of the loop once again.

◆ This time <u>sqnumber</u> is set to 9 * 9 = 81, and the values 9 81 are printed.

◆ Then <u>number</u> increases to 10; this time the condition controlling the loop is false because 10 is not less than or equal to 9.

◆ Therefore, we do not enter the body of the loop again. Instead, we continue with the next statement in the program.

You should appreciate the control that a **for** loop gives us. The series of instructions inside the body of the loop is written only once but executed several times. A large part of the power of a computer comes from the ability to repeat a calculation for different values. Each instruction appears just once in the program but can be executed six or 100 or any number of times. In Section 7, we will talk more about **for** loops, and we will use this construct in almost all of our later programs.

TWO WAYS TO TRACE A PROGRAM

Trace this example through again until you are completely convinced that it works. Do this on all of your programs before you run them. You will be amazed at how many errors can be caught (and then corrected). In fact, short of actually running the program, there is no better way to see if it is correct.

As you do the trace, do not attempt to keep track of the values of the variables in your head. Instead, do one of two things. You can draw a box for every variable and at each step use it to hold the current value (see Figure 1-1). This is how the computer actually works since it keeps track of only the current value of a variable.

The other method of tracing is to draw a series of columns down a page, one column per variable. At the top of the column, put the name of the variable. Underneath the name, keep a record of what is stored in the variable by writing down each new value assigned (see Figure 1-2). The advantage of this method is that you have a complete record of the program trace.

You are welcome to use whichever method of tracing you prefer, but you should definitely use pencil and paper, rather than just your memory.

FIGURE 1-2   Another method of tracing a program

number	sqnumber	
–	–	initially
4	–	after the **for** loop header sets <u>number</u> to 4
4	16	after computing <u>sqnumber</u> the first time
5	16	after incrementing <u>number</u> to 5
5	25	after computing <u>sqnumber</u> with 5 as the value of <u>number</u>
6	25	
6	36	
7	36	...
7	49	
8	49	
8	64	
9	64	
9	81	after computing <u>sqnumber</u> with the final value for <u>number</u>
10	81	at the end of the **for** loop (note that <u>number</u> increases to 10, but we do not use this value to compute <u>sqnumber</u>)

SECTION 6 ENRICHMENT: RUNNING A C++ PROGRAM; SOFTWARE DEVELOPMENT CYCLE

Now that we have shown a complete C++ program, we will describe how to run it on an actual computer. We will also describe the parts of the software development cycle.

CAUTION The details of how to run a program may vary greatly from computer to computer, and even from one computer center to another. Be sure to find out the precise rules that govern your installation. If you are using this text in class, your instructor will probably distribute these rules.

We will assume that you are using C++ on a personal computer or workstation. Typically, a person communicates with a personal computer through a keyboard and monitor with programs and data stored on either a hard disk, a floppy disk, or on a flash drive.

ENTERING A PROGRAM WITH A TEXT EDITOR

The first step is to enter your program into the computer using the keyboard. You must use a text editing system to enter the program. There are a large number of text editors; most likely, the compiler you use will come packaged with an editor.

WARNING You cannot use a word processing program like MS Word to enter programs; word processing programs put all sorts of codes in the file that will confuse the compiler.

TYPING A C++ PROGRAM

A program consists of a series of lines. A *line* is a group of characters ended by pressing the <Return> or <Enter> key. Each statement of your C++ program should start on its own line. If a statement is too long, it can continue on the next line. Simply stop at some convenient point (not in the middle of a word or a string—try to stop after a blank or comma) and put the rest of the statement on the next line; indent the second line to make it easier to read. If the statement requires a semicolon at the end, place it after the entire statement, not at the end of the first line. When the computer reads the first line, it will know that the statement is not finished and continue reading. When the computer sees the semicolon, it will know the statement is complete.

You will rarely have to continue onto a new line because most C++ statements fit comfortably on a single line. However, in certain circumstances, you should purposely spread a statement out over several lines for readability. For example, technically a **for** loop is a single statement, but you should always separate the body from the header by putting each on a new line.

Actually, C++ allows you more freedom in entering text than we have implied. Each statement does not have to start on a new line. (However, a program is usually much more readable if it does.) Two or more C++ statements can be put on the same line, separated by a semicolon.

STYLE WORKSHOP You will save room if you put two or more statements on a line, but, in the long run, you will cause yourself grief because it will be much harder to get your programs to work if they are difficult to read. Furthermore, you will probably make more typing errors, and each error may be harder to locate and correct on a line with two or three statements. Therefore, we recommend that you put one statement per line.

Two small assignment statements can often be put on the same line without any confusion. For example, if x and y are both to be set to 0, then most people won't mind if you write the statements like this:

x = 0; y = 0;

Observe that each statement ends in a semicolon. Obviously, the semicolons are crucial in telling the compiler where one statement ends and the next one starts. In fact, with the proper use of semicolons, you can put any number of C++ statements on the same line; however, the <u>#include</u> directive must appear on its own line.

Here is another version of Program 1, rewritten with no extra spaces. Note that the comment has also been eliminated.

```
#include <iostream>
using namespace std;int main(){int number,sqnumber;for(number=4; number<=9;
number=number+1){sqnumber=number*number;cout<<number<<sqnumber<<endl;}
return 0;}
```

Although the program is perfectly valid from the compiler's point of view, it is essentially unreadable by a person. As a general rule, you should never combine a large statement with anything else since a person is likely to overlook any smaller statements. For example, it is easy to lose the assignment statement in this line:

```
cout << "help is close, so keep hanging on" << endl; x = 0;
```

INDENTING STYLE

A C++ statement can appear anywhere on a line, but you should follow a consistent set of guidelines when typing your program. Here are the rules that we will follow:

◆ We will start the first comment, describing what the program does, in column 1.

◆ The lines specifying the include file(s) to be used with a program will also start in column 1, as will the line containing **int** main().

◆ The opening brace will be in column 1; at the end of the program, the closing brace will also be in column 1.

◆ Inside the action portion of a program, we will indent all statements five spaces. Some C++ programmers use the Tab key to indent. Depending on the system you are using, this will indent up to eight spaces, which may be too much.

◆ In addition, we will indent the statements in the body of a **for** loop five spaces. Once again, you may want to use the Tab key.

◆ If the body of the loop is a compound statement, the closing brace will appear directly underneath **for**. Because the body of the loop has been indented, there will be nothing in the direct line between the closing brace and **for**.

Here is a sketch of this indenting style (other rules will be given later):

```
col. 1
↓

// first comment
#include <iostream>
using namespace std;
int main()
{
     int ...

     for ( ... ) {
          ...
     ↑
col. 6    ↑
     ↓    col. 11
     }
}
```

STYLE WORKSHOP   While indenting is not strictly necessary, it will make your program much more readable and is considered an important aspect of good programming style. Please follow these rules or some other easy-to-read method. Above all, be consistent. Indent all statements in a loop one tab position, for instance; don't indent some but not others. You should not indent too much because statements will be hard to read when they seem to run off the right-hand side of the screen. The time you spend getting your program to look nice is an excellent investment.

SAVING, COMPILING, AND RUNNING A PROGRAM

After writing a C++ program, you will want to save it, compile it, and then run it. How to do these things is system-dependent. If you are using some other system, your instructor will probably give you directions.

SAVING A PROGRAM

After you have finished typing your C++ program, *you must save it before doing anything else.* In fact, you may wish to save your program several times while you are writing, just in case something happens. Saving allows you to work on your program later if it needs revision.

When you are typing the program, it is stored in the memory of the computer in RAM. Things in RAM are volatile; they will disappear when the power is shut off. If someone pulled out the plug of your computer, or if a lightning storm knocked out the power, or even if the machine had some mechanical glitch, you might lose all the material you just typed in. In addition, an error in the program might cause the system to crash.

For all these reasons, it is important to save your program. **Saving** means copying the program from the memory of the machine (its short-term memory, to use a human term) to a disk (its long-term memory). Once you have saved your program to a disk, you can reuse it, change it, or carry it from one machine to another (if it is on a floppy disk or a flash drive).

Whatever system you use, the best way to prevent problems is to follow this rule:

Always Save Your Program Before Running It.

If something goes wrong, at least you won't have to worry about losing your work.

COMPILING A PROGRAM

Once your program has been saved, you are ready to compile and then run it. When you compile your program, you are invoking the **compiler**, a special program that will translate your program into **machine language**, the language that the machine understands.

ERROR CORRECTION AND RECOMPILATION

During compilation, the compiler may find errors which make it unable to translate your program. A large part of the software development process is finding and correcting errors; this process, known as **debugging a program**, is discussed in more detail in Chapter 2. Look carefully at the error messages, which will identify the type of error and the line number where it occurred; you should easily be able to see what is wrong most of the time. If not, ask your instructor for assistance. (However, if there are many errors, some of the error messages may be misleading. In that case, concentrate on fixing the first few.) Correct the errors using your editor and then recompile the program. Continue this cycle until your program compiles with no errors. Don't be discouraged if this process takes quite a while. No one always writes error-free code; your goal should be to find and correct most errors before you compile the program, and to correct the others without making more.

RUNNING A PROGRAM (PROGRAM EXECUTION)

Once your program has compiled successfully, a copy in machine language is stored on the disk. Now you can **execute** or **run** your program, which means to let the instructions you wrote actually control the machine.

SELF-CHECK 1-8

1. If a statement continues for more than one line, how does the compiler know that it is not finished at the end of the first line?
2. What is the difference between compiling and running a program?
3. What is a text editor?

SOFTWARE DEVELOPMENT CYCLE

Suppose you look at your output, and it is wrong. The computer didn't make a mistake; you did. You have to figure out what is wrong with your program, correct the error, and go through the process we've outlined again until the output is correct.

Writing computer programs (also called **software**) is often a lengthy process. Multimillion dollar companies that write software go through the same process, called the **software development cycle**, that you must follow when creating a program. Let's look at some of the steps in the process; you will become more familiar with them as you go along.

The process starts with a statement of the problem.

♦ Sometimes the problem statement is not perfectly clear, and you will need to check with the person who wrote it (for now, your instructor) to determine exactly what is required.

♦ You must analyze the problem statement, determining what the program is to do, what input it gets, what output it produces, and what process will get from the input to the output. Be sure you understand all these things before you go on.

♦ You then need to write pseudocode for the program.

♦ Next you will write the program from the pseudocode.

♦ After typing in, editing, and saving the program, you will compile it. There will probably be errors, and you must correct them and recompile the program.

♦ Once the program compiles correctly, you will run it. There may be errors in the output, which means there are errors in the program. You must correct the errors and recompile the program.

As your programs get more complicated, you will need to do program testing. This involves running the same program with different data until you are certain that it works in all cases.

Once the program and its output are correct, you will submit it to the person who requested it. You may find that the program does not meet the specifications (in other words, it doesn't work in all cases, or it does something other than what it is supposed to do, or the output isn't readable). In that case, you may have to make further modifications and go through the process again until the program is satisfactory.

Now you are ready to run your first program. Good luck!

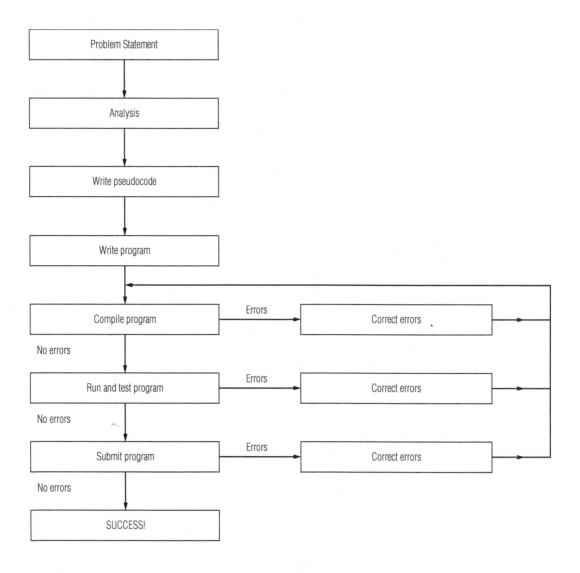

SELF-CHECK 1-9

1. What are the steps in the software development cycle?

2. Which steps have we done for you in Program 1?

3. Which will you have to do on your own?

SECTION 7   MORE DETAILS: COMMENTS, ARITHMETIC OPERATIONS, IDENTIFIERS, for LOOPS

In this section, we will go into a little more depth on some topics that have been introduced earlier in this chapter.

SECOND FORMAT FOR COMMENTS

C++ has a second format that can be used for a comment. (This format is a carryover from the language C, which did not allow the // form of a comment.) This type of comment begins with /* and ends with */. The symbols /* and */ are called **comment delimiters**, because they delimit or mark the beginning and end of the comment. Between them we can put any message we want, including abbreviations, misspelled words, and so on, because the C++ compiler ignores everything between the comment delimiters. This format is especially useful for comments which extend over more than one line.

CAUTION If, by mistake, you start a comment with /* but forget to end it with */, the compiler will think the rest of your program is part of the comment. More precisely, it will skip from the beginning of the comment until either the end of the next comment or the end of the entire program, whichever comes first. Anything in between will be ignored. This usually has a catastrophic effect on your program and may cause misleading error messages. Always be sure you end each and every comment of this type in your program.

STYLE WORKSHOP Because this type of comment is somewhat prone to mistakes, we will use the other. (However, the older C form is sometimes useful in getting rid of the mistakes in a program—you can comment out a section of text, even one that includes // comments.

ARITHMETIC OPERATIONS IN C++

We have been using the words "operator" and "operation," and it might be helpful to explain their meaning in C++. An **operation** is a way of combining objects, usually one or two at a time, to form something new; the **operator** is the symbolic representation of the operation. For example, addition is an operation, and the operator + represents addition in C++. The objects are normally numbers or characters, but they can also be other things, as we will see later. The simplest operations are those that work with numbers. We will call these **arithmetic operations**.

A number of arithmetic operations are available in C++. Addition and multiplication are two simple operations that have been used in Program 1, with + used for addition and * for multiplication. Even though many symbols can be used in arithmetic or algebra to denote multiplication [e.g., we can use $a \cdot b$, $a \times b$, ab, or $a(b)$], an asterisk, as in $a * b$, is the only way to indicate multiplication in C++. Subtraction is also easy, just $a - b$.

Division in arithmetic is normally $\frac{a}{b}$ or $a \div b$, but in C++, division is indicated by a slash (/). More precisely, a/b means a divided by b. Here are some examples:

◆   If a is 10 and b is 5, then a/b is 2.

◆   If a is 11 and b is 4, then a/b is 2 (the fractional part of the answer is lost).

◆   If a is 10, then $a/4.0$ is 2.5 (in this case, the entire answer is kept).

◆   If a is 4, then $10.0/a$ is 2.5 (the entire answer is kept).

◆   If dist is 3.6 and hours is 2.4 (in the next chapter, we will discuss how variables can hold such values), then dist/hours is 1.5.

In these examples, the result of division, called the quotient, is sometimes an integer and sometimes not. If either (or both) operand is not an integer (e.g., 10.6/2.3, 10.6/2, or even 10/2.0), the division will work as it does in arithmetic, and the quotient will have decimal places. However, if one integer is divided by another, C++ uses **integer division** to find the quotient. This value is always an integer since any fractional part of the quotient is chopped off.

Because the fractional part of the answer is lost in integer division, C++ has a **modulus** or **remainder operator**, denoted by %, that will give the remainder when one integer is divided by another. For example, if $\underline{c}$ is 10 and $\underline{d}$ is 6, then $\underline{c}$ % $\underline{d}$ is 4. As another example, 26 % 5 is 1. Also 5 % 6 is 5. In general, $\underline{x}$ % $\underline{y}$ gives the remainder when $\underline{x}$ is divided by $\underline{y}$. (The calculations can be tricky if one or both of the values is negative. See Exercise 11 for more details.) Of course, for both of these operations (/ and %), it is understood that the second operand cannot be 0 to avoid the obvious problem of dividing by 0.

Table 1-1 summarizes these operations. Note that arithmetic operators can be surrounded by any number of blanks (including none, as in $\underline{y}$ + $\underline{z}$). In our programs, we will usually include a single blank on each side if it improves readability.

In Chapter 2, we will add several other arithmetic operations to this list. We will also study further properties, including how to combine them to form complex expressions.

SELF-CHECK 1-10

1. What is the result of each of these division operations?

   a. 6/3   c. 5/6   e. 6/4.

   b. 6/4   d. 199/100   f. 199/100.

2. What is the result of these operations?

   a. 6 % 3   c. 5 % 6   e. 200 % 100

   b. 6 % 4   d. 199 % 100   f. 201 % 100

IDENTIFIERS

An **identifier** is a name for a variable or function. In C++, the following characters are valid as part of an identifier name:

◆ letters, either lowercase or uppercase;

◆ the digits 0–9; and

◆ the underbar symbol (_).

TABLE 1-1 Arithmetic Operations in Arithmetic and in C++

Operation	Arithmetic	C++	Other C++ Examples	
Addition	$\underline{a}$ + $\underline{b}$	$\underline{a}$ + $\underline{b}$	$\underline{age}$ + 1	$\underline{sum}$ + $\underline{tax}$
Subtraction	$\underline{a}$ − $\underline{b}$	$\underline{a}$ − $\underline{b}$	10 − $\underline{rate}$	$\underline{ht}$ − $\underline{wt}$
Multiplication	$\underline{a} \cdot \underline{b}$, $\underline{ab}$, $\underline{a}(\underline{b})$	$\underline{a}$ * $\underline{b}$	2*$\underline{pay}$	$\underline{mass}$ * $\underline{veloc}$
Division	$\underline{a} \div \underline{b}$ or $\frac{a}{b}$			
quotient		$\underline{a}$ / $\underline{b}$	$\underline{age}$/12	$\underline{dist}$/$\underline{hours}$
remainder (or modulus)		$\underline{a}$ % $\underline{b}$	$\underline{value}$ % 10	$\underline{months}$ % $\underline{yrs}$

An identifier name is a series of one or more valid characters. The first character must be a letter or the underbar symbol, but the remainder can be letters, digits, or underbars. Any other symbols are illegal in an identifier name.

We will only use underbars when the name is long, and the underbar improves readability (e.g., largest_grade). Unfortunately, the various C++ compilers differ in the rules for the length of a valid identifier name. Certain versions of C++ restrict identifiers to just eight characters; others allow them to be any size. In general, we will use large names when it is convenient.

You are allowed to use any combination of capital and lowercase letters in a C++ program. In fact, a single identifier name can contain a mixture of the two (e.g., Rate). However, please note the following warning!

CAUTION Unlike many other languages, C++ distinguishes between capital and lowercase letters, so RATE, rate, and Rate do not refer to the same identifier. Technically you can use all of these in your program, and they will be considered different. Obviously, this can lead to a tremendous amount of confusion. Later in this section, we will recommend how to use capital and lowercase letters to eliminate confusion.

EXAMPLE 1-6   Here are some valid names:

> a, a1, sales1995, rate, sumoftestgrades, r2d2, student_avg, PI

Here are some invalid ones, with the reason in parentheses:

new sum	(a blank in the middle)
test-grade	(a minus sign in the middle)
96sales	(a digit as the first symbol instead of a letter)
entry#	(an illegal symbol, the #, in the name)

KEYWORDS

There are three general categories of identifiers in C++: keywords, standard identifiers, and programmer-defined identifiers. Let's go through these one by one. Certain words in a C++ program must be used in specific places and have a particular meaning in that context. For example, here are two words that appeared in our first program: **int** and **for**. These special words are called **keywords**, which means that they cannot be used by the programmer in any other way. For example, in our program, we could not use a variable named **int** or **for**.

STANDARD IDENTIFIERS

Other words have a special meaning in the language, but a programmer is allowed to override it by using them as the names of variables or in other places. These words are called **standard identifiers**. In almost all cases, standard identifiers are names of functions in the standard library (see Chapter 2, Section 5), but there are a few others.

Standard identifiers have their predeclared meaning unless the programmer explicitly uses their name for some other purpose in the program. For example, cout is not a keyword, but it does have a special meaning. A programmer could declare a variable with the name cout, and this new meaning would take precedence over its predeclared meaning. (This means that cout could no longer be used to print a line of output.) A programmer could use the name cout for some other purpose, but it is hard to imagine what is gained. Therefore, we recommend that you do not use standard identifiers for anything other than their intended purpose unless you have a compelling reason.

PROGRAMMER-DEFINED IDENTIFIERS

All other identifiers are **programmer-defined** or **user-defined**. For these identifiers, the user must give an explicit declaration. The programmer-defined identifiers we used in our first program are number and sqnumber.

The same identifier cannot have two meanings in any one main program or function (we will talk more about functions later). For example, if a variable is named query, then nothing else in the main program can have that name. If the name of a standard identifier such as cout is used as a programmer-defined name, it is not possible to use its predeclared meaning.

STYLE WORKSHOP In this text, we will use certain conventions to write identifiers. Keywords and standard identifiers will always be written in lowercase letters (e.g., **int** or cout). Programmer-defined identifiers will also be written in lowercase letters (e.g., number or sqnumber). Capitals will be reserved for a special purpose, to be explained later.

In a program or display, we will use a special typeface for keywords, standard identifiers, and programmer-defined identifiers. In the body of the text, identifiers will be written in a similar typeface. For example, we would write *number* = *number* + *1* in the middle of a paragraph.

When you are typing your program, everything that you enter must be in the same typeface. You may wish to adopt conventions of capitalization or naming which improve readability. The most important thing is to be consistent.

SELF-CHECK 1-11

1. What are the rules for a valid identifier name?
2. What are the differences among keywords, standard identifiers, and programmer-defined identifiers? Give an example of each in Program 1.
3. Are programmer-defined identifiers usually written using uppercase or lowercase letters?

A for LOOP USING DECREMENT

As a way of introducing some of the additional power of a **for** loop, let's try one modification of Program 1. If we wanted the table of values for number and sqnumber to be printed out in reverse order, from 9 81 at the top to 4 16 at the bottom, there are many ways to do this. Most of them are too advanced for this chapter. However, there is a simple modification (called a **decrement** rather than an increment) to the **for** loop that will accomplish this.

To decrement using a **for** loop, no changes have to be made in the body of the loop. All we have to do is change the **for** loop header. Start the control variable at a higher value than the final one. In addition, change the condition that controls when to execute the body of the loop: it should allow executing the body of the loop if the control variable is greater than or equal to the final value. Finally, rather than incrementing the control variable each time through the loop, decrement instead. In particular, the statement *number* = *number* − *1* will cause the value of number to decrease each time through the loop. The new **for** loop will execute for number having the values 9, 8, 7, 6, 5, and 4. After the value 4 has been processed, <u>number</u> will decrease to 3; the test condition will now be false, and the loop will terminate. Of course, we should also alter the comment at the top of the program to indicate the change.

EXAMPLE 1-7

Here is the complete program using a decrement loop. We will not bother tracing this version (which we will call <u>prog1d.cpp</u>), although you may find it useful to do that yourself.

```cpp
// Program prog1d.cpp:
//    print the numbers from 9 to 4
//    and their squares
#include <iostream>
using namespace std;
int main()
{
    int number,sqnumber;
    for (number = 9; number >= 4; number = number - 1) {
        sqnumber = number * number;
        cout << number << " " << sqnumber << endl;
    }
    return 0;
}
```

MORE EXAMPLES OF for LOOP HEADERS

Two special cases of **for** loop headers are worth noting. If we use the type of loop discussed in this chapter, and if the starting value is the same as the last value to be processed, the body of the **for** loop will be executed only once, with the control variable having that common value.

EXAMPLE 1-8

The loops shown below will both print the number 5.

```cpp
for (i = 5; i <= 5; i = i + 1)          for (i = 5; i >= 5; i = i - 1)
    cout << i << endl;                      cout << i << endl;
```

Finally, if the test controlling the loop is false initially, then the body of the loop will not be executed at all.

EXAMPLE 1-9

The loops shown below do not print anything since neither <u>cout</u> statement will ever be executed. (See if you can predict what value <u>i</u> will have when each loop ends.)

```cpp
for (i = 6; i <= 5; i = i + 1)          for (i = 5; i >= 6; i = i - 1)
    cout << i << endl;                      cout << i << endl;
```

The header of a **for** loop can be more complicated than the ones we have used so far. Consider the following example:

EXAMPLE 1-10

We can have a **for** loop that looks like this:

```cpp
for (i = 1, j = 7; i <= j; i = i + 3, j = j + 1)
    cout << i << " " << j << endl;
```

The header has two initialization statements, separated by a comma, plus two increment statements, also separated by a comma. This loop starts by performing both initializations; then the values of i and j are compared. If the value of i is less than or equal to the value of j, the body of the loop is executed, and both increments are done. The test controlling the loop determines whether to execute the body again. If the body is executed, the increments, the test, and so on will follow.

In the body of the loop shown above, the following pairs of values of i and j will be printed:

```
1 7
4 8
7 9
10 10
```

Then i will increment to 13, and j will become 11. These values of i and j will cause the loop to terminate because i is not less than or equal to j.

THE GENERAL FORM OF A for LOOP

C++ has an even more general form of a **for** loop. In this general form, the initialization and update steps (note that we generalize from "increment" to "update"—more on this below) can consist of any number of individual C++ statements, separated by commas. However, there must still be just one test controlling the loop.

General Form of a for Loop

> for *(initialization statement(s)*;*controlling condition*; *update statement(s))*
>   *body of the loop*

Let's describe how this general form is executed.

♦   First, all of the initialization statements are performed. In case there are two or more initialization (or update) statements, they are performed from left to right.

♦   Then the controlling condition is checked. If it is true, the statement(s) in the body of the loop are executed.

♦   After the body of the loop, all of the update statements are executed, and the controlling condition is checked again. If the condition is true, the body of the loop is executed again, the update statements are executed, the condition is checked again, and so on.

The loop continues as long as the condition is true. The loop will terminate when the controlling condition becomes false.

In the general form of the **for** loop header, we use the term *update statements*, rather than *increment statements*. Statements in this portion of the header are not limited to increments or decrements. They can, in fact, be any C++ statements whatsoever. However, in almost all cases, there is just one statement included, and that one statement changes the value of a variable used to control the loop.

SHORTHAND FOR INCREMENTS: ++ AND − −

Because increment statements are so common, C++ has a shortcut form that is almost always used. In the line below, the statement on the right is an abbreviation for the statement on the left.

i = i + 1;   **can be replaced by**   i++;

Actually, the abbreviated form becomes much more useful if the name of the variable is large, rather than very short like i. For example, compare these two statements:

verylongname = verylongname + 1; **compared to** verylongname++;

Another advantage of this form comes when it is used as part of larger C++ constructs. In later chapters, we will see how to use the increment operator in these situations.

EXAMPLE 1-11 As a simple example, we will show how to use the increment operator in a **for** loop header:

```
for (number = 4; number <= 9; number++)
```

In the same way, subtracting one from a variable can be abbreviated by using the decrement operator −−. For example, these two statements are equivalent:

number = number − 1; **and** number−−;

EXAMPLE 1-12 Once again, here is an example using a **for** loop header:

```
for (number = 9; number >= 4; number--)
```

Finally, the increment and decrement operators can also appear to the left of the variable name. In the case of a simple assignment statement (e.g., as part of a **for** loop header), these three statements have the same meaning:

i++; ++i; i = i + 1;

However, if the increment or decrement operator is used as part of a larger expression, there can be differences in meaning.

SELF-CHECK 1-12

1. In a decrement version of a **for** loop, what happens to the control variable each time through the body of the loop?

2. How many statements are allowed to appear in the initialization or update portion of a **for** loop header? How many are allowed in the test portion?

3. What does the statement i++ mean? What does ++i mean? What about i−−?

SUMMARY

BASIC CONCEPTS

1. The computer programs in this text are written in the language called C++. Several versions of C++ are available.

2. Comments should be used to explain (to a person, not the computer) what the program is designed to do. Comments are ignored by the compiler but are printed with the program. The symbols // indicate the start of the comment; everything else on that line is considered to be part of the comment. Every program should have a comment at the top explaining what the program does. As a carryover from C, C++ has another form of comment; a comment of this type is enclosed within comment delimiters (/* and */).

3.   The lines below, called compiler directives, are usually included at the beginning of every C++ program:

```
#include <iostream>
using namespace std;
```

These directives, although not strictly a part of the C++ language, allow the program to access information about certain functions from the standard library. The header file iostream.h contains information about the output stream cout. The line "using namespace std;" allows using shortcuts when naming items from C++ libraries. A compiler directive must start in column 1, and it cannot be followed by anything else on the same line.

4.   A C++ program is composed of individual C++ statements. The first line of C++ code in a program, sometimes called the main program header, is

```
int main()
```

5.   Each complete C++ statement (except for comments and directives, which are not technically C++ statements) must end in a semicolon. If a statement is too long to fit on a single line, it can be continued on the next line, with a semicolon at the end of the entire statement.

6.   For clarity, each statement should start on a new line. Actually, two or more statements can be put on a single line, separated by a semicolon. However, a program will normally be more readable and easier to understand if no more than one statement is on any line. Consistent use of indentation and alignment also makes a program more readable.

PSEUDOCODE AND ALGORITHMS

7.   Pseudocode, consisting of statements which are a mixture of English and C++ code, is an intermediate step in writing a program. Pseudocode is an aid in writing the program and also a guide to following it once it is written.

8.   Pseudocode comes from the English-language description of a program. Then the C++ program is written from the pseudocode. This two-step process is almost always easier than going directly from English to C++.

9.   Standard mathematical notation is allowed in pseudocode, including exponents, the symbol for square root, and so on. These must all be translated into C++ when the program is written.

10. An algorithm is a step-by-step explanation of a process that is precise enough to be expressed in pseudocode and then developed into a program.

IDENTIFIERS

11. Almost any combination of letters and digits (starting with a letter or underbar) that fits on a single line is a valid identifier name; certain versions of C++ have further restrictions—for example, on the length of the name. Capital and lowercase letters can both be used in an identifier name. However, the compiler will consider an uppercase letter to be distinct from the corresponding lowercase one. For example, alpha and Alpha are two different identifiers. For consistency, we will use only lowercase for variable names.

12. A number of identifiers (e.g., **for** and **int**) have special meanings in C++. These are called keywords and should always be used with their intended meaning.

13. Other identifiers (e.g., <u>cout</u>) have a predeclared or standard meaning, but a programmer can override it by using them in some other way. However, it is recommended that a programmer use these identifiers only in the standard way.

14. An identifier that is neither a keyword nor a standard identifier is called a programmer-defined identifier.

FORMAT OF A C++ PROGRAM

15. The header or top line of a program is followed by a series of declarations, which tell the compiler which programmer-defined identifiers are being used. The declarations are followed by the main body of the program. The declarations and main body form the action portion of the program. The entire action portion is surrounded by a pair of braces ({ and }).

16. Here is a diagram of the form that a C++ program should follow:

```
// ...              comment describing the job of the program
#include ...        reference to functions from the standard library
using name...       allows naming shortcuts
int main()          main program header
{                   start of the action portion of the program
    int ... ;       declarations
    ...             statements to accomplish the program's task
    return 0;
}                   end of the main program
```

VARIABLES, ASSIGNMENT STATEMENTS, AND ARITHMETIC OPERATIONS

17. A variable is a type of identifier that holds information during the execution of a program. Every variable in C++ must be declared explicitly by associating the name of the identifier with a data type. The simplest data type is **int**, short for integer, which allows a variable to hold integer values only. Here is a declaration for two integer variables named <u>alpha</u> and <u>beta</u>:

```
int alpha,beta;
```

18. A variable does not have a value until the computer is told explicitly to put something into that storage location, typically through an assignment statement. An assignment statement has this general form:

```
varname = expr;
```

This is executed by evaluating the expression (<u>expr</u>) on the right-hand side of the assignment symbol (=) and then assigning this value to the variable (<u>varname</u>) on the left-hand side.

19. The standard arithmetic operations of addition (+), subtraction (–), and multiplication (*) are available in C++. Several types of division are also available. The symbol / is used to divide one number by another. For example, 7/2 is 3; 7/2 is 3.5. The modulus or remainder operator % gives the remainder when one integer is divided by another; x % y gives the remainder when x is divided by y (e.g., 7 % 2 is 1).

OUTPUT STREAM: <u>cout</u>

20. The output stream <u>cout</u> can be used to print the value of one or more variables. For example, the line below will print the value of <u>x</u>, one space, and then the value of <u>y</u>. The output statement after this will print on a new line because of the stream manipulator <u>endl</u>.

```
cout << x << " " << y << endl;
```

21. Putting a message inside quotation marks creates a literal string (e.g., "help"). The <u>cout</u> output stream, together with the insertion operator (<<), can then be used to print the string. For example, ***cout << "help"*** prints the string "help."

22. The general form to use with <u>cout</u> is this (the insertion operator and then the literal string or expression can be repeated any number of times):

```
cout << literal string or expression ... ;
```

LOOPS

23. Statements are normally executed sequentially. However, a loop can modify this order. In general, a loop contains a series of statements that are written once but can be executed repeatedly.

24. A common programming technique is incrementing a variable, which means to increase its value (usually, but not always, by 1). Incrementing allows us to get the next in a series of values as we progress through a loop. The way to increment the variable <u>varname</u> by <u>increment value</u> is:

```
varname = varname + increment_value;
```

25. C++ has a number of different loop structures. The one that is used first in the text is a **for** loop, which allows a series of instructions to be executed a specified number of times.

26. One simple form of a **for** loop is the following:

```
for (index = start; index <= limit; index = index + 1)
    statement;
```

Here <u>index</u> is used as the control variable or **for** loop index; <u>start</u> is the starting or initial value for <u>index</u>; <u>limit</u> is the final or limiting value for <u>index</u>; *statement* is a single C++ statement. Each time through the body of the loop, the value of the control variable is increased by 1. The body of the loop consists of one single statement, but this can be modified by using a compound statement, as described in paragraph 28.

27. This **for** loop is executed as follows: <u>index</u> is initialized to <u>start</u> and compared to <u>limit</u>. If <u>index</u> is less than or equal to <u>limit</u>, then the one statement constituting the body of the loop is executed with <u>index</u> equal to <u>start</u>. Each time the body of the loop is completed, <u>index</u> is incremented by 1, and the process is repeated. That is, the new value for <u>index</u> is tested against <u>limit</u>; if it is less than or equal to <u>limit</u>, then the body is executed again. The loop continues until the condition controlling it is false (in this case, when <u>index</u> is not less than or equal to <u>limit</u>). When that occurs, the **for** loop is terminated, the body of the loop is not entered, and the next statement in the program is executed.

28. Some variations are allowed in the general form of a **for** loop. For example, by using a compound statement, which consists of a pair of braces around a group of statements, a programmer can include any number of C++ statements in the body of the loop. In the example below, *statement-1, statement-2, ..., statement-n* will be done each time the body of the loop is executed.

```
for (index = start; index <= limit; index = index + 1) {
    statement-1;
    statement-2;

    ...

    statement-n;
}
```

29. The general form of a **for** loop allows any number of initialization statements, one controlling condition, and any number of update statements:

    for *(initialization statement(s); controlling condition; update statement(s))*
        body of the loop

    First, all of the initialization statements are performed. Then the controlling condition is checked. If it is true, the statement(s) in the body of the loop are executed. Finally, all of the update statements are executed, and the controlling condition is checked again. The loop continues as long as the condition is true. The loop terminates when the controlling condition becomes false.

SOFTWARE DEVELOPMENT CYCLE: SAVING, COMPILING, AND RUNNING A PROGRAM

30. As part of the software development cycle, a programmer should do the following: analyze a problem, come up with an algorithm and express it in pseudocode, and write a program to translate the pseudocode into a programming language. The program should then be typed in, saved, compiled, run, and tested. The details of how to do these steps vary from system to system.

INCREMENT AND DECREMENT OPERATORS

31. Because increment and decrement statements are so common, C++ has shorthand operators that are often used. The statements on the right are an abbreviation for the ones on the left.

`number = number + 1;`	**becomes**	`number++;`
`number = number - 1;`	**becomes**	`number--;`

32. The increment and decrement operators can be used in a **for** loop header. For example, here is another way to write the header in paragraph 28:

    ```
    for (index = start; index <= limit; index++)
    ```

    This form will be used in almost all our later programs.

EXERCISES

For each exercise, assume that all variables have been declared to have data type **int**. If you are asked to write a program, be sure to include comments. In the exercises, when we give a complete C++ program, we usually omit comments.

TRACING EXERCISES

1. For each of the following series of C++ statements, trace what happens as the section of code is run. That is, show what value is stored in each variable as each step is executed. You can use either of the tracing methods in Section 5.

    a.
    ```
    y = 2;
    x = y + 1;
    y = y + 1;
    x = 4;
    ```

    b.
    ```
    numb = 5;
    cbnumb = numb * numb * numb;
    sqnumb = numb * numb;
    ```

   c. `w = 6;`
     `w = w + 1;`
     `q = 2 * w;`

   d. `rate = 7;`
     `time = 5;`
     `junk = rate - time;`
     `dist = rate * time;`

   e. `for (x = 6; x <= 10; x = x + 1)`
        `y = x * 2;`

   f. `s = 0;`
     `for (i = 1; i <= 5; i = i + 1)`
        `s = s + i;`

2. For each of the following C++ programs, show what is printed.

a.
```cpp
#include <iostream>
using namespace std;
int main()
{
    int x,y;

    y = 2;
    x = y + 1;
    cout << x << " " << y << endl;
    y = y + 2;
    x = 5;
    cout << x << " " << y << endl;
    return 0;
}
```

b.
```cpp
#include <iostream>
using namespace std;
int main()
{
    int numb,cbnumb;

    numb = 4;
    cbnumb = numb * numb * numb;
    cout << numb << " "
         << cbnumb << " "
         << numb*numb << endl;
    return 0;
}
```

c.
```cpp
#include <iostream>
using namespace std;
int main()
{
    int w,q;

    w = 6;
    w = w + 3;
    q = 4 * w;
    cout << w << " " << q << endl;
    return 0;
}
```

d.
```cpp
#include <iostream>
using namespace std;
int main()
{
    int rate,time,dist,junk;

    rate = 7;
    time = 3;
    junk = rate + time;
    dist = rate * time;
    cout << rate << " " << time
         << " " << junk << " "
         << dist << endl;
    return 0;
}
```

e.
```cpp
#include <iostream>
using namespace std;
int main()
{
    int x,y;

    for (x = 6; x <= 10; x++) {
        y = x * 5;
        cout << x << " "
             << y << endl;
    }
    x = 8;
    cout << x << " "
         << y << endl;
    return 0;
}
```

f.
```cpp
#include <iostream>
using namespace std;
int main()
{
    int i,s;

    s = 0;
    for (i = 1; i <= 7; i++)
        s = s + i;
    cout << s << endl;
    return 0;
}
```

3. a. The traces in Exercise 1(a)–(d) are much shorter than those for parts (e) and (f). Why is this true? [*Suggestion:* What new instruction is used in parts (e) and (f)?]

   b. In Exercise 1(b), would it be legal to write either cbnumb = numb * numb or sqnumb = numb * numb * numb? If so, is it a good idea? If it is illegal, explain why.

4. Assume that the variables x, y, z, and w of type **int** have the values shown below (for each part of this exercise, start from these initial values). As each step is executed, show what is stored in each variable.

   ```
   x = 7;   y = 6;   z = 1;   w = 4;
   ```

   a. z = x / y;   b. x = y / w;   c. x = x + 1;   d. w = y − w;
      w = x % y;   z = y % w;   y = x + 1;   z = y / x;
                                              z = x * y;

5. Each part of this question contains two similar series of statements. However, there is a significant difference in each part between the two series. Trace each part step by step and show what is printed. Be sure that you understand the difference between (i) and (ii) in each part.

   a. (i) numb = 9;   (ii) numb = 9;
          cout << 2 * numb;   numb = 2 * numb;
          cout << endl << numb;   cout << numb;

   b. (i) numb = 3;   (ii) numb = 3;
          cout << numb;   numb = numb + 1;
          numb = numb + 1;   cout << numb;

   c. (i) x = 5;   (ii) x = 5;
          x = x + 1;   y = x;
          y = x;   x = x + 1;
          cout << x << " " << y;   cout << x << " " << y;

6. Show what is printed by each of the following **for** loops.

   a. for (i = 1; i <= 8; i++) {   b. for (i = 8; i >= 1; i--) {
          k = 9 - i;   k = i;

          m = 2 * k;   m = 2 * k;

          cout << i << " " << k   cout << i << " " << k
               << " " << m << endl;   << " " << m << endl;

      }   }

ANALYSIS EXERCISES

7. Here is a list of possible names for variables in C++. Which are legal names for your particular compiler? Which are illegal names? If a name is illegal, explain why (e.g., it starts with an illegal character).

   a. beginend   h. 5
   b. space1999   i. one_2
   c. 1999_space   j. 2one
   d. p qrs   k. help+me
   e. IBM   l. abc...xyz (with ... in the name)
   f. i.b.m.   m. for
   g. iNtEL   n. fore

o. `zyxwvutsrqponmlkjihgfedcba`	u. `number1`
p. `upto`	v. `_a`
q. `downto`	w. `a_`
r. `legal`	x. `FOR`
s. `legal?`	y. `1x`
t. `#1`	z. `x1`

8. Here is the final version of Program 1 from Section 5 (with just one line from the top comment). The numbers to the left of the statements are for our discussion only, to make it easier to refer to individual statements. They are not part of the C++ program and should not be included when you type the program. Answer the questions below the program.

```
1. // Program prog1b.cpp:
2. #include <iostream>
3. using namespace std;
4. int main()
5. {
6.      int number,sqnumber;
7.
8.      for (number = 4; number <= 9; number = number + 1) {
9.           sqnumber = number * number;
10.          cout << number << " " << sqnumber << endl;
11.     }
12.     return 0;
13. }
```

a. Line 1 is a comment. What is its purpose?

b. Line 2 says that we want to include something in our program. What will we include? Why do we want to include it?

c. Line 4 is called the main program header. What does it tell the compiler?

d. Line 5 consists of a single piece of punctuation, the opening brace ({). What does this symbol mean?

e. Line 6 is a declaration, which sets aside space for the variables (whose names are?) and tells what type of information they will hold (what type?).

f. Line 7 is blank. Why is it included?

g. Line 8 sets up a **for** loop, which will process successive values of <u>number</u> from 4 to 9. What is the control variable of this loop? The initial value? What is the condition used to control the loop? What is the last or limiting value to be processed? What does the control variable increase by each time? Line 8 does not end in a semicolon since the statement is not yet complete (why not?). What does the opening brace at the end of this line indicate to the compiler?

h. How many things do we want to do in the body of the loop? Lines 9 and 10 contain the statements that are to be executed each time through the body of the **for** loop. What type of statement is line 9? What value does it give to <u>sqnumber</u>?

i. What is the purpose of line 10? What does it print? What is the purpose of the symbols <<? What is the string inside quotation marks called? What is the purpose of <u>endl</u>?

j. Line 11 uses a closing brace (}) to indicate the end of the series of statements that we want to include inside the body of the **for** loop. What is the brace aligned under? Why doesn't this line end in a semicolon?

k. Line 12 marks the logical end of the program. What does the 0 signify? What would a *return 1* mean?

l. Line 13 consists of a closing brace. What other symbol is this closing brace matched with? What line is that symbol on? What is the purpose of line 13? What is the difference between the logical end and the physical end of a program?

9. When the program below was compiled, there was an error message. What was the error message? How should the program be fixed to correct this error?

```
#include <iostream>
using namespace std;
int main()
{
    int Numb;
    numb = 1;
    return 0;
}
```

10. In Section 7, we described rules used by a compiler to determine if two identifier names are identical. Decide if each of the following possible names for variables is valid on your system. Also determine if two or more of these names will be considered identical by your compiler.

a. xxxxxxxxxxxxxxxxxxxxxxxxx (writing x 25 times)

b. xxxxxxxxxxxxxxxxxxxxxxxxxxxxxxxxxxx (writing x 35 times)

c. xxxxx...xxxx (writing x 75 times)

d. xxxxx...xxxx (writing x 150 times)

11. In most cases, the operations of / and % are used with positive integers. However, they are defined for negative values as well. Make up a series of little programs that allow you to discover the rules your compiler follows for negative values. For example, write a program that determines the value of –1 % 5, 9 / –2, –7 % –3, or –5 / 4. Construct a chart summarizing the rules. *Warning:* The rules may vary slightly from one C++ compiler to another. Therefore, most programmers avoid using these special cases in a program that may eventually run on some other compiler.

12. The program below has many errors in it. Try to find and correct all of them. Some of them are foolish, like leaving off a semicolon. Others are things like misspelled words, and so on. When you think you have found all the errors, run the program to see if you missed any. An error in a program is called a **bug**. Getting a program to work correctly by making sure there are no mistakes in it is called **debugging**. You will learn much more about debugging as you write more programs.

```
/* comant is ok {;
#includ <iostream>;
using myspace: standard;
void main
{
    ints x,y;
    x + 1 = 4;
    y = y + 1;
    x = 3y + 5x
    cout << x,y)
    return 0;
```

EXERCISES TO MODIFY PROGRAM 1

13. In Section 3, we gave a version of Program 1 which did not use a **for** loop; in this version, we explicitly assigned the values 4, 5, 6, 7, 8, and 9 to number. In Section 4, we started to write another version of Program 1 which did not use a **for** loop; in this version, we incremented number to hold each of the values from 4 to 9.

    a. Assume that we want the squares of the numbers from 4 to 59. How many more statements are needed? Assume that we continue to write the program using one of the versions without a **for** loop.

    b. Repeat part (b) with the assumption that the program will print the squares of the numbers from 4 to 159, instead of 4 to 59.

    c. What can you conclude about the power of a **for** loop?

14. In this and the next few exercises, we will modify the **for** loop version of Program 1. The first modification is very simple. We put the sqnumber = number * number statement after the cout. Rewrite the program with this modification. Then describe what happens if we run the new program. (*Suggestion*: The program runs, but the answers are very strange.)

15. Show how to modify Program 1 so that it prints the squares (only the squares, not the numbers themselves) of all the numbers from 1 to 12. The new program should print

    ```
    1 4 9 16 25 ... 144
    ```

16. Modify Program 1 so that it prints the numbers from 4 to 9, together with each number's square and cube. For example, it starts by printing

    ```
    4 16 64
    ```

17. Modify Program 1 so that it prints the numbers from 4 to 9, together with the square of the number, the cube of the number, two times the number, and three times the number.

18. Modify Program 1 so that it prints the even numbers from 4 to 20 and their squares—i.e., 4 16, 6 36, 8 64, up to 20 400. (*Suggestion*: If the variable i increases by 1, then 2 * i increases by 2. Or, as an alternative, as part of the **for** loop header, you can have i itself increase by 2.)

19. Modify the program from Exercise 18 so that it prints the even numbers from 4 to 20 and their squares, and then the odd numbers from 5 to 19 and their cubes. (*Suggestion*: Use two loops, one for each part.)

20. Modify Program 1 so that it prints the numbers from 4 to 9 and their squares, except that the square is printed only for numbers greater than 5. The output should be

    ```
    4 5 6 36 7 49
    ```

    Note that 4 and 5 print, but their squares do not. (*Suggestion:* Treat 4 and 5 separately outside of a loop.)

PROGRAMMING PROJECTS

21. Write a program that prints all of the numbers less than 2000 that are evenly divisible by 10. The first few numbers are 10 20 30 ....

22. Write a program that prints all of the numbers that are evenly divisible by 10. Of course, you won't be able to find all of them, but see how many you can print before there is a problem.

23. a. Without using a loop, write a program that prints your name twice and has three blank lines between the two lines of output.

    b. Repeat part (a), but this time write your name five times.

    c. Repeat part (a), but this time write your name 100 times. Does it make sense not to use a loop for this version?

24. Write a program that prints the numbers from 1 to 100 with five values per line, two blank spaces between values. The last few lines will look like this:

```
 . . .
91 92 93 94 95
96 97 98 99 100
```

25. a. A computer programmer wants to give her boyfriend several pieces of candy every day during June, starting with six on the first day and increasing by five more pieces each day. Write a program that prints the days of the month (the numbers from 1 to 30), together with the number of pieces of candy to be given on that day.

    b. Modify the program from part (a) so that it begins with <u>start</u> pieces of candy on the first day and goes up by <u>increase</u> number of pieces per day; you will give <u>start</u> and <u>increase</u> values at the beginning of the program.

26. Go through the earlier exercises that ask you to write programs. Solve each exercise by first writing pseudocode, then writing the program from the pseudocode. If you have already written programs for some of these exercises, compare how easy it was to write the original programs with how easy it is to write them from pseudocode. What conclusions can you draw?

EVALUATING AN EXPRESSION

PROBLEM: The Registrar's Headache

SYNTAX CONCEPTS: double, **float**, and **char** data types; printing messages, arithmetic precedence rules, **if** statement, relational operators, compound assignment operators, standard library of functions

PROGRAMMING CONCEPTS: evaluating an expression, branching, creating readable output

CONTROL STRUCTURES: if statement

PROBLEM-SOLVING TECHNIQUES: debugging

HOW TO READ CHAPTER 2

OUTLINE:

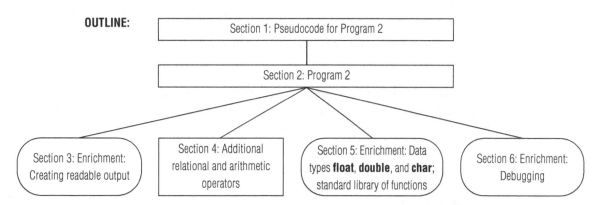

INTRODUCTION AND STATEMENT OF THE PROBLEM

INTRODUCTION

This chapter shows how to write a program to evaluate a complex mathematical expression. In the process, it presents the C++ precedence rules. It discusses relational operators and introduces the idea of branching—executing one statement or another, depending on the value of an expression. Chapter 2 also uses real numbers (data types, **double**, and **float**) and the standard library of functions. It discusses how to create readable output and introduces debugging. In the process of writing Program 2, we reiterate and consolidate ideas introduced in Chapter 1.

STATEMENT OF THE PROBLEM

Our second problem starts with a story. At University A, sections of a certain class fill very quickly because of the popularity of Professor B. To determine if a student can enter a closed section, the registrar uses the student's grade point average (which we will call gpa) to evaluate a complicated mathematical formula, which we will signify by **result = formula(gpa)**. If the value of the formula is high enough, the student gets into the section.

Until recently, the registrar asked for the student's gpa, plugged it into the formula **result = formula(gpa)**, then said either "Congratulations" or "Sorry." Because of the large number of students involved, the registrar has become increasingly busy and has decided to computerize part of the process (in the exercises, you will be asked to program other parts as well) by constructing a chart showing various values for the grade point average and the formula. This way, when a student comes in, the registrar can simply look up the average in the table and find the correct answer to the formula instead of recomputing it each time.

PROBLEM 2 Write a complete C++ program to produce a table for the registrar's formula, starting at gpa = 0.00 and going up to gpa = 4.00, increasing by 0.50 each time.

$$result = \frac{gpa^3 + 7gpa - 1}{gpa^2 - \dfrac{gpa + 5}{3}}$$

Next to each value of <u>result</u> that is greater than or equal to 0, print the message "Admit."

If you don't know how to evaluate the formula, don't worry. The computer will do that task for you. All you have to do is write the formula in a form that the computer can understand.

Keep in mind that the story is whimsical. We are simply trying to describe a problem that lets us introduce the question of evaluating a formula in C++.

SECTION 1   PSEUDOCODE FOR PROGRAM 2

STARTING THE PROGRAM

Just as in Chapter 1, we are to write a complete C++ program to solve this problem. This time the calculations are more complex, and it is more reasonable to do them on a computer. However, as before, we will not start writing code immediately. Instead, we will think through the problem and devise pseudocode for the solution. First, we will analyze the statement of the problem and determine what the program has to do and what output it produces. It's easier to start with the output.

The problem statement says to produce a table of values. This clearly implies that we want to print some results. The formula in the problem computes a relationship between each value of gpa and <u>result</u>: For each value of gpa, the formula will produce a value for <u>result</u>. To create a table, we should print both values. Analyzing the output this way gives us two lines of pseudocode:

compute result = *the formula applied to* gpa
print gpa, result

Notice that we haven't gone into the details of how to write the formula in C++. The pseudocode doesn't need to be carried to that level since it is just an outline of what we plan to do.

These two lines of pseudocode are sufficient for one value of gpa, but the problem statement says to compute result for a number of values, starting at 0.00 and ending at 4.00, increasing each time by 0.50. This suggests that we need a loop structure, which leads to the next version of the pseudocode:

for values of gpa *from 0.00 to 4.00, increasing by 0.50*
    compute result = *the formula applied to* gpa
    print gpa, result

The last part of the problem statement says to print a message next to each value of result that is greater than or equal to 0. Let's try to make this more precise. After printing each set of gpa and result values, we want to determine if result is greater than or equal to 0. If it is, we want to print the word "Admit" and continue processing with the next value of gpa. If result is less than 0, we will just continue processing. Let's write a question as part of our pseudocode, using the mathematical symbol for "greater than or equal to":

for values of gpa *from 0.00 to 4.00, increasing by 0.50*
    compute result = *the formula applied to* gpa
    print gpa, result
    is result ≥ 0?
        print "Admit"

That's it. It almost looks like a C++ program already, largely because of the indenting. It is customary and helpful when writing pseudocode to indent as you would in a program. Then it is clear how the parts of the pseudocode go together in the translation.

SECTION 2 **WRITING PROGRAM 2; THE if STATEMENT**

STARTING THE PROGRAM

Now that we've written the pseudocode, let's start on the C++ code. The first few lines are not shown in the pseudocode since it deals only with the action part of the program. These lines will be exactly the same as for our first program, except for the comment.

```
// Program prog2a.cpp:
//   creates a table to evaluate a formula based on values of
//   gpa in the range from gpa = 0.00 to 4.00 in units of 0.50
#include <iostream>
using namespace std;
int main()
{
```

NEW DATA TYPE: double

Now we need a declaration of the variables and their data types. We have already decided to use gpa and result for the names of the variables.

Next let's see what kind of values gpa and result hold in this program. The index gpa starts at 0.00, then becomes 0.50, 1.00, 1.50, …, 3.50, 4.00. Some of these values can be represented as integers, but others cannot. Therefore, gpa cannot have data type **int**. To allow for the decimal places, we will declare gpa to have data type **double**. This data type allows gpa to hold a real number, one that may contain decimal places. Clearly, the result of the formula (the value stored in result) will not be an integer in all cases, so we will give result data type **double** as well. Here is the declaration:

```
double gpa, result;
```

SETTING UP THE for LOOP FOR PROGRAM 2

The pseudocode makes it obvious that we want to use a **for** loop in this program. The initial value we want is 0.00, the final value is 4.00, and the increment is 0.50. Since we want gpa to start at 0.00, we initialize it in the header:

```
for (gpa = 0.00; ... ; ...)
```

The **for** loop should use all values of gpa up to and including 4.00, so we can continue the **for** loop header with the following condition:

```
for (gpa = 0.00; gpa <= 4.00; ...)
```

Finally, the pseudocode says that we want to increment the value of gpa by 0.50 each time, so we complete the **for** loop header like this:

```
for (gpa = 0.00; gpa <= 4.00; gpa = gpa + 0.50)
    compute result = the formula applied to gpa
    print gpa, result
    is result ≥ 0?
        print "Admit"
```

THE BODY OF THE LOOP

Since we must give result a value and also do some printing, the loop body will consist of several statements and should be surrounded by a pair of braces. Inside the loop, the variable result should be set to whatever the formula works out to be for a given value of gpa. For now, we will simply write the assignment statement as result = *formula*, where *formula* stands for the C++ translation of the formula. Since the details of this translation are tricky, we will come back to it later.

STYLE WORKSHOP Don't think that this is a poor way to program. It is very common to sketch the basic outline of a program or part of one, then fill in the details later. Chapter 4 discusses this idea further.

PRINTING VALUES OF TYPE double

After computing result, the pseudocode says to print gpa and result. We can use the following line to print the values of gpa and result, with each pair of values on a new line:

```
cout << gpa << "   " << result << endl;
```

There are three blanks in the quotation marks, which will cause three spaces to print between the numeric values. As usual, there will be no blanks between the items unless we specifically enter them. Assuming that gpa has the value 2.0 and result has the value 12.6, the following will print:

```
2   12.6
```

Notice that C++ prints only the decimal places necessary to represent the value of the number accurately. As we will see in Chapter 3, it is possible to specify the number of decimal places to print.

THE LOOP SO FAR

Let's look at the loop so far:

```
for (gpa = 0.00; gpa <= 4.00; gpa = gpa + 0.50) {
    result = formula;
    cout << gpa << "   " << result << endl;
    is result ≥ 0?
        print "Admit"
}
```

SELF-CHECK 2-1

1. Could the variables gpa and result instead be called number and sqnumber?

2. Why can't we increment by writing gpa++? (*Hint*: What does the ++ operator do?)

3. What will be printed by the following if num1 has the value 234.5230 and num2 has the value −4.7600?

```
cout << num1 << " " << num2;
```

MAKING DECISIONS USING A CONDITIONAL OR if STATEMENT

The pseudocode says to print the word "Admit" whenever the value of result is positive or zero. If result is less than 0, we don't want to print. In either case, we want to go to a new line and continue processing with the next value of gpa. In C++, a **conditional** or **if** statement is used to ask a question or make a decision, and cout is used to print a message. The pseudocode translates to the following C++ code:

```
if (result >= 0)
    cout << " Admit";
cout << endl;
```

Let's first look at the **if** statement. Up until now, all our programs have been written so that each statement executes each time the program runs. Most programs, however, need more than that. A conditional or **if** statement allows a program to **branch**, which means to allow the path of execution to go in one of two directions, depending on a specific condition. Some statements will be executed, and others will not, depending on the condition's value.

In a conditional statement, the keyword **if** is followed by some condition (which must be in parentheses) that evaluates to either true or false. Usually, the condition compares two items using a **relational operator**; in the example, that operator is >= (with no space between the two symbols), which means "greater than or equal to."

♦ If the condition is true, we execute the statement that follows [in this case, ***cout << "Admit";***], and continue processing.

```
result = 3.0;
if (result >= 0)
    cout << " Admit";
cout << endl;
```

♦ If the condition is false, we simply skip that statement and "fall through" to the next instruction.

```
result = -1.0;
if (result >= 0)
    cout << " Admit";
cout << endl;
```

In the example above, if <u>result</u> is greater than or equal to 0, we print the word "Admit," but if <u>result</u> is less than 0, we don't. Instead, we proceed to the next statement, which sends the cursor to a new line in all cases.

General Form of an if Statement

```
if (cond)                        // no semicolon here
    stmt-1;                      // end of if statement
stmt-2;                          // next statement
```

The keyword **if** is followed by a condition (*cond*), in parentheses. As shown in Figure 2-1, *cond* is evaluated; if it is true, we execute *stmt-1*; if *cond* is false, we skip *stmt-1*. In either case, we continue with *stmt-2*, which follows the **if** statement.

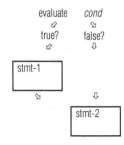 **CAUTION** Do not put a semicolon after the **if** condition since the **if** statement is not yet complete. Here is an example of the error:

```
if (cond);
    stmt-1;
stmt-2;
```

If by accident you put a semicolon after the **if** condition, the **if** statement terminates at that point. The condition is tested, but nothing happens, and the following statement (*stmt-1*) is executed in all cases (see Exercise 21).

STYLE WORKSHOP It is considered good style in C++ to put the **if** condition on one line and the statement to be executed, *stmt-1*, on the next line, indented several spaces or one tab position.

TRACING PROGRAM 2

Let's look at the entire loop to verify that it works.

```
for (gpa = 0.00; gpa <= 4.00; gpa = gpa + 0.50) {
    result = formula;
    cout << gpa << " " << result;
    if (result >= 0)
        cout << " Admit";
    cout << endl;
}
```

FIGURE 2-1 Flow of control using an **if** statement

```
         evaluate    cond
            ↙          ↘
          true?       false?
            ↙            ↓
       ┌─────────┐
       │ stmt-1  │
       └─────────┘
            ↘            ↓
                    ┌─────────┐
                    │ stmt-2  │
                    └─────────┘
```

PROGRAM TRACE

◆ Initially, <u>gpa</u> gets the value 0.00. This value is less than or equal to 4.00, and we enter the body of the loop. The value 0.00 is used to compute a value for <u>result</u>, and we print <u>gpa</u> and <u>result</u>. Then we test to see if the value computed for <u>result</u> is greater than or equal to 0. If it is, we print "Admit"; otherwise we skip that line. In either case, we go to a new line in the output.

◆ Next we return to the header of the **for** loop, where we increment the value of <u>gpa</u> by 0.50 to 0.50 and then test the new value against 4.00. Since <u>gpa</u> is less than or equal to 4.00, we enter the body of the loop. There we compute a new value of <u>result</u>, print, test it, and again return to the loop header to increment <u>gpa</u>, this time to 1.00.

◆ Eventually, we print 4.00 ... (where ... is the value of <u>result</u> when <u>gpa</u> = 4.00) and check the value of <u>result</u>. Then <u>gpa</u> increases to 4.50, which is greater than 4.00, so we fall out of the loop.

ENDING THE PROGRAM

After the loop, we could just end the program. But let's first print a message that the table is finished:

```
cout << "The table is finished" << endl;
return 0;
}
```

This message, called a trailer message, is helpful to both the programmer and the user. It signals to the programmer that the program has run to completion and has not become stuck in the middle. To the user, it signals that the output is finished, and no pages are missing.

SELF-CHECK 2-2

1. What is the difference between the output of the two lines shown below?

```
int help;
help = 3;
cout << help;
cout << "help";
```

2. What is the purpose of an **if** statement?

3. What is wrong with the following **if** statement?

```
if x < 7
    cout << "less";
```

WRITING THE FORMULA IN C++

Our program is almost complete, but we still have a major task to work on: we have not expressed the formula in C++. Using the symbols for arithmetic operations from Chapter 1, Section 7, we can produce a first approximation of the correct formula. Recall that the formula looks like this:

$$result = \frac{gpa^3 + 7gpa - 1}{gpa^2 - \dfrac{gpa + 5}{3}}$$

By a straightforward translation, this becomes the following in C++:

```
result = gpa * gpa * gpa + 7 * gpa - 1 / gpa * gpa - gpa + 5 / 3; // incorrect
```

PRECEDENCE: THE ORDER OF OPERATIONS

This is not, however, a correct translation, because it ignores precedence of operations, which is the order in which arithmetic operations are performed when an expression contains two or more operators. For example, in the original mathematical formula, the entire numerator is divided by the entire denominator; division is the last step. But in the C++ formula as written, the + between gpa and 5 is the last step (you will see why shortly). We want to instruct the computer to execute operations in the correct order.

To do this, we have to determine what order C++ uses if we do not specify the precedence—that is, the natural or default order of operations in C++. Table 2-1 summarizes the precedence of basic arithmetic operations in C++.

Note that these rules are identical to the ones for arithmetic (e.g., $2 + 3 \times 4$ is $2 + 12 = 14$). In arithmetic, however, the meaning is usually made clear by the way we write the formula: for example, in the expression $3 - 2x$, we know to multiply 2 by x before subtracting it from 3.

EXAMPLE 2-1

In what order are the following C++ expressions evaluated?

    a. `a * 3 - b`
    b. `x + 1 / 2`

In expression (a), multiplication is done before subtraction:

    `a * 3 - b`

    first   second

In expression (b), division is done before addition

    `x + 1 / 2`

    second   first

C++ has two uses for the minus sign, as does standard arithmetic. One use is subtraction (e.g., $5 - 3$). The other is **unary minus** (e.g., -7), so called because it has one operand. Similarly, C++ has two uses for the plus sign. There is addition, and there is **unary plus** (e.g., $+7$). Unary minus (sometimes called negation) and unary plus have precedence over all other arithmetic operators.

EXAMPLE 2-2

What is the value of this expression?

    `6 * -4`

It evaluates to -24. The 4 is negated, then multiplied by 6.

TABLE 2-1   The Arithmetic Precedence Rules

higher precedence (done first)	`*  /  %`
lower precedence (done last)	`+  -`

ASSOCIATIVITY

There is another concept, called **associativity**, that accompanies precedence. Associativity determines which has priority if two operators with the same precedence are next to each other.

◆ For the binary operators (*, /, %, +, and –), associativity is left to right.

◆ For the unary operators (unary minus, unary plus, ++, and −−), associativity is right to left. (This is quite rare.)

In an expression like a / b * c or a – b + c, where both operations have the same precedence, the one on the left has priority over the one on the right because of associativity.

EXAMPLE 2-3

Evaluate the following program sequence:

```
int a,b,c,ans;
a = 3;
b = 4;
c = 24;
ans = c / b * a;
```

In this case, first c is divided by b to yield 6; this value is multiplied by a to give 18. The value 18 is assigned to ans.

THE C++ ARITHMETIC PRECEDENCE RULES

Table 2-2 summarizes the arithmetic precedence rules in C++, including associativity.

Example 2-4 shows an expression where both precedence and associativity rules are used:

EXAMPLE 2-4

$5 - 3 + 2 * 6 / 2$ evaluates to 8 in the order shown:
$5 - 3 + 12 / 2 =$
$5 - 3 + \quad 6 \quad =$
$\quad 2 \; + \; 6 \quad = 8$

If the precedence rules do not correspond to the order in which we want things to be done, the way to override them in C++ is the same as in arithmetic—use parentheses. For example, we can write $y = a/(b + 3)$ in order to add before dividing.

Table 2-2   The C++ Arithmetic Precedence Rules with Associativity Rules

					Associativity
highest precedence (done first)	unary minus	unary plus	++	−−	right to left
		* / %			left to right
lowest precedence (done last)	+ –				left to right
Operators on the same line have the same precedence					

EXAMPLE 2-5   x * 2 + 1 says to multiply x by 2, then add 1.

x * (2 + 1) says to add 2 + 1, getting 3, then multiply by x.

Inside a pair of parentheses, the same precedence rules apply.

EXAMPLE 2-6   How do we evaluate this C++ expression?

```
5 * (3 + 4 / y)
```

The first operation performed is division, followed by addition. Once the expression inside the parentheses has been evaluated, multiplication is done.

SELF-CHECK 2-3

1. What does "precedence of operations" mean?
2. What happens if two operations with the same precedence occur next to each other in an expression?
3. How can you override the normal order of precedence?

APPLYING THE RULES TO PROGRAM 2

Now let's return to our formula. We wrote it as

```
result = gpa * gpa * gpa + 7 * gpa - 1 / gpa * gpa - gpa + 5 / 3;
                                                              // incorrect
```

In Exercise 4, you are asked to trace the precise order in which this is evaluated in C++ and the sequence in which the original mathematical formula would be evaluated. It should be clear that they are not the same.

As a first step to correcting this problem, we can put parentheses around the numerator and denominator:

```
result = (gpa * gpa * gpa + 7 * gpa - 1) / (gpa * gpa - gpa + 5 / 3);
                                                              // incorrect
```

This will guarantee that division is performed last. Curiously, despite the length of this expression, this simple use of parentheses is almost enough. You should verify that the numerator is correct, but the denominator must be fixed. We want **gpa + 5** to be divided by 3, not just 5 divided by 3, so we need another pair of parentheses around **gpa + 5**. No other parentheses are needed since the operations are now in the correct sequence. Here is the correct C++ translation:

```
result = (gpa * gpa * gpa + 7 * gpa - 1) / (gpa * gpa - (gpa + 5) / 3);
                                                              // correct
```

STYLE WORKSHOP   We really shouldn't say that this is *the* correct translation because many others are equally valid. For example, another correct formula comes from adding extra parentheses within the existing ones, making the numerator into this: **((gpa * gpa * gpa) + (7 * gpa) − 1)**, and so on. In fact, we could put in so many parentheses that there would be no need to remember the precedence rules, but this isn't a good idea. First, the extra parentheses make the formula hard to read. Second, if you are not careful, you may put in an extra (or), or leave one out. Any of these mistakes will cause an error in your program. Use parentheses only when you must—when you want to override the normal rules of precedence. Of course, if you are in doubt, an extra pair in the right place (always a pair) won't hurt.

We could also have omitted all the blank spaces in the C++ version of the formula, but it would be much harder to read. We often insert extra blanks in C++ statements for readability. We have inserted some extra blank lines into the final version of the program for the same reason.

We can now substitute our C++ statement for the one that reads <u>result</u> = *formula* to get an almost complete version of Program 2.

PROGRAM 2 WITH THE FORMULA

Here is Program 2 with the complete formula:

  PROGRAM LISTING

```
// Program prog2a.cpp:
//   creates a table to evaluate a formula based on values of
//   gpa in the range from gpa = 0.00 to 4.00 in units of 0.50
#include <iostream>
using namespace std;
int main()
{
    double gpa,result;

    for (gpa = 0.00; gpa <= 4.00; gpa = gpa + 0.50) {
        result = (gpa * gpa * gpa + 7 * gpa - 1) /
                 (gpa * gpa - (gpa + 5) / 3);
        cout << gpa << " " << result;
        if (result >= 0)
            cout << " Admit";
        cout << endl;
    }
    cout << "The table is finished" << endl;
    return 0;
}
```

Although it appears that we are finished with Program 2, we can still make improvements. To see why, let's take a look at the output from this program.

OUTPUT FROM PROGRAM 2 SO FAR

Figure 2-2 shows the output from this version of Program 2 (prog2a.cpp). If you can't tell what it means, that is probably because we haven't labeled or identified the output. We will fix some of the problems in the next section.

FIGURE 2-2   Output from Program 2 (Version prog2a.cpp)

```
0    0.6 Admit
0.5   -1.65789
1    -7
1.5   154.5 Admit
2    12.6 Admit
2.5   8.56667 Admit
3    7.42105 Admit
3.5   7.04867 Admit
4    7 Admit
The table is finished
```

SELF-CHECK 2-4

1. In what order will the operations in each of the following C++ expressions be evaluated? What will the value of each expression be if $p = 4$, $q = 7$, $r = 3$, and $s = 5$?

    a. `(p - q) + (r - s)`   b. `p - (q + r) * s`

2. Which is a correct C++ translation of the right-hand side of the following equation? If more than one is correct, which is preferred?

    $$y = \frac{p + q \times r - s}{p + q}$$

    a. `(p + q) * (r - s) / (p + q)`   b. `((p + q) * (r - s)) / p + q`

    c. `(p + q * r - s)/(p + q)`   d. `((p + (q * r) - s)) / (p + q)`

    e. `p + (q * r) - s / p + q`   f. `(p + q * r - s) / p + q`

SECTION 3 ## ENRICHMENT: CREATING READABLE OUTPUT

Even though we have written the last line and the formula, we are not quite finished with Program 2. One thing a programmer must always consider is the readability of the output. The output from our program is messy and unclear, but we can fix it by improving the printing. We will identify the columns in the output, put a heading on the table, fix the position of the word "Admit," and put in blank lines. The purpose is to make the output clear to the person who uses the program. This is necessary because, when you write professional programs, the user will normally be someone else.

PRINTING MESSAGES TOGETHER WITH VALUES

The output from this program is a little confusing. In Program 1, it was easy to see that the value of sqnumber was the square of number, but it is more difficult to see the correspondence between gpa and result. It would be clearer to have next to each number an indication of what it represents. For example, ***gpa = 0 result = 0.6*** is more readable than just 0 0.6. To print the messages "gpa =" and "result =" to the left of the numbers, send these literal strings to cout. Let's see how this works.

In Program 1, we used cout to print the values of number and sqnumber, with a single space between the values. In fact, we can combine numeric values with any sequence of characters surrounded by quotation marks. For example, we can print the following line which is a combination of messages:

```
number = 4       sqnumber = 16
```

To do this, we could send the messages "number = " and "sqnumber = " to cout.

```
cout << "number = " << number << " sqnumber = " << sqnumber;
```

The computer would make the same substitutions as before—putting in the values of number and sqnumber. Thus, it would print the following line:

```
number = 4       sqnumber = 16
```

STYLE WORKSHOP Note that we usually include blanks in messages to separate the words from the surrounding values. We insert as many blanks at the end (or the beginning) of the message as needed to make the final output easy to read.

Now let's apply this technique to Program 2. Our new print statement looks like this:

```
cout << "gpa = " << gpa << " result = " << result;
```

On the output screen, the messages inside the quotation marks appear exactly as they do in the C++ statement, combined with the values of gpa and result. The first line of output will look like this:

```
gpa = 0 result = 0.6
```

If we change the statement used in prog2a.cpp to what is shown above and leave everything else exactly the same, the output is shown in Figure 2-3.

This is certainly an improvement over just printing numerical values for gpa and result. We should always label our output so that the user knows what has been printed.

PRINTING A HEADING ON THE OUTPUT

Let's go further in improving the output. So that the user knows what this table is, we'll print a message at the very start, saying that this is a table of function values. For clarity, we want to leave a blank line before printing the first values of gpa and result. All it takes is this:

```
cout << "Table of Function Values" << endl << endl;
```

STYLE WORKSHOP Printing a heading on the output is good programming style and is necessary even if there is already a comment saying the same thing. The comment is associated with the listing of the program, while the heading is associated with the output.

We have seen that a print statement *after* the loop (e.g., **cout** << *"The table is finished"*) prints the message once, after the loop is completed. A print statement *inside* the loop (e.g., **cout** << *"gpa = ... "*) prints each time the loop is executed. Obviously, printing *before* a loop prints once before the loop begins. This is what we want, a message that appears as the first line of the output. Let's insert the new statement right after the declaration:

FIGURE 2-3   Output from Program 2 with messages

```
gpa = 0 result = 0.6 Admit
gpa = 0.5 result = -1.65789
gpa = 1 result = -7
gpa = 1.5 result = 154.5 Admit
gpa = 2 result = 12.6 Admit
gpa = 2.5 result = 8.56667 Admit
gpa = 3 result = 7.42105 Admit
gpa = 3.5 result = 7.04867 Admit
gpa = 4 result = 7 Admit
The table is finished
```

```
double gpa,result;

cout << "Table of Function Values" << endl;
for (gpa = 0.00; gpa <= 4.00; gpa = gpa + 0.50) {
    result = (gpa * gpa * gpa + 7 * gpa - 1) /
            (gpa * gpa - (gpa + 5) / 3);
    cout << "gpa = " << gpa << " result = " << result;
    if (result >= 0)
        cout << " Admit";
    cout << endl;
}
```

DOUBLE-SPACING AND ITS VARIANTS

Each <u>endl</u> makes the cursor go to the beginning of a new line. It is possible to double space by using two <u>endl</u>'s, triple space by using three <u>endl</u>'s, or stay on the same line after printing by omitting <u>endl</u>. An <u>endl</u> can be printed at the beginning of a line of output or at the end.

The line below will print the heading "Table of Function Values" and then go to the beginning of a new line twice, thus skipping a line. This has the effect of double spacing, and improves the appearance of the output.

```
cout << "Table of Function Values" << endl << endl;
```

We will now improve the line spacing before the trailer message. "The table is finished" prints right under the values above it; it would look nicer if we were to skip a line before printing it, as follows:

```
cout << endl << "The table is finished" << endl;
```

This revised statement causes the cursor to move to a new line before printing the message and again afterward.

COLUMN HEADINGS

Let's make one further modification. Instead of having messages and values printed across the page, we can make a neat table of <u>gpa</u> and <u>result</u> values and messages. In fact, we can make column headings for the table, eliminating the need for the messages "gpa = " and "result = ".

Column headings should be printed once—before the loop starts but after the message announcing the table. Here are statements to print the headings, including some blank lines to improve readability:

```
cout << "Table of Function Values" << endl << endl;
cout << "Grade Point Average   Value of Formula   Status"
        << endl << endl;
```

The extra blanks in the headings space the words across the page.

STYLE WORKSHOP It is much more informative to have column headings reading "Grade Point Average" and "Value of Formula" rather than "gpa" and "result." In fact, printing a heading that describes the variable is usually better than printing just the variable's name.

Now, inside the loop, we can print several lines of output with these statements:

```
cout << "         " << gpa << "                " << result;
if (result >= 0)
    cout << "          Admit";
cout << endl;
```

Note that we no longer print "gpa = " or "result = " each time through the loop. Instead, the numerical values should be aligned under the appropriate headings. We will also have, on some of these lines, the word "Admit" in the column headed "Status."

We have added a number of blanks in the statement which prints the values of <u>gpa</u> and <u>result</u> and the one which prints the message "Admit." This way the values will print neatly aligned under their headings.

PROGRAM 2 WITH PRINTING CHANGES

Let's take a look at the whole program with all the printing changes we have made: a title on the output, column headings, and neatly spaced columns.

🖥 PROGRAM LISTING

```
// Program prog2b.cpp:
//    creates a table to evaluate a formula based on values of
//    gpa in the range from gpa = 0.00 to 4.00 in units of 0.50
#include <iostream>
using namespace std;
int main()
{
     double gpa, result;

     cout << "Table of Function Values" << endl << endl;
     cout << "Grade Point Average   Value of Formula   Status"
          << endl << endl;
     for (gpa = 0.00; gpa <= 4.00; gpa = gpa + 0.50) {
          result = (gpa * gpa * gpa + 7 * gpa - 1) /
                    (gpa * gpa - (gpa + 5) / 3);
          cout << "          " << gpa << "                    "
               << result;
          if (result >= 0)
              cout << "              Admit";
          cout << endl;
     }
     cout << endl << "The table is finished" << endl;
     return 0;
}
```

OUTPUT FROM PROGRAM 2 SO FAR

Figure 2-4 shows the complete output from <u>prog2b.cpp</u> (the appearance is still odd, but we'll take care of that in the next version).

THE TAB CHARACTER

Now let's resolve the final problem in the appearance of the output. Because the values of <u>gpa</u> and <u>result</u> printed with different lengths, the remaining columns of values are not aligned. Inserting blanks in the literal string won't help, because the number of blanks needed will vary. However, C++ provides the **tab character**, '\t'. The tab character consists of two keystrokes, a backslash followed by a 't'. (See the paragraph on Escape Sequences in this section for more explanation.) Printing '\t' causes the cursor to move to the next tab position before printing. The tab character can stand alone or be part of

FIGURE 2-4   Output from Program 2 (Version <u>prog2b.cpp</u>)

```
Table of Function Values

Grade Point Average    Value of Formula    Status

          0             0.6               Admit
          0.5          -1.65789
          1            -7
          1.5           154.5                Admit
          2            12.6               Admit
          2.5           8.56667              Admit
          3            7.42105            Admit
          3.5           7.04867              Admit
          4            7                 Admit

The table is finished
```

a string. This feature is very useful for aligning output in columns. (A character in C++ is enclosed in single quotation marks; see Section 5 for more information on the **char** data type.)

Here's how we can use tabs in Program 2. Instead of printing long strings of blanks, use the tab character. Notice that the tab character can be printed independently or included in a literal string:

```
cout << gpa << '\t' << result;
cout << "\tAdmit";
```

In the final version of Program 2, we have used tabs to align the output. Sometimes we needed more than one tab to align the values under the headings. To see if you understand how tabs work, figure out what is printed by the following:

```
cout << "\tFirst\tSecond\tThird" << endl << "Fourth";
```

It prints

```
      First   Second   Third
Fourth
```

SELF-CHECK 2-5

1. What is the difference between the comment at the beginning of the program and the heading printed with the table? Who will see the comment? Who will see the heading?

2. What is the advantage of column headings over messages printed with the output values?

3. How can you go to a new line before printing a message?

COMPLETE PROGRAM 2 AND OUTPUT

Here is the final version of Program 2 with the formula and all the printing improvements.

PROGRAM LISTING

```
// Program prog2c.cpp:
//   creates a table to evaluate a formula based on values of
//   gpa in the range from gpa = 0.00 to 4.00 in units of 0.50
#include <iostream>
using namespace std;
```

```cpp
int main()
{
    double gpa, result;

    cout << "\t\tTable of Function Values" << endl << endl;
    cout << "Grade Point Average\tValue of Formula\tStatus"
         << endl << endl;

    for (gpa = 0.00; gpa <= 4.00; gpa = gpa + 0.50) {
        result = (gpa * gpa * gpa + 7 * gpa - 1) /
                     (gpa * gpa - (gpa + 5) / 3);
        cout << '\t' << gpa << "\t\t" << result;
        if (result >= 0)
            cout << "\t\t\tAdmit";
        cout << endl;
    }
    cout << endl << "The table is finished" << endl;
    return 0;
}
```

Figure 2-5 shows the output from prog2c.cpp. Notice how the output is now neatly aligned in columns.

ESCAPE SEQUENCES

The computer uses the \ symbol to distinguish between the 't' that is the tab character and the 't' that might occur anywhere in the string. The symbol \ is called the **escape character** and tells the computer to treat the next character as special. (We call a sequence like \t an **escape sequence**.) We can use the escape character to tell the computer to print characters which otherwise would be unprintable, like %, ", and \ itself. To print any of these special formatting characters, simply precede it with a backslash. Here is an example:

```cpp
cout << "\% \\ \" " << endl;
```

The cursor goes to a new line after the program prints the following:

```
% \ "
```

FIGURE 2-5 Output from Program 2 (Version prog2c.cpp)

```
                Table of Function Values

   Grade Point Average      Value of Formula       Status

           0                0.6                  Admit
           0.5              -1.65789
           1                -7
           1.5              154.5                Admit
           2                12.6                 Admit
           2.5              8.56667              Admit
           3                7.42105              Admit
           3.5              7.04867              Admit
           4                7                    Admit
   The table is finished
```

TABLE 2-3   Common Escape Sequences in C++

\n	the newline character (line feed)
\t	the tab character
\b	the backspace character
\"	double quote
\\	backslash
\%	the percent sign
\0	null character
\a	BEL (makes an audible signal)
\f	formfeed (new page on printer)
\r	carriage return character

For compatibility with the C language, C++ also has the **newline character**, represented by the escape sequence *n*. It can be printed directly or used as part of a literal string and performs the same function as <u>endl</u>.

Table 2-3 shows the escape sequences commonly used in C++.

Here is an example using some of the escape sequences:

```
cout << "\n\t\"Table of Function Values\"";
```

This prints the following one tab position in on a new line:

```
"Table of Function Values"
```

SELF-CHECK 2-6

1.   What is an escape sequence?
2.   What symbol introduces an escape sequence?
3.   What escape sequence is used to control spacing in Program 2?

SECTION 4   RELATIONAL OPERATORS, COMPOUND ASSIGNMENT OPERATORS

In a condition, values are compared using relational operators. In this section, we will introduce the remaining relational operators and discuss their precedence. In addition, we will introduce several new arithmetic operators.

RELATIONAL OPERATORS

We used an **if** statement in Program 2 to determine whether to print the word "Admit." In that case, we wanted to print the message under these circumstances:

```
if (result >= 0) ···
```

TABLE 2-4 The Relational Operators

Symbol	Meaning	Example
<	less than	a < b
>	greater than	num > 4
<=	less than or equal to	x + 1 <= 12
>=	greater than or equal to	result * 3 >= 3.5 − w
==	equal to	sqnumber == 16
!=	not equal to	answer != 7

The operator >= means "greater than or equal to." To print the message if <u>result</u> is "less than or equal to 0," we would use the operator <=.

```
if (result <= 0) ...
```

A number of operators can be used to represent the relationship between values; they are called **relational operators**. Table 2-4 shows the relational operators available in C++.

Two of these may surprise you. First, the operator to test equality, called the **logical equals** operator, is ==. This is not the same as the = used in mathematics to compare two values. C++ uses the = symbol for assignment, but it uses == for comparison.

Second, the != operator is also different from the symbol used in mathematics (≠). In C++, you can think of ! as standing for "not," so != is "not equal."

These relational operators can be used wherever your program requires a condition. Obviously, an **if** statement uses a condition, and there is another one in Program 2 (and also in Program 1). To find them, let's look again at the **for** loop headers:

```
for (number = 4; number <= 9; number++)          (from Example 1-11)
for (number = 9; number >= 4; number-)           (from Example 1-12)
for (gpa = 0.0; gpa <= 4.0; gpa = gpa + 0.50)     (from Program 2)
```

Right in the middle of each **for** loop header is a condition—the one that determines whether or not we are finished executing the loop. Although conditions using <= or < are probably the most common in **for** loops, others are also possible. Some are explored in the exercises.

INCREMENT AND DECREMENT OPERATORS

These **for** loop headers give us the perfect opportunity to explore other operators in C++. Let's look at the third part of the header, the increment. Chapter 1 introduced the increment operator ++, used in <u>number</u>++ to increase the value of <u>number</u> by 1. An expression like <u>number</u>++ can be used in the header of a **for** loop or as a separate statement. In Chapter 1, you also saw the decrement operator, −−, used in the second **for** loop above to decrement <u>number</u>. The ++ and −− are unary operators, with the same precedence as unary minus and unary plus and the same associativity, right to left. Because their use can be complex, we will employ these operators for now only in simple increment and decrement statements and **for** loop headers.

CAUTION It is not possible to increment or decrement an expression or a constant. Both of the following examples are illegal in C++:

```
(x + y)++;                              // illegal
4--;                                    // illegal
```

Only a variable can be incremented or decremented.

COMPOUND ASSIGNMENT OPERATORS: +=, –=, *=, /=, %=

The loop header from Program 2 does not use ++; we cannot increment gpa with the ++ operator because ++ always increments by 1, and we need to increase gpa by 0.50. However, using another operator, we can replace *gpa = gpa + 0.50* with the following:

```
gpa += 0.50;
```

The += is a **compound assignment operator** which combines addition and assignment. The operator says to take the value of the variable to its left and add to it the value to the right. This is exactly the same as *gpa = gpa + 0.50*. The **for** loop header for Program 2 could be rewritten this way:

```
for (gpa = 0.0; gpa <= 4.0; gpa += 0.50)
```

STYLE WORKSHOP Since we can also use the += operator to increment by 1, we have four equivalent statements:

```
number = number + 1;          is equivalent to
number += 1;                  is equivalent to
number++;          .          is equivalent to
++number;
```

Experienced C++ programmers usually use number++ (except when other factors require ++number).

Let's look at a few more examples using the += operator.

EXAMPLE 2-7 We can write a **for** loop to print all the numbers between 10 and 500 which are divisible by 10.

```
for (number = 10; number <= 500; number += 10)
    cout << number << endl;
```

EXAMPLE 2-8 Here is a loop to add 6 to each value of result computed by the formula in Program 2.

```
for (gpa = 0.0; gpa <= 4.0; gpa += 0.50) {
    result = formula;
    result += 6;
    ...
}
```

It should be noted that += is not the only compound assignment operator in C++. There are similar operators for subtraction (–=), multiplication (*=), division (/=), and remainder (%=). Addition and subtraction are by far the most common. All of these compound operators have the same precedence as the assignment operator; this precedence is lower than that of any arithmetic or relational operator. All assignment operators associate right to left.

From here on, we will use the ++, –, +=, and –= operators quite regularly since they are standard in C++.

MORE ON THE C++ ARITHMETIC PRECEDENCE RULES

Table 2-5 expands Table 2-2 by summarizing the arithmetic precedence rules for all the operators seen so far.

TABLE 2-5   Precedence of Arithmetic, Assignment, and Relational Operators

		Associativity
highest precedence (done first)	– (unary) + (unary) ++ – –	right to left
	* / %	left to right
	+ –	left to right
	< <= > >=	left to right
	== !=	left to right
lowest precedence (done last)	= += –= *= /= %=	right to left

SELF-CHECK 2-7

1. What relational operator represents each of the following?

    a. greater than   b. not equal to

    c. less than   d. greater than or equal to

2. What is wrong with this **if** statement? (*Note*: This statement will *not* generate an error message.)

    ```
    if (x = 4)
        cout << x;
    ```

3. Write each of the following using a compound operator if possible:

    a. `sum = sum + num;`   b. `count = count + 1;`

    c. `result = result % 4;`   d. `numleft = numleft - 1;`

    e. `avg = num / count;`   f. `result = result * 2;`

SECTION 5 **DATA TYPES float, double, AND char; REAL AND MIXED-MODE ARITHMETIC; STANDARD LIBRARY OF FUNCTIONS**

DATA TYPES float AND double, AND THE RANGE OF VALUES OF FLOATING POINT NUMBERS

In C++, **double** is the primary data type for real numbers. This data type permits decimal places; in addition, it can represent numbers that are extremely large or small. C++ relies on the individual compiler and its implementation on a specific machine to determine the limits of data types. The range of numbers that can be represented by data type **int** is about five billion; type **long int** (usually abbreviated as **long**) has an even larger range of integers.

A variable with data type **double** can store a much wider range of values and includes numbers with many decimal places. The exact range varies from compiler to compiler, but almost all allow numbers like positive or negative values ranging from 1.0×10^{-30} to 1.0×10^{30}, which are infinitesimal and enormous, respectively. Exercise 13 asks you to determine the range of data types **int** and **double** on your own system.

STYLE WORKSHOP C++ has another data type, **float**, which can also hold floating point numbers but in a smaller range. Although our numbers fit comfortably into variables of type **float**, we always use the larger type **double** as is commonly done in C++ for efficiency.

ARITHMETIC USING REAL NUMBERS

Arithmetic using real numbers is similar to integer arithmetic, except for the operation of division. Arithmetic with values of type **double** uses the same operators as integer arithmetic: +, −, *, and /. However, since the / operator yields a result with decimal places, the % operator is not necessary and does not make sense for real numbers. Here are some examples:

◆ If a is 4.5, a + 10 is 14.5

◆ If a is 10, then a/4.0 is 2.5 (because 4.0 is a real number)

◆ If a is 4, then 10.0/a is 2.5

◆ If dist is 3.6 and hours is 2.4, then dist/hours is 1.5.

MIXED MODE ARITHMETIC

In the first three examples above, the operands had different types: one was an integer and one a real number. This is called mixed-mode arithmetic. In mixed-mode arithmetic, the more restrictive type is "promoted" to the less restrictive type in order to perform the operation. Type **int** (most restrictive, because it can't hold decimal values) is thus promoted to **float** or **double** to perform the operation. This way it is possible to add 10 and 4.5, yielding 14.5.

We can assign an integer value to a variable with type **double** or type **float** without any problem. For example, if num has type **double**, we can write **num = 16,** assigning the integer 16 to a variable with data type **double**. It is also legal to assign a real number to a variable of type **int**, but any decimal portion is lost. Example 2-9 shows what happens.

EXAMPLE 2-9   Suppose that we assign real number num to answer, an integer variable:

```
double num;
int answer;

num = 1.6;
answer = num;
cout << "num is " << num << " and answer is " << answer << endl;
```

This prints the following:

```
num is 1.6 and answer is 1
```

In C++, if either (or both) operand in a division is a real number (e.g., 10.6/2.3, 10.6/2, or even 10/2.0), the quotient will have decimal places.

What happens to the decimal places after the division, however, is dependent on how the result is used. If the result is printed directly, using cout, the decimal places will print:

```
cout << 10/4.0;   will print 2.5
```

If the result of the division is assigned to a variable, the type of the destination variable determines what happens to the decimal places. Example 2-10 illustrates the difference.

EXAMPLE 2-10

```
int     result, num;
double fract, val;

num = 10;
val = 4.0;

fract = num / val;
result = num / val;
```

In this example, <u>fract</u> can hold the decimal places resulting from the division and will get the value 2.5; <u>result</u> cannot hold the fractional part of the number, and it will be assigned the value 2.

SELF-CHECK 2-8

1. What two data types in C++ represent real numbers? Which one is used in this text?
2. What is mixed-mode arithmetic?
3. When will the result of a division yield decimal places?

STANDARD LIBRARY OF FUNCTIONS (cmath.h)

In addition to the five standard arithmetic operations (+, −, *, /, and %), C++ offers simple functions to perform other mathematical operations. These functions save us a lot of calculation; instead, the computer does most of the work. For example, sometimes we need the square root of a number. C++ has a function called <u>sqrt( )</u> that automatically finds the square root.

EXAMPLE 2-11

What value is given to the variable <u>root</u>?

```
double w, root;

w = 12;
root = sqrt(w + 7);
```

The expression <u>sqrt(w + 7)</u> finds the square root of <u>w + 7</u>. Since <u>w</u> has the value 12, the <u>sqrt( )</u> function finds the square root of 19 (which is 4.36) and assigns it to <u>root</u>.

The function <u>sqrt( )</u> is called a **library function** because its instructions are stored in a library. (*Note*: In C++, when referring to the name of a function, it is customary to use parentheses after the name; this distinguishes the name of a function from other types of identifiers.) The collection of these functions is called the **standard library of functions** or the C++ standard library.

The expression which invokes a function from the standard library is known as the **call to the function** or a **function call**. Typically, the function call specifies two things: the name of the function and the value or values on which the function should operate, as shown in Figure 2-6.

FIGURE 2-6   A call to a library function

```
root = sqrt(w+7);
         ↗     ↖
    function  value on which
    name      sqrt() should operate
```

A call to a library function can be placed on the right-hand side of an assignment statement, in a cout expression, or anywhere that an expression can occur. For example, here are some C++ statements that use library functions (we will explain ceil( ) and floor( ) in a moment):

```
a = sqrt(b);
cout << ceil(realnum);
z = x + floor(w);
```

In addition to sqrt( ), there are many other library functions. A useful one is abs( ). The expression abs(x) finds the absolute value of the integer x, which in mathematics is written |x|. A call to abs( ) always returns a positive or 0 answer.

EXAMPLE 2-12

```
abs(0)     = 0
abs(4)     = 4
abs(-4)    = 4
abs(-4.34)  result depends on system: it may not work, or it may
               yield 4 or 4.34 (see below)
```

For numbers with type **float** or **double**, we use the corresponding function, fabs( ), to compute the absolute value of a floating point number:

```
fabs(-4.34) = 4.34
```

However, in some C++ compilers, abs( ) works in exactly the same way as fabs( ). The best advice we can give is that you should be careful and check exactly what your compiler does if abs( ) is used with a floating point value.

```
fabs(-4.34) = 4.34
```

The library contains trigonometric functions such as sin( ), cos( ), and tan( ) to find the sine, cosine, and tangent of an angle that is measured in radians, and floor( ) and ceil( ), which convert a **float** or **double** value to the next lower or higher integer. (The floor( ) function is usually not necessary in simple assignment statements since assigning a value of type **double** to an integer automatically cuts off the decimal places.)

EXAMPLE 2-13

```
int bot,top;

bot = floor(4.78);          // same as bot = 4.78
top = ceil(9.3);
```

The variable bot gets the value 4; the variable top gets the value 10.

Another useful numeric task, related to floor( ) and ceil( ), is rounding. C++ does not have a library function to round a number to the closest integer; however, the simple addition technique illustrated in Example 2-14 will do the trick.

EXAMPLE 2-14

To round a real number to the closest integer, you can write this:

```
int intnum;
double realnum;

. . .

intnum = realnum + .5;
```

If the fractional part of <u>realnum</u> is less than .5, then adding .5 to it does not affect the integer part. For example, if <u>realnum</u> is 3.4, adding .5 gives 3.9; the 3 remains the same. Assigning the result to an integer truncates the fractional part so that <u>intnum</u> gets the value 3. If, on the other hand, the fractional part of <u>realnum</u> is greater than or equal to .5, adding .5 to it raises the number to the next integer. For example, if <u>realnum</u> is 3.6, adding .5 produces 4.1, and the assignment gives <u>intnum</u> the truncated value 4.

To use any of the library functions which work with floating point numbers [essentially all but <u>abs( )</u> and an integer version of <u>sqrt( )</u>], there has to be another line at the beginning of your program. Notice that each <u>#include</u> directive must appear on its own line; it cannot be combined with anything else. This new line tells the compiler to include a file with information about the math library functions. If you try to use these functions without including this line, you will either get an error message or a very strange result (e.g., your program may say that <u>sqrt(7)</u> is a negative number!).

```
#include <iostream>
#include <cmath>
using namespace std;
int main()
...
```

The C++ library contains functions for more than mathematical tasks, as we will see in the later chapters. In Chapter 5, we will learn how to write our own functions.

DATA TYPE char

C++ has another simple data type. It is **char**, which stands for character. A variable of this data type can hold any one character (e.g., 'a' or ' ' or '?'). A character is essentially anything that can be typed—a number, letter, space, period, or symbol. In addition, special characters like the tab character '\t' (used earlier in this chapter) and newline character '\n' (which can be used in place of <u>endl</u>) are values of type **char**. The Appendix contains a list of all the printable characters that can be used in C++. Note that values of type **char** are enclosed in single quotation marks, while literal strings are enclosed in double quotation marks. Example 2-15 shows the declaration for a variable <u>letter</u> of type **char** and some statements using **char** variables and values.

EXAMPLE 2-15

```
char letter;

letter = 'a';
if (letter != 'b')
    cout << "letter has the value " << letter << '\n';
```

Since <u>letter</u> is not equal to 'b', this example prints the following:

```
letter has the value a
```

Data type **char** is actually a subset of data type **int**. Each **char** value has a number associated with it, called its **ASCII value**; the ASCII values for characters range from 0 to 255. We could change the declaration in Example 2-15 to the following without altering the code:

```
int letter;
```

For a while, we will use characters only as part of strings to be printed, since a variable of type **char** by itself is not very useful (it can hold only one character).

SELF-CHECK 2-9

1. What does the sqrt( ) function do?
2. What is the purpose of the line **#include <cmath>**?
3. What data type would you use to hold each of the following?
   a. the distance from the sun to the earth   b. the value of pi
   c. a letter grade (A, C, etc.)   d. your IQ score

SECTION 6   ## ENRICHMENT: DEBUGGING

This section will introduce an important problem-solving technique, called **debugging**. An error in a program is often called a "bug." Debugging is the process of finding and removing errors from a program without creating new ones. Since a program rarely works perfectly the first time it is run, debugging is one of the most important programming skills. The various types of errors that a program might have include compilation, execution, and logic errors.

COMPILATION ERRORS

A **compilation error** is one caught by the compiler while it is translating your program into machine language before running it. Compilation errors caused by mistakes in the syntax or form of a statement are called **syntax errors**. These errors are caught in the first phase of compilation. Here are some examples of syntax errors with the particular mistake identified in parentheses:

```
fir(i = 1; i < 5; i++)     (misspelled keyword)
a = (b + 1/3;              (missing right parenthesis)
x + 3 = 5;                 (expression on the left of an assignment statement)
x = 5                      (missing semicolon)
```

Errors discovered in the second phase of compilation are called **linker errors**. This phase is handled by the linker, the program that connects your program with the standard libraries. If you use a library function, the compiler looks for it in the standard library during the link phase of compilation. If it doesn't find the function (either it doesn't exist or you have misspelled its name), the linker gives you an error message. Here is an example of a linker error:

```
cuot << num;               (The linker tries to find a declaration for cuot,
                              which doesn't exist; cout is misspelled.)
```

Figure 2-7 shows a program with several errors. Some lines are numbered so that we can refer to specific errors as we discuss the kinds of messages they generate.

If your program has a compilation error, the compiler will indicate the type. The compiler finds several different types of compilation errors in the program shown in Figure 2-7:

1. a misspelled identifier (cut instead of cout)
2. a missing left parenthesis before the first gpa
3. an identifier in the wrong case (GPA instead of gpa)
4. a missing semicolon at the end

Sometimes the compiler cannot figure out what the programmer intended. For example, if a parenthesis is missing in an expression, the compiler doesn't know where it should go. The compiler might misinterpret the missing opening parenthesis in the formula above as a missing semicolon, but

FIGURE 2-7   A sample program (prob2err.cpp) with compilation errors

```
      // Program prog2err.cpp:
      //   creates a table to evaluate a formula based on values of
      //   gpa in the range from gpa = 0.00 to 4.00 in units of 0.50
      #include <iostream>
      using namespace std;
      int main()
      {
            double gpa,result;

1.          cut << "Table of Function Values" << endl << endl;
            cout << "Grade Point Average   Value of Formula   Status"
                  << endl << endl;

            for (gpa = 0.00; gpa <= 4.00; gpa = gpa + 0.50) {
2.                result = gpa * gpa * gpa + 7 * gpa - 1) /
                              (gpa * gpa - (gpa + 5) / 3);
3.                cout << '\t' << GPA << "\t" << result;

                  if (result >= 0)
                        cout << "\tAdmit";
4.                cout << endl
            }
            cout << endl << "The table is finished" << endl;
            return 0;
      }
```

making the compiler's suggested correction would result in a different error. Correcting errors without careful thought can cause serious problems in the program. Be sure to determine what is really wrong before you fix an error and rerun the program.

The compiler may also generate warnings, which are normally less serious than errors. Some (but not all) warnings can be ignored, but this is not a good habit to get into.

After reading the error messages, correct the mistakes, save, and recompile the program. When all errors have been removed, your program should compile correctly.

EXECUTION ERRORS

The next kind of error, an **execution error**, is not caught by the compiler. Instead, it is detected once the program is running, which is why it is sometimes called a **run-time error**. As an example, suppose that your program attempts to divide by a variable whose value is zero. The compiler will not object to this expression, but the computer will be unable to execute it. Your program will normally stop at the error and display an error message.

While compilation errors are often only typing mistakes, execution errors can be much more serious and require careful thought to correct. If the error is very serious, the machine may "hang" completely; you won't get an error message, nor will you be able to get out of C++ or into the editor—you may not be able to do anything but shut off the machine. If this happens, don't panic; there are solutions. To avoid disaster, follow the rule we stated in Chapter 1:

ALWAYS SAVE YOUR PROGRAM BEFORE RUNNING IT.

LOGIC ERRORS

The last type of error, a **logic error**, is the hardest to catch. Each individual statement in a program may be valid in C++ and thus acceptable to the compiler. The program may run without causing any execution errors, but the answers may be wrong. This type of error is called a logic error. A logic error may be something simple—for example, initializing a variable to 1 instead of 0, or multiplying by 2 instead of 3, or using an incorrect formula—but it can also be a basic mistake in the logic of the program. Such a mistake is hard to find and correct, since it won't generate an error message. The programmer has to catch logic errors by critically examining the output and testing the program on all possible sets of data.

Be aware, too, that many statements that look like compilation errors are actually valid C++ statements. For example, the statement shown below is not a compilation error, although someone probably used the wrong symbol for assignment:

```
x == x + 3;
```

Unfortunately, this is a valid statement in C++, even though it will not assign a value to x.

HOW TO DEBUG A PROGRAM

To debug a program, first check for compilation or execution errors, perhaps compounded by inappropriate "corrections" by the compiler. Second, verify that the program you actually ran matches what you want it to be; that is, make sure that you have not made any typing errors.

If these two steps do not produce any explanations for the problem, then trace the program step by step once again (you should have done that first before you ran it). As we did in Chapter 1 (see Figures 1-1 and 1-2), have a box or position for each variable and be careful to use the current value of that variable at all times. Make sure that you go step by step; do not skip or add anything. In almost all cases, a detailed trace will locate the problem.

Finally, the best way to eliminate a bug is not to include it in the first place. Theoretically, at least, if a program is written correctly the first time, there is no need to debug it. What this means is that you should be extremely careful in planning your original solution to the problem, writing the program, and hand simulating it before you run it. If this is done, and the rules for good style are followed, most mistakes will be caught before they do any damage.

To be honest, we must admit that debugging is really an art, not a science. Most programmers develop their own approach to it, just as they develop their own programming style. Later on, we will suggest some things to make debugging easier. (Exercise 24 gives you practice in finding errors of all three types.)

SELF-CHECK 2-10

1. What is a compilation error? Give three examples.
2. What is an execution error? Give an example.
3. What is a bug? What is debugging?

SUMMARY

EVALUATING AN EXPRESSION

1. A C++ program can evaluate a complicated mathematical expression, as shown in the sample problem in the text. The programmer does not have to be able to evaluate the expression by hand but only express it in C++.

DATA TYPES: **float**, **double**, AND **char**

2. A variable declared to have data type **double** or **float** can store numbers with decimal places, or more generally, numbers in scientific notation. The exact range depends on the compiler, but it almost surely can hold positive or negative values from 1×10^{-30} to 1×10^{30}.

3. A variable declared to have data type **double** or **float** can be assigned a value in any format: an integer value, a real number in decimal format (e.g., 1., .1, or 0.1), or a value in scientific notation. A real number can be expressed using either an exponent or a decimal point or both (e.g., 314e-2 or 3.14 or 31.4e-1).

4. A variable with data type **double** or **float** is printed with as many decimal places as are needed to represent the value of the number, although it is also possible to modify the number of decimal places.

5. A variable with type **char** can hold a single character, like 'a' or '*'. It is possible to use variables and values of type **char** in conditions and assignment statements.

CONDITIONAL OR **if** STATEMENTS

6. A conditional or **if** statement makes a decision. The general form of a conditional statement (where *cond* is a condition that evaluates to true or false and *stmt-1* is any C++ statement) is

```
if (cond)
    stmt-1;
```

If *cond* is true, then *stmt-1* is executed. If *cond* is false, then *stmt-1* is skipped.

7. In a condition, two expressions can be compared using a relational operator, like <, >, <=, >=, ==, or !=. To test for equality in a condition, use the logical equals operator (==), not the assignment symbol (=). To test for inequality, use !=.

SENDING MESSAGES AND VALUES TO cout

8. Messages and values can be combined in the output string sent to cout. In addition, endl and characters like '\t' (tab character) and '\n' (newline character) can be printed to shape the appearance of the output.

9. Here is an example:

```
int first;
double second;
...
cout << "first number = " << first
    << " and second number = " << second << endl;
```

When this is executed, the value of first and the value of second will be printed, together with messages. After the line of output is printed, the cursor goes to a new line. For example, if first has the value 12 and second has the value 86.35, the statement prints the following:

```
first number = 12 and second number = 86.35
```

10. A blank line is produced in the output by using **cout << endl** (or *cout* << '*\n'*). Double or triple spacing, indenting, and printing in columns are done by judicious placement of endl and the tab character.

11. The \ character can be used to print tabs, newlines, or control characters like %, ", and \; simply place the \ character immediately in front of the control character to be printed. The combined symbol (e.g., \t) is called an escape sequence.

COMPOUND ASSIGNMENT OPERATORS

12. C++ has compound assignment operators, which do arithmetic and assignment in one operation. These operators are +=, −=, *=, /=, and %=. For example, to add 3 to y and store the result in y, simply say this:

```
y += 3;
```

The compound addition and subtraction operators are more commonly used than the others.

PRECEDENCE OF OPERATIONS

13. The C++ arithmetic precedence rules determine the order in which arithmetic operations are performed in an expression. Operations with higher precedence or priority are done before those with lower precedence.

14. Unary minus, ++, and −− have the highest precedence, followed by multiplication and the two division operations (/ and %), followed by addition and subtraction. The assignment operators have lowest precedence. Parentheses can override these rules.

15. When operators of equal precedence occur next to each other in the same expression, the operation to be performed first is determined by associativity. Arithmetic operators (*, /, %, +, and −) associate left to right. The unary operators (−, +, ++, and −−) and the assignment operators (=, +=, −=, *=, /=, and %=) associate right to left. Parentheses can override these rules.

FUNCTIONS FROM THE STANDARD LIBRARY

16. C++ has a number of standard or library functions to compute many mathematical functions. These include sqrt( ) for square root, abs( ) for absolute value, and fabs( ) for floating point absolute value. In addition, there are trigonometric functions, like sin( ), cos( ), and tan( ), among others. Most mathematical functions cannot be used without adding the line **#include <cmath>** at the beginning of the program.

17. The expression that invokes a standard function is known as the call to the function. The call specifies the name of the function as well as the value(s) on which the function should operate.

DEBUGGING

18. A mistake in a program is called a bug. The process of eliminating mistakes so that a program runs correctly is called debugging. Debugging is one of the most important skills for a programmer because very few programs work perfectly the first time they run.

19. A compilation error is one that is caught by the compiler before a program runs. Many compilation errors are simple typing mistakes—misspelling a keyword or omitting required punctuation. The programmer must always correct a compilation error before rerunning the program.

20. Some compilation errors show up as linker errors. For example, a linker error occurs if you misspell the name of a library function like sqrt( ). Some C++ compilers also produce warnings, which are not as serious as errors. Some warnings can be ignored.

21. An execution error is caught not during compilation but while the program is running. For example, an attempt to divide by 0 causes an execution error.

22. A logic error is a mistake that is not caught during either compilation or execution but that causes wrong answers. A logic error may be something simple, such as a typing mistake that creates a valid statement but yields incorrect answers. It can also be caused by an error in the basic logic of a program.

EXERCISES

TRACING EXERCISES

1. Trace each of the following C++ programs step by step. Show exactly what each program prints.

   a.
   ```cpp
   #include <iostream>
   using namespace std;
   int main()
   {
       int p,b;

       for (b = 2; b <= 6; b++) {
           p = 2 * b + 3;
           cout << b << " " << p << endl;
       }
       return 0;
   }
   ```

   b.
   ```cpp
   #include <iostream>
   using namespace std;
   int main()
   {
       int x,y;

       for (x = 15, y = 4; x >= 0; x -= y, y += 3)
           cout << x << " " << y << endl;
       return 0;
   }
   ```

   c.
   ```cpp
   #include <iostream>
   using namespace std;
   int main()
   {
       int s,t;

       t = 0;
       for (s = 8; s >= 4; s -= 3) {
           if (s > t)
               t += 3;
           if (s <= t)
               s += 2;
           cout << s << " " << t << endl;
       }
       return 0;
   }
   ```

d.
```cpp
#include <iostream>
#include <cmath>
using namespace std;
int main()
{
      int x,y,z;

      x = -3;
      y = 1;
      z = 2;
      if (abs(x + z) > abs(y))
           cout << " no ";
      if (abs(x) + abs(z) > abs(y))
           cout << " no ";
      cout << " maybe ";
      return 0;
}
```

e.
```cpp
#include <iostream>
#include <cmath>
using namespace std;
int main()
{
      double b;
      int a;

      cout << "number\tsquare root" << endl;
      for (a = 0; a <= 6; a++) {
           b = sqrt(a);
           cout << a << '\t' << b << endl;
      }
      return 0;
}
```

f.
```cpp
#include <iostream>
using namespace std;
int main()
{
      int c;
      double d;

      cout << "number\treciprocal\tcheck" << endl;
      for (c = 1; c <= 8; c++) {
           d = 1.0 / c;
           cout << c << '\t' << d << '\t' << c*d << endl;
      }
      return 0;
}
```

g.
```cpp
#include <iostream>
using namespace std;
 int main()
  {
      double n,v;
```

```
        for (n = .4; n < 3.6; n += 1.2) {
            v = n * .5 + 1.7;
            cout << n << " " << v << endl;
        }
        return 0;
    }
```

h. ```
   #include <iostream>
   using namespace std;
   int main()
   {
       double x,y;

       for (x = 17.5; x >= .5; x -= 4.5)
           cout << x << " " << y << endl;
       return 0;

   }
   ```

2. For each of the following series of C++ statements, try to describe in words what is accomplished (e.g., the larger of x and y is put into max and then max is printed; or x is multiplied over and over by 2 until it is more than 30, etc.). For parts (a)–(c), (f), and (g), assume that x and y have been given certain values. All variables have data type **int**.

   a. ```
      if (x > y)
          max = x;
      if (x <= y)
          max = y;
      cout << max;
      ```

   b. ```
      if (x > y)
          ans = x;
      if (x < y)
          ans = y;
      if (x == y)
          ans = 1;
      ```

   c. ```
      hold = 5;
      if (x == y)
          hold = x;
      if (x < y)
          hold = y;
      ```

   d. ```
      for (x = 1; x < 100; x *= 2)
          if (x < 50)
              x *= 2;
      ```

   e. ```
      for (x = 0; x < 15; x += 4)
          if (x == 8)
              cout << x;
      ```

   f. ```
      for (x = 0; x < 15;) {
          x = x + y;
          if (x < y)
              x = y;

      }
      ```

   g. ```
      if (x == y)
          cout << x;
      if (x != y)
          cout << y;
      ```

   h. ```
      for (x = 0; x <= 6; x++) {
          y = x + 4;
          if (y == 10)
              cout << "done";

      }
      ```

3. For each of the following C++ statements, show the exact order in which the operations are performed. Assume that all variables have data type **double**, and these are the initial values: a = 5, b = 6, c = 3, d = 2, and e = 2. Where necessary, use the results of previous statements to provide values for the variables.
      ```

```
a. f = -a + b * c / 3 * d + e;        b. g = -a + b * c / (3 * d) + e;
c. h = 4 * (a - 1) * (c / (b * d));   d. i = 4 * a - 2 * c / b * d;
e. p = -a - b + c * d;                f. b = -(a - b + c) * d;
g. r= -b - p + 5;                     h. s = 2 * b / c + 3;
i. t = 2 * (b / c) + 3;               j. u = (2 * b) / c + 3;
k. v = 2 * b / (c + 3);               l. w = b * (d + 2) / c;
m. x = 8 * s - t;                     n. y = 100 * v + 10 * w - u;
```

4. a. Here is the original C++ translation of the formula used in Problem 2:

```
result = gpa * gpa * gpa + 7 * gpa - 1 / gpa * gpa - gpa + 5 / 3;
```

Show step by step the order of operations that would be followed to evaluate the formula as written. Is this a correct C++ translation of the mathematical formula for Problem 2?

b. Here is the final C++ translation of the formula:

```
result = (gpa * gpa * gpa + 7 * gpa - 1) / (gpa * gpa - (gpa + 5) / 3);
```

Show the order of operations step by step. Is this a correct C++ translation?

MISCELLANEOUS EXERCISES

5. What is the purpose of a trailer message?

6. Which operation has higher precedence, addition or multiplication? What about addition or sub-
    traction? Multiplication or division?

7. In what order will the operations in each of the following expressions be evaluated? What is the
    value of each expression if $p = 4$, $q = 7$, $r = 3$, and $s = 5$?

```
a. p - (q + r) - s        b. q % p - r + 5
c. p - q + r * s          d. q % (p - r) + 5
e. p + q + r + s          f. p + q * r - s
g. p - q + r - s          h. q % p - r + 5
i. p * q + r * s          j. s / r + q / p
```

8. Which is a correct C++ translation of the right-hand side of the following equation? If more than
    one is correct, which is preferred?

$$y = \frac{(p + q) \times r - s}{p + q}$$

```
a. (p + q) * r - s / p + q          b. ((p + q) * (r - s)) / (p + q)
c. ((p + q * r) - s)) / (p + q)     d. (p + q * r - s) / (p + q)
e. ((p + q) * r - s) / (p + q)      f. (((p + q) * r) - s) / (p + q)
```

9. Translate each of these mathematical formulas into C++. Try to use parentheses only when necessary.

a. $x = \dfrac{-b + \sqrt{b^2 - 4ac}}{2a}$ b. $y = \dfrac{1 - x}{2 - x}$

c. $z = x^2 + 3y$ d. $p = |b - r| - |r + b|$

e. $e = mc^2$ f. $c = 2t^3 / 8x$

g. The area, <u>a</u>, of a trapezoid is one half the height, <u>h</u>, times the sum of the bases, <u>b1</u> and <u>b2</u>.

h. <u>k</u> is the sine of angle <u>a</u> plus the cosine of angle <u>b</u> plus the tangent of angle c.

10. Show several formats combining variables, <u>endl</u>, and tabs that will produce the output in each part. Assume that all numbers are printed from variables specified in the following declaration, where <u>a</u> = 10, <u>b</u> = 20, c = 30, and <u>d</u> = 40:

    ```
    int a,b,c,d;
    ```

    a. 10 20 30 40   b. 10 20   c. 10 20
                               30 40   (blank line)
                                                       30
                                                       40

    d. 10   e. 10   20   30   (one tab position apart)
       20   40
       30
       40

11. Show what is printed by each of the following:

    a. `cout << "The cat" << endl << "stepped over" << endl`
           `<< "the jam closet" << endl;`
    b. `cout << endl << endl << "TADA" << endl << endl;`
    c. `cout << "\"\%\n";`
    d. `num = 5;`
       `cout << num << "\%\n";`
    e. `cout << "\"Big deal,\" she said." << endl;`
    f. `x = 3;`
       `y = 4;`
       `cout << x << '\t' << y << endl;`

12. Each of the following program segments is preceded by a comment that describes what we would like to accomplish. Try to use these data values to see if the segment works in all cases. If it does not work, explain exactly what happens and show how to amend it so that it does always work.

    a. `// set z to the square root of w`

       `int w;`
       `double z;`

       `z = 0.5 * w;`   (try <u>w</u> = 4, <u>w</u> = 8)

    b. `// if x is negative, print the word negative`
       `// otherwise print non-negative`
       `int x;`

       `if (x < 0)`
           `cout << "negative";`
       `if (x > 0)`
           `cout << "non-negative";`   (try <u>x</u> = −2, <u>x</u> = 0, <u>x</u> = 5)

    c. `// add 4 to x if x is negative; otherwise add 2`
       `int x;`
       `if (x < 0)`

```
        x = x + 4;
    if (x >= 0)
        x = x + 2;                          (try x = –6, x = –2, x = 0, x = 3)
```

d. `// if x is larger than 12, print x; otherwise print 12`

```
    int x,ans;

    ans = 12;
    if (x > 12)
        ans = x;
    cout << ans;                            (try x = 5, x = 12, x = 20)
```

e. `// find the smallest integer whose`
`// square is greater than y`

```
    int number,test,y;

    test = 0;
    for (number = 1; test <= y; number++)
        test = number * number;
    cout << number - 1 << " is the smallest" << endl;
                                            (try y = 4, y = 5, y = 26)
```

13. Write a program which will test the limits of data types **int**, **float**, and **double** on your system. [*Suggestion*: Use a loop to print out successively larger (and smaller) values until you find one that is nonsense; for example, the value may suddenly change sign from positive to negative. Narrow in on the exact value that is the limit in each direction.] Your C++ compiler comes with a file, called limits.h, which defines the limits of each data type on your system. You might want to compare your results to the values in the file.

14. a. Write a program which will print your name, then two blank lines, then your name, etc., a total of four times. Write the program two ways: first without using a loop, then using a **for** loop to repeat a series of instructions four times.

    b. Repeat part (a) but have your name print ten times.

    c. Repeat part (a) but have your name print 100 times.

    d. Which part(s) of this exercise are you willing to do? Which part(s) don't you want to do? Why? What can you conclude about the power of the **for** loop?

15. In Program 2, result and gpa were declared to have data type **double**. Was this actually necessary? What would happen if result or gpa had data type **int**? To test your answer, run three new versions of Program 2: one in which result has data type **int**, and gpa has data type **double**; one in which result has data type **double**, and gpa has data type **int**; and one in which they both have data type **int**. Will all of these work?

MODIFYING AND EXTENDING PROGRAM 2

16. The registrar with whom we began this chapter has been told more precisely how to evaluate a student's enrollment status. If the formula results in a positive value, the student should be allowed to enroll; if the value is negative, the student should be turned away; if the value is 0, the student must see the professor personally. Modify Program 2 so that it prints an appropriate message ("accepted," "rejected," or "see professor") next to each value of result.

17. Assume that the registrar's instructions in Exercise 16 are not good enough. Modify the program to shift the cutoff point. It should print "accepted" if the value of the formula is greater than 5,

"rejected" if it is less than 5, and "see professor" if it is exactly 5. Then modify it again so that 10 is the cutoff. Finally, have −5 as the cutoff point.

18. Most students coming to the registrar will not have a grade point average (gpa) that is exactly 2.00 or 2.50 or something similar. Modify Program 2 so that it can handle other values of gpa. Do this by using the gpa value in the table as the center of a range. For example, all values of the average from 0.00 to 0.24 are covered by the entry for 0.00; values from 0.25 to 0.74 are covered by the entry for 0.50, etc. To do this, modify the printout so that next to each gpa average is the range of values it covers. For example,

Average	Range Covered	Value of Formula
0.000000	0.00 - 0.24	0.600000
0.500000	0.25 - 0.74	-1.657895

19. Modify Program 2 so that it keeps track of (a) the lowest value of result ever obtained by the formula, and (b) the gpa value which led to the lowest result. There are two ways to interpret this. First, it can mean the smallest absolute value so that, for example, 0.23 is lower than −2.17. It can also mean that all negative values are lower than all positive ones. Write two programs, one for each interpretation.

20. One exercise in Chapter 1 asked you to rewrite Program 1 without a loop by using each value of number explicitly. This would also be possible in Program 2, but it would be much more tedious. Describe how to do it and explain why it is much worse in Program 2.

DEBUGGING EXERCISES

21. The following **if** statement does not generate an error message. Nonetheless, it is probably not what the programmer wants. Can you figure out what the statement does? What is wrong with it if the intention is to print the word "less" if x is less than 7?

```
if (x < 7);
    cout << "less";
```

22. What is wrong with the following **if** statement? Will it generate an error message?

```
if (x < 7)
    cout << "x is greater than 7";
```

23. Exercise 12 in Chapter 1 asked you to find and correct a number of errors in a program. Go back to that program and determine the type (compilation, execution, or logic) of each error. In some cases, this distinction is not clear-cut. See if you can find any errors that can be interpreted as either compilation or logic.

24. The following program has many bugs in it. Try to find them and identify the type (compilation, execution, or logic) of each error.

```
// do various calculations, including
/ finding the perimeter of a rectangle
include iostreem;
ussing name standard;
void mane{}
    integer x;
    y: double;
    int perimeter;length;width;
```

```
        {
            x == 4.0;
            y = .5 * 3 \ (x - 4);
            if x = 5
                cout << 'five'
            2y = x + (5 + 4 % 3;
            perimeter = length + width * 2;
            cout perimeter,length,width" endl)
        };
```

25. Write a program that uses the library function sqrt( ), but omits the **#include <cmath>** directive. If it compiles on your system, test it by finding sqrt(4), sqrt(9), and then sqrt(7) and sqrt(8). What happens?

PROGRAMMING PROJECTS

26. Write a program that prints a table of the numbers from 1 to 50, together with the square, cube, and square root of each. Include appropriate column headings.

27. a. Write a program that prints a table of the angles from 0 to 180 degrees, together with the radian measurement, the sine, and the cosine of each angle. Recall that 180 degrees is equal to pi radians. Give pi the value 3.14159 and use the library functions sin( ) and cos( ).

    b. Modify the program from part (a) so that it also prints the tangent of each angle. (*Note*: This may cause an execution error if you attempt to find tan(90°), which is undefined.)

28. Write a program that prints a table of numbers from 1 to 50. Next to each number should be the logarithm to the base e (natural log) of the number and e raised to the number as exponent. Use the library functions log( ) (for natural log) and exp( ) (for e raised to the number as exponent).

29. Write a program that prints two conversion tables to change temperatures in Fahrenheit (F) to temperatures in Celsius (C) and vice versa. One formula is $F = (9/5)C + 32$. (What is the other formula?) One table should list the Fahrenheit values from −50 to 250 in steps of 10, together with the Celsius equivalent. The other should list Celsius values from −50 to 150 in steps of 5, together with the Fahrenheit equivalents.

30. Write a program that finds and prints the values of ans for values of num from 1 to 6 in increments of .25 (1, 1.25, 1.50,…), based on the following formula:

$$ans = \frac{(num + 2)^2 - |num - 7|}{\dfrac{num + 3}{14}}$$

31. Write a program that finds and prints the values of result for all even values of y from 2 to 16, using the following formula:

$$result = \frac{(y - 1) + (y + 4)^3}{y - \dfrac{1}{y}}$$

READING A SET OF DATA

PROBLEM: A Simple Payroll Program

SYNTAX CONCEPTS: **while** loop, <u>cin</u>, precision, **if-else** statement, conditional operator (?:), standard I/O streams, <u>cerr</u>

PROGRAMMING CONCEPTS: reading data, interactive data entry, using a trailer value, structured read loop, counting, selecting one of two alternatives, sending output to a file, reading data from a file, redirecting output to a file, running a program from the command line

CONTROL STRUCTURES: **while** loop, **if-else** statement, conditional expression

HOW TO READ CHAPTER 3

OUTLINE:

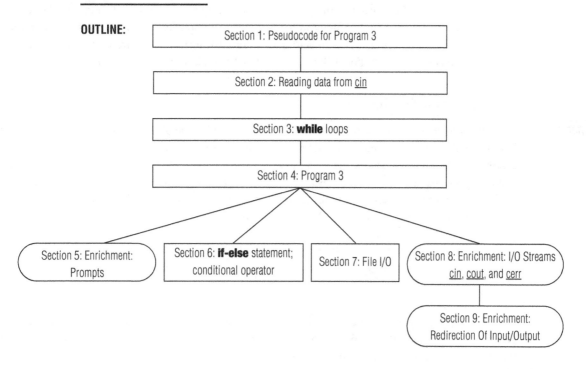

Section 1 provides a pseudocode solution to Problem 3. Sections 2 and 3 introduce a number of new C++ features, including <u>cin</u> and the **while** loop, which will be used in Program 3. Section 4 uses the new features to write Program 3. Section 5, an enrichment segment, discusses prompts, which are crucial for interactive input. Section 6 introduces the **if-else** statement, which generalizes the **if** statement used in Programs 2 and 3. Sections 7, 8 and 9 introduce various ways of doing I/O, including using files, and separating I/O streams and sending prompts to the screen while sending output to the printer or to a file. It is recommended that all students be introduced to the concepts in Section 7 (File I/O), and that the instructor introduce Sections 8 (I/O Streams) and 9 (Redirection of I/O) depending on the environment within which the course is being taught.

INTRODUCTION AND STATEMENT OF THE PROBLEM

INTRODUCTION

Our programs so far have been unrealistic, not just because they are too simple but also because each program is completely self-contained; all the information needed to solve the problem is already known. The first program had built into it the starting point (4), the ending point (9), and the operation to perform (squaring). The second program knew the starting (0) and ending (4) points, the increment (0.50), and the formula to use (result = ...). Nothing further had to be supplied to either one.

A program's being totally self-contained may seem like an advantage, but it is really a fault. Programs 1 and 2 each work for a single, specific problem with a specific set of values; however, neither works for a general set of problems or even on another set of values. A more realistic (and more useful) program would allow some values to be specified as the program is running. This gives it much more flexibility because many different types of problems can be handled.

The simplest way of entering data is to type values into the computer as the program requests them. This process, which is the focus of this chapter, is called **reading in data**. We will explain how to enter data from the keyboard, and in the process, we will introduce the concept of interactive data entry. The new values specified as the program is executing are called **input data**, or just **input** or **data**. The ability to read in data adds immeasurably to the power and usefulness of a computer. Another method of entering data is to set up an external file (when you are using a personal computer, the file is usually stored on a floppy or hard disk) and have the computer read from that file.

STATEMENT OF THE PROBLEM

PROBLEM 3   Write a complete C++ program to do the following: Read in data about an employee of a company. The data will contain the employee's ID number, hours worked in a week, and rate of pay per hour. Compute the employee's pay for the week, which is equal to hours times rate. Print the relevant information about this employee. Then repeat the same steps for the other employees until all have been processed. Count the number of employees processed and print the total at the end.

Two typical groups of data might be the following:

```
1234      35      14.20
2345      11.3     5.87
```

Note that the same payroll program can work for many different groups of employees. To keep the program flexible, we will not specify the particular values for the ID number, hours, and rate within the program. That would limit us to just one group.

SECTION 1   PSEUDOCODE FOR PROGRAM 3

TRANSLATING THE PROBLEM STATEMENT

According to the description of the problem, we want to read in data containing an employee's ID number, hours worked, and rate of pay. Reading in data means getting information from outside the program during execution. In the case of interactive data entry, the information is typed in from the keyboard. We have already learned one way of giving a value to a variable—the assignment statement; reading in a value is another. We want to read in the employee's ID number, the hours worked, and the rate of pay. With an obvious choice of names for the variables, we can write the following in pseudocode:

> *read* id
> *read* hours
> *read* rate

We are also told to compute the employee's pay for the week. We could write this in pseudocode as "*compute* pay," but it is simple enough to put directly in C++:

> pay = hours * rate;

Next we print the information about the employee:

> *print relevant information*

Finally, we must count the employee:

> *count this employee*

This ends what is to be done for one employee. Then the problem statement says to do the same for the other employees. Remember from Chapter 1 that any time an action must be repeated numerous times, it makes sense to use a loop. After the loop terminates, we will print the total number of employees.

Putting all this together, here is the first version of the pseudocode for this problem:

> *do the following for each employee*
> > *read* id
> > *read* hours
> > *read* rate
> > pay = hours * rate;
> > *print relevant information*
> > *count this employee*
> *print total number of employees*

This is not the final pseudocode version of this program, but we will refine the pseudocode as we write Program 3.

SELF-CHECK 3-1

1. What is the purpose of reading in data?
2. What is interactive data entry?
3. What wording in a problem statement signals that we should use a loop?

SECTION 2   READING DATA FROM cin

INTERACTIVE DATA ENTRY

Data read by a program can come from two places: the keyboard or a data file (see Section 7). Initially, our programs will read data from the keyboard, entered by **interactive data entry,** so called because the user interacts with the computer. The programmer writes the program so that the computer asks for data when it is ready to read. After the user types in the requested data values, the computer reads them and then goes ahead with the program.

READING FROM cin

According to the pseudocode, the program starts by reading the ID number, hours, and rate of pay for each employee. However, we need a way to read in data in C++.

We will read in values from <u>cin</u>. Just as <u>cout</u> is an output stream, <u>cin</u> is an **input stream** (actually it is an object of class <u>iostream</u>, as is <u>cout</u>). We use the **extraction operator** (>>) to get a value from the stream and place it into the variable whose name follows the operator.

We can refine the pseudocode from Section 1 to the following:

```
cin >> id;
cin >> hours;
cin >> rate;
```

When reading from <u>cin</u>, the computer pauses, waiting for a value. Once the user types in a value, followed by <Enter>, the program resumes, reads the value and copies it into the specified variable. The new value read in from <u>cin</u> replaces any previous value held by the variable. In that sense, reading from <u>cin</u> is similar to using an assignment statement.

EXAMPLE 3-1   Assume we want to read an integer into the variable <u>num</u> and then print out this value. The following code will do it:

```
int num;
cin >> num;
cout << num;
```

Suppose that the user types in the value 1234, followed by <Enter>, when the machine pauses to read from <u>cin</u>. The machine reads 1234 and stores it in <u>num</u>, replacing what was previously there, as shown in Figure 3-1.

EXAMPLE 3-2   Let's read in the length and width of a rectangular room and then compute and print the area. The dimensions of the room may have decimal places, so the variables must have type **double**:

```
double length,width,area;
cin >> length;
cin >> width;
area = length * width;
cout << area;
```

Assume the user types in 14.5 for the length and 12.4 for the width. The first statement reads 14.5 from <u>cin</u> and stores it in <u>length</u>. The second reads 12.4 and stores it in <u>width</u>. The value 179.8 is computed, stored in <u>area</u>, and then printed.

FIGURE 3-1   Effect of reading from <u>cin</u> in Example 3-1

```---- ```	user types 1234	```1234```
<u>num</u> initially		<u>num</u> after reading from cin

FORM OF AN EXPRESSION THAT READS FROM cin

A statement that reads from <u>cin</u> can be used to read a value into one or more variables.

A statement that reads from cin starts with the identifier <u>cin</u>, followed by the **extraction operator** >> followed by the name of a single variable. For example, we can use the following:

```
cin >> number;
```

This extracts a value from the input stream <u>cin</u> and sends the value to the storage location <u>number</u>.

To read values into more than one variable, add an operator and a name for each variable, as described below.

General Form Showing Reading from <u>cin</u> to Give Values to Several Variables

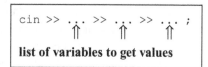

GUIDELINES FOR READING FROM cin

♦ The statement starts with the name of the I/O stream, <u>cin</u>.

♦ The name cin is followed by the extraction operator >> and then by the first variable which should get a value.

♦ This can be followed by additional variable names, each one preceded by the extraction operator.

Here's an example that reads three integer values into the variables <u>first</u>, <u>second</u> and <u>third</u>:

```
int first,second,third;
cin >> first >> second >> third;
```

To enter the data needed, the user types three separate values, each followed by a space, a tab, or the <Enter> key.

MATCHING THE DATA TO THE VARIABLES

When entering data, you should be careful to enter the data values in the correct order, or your program will fail to work properly. For example, take these statements that read from <u>cin:</u>

```
int intnum;
double realnum;
cin >> intnum;
cin >> realnum;
```

To match this order, the first value entered should be an integer, to be read into <u>intnum</u>, and the next value should be in numeric format, either integer or real, to be read into <u>realnum</u>. If the user enters 7 and 3.6, they will be stored as shown in Figure 3-2.

FIGURE 3-2 Reading values into two variables

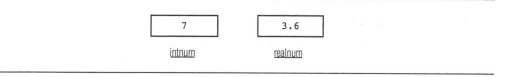

An integer value can be read into a variable with type **float** or **double**, but not vice versa. For example, if 7 is read into a variable of type **double**, then it will be stored as 7.0. However, if you attempt to read 3.6 into an integer variable, the value 3 will be stored in the variable, but the extraction operator will stop reading at the decimal point, which is not part of an integer value. What happens to the .6 depends on the next variable that is supposed to get a value. If the variable has type **float** or **double**, it will get the value 0.6. If the variable has type **int**, the program will not change the value of the **int** variable, producing unpredictable results, depending on the compiler you are using. In fact, attempting to read anything other than a numeric value into a variable with a numeric data type will cause unpredictable results.

WHY READ IN DATA?

Before concluding, we need to make sure you understand why we read data into a program. Running a C++ program once or even two or three times takes only a few seconds. Because of this, some students don't appreciate why reading in data is such a powerful tool. Instead of reading a value into a variable, they write an assignment statement. When the data values change, those same students just change the values on the right-hand side of each assignment statement and rerun the program. They don't understand what is wrong with this technique.

As you write more programs, the answer will become clear. First of all, each time you change the statements, you must recompile the program before you run it. In contrast, if you read in data, you can run the exact same program. When you are writing a small program, you do not mind the extra compilation time. However, as your programs get longer, compilation takes more time.

Worse, every time you change a program, you introduce the possibility of mistakes, either through the change you make or as a side effect (e.g., accidentally erasing a line or even a single character). The last thing an experienced programmer wants to do is alter a working program.

Another important factor is the way your program will be used. Right now, you are the writer and the user of the program. If you need to change the data, you know exactly what to do. But in another environment, the programs you write will be used by others who won't know how to change your program. In fact, if you write a program for someone else, you may not even want to give them the C++ code for security reasons—you may not want them to know how the code works, or have them mess up your program. To prevent them from seeing or changing the code, you can give them a previously compiled version of the program. Computer games and word processing programs are distributed this way. All the user does is run the program.

Then there are issues about the amount of data that a program requires and the way the sets of data are used. If you run a program two or three times using different data values, you may not find it a chore to change the values for each run (a **run** is a single execution of the program). However, suppose you are running Program 3 for a large company with 500 employees. You wouldn't want to change the program code, enter new values, and rerun the program 500 times. Allowing the program to read in data values as it needs them saves the user an enormous amount of time.

Finally, the results from your program may depend upon more than one set of data values. For example in Program 3, we count the number of employees. We can do this only if we read in the data; if we ran the program once for each employee, the count would remain at 1. For all these reasons, reading in data is one of the most important features of any programming language.

SELF-CHECK 3-2

1. What is the purpose of reading from <u>cin</u>?

2. What is the name for the >> symbol?

3. Give several reasons for reading data into a program.
4. What is the potential hazard of changing a working program?

SECTION 3   THE while LOOP

In this section, we will refine the pseudocode from Section 1. We will also introduce an important new control structure, called a **while** loop, together with a **trailer value** (also called a **flag** or **sentinel** value) used when reading in data.

USING A LOOP IN PROGRAM 3

Unlike the loops in Programs 1 and 2, the loop in Program 3 doesn't seem to have a starting point, stopping point, or increment value. All the pseudocode says is *"do the following for each employee."* We could try to number the employees and use a **for** loop; however, that would violate the spirit of what we want to do, which is to read in employee information until we get to the end of the list. Fortunately, C++ has another type of loop, called a **while** loop, that will work perfectly here.

THE while LOOP

The **while** loop allows us to continue processing (looping), depending upon a condition whose value usually changes within the loop. It specifies no increment value but continues as long as the condition is true.

General Form of the while Loop

```
while (cond)              // header of the loop
      body of the loop    // body of the loop
```

The top line of the **while** loop, called the **header**, contains the keyword **while**, followed by a condition in parentheses; *cond* is any condition that evaluates to true or false; *body of the loop* is a single C++ statement.

HOW A while LOOP WORKS

The body of the loop is executed until the condition becomes false. Each time through the loop, including the first, the condition is evaluated.

◆ If the condition is true, the body of the loop is executed. When the computer reaches the end of the body, it goes back to the header and evaluates the condition again.

◆ If the condition is false, the body of the loop is skipped, and the statement after the body is executed.

Because the condition is at the top of the loop, if it is false immediately, the body of the loop is never executed. If the condition is always true, the loop executes forever. A loop that continues forever is called an **infinite loop**. (Exercise 53 discusses infinite loops in more detail.)

TABLE 3-1   Results of **while** condition values

Value of the while Condition	Result
true	execute body of loop
false	skip body of loop
never true	never enter body of loop
never false	infinite loop

Table 3-1 illustrates what happens in a **while** loop under various conditions. Example 3-3 shows a very simple **while** loop.

EXAMPLE 3-3

```
num = 0;
limit = 10;
while (num < limit)
      num++;
```

This loop requires initial values for <u>num</u> and <u>limit</u>. As long as <u>num</u> is less than <u>limit</u>, the loop body will be executed. In this case, the loop executes 10 times, with <u>num</u> having the values 0, 1, …, 9; when <u>num</u> becomes 10, the condition <u>num</u> < <u>limit</u> is false, and the loop terminates.

CAUTION Do not place a semicolon after the condition:

```
while (num < limit);
      num++;
```

If you do, the loop terminates at the semicolon, and the body of the loop contains nothing. This may cause an infinite loop during execution (why?).

A while LOOP WITH A COMPOUND STATEMENT

If more than one statement is to be executed in the body, this format must be used:

General Form of a while Loop with a Compound Statement

```
while (cond) {
      stmt-1;
      stmt-2;        // body of the loop
      . . .
      stmt-n;
}
```

The braces are used the same way they were in a **for** loop when the body of the loop is a compound statement. A semicolon is not necessary following the closing brace.

EXAMPLE 3-4

Assume that we want to print all the powers of 2 less than 1000. When we fall out of the loop, we want to print a message and continue with another part of the program. Here is a **while** loop to accomplish this task:

```
power = 1;                    // this is the first power of 2
while (power < 1000) {
      cout << power << endl;
      power *=2;
}
cout << "These are all the powers of 2 less than 1000";
```

Initially, <u>power</u> is given the value 1; the **while** condition (<u>power</u> < 1000) is true, so we enter the body of the loop, where we print 1, which is the first power of 2 (2^0). We multiply <u>power</u> by 2, giving it the new value of 2 (remember that <u>power</u> *= 2 is shorthand for <u>power</u> = <u>power</u> * 2). After the body of the loop executes, we go back to the header, where we test the condition again. Since <u>power</u> is still less than 1000, we enter the body of the loop again, print 2, and compute the new value 4 for <u>power</u>.

This series of actions—printing the old value, computing a new value, and testing the condition— is repeated until <u>power</u> gets the value 1024. This time when we test the condition (<u>power</u> < 1000), it is false, and we fall out of the loop. The output from this section of code looks like this:

```
1
2
4
8
16
32
64
128
256
512
These are all the powers of 2 less than 1000
```

USING A while LOOP IN PROGRAM 3; A TRAILER OR PHONY DATA VALUE

Let's look at the pseudocode for Program 3. It says "*do the following for each employee.*" We will implement this using a **while** loop. Inside the loop, we are told to read <u>id</u>, read <u>hours</u>, and read <u>rate</u>. Translating this, we get the following (the header is still in pseudocode):

```
while (there are employees to process) {
    cin >> id;
    cin >> hours;
    cin >> rate;
    pay = hours * rate;
}
```

Unfortunately, this section of code has a fatal flaw: there is no way to stop the looping process. This is an infinite loop! The program needs to stop looping when there are no more employees and it runs out of data.

We have to find a way to tell the computer that we have run out of data. A person would see that there is nothing left, but a computer doesn't notice things. It doesn't know which employee is the last one.

There are many ways to tell the computer that it has reached the end of a set of data, but the one that we will use is called a **trailer**, a **sentinel**, or more picturesquely, a **phony** data value. As the name suggests, our last value will not contain real employee information. Instead, it will signal the computer that the set of data is complete. (<u>Note</u>: A trailer is an older technique, no longer used by professional programmers except under very specific circumstances; however, it is a simple introductory method. In Chapter 7, we introduce reading until end of file, which is a more common method of handling the end of a data set.)

The last or phony value does not look different from the others but will be treated in a special way by our program. When the program reads this data value, it will fall out of the loop instead of processing the value. Picking a phony value is tricky because it must be a value which can't possibly occur in the set of data. We might use an employee who has worked 0 hours, or one whose rate of pay is 0, but it is conceivable that these values could occur. It is safer to use a phony ID number as our signal; even then, a number like 9999 or 0000 might be an actual ID. The trailer value must be something, such as a negative number, that can't possibly occur. In fact, let's use a negative number as our signal in Program 3.

In the program, we must test each value of <u>id</u> which has been read in to see if it is not negative. The best place to test the <u>id</u> value is before computing the pay for an employee so that we don't waste time with a phony employee. We must insert a question into the pseudocode to represent this test, in the header of the loop. Let's revise the first line of the pseudocode to include this condition:

```
while (id is not negative) {
    cin >> id;
    cin >> hours;
    cin >> rate;
    pay = hours * rate;
    print relevant information
    count this employee
}
print total number of employees
```

This pseudocode is quite close to C++, and we will write the program from this version.

SELF-CHECK 3-3

1. What value of the condition in the **while** loop header
   a. causes the body of the **while** loop to be executed?
   b. causes the **while** loop to terminate?
2. a. What happens if the condition of a **while** loop is initially false?
   b. What happens if the condition of a **while** loop never becomes false?
3. What is the purpose of a trailer value?

SECTION 4 WRITING PROGRAM 3

In this section, we will use the pseudocode and the topics introduced in the last few sections to write Program 3.

PROGRAM HEADER

Let's take another look at the pseudocode, as revised in Section 3.

```
while (id is not negative) {
    cin >> id;
    cin >> hours;
    cin >> rate;
    pay = hours * rate;
    print relevant information
    count this employee
}
print total number of employees
```

Looking at the pseudocode, we know how to translate everything into C++. Here are the first few lines:

```
// Program prog3a.cpp:
// payroll program—reads in an ID number, hours worked,
// and rate of pay, and computes the weekly pay,
// using interactive data entry
#include <iostream>
using namespace std;
int main()
```

DECLARING THE VARIABLES

Let's see what variables we have to declare. Even though the pseudocode does not explicitly say to declare variables, we can see which were used: id, hours, rate, pay, and a variable to count employees. We'll start with id. Assuming that the employees' ID numbers are integers, rather than decimal numbers, we use the following declaration:

```
int id;
```

In contrast, the variables hours, rate, and pay will not be integers in all cases because that would mean ignoring all the decimal positions. Certainly someone who has a pay rate of $5.75 an hour doesn't want to lose 75 cents! We will declare these variables to have data type **double**.

```
double hours,rate,pay;
```

We are also asked to count the number of employees. An appropriate name for this variable might be numemps. Since the number of employees is not going to have decimal places, it makes sense to use data type **int** for numemps, so we use the following declaration:

```
int numemps;
```

Here is the complete declaration for this program:

```
int id,numemps;
double hours,rate,pay;
```

STYLE WORKSHOP Note that we have combined the variables of type **int** and put them on a different line from the variables of type **double**. This helps make the declaration part of the program more readable.

USING A while LOOP TO READ THE DATA

Now let's translate our loop header into C++. We want to repeat the body of the loop "*while* (id *is not negative*)." When id is less than 0, we want to fall out of the loop. Translated into C++, the header becomes the following:

```
while (id >= 0)
```

Then, since all the indented statements are part of the loop body, it should be obvious that we need a pair of braces. Here is the code so far:

```
while (id >= 0) {
    cin >> id;
    cin >> hours;
    cin >> rate;
    pay = hours * rate;
```

```
        print relevant information
        count this employee
}
print total number of employees
```

You may have noticed that there is going to be a problem testing the condition; we will come back to it after writing the rest of the body of the loop.

COMPUTING THE EMPLOYEE'S PAY AND PRINTING THE RESULTS

The code for computing the pay has already been translated into C++, as follows:

```
pay = hours * rate;
```

Next we print the information about this employee. Up till now, we have been vague on exactly what should be printed. Now we must be a little more specific. We will certainly print the employee's pay, but we also need to identify the person. At a minimum, then, we should print id and pay. However, the job of checking our program is much easier if we also print hours and rate. Then a few simple cases can be checked by hand to verify accuracy. We should also include some messages to make the output more readable. Let's say we would like to print results like this:

```
Employee 1234 worked 35.0 hours at a rate of $14.20, earning $497.00
```

The following statement will do that nicely (except for printing two decimal places for the dollar amounts, which we'll take care of later):

```
cout << "Employee " << id << " worked " << hours
    << " hours at a rate of $" << rate << " earning $"
    << pay << endl << endl;
```

FIXING THE FATAL FLAW

Let's look at what we have so far:

```
while (id >= 0) {
    cin >> id;
    cin >> hours;
    cin >> rate;
    pay = hours * rate;
    cout << "Employee " << id << " worked " << hours
        << " hours at a rate of $" << rate << " earning $"
        << pay << endl << endl;
    count this employee
}
print total number of employees
```

As we mentioned, there is one big problem with this version of the program. The very first line asks us to compare the value of id with 0, but we haven't given id a value yet. It only gets its value inside the body of the loop, after the condition in the header is tested. However, we should never test the value of a variable before it has been initialized. Instead, we should read id outside the loop, before the test. Then, if id is not greater than or equal to 0, we can read hours and rate inside the loop. Here is a revision of what we have so far:

```
cin >> id;
while (id >= 0) {
```

```
        cin >> hours;
        cin >> rate;
        pay = hours * rate;
        cout << "Employee " << id << " worked " << hours
            << " hours at a rate of $" << rate << " earning $"
            << pay << endl << endl;
        count this employee
    }
    print total number of employees
```

We aren't done yet. Now that we have moved ***cin >> id*** outside the loop, this program won't let us read the ID number for any employee but the first. Trace through the indented statements, those which form the body of the loop; you'll see that there isn't any place where we read in an ID number. You may think we can use the ***cin >> id*** that comes before the loop. However, when we return to the top of a loop, we start at the header; we never repeat lines that come before the beginning. Therefore, id will continue to have the same value, and the loop will be infinite.

One solution is to insert another statement to read the ID number of each employee after the first. We can't put it inside the loop with the statements that read hours and rate because we have read the ID number of the first employee by the time we enter the loop. The only place to put it is at the bottom of the loop after processing the previous employee completely. At that point, we are ready to start reading data for the next employee.

```
    cin >> id;
    while (id >= 0) {
        cin >> hours;
        cin >> rate;
        pay = hours * rate;
        cout << "Employee " << id << " worked " << hours
            << " hours at a rate of $" << rate << " earning $"
            << pay << endl << endl;
        count this employee
        cin >> id;
    }
    print total number of employees
```

THE STRUCTURED READ LOOP

The type of loop that reads data once outside the loop and again inside at the bottom is called a **structured read loop**. In this type of loop, once we have read in each ID value, the next action is to check if this is the last (or phony) piece of data. In this case, the variable id is checked to see whether it holds a negative value. If the first value read into id is negative, we will never enter the body of the loop, but instead skip to the statements that follow. If the value read into id is non-negative, the body of the loop will execute. In the exercises and later chapters, we will explore more reasons for using a structured read loop.

PROGRAM TRACE Let's trace this loop with the following three ID numbers (plus associated data):

```
1234
2345
-1
```

◆ In response to the first read statement, the user types in 1234.

◆ This value is placed in <u>id</u> and compared to 0.

◆ Since it is greater than 0, the computer enters the body of the loop, where the user is prompted to enter values for <u>hours</u> and <u>rate</u>.

◆ Next the program computes <u>pay</u>, prints the values and messages specified in the <u>cout</u> statement, and counts the employee. This finishes the first employee.

◆ In response to the *cin >> id* at the bottom of the loop, the user types in 2345.

◆ This gives <u>id</u> a new value which is tested when the computer checks the condition in the loop header.

◆ Since the new value of <u>id</u> is again greater than 0, the computer again enters the body of the loop to read and process this employee's information. The machine computes and prints <u>pay</u> and counts this employee. This finishes the second person.

◆ Then the program asks for an ID number for the next employee. This time the user enters −1.

◆ When the computer tests this value in the loop header, the condition (<u>id</u> >= 0) is false, the loop terminates, and the program prints the number of employees processed. The program does not read <u>hours</u> and <u>rate</u> nor compute <u>pay</u> for the phony employee.

ALL OVER BUT THE COUNTING: COUNTING THE NUMBER OF EMPLOYEES

There is one last piece of pseudocode. The problem says to count each employee as the pay is processed and print the total number of employees at the end. Let's develop an algorithm for counting a series of items.

AN ALGORITHM FOR COUNTING

To count something, initialize a variable to zero. Each time the event happens, increment that variable by one. At the end, the variable holds the number of times the counted event happened, and that value can be printed.

```
count = 0;
while ( ... ) {
    // event happens
    count++;
}
print count
```

When the event occurs once each time through a loop, initialize the counting variable to zero outside the loop and increment it by one each time through. When the loop terminates, the variable has the count of the times through the loop, which is also the number of times the counted event happened.

Based on the algorithm, we must have a variable—traditionally called a **counter**—whose value represents the number of items (in this case, employees) we are counting. The variable <u>numemps</u> has already been declared for this purpose.

◆ At the beginning of the program, before the loop, no employees have been processed. This tells us to initialize <u>numemps</u> to 0 before the loop.

◆ We should increment the value of <u>numemps</u> by one each time through the loop, after completely processing an employee. That should happen after we complete the printing but before we read the next ID.

Now we can translate "*count this employee*" in Problem 3 into the following:

```
numemps = 0;              // initial value
for each employee ...
    numemps++;            // increment each time through the loop
```

Doing this in Program 3 gives us the following:

```
numemps = 0;
cin >> id;
while (id >= 0) {
    cin >> hours;
    cin >> rate;
    pay = hours * rate;
    cout << "Employee " << id << " worked " << hours
         << " hours at a rate of $" << rate << " earning $"
         << pay << endl << endl;
    cin >> id;
    numemps++;
}
print total number of employees
```

After the **while** loop has processed all the employees, we should print the final value of numemps, together with an appropriate message. The final line of pseudocode translates as follows:

```
cout << "We processed " << numemps << " employees" << endl;
```

INITIALIZATION IN THE DECLARATION

There is a handy modification of the way we have declared and initialized numemps. Instead of writing the declaration and the initialization separately, we can put the initial value in the declaration:

```
int id, numemps = 0;
```

This combined statement gives the value of 0 only to numemps, not to id. If a variable is initialized in the declaration, the assigned value is just a starting one. The variable's value can still change during the program.

(ALMOST) COMPLETE PROGRAM 3

Here is our complete program, prob3a.cpp, now that we have translated all the pseudocode:

🖳 PROGRAM LISTING

```
// Program prog3a.cpp:
// payroll program - reads in an ID number, hours worked,
// and rate of pay, and computes the weekly pay,
// using interactive data entry
#include <iostream>
using namespace std;
int main()
{
    int id, numemps = 0;
    double hours, rate, pay;
```

```
cin >> id;
while (id >= 0) {
    cin >> hours;t
    cin >> rate;
    pay = hours * rate;
    cout << "Employee " << id << " worked " << hours
        << " hours at a rate of $" << rate << " earning $"
        << pay << endl << endl;
    numemps++;
    cin >> id;
}
cout << "We processed " << numemps << " employees" << endl;
return 0;
}
```

Having assembled the parts, we have a working program that reads in the data, computes the pay, and prints out the results. In fact, you may want to run the program at this point to see how it works. Figure 3-3 shows what appears on the screen after running the program for the two employees listed in the statement of the problem. As you can see, there are still a few issues to resolve, which we will discuss in Section 5.

FIGURE 3-3 Output from <u>prob3a.cpp</u> for original two employees

```
1234
35
14.20
Employee 1234 worked 35 hours at a rate of $14.2 earning $497

2345
11.3
5.87
Employee 2345 worked 11.3 hours at a rate of $5.87 earning $66.331

-1
We processed 2 employees
```

SELF-CHECK 3-4

1. When computing <u>pay</u>, does it make any difference if we use <u>rate</u> * <u>hours</u> instead of <u>hours</u> * <u>rate</u>?

2. In a structured read loop, why do we read into the same variable twice?

3. Why do we start counting the number of employees at 0? Can you think of a circumstance where you might begin counting at another value, say 10?

SECTION 5 ENRICHMENT: IMPROVING THE INPUT/OUTPUT—PROMPTS AND PRINTING

This section introduces prompts for interactive data entry. In addition, it explains field width and decimal precision for printing values of type **double**. These are enhancements to the basic program developed in Section 4.

PROMPTS AND INTERACTIVE DATA ENTRY

If you ran the program from Section 4, you may have noticed something strange. It's hard to know when the machine is ready for the data. When you run the program in this form, the computer doesn't tell you when to type in the data or which piece of data to type in at any given point.

Actually, when the computer executes the statement that reads from cin, the cursor appears on the screen. The presence of the cursor is the signal that the computer is waiting for you to type in data. The program does not continue until you type something. However, even if you remember what the cursor means, you may not remember which value is needed at that moment. More importantly, some other person may be running your program, and that person won't have a clue what to do.

To make it easier for the user, the computer should issue a **prompt**, which is a request for information. The prompt appears on the screen as the result of sending a message to cout (or to cerr—see below). The user's response is to type in the data. What the user types in is read right from the keyboard into the variable mentioned in the statement that reads from cin. You can think of this format as an interactive question and answer session: The computer asks a question, and the user provides the answer.

Let's begin with a simple example.

EXAMPLE 3-5

Suppose you want to write a program that will read in a number (to be stored in number) and print out its square (sqnumber). You would first have to write a prompt to tell the user to enter a number to be squared. Then you would include the statements to read that number, square it, and write the results on the screen.

```
cout << "Please enter a number> ";
cin >> number;
sqnumber = number * number;
cout << "The square of " << number << " is " << sqnumber << endl;
```

As a result of running this code, the following prompt appears on the screen, followed on the same line by the cursor (indicated by the underbar in the display):

```
Please enter a number> _
```

As the input value is typed, it appears immediately after the prompt on the same line. At this point, if the user types in 5 and then presses <Enter>, number will hold 5, and sqnumber will later be set to 25.

USING PROMPTS IN PROGRAM 3

Now let's see where we need to add prompts to Program 3. We have to put a prompt before each statement that reads from cin. As a first step, use the following simple prompts (the first one is also used with the cin at the bottom of the loop):

```
cout << "Enter the employee's ID number> ";
cin >> id;
...
cout << "Enter the hours worked> ";
cin >> hours;
cout << "Enter the rate of pay> ";
cin >> rate;
```

Each prompt appears on the screen directly before the cursor. The prompt gives the user information about which data value to enter for the input statement that follows. We have ended each prompt with a right arrow and a blank; the arrow is meant to focus the user's attention, and the blank separates the data value from the prompt for easy reading. Of course, there are other possible formats that you may find more useful.

IMPROVING THE PROMPTS

We need to consider whether these prompts are adequate. They do tell the user when to enter the data, but they don't give enough information about the basic nature of the program and how it runs. The following set of messages, inserted at the beginning of the program, solves the problem:

```
cout << "This program computes an employee's pay" << endl;
cout << "Enter ID number, hours worked, and rate of pay" << endl;
cout << "First, enter the employee's ID number" << endl;
cout << "To stop, enter a negative value as the employee's ID number> ";
```

STYLE WORKSHOP If typing a long prompt seems like a pain, remember that someone using an interactive program probably doesn't have a printout or program listing. There are no comments to explain the program to the user. One complaint people have about programs they purchase is that they are too hard to use. You should try to make every program you write easy to use.

Notice that the first three lines are not really prompts but informational messages. We terminate them with <u>endl</u>. The last line before the user enters the ID number is a true prompt and does not end with <u>endl</u>; this allows the user to enter the data value on the same line as the prompt.

SELF-CHECK 3-5

1. Why does the person entering data need explanatory messages and prompts?
2. What happens if you put in a statement that reads from <u>cin</u>, but you forget to put in a prompt?
3. What happens if you put in a prompt but forget to follow it with a statement that reads from <u>cin</u>?

PRINTING NUMBERS NEATLY: FIELD WIDTH AND DECIMAL PRECISION

We are not quite finished. We still have to take care of some of the printing details. According to our payroll report, employee 2345 is about to get a paycheck for $66.331. This format is not going to make employee 2345 (or his bank) happy. Fortunately, C++ can print real numbers in our more familiar notation.

Unless we specify otherwise, C++ prints real numbers with up to six significant digits. The number of digits appearing after the decimal point is determined by the number of digit positions left after printing the integer part of the number (as well as by the value of the number itself). We need some way to specify the number of decimal places, regardless of how many significant digits may be left.

For now, we'll just introduce the necessary steps, without a great deal of explanation of why they work as they do. Add these two lines to a program in which you want to print real values with two decimal places:

```
cout.setf(ios::fixed,ios::floatfield);
cout.precision(2);
```

The first line tells the computer that we want the line <u>cout.precision( )</u> to specify the number of decimal places, rather than the number of significant digits. After this is done, the line <u>cout.precision(2)</u> specifies that we want floating point numbers to print with two decimal places. Once set, this value holds for the rest of the program, or until another call to <u>cout.precision( )</u> changes it to a different value. [Briefly, <u>precision( )</u> is a member function of the class <u>iostream</u>, of which <u>cout</u> is an object, and a call to that function means asking it to perform a task.]

EXAMPLE 3-6　Suppose we have a variable named <u>num</u>. Here is the declaration followed by a statement to print the value:

```
double num = 2143.67645;

cout << num;
```

The output from this (in at least one compiler) will be 2143.68, with a total of six positions and two decimal places.

However, we can print a different number of decimal places by adding the lines specified above:

```
cout.setf(ios::fixed,ios::floatfield);
cout.precision(2);
cout << num << endl;
cout.precision(4);
cout << num << endl;
```

The output from this is the following:

```
2143.68
2143.6765
```

Note that the values are rounded up, first to two decimal places and then to four decimal places.

EXAMPLE 3-7　Suppose <u>hours</u> has the value 26.25. How will it print given these calls to <u>cout.precision( )</u>?

```
cout.setf(ios::fixed,ios::floatfield);
cout.precision(1);
cout << hours << endl;
cout.precision(2);
cout << hours << endl;
```

The first call to <u>cout.precision( )</u> causes <u>hours</u> to be printed with one decimal place: 26.3. The second call changes the number of decimal places to two, so <u>hours</u> prints with two decimal digits: 26.25.

WARNING　If you omit the call to <u>cout.setf( )</u>, the call to <u>cout.precision( )</u> will specify the number of significant digits, rather than the number of decimal places. Consider the following two lines [without a call to <u>cout.setf( )</u>]:

```
cout.precision(3);
cout << 14.3678;
```

The lines shown above will print 14.4 (three significant digits), not 14.368 (three decimal places).

FORMATTING OUTPUT FOR PROGRAM 3

Returning to Program 3, let's figure out how to print the values in a nice format. For simplicity, we'll print all values of type **double** with two decimal places. The final version looks like this:

```
cout.setf(ios::fixed,ios::floatfield);
cout.precision(2);
cout << "Employee " << id << " worked " << hours
    << "hours at a rate of $" << rate << " earning $"
    << pay << endl << endl;
```

Suppose <u>id</u> has the value 4444, <u>hours</u> has the value 15.3, and <u>rate</u> has the value 12.36. The lines above print the following:

```
Employee 4444 worked 15.30 hours at a rate of $12.36, earning $189.11
```

SETTING THE FIELD WIDTH: width( )

Occasionally (especially when printing values in columns), it is very useful to set a specific field width for the values to be printed, and to align the values within those columns. To specify the exact number of character positions a value should occupy when it is printed, use a call to <u>cout.width( )</u>, another member function of the <u>iostream</u> class, as shown in Example 3-8a.

EXAMPLE 3-8a   In Program 2, we wanted to print the values of <u>gpa</u> and <u>result</u> neatly aligned in columns; here are two of those sets of values:

```
1.5  154.5
2    12.6
```

In Chapter 2, we created columns by using tabs, but a nicer way is to use calls to <u>cout.width( )</u> inside the loop:

```
cout.width(10);
cout << gpa;
cout.width(10);
cout << result;
```

The values would print as shown below, right-aligned in columns 10 spaces wide:

```
  1.5       154.5
    2        12.6
```

WARNING   A call to <u>cout.width( )</u> applies only to the very next value to be printed. It doesn't even apply to two values printed in the same <u>cout</u>. This is different from calls to <u>cout.precision( )</u> and <u>cout.setf( )</u>, which stay in effect for the rest of the program.

LEFT AND RIGHT ALIGNMENT

Once you have specified a field width using <u>cout.width( )</u>, you can also specify whether you want the value left or right aligned within its field. Left aligned means starting in the far left position in the field; right aligned means ending in the far right position. Right alignment, shown in Example 3.8, is the default.

To set alignment, use a call to <u>cout.setf( )</u>, specifying left or right alignment:

```
cout.setf(ios::left);    // aligns left
cout.setf(ios::right);   // aligns right
```

The value set in this way remains in effect for the rest of the program, or until the next call that overrides it. The output in Example 3.8a illustrates right alignment, which is the default. Example 3-8b illustrates left alignment.

EXAMPLE 3-8b

```
cout.setf(ios::left);
cout.width(10);
cout << gpa;
cout.width(10);
cout << result;
```

This produces the following output:

```
1.5          154.5
2            12.6
```

SELF-CHECK 3-6

1. How can we print each of the following values exactly as shown?

   a. 13.5   b. −452.67   c. 455.2098

2. How can we print these numbers right aligned in a field of 20 spaces, with three decimal places apiece?

   162.45   298.765

SPLITTING WHAT WE SEND TO cout

Often what we want to send to <u>cout</u> is too long to fit on one line, especially with the appropriate indenting. When we look at the program, the line will run off the edge of the screen; when we print the output, the line will run over onto the next one, ruining the careful indenting. The program will still compile and run, but it is hard to read, both on screen and on paper.

When a line is too long to fit, it makes sense to break it up over two or more lines, as we did in Program 3:

```
cout << "Employee " << id << " worked " << hours
    << " hours at a rate of $" << rate << " earning $"
    << pay << endl << endl;
```

We have split the line carefully, between the items on the list, not in the middle of an item. It doesn't matter whether the << operator goes on the same line as the item to which it applies. You cannot, however, split a string over two lines, since that is a compilation error in C++.

If a string you want to print with <u>cout</u> is too long, the best solution is to divide the string into two separate strings. Here is one possible way:

```
cout << num << " followed by a string which is too long "
    << "to fit on one line" << endl;
```

These two strings will print the same way as if they had been combined in the <u>cout</u> statement.

Note that we have indented the continued lines of the statement that has been broken up. This is important to keep the program readable.

COMPLETE PROGRAM 3

Now we really are finished. We can rewrite the entire program with field widths and the full set of prompts:

 PROGRAM LISTING

```cpp
// Program prog3b.cpp:
// payroll program - reads in an ID number, hours worked,
// and rate of pay, and computes the weekly pay,
// using interactive data entry
#include <iostream>
using namespace std;
int main()
{
    int id,numemps = 0;
    double hours,rate,pay;

    cout.setf(ios::fixed,ios::floatfield);
    cout.precision(2);

    cout << "This program computes an employee's pay" << endl;
    cout << "Enter ID number, hours worked, and rate of pay"
        << endl;
    cout << "First, enter the employee's ID number" << endl;
    cout << "To stop, enter a negative value as the employee's ID number> ";
    cin >> id;
    while (id >= 0) {        // read until user enters a negative value
        cout << "Enter the hours worked> ";
        cin >> hours;
        cout << "Enter the rate of pay> ";
        cin >> rate;
        pay = hours * rate;
        cout << "Employee " << id << " worked " << hours
            << " hours at a rate of $" << rate << " earning $"
            << pay << endl << endl;
        cout << "Enter the employee's ID number, negative to stop> ";
        cin >> id;
        numemps++;
    }
    cout << "We processed " << numemps << " employees" << endl;
    return 0;
}
```

TRACING PROGRAM 3

Before we run this final version of the program, we should trace it just to make sure it is correct. You should do this with every program you write.

For simplicity, assume that the data values to be typed in are the two sets discussed before and a phony ID number, where each individual value is entered in response to a prompt. These are the three sets of values:

```
1234    35      14.20
2345    11.3     5.87
-1
```

PROGRAM TRACE Now let's trace our program on this set of data.

♦ The program begins by setting <u>numemps</u> to 0, prints some introductory messages, and continues by prompting the user to enter an ID number.

♦ The user types 1234, which is read from the keyboard, and <u>id</u> gets this value. Then <u>id</u> is compared to −1. The two numbers are not equal, so we enter the body of the loop.

♦ Inside the loop, the computer again prompts the user to enter two more values and reads these values, one into <u>hours</u> and one into <u>rate</u>. We find these values stored in the variables:

1234	35.0	14.20	
<u>id</u>	<u>hours</u>	<u>rate</u>	<u>pay</u>

The variable <u>pay</u> has no value yet because we did not read anything into it, and we have not yet computed its value. Then <u>pay</u> is calculated as 35.0 x 14.20 and set to 497.00.

1234	35.0	14.20	497.00
<u>id</u>	<u>hours</u>	<u>rate</u>	<u>pay</u>

We print the following:

> Employee 1234 worked 35.00 hours at a rate of $14.20, earning $497.00

Then we increment <u>numemps</u> to 1, indicating that we have processed one employee.

♦ Next, after again prompting the user, we read another employee's ID number, giving <u>id</u> the value 2345. We return to the loop header, where we find that the value for <u>id</u> is not equal to −1.

♦ We enter the body of the loop and read two more data values, setting the variables to the following (after we recompute <u>pay</u>, which is now 11.3 x 5.87 = 66.33):

2345	11.3	5.87	66.33
<u>id</u>	<u>hours</u>	<u>rate</u>	<u>pay</u>

The printout looks like this:

> Employee 2345 worked 11.30 hours at a rate of $5.87, earning $66.33

The computer again increments <u>numemps</u>, making it equal to 2.

♦ Then we prompt for and read in the third (and last) ID number, making <u>id</u> hold the value −1. We return to the loop header.

♦ This time when we compare, we find that <u>id</u> is equal to −1, so we fall out of the loop. We never read values for <u>hours</u> and <u>rate</u> or compute the <u>pay</u> for the phony employee, nor do we count that person. When we fall out of the loop, we print the final count of employees:

> We have processed 2 employees

Then we end the program.

In our trace, we analyzed three employees, two real and one phony. We could, of course, process many more; we could also run the program many times with different data values; this is the flexibility built into a program which reads in data. This completes Program 3.

SELF-CHECK 3-7

1. What happens in Program 3 if the user types in −1 as the first ID number?
2. Why didn't we read in a value for <u>pay</u>?
3. What will happen if you write this?

```
cout << "Today is
     Tuesday" << endl;
```

SECTION 6   THE If-else STATEMENT AND THE CONDITIONAL OPERATOR

There is a very powerful C++ feature that we did not need in Program 3 which will be helpful in modifying the basic program—for example, if we want to pay overtime to an employee who works more than 40 hours in a week or compute tax to be withheld.

CHOOSING ONE OF TWO ALTERNATIVES

Before we show how to use the new feature, let's investigate the alternative to its use. Consider this problem: We want to find the larger of <u>x</u> and <u>y</u>, put it in <u>max</u>, and print it. Figure 3-4 diagrams the problem. How can we translate this into C++? The program should determine which path to follow, execute the appropriate statement, and finally link up the two paths to print.

TWO POSSIBLE SOLUTIONS

First, we can initially assume that one case holds (e.g., that <u>y</u> is larger); if this is wrong, we'll make a modification.

```
max = y;
if (x > y)
    max = x;
cout << max << endl;
```

FIGURE 3-4   Diagram to find the larger of <u>x</u> and <u>y</u>

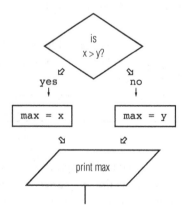

To see if this works, we don't have to try all possible combinations of x and y. We can test a representative sample of cases. In this example, there are two cases: x > y and x <= y. If we want to be meticulous, we can split this into three cases: x > y, x < y, and x = y.

PROGRAM TRACE Let's make up data to test these three cases, say x = 5 and y = 3; x = 4 and y = 6; and x = 7 and y = 7.

♦ If x = 5 and y = 3, we start by setting max to 3. The **if** condition is true, so max is reset to 5, and this value prints.

♦ If x = 4 and y = 6, max starts at 6. The **if** condition is false; we skip the max = x statement and print 6.

♦ If x = 7 and y = 7, max starts at 7; we skip the max = x statement and print 7.

All possible paths work correctly, which means that this is a correct translation, except that it is doing wasted work, since max is initially set to y even if it should be x. Also, this solution does not match the diagram, which says to choose one thing or the other, but not both.

Let's try another method. If the answer to the question is true (i.e., if x > y), we set max to x. If it's false, or more precisely if the reverse is true (if x <= y), we set max to y.

```
if (x > y)
    max = x;
if (x <= y)
    max = y;
cout << max << endl;
```

We leave it to you see whether this translation works in all cases for this problem. (It won't work if the first path modifies the outcome of the original question—see Exercise 7.) We are also asking two questions while the diagram says to ask only one, so again the C++ code does not match the diagram.

THE if-else STATEMENT

Our final method of translating the diagram works in all cases, does not use any extraneous statements, is more efficient, and is much closer to the spirit of the original diagram, which says to ask a question and then do one thing or another, but not both. Neither of the previous methods followed this basic outline, but the **if-else statement** does. The **if-else** statement provides two paths and allows us to execute exactly one of them, depending on the value of the condition. Example 3-9 is a solution using **if-else**. Note the indenting, which is not absolutely necessary but improves readability.

EXAMPLE 3-9 Here is the preferred solution to the problem of finding the larger of x and y:

```
if (x > y)
    max = x;
else
    max = y;
cout << max << endl;
```

PROGRAM TRACE

♦ If x = 5 and y = 3, the **if** condition is true; we execute the statement after the condition and set max to 5. The **else** statement is skipped when the condition is true. The cout prints 5.

♦ If x = 4 and y = 6, the **if** condition is false; as usual we skip the statement after the condition. However, now we do execute the **else** statement, which sets max to 6. The cout prints 6.

♦ If x = 7 and y = 7, the **if** condition is false; we skip the statement after the condition; the **else** statement sets max to 7 which is then printed.

All three cases give the correct answer, so this method works.

STYLE WORKSHOP This choice of one of two alternatives is extremely common in programming. The **if-else** statement is considered the best way to translate this choice into C++. Among other things, it is more efficient: it does not waste time making extra assignments or unnecessary comparisons. You should, however, appreciate the diverse ways C++ can translate this relatively simple diagram. As we go on, we will find that our major concern is not finding one way to do something but choosing among many methods.

THE GENERAL FORM OF if-else

Figure 3-5 diagrams the general form of the **if-else** statement.

This translates into C++ as follows:

General Form of if-else

```
if (cond)
      stmt-1;
else
      stmt-2;
stmt-3;
```

If *cond* is true, do *stmt-1*; if *cond* is false, do *stmt-2*. In all cases, do *stmt-3*.

STYLE WORKSHOP This format for the **if-else** statement is the most commonly used: indent the statement after the condition five spaces (or one tab position), and align the word **else** under the word **if**. Although you may see other formats, this is the one we consider to be better C++ style.

EXECUTING MORE THAN ONE INSTRUCTION IN AN if STATEMENT

We often want to do two or more things if the condition is true or if it's false. Suppose we want to find both the larger and smaller of x and y from Example 3-9, putting the larger in max and the smaller in min. Figure 3-6 illustrates the problem:

  C++ limits us to executing a single statement in case the **if** condition is true and another single statement in case the condition is false. Fortunately, we can modify this rule to execute more than one instruction. As usual, C++ uses a pair of braces to solve this problem. If either part of the **if-else** statement contains more than one statement, then braces must be used to form a compound statement.

FIGURE 3-5 Diagram of **if-else**

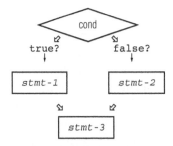

FIGURE 3-6   Diagram to find the larger and smaller of x and y

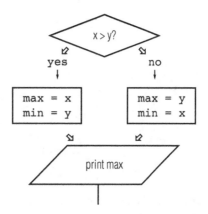

If we employ this new construction, we can find values for both the larger and smaller using a single **if-else** statement, as shown in Example 3-10.

EXAMPLE 3-10   This section of code uses compound statements to find both the larger and smaller of x and y.

```
if (x > y) {
     max = x;
     min = y;
}
else   {
     max = y;
     min = x;
}
cout << "max = " << max << " and min = " << min << endl;
```

General Form of if-else with Compound Statements

```
if (cond) {
     stmt-1;
     stmt-2;
     . . .
}
else {
     stmt-3;
     stmt-4;
     . . .
}
```

STYLE WORKSHOP We prefer this style of indenting. However, some C++ programmers like to align the braces in one of these ways:

```
if (cond) {                          if (cond)
    stmt-1;                          {
    stmt-2;                              stmt-1;
} else {                                 stmt-2;
    stmt-3;                          }
    stmt-4;                          else
}                                    {
                                         stmt-3;
                                         stmt-4;
                                     }
```

Most C++ programmers tend to be ardent advocates of one style of indenting and/or placement of braces. Your instructor may prefer a style different from ours. It is important to be consistent in whatever style you use.

REORGANIZING THE if-else

Statements which appear in both clauses of an **if-else** do not belong in either. These statements will be executed on each branch of the **if-else**; therefore, they should either precede or follow the entire construct. Example 3–11 illustrates this point.

EXAMPLE 3-11   The following **if-else** statement has identical statements in both clauses:

```
if (x > y) {
    cout << x << " " << y << endl;
    max = x;
    min = y;
    cout << "larger is " << max << " and smaller is " << min << endl;
}
else {
    cout << x << " " << y << endl;
    min = x;
    max = y;
    cout << "larger is " << max << " and smaller is " << min << endl;
}
```

The identical statements should be moved out of the **if-else**; depending on the context, they can be moved prior to or after the **if-else**, as shown here:

```
cout << x << " " << y << endl;
if (x > y) {
    max = x;
    min = y;
}
else {
    min = x;
    max = y;
}
cout << "larger is " << max << " and smaller is " << min << endl;
```

USING if-else TO MODIFY PROGRAM 3

Let's practice the **if-else** statement by modifying Program 3 to perform an additional task. Rather than simply computing an employee's pay, let's also figure the tax. The tax rate is not flat but has two levels. For employees who earn less than $300 a week, the tax is 15 percent of the pay; for all other employees, it is 28 percent. The net pay is the pay minus the tax.

Obviously, we should compute the tax after pay. Fifteen percent of pay is 0.15 * pay, and 28 percent is 0.28 * pay. To obtain the net pay, we want to subtract the appropriate amount from the employee's pay for withholding tax. To do this, we add two new variables: tax and netpay. The variable tax stores the amount to withhold; netpay is the employee's weekly pay after taxes. A new test will determine which value to store in tax; then we will subtract tax from pay to get netpay.

```
double tax,netpay;
...
pay = hours * rate;
if (pay < 300)
    tax = 0.15 * pay;
else
    tax = 0.28 * pay;
netpay = pay - tax;
```

We can insert these new statements into the version of Program 3 from Section 5 to produce a complete program that computes netpay and tax and prints both. Notice that we now double-space after printing tax and netpay, so that the program skips an extra line between employees.

PROGRAM LISTING

```
// Program prog3c.cpp:
// payroll program - reads in an ID number, hours worked,
// and rate of pay, and computes the weekly pay, after taxes,
// using interactive data entry
#include <iostream>
using namespace std;
int main()
{
    int id,numemps = 0;
    double hours,rate,pay;
    double tax,netpay;

    cout.setf(ios::fixed,ios::floatfield);
    cout.precision(2);

    cout << "This program computes an employee's pay" << endl;
    cout << "Enter ID number, hours worked, and rate of pay" << endl;
    cout << "First, enter the employee's ID number" << endl;
    cout << "To stop, enter a negative value as the employee's ID number> ";
    cin >> id;
    while (id >= 0) { // read until user enters a negative value
        cout << "Enter the hours worked> ";
        cin >> hours;
        cout << "Enter the rate of pay> ";
        cin >> rate;
        pay = hours * rate;
```

```
            if (pay < 300)
                tax = 0.15 * pay;
            else
                tax = 0.28 * pay;
            netpay = pay - tax;
            cout << "Employee " << id << " worked " << hours
                << " hours at a rate of $" << rate << " earning $"
                << pay << endl;
            cout << "tax withheld was $" << tax
                << " leaving net pay of $" << netpay << endl << endl;

            cout << "Enter the employee's ID number, negative to stop> ";
            cin >> id;
            numemps++;
        }
        cout << "We processed " << numemps << " employees" << endl;
        return 0;
}
```

SELF-CHECK 3-8

1. When should you use an **if-else** instead of just an **if** statement?
2. What should you do with a statement that is executed on both branches of an **if-else**?
3. Will the action following the **if** condition ever be executed together with the action following the **else**?

THE CONDITIONAL (?:) OPERATOR

C++ has another operator which is useful in selecting one of two alternatives. It is the **conditional operator**, whose symbol is ?: (a question mark followed by a colon). Let's use the conditional operator to assign the larger of x and y to max. Here is how we did it at the beginning of this section using **if-else**:

```
if (x > y)
    max = x;
else
    max = y;
```

The conditional operator allows us to write this as a single assignment statement which gives max a value using a **conditional expression** as its right-hand side:

```
max = x > y ? x : y;
```

Let's take a closer look.

♦ The conditional expression begins with the condition x > y, the same as in the **if** statement above, and has the same meaning: to test the relationship between x and y.

♦ The condition is followed by the ? symbol [you can think of x > y ? as saying "is (x > y)?"].

♦ The ? symbol is followed by two possible values for the expression, separated by a colon.

   To the left of the colon is the value of the expression if the condition is true.

   To the right of the colon is the value of the expression if the condition is false.

♦ After the entire expression is evaluated, its value will be assigned to max.

PROGRAM TRACE

♦ If x is 9 and y is 5, the condition is true, the expression gets the value 9, and max is assigned that value.

♦ If x is 12 and y is 23, the condition is false, the expression gets the value 23, and max is assigned that value.

♦ If x and y are both 10, the condition is false, the expression gets the value of y or 10, and max is assigned that value.

It is not necessary to assign the result of the conditional operator to a variable. We can put an expression involving the conditional operator anywhere we would use any other expression. The following statement simply prints the result which we assigned to max in the last example:

```
cout << "the larger number is " << x > y ? x : y;
```

General Form of the Conditional Expression

expr1 ? *expr2* : *expr3*
expr1 is a condition that evaluates to true or false
    if *expr1* is true
        expr2 is the value of the conditional expression
    else
        expr3 is the value of the conditional expression

USING A CONDITIONAL EXPRESSION IN PROGRAM 3

Let's use a conditional expression to compute tax in prog3c.cpp. We want to replace the **if-else** statement that computes tax in prog3c.cpp:

```
if (pay < 300)
    tax = 0.15 * pay;
else
    tax = 0.28 * pay;
```

The following conditional expression does the same thing as **if-else**:

```
tax = pay < 300 ? 0.15 * pay : 0.28 * pay;
```

If this is hard to read, we can use parentheses to make it clearer:

```
tax = (pay < 300) ? (0.15 * pay) : (0.28 * pay);
```

This statement says that if pay is less than 300, the value of the expression is 0.15 ∗ pay. If pay is greater than or equal to 300, the value of the expression is 0.28 ∗ pay. In either case, the value of the expression is assigned to tax.

STYLE WORKSHOP The conditional expression has several advantages over the **if-else** format. It is more versatile because it can be used as part of another expression. Also, as seen above, the conditional expression emphasizes that we are assigning a value to tax (or to max), whereas the **if-else** obscures this. On the other hand, we can execute more than one statement in each branch of an **if-else**, which gives it more power in most other circumstances.

SELF-CHECK 3-9

1. Does the result of a conditional expression have to be assigned to a variable?

2. a. What is to the left of the ? symbol in a conditional expression?

   b. What is to the left of the : symbol in a conditional expression?

   c. What is to the right of the : symbol in a conditional expression?

3. What is the value of each of the following conditional expressions?
   a. `3 > 4 ? 9 : 10;`
   b. `9 < 11 ? 0 : 1;`
   c. `8 == 8 ? 1 : 0;`

SECTION 7 ▪ FILE I/O

YUCKY OUTPUT

You may have discovered that the output from prog3c.cpp is messy. Now that we have interactive data entry, all sorts of things are competing for space on the screen: prompts, the data typed in by the user, and the output. The screen for prog3c.cpp looks like Figure 3-7 (and may be worse if there are other things on the screen before we run the program):

STYLE WORKSHOP   To most experienced programmers, this output is unattractive and almost unreadable. More importantly, consider what will happen if there are more than two employees: the information will scroll off the top of the screen. We won't be able to look at all the output at the end of the program or print it, either. What we really want is a neatly printed payroll report with just the computed results, without prompts and data.

MULTIPLE SOLUTIONS

There are several solutions to fixing the appearance of the output. This section solves the problem by sending the output of the program to a file. Sections 8 and 9 solve the problem by using two separate output streams.

FIGURE 3-7   Screen output for prog3b.cpp

```
This program computes an employee's pay.
Enter the ID number, hours worked, and rate of pay
First, enter the employee's ID number
To stop, enter a negative value as the employee's ID number> 1234
Enter the hours worked> 35
Enter the rate of pay> 14.20
Employee 1234 worked 35.00 hours at a rate of $14.20 earning $497.00
tax withheld was $139.16 leaving net pay of $357.84

Enter an ID number, negative to stop> 2345
Enter the hours worked> 11.3
Enter the rate of pay> 5.87
Employee 2345 worked 11.30 hours at a rate of $5.87 earning $66.33
tax withheld was $9.95 leaving net pay of $56.38

Enter an ID number, negative to stop> -1
We processed 2 employees
```

In this section, we'll show how to allow Program 3 to send its computed results directly to a file while the interactive data entry prompts and the input data remain displayed on the screen. First, we have to see how to use files for output (and for input as well).

USING FILES FOR INPUT AND OUTPUT

Reading from or printing to a file requires some extra steps in your program. The program shown in Figure 3-8 uses both file I/O and stream I/O. We will separate out the important features below.

FILE STREAM FSTREAM

To use files in C++, you must add another #include statement at the beginning of the program. While *#include <iostream>* permits use of the functions that work with iostreams like cin, cout, and cerr, it is necessary to add *#include <fstream>* to allow use of the functions that work with files.

OPENING AND NAMING THE FILE: USING ifstream AND ofstream

To use a file in C++, you must declare and open the file. This is done by specifying the name of the file on the disk, and associating the name of the disk file with the name by which the file will be called in the program. (Declaring the file can be done in combination with opening the file, or separately; we will show both ways.) For output, this association is done using ofstream: the line below declares the file object outfile, associates the internal name outfile with the file on disk called "p3.out", and opens that file:

```
ofstream outfile("p3.out");
```

For input, declaring the file is done using ifstream; the line below associates the internal name infile with the actual file on disk called "p3.dat". This statement declares the input file named infile and opens it:

```
ifstream infile("p3.dat");
```

FIGURE 3-8   A program that uses file I/O and stream I/O

```
#include <iostream>
#include <fstream>
using namespace std;
int main()
{
    int x,y;
    ofstream outfile("output.out");
    ifstream infile("input.in");

    cout << "This output will go to the screen" << endl;
    outfile << "This output will go to the output file" << endl;

    cin >> x;                           //This will read from the keyboard
    infile >> y;                        //This will read from the file

    cout << x << " " << y << endl;      // this will write to the screen
    outfile << x << " " << y << endl;   // this will write to the file

    outfile.close();
    infile.close();
    return 0;
}
```

The internal name for a file may be anything you wish, but it is customary to use names that reflect the use of the file (<u>infile</u>, <u>outfile</u>, <u>data</u>, etc.). When specifying the external name, you should give the full name by which the file is known in the system (for example, if file "p3.dat" is on your a: disk, you must say "a:p3.dat").

CAUTION For Windows and DOS users: To use a file in a subdirectory, prefix the path separator (\) with the escape character (also \) so that C++ will correctly identify the path character; for example, "c:\\homework\\p3.dat". In Unix, which uses the / character for directory paths, this is not a problem.

USING A SEPARATE CALL TO open( )

The statements on the previous page do two things: they declare the internal name (<u>infile</u> or <u>outfile</u>), and they associate the internal name with the external name ("p3.dat" or "p3.out"). It is also possible to separate opening the file from the declaration, using the file stream member function <u>open( )</u>:

```
ifstream infile;
ofstream outfile;

infile.open("p3.dat");
outfile.open("p3.dat");
```

This is particularly useful when you want to open a file more than once in a program, or when you want to use a file in several functions in a program (see Chapter 5).

LOCATION OF DECLARATION

Declaring the file may be done inside the main program as shown in these examples, or it may be done above main. Declaring the file above main makes the file available for use in the main program as well as in other functions the program uses (see Chapter 5). The file must be opened before the first use of the file. Do not open a file more than once (unless you close it in between), because each call to <u>open( )</u> starts reading or writing over again at the beginning of the file.

CLOSING FILES

When you are finished using a file, you should close it, as shown below. The system will generally close the file if you don't explicitly close it, but failure to close a file can cause problems, and you should get into the habit of explicitly closing all files.

```
infile.close();
outfile.close();
```

USING AN OUTPUT FILE

Once a file has been opened, you can write to it by substituting its name where you would have used <u>cout</u>. The following statement writes the value of <u>num</u> to the file known internally as <u>outfile</u>.

```
outfile << num;
```

Example 3-12 summarizes the steps needed to use a file for output.

EXAMPLE 3-12   Here are the steps needed to send output to file "p3.out":

```cpp
#include <iostream>
#include <fstream>                          // allow use of functions to work with files
using namespace std;
int main()
{
    int num = 15;
    ofstream outfile("p3.out");            // open file "p3.out" and call it outfile
    outfile << num;                        // write the value of num to the file
    outfile.close();                       // close the file
    return 0;
}
```

SOLVING THE PROGRAM 3 PROBLEM: SENDING OUTPUT TO A FILE

The program below solves the problem of output in Program 3. The program sends prompts to the screen by writing to <u>cout</u>; it reads input from <u>cin</u>, and that input is echoed to the screen. The output—the actual computed results—are sent to a file on disk.

PROGRAM LISTING

```cpp
// Program prog3d.cpp:
// payroll program - reads in an ID number, hours worked,
// and rate of pay, and computes the weekly pay, after taxes,
// reading data from cin and sending output to a file
#include <iostream>
#include <fstream>
using namespace std;
int main()
{
    int id, numemps = 0;
    double hours, rate, pay;
    double tax, netpay;

    ofstream outfile("p3.out");

    outfile.setf(ios::fixed, ios::floatfield);
    outfile.precision(2);

    outfile << "\t\t\tPayroll Report" << endl << endl;

    cout << "This program computes an employee's pay" << endl;
    cout << "Enter ID number, hours worked, and rate of pay"
         << endl;
    cout << "First, enter the employee's ID number" << endl;
    cout << "To stop, enter a negative value as the employee's ID number> ";

    cin >> id;
    while (id >= 0) { // read until user enters a negative value
        cout << "Enter the hours worked> ";
        cin >> hours;
        cout << "Enter the rate of pay> ";
```

```
        cin >> rate;
        pay = hours * rate;
        if (pay < 300)
            tax = 0.15 * pay;
        else
            tax = 0.28 * pay;
        netpay = pay - tax;
        outfile << "Employee " << id << " worked " << hours
                << " hours at a rate of $" << rate << " earning $"
                << pay << endl;
        outfile << "tax withheld was $" << tax
                << " leaving net pay of $" << netpay << endl << endl;
        cout << "Enter the employee's ID number, negative to stop> ";
        cin >> id;
        numemps++;
    }
    outfile << "We processed " << numemps << " employees" << endl;
    outfile.close();
    return 0;
}
```

This version of the program produces the results shown in Figure 3-9.

USING AN INPUT FILE

We've solved our last issue with Program 3, but we still should see how to read in data values from an input file. As we discuss later in this section, it is often easier and more convenient to read data from a file than from a keyboard. (You must create the data file before you read from it, by opening a file, typing in the data values, and saving the file.)

Once a file has been opened, you can read from it by substituting its name where you would have used <u>cin</u>. The following statement reads a value from the file known internally as <u>infile</u> and puts the value into <u>num</u>.

```
infile >> num;
```

Example 3-13 summarizes the steps necessary to use a file for input.

EXAMPLE 3-13   Here are the steps necessary to read data from file "p3.dat":

```
#include <iostream>
#include <fstream>                    // allow use of functions to work with files
using namespace std;
int main()
{
    int num;
    ifstream infile("p3.dat");    // open file "p3.dat" and call it infile

    infile >> num;                    // read a value for num from the file

    infile.close();               // close the file
    return 0;
}
```

FIGURE 3-9A   Screen output for prog3d.cpp

```
This program computes an employee's pay.
Enter the ID number, hours worked, and rate of pay
First, enter the employee's ID number
To stop, enter a negative value as the employee's ID number> 1234
Enter the hours worked> 35
Enter the rate of pay> 14.20

Enter an ID number, negative to stop> 2345
Enter the hours worked> 11.3
Enter the rate of pay> 5.87

Enter an ID number, negative to stop> -1
```

FIGURE 3-9B   File output for prog3d.cpp

```
Employee 1234 worked 35.00 hours at a rate of $14.20 earning $497.00
tax withheld was $139.16 leaving net pay of $357.84

Employee 2345 worked 11.30 hours at a rate of $5.87 earning $66.33
tax withheld was $9.95 leaving net pay of $56.38

We processed 2 employees
```

PROGRAM 3 USING FILE I/O (ALL OPERATING SYSTEMS)

Here is a final version of Program 3 that reads input from a file and sends output to a file. This version of the program will work in all operating systems.

Note that all references to cin are changed to infile. Any references to cout are changed to outfile. (This includes the calls to setf( ) and precision( ), which now must define the output as it appears in the output file, not in cout.) Prompts are omitted; they are not necessary (and in fact are wasteful) once we are reading from a data file.

PROGRAM LISTING

```cpp
// Program prog3e.cpp:
// payroll program - reads in an ID number, hours worked,
// and rate of pay, and computes the weekly pay, after taxes,
// reading data from a file and sending output to a file
#include <iostream>
#include <fstream>
using namespace std;
int main()
{
    int id,numemps = 0;
    double hours,rate,pay;
    double tax,netpay;

    ifstream infile("p3.dat");
    ofstream outfile("p3.out");

    outfile.setf(ios::fixed,ios::floatfield);
```

```
        outfile.precision(2);

        outfile << "\t\t\tPayroll Report" << endl << endl;
        infile >> id;
        while (id >= 0) {                  // read until user enters a negative value
            infile >> hours;
            infile >> rate;
            pay = hours * rate;
            if (pay < 300)
                tax = 0.15 * pay;
            else
                tax = 0.28 * pay;
            netpay = pay - tax;
            outfile << "Employee " << id << " worked " << hours
                    << " hours at a rate of $" << rate << " earning $"
                    << pay << endl;
            outfile << "tax withheld was $" << tax
                    << " leaving net pay of $" << netpay << endl << endl;
            infile >> id;
            numemps++;
        }
        outfile << "We processed " << numemps << " employees" << endl;
        infile.close();
        outfile.close();
        return 0;
}
```

ADVANTAGES OF USING FILES

Is useful to discuss just why working with files is so important. There are a number of advantages to using a file for input, and there are a number of advantages to using a file for output.

ADVANTAGES OF USING A FILE FOR INPUT

First, let's talk about using a file for input. If you are trying to get a program to work, you may have to run the program over and over. If you are using the keyboard to enter values, this could mean typing in the same data values many times. On the other hand, if you use a data file for input, the data file is typed in advance, not while the program is running, The values in the file are typed in only once, no matter how many times the program is run. This saves you from retyping the same values while you are debugging your program

In some of the later programs, there may be many paths through the program, and each path should be tested to make sure that the program works in all cases. This may mean you need to enter many different sets of values, which could be tedious to type in over and over from the keyboard. In addition, the same data file can be used for several different programs. For example, one program can find the average of the set of data values in a file. Another program can put these same data values into ascending order. (This is called sorting a set of data; it will be discussed in a later chapter.) Your instructor may want to create a file of data values; that same file can be used to test every student's program. Finally, in a commercial program, the actual data set used could be much too large for the values to be entered one at a time as the program is executing.

ADVANTAGES OF USING A FILE FOR OUTPUT

There are also advantages to using a file for output, instead of having all output go to the screen. One advantage of using a file for output is that the output file is permanent. If you send output to the screen, then you will usually need some method of printing a copy of what is on the screen before the output window is closed. But if you send the output to a file, the output file is still available after the program ends. Second, the output file can be permanently stored on a hard drive, or the output file can be on a diskette or flash memory which can be carried from place to place. Third, the output file can include any number of lines; it is not limited to the size of the output window. In addition, if you use an output file, your program can send some output to the screen (for example, prompts) and some to the output file (for example, results computed by the program), making the output easier for the user to read. Finally, the output from one program can then be used as an input file for another program.

SECTION 8 ## ENRICHMENT: I/O STREAMS cin, cout, AND cerr

The following section introduces standard I/O streams, and proposes using cerr as part of the solution to improving the output from Program 3. All students should be introduced to cerr and the concept of separate output streams. Section 8 works closely with Section 9, on redirection and piping of output. In Windows, redirection is permitted only when running the program from the Command prompt.

OUTPUT FROM PROGRAM 3

If you skipped Section 7, go back and read the section entitled Yucky Output, and look at the output shown in Figure 3-7. Briefly, the problem is that prog3b.cpp sends everything to the screen: prompts, copies of the data values entered, and computed results. It's too long and pretty messy. Section 7 showed how to solve the problem using files. This section, and the next, provide another option.

STANDARD INPUT/OUTPUT STREAMS cin, cout, and cerr

We would like to allow Program 3 to send its computed results directly to the printer or to a file while the interactive data entry prompts and the input data remain displayed on the screen. We can do that by splitting the program's output and sending it to two different standard output streams.

C++ has three **standard input/output streams**: cin, cout, and cerr. The input stream cin refers to the place from which C++ reads input values; by default, C++ reads from the keyboard, and the values typed in are echoed to the screen. The output stream cout refers to the place to which C++ sends output messages; by default, C++ sends output to the screen. We have already used cin and cout.

The second output stream cerr refers to the place to which C++ sends error messages; by default, that is also the screen. Normally the output to cout and cerr, as well as the echo of values typed into cin, are mixed together, as shown in Figure 3-10.

Unless you do something like redirection or piping (see Section 9) to separate the destination of the I/O streams, you won't see any difference between sending output to cout and sending it to cerr. The difference between the two, however, is at the heart of solving the problem of the output from Program 3.

FIGURE 3-10 Screen as destination for <u>cout</u>, <u>cerr</u>, and echo of <u>cin</u>

Default:
```
cerr << "Enter num> " << endl;
cin >> num;
cout << "num is " << num << endl;
```

```
Enter num>
123
num is 123
```

screen

FIGURE 3-11 screen, after redirection of <u>cout</u>

When cout is redirected elsewhere:
```
cerr << "Enter num> " << endl;
cin >> num;
cout << "num is " << num << endl;
```

```
Enter num>
123
```

num is 123

screen

printer or
output file

It is possible to send <u>cout</u> to a different location, such as to the printer or to a file. Unix uses piping to send output to the printer and redirection to send output to a file; DOS uses redirection for both. Windows allows redirection to a file or to the printer (but not to a printer that uses a USB port). With redirection or piping, anything sent to <u>cout</u> goes to the new location. In DOS and Unix, this redirection of <u>cout</u> does not affect <u>cerr</u> or the echo of <u>cin</u> which still go to the screen, as shown in Figure 3-11.

SELF-CHECK 3-10

1. What is an input stream?
2. What is an output stream?
3. a. What is the default destination of <u>cout</u>?
   b. What is the default destination of <u>cerr</u>?
   c. What is the default source of <u>cin</u>?

SEPARATING THE PROMPTS FROM THE OUTPUT

In Program 3, we want to divide the output between a file (or the printer) and the screen. The actual computed results of our program should go to <u>cout</u>, which can be redirected to a file (or to the printer). We can then send the prompts to <u>cerr</u>, which continues to go to the screen. (The prompts are worthless to the user if they don't go to the screen, because they aren't visible on the screen as a guide to entering data values.)

You may wonder why we send prompts, which are not errors, to <u>cerr</u>. Despite its name, <u>cerr</u> is simply a second available output stream; we can use it for any output which we intend to go to the screen.

This means that the lines that print the computed <u>pay</u>, <u>tax</u>, and <u>netpay</u> for each employee should go to <u>cout</u>:

```
cout << "Employee " << id << " worked " << hours
        << " hours at a rate of $" << rate << " earning $"
        << pay << endl;
cout << "tax withheld was $" << tax
        << " leaving net pay of $" << netpay << endl << endl;
```

The final line that prints the employee count should also send its output to the file (or to the printer) rather than to the screen with the prompts and input values:

```
cout << "We processed " << numemps << " employees" << endl;
```

While we are producing neat output, it would be a good idea to add a heading at the top. We can do this just as we did in Program 2, by printing a message. This time we will send it to <u>cout</u> so the message appears with the rest of the output. A good heading might be "Payroll Report." Here is the line to print this heading, roughly centered by using three tabs, followed by a blank line:

```
cout << "\t\t\tPayroll Report" << endl << endl;
```

The rest of the lines currently going to <u>cout</u> are prompts, and they should appear on the screen so that the user knows what to type in. We should make their destination <u>cerr</u>; when <u>cout</u> is redirected, <u>cerr</u> continues to go to the screen. Here is the revised Program 3 with these modifications.

PROGRAM LISTING

```cpp
// Program prog3f.cpp:
// payroll program - reads in an ID number, hours worked,
// and rate of pay, and computes the weekly pay, after taxes,
// using interactive data entry and cerr for prompts

#include <iostream>
using namespace std;
int main()
{
    int id, numemps = 0;
    double hours, rate, pay;
    double tax, netpay;

    cout.setf(ios::fixed, ios::floatfield);
    cout.precision(2);

    cout << "\t\t\tPayroll Report" << endl << endl;
    cerr << "This program computes an employee's pay" << endl;
    cerr << "Enter ID number, hours worked, and rate of pay"
        << endl;
    cerr << "First, enter the employee's ID number" << endl;
    cerr << "To stop, enter a negative value as the employee's ID number> ";
    cin >> id;
    while (id >= 0) {             // read until user enters a negative value
        cerr << "Enter the hours worked> ";
        cin >> hours;
        cerr << "Enter the rate of pay> ";
        cin >> rate;
        pay = hours * rate;
        if (pay < 300)
            tax = 0.15 * pay;
        else
            tax = 0.28 * pay;
        netpay = pay - tax;
        cout << "Employee " << id << " worked " << hours
            << " hours at a rate of $" << rate << " earning $"
```

```
                            << pay << endl;
                cout << "tax withheld was $" << tax
                    << " leaving net pay of $" << netpay << endl << endl;
                cerr << "Enter the employee's ID number, negative to stop> ";
                cin >> id;
                numemps++;
            }
            cout << "We processed " << numemps << " employees" << endl;
            return 0;
    }
```

After these changes, and when output is redirected, the output sent to <u>cout</u> appears as shown in Figure 3-12a, while all other output continues to go to the screen, as shown in Figure 3-12b.

CAUTION Remember that the output will be divided as shown above *only* if you redirect <u>cout</u>, as explained in Section 9. We recommend that you postpone redirecting output until your program is completely debugged. In other words, send all of your output to the screen until you are sure the program is working; then, by redirection, send the computed results to a file or to the printer. Displaying everything until the program is debugged saves a lot of time tracing the program. Furthermore, if there is the possibility of an infinite loop, displaying your output may save a lot of paper!

STYLE WORKSHOP The format in which we have displayed the output is simple and works for programs with small amounts of output. However, it is not as easy to read as output aligned in columns with headings, like the results of Program 2. The output from our payroll program would be much easier to read if it looked like Figure 3-13.

You should begin to experiment with ways to produce neat, clean output from a program, utilizing tabs, blanks, and field widths to create columns and headings. Exercise 38 asks you to rewrite Program 3 to produce the output in Figure 3-13. Be aware that you must eliminate the prompts to make the output this neat.

FIGURE 3-12A   Output to <u>cout</u> when separated from prompts and input

```
                        Payroll Report
Employee 1234 worked 35.00 hours at a rate of $14.20 earning $497.00
tax withheld was $139.16, leaving net pay of $357.84

Employee 2345 worked 11.30 hours at a rate of $ 5.87 earning $66.33
tax withheld was $9.95 leaving net pay of $   56.38

We have processed 2 employees
```

FIGURE 3-12B   Screen, containing prompts and input values

```
This program computes an employee's pay.
Enter the ID number, hours worked, and rate of pay
First, enter the employee's ID number
To stop, enter a negative value as the employee's ID number> 1234
Enter the hours worked> 35
Enter the rate of pay> 14.20

Enter an ID number, negative to stop> 2345
Enter the hours worked> 11.3
Enter the rate of pay> 5.87

Enter an ID number, negative to stop> -1
```

FIGURE 3-13   Suggested improved output from Program 3

```
                        Payroll Report
   Emp. ID    Hours Worked    Pay Rate    Pay        Tax        Netpay
   1234         35.00         $14.20      $497.00    $139.16    $357.84
   2345         11.30         $ 5.86      $ 66.33    $  9.95    $ 56.38
         We have processed 2 employees
```

SELF-CHECK 3-11

1. Is <u>cerr</u> reserved for error messages?
2. Why is it foolish to send prompts to the printer?

SECTION 9 ENRICHMENT: REDIRECTION OR PIPING OF INPUT/OUTPUT

The following section introduces redirecting (or piping) output to a file (or to the printer) while still sending the prompts to the screen. *Note:* We will use the term "redirection" loosely in this section to include the idea of piping.

REDIRECTION AND PIPING OF OUTPUT

We can send output directly to a file on disk (or to the printer) using **redirection** (in DOS, Windows, and Unix) or **piping** (in Unix). Redirection or piping sends <u>cout</u> to a different destination than the screen. In most circumstances, output sent to <u>cerr</u> and the echo of values typed into <u>cin</u> are still sent to the screen.

Sending output to a file on disk is often quite useful. It may be necessary in an environment where printers are shared (as in a computer lab). It is also valuable when the output is lengthy, or when the programmer wants to examine the output, then use it as input to another program.

HOW TO REDIRECT OR PIPE cout

We first illustrate redirection or piping of just <u>cout</u>.

IN WINDOWS OR DOS

Redirection requires you to run your program from the command prompt (also called the DOS prompt). First, compile the program. Then do one of the following:

1. **In Windows XP,** go to the Start menu, select Run and type the word command. This will open a command window.

   In Windows98, go to the Start menu, select Programs | MS-DOS Prompt. This will open a DOS window.

   In DOS, first Make the program (compile and link at once). Then select File | Exit to DOS.

2. Next change to the folder in which your program is located. For example, if your programs are stored in C:\myprograms, type in

   ```
   cd \my programs <Enter>
   ```

If your programs are stored on a floppy disk in the a: drive, type this:

```
a: <Enter>
```

If your programs are stored on a flash drive, type the name of the drive and then <Enter>.

REDIRECTION TO A FILE (IN BOTH WINDOWS AND DOS)

Run the program by typing the name of its executable file, followed by the output redirection symbol (>) and a name you have picked for the output file, such as p3.out.

For example, if the program is named prog3.cpp, the executable file is prog3.exe, and you type the following to redirect output to a file p3.out:

```
prog3 > p3.out
```

The output file will be in the same folder as your program. Open it in your editor and print it.

NOTE

Without redirection, you can run your program from the command line (after compiling it) simply by typing its name at the prompt:

```
prog3
```

REDIRECTING TO THE PRINTER

To send the output to the printer, substitute prn in place of the file name.

```
prog3 > prn
```

WARNING (for Windows) In newer versions of Windows, redirection of output to the printer is very problematic; sending output to a file is the best solution.

IN UNIX

If you are running gcc or g++ under Unix, you can send the output to the printer by piping, or to a file by redirection. Either is a simple modification of the way you have always run the program: typing the name of the executable file at the prompt.

PIPING TO THE PRINTER

To pipe the output to the printer, type the name of the executable file, followed by the pipe symbol (the upright bar: |) and the Unix filter program lpr.

For example, if the program is named prog3.cpp, the executable file is a.out, and you type the following to pipe the output to the printer:

```
a.out | lpr
```

REDIRECTING TO A FILE

To send the output to a file, you must use redirection.

Type the name of the executable file, followed by the output redirection symbol (>) and the name of the file to be created:

```
a.out > outfile
```

REDIRECTION OF INPUT

One other item is important while we are discussing input and output. Just as we can redirect output to a file, we can also redirect input to come from a data file on a disk rather than the keyboard. The values in a data file are typed in only once. This saves you from typing in the same values over and over while you are debugging your program. In addition, the process of testing a program usually means entering many different sets of values to make sure that the program works in all cases, but it is essential to test each new version on the same sets. (We will discuss testing your program in more detail later. Your instructor may want to create a set of data values to test each student's program.) Finally, in commercial programs, data sets are much too large for the values to be entered one at a time.

For all these reasons, it is often convenient to redirect <u>cin</u>. Input can be redirected even if your program sends prompts to the screen; the prompts appear, but the computer no longer waits for you to type in data since the values are coming from a file. (Of course, if redirection is your permanent way of entering data, the prompts aren't necessary.) Here's how to redirect <u>cin</u> in the two environments; do everything explained above for redirecting output. But at the last step, type the following to read data from a file called <u>p3.dat</u>:

```
prog3 < p3.dat
```

REDIRECTING BOTH INPUT AND OUTPUT

It is possible to redirect both <u>cin</u> and <u>cout</u> at the same time. Here's what you would type at the prompt to redirect <u>cin</u> to come from <u>p3.dat</u> and also to send <u>cout</u> to a file <u>p3.out</u>:

```
prog3 < p3.dat > p3.out
```

SELF-CHECK 3-12

1. What does redirection mean? What does piping mean?
2. How do you specify the printer in the system you are using?
3. If you redirect input, where does the data come from?

SUMMARY

READING DATA

1. As a C++ program is executing, it can read values from a set of data. The same program can be run with different data, leading to much more flexibility.

2. The set of data is the group of values that will be read into a specific program. It is not part of the C++ program but will be input as requested from outside while the program is running. In our first few programs, we will enter data from the keyboard. This is called interactive data entry.

3. A phony value or piece of data (sometimes called a sentinel or trailer) indicates the end of a set of data. This phony value can be a special one as a signal that it is the last value. For example, a phony value for <u>id</u> marks the end of data in Program 3.

THE **while** LOOP

4. A **while** loop can be used as an alternative to a **for** loop. A **while** loop allows a program to repeat a series of statements without specifying an exact initial value or increment.

5. Here is the general form of a **while**, where <u>cond</u> is a condition that evaluates to either true or false. If only one statement is included in the body of the loop, the { and } lines can be eliminated.

```
while (cond) {
    stmt-1;
    stmt-2;
    ...
    stmt-3;
}
```

6. The **while** loop is executed as follows: The condition *cond* is evaluated. If it is true, the body of the loop is executed. Then *cond* is evaluated again, and the process is repeated. The body of the loop is executed each time the condition is true. If the condition becomes false, the loop is terminated, the body is not executed, and the program goes on to the statement after the loop.

7. If the condition of a **while** loop is never true, the loop is never entered. If the condition of a **while** loop never becomes false, the loop never terminates. This is called an infinite loop.

READING FROM <u>cin</u>

8. By reading from the input stream <u>cin</u>, a program can read a data value for one or more variables from the keyboard. By reading in values, a program becomes much more useful because it can be run on many different sets of data without changes or recompiling.

9. Values entered as data may be separated by blanks, tabs, or <Enter>. When reading from <u>cin</u> using the extraction operator (>>), the computer reads past all these characters while trying to find a value for a numeric variable. The program does not continue until each included variable has been given a value.

PROMPTS

10. A prompt is a message displayed on the screen as the result of sending a message to <u>cout</u> (or <u>cerr</u>). The prompt tells the user when to enter a data value. Here is an example of a prompt, followed by reading from <u>cin</u>.

```
cout << "Enter a number> ";
cin >> number;
```

STRUCTURED READ LOOP

11. A structured read loop reads in data while testing for a final value. The general form of a structured read loop is shown below, where *cond* is a condition that depends upon the value read from <u>cin</u>.

```
cin >> id;
while (cond) {
    // process ID
    ...
    cin >> id;
}
```

DECIMAL PLACES AND FIELD WIDTHS

12. A value of type **double** or **float** will normally be printed with up to 6 significant digits; however, this can be changed.

13. It is possible to specify the number of decimal places to print by inserting two lines in the program:

```
cout.setf(ios::fixed,ios::floatfield);
cout.precision(2);
```

The first line says that the next line will specify the number of decimal places, rather than the number of significant digits. Then the second line says to print all real numbers with two decimal places. The value to be printed is rounded to the nearest decimal place. The number of decimal places set by a call to cout.precision( ) holds for the rest of the program, or until overridden by another call to cout.precision( ).

14. A call to cout.width( ) can be used to specify the number of spaces to use to print a real value. This can be used to print numbers in columns. A call to cout.width( ) specifies the size of the field in which to print just the next value (it does not hold for the rest of the program). The following call says to print a value in a field of 10 spaces.

```
cout.width(10);
```

15. Once a field width has been established, values are by default right-aligned in the field. It is possible to specify left or right-alignment by calls to cout.setf( ):

```
cout.setf(ios::left);
cout.setf(ios::right);
```

Each of these applies until the end of the program or until overridden.

THE **if-else** STATEMENT

16. The **if-else** construction can select one of two alternatives. The general form is

```
if (cond)
    stmt-1;
else
    stmt-2;
```

If the condition *cond* is true, then statement *stmt-1* is executed; if *cond* is false, then statement *stmt-2* is executed instead. One of the two (but never both) statements is executed each time the **if-else** statement is encountered.

17. In general, C++ allows only a single statement to be executed on either path through a conditional statement. However, by using a pair of braces (i.e., a compound statement), a programmer can include as many statements as necessary on either path. Here is an example with two statements in one case and three in the other:

```
if (condition) {
    st-1;
    st-2;
}
else {
    st-3;
    st-4;
    st-5;
}
```

If *condition* evaluates to true, statements *st-1* and *st-2* are executed; if *condition* evaluates to false, statements *st-3*, *st-4*, and *st-5* are executed.

THE CONDITIONAL OPERATOR

18. The conditional (?:) operator is another method of selecting one of two alternatives and is used in a conditional expression. The general form of the conditional expression is

cond ? *true option* : *false option*

If *cond* is true, the conditional expression has the value of *true option*; otherwise, it has the value of *false option*. A conditional expression can be used anywhere any other expression is valid; the resulting value can be assigned to a variable or simply printed. Here are two examples:

```
y = a < b ? a : b;
cout << a <= b ? "a is less" : "a is equal or greater" << endl;
```

FILES FOR INPUT/OUTPUT

19. With the addition of a few statements, a program can directly read from and write to files on disk. Here are the steps necessary to read a value from one disk file and write that value to another file:

```
#include <iostream>
#include <fstream>                    // new include directive
using namespace std;
int main()
{
    int x;

    ofstream outfile("px.out");       // open files
    ifstream infile("px.in");

    infile >> x;                       // read x from file infile
    outfile << x;                      // write x to file outfile

    outfile.close();                   // close files
    infile.close();
    return 0;
}
```

INPUT/OUTPUT STREAMS: cin, cout, AND cerr

20. C++ has three standard input/output streams. Standard input or cin comes, by default, from the keyboard. Standard output or cout goes, by default, to the screen. Standard error or cerr also goes, by default, to the screen.

21. In a single program, you can direct some output to the screen and some to the printer or to a file. Typically, prompts are directed to the screen, and the computed values are directed a file or to the printer.

REDIRECTION AND PIPING OF INPUT/OUTPUT

22. When a program's output is redirected to the printer, output sent to cout goes to the printer; any output sent to cerr continues to go to the screen.

23. To redirect input or output in Windows, you must run the program from the command window. Use the output redirection symbol (>), followed by a filename to redirect output to a file on a disk.

    redirecting to a file on disk

    ```
    progx > c:px.out
    ```

24. To use redirection or piping in Unix, run the program as usual from the prompt. To pipe output to the printer, use the pipe symbol (the upright bar: |) and the Unix filter program lpr. To send output to a file, use the redirection symbol (>) and the name of the output file to be created.

piping to a file on disk   **redirecting to the printer**

```
a.out | outfile
```
```
a.out > lpr
```

25. In Windows or Unix, it is possible to redirect input so that it comes from a file on a disk rather than the keyboard. (In Windows, this must be done from the command window.) To redirect input, use the input redirection symbol (<), followed by the name of the file which contains the data; for example, if the program is named <u>progx</u>, the following statement reads data from the file <u>px.dat</u>:

Windows   **Unix**

```
progx < px.dat
```
```
a.out < px.dat
```

EXERCISES

TRACING EXERCISES

1. Trace each of these C++ programs step by step. Show exactly what is printed by each program.

   a.
   ```cpp
   #include <iostream>
   using namespace std;
   int main()
   {
       int p, q=2;

       cout << "q p " << endl;
       while (q <= 6) {
           p = 2 * q + 3;
           cout << q << " " << p
               << endl;
           q +=2;
       }
       return 0;
   }
   ```

   b.
   ```cpp
   #include <iostream>
   using namespace std;
   int main()
   {
       int x=15,y=4;

       cout << "x y" << endl;
       while (x >= 0) {
           x = x - y;
           y = y + 3;
       }
       cout << x << " " << y;
       return 0;
   }
   ```

   c.
   ```cpp
   #include <iostream>
   using namespace std;
   int main()
   {
       int s=8, t=0;

       while (s >= 4){
           if (s > t)
               t += 3;
           if (s <= t)
               s += 2;

           cout << s << " " << t
               << endl;
           s -= 3;
           cout << s << " " << t
               << endl;
       }
       return 0;
   }
   ```

   d.
   ```cpp
   #include <iostream>
   using namespace std;
   int main()
   {
       int x=-3,y=1,z=2;

       while (x < z) {
           if (abs(x + z) > abs(y))
               cout << " no ";
           if (abs (x) + abs (z) > abs (y))
               cout << " no ";
           cout << " maybe ";
           x++;
           z--;
       }
       return 0;
   }
   ```

e.
```cpp
#include <iostream>
#include <cmath>
using namespace std;
int main()
{
double b;
    int a=0;

    cout << "number ";
    cout << "square root ";
    while (a <= 6) {
        b = sqrt(a);
        cout << a << " " << b
            << endl;
        a += 1;
    }
    return 0;
}
```

f.
```cpp
#include <iostream>
using namespace std;
int main()
{
    int c=1;
    double d;

    cout << "number reciprocal";
    cout << " check" << endl;
    while (c <= 8) {
        d = 1.0 / c;
        cout << c << '\t' << d
            << '\t' << c*d << endl;
        c += 1;
    }
    return 0;
}
```

2. What is the value of <u>ans</u> at the end of the following **if-else** statement?
```cpp
num1 = 12;
num2 = 14;
if (num1 + 3 < num2 - 2)
    ans = num1 - 9;
else
    ans = num1 + num2;
```

3. What is printed by the following section of code?
```cpp
int num=9,x=12;

if (num >= x) {
    num = x;
    x = num - 2;
}
else {
    x = num;
    num += 3;
}
cout << "num = " << num << " and x = " << x << endl;
```

4. What is wrong with the following loop?
```cpp
x = 4;
while (x < 5);
    cout << x << endl;
```

5.   a. When reading data, which of the two—<u>cout</u> or <u>cin</u>—causes a message to appear on the screen?

      b. Which of the two causes the computer to stop and wait for the user to type in a value?

      c. Which of the two lines below could be eliminated? Why?
```cpp
cout << "Enter a number> ";
cin >> num;
```

6. A program is said to be **user friendly** if it is easy to understand and use. What techniques help to make a program user friendly?

7. a. What is wrong with the following code?

```
if (x > 100)
    x -= 10;
if (x < 100)
    x -= 17;
cout << "x is now " << x << endl;
```

   b. Rewrite the code above using an **if-else**.

8. What is wrong with the following **if-else** statement? Note that it is not a simple syntax error—it *will* compile. Fix the error.

```
if (x = y)
    z = x + 1;
else
    z = x + 2;
```

9. Suppose we have the following **if-else** statement. If the code prior to it gives values only to x and y, can we rely on p or z having a value (other than garbage) in the statement that writes to cout?

```
if (x < y)
    p = x;
else
    z = x;
cout << p << " " << z << endl;
```

10. For each of the following series of C++ statements, try to describe in words what is accomplished (e.g., the larger of x and y is put into max, and then max is printed; or x is multiplied over and over by 2 until it is more than 30). For parts (a)-(c), (f), and (g), assume that x and y have already been given values. All variables have data type **int**.

a.
```
if (x > y)
    max = x;
else
    max = y;
cout << max << endl;
```

b.
```
if (x > y)
    ans = x;
else
    ans = y;
if (x == y)
    ans = 1
```

c.
```
hold = 5;
if (x == y)
    hold = x;
else
    hold = y
```

d.
```
x = 1;
while (x < 100) {
    if (x < 50)
        x *= 2;
    x *= 2
}
```

e.
```
x = 0;
while (x < 15){
    x = x + 4;
    if (x == 8)
        cout << x << endl;
}
```

f.
```
x = 0;
while (x < 15) {
    x = x + y;
    if (x < y)
        x = y;
}
```

g.
```
if (x == y)
     cout << x;
else
cout << y;
cout << endl;
```

h.
```
x = 0;
while (x <= 6) {
     y = x + 4;
     if (y == 10)
          cout << "done" << endl;
     x += 1;
}
```

11. What is printed by the following?
```
x = 10;
if (x < 8)
     y = x + 3;
else
     y = x - 2;
cout << "y = " << y << endl;
```

12. What is wrong with this **if-else** statement? Fix the errors.
```
if (x < y);
     z = x + 1
else
     z = x + 2;
```

13. What is the value of <u>num</u> at the end of this **if-else** statement?
```
int y = 4;
if (y >= 7)
    num = 12;
else
    num = 18;
```

14. The segment below is designed to subtract 5 from the larger of the two numbers, <u>x</u> and <u>y</u>, and also add 5 to the smaller.

    a. Does the segment accomplish this task in all cases? For example, what happens if <u>x</u> is 5 and <u>y</u> is 6? What if <u>x</u> is 6 and <u>y</u> is 5?

    b. Rewrite the segment so that it does work in all cases. (*Hint*: You may want to use one or more pairs of braces.)

```
int x,y;
  ...
if (x > y)
     x -= 5;
else
     y -= 5;
if (x > y)
     y += 5;
else
     x += 5;
  ...
```

15. The following program is preceded by a comment that describes the goal. Try to use the data to see if the segment works in all cases. If it does not, explain exactly what happens and show how to amend it so that it does always work.

```
// find the smallest integer whose
// square is greater than y
#include <iostream>
using namespace std;
int main()
{
    int number=0,test=0,y;

    while (test <= y) {
        number++;
        test = number + number;
    }
    cout << number << " is the smallest" << endl;
    return 0;

}
```
(try y = 4, y = 5, y = 26)

16. Assume that the user types in these values as requested:

    5   7   -3   4   10   -1   7   0

Trace step by step the execution of the following program as it reads the data. Show exactly what is printed.

```
#include <iostream>
using namespace std;
int main()
{
    int x;

    cout << "Please enter a number> ";
    cin >> x;
    while (x != 0) {
        if (x < 0)
            cout << "\tnegative" << endl;
        if (x > 0)
            cout << "\tpositive" << endl;
        if (x > 5)
            cout << "\tmore" << endl;
        else
            cout << "\tless" << endl;
        cout << "Please enter another number> ");
        cin >> x;
    }
    return 0;
}
```

17. This exercise uses material from Section 8. Assume that the user types in these values as requested:

    10   -1   -1   -7   0   -1   4   14   4   6   13   5   9   0   42   42

Trace step by step the execution of this program. Assuming <u>cout</u> is redirected to the printer, show exactly what is printed and where it appears (screen or printer).

```cpp
#include <iostream>
using namespace std;
int main()
{
    int x,y;

    cerr << "Please enter an integer> ";
    cin >> x;
    cerr << "Please enter another integer> ";
    cin >> y;
    while (x != y) {
        cout << x << " " << y;
        if (x > y)
            cout << "\t" << x << endl;
        else
            cout << "\t" << y << endl;
        cerr << "Please enter two more integers> ";
        cin >> x;
        cin >> y;
    }
    cout << endl << "Finished" << endl;
    return 0;
}
```

18. Assume that the user types in consecutive numbers, starting from 1, as data for each of the following programs. Trace step by step what is in the variables x, y, and z as each program is executed.

    a.
    ```cpp
    #include <iostream>
    using namespace std;
    int main()
    {
        int x,y,z;

        cout << "Enter a number";
        cin >> x;
        while (x < 6) {
            cout << "Enter 2 numbers> ";
            cin >> y;
            cin >> z;
            cout << y << " " << z << endl;
            cout << "Enter 2 numbers> ");
            cin >> z;
            cin >> x;
            cout << z << " " << x << endl;
            cout << x << endl;
        }
        cout << "Enter a number> ";
        cin >> y;
        cout << y << endl;
        cout << "Enter 3 numbers> ";
        cin >> x;
    ```

```
        cin >> y;
        cin >> z;
        cout << x << " " << y << " " << z << endl;
        return 0;
    }
```

b.
```
    #include <iostream>
    using namespace std;
    int main()
    {
        int i,x,y,z;

        for (i = 1; i <= 3; i++) {
            cout << "Enter 3 numbers> ";
            cin >> x;
            cin >> y;
            cin >> z;
            cout << x << " " << y << " " << z << endl;
            cout << "Enter 2 numbers> ";
            cin >> y;
            cin >> z;
        }
        cout << y << " " << z << endl;
        return 0;
    }
```

19. The next two exercises use material from Sections 7 and 8. Assume that the user enters the data values below on four lines as needed (or that the data values come from a file where <u>cin</u> has been redirected). Trace step by step the values that are read into the variables <u>a</u>, <u>b</u>, <u>c</u>, and <u>d</u>. Assuming <u>cout</u> is redirected to the printer, show exactly what is printed by this program.

```
    #include <iostream>
    using namespace std;
    int main()
    {
        double a,b,c;
        int d;

        cout.setf(ios::fixed,ios::floatfield);
        cout.precision(2);

        cerr << "Enter the first line of numbers> ";
        cin >> a >> b >> c >> d;
        cout << a << " " << b << " " << c << " " << d << endl;
        cerr << "Enter the second line of numbers> ";
        cin >> a;
        cerr << "Enter the third line of numbers> ";
        cin >> a >> b >> c;
        cout << a << " " << b << endl;
        cout.precision(1);
        cout << " " << c << " " << d << endl;
        cerr << "Enter the fourth line of numbers> ";
        cin >> b >> c >> d;
```

```
        cout.precision(2);
        cout << a << " " << b << endl;
        cout.precision(1);
        cout << " " << c << " " << d << endl;
        return 0;
    }
    1.35   2.1  -9.2   13
    15
    123.45  0  678
    12.39  -5  5
```

20. a. Assume that the declaration for variable c in Exercise 19 is changed from type **double** to **int**. Does this affect the execution of the program? How does it affect the values printed out?

    b. Assume that all four variables are declared to have data type **double**. What effect does this have on the printout?

    c. Assume that by mistake the last line is typed as 12.39 –55, with no space between the two 5s. How does this affect the program?

21. For each number, determine what call to cout.precision( ) to use to print the value in the format shown.

    a. 276.345   b. -8314.5678   c. 52.676
    d. -.00003   e. .000076   f. 1.14151617
    g. 567.3   h. 493.888   i. -9.4
    j. -19.6475   k. -203.2

    Write a program to test whether your answers are correct.

22. Here are some possible values of a variable num with type **double**. For each, write calls to cout.setf( ) and cout.precision( ) to produce the following formats.

    a. 42   b. -6.8   c. 0.1   d. 371.00
    e. 6174.55   f. 0.0999   g. -0.00008 h. 1000.056

23. Write statements to print the numbers in question 21 in columns. First print the numbers right-aligned. Then write statements to print the numbers left-aligned in the columns. Make sure the width is sufficient to print all significant digits.

QUESTIONS ABOUT AND MODIFICATIONS TO PROGRAM 3

24. In Program 3, why don't we read in the pay for each employee?

25. a. Why isn't 0000 or 9999 a good trailer value for Problem 3?

    b. Instead of using a trailer value, why don't we just set up a **for** loop to read in 25 employees? Or 15?

26. What happens in Program 3 if the user forgets to enter a negative number as the last ID number, but enters something like 1111?

27. Here is a poor solution to fixing the flaw in the first version of the loop used to solve Problem 3. What is wrong with this solution? If you cannot see what's wrong, the questions below will help you.

```
    id = 0000;
    while (id >= 0) {
        cin >> id;
```

```
        cin >> hours;
        cin >> rate;
        pay = hours * rate;
        cout << "Employee " << id << " worked " << hours
            << " hours at a rate of $" << rate << " earning $"
            << pay << endl;
        count this employee
    }
    print total number of employees
```

a. To use this solution, how many employees would there have to be, at a minimum?

b. If we used this format, how much information would have to be provided for the phony employee?

c. If we used this format, what information would be printed for the phony employee?

28. In Program 3, we said that we needed to provide a phony value only for <u>id</u>, not for <u>hours</u> and <u>rate</u>, since we used three different <u>cin</u> statements to read in the data. However, if we use a single <u>cin</u> to read in all three values at once, then we should provide phony values for <u>hours</u> and <u>rate</u> as well. Why? Show how to do this. Indicate the changes that are necessary in the pseudocode and then in the program.

29. Modify Program 3 so that, after reading the last piece of data, it prints a message at the end indicating that the payroll is completed.

30. Modify Program 3 so that, in addition to computing each employee's pay, it also prints a summary at the end. This summary should print after it reads the last value and should include the total number of employees, the total number of hours worked, and the total amount of pay. Print this information several lines below the output for the final employee.

31. a. Modify Program 3 so that, after reading the phony value, it prints out the ID number of the employee with the highest pay rate. (*Suggestion*: Have the program keep track of the highest rate of pay as it goes along, and change this value when appropriate.)

   b. Modify the program from part a. to keep track also of the employee working the most hours and the one with highest weekly pay. Print this information at the end.

32. Modify Program 3 so that each employee is paid overtime for any hours above 40. Overtime is one-and-a-half times the normal rate. For example, if an employee earning $5.00 per hour works 48 hours, the first 40 are paid at $5.00, and the extra 8 hours are paid at $5.00 x 1.5 = $7.50 per hour.

33. Modify Program 3 so that social security and state income taxes are withheld from each employee's pay. Assume that the social security tax is 9 percent of weekly pay, and that state income tax is $10.00 if the pay is less than $100.00 (with the exception given below) and $20.00 if the pay is $100.00 or more. However, the state tax is never more than the base pay minus social security tax (e.g., if the base pay is $5.00, then the social security tax is $.45, and the state income tax is $5.00 − $0.45 = $4.55, not $10.00). Print each employee's base pay, taxes, and net pay after taxes.

34. Modify Program 3 so that it reads in a fourth piece of information for each employee, either the number 1, meaning "union," or the number 0, meaning "nonunion." Use this information to determine the employee's union dues, which are 10 percent of the pay for members and 0 for nonunion workers. Print each employee's union status, dues, and net pay after dues.

35. Modify the preceding program to include the overtime rate for hours above 40 for union members only. Nonunion workers will be paid at their standard rate regardless of the number of hours.

36. Modify Program 3 so that it reads in a fourth piece of information for each employee, an integer representing the number of dependents. An employee will pay a state tax of 10 percent on the modified pay, which is the base pay minus 10 times the number of dependents. The state tax should be 0 for an employee whose modified pay is negative (e.g., if the base pay is $35.00, and there are four dependents). For each employee, print the number of dependents, the modified pay, and the state tax.

37. In Program 3, we wrote the prompts without <u>endl</u> so that the data value typed in by the user appeared on the same line as the prompt. As we noted, another common technique is to include <u>endl</u> in each prompt. What effect does this have? Rewrite Program 3 using <u>endl</u> in each prompt and run the new program to check your answer.

38. Modify Program 3 so that it produces output in columns with headings, as shown in Figure 3-13.

39. Modify Program 3 so that it reads in two initials (<u>first</u> and <u>last</u>) to identify each employee, rather than an ID number. What can you use as a phony value? Should you test <u>first</u> or <u>last</u>?

MODIFICATIONS OF OTHER PROGRAMS

40. a. Write a complete C++ program to do the following: The program will read a number such as 3.10 or 2.50 which represents a student's grade point average (<u>gpa</u>). Using this value for <u>gpa</u>, the program will calculate the corresponding value of the registrar's formula given in Chapter 2. The program will print the student's <u>gpa</u> and the value of the formula.

    b. Modify this program so that, after finishing with the first student, it reads a new value of <u>gpa</u> for another student. Compute the formula for this <u>gpa</u> and print the results. Repeat this process until the program reads a negative <u>gpa</u> value (e.g., −2.35). This negative value will signal that the set of data is complete.

41. a. Modify your program for Chapter 2, Exercise 18, so that, after printing the table of interval values for <u>gpa</u> (e.g., 3.25 to 3.74 covered by 3.50), your program reads a value for <u>gpa</u> from the data. The program should determine which line of the table applies (e.g., if <u>gpa</u> is 3.47, the program should print "Use the 3.50 value in the table above."). Repeat this process for a series of numbers.

    b. Compare the method used in part (a) of this exercise to the one in Exercise 40(b). What are the advantages and disadvantages of the two approaches? Which would be better to use if the formula were relatively simple (e.g., *result = gpa * 3 + 5*)? Which would be better on an extremely complex formula that was difficult to compute? What if you expected one or two students? What if you expected several thousand?

42. Modify Program 2 so that it keeps track of how many formula values are positive, how many are negative, and how many are zero. After the last line of the table, print the number of each type found.

43. Modify Program 2 so that it keeps track of (a) the highest value of <u>result</u> ever obtained by the formula, and (b) the <u>gpa</u> value which led to the highest outcome. After printing the last line of the table, print these <u>gpa</u> and <u>result</u> values.

44. a. Modify Program 2 so that the values print left-aligned in their columns.

    b. Modify Program 2 so that the formula values print with two decimal places.

45. Modify Program 2 so that it uses a **while** instead of a **for** loop. Which version is clearer?

46. Go through the exercises in Chapters 1 and 2 that ask you to write programs. Solve each exercise by first writing pseudocode, then writing the program from the pseudocode. If you have already written programs for some of these exercises without pseudocode, compare how easy or difficult it is to write them now from pseudocode. What conclusions can you draw?

47. Modify Programs 1 and 2 to make them interactive. What data will you ask the user to enter? What prompts will you need?

48. Go through the exercises in Chapters 1 and 2 that ask you to write programs. In each case, if it makes sense, rewrite the program so that it is interactive. What data will you ask the user to enter? What prompts will you need?

MISCELLANEOUS EXERCISES

49. Why is it a disadvantage for a program to be completely self-contained?

50. What symbols are you allowed to use in pseudocode?

51. In Section 4, we said that the variable <u>count</u> will *always* contain the number of employees. This statement about <u>count</u> is an example of a **loop invariant**, an assertion which is always true when the condition in the loop is tested; it is also true after the loop has terminated.

Here is a loop, followed by some examples of loop invariants:

```
sum = 0;
i = 0;
while (i <= 100) {
      i++;
      sum += i;
}
cout <<"i = " << i << " and sum = " << sum << endl;
```

1) $i <= \underline{sum}$

2) $\underline{sum} >= 0$

3) <u>i</u> is equal to the number of times we have processed the loop body

4) <u>sum</u> is equal to the sum of the <u>i</u> values processed so far (i.e., $0 + 1 + \cdots + \underline{i}$)

Trace the following loops; which of the statements that follow are loop invariants for that loop?

```
a. y = 1;
   x = 0;
   while (x < 10) {
         x += 2;
         y *= x;
   }
   cout << x << " " << y << endl;
```

   i. $\underline{x}$ is equal to 10   iv. $\underline{x} < \underline{y}$

   ii. $\underline{x} < 10$ v. $\underline{x}$ is even

   iii. $\underline{x}$ is not equal to $\underline{y}$ vi. $\underline{y}$ is even

```
b. x = 0;
   y = 1;
   while (x != 16) {
         x++;
         y *= 2;
   }
   cout << x << " " << y << endl;
```

i. $\underline{x} < 16$ vi. $\underline{y}$ is even

ii. $\underline{x}$ is not equal to 16   vii. $\underline{y} = \underline{x}^2$

iii. $\underline{x}$ is not equal to $\underline{y}$ viii. $\underline{y} = 2^x$

iv. $\underline{x} < \underline{y}$ ix. $\underline{y} < 32767$

v. $\underline{x}$ is odd

52. In Section 6, we introduced the **if-else** construction and diagrammed the flow of control using a **flowchart**. Like pseudocode, a flowchart is another intermediate step to translate the English statement of the problem into C++. Most people nowadays use pseudocode instead of flowcharts, but there are occasions, like showing the flow of a nested **if** statement (see Chapter 6), where a flowchart can be helpful. Unfortunately, in other cases, flowcharts actually obscure what is happening in the program, which is why they have lost popularity.

    The flowchart in Section 6 used only a few of the common symbols. Figure 3-14 shows some of the available ones:

    Figure 3-15 is a flowchart for Program 3, first version, using these symbols. Notice that the flowchart does not include declarations or comments.

    a. Draw a flowchart for Program 1. (This is obviously not the normal order; you write the program from the flowchart, not vice versa.)

    b. Draw a flowchart for Program 2.

    c. Draw a flowchart for Program 3 (the last version).

    d. Draw flowcharts for the code shown in Exercises 1-4, 9, 11, and 12. Which C++ constructs are difficult to represent in a flowchart?

    e. Write pseudocode for the code shown in Exercises 1-4, 9, 11, and 12, and compare it with the flowchart. In each case, which is easier to follow?

53. If you are in an infinite loop that contains print statements, you will know that you are in an infinite loop because you will see lines and lines of output; if you are in an infinite loop without any print statements, you may just see a frozen screen. Write a simple program that contains an infinite loop (a program containing the loop below will do the trick).

FIGURE 3-14   Flowchart symbols

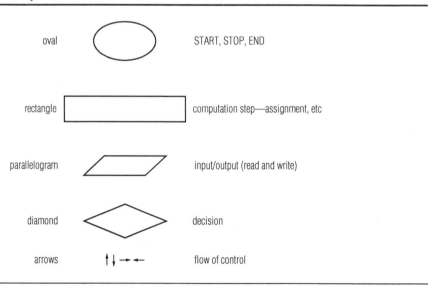

oval		START, STOP, END
rectangle		computation step—assignment, etc
parallelogram		input/output (read and write)
diamond		decision
arrows		flow of control

FIGURE 3-15 Flowchart for Program 3 (first version)

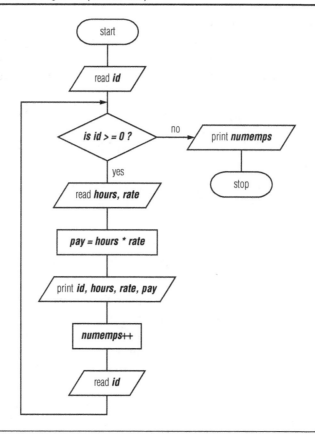

```
i = 0;
while (1 == 1) {
      i++;
      cout << i << endl;
}
```

Then run the program and see what happens. Try to break out of the loop. Now remove the line that writes to cout and see what happens. Again, try to break out of the loop (it should work the same way). Did you know what was wrong when the infinite loop occurred?

54. Anything that can be done with a **for** loop can also be done using a **while** loop, and vice versa. In fact, some programmers prefer to use a **while** loop whenever a series of steps must be repeated. For example, the **for** loop on the left (which executes the body of the loop ten times, for i having values from 1 to 10) can be replaced by the **while** loop on the right.

```
for (i = 1; i <= 10; i++) {            i = 1;
     body of the loop                  while (i <= 10) {
}                                            body of the loop
                                             i++;
                                        }
```

a. Show how we could have used a **for** loop in Program 3.

b. Go through the earlier exercises which asked you to use **while** loops and show how to solve them using **for** loops.

c. Show that anything that can be done with a **for** loop can be done with a **while** loop, and vice versa.

PROGRAMMING PROJECTS

55. Write a complete C++ program to do the following: Use a **while** loop to read in a series of numbers and print each number with its square and its cube. Put column headings on the output. Let 0 indicate the end of the input data. (Be careful of the limit on data type **int** in PC-based compilers; some squares or cubes may require a data type that can hold larger values.)

56. Write a complete C++ program to do the following: Read in a series of positive numbers and print each number with its square and its square root. Put column headings on the output and format the square roots to have four decimal places. Let any negative number signal the end of the input data.

57. Write a complete C++ program to do the following: Read in a series of positive and negative values. Print the numbers and their absolute values. Put column headings on the output. Let 0 indicate the end of the input data.

58. A prime number is one which has no divisors but itself and 1. Write a complete C++ program to read in a series of numbers and determine if each is prime. If it is, print "prime"; otherwise, print a list of its divisors.

59. Write a complete C++ program to do the following: Read in information about the customers of the Handy Hardware Company. For each one, the data consists of a customer number, the current dollar amount of orders placed, and the current dollar amount of orders paid for. For each customer, compute the balance due. If the amount is negative, print a message saying, "Credit." If the amount is positive, print a message saying, "Amount owed." Consider a zero balance positive.

   When you have read in the information about all the customers, print the company totals: total dollar amount of orders placed, total dollar amount of orders paid for, and total balance due the company. (Should all three be computed the same way?)

60. Write a complete C++ program to do the following: Read in information about the students in the graduating class at Science Tech. For each one, there is a student ID number and a grade point average in the range of 0.00 to 4.00. Your program should determine whether each student can graduate and if it is with honors. Print each student's ID number and grade point average. If the grade point average is 2.0 or better, print "Graduate" next to it. If it is less than 2.0, print "Sorry." If it is 3.5 or better, print "Honors" next to the word "Graduate."

   After processing all the students, print four totals: the total number of students, the number graduating, the number graduating with honors, and the number who are not graduating. (Do all of these totals have to be summed?)

61. Write a complete C++ program to do the following: Read in a series of numbers, each of which can contain decimal places. Print each number as it is read in. Determine whether each number is positive, negative, or zero, and print "positive," "negative," or "zero" next to it. Keep track of how many numbers are positive, negative, and zero and print these counts at the end, together with appropriate messages. Since all numbers are acceptable, pick any one you wish to signal the end of the data.

62. Write a C++ program, including comments, to compute statistics for how students did on an exam. The program should compute various things about a student, and print all the results. Then the program repeats the process for each new student until the entire set of data has been completed.

a. The program reads in the ID number of a student [see step g. below] and then the number of right answers and the number of wrong answers. (The total number of questions on the test is 50.) For example, the program could read in the following:

    1234 20 5 (ID number 1234 has 20 right and 5 wrong)

b. The program computes and prints the total number of questions answered plus the number omitted (which is simply 50 minus the number answered). The number right plus the number wrong will never be more than 50 [see optional a. below].

c. The program computes the student's correct answer percentage, which is a decimal value between 0 and 1. The correct answer percentage is the number of right answers divided by the number of questions answered. [The student always answers at least one question—see optional b.] For the data values shown for ID number 1234 above, the correct answer percentage is 20 / 25 = 0.800. The program should print this out as shown, with three decimal places.

d. The program also assigns the student a numerical grade on the exam. The numerical grade is the number of right answers times 2 (ignoring the wrong answers). For example, ID number 1234 got a numerical grade of 40 on the exam (20 right x 2). The program prints the student's grade.

e. The program determines if the student had more right than wrong answers, the same number of each, or more wrong than right answers. In each case, it prints an appropriate message.

f. The program determines if the student omitted ten or more questions. It prints a message with this information.

g. Then the program skips a few lines and repeats the entire process for the next student until the last student is finished. (You must decide how to recognize the last student.)

h. At that point, print the total number of students in the class (you must keep track of this as the program executes) and stop.

Data: Be sure to read in data for at least 12 students. Make sure that you have at least two with the same number right and wrong, at least two with more wrong than right, and at least two with more right than wrong. Include a student with all wrong answers and one with all right answers (but not 50 right). Have some students who don't omit anything and some who omit almost all the questions.

Output: Here is a complete set of output for two typical students:

```
id 1234                          id 7890
12 right 13 wrong                30 right 15 wrong
total answered 25                total answered 45
number omitted is 25             number omitted is 5
grade is 24                      grade is 60
more wrong than right            more right than wrong
correct answer pct. is 0.480     correct answer pct. is 0.667
10 or more omitted               less than 10 omitted
```

Optionals:

a. If a student answered more than 50 questions, print an error message, skip the rest of the processing, and go on to the next student.

b. Make sure that you do not divide by 0 if the student answered no questions (everything was omitted). Print a special message and go on to the next student.

c. Keep track of the student with the best correct answer percentage and the one with the highest grade. (These do not have to be the same—to test, make sure they are different.) Print these out at the end.

63. Write a complete C++ program, including comments, to compute a weekly payroll. The program reads in information for each of the employees of a company and then prints the results. After processing the last person, the program prints the total number of employees. The program does the following for each employee:

a. First, it reads in the data values for this employee. Each employee has a three-digit identification number (an integer from 100 to 999), hours worked, rate of pay, and union status (1 if the employee is in the union, 0 if not). For example, here are data values for two typical workers:

123　46　　6.50　1　(ID number 123 is in the union)
456　32.12　3　　0　(ID number 456 is nonunion)

b. The program computes the weekly pay, which comes from the following formula (this includes an overtime bonus of time and a half for each hour over 40):

if hours are less than 40, weekly pay is hours times rate

but

if hours are 40 or more, weekly pay is 40 times the rate plus the number of overtime hours times 1.5 times the rate

For example, ID number 123 would get $40 * 6.50 + 6 * 1.5 * 6.50$.

ID number 456 would get $32.12 * 3$.

c. The program computes the union dues, which are 10 percent of the weekly pay for union members, and $5 ($5, not 5 percent) for nonunion employees. [You can assume that the only values for this variable are 1 (union) and 0 (nonunion). See optional b. below.]

d. The program computes net pay, which is weekly pay minus union dues.

e. The program prints all of the data values read in and the words "union" or "nonunion," plus each item that has been computed (weekly pay, union dues, net pay). Make sure that all money amounts have exactly two decimal places. You can put dollar signs in, but it is not necessary.

f. Then the program skips three lines and goes to the next employee.

After the last person has been read, the program should print the total number of employees that have been processed. (This count should not include a phony employee used to end the set of data.)

Your program must determine when the last employee has been read. Explain how to do this in a comment.

Output Format: Here is a sample set of output for one employee (messages can vary):

employee 123 worked 46.0 hours at 6.50 per hour union member
weekly pay 318.50 union dues 31.85 net pay 286.65

Data: Have at least ten employees. Make sure that at least four are union and four are not. Make at least four overtime and four not (and cover all possible combinations).

Make sure that most of your values are integers (so that you can check the calculations by hand) but a few have decimal places (e.g., 6.50 per hour or 30.5 hours).

Optionals:

a. Determine the total weekly payroll (for all employees added together). Print this at the end.

b. If a person's union status is not one of the allowed values (union or nonunion), print an error message. Do not subtract anything for union dues.

64. Write a complete C++ program, including comments, to compute baseball statistics. The program computes various things about a team and prints everything out. Then it repeats the process for each new team until the entire set of data has been completed.

a. The program reads in the ID number of a team [see step e. below]. It reads the number of wins and the number of losses. For example, it could read in the following:

1234 5 7 (team 1234 has 5 wins and 7 losses)

b. The program computes (and prints) the total number of games played, which is simply the number of wins plus the number of losses. If the total is exactly 20, the program prints a message saying the season is finished. If the total is less, the program prints how many games are left. No team has played more than 20 games. For example, for the team above, the total number of games played is 12, and there are 8 games left (20 − 12).

c. The program computes the team's winning percentage, which is a decimal value between 0 and 1. The winning percentage is the number of games won divided by the number of games played. For the team above, the winning percentage is 5 / 12 = 0.41667. The program prints this out as shown, with exactly five decimal places.

d. The program computes how much the team is above or below 0.50000. This is defined as follows:

If the team has won more games than it has lost (or if these are equal), the amount above 0.50000 is the number of wins minus the number of losses. Otherwise, the amount below 0.50000 is the number of losses minus the number of wins. This value should be printed with an appropriate message (saying if this is games above or below 0.50000).

For example, the team above is 2 games below 0.50000 (5 is less than 7, and 7 − 5 = 2).

e. Then the program skips a few lines of output and repeats the entire process for the next team until it reaches the last one. (You must decide how to recognize the last team.) At that point, print the total number of teams in the league and stop.

Data: Be sure to read in data for about eight to ten teams. Make sure that at least three teams have completed their season and three have not. Have at least two teams with more wins than losses, one with an even record, and two with more losses.

Output: Here is a complete set of output for a typical team:

```
team 9867
4 wins 16 losses
total number of games played is 20
the season is finished
the winning percentage is 0.20000
the team is 12 games below 0.50000
```

Optionals:

a. Compute the team's record if it wins all of the remaining games (give the winning percentage and games above/below 0.50000) and the record if it loses all of them.

b. Keep track of the team with the best winning percentage and the one which is the most games above 0.50000. Print these out at the end.

65. Write a program that assigns a student a letter grade based upon exam marks. First, read in the student's ID number. This should be an integer. Then read in the student's exam marks (since they can have decimal places, e.g., 87.5, the marks must be declared as **double**). Use a trailer value to indicate the end of the grades (−1 is a good value for this trailer) to allow a student to have taken an arbitrary number of exams.

    Once the grades have been read in, calculate the student's average (the sum of the exams divided by the number). Finally, based upon the average, assign a letter grade using the standard grading scale:

90 and above	A
80 and above	B
70 and above	C
60 and above	D
below 60	F

    Your program should print out the student number, the number of exams taken and their marks, the average, and the final grade. Try to make the output readable; for example:

    ```
    Grade report for student 122

    4 exams taken:

    Exam: 90
    Exam: 93.5
    Exam: 86
    Exam: 84
    _____

    Student's average is 88.375
    Grade is B
    ```

    Run this program for several students, making sure that your data values produce at least one with each grade from A through F.

66. You have just been hired director of programming at the TooHeavy Hauling Company. Your first assignment is to write a program that calculates shipping information for the company and reports the results to the dispatcher.

    The program reads in a sequence of truck shipment orders. Each order consists of three carton weights (all shipments consist of exactly three containers). Assign a truck category to the shipment based upon its total weight, according to the following table.

Category	Weight Limit	Shipping Cost
1	2,000 lbs	$50
2	5,500 lbs	$100
3	10,000 lbs	$135
4	14,000 lbs	$200

    If no truck is capable of carrying the shipment (its total weight exceeds the maximum load), issue a message to the dispatcher (see the Output section). Use a trailer value of −1 to indicate the end of the set of data.

Output:

The output serves as a report to the company's shipping dispatcher, who is required to sign off on each shipment prior to loading and dispatching the truck. All data should be printed: the individual and total weights, the resulting category (or an error message if the shipment is too large), and the shipping cost. The total number of shipments should be appear at the end.

Test Data:

Use the following test data:

200	300	400
1000	1	1000
1000	900	0
1000	1000	100
2000	2000	1600
2000	2000	1500
3000	3000	3000
3400	3400	3400
3334	3333	3333
4000	4000	5500
5000	5000	5000
4000	5000	5000
0	0	0
1	2	3
9000	5000	0
5000	1	9000
-1		

Optionals:

a. Assign each shipment an identification number, beginning with 1. Print this number with the other information about the shipment.

b. Print the total cost for all shipments at the end of the report (you may want to read about summation in Chapter 4).

c. Assume trucks can travel 500 miles per day. Add another piece of data to each shipment order—the distance. Using the shipping cost as a daily rate, calculate and output the total for each shipment. (You have to modify the input data by adding the distance; leave the rest the same.)

d. Allow an arbitrary number of containers per shipment (you need a second trailer value and have to modify the format of your data).

e. If the shipment is heavier than the maximum weight, rather than issuing an error message, break it up into two or more sections.

SUMMATION, STEPWISE REFINEMENT, AND NESTED LOOPS

PROBLEM: The Sultan's Gift—The Sum of the Squares of the Numbers from 1 to 30

SYNTAX CONCEPTS: defining a constant, nested loops

PROGRAMMING CONCEPTS: summing a series of terms, using a constant, reading a limit value, programming style

CONTROL STRUCTURES: nested loop

PROBLEM-SOLVING TECHNIQUES: stepwise refinement, top-down programming, structured programming

HOW TO READ CHAPTER 4

OUTLINE:

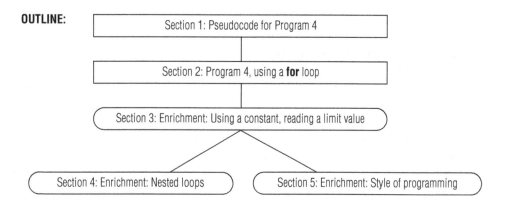

Chapter 5, Section 3 depends upon the material in sections 2 and 3; Chapter 5, Section 6 depends upon the material in Section 4.

INTRODUCTION AND STATEMENT OF THE PROBLEM

This chapter introduces several key ideas. We solve a rather straightforward problem—finding the sum of the squares of the numbers from 1 to 30. The method of summation introduced in the solution will be employed in later problems. Even more important are the programming and problem-solving techniques discussed in this chapter. The most essential of these is a method of attacking a problem called stepwise refinement or top-down programming. Most people working in the field agree that this method, possibly combined with others discussed later, offers the best approach to solving complex problems. After solving Problem 4, we introduce the nested **for** loop.

PROBLEM 4

The Sultan of RedValley has decided to give his daughter, who was born on the last day of June, a special birthday gift. On the first day of June, he will give her 1 (1 times 1) diamond; on the second day, he will give her 4 (2 times 2) diamonds; and so on, until the last day of June, when he will give her 30 times 30 diamonds. The sultan has asked you to determine the total number of diamonds he needs. Write a C++ program to find the number.

SECTION 1   **PSEUDOCODE FOR PROGRAM 4**

In this section, we will develop an algorithm and a pseudocode solution to Problem 4. Much more important than the pseudocode is the method we use to develop it. This method, called **top-down programming** or **stepwise refinement**, is perhaps the single most important problem-solving tool.

FIRST APPROXIMATION, USING PSEUDOCODE

The number of diamonds the sultan needs is 1^2 for the first day, 2^2 for the second day, to 30^2 for the last day. The total number is equal to the sum of the squares of the numbers from 1 to 30 (the sum of the first 30 squares). Therefore, the program must compute $1^2 + 2^2 + 3^2 + \cdots + 29^2 + 30^2$.

The first version of the pseudocode for Problem 4 is

find the sum of the first 30 squares
print the sum

THE METHOD OF STEPWISE REFINEMENT

Some people would argue that this pseudocode is slightly silly. In some ways, they are right, but the pseudocode does have a purpose. It gives us a starting point for the method of stepwise refinement.

We take this first crude pseudocode and break it up into individual steps. Once the sum has been computed, printing is easy. (Simple steps like this can be put aside while we refine the more complicated ones.) The only line we must refine is the computation itself (*find the sum of the first 30 squares*).

To compute the sum of the first 30 squares, we need an algorithm for summing a series of terms. A simple-minded approach is the following:

```
sumofthesquares = 1 * 1 + 2 * 2 + 3 * 3/+ ... + 30 * 30;
```

Before we dismiss it, let's analyze this. First, we can't use the ellipsis (…) in C++; a person knows how to fill in the dots, but the computer doesn't.

We could write out each of the 30 terms explicitly, but that has us doing most of the work and is certainly not the best method of solving the problem. We want to find a way to instruct the computer to generate and add the terms (first 1 * 1, then 2 * 2, etc.) without our having to write each one out individually.

DEVELOPING AN ALGORITHM FOR FINDING THE SUM OF A SERIES OF SQUARES

There is a simple algorithm for adding a series of terms. In our particular case, assume that we have already computed the sum of the first 29 squares. If we have this number, to get the sum of the first 30 squares, we can add 30 squared (30 * 30) to it.

$$\text{the sum of the first 30 squares} = \text{the sum of the first 29 squares} + 30^2$$

We still have a problem: to compute the sum of the first 29 squares. If we have the sum of the first 28 squares, we can get the sum of the first 29 squares by adding 29 * 29.

$$\begin{array}{ccc} \text{the sum of the first} \\ \text{29 squares} \end{array} = \begin{array}{c} \text{the sum of the first} \\ \text{28 squares} \end{array} + \ 29^2$$

Continuing this way, we eventually have

$$\begin{array}{c} \text{the sum of the first} \\ \text{2 squares} \end{array} = \begin{array}{c} \text{the sum of the first} \\ \text{1 squares} \end{array} + \ 2^2$$

$$\begin{array}{c} \text{the sum of the first} \\ \text{1 squares} \end{array} = \begin{array}{c} \text{the sum of the first} \\ \text{0 squares} \end{array} + \ 1^2$$

Finally, the sum of the first 0 squares is 0, of course:

the sum of the first 0 squares = 0

Once we have this place to start, we can compute the sum of the first 1 squares, the sum of the first 2 squares, …, the sum of the first 30 squares, by using these formulas. Notice the order in which we add terms. We start from 0, then add 1 squared, then 2 squared, …, then add 30 squared, even though the formulas started at 30 squared and went down.

Algorithm for finding the Sum of a Series of Terms

To find the sum of a series of terms: Start a sum at 0. At each step, add one new term (in our case, first 1 squared, then 2 squared, …, then 30 squared) to the sum of the terms already processed.

The method of adding a new term to an existing sum is a generalization of the relatively simple incrementing we used in earlier chapters. For example, in Chapter 2, we repeatedly added 0.5 to the old value of gpa to process values from 0 to 4.0; in Chapter 3, we repeatedly added 1 to the old value of numemps to count the number of employees. In this chapter, we are using a variable to hold the sum of an entire series of terms and repeatedly adding a new term to the sum. In later programs, we will use this same idea in many other situations.

FURTHER REFINEMENTS OF THE PSEUDOCODE

Let's be more precise about our algorithm. In other words, let's *refine* the solution further. Start by initializing a variable called sum to 0. At each step, add a new term to the running sum of what has been added so far. Here is the pseudocode for adding a series of terms and printing the sum:

```
sum = 0;
for each item from the first to the last
    add a new term to sum
    get the next item
print the sum
```

It is clear we have made significant progress. What does each new term look like? The first is 1 squared, the second is 2 squared, and the last is 30 squared. In general, each term is the next integer squared. This suggests that we use a variable item to represent the integer we are up to and item * item as our new term. (Be sure you understand the difference between the counter item and the term item * item.) The key step is to add the next term to the running sum of the squares so far. To express this, use the following statement:

```
sum = sum + item * item;
```

Before the first new term is added, initialize item to 1. Before each term is added to sum, test to see if another term should be added. To do this, ask if item is less than or equal to 30. If it is not, then we have summed all the terms and are ready to print the value of <u>sum</u>. This is leading us in a natural way toward a **for** loop. Recall that in a **for** loop, initialization, comparison, and incrementing are all specified in the header.

FINAL PSEUDOCODE AND REVIEW OF THE METHOD

Putting all the pieces together, we get our next refinement of the pseudocode:

```
sum = 0;
```
for each value of item from 1 to 30
```
      sum = sum + item * item;
```
print the sum

The phrasing for the header of the loop has changed slightly in each refinement of the pseudocode as the **for** loop structure emerged. In this section of pseudocode, we have a starting value for <u>item</u> (1), a limiting value (30), and a method for changing <u>item</u> each time through the loop. Therefore, we use <u>item</u> as the control variable or index of the loop. If we use a **for** loop, we do not need a separate step to initialize <u>item</u>; we do not need a separate step to compare <u>item</u> to the limit; and we do not need a separate step to increment <u>item</u> by 1. All these things are taken care of automatically. We will make the **for** loop explicit in the next version.

```
sum = 0;
for (item = 1; item <= 30; item++)
      sum = sum + item * item;
```
print the sum

By this point, the last line, which you should certainly know how to translate into C++, is the only one left in pseudocode. This means that we can write the C++ program from the pseudocode.

NOTE

All our previous programs have used some type of loop. However, this program is the first in which the loop as a single unit has a distinct purpose. In earlier programs, each pass through the loop accomplished something, and the loop repeated this series of calculations for different values. In this program, the entire loop computes a single value.

Here is a summary of stepwise refinement:

HIGHLIGHTS

◆ Start from a rough solution to the problem with certain steps still vague.

◆ Ignore the clear steps and concentrate on the vague ones, breaking each of them down into further steps and making it more precise as you go.

◆ Continue the process for each new step until everything is clear.

As we have seen, pseudocode fits very nicely with stepwise refinement. Pseudocode can be refined and made more precise in a step-by-step fashion until all the pseudocode has been translated into C++. In addition, the pseudocode used at one stage of the development process often serves as a comment at the next stage.

SELF-CHECK 4-1

1. In using stepwise refinement to write a program, what purpose does a rough solution to the problem serve? How do we refine that rough solution?

2. In order to sum a series of terms, what value initializes the variable which holds the sum? If we have to form a product of terms, to what value should that product be initialized?

SECTION 2 PROGRAM 4 (FIRST VERSION)

WRITING THE PROGRAM FROM THE PSEUDOCODE

It is time to write the program from the pseudocode. Theoretically, we could use any version, but it is clearly better to use the final refinement. If we have followed stepwise refinement, this last step of writing the program should be extremely easy because the pseudocode is so precise. As usual, the first few lines are standard, although they do not appear in the pseudocode.

```
// Program prog4a.cpp:
// find the sum of the first 30 squares
#include <iostream>
using namespace std;
int main()
{
```

Next is the declaration of variables. From the pseudocode, we see that <u>item</u> and <u>sum</u> must be declared. We know that each holds only integer values. In addition, we can see that <u>sum</u> is initialized to 0 in the first line of code. Thus, we can use the following declaration statement and also take care of initialization:

```
int item, sum = 0;
```

After the declaration is the action portion of the program. We use the last refinement of the pseudocode from Section 1. Because the body of the **for** loop is a single assignment statement, it is not necessary to use another set of braces inside the loop. We have used the compound assignment operator += (see Chapter 2, Section 3) to simplify the assignment statement.

```
for (item = 1; item <= 30; item++)
    sum += item * item;
cout << sum << endl;
```

If you recall, <u>sum</u> += <u>item</u> * <u>item</u> means that the new value for <u>sum</u> is set to the old value plus the term <u>item</u> * <u>item</u>.

Once we leave the **for** loop, <u>sum</u> holds the sum of the first 30 squares. At that point, all we have to do is print the final answer. In the pseudocode, we simply printed <u>sum</u>. However, in the C++ program, we will print a message with the value of <u>sum</u>. It is perfectly reasonable to make minor changes like this in the final program. Here is the statement we use:

```
cout << sum << " is the sum of the first 30 squares" << endl;
```

COMPLETE PROGRAM 4 (FIRST VERSION)

Here is the complete program:

PROGRAM LISTING

```
// Program prog4a.cpp
// find the sum of the first 30 squares
#include <iostream>
using namespace std;
int main()
{
    int item, sum = 0;

    for (item = 1; item <= 30; item++)
```

```
        sum += item * item;
    cout << sum << " is the sum of the first 30 squares" << endl;
    return 0;
}
```

TRACE OF PROGRAM 4

The program was quite simple once we refined the problem. Let's trace the program to make sure it is correct.

PROGRAM TRACE

♦ The variable sum is initialized to 0. When the **for** loop starts, item is given the value 1. Inside the loop, item * item = 1 * 1 is added to sum, making it 0 + 1 = 1.

♦ Then item is increased by 1 to 2. This time through the loop, 2 * 2 = 4 is added to sum, giving 1 + 4 = 5.

♦ Then item increases to 3; we add 3 * 3 to sum, and so on.

♦ Eventually, item increases to 30, and we add 30 * 30 = 900 to sum, giving a total of 9455. (See Exercise 16 for a simple way to compute the sum of the first 30 squares and check the answer from the program.)

♦ We increase item to 31, making the condition controlling the loop now false.

♦ The loop ends, and we continue with the next statement in the program, which sends output to cout. This displays the following line of output:

```
9455 is the sum of the first 30 squares
```

SELF-CHECK 4-2

1. When we translate pseudocode from the stepwise refinement process into C++, which refinement(s) can be used? (The original? The first refinement? Etc.)

2. Of the refinements, which one is closest to C++?

3. In Program 4, why does each variable hold only integer values?

SECTION 3 ENRICHMENT: OTHER VERSIONS OF PROGRAM 4—DECLARING A LOOP INDEX, DEFINING A CONSTANT, AND READING DATA

In this section, we will give several other versions of Program 4 that introduce other features of C++ and also make the program more useful. The first version shows a common C++ technique for declaring the index of a **for** loop. The next version introduces a constant and uses it to control the **for** loop. The last version reads in a data value to control the loop.

DECLARING A LOOP INDEX

Our first variant introduces a feature of C++ that is intended to enhance the modularity of program code. In prog4a.cpp, the variable item is used only as the loop index; it controls how many times the loop executes. This **for** loop index has no use in the program either before or after the loop. If a variable is used in this manner in a C++ program, it is customary to declare it directly in the loop header, rather than at the beginning of the program.

A variable declared inside a **for** loop header has no meaning anywhere in the program except within that loop.

To declare a loop index in the loop header, simply supply the data type (in this case, **int**) of the variable directly before the first use of the variable name. Once we make this change, the new version of the program (which we will call <u>prog4b.cpp</u>) looks like this:

 PROGRAM LISTING

```cpp
// Program prog4b.cpp:
// find the sum of the first 30 squares
#include <iostream>
using namespace std;
int main()
{
    int sum = 0;

    for (int item = 1; item <= 30; item++)
        sum += item * item;
    cout << sum << " is the sum of the first 30 squares" << endl;
    return 0;
}
```

MODIFYING THE PROGRAM FOR A DIFFERENT NUMBER OF SQUARES

Although the program shown in Section 2 seems to work perfectly, there are certainly ways to modify and improve it. What if the Sultan's friends want to use the program for their own children who might be born on a different day of the month, instead of the thirtieth? For example, the Sultan of Swat might have a child who was born on May 27; he would need the sum of the first 27 squares. We could not use Program 4 as currently written to compute that sum since it works only for the first 30 squares.

We can modify the program to work for the first 27 squares by making a few simple changes. The most obvious one is the limiting value in the **for** loop, which must be changed from 30 to 27. A less obvious, but still important, change is the message at the end of the program. We are computing the sum of the first 27 squares, so we don't want a message saying this is the sum of the first 30 squares. Similarly, we should change the comment at the top of the program.

Once we make these changes, the new version of the program (which we will call <u>prog4c.cpp</u>) looks like this:

PROGRAM LISTING

```cpp
// Program prog4c.cpp:
// find the sum of the first 27 squares
#include <iostream>
using namespace std;
int main()
{
    int sum = 0;

    for (int item = 1; item <= 27; item++)
        sum += item * item;
    cout << sum << " is the sum of the first 27 squares" << endl;
    return 0;
}
```

DEFINING A CONSTANT

This way of modifying the program is not bad, but other ways are considered more "elegant." The new methods also introduce some important C++ features.

It would be nice to isolate the material that is being changed (the number of squares we want to sum) from the rest of the program, which essentially stays. Rather than making a series of changes throughout the program, with the possibility of forgetting one or more, we would like to restrict what must be modified to just one portion.

There are many ways to do this, but one of the simplest introduces a **constant identifier** or just a **constant**. While the value of a variable can change in a program, the value of a constant is fixed. To use a constant in this program, we simply replace 30 or 27 or 35 or another particular value by a constant which we call <u>NUMBERTOSUM</u>. The definition for this constant gives it a value that can be used any number of times in the program. If we decide to change this value, we need only alter the definition for the constant and recompile the program. For example, we can include the following:

```
const int NUMBERTOSUM = 30;
```

In order to make the value of a constant available for use anywhere in the program, it is customary to place constant definitions outside the main program, above **int** <u>main()</u>. Something defined outside the main program is called **global** to the program. If a constant is defined in the main program, it is called **local** to the main program, and its use is limited to the main program.

STYLE WORKSHOP By convention, C++ programmers usually use capitals for the name of a constant; this distinguishes constants from variables, which typically have lowercase letters. Recall our discussion in Chapter 1, Section 2 about being consistent with identifier names.

General Form of Constant Definition

The general form of a constant definition is the following:

const *datatype name* = *value;*

Every time *name* occurs in a program, it is replaced by *value* (which has type *datatype*).

EXAMPLE 4-1 Here is a program segment that defines a constant called <u>LIMIT</u> and uses it in several comparisons:

```
#include <iostream>
using namespace std;
const int LIMIT = 50;
int main()
{
    int a,b;

    ...
    if (a > LIMIT)
        ...
    if (b > LIMIT)
        ...
}
```

When this program is compiled, every occurrence of the identifier <u>LIMIT</u> in the body of the program is replaced by the value 50. However, if <u>LIMIT</u> occurs as part of a larger word (<u>LIMITATION</u>) or in a literal string [e.g., *cout << "you reached the LIMIT")*], it will *not* be replaced.

USING A CONSTANT IN PROGRAM 4

In Program 4, we want to use the constant <u>NUMBERTOSUM</u> to stand for the number of squares to be summed. If we want to compute the sum of the first 30 squares, then the definition for the constant <u>NUMBERTOSUM</u> is this:

```
const int NUMBERTOSUM = 30;
```

If we want to sum 27 squares, then the definition is this:

```
const int NUMBERTOSUM = 27;
```

Any number of squares can be handled by using an appropriate constant—by changing the value after the identifier <u>NUMBERTOSUM</u>.

As to the rest of the program, instead of a particular value, say 30 or 27, as the limit of the **for** loop, we use <u>NUMBERTOSUM</u>. In the same way, we can replace the printout at the end of the program by a slightly longer one which uses the value of the constant <u>NUMBERTOSUM</u> to produce a message indicating how many squares we have summed.

```
cout << sum << " is the sum of the first " << NUMBERTOSUM
    << " squares" << endl;
```

As a simple example, if <u>NUMBERTOSUM</u> has the value 3, then the sum of the first three squares is $1 + 4 + 9 = 14$. The entire line of output looks like this:

```
14 is the sum of the first 3 squares
```

PROGRAM 4 USING A CONSTANT

Here is the complete new version of the program (which we will call <u>prog4d.cpp</u>). Notice that we also changed the comment at the beginning.

🖥 PROGRAM LISTING

```
// Program prog4d.cpp:
// compute the sum of the first NUMBERTOSUM squares
// with NUMBERTOSUM defined as a constant
#include <iostream>
using namespace std;
const int NUMBERTOSUM = 30;
int main()
{
    int sum = 0;

    for (int item = 1; item <= NUMBERTOSUM; item++)
        sum += item * item;
    cout << sum << " is the sum of the first " << NUMBERTOSUM
        << " squares" << endl;
    return 0;
}
```

If we decide to modify the program to handle the sum of the first 27 or 15 squares, all we need to change is the definition of the constant. Note that the value of a constant is fixed for each particular run of a program. However, we can change its value, recompile the program, and then rerun it with the new value.

Before we finish, we must note one restriction on the program. As we mentioned earlier, there is a limit on the size of a value stored in a variable whose data type is **int**, though that limit might be quite large. Because of this limit on the value stored in <u>sum</u>, there is a limit (which also may be large) on the number of squares that can be summed. (See Exercise 14 for more details.)

SELF-CHECK 4-3

1. If a variable is declared in the header of a **for** loop, where in the program can it be used? Where can't it be used?

2. What technique makes a constant identifier name look different from a variable identifier name? What word occurs in the definition of a constant that does not occur in the declaration of a variable? What is the major advantage of using a constant in a program?

3. If we are using a constant, how can it be changed to some other value? Why is it necessary to recompile the program after changing the value of a constant?

READING THE NUMBER OF SQUARES FROM A LINE OF DATA

Actually, the program we have just presented is still too limited because the constant must be specified in advance. We must know which particular value the sultan wants to use as the number of squares to be summed. Once the program is written, it cannot be used for any other calculation without modifying it each time. As you write more programs, you will learn to appreciate a point discussed in Chapter 3: the last thing a programmer wants to do is modify a working program every time it runs. Anytime you change a program, even in the most elementary way, you introduce the possibility of an error.

As we noted in Chapter 3, a program can be made more flexible by reading in values (input data) as it is running. In this program, we can specify the number of squares to be summed as a variable (which we call <u>numbertosum</u>—note the lowercase since it is now a variable) rather than a constant. The same program, without any change whatsoever, can then sum any number of squares by reading in a data value for the variable <u>numbertosum</u> and letting this value control the **for** loop.

Let's make this idea more precise. First, we declare <u>numbertosum</u> to be a variable with data type **int** rather than a constant. Then we use <u>cin</u> to read in a value for the new variable <u>numbertosum</u>. As you know by now, whenever we ask the user to supply some data, there should be a prompt. We should print a message asking the program user to type in a number. The following two lines do these things:

```
cout << "type in the number of squares to be summed> ";
cin >> numbertosum;
```

The rest of the program for this version is the same.

STYLE WORKSHOP It is important to notice that since <u>numbertosum</u> is a variable used in the main program, we place its declaration inside the main program. Constants should be declared outside of main, but not variables. The use of global variables, except in very limited circumstances, is dangerous and should be avoided.

THIRD VERSION OF PROGRAM 4 (USING A VALUE READ FROM A LINE OF DATA)

Here is the entire program (which we will call <u>prog4e.cpp</u>), rewritten so that it reads in a limit value:

💻 **PROGRAM LISTING**

```
// Program prog4e.cpp:
// compute the sum of the first numbertosum squares
// with numbertosum read from a line of data
#include <iostream>
using namespace std;
int main()
{
    int sum = 0;
    int numbertosum;

    cout << "type in the number of squares to be summed>> ";
    cin >> numbertosum;

    for (int item = 1; item <= numbertosum; item++)
        sum += item * item;
    cout << sum << " is the sum of the first " << numbertosum
        << " squares" << endl;
    return 0;
}
```

Note that this version can be used to find the sum of any number of squares (within the limits of the value we can store in <u>sum</u>). The program doesn't have to be changed to find any particular number of squares. All we need to do is read this particular number in as a data value.

SELF-CHECK 4-4

1. What is the advantage of reading in a limit value as data? Will the program have to be changed if we want to use a different limit value?

2. If the limit value is read in, is it necessary to recompile the program each time we use a different data value?

3. If not, what has to be done to have the program read in a new data value?

SECTION 4 **ENRICHMENT: USING A NESTED LOOP**

To give us more practice with loops, this section focuses on one long example—a program to construct a multiplication table. As we develop and refine the pseudocode for this program, we will continue to use stepwise refinement. The solution will also introduce the nested **for** loop construction.

EXAMPLE 4-2

Write a program to produce a multiplication table that covers the numbers from 1 to 10. For example, one row of the table will show 3, followed by the first 10 multiples of 3 (3 6 ⋯ 27 30); another row will show 8 followed by the multiples of 8 (8 16 ... 72 80), and so on. Here are a few rows from the table:

1	1	2	3	4	5	6	7	8	9	10
2	2	4	6	8	10	12	14	16	18	20
3	3	6	9	12	15	18	21	24	27	30

FIRST VERSION OF THE PSEUDOCODE

Recall that stepwise refinement starts from a rough pseudocode solution, refines those pieces which are not precise, and continues until it is easy to translate everything into C++. Here is a very rough solution to the problem:

> *print the headings at the top of the page*
> *construct each row of the multiplication table*
> *print the table*

REFINEMENT OF THE FIRST VERSION

This first approximation is over-simplified but provides a place to start. We need to elaborate on the top line *(print the headings at the top of the page)* and discuss how to print the table, but the most important thing is the middle statement *(construct each row of the multiplication table)*, so we refine it next. Each row of the multiplication table consists of the multiples of a given number, for example, 3, which we will call the multiplicand. For each multiplicand <u>m1</u> from 1 to 10, we need a set of the multiples of <u>m1</u>; more precisely, we need <u>m1</u> times each multiplier from 1 to 10—<u>m1</u> times 1, <u>m1</u> times 2, ..., <u>m1</u> times 10. Using this idea, here is a refined pseudocode solution:

> *print the headings at the top of the page*
> *for each multiplicand* m1 *from 1 to 10*
> > *print a line of output showing*
> > m1 *times each multiplier from 1 to 10*

FORMAT OF THE OUTPUT

Now let's be precise about the format of the output. On the top of the page, we want to print headings. They consist of a message saying this is a multiplication table, an 'X' standing for multiply, plus column headings of the multipliers from 1 to 10. Our answers will appear underneath them. For example, in row three (which contains the multiples of 3), the fifth column has the value 15 (which is 3 × 5). Here is the last version of the pseudocode:

> *print a line introducing the table*
> *print a line of multipliers from 1 to 10*
> *for each multiplicand* m1 *from 1 to 10*
> > *start a new line of output by printing* m1
> > *for each multiplier* m2 *from 1 to 10*
> > > *print* m1 ** m2 under the heading for* m2

STARTING THE PROGRAM

To start, here is the main comment which explains the purpose of the program, followed by the program header.

```
// Program mult.cpp:
// construct a multiplication table,
// showing the first 10 multiples of the numbers from 1 to 10
#include <iostream>
using namespace std;
int main()
```

Now we must write the body of the program. From the pseudocode, we need to declare two variables, m1 and m2, of data type **int**; however, these variables will be the indexes of **for** loops, and we will therefore postpone their declaration until the loop header. Next come the printouts needed for the first few lines of output. (See Exercise 13 for a way to print the last line of the heading using a **for** loop.)

```
{
    cout << "This is a Multiplication Table, from 1 to 10";
    cout << endl << endl;
    cout << " X    1    2    3    4    5    6    7    8    9    10"
    cout << endl;
```

These statements produce the following lines of output:

```
This is a Multiplication Table, from 1 to 10

 X    1    2    3    4    5    6    7    8    9    10
```

PRINTING A ROW OF THE MULTIPLICATION TABLE FOR EACH MULTIPLICAND

Now we are ready to start producing the values in the chart. The next part of the pseudocode starts like this:

for each multiplicand m1 *from 1 to 10*

It is logical to use a **for** loop, with m1 as the index, to translate this into C++.

```
for (int m1 = 1; m1 <= 10; m1++)
```

Within the body of this loop, we want to start a new line of output by printing the value of m1 on the left.

```
cout << endl << m1;
```

This should be followed by the multiples of m1 (for each multiplier m2 from 1 to 10). Each multiple should be aligned under its corresponding column heading.

When we printed the column headings, we mentioned each value from 1 to 10 explicitly in the line of output. But now, to handle all the multipliers, we use another **for** loop. This second **for** loop has a second variable, called m2, as its index.

```
for (int m2 = 1; m2 <= 10; m2++)
    cout << m1 * m2;
cout << endl;
```

To handle the alignment, we print each multiple using a field width of five (see Chapter 3, Section 5). To do this, we'll insert <u>cout.width(5)</u> into the program. Since a call to this function applies only to the next value printed, we'll actually have to put this call into the program in two places, right before printing each value of <u>m1</u> and before printing each value of <u>m1</u> * <u>m2</u>. By default, the values will be right-aligned within the columns, which is what we want.

We use <u>endl</u> twice in the program, to make sure that each row of the multiplication table starts on a new line and to double space the lines of the table.

COMPLETE PROGRAM

Let's take a look at the entire program:

 PROGRAM LISTING

```
// Program mult.cpp:
// construct a multiplication table,
// showing the first 10 multiples of the numbers from 1 to 10
#include <iostream>
using namespace std;
int main()
{
    cout << "This is a Multiplication Table, from 1 to 10";
    cout << endl << endl;
    cout << " X    1    2    3    4    5    6    7    8    9   10"
        << endl;
    // nested loop to print the table
    for (int m1 = 1; m1 <= 10; m1++) {
        cout << endl;
        cout.width(5);
        cout << m1;
        for (int m2 = 1; m2 <= 10; m2++) {
            cout.width(5);
            cout << m1 * m2;
        }
        cout << endl;
    }
    return 0;
}
```

NESTED for LOOP

Note that we have one **for** loop contained within another. This construction is called a **nested for loop**. One **for** loop uses <u>m1</u> as its index, and the other has <u>m2</u>. The <u>m2</u> **for** loop is completely contained within the <u>m1</u> **for** loop, forming a nested loop. The <u>m1</u> loop contains a number of statements which are inside the <u>m1</u> loop but before the <u>m2</u> loop; it contains the entire <u>m2</u> loop, and it contains a statement which is inside the <u>m1</u> loop but after the end of the <u>m2</u> loop. See Figure 4-1. When the program runs, the inner or <u>m2</u> loop will be executed completely every time we pass through the body of the outer or <u>m1</u> loop.

FIGURE 4-1 A nested for loop

```
for(int m1 = 1;...){
   ...
   for(int m2 = 1;...)
         cout << ...;
   ...
}
```
m2 loop m1 loop

NOTE

When we discussed Program 4, we remarked that the **for** loop computed a single value. Similarly, we can analyze the loops in this program. The inner loop computes a row of the multiplication table. The outer loop repeats this process for a series of values. The nested loop as a whole computes and prints a single item—a complete multiplication table.

TRACING THE PROGRAM

In order to study a nested loop, we will trace the entire program.

PROGRAM TRACE First, the computer prints the headings before either loop begins.

♦ The m1 loop starts by setting m1 to 1. Inside the body of the m1 loop, we skip a line, then print the value of m1 (1), ready to continue printing on the same line.

♦ At this point, the m2 loop begins, with m2 initialized to 1. Inside the m2 loop, we print 1 (since 1 * 1 = 1).

♦ Then m2 is incremented to 2 (with m1 still at 1). On the same line, we print 2 (1 * 2 = 2).

♦ Then m2 is incremented to 3, we print 3, and so on.

♦ Eventually, m2 becomes 10, and we print 10. When m2 becomes 11, the condition m2 <= 10 is false, and the m2 loop is completed.

The next statement to execute is *cout << endl*, which ends this line of output. At this point, we have completed one entire pass through the m1 loop and printed a line corresponding to the multiplication table for the multiplicand 1.

♦ We now start the next pass through the m1 loop, this time with m1 equal to 2. The first thing we do is skip a line because of the statement *cout << endl*, which starts the body of the m1 loop.

♦ Then we start a new m2 loop, with m2 starting over again at 1. Inside this m2 loop, we run through all values of m2, from 1 to 10, each time printing the value of the multiplicand m1 (which is 2) times the current value of m2.

♦ Eventually, m2 becomes 10, and we print 20. When m2 becomes 11, the condition m2 <= 10 is false, terminating the m2 loop.

After the m2 loop, we execute the statement *cout << endl*, which ends this line of output and the second pass through the m1 loop. This pass prints a multiplication table for the multiplicand 2, listing all the multiples of 2, from 2 * 1 to 2 * 10.

Similarly, we will have a pass through the m1 loop for each remaining value of m1, first printing the multiples of 3, then those of 4, and finally the multiples of 10. Let's pick up the trace here: For the last multiple to be printed, m2 also has the value 10, and we print 100. Then m2 is incremented to 11, so we fall out of the m2 loop. But then m1 is incremented to 11, and the condition m1 <= 10 is also false, so we fall out of the entire nested loop.

OUTPUT FROM THE PROGRAM

The output from this program looks like this:

```
This is a Multiplication Table, from 1 to 10
 X     1     2     3     4     5     6     7     8     9    10
 1     1     2     3     4     5     6     7     8     9    10
 2     2     4     6     8    10    12    14    16    18    20
 3     3     6     9    12    15    18    21    24    27    30
 4     4     8    12    16    20    24    28    32    36    40
 5     5    10    15    20    25    30    35    40    45    50
 6     6    12    18    24    30    36    42    48    54    60
 7     7    14    21    28    35    42    49    56    63    70
 8     8    16    24    32    40    48    56    64    72    80
 9     9    18    27    36    45    54    63    72    81    90
10    10    20    30    40    50    60    70    80    90   100
```

SELF-CHECK 4-5

1. In a nested **for** loop, can the same control variable be used for both loops? Should it be used for both loops?

2. In this program, what is the body of the m1 loop?

3. What is the body of the m2 loop?

MORE ON THE NESTED for LOOP CONSTRUCTION

We have seen that one **for** loop can appear within the body of another, producing a nested construction. There are many ways to include statements within a nested loop. Let's investigate a number of possible positions where statements can appear and discuss how many times each statement is executed. The exact position of a particular statement will, of course, depend upon its role in a program.

STATEMENTS OUTSIDE THE NESTED LOOP

In a nested loop, the inner loop is executed one complete time for each pass through the outer loop. Statements before the start of a nested **for** loop are executed once, before the entire nested loop begins; statements after the end of the loop are executed once, after the loop ends. See Figure 4-2.

As an example, we can print a heading at the start of the output and a second message after a computation is completed.

FIGURE 4-2   Statements before or after a nested **for** loop

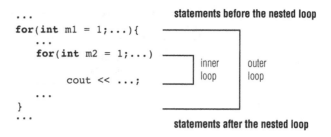

```
...                          statements before the nested loop
for(int m1 = 1;...){
    ...
    for(int m2 = 1;...)              inner      outer
                                     loop       loop
        cout << ...;
    ...
}
...                          statements after the nested loop
```

FIGURE 4-3   Statements between the loops of a nested **for** loop

```
for(int m1 = 1;...){                          inside the
    ...                                       outer loop
    for(int m2 = 1;...)           inner       but not      outer
                                  loop        in the       loop
        cout << ...;                          inner loop
    ...
}
```

EXAMPLE 4-3

In the following code, each message prints one time, regardless of what statements appear within the loops. (In this example, we are assuming the j loop is the only statement within the body of the i loop; therefore, the i loop does not need braces.)

```
cout << "this heading appears before the nested loop output" << endl;
for (int i = 1; i <= 5; i++)
    for (int j = 1; j <= 4; j++)
        ...
cout << "this message appears after the nested loop output" << endl;
```

STATEMENTS BETWEEN THE TWO LOOPS

Any statement that comes before the inner loop starts or after it ends (like the statement ***cout << endl*** in Example 4-4) is executed once for each pass through the outer loop. This includes the inner loop, which is executed completely each time through the outer loop. See Figure 4-3.

EXAMPLE 4-4

Here is an example that prints a blank line before the inner loop begins. The blank line is printed each time we go through the body of the outer (or i) loop; in this case, it prints five times. The entire inner (or j) loop also executes five times, with i having the values from 1 to 5.

```
for (int i = 1; i <= 5; i++) {
    cout << endl;
    for (int j = 1; j <= 4; j++)
        ...
}
```

STATEMENTS INSIDE BOTH LOOPS

A statement inside the body of the inner loop (which is also inside the outer loop) is executed on each pass through the inner loop. The number of times this statement executes is equal to the number of passes through the outer loop times the number of passes through the inner loop.

FIGURE 4-4   Statements inside both loops of a nested for loop

```
for(int m1 = 1;...){
    ...
    for(int m2 = 1;...) {
            ...     statements inside
            ...     both loops
    }
}
```

inner loop   outer loop

(See Figure 4-4.) As an example, program <u>mult.cpp</u> has a statement which multiplies both **for** loop indices to produce an element of the multiplication chart. This statement is executed 100 (10×10) times.

EXAMPLE 4-5   Here is an example showing a print statement inside the inner loop. This statement is executed 5 * 4 = 20 times.

```
for (int i = 1; i <= 5; i++)
    for (int j = 1; j <= 4; j++)
        cout << ...;
```

Finally, a **while** loop can replace either or both of the **for** loops in a nested loop. See Exercise 12.

SELF-CHECK 4-6

1. In Example 4-4, show exactly what value i has each time the line containing <u>cout</u> is executed.

2. In Example 4-5, show exactly what values i and j have each time the line containing <u>cout</u> is executed.

3. In a nested **for** loop, what happens after the condition controlling the inner loop becomes false? What happens after the condition controlling the outer loop becomes false?

SECTION 5 ENRICHMENT: RECOMMENDATIONS ON STYLE; STRUCTURED PROGRAMMING

In earlier chapters, we made some recommendations on style of programming. This section will summarize previous points and add new ideas. The general set of rules that we follow is called **structured programming.**

Originally, structured programming referred to the use of certain control structures and the avoidance of others (notably, avoiding the **goto** statement, which is discussed briefly in Chapter 6, Section 7). Structured programming emphasized these three control structures:

♦   sequence—executing statements in order

♦   selection—choosing one of two alternatives

♦   iteration—repeating a series of instructions

Nowadays, almost all programmers use preferred control structures, and the term "structured programming" usually refers to the style issues discussed in this section. Let's start by reviewing things we did to make program <u>mult.cpp</u> more readable.

COMMENTS

First, we included comments. It is better to include a few large comments rather than several short ones; a comment for every single C++ statement is counterproductive. For example, the lines below do not require comments; those shown are superfluous and make the program harder to read.

```
x = 0;              // set x to 0
y = 1;              // set y to 1
z = x + y;          // add x and y together
```

There should always be a comment at the beginning to describe the purpose of the program. After that point, include a comment if you think it will help a person reading the program to understand something. For example, in program <u>mult.cpp</u> we put a comment before the nested loop. Because this program is so short, it is not necessary to include additional comments. In other programs, we might decide to include more. For example, if we were doing something complicated in the middle of a program, we would include a comment to explain the method, or if the program had a nested loop which needed more explanation, we would explain it in a comment.

STYLE WORKSHOP

Here are three suggestions on where to use comments:

♦ at the beginning of a program

♦ at the start of each major unit of a program (e.g., a nested loop as in <u>prog5a.cpp</u> or a function as discussed in the next chapter)

♦ whenever it is helpful to explain a technique or method

Regardless of where a comment is located, several things make it more readable. A large comment can be placed on two or more lines instead of one long line, and the comment can be written in a way that draws attention to it. (See Chapter 5, Section 6.) The object is to make the comment more visible to a person glancing over the program. Obviously, you should make sure your comment is worthwhile. It should be possible to read only the comments and get some understanding of how the program works; it should also be possible to read the program without the comments getting in the way.

MNEMONIC NAMES

One should always be careful to use meaningful or **mnemonic names** for identifiers. For example, in Program 1, we called the variables <u>number</u> and <u>sqnumber</u>; in Program 2, we used <u>gpa</u> and <u>result</u> rather than simply <u>x</u> and <u>y</u>; in Program 3, we used <u>hours</u>, <u>rate</u>, and <u>pay</u>. In <u>mult.cpp</u>, <u>m1</u> and <u>m2</u>, although not as mnemonic as some of our other choices, were probably enough to describe the purpose of the variables. As an additional aid to the reader, the comment at the top of the main program or a function can list each variable and its use, or this can be done in the declaration statement.

EXAMPLE 4-6 For example, we could use the following declaration in <u>prog3.cpp</u>:

```
double hours;       // the hours worked in a week
double rate;        // the rate of pay per hour
double pay;         // the weekly pay
```

However, using appropriate names for variables might make such comments unnecessary.

Using comments in this way reinforces a point we made in Chapter 1. Every variable in a program should serve a specific purpose. Mentioning this purpose in a comment helps you understand the variable's role in your program. Of course, these detailed comments should supplement, rather than replace, mnemonic names. Don't use sloppy names like x and y just because you have comments explaining their roles.

Some programmers prefer to be consistent in their variable names. For example, they may always use i or j as the index of a **for** loop (or chr as the name of a variable which holds characters), even though these are not very useful names. This is largely a matter of taste, and you can experiment as you develop your own programming style.

SPACING AND INDENTATION

The physical layout of a program is important for clarity. Remember our previous warning against writing more than one statement per line. The only possible exception (and this should be avoided) is two or more very short assignment statements on the same line. In addition, we suggest that you purposely include blank lines in your program to separate and draw attention to things. For example, a comment could be surrounded by blank space to set it off from code. Any statement or group of statements (e.g., declarations) can be accented this way. Blank lines are ignored by the compiler but are very helpful to the reader.

Statements in a program should be indented consistently. For example, the statements inside a **for** or a **while** loop should be indented. If a program uses the **if-else** construction, the keywords **if** and **else** should be aligned, and so on.

Although the advantage in following these rules is slight in a short program, a large program written this way is much easier to follow. The precise details of where to put a blank line and how to align statements are not important. What is important is clarity.

READABLE OUTPUT

Often a programmer devotes a lot of time to making sure that a program works perfectly but forgets about the output. Most people look at the output, not the program. No matter how clear the code is, if the output is a meaningless stream of numbers, the program is useless.

In addition to a comment inside the program, be sure to include headings or messages in the output to explain the various values. For example, if a program finds the sum of the first 30 squares, this should be mentioned in the output. If the program computes an employee's weekly pay, this fact should be part of the printed output. If a program evaluates a mathematical formula, the program should print a message saying this. (Perhaps even the formula can be printed if it is relevant to the results.) Some programmers go to the opposite extreme and print everything (even a copy of the prompts requesting interactive I/O). This makes it hard for the reader to see what is important, but it is better to have an extra line of output than to omit a necessary one.

DEBUG PRINTOUT

In Chapter 2, Section 6, we gave some recommendations on debugging a program. There is an important concept, called **debug printout**, that we did not mention at that time. If a program is not working, it is helpful to insert a few extra print statements at key points. These extra output statements give the programmer further information about executing the program—the values of intermediate calculations, the status of loop control variables, or the results of function calls.

In the multiplication table program, suppose we want to make sure that all possible multiplications are being produced. It may be helpful to print the values of m1 and m2 inside the nested **for** loop.

EXAMPLE 4-7   Here is some code that includes debug printout:

```
// nested loop to print the table
for (int m1 = 1; m1 <= 10; m1++) {
    cout << endl;
    cout.width(5);
    cout << m1
    for (int m2 = 1; m2 <= 10; m2++) {
        cout << "m1 and m2 are: " << m1 << " " << m2
            << endl; // debug printout
        cout.width(5);
        cout << m1 * m2;
    }
    cout << endl;
}
```

Let's consider one last example from Program 4 (calculating the sum of the squares of the numbers from 1 to 30): To check that the calculation is correct, we can print the value of <u>sum</u> each time through the loop instead of just once at the end.

EXAMPLE 4-8   Here is the **for** loop from the first version of Program 4 rewritten with the extra debug printout statements:

```
cout << "before the loop" << endl;
for (int item = 1; item <= 30; item++) {
    sum += item * item;
    cout << "after " << item << " terms, the sum is " << sum << endl;
}
cout << endl << "after the loop the final sum is " << sum << endl;
```

These suggestions show that debug printout gives the programmer extra information to eliminate programming bugs. In most cases, the more debug printout you include, the easier it is to locate a bug. Of course, you usually remove the statements that generate the debug printout once the error has been found and corrected. Or you may decide to include the "quick and dirty" debug printout statements, cleaned up a little, as part of the final output from the program.

AVOID CLEVER CODE

In the 1950s and 1960s, when computing was still in its infancy, programmers vied with each other to produce "clever code" to solve a problem in a tricky or unexpected way. Believe it or not, a program incomprehensible to anyone else was considered to be "better" than an easily understood one.

As the field has matured, this attitude has been replaced by an emphasis on readability and clarity. However, some programmers, especially if they are trying to impress someone, still use a tricky or clever style.

EXAMPLE 4-9   Can you figure out what the code below is designed to do?

```
int x,y,z,w;
...
if (x > y)
    z = 0;
```

```
else
    z = y - x;
w = x + z;
```

_____ It computes the larger of the two numbers x and y. See if you can determine how.

Naturally, a program using tricks like this is almost impossible to debug or modify by anyone other than the original programmer (even he or she may not remember how things work after a period of time).

STYLE WORKSHOP Avoid tricks. If you have two ways of doing something, a clear but slightly less efficient method and a tricky one, it is almost always better to use the clear version. A programmer's time is usually much more valuable than a machine's.

DOCUMENTATION

A program written in a good style is still almost worthless unless people can use it. The information required to use a program is called **documentation**. In the business or commercial world, a program is not considered complete until it has documentation. The following information should be included in a program's documentation:

♦ a statement of what problem the program is designed to solve

♦ pseudocode (or some other outline of how the program works)

♦ a listing of the program, including a good set of comments

♦ a set of instructions with any special information needed to run the program (e.g., a special format for the data)

♦ a complete set of test cases (trying all possible paths in the program), together with sample output

STYLE WORKSHOP As programs grow larger and larger, documentation becomes even more crucial. These rules for developing good programming style are by no means complete. There is no universal agreement in the field of programming on what constitutes good style, just as there is none in English. However, most programmers would agree with our recommendations. There is another advantage to following these rules on style: A program which obeys the rules is almost always easier to debug than one that doesn't follow consistent rules.

SELF-CHECK 4-7

1. What is structured programming?
2. What things improve the physical appearance of a program?
3. What are the major parts of the documentation accompanying a program?

SUMMARY

STEPWISE REFINEMENT AND TOP-DOWN PROGRAMMING

1. Stepwise refinement and top-down programming are useful in solving a complex problem. Stepwise refinement starts with pseudocode that may be only a rough approximation to the final solution of the problem. Any steps that are vague are subdivided and made more precise as the solution is refined. This process is repeated until all steps are clear and can be translated easily into C++.

2. When refining the solution to a problem by top-down programming, questions of detail can be postponed until overall structural decisions have been resolved. Pseudocode shows the successive refinements.

SUMMING A SERIES OF TERMS

3. A series of values or terms of a formula can be added together by the following algorithm: Initialize a sum to 0; each time through a loop, add a new term to the sum; repeat the loop until all terms have been added to the running total. At the end of the loop, this total is the sum of the entire series of terms.

4. In previous chapters, the purpose of a loop has been to repeat a series of calculations several times. In Program 4, the entire **for** loop has a single purpose—to compute the sum of a series of terms. Similarly, in mult.cpp, the purpose of the nested loop is to compute a multiplication table.

DECLARING A LOOP INDEX

5. It is customary in C++ to declare the index of a **for** loop inside the loop header. A variable declared in this location has meaning and value only within the loop. Here is a loop with the index declared in the header:

```
for (int i = 1; i < 10; i++)
     cout << i;
```

The variable i cannot be used outside of this **for** loop, unless it is declared again as the index of another loop.

CONSTANTS

6. The value of a variable can change as a program is executing. However, the value of a constant is fixed by a definition. The general form of the definition for a constant is:

```
const type name = value;
```

7. The compiler replaces every occurrence of the constant identifier *name* by the value *value*. For example, in the program using these constant definitions, every occurrence of NUMB is replaced by the value 7, while EPSILON is replaced by 0.00001.

```
const int NUMB = 7;
const double EPSILON = 0.00001;
```

READING IN A LIMIT VALUE

8. The limit value controlling the number of times a **for** loop is executed can be read in from a set of data. Reading a value (as opposed to using a constant to control the loop) gives the program more flexibility because the same program can be used to compute several different results.

NESTED **for** LOOPS

9. One **for** loop can be completely contained or nested within another. Each pass through the outer loop leads to a complete execution of the inner loop. When the program finishes a complete pass through the inner loop, it starts a second pass through the outer loop, and so on. This process continues until completion of the last pass through the outer loop.

10. Any statement that appears before the nested loop begins or after it ends is executed once. Any statement which is inside the outer loop but not contained in the inner loop is executed once for each pass through the outer loop. Any statement which is inside the inner loop is executed once for each pass through the inner loop. The entire inner loop is executed once for each pass through the outer loop.

11. This example illustrates some of these ideas:

```
int count;

cout << "counts for each pass" << endl;
for (int i = 1; i <= 10; i++) {
    count = 0;
    for (int j = 1; j <= 5; j++)
        count++;
    cout << count << " for pass " << i << endl;
}
cout << "finished processing" << endl;
```

The first and last printouts are done once; the initialization of <u>count</u> and the printout of <u>count</u> plus <u>i</u> are each done ten times; the increment of <u>count</u> is done 10 * 5 = 50 times. However, note that <u>count</u> is reset to 0 between the two loops and thus never gets a value above 5.

STRUCTURED PROGRAMMING

12. Structured programming is the name of the currently accepted style of programming. Structured programming encourages the use of comments, meaningful identifier names, consistent spacing, indentation, readable output, and proper documentation. It discourages tricky code.

13. Comments are perhaps the single most important aspect of good style. They help someone to read the program. A person should be able to read the comments without getting bogged down in the details of a program and read the program without being annoyed by the comments.

14. Any good program must be accompanied by documentation explaining its use. This documentation can include a statement of the problem, pseudocode, a program listing with comments, a set of instructions for using the program, and sample output from a complete set of test data.

EXERCISES

TRACING EXERCISES

1. For each of these program segments, show what is printed. All variables have data type **int**.

```
a. sum = 0;
   for (int i = 1; i<= 10; i++)
       sum += i;
   cout << "the sum is " << sum << endl;
```

```
b. count = 0;
   for (int i = 1; i <= 10; i++)
       count++;
   cout << "the count is "
               << count << endl;
```

```
c. cin >> a;
   cin >> b;
   sum = 0;
   for (int i = a; i <= b; i++)
       sum += i;
   cout << "from " << a << " to " << b << " the sum is " << sum << endl;
```

Answer part (c) three times. First, assume that the set of data consists of the two numbers 3 5; then answer the question assuming that the set of data is 1 6; then assume it is 5 5.

2. Show exactly what is printed by the following program segment. All variables have data type **int**.

```
sign = 1;
sum1 = 0;
sum2 = 0;
for (int i = 1; i <= 7; i++)   {
    sum1 -= sign * i;
    sum2 += sign * i * i;
    sign *= -1;
    cout << i << " " << sum1 << " " << sum2 << " " << sign << endl;
}
cout << "at the end:" << endl;
cout << sum1 << " " << sum2 << " " << sign << endl;
```

3. Show what is printed by the following program.

```
#include <iostream>
using namespace std;
int main()
{
    int sign = 1, x = 5, y = 1;

    for (int k = 1; k <= 5; k++) {
        x = y - sign * y;
        y++;
        sign *= -1;
        cout << k << " " << x << " " << y << " " << sign << endl;
    }
    cout << x << " " << y << " " << sign << endl;
    return 0;
}
```

4. Show what is printed by each of the following:

a. ```
int n;
   . . .
for (int j = 1; j <= 3; j++)
    for (int i= 1; i <= 4; i++) {
        n = 10 * i + j;
        cout << i << " " << j << " " << n << endl;
    }
cout << endl << "done" << endl;
```

b. ```
int n;
   . . .
for (int i = 1; i <= 4; i++)
    for (int j = 1; j <= 3; j++) {
        n = 10 * i + j;
        cout << i << " " << j << " " << n << endl;
    }
cout << "done" << endl;
```

5. Show what is printed by the following program:

```
#include <iostream>
using namespace std;
const int LIMIT = 10;
int main()
{
    int sum;

    for (int i = 1; i <= LIMIT; i++) {
        sum = 0;
        for (int j = 1; j <= i; j++)
            sum += j;
        cout << "When i equals " << i << " the sum is "
            << sum << endl;
    }
    return 0;
}
```

On the line defining the constant <u>LIMIT</u>, replace 10 by each of the following and repeat the program:
(a) 5   (b) 7   (c) 11   (d) 12

6. What is a good name for a variable whose purpose is to

   a. hold the numbers from 1 to 100
   b. count how many negative numbers are read in
   c. hold a four-digit student ID number
   d. hold the average of a series of test scores
   e. hold the sales of a company for January

7. In each of the following, what is wrong with the indenting and aligning? Fix each one.

```
a. for (int i = 1; i <= 4; i++)
        sum = ...
        cout << ...;
```

```
b. for (int i = 1; i <= 4; i++)
   sum = ...
   cout << ...;
```

```
c. if (hours < 40) pay = hours * rate;
        else pay = hours * rate + (hours - 40) * rate * 0.5;
```

```
d. for (int row = 1; row <= 5; row++) {
   col = 1;
   while (col <= 4) {
   cout << row << " " << col << endl;
   col++;
   }
   }
```

```
e. if (x < 0) cout << "yes"; else cout << "no"; cout << endl;
```

MODIFICATIONS OF PROGRAM 4

8.   a. Write a loop to find the sum of the numbers from 1 to 100.
     b. Write a loop to find the sum of the even numbers from 10 to 200.
     c. Write a loop to find the sum of the cubes of the numbers from 1 to 10.

9. Rewrite the loops in Exercise 8 using constants to control them.

10. There is still some trouble with the solution to Problem 4 at the end of Section 3. Assume that we want to compute the sum of the first 7 squares, the sum of the first 5 squares, the sum of the first 27 squares, and the sum of the first 8 squares. It seems that we have to run the program four times, each one with a new value for the number of squares (n) to be summed. However, there is a better solution.

    Modify the program so that, after reading and processing completely one particular value for n, it reads another number representing a new value for n and starts all over again. For example, the set of data may contain 8 12 7. This directs the program to read 8 into n and find the sum of the first 8 squares; then the program goes back to the beginning (you must decide where), reads 12, and computes the sum of the first 12 squares; then it reads 7 and repeat the entire process for the first 7 squares. (If one of the n values you use is greater than 40, see Exercise 15.)

    You must also provide a way to detect the end of data (perhaps use a trailer, such as a negative value). Note that this program contains two loops, one within the other. The inner loop finds the sum of the first n squares; the outer loop processes several values of n.

11. Rewrite Program 4 using a **while** instead of a **for** loop. Rewrite Program 4 without using any loops (by taking care of each number individually). Compare the three versions. Which is the easiest to understand? Which is the longest? Which is the easiest to modify?

12. Repeat Exercise 11 for the multiplication table program in Section 4. That is, compare the original version using one **for** loop inside another to versions which use a **while** loop for the inner, outer, or both loops.

13. Modify the column headings in the multiplication table program so that the list of multipliers from 1 to 10 is printed with a **for** loop instead of mentioning each number explicitly.

ANALYSIS EXERCISES

14. In arithmetic, the sum of a series of integer terms is always an integer, regardless of how many terms are added together. In C++, this may not always be true because of the restrictions on the size of a variable of type **int**. (This value depends upon your particular compiler.)

    a. If you sum the first 30 squares, will each term be less than the maximum integer value? Will the sum of the terms be less than this maximum?

    b. If you sum the first 100 squares, will each term be less than the maximum? Will the sum of the terms be less?

    c. If you sum the first 5000 squares, will each term be less than the maximum? Will the sum of the terms be less?

    d. See if you can determine the maximum number of squares that can be summed before the sum is more than the maximum integer value. (*Suggestion*: Write a program to solve this problem.)

    e. See if you can determine the largest number whose square is less than the maximum. Why is this much easier than part (d)?

15. In addition to data type **int**, C++ has two other integer data types called **long int** (abbreviated as **long**) and **short int** (abbreviated as **short**).

    a. On your system, what is the largest value that can be stored in a variable of type **long**? Repeat Exercise 14 for a variable of this data type.

    b. Do the same for type **short**.

16. There is a simple mathematical formula to check the calculations obtained by the programs in this chapter. The sum of the first $\underline{n}$ squares is given by the expression:

$$1^2 + 2^2 + \cdots + \underline{n}^2 = \underline{n} * (\underline{n} + 1) * (2 * \underline{n} + 1) / 6$$

For example, if $\underline{n}$ is 2, then $1 * 1 + 2 * 2 = 5$, and $2 * 3 * 5 / 6 = 5$ as well.

Modify the version of the program at the end of Section 3 (prog4a.cpp) so that it computes a check on the sum. After adding up the first $\underline{n}$ squares, the program should set a variable called check to *n* * *(n+1)* * *(2n+1)* / *6*. The program should then compare sum to check and print a message explaining whether they agree. *Warning*: If you are computing the sum of a large number of squares (e.g., $\underline{n} > 40$), the variables sum and check may hold values larger than the maximum (see Exercise 14). Therefore, you may want to change these variables to have data type **double** or **long** rather than **int**.

17. This exercise explores what can occur in a nested **for** loop when both loops use the same name for the loop control variable. It also illustrates one of the reasons for declaring a loop index in the loop header: to avoid problems such as these. In each part, show what is printed by inserting the nested **for** loop into the basic program below. Then rewrite each part so that the inner loop uses a new control variable, j. (What else must be done to the program?)

```
#include <iostream>
using namespace std;
int main()
{
    int i;

    // insert nested for loop here

    return 0;
}
```

a. `for (i = 1; i <= 5; i++)`
     `for (i = 1; i <= 5; i++)`
         `cout << " i is: " << i << endl;`

b. `for (i = 1; i <= 5; i++)`
     `for (i = 4; i <= 7; i++)`
         `cout << " i is: " << i << endl;`

c. `for (i = 4; i <= 7; i++)`
     `for (i = 1; i <= 5; i++)`
         `cout << " i is: " << i << endl;`

PROGRAMMING PROJECTS

18. a. Write a program to do the following: Read in a series of numbers from a set of data. Print each number as you read it in. When the sum of the numbers becomes 100 or more, print a message saying that a total of 100 has been reached and stop processing. However, if you read the number 17 before reaching 100, print a message giving the sum so far and terminate the program at that point.

b. Modify the program from part (a) so that it also prints the number of values used to obtain the sum. Do this for either case—whether or not you actually reach 100.

19. Write a program which reads in a number $\underline{n}$ from the data, then compute the sum of the first $\underline{n}$ integers—that is, $1 + 2 + \cdots + \underline{n}$. As a check, this sum should be *n(n + 1)/2*. After processing the first value of $\underline{n}$, the program should go back to read in a new value and repeat the calculation. Repeat the entire process until the set of data is exhausted.

20. Write a program that reads in a number $\underline{n}$ from the data, then compute the sum of the first $\underline{n}$ cubes, $1^3 + 2^3 + \cdots + \underline{n}^3$. Continue the processing until the set of data is exhausted. As a check, the sum should be *(n * (n + 1)/2)²*. Also see Exercise 14.

21. Write a program that reads in a number $\underline{k}$ from the data, then computes the sum of the first $\underline{k}$ powers of $\underline{k}$ (that is, the sum of the powers of $\underline{k}$ from $\underline{k}^1$ to $\underline{k}^k$). For example, if $\underline{k}$ is 2, it computes the sum of $\underline{k}^1 + \underline{k}^2$, but if $\underline{k}$ is 3, it computes $\underline{k}^1 + \underline{k}^2 + \underline{k}^3$. Is there a simple check for this problem?

22. Write a program that reads in $\underline{n}$ from the data, then compute the sum of the first $\underline{n}$ even numbers and the sum of the first $\underline{n}$ odd numbers. For example, if $\underline{n}$ is 3, then it computes $2 + 4 + 6 = 12$ as the sum of the first three even numbers, and $1 + 3 + 5 = 9$ as the sum of the first three odd numbers. The checks are *n * (n + 1)* for the sum of the first $\underline{n}$ even numbers, and $\underline{n}$ * $\underline{n}$ for the sum of the first $\underline{n}$ odd numbers.

    Repeat the calculations for a series of values of $\underline{n}$. Here is a possible method: In the program, use two separate loops, one for even numbers and the other for odd. In each loop, you have to be careful to skip over odd when adding even (and even when adding odd).

23. Write a program to read in two numbers, $\underline{x}$ and $\underline{n}$, and then compute the sum of this geometric progression:

    $$1 + x + x^2 + x^3 + \cdots + x^n$$

    For example, if $\underline{n}$ is 3 and $\underline{x}$ is 5, then the program computes $1 + 5 + 25 + 125$. Print $\underline{x}$, $\underline{n}$, the sum, and the check given here, together with appropriate messages. The check for the sum is

    $$\frac{x^{n+1} - 1}{x - 1} \qquad \text{(the check cannot be used if } \underline{x} \text{ is 1)}$$

    Repeat the process for a series of numbers.

24. Modify the program from Exercise 23 to do some error checking. For example, the formula does not make sense for negative exponents—if $\underline{n}$ is less than 0. Have your program print an error message if $\underline{n} < 0$, then go back and read in the next pair of numbers without computing the sum. Are any values of $\underline{x}$ also illegal? If so, test for them, too.

25. a. Introduce error checking into some of the earlier exercises. For example, if we are computing the sum of the first $\underline{n}$ cubes, what constitutes bad data? If you find bad data, print a message, then go on to the next value.

    b. Do the same for some of the exercises from Chapter 3. (What would be bad data in a payroll program?)

26. a. Write a program to do the following: For each number $\underline{n}$ from 1 to 40, find the sum of the squares of the numbers from 1 to $\underline{n}$. That is, compute $1 * 1 + \cdots + \underline{n} * \underline{n}$ (see Exercise 15 for a way to check this calculation).

    b. Modify your program from part (a) so that it computes the sum of the cubes of the numbers from 1 to $\underline{n}$. (Exercise 20 has a check.)

27. The Fibonacci series consists of the numbers 1, 1, 2, 3, 5, 8, 13, ... The first two terms are both 1; thereafter, each term is the sum of the two previous ones ($8 = 3 + 5$, $13 = 5 + 8$).

Write a program to read a value n, then compute and print the values of the first n terms of the Fibonacci series. (*Suggestion*: You have to keep track of the last term and the next-to-last term and update them at the appropriate time.)

28. The factorial of a number n, written n!, is defined as follows:

    n! = 1 * 2 * ⋯ * (n – 1) * n (and 0! = 1)

    For example, 5! = 1 * 2 * 3 * 4 * 5 = 120; 3! = 1 * 2 * 3 = 6.

    a. Write a program to do the following: Read in a number n, then compute n!. [*Suggestion*: Use a **for** loop to compute the product (just as we used a **for** loop to compute a sum) with an appropriate initialization and multiplication step.]
    b. Write a program that computes a table of the numbers from 1 to n, together with the factorial of each number. For example, if n is 7, then it should print (each pair on a new line)

1	1	2	2	3	6	4	24	5	120	6	720	7	5040

    c. Modify your program from part (a) so that it reads in a series of values for n and computes n! for each value (use a negative value as a trailer).

29. Compare the efficiency of the programs from Exercise 28, parts (b) and (c). (First, you have to specify some way of measuring program efficiency. For example, you can see which program executes fewer instructions.) If you want to compute a large number of consecutive factorial values, which is the more efficient method? If you only want one or two widely spaced factorial values, which is more efficient?

30. a. One of the sultan's friends, the Lord of Flatbush, is relatively poor. He has only 1000 diamonds to give to his child. Write a program which determines the maximum number of days when the Lord of Flatbush can distribute diamonds (assuming that he gives 1 * 1 on the first day, 2 * 2 on the second day, and so on).
    b. Write a program which starts by asking the Lord of Flatbush exactly how many diamonds he has. Then the program determines how many days he can distribute them.

31. The Sultan of RedValley wants to give his son, who was born on the last day of April, a special birthday present, lasting through the entire month. On the first day, he wants to give his son one diamond. On the second day, two diamonds, then four on the next day, and so on. Each day he gives twice as many diamonds as the day before.

    a. Write a program to print the number of diamonds given on each day in April. (*Suggestion*: Can a variable of type **int** hold the number of diamonds? See Exercises 14 and 15.)
    b. Modify the program from part (a) so that on each day, it also prints the total number of diamonds given so far.

32. Combine the program from Exercise 31 with the original program for Problem 4. On each day of the month, print how many diamonds the son is getting, how many the daughter is getting, and the total number received by each child so far.

33. This exercise asks you to write a series of programs to help a scientist analyze the results of some laboratory experiments.

    a. The first program should do the following: Read in ten values, each representing the weight of a mouse in grams (e.g., 145.34 or 421.23). Find the average of the ten readings.
    b. Modify the program from part (a) so that it reads in two values for each mouse, the weights before and after it is fed a special diet. For each mouse, find how much weight it has gained or lost. Find the average weight before and after the diet.

    c. Modify the program from part (b) so that it also prints how many mice gained weight, how many lost weight, and how many stayed the same.

34. Modify the program from Exercise 33 part (c) so that the experiment is repeated for a series of mice (not necessarily ten) until a negative value is entered for a weight. For example, if the experiment has been conducted on eight mice, there would be a total of 16 weight readings, followed by a negative value to signal the end of the set of data.

35. a. Modify the program from Exercise 33 part (c) so that the experiment is repeated for five groups of mice with ten readings in each group. After processing each group of ten, print what is requested in Exercise 33. After processing all five groups, print the overall average, plus the total number of mice which gained weight, the total number which lost weight, and the total number which stayed the same.

    b. The program in part (a) uses five groups of ten readings. Modify it to read in groups of ten until a negative value is entered for the first weight in the group. At that point, print the final totals.

36. A team of social scientists conducts an experiment in which they ask a group of a hundred people to estimate the average family income in their community. Write a program to analyze the results of the survey. First, read in a value representing the actual average family income in the community (e.g., 23456.67). Then read in a series of 100 values, representing the estimates. For each estimate, compute how far it is either above or below the actual value. Compute the average of the estimates. Compute how far the average is from the actual value.

37. Modify the program from Exercise 36 so that it also determines which estimate is closest to the average and which one is farthest from the average. (*Hint*: To do this, you need an algorithm to determine the largest or smallest value in a group of numbers.)

FUNCTIONS

PROBLEM: Sum of Squares (Revisited)

SYNTAX CONCEPTS: functions, parameters, function definition, **return** statement, function declaration or prototype, type **void**, reference parameters

PROGRAMMING CONCEPTS: driver program

CONTROL STRUCTURES: function call and return, void function, parameterless function

PROBLEM-SOLVING TECHNIQUES: using functions, shifting details to functions, modular programming, I-P-O comments

HOW TO READ CHAPTER 5

OUTLINE:

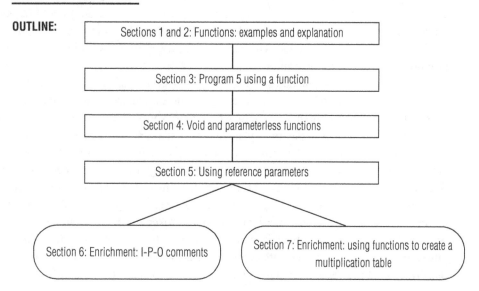

Sections 1, 2, 4, and 5 are the crucial ones in this chapter. It is possible to cover any of Sections 4–7 without doing Section 3.

INTRODUCTION AND STATEMENT OF THE PROBLEM

The problem for this chapter should look familiar since Problem 5 is identical to the problem used in Chapter 4. Instead of concentrating on a new problem, we are purposely spending most of this chapter introducing an extremely powerful C++ feature, called a function. Then we will use a function to solve Problem 5. A number of other sections supply more details about functions and how to use them.

PROBLEM 5   Write a C++ program to read a data value n̲. Then find the sum of the squares of the numbers from 1 to n̲ (the sum of the first n̲ squares). Print the sum of the squares.

SECTION 1   FUNCTIONS

This section introduces what is perhaps the single most important feature of the C++ language: functions. This feature is used over and over in later programs. In Section 1, we begin by reviewing and expanding our knowledge of standard library functions like sqrt( ).

THE CONCEPT OF A FUNCTION

In Chapter 4, we gave a number of versions or modifications of Program 4. In this chapter, there is one last modification: rewriting the program (now called Program 5) using a **function**. Before we actually rewrite Program 5, we need to discuss functions.

Each version of Program 4 centered around a series of instructions to calculate the sum of a given number of squares. A series of instructions with one specific purpose is called a **module**. A module can be written directly in the main program, as in Chapter 4, but there is another method. We can write a function that consists of the module. Then, in the main body of the program, a single instruction (known as the **call to the function**) utilizes this function in a particular situation. Another example is the portion of Program 3 which computes and prints payroll information for a single employee. The details of the payroll calculation (base pay, taxes, etc.) could be computed in one module, and the details of the printout handled in another. We can write each module as a separate section of code, called a function. The main body of the program would contain a call to the calculation function and one to the printout function. See Figure 5-1.

The concept of using modules is actually very widespread. Just about any large program can be broken up into a series of well-defined tasks or modules. Then a separate function can be written for each. After you have written a few larger programs, you will find they tend to use the same little pieces over again. For example, once you have written a function to read in a set of data, this module can be saved for reuse in other programs. If you have a function to print the results of a series of calculations, you may be able to reuse it too. A large program can be divided into a series of reusable functions (this process is called **modularization**). Instead of starting from scratch to solve each problem, the programmer can plug in one or more previously written functions. In a business or commercial environment, once a program has been broken down, different programmers can work on separate functions, then combine their little pieces to solve the entire problem. The actual implementation of these ideas using separate compilation is beyond your current programming abilities (it is usually covered in a second programming course), but you can start to think in these terms.

FIGURE 5-1   Using functions in Program 3

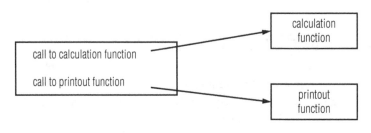

We already introduced the concept of a function with library functions like sqrt( ). We don't know what the statements inside the sqrt( ) function look like—we just issue a call to tell sqrt( ) what to work on. For example, we could write the following in a main program:

```
y = sqrt(w);
```

This call tells the sqrt( ) function to find the square root of w, storing the answer in the variable y.

ADVANTAGES OF FUNCTIONS

There are two main advantages to using a function. First, we can separate the mechanics of a function from its particular use in a larger program. For instance, in the example above, the main program does not have to specify the individual steps in finding the square root. It simply issues a call or request to the sqrt( ) function. In that call, the main program has to specify the value for which it wants to find the square root. This extra information sent to the function is called a **parameter** (in the example, it is w). Figure 5-2 shows another example; in this one, a function performs the command "shop." The extra information, which is substituted for the blank in the function, is the type of shopping to perform.

When writing the main program, we can concentrate on it, without having to worry about details which are contained in the function. As you can guess, this ties in well with top-down programming and stepwise refinement stressed in Chapter 4. Instead of refining a particular calculation or module down to the last detail in a main program, we specify the call to the function but leave the particular steps for the function. A person who wants just an overview looks at the main program; to see the specific details, the person looks at the function.

Another advantage of a function is that the set of instructions specifying the task performed by the function is written just once but can be used any number of times. For example, we can compute the square root of w and then the square root of z + 27 simply by issuing two calls with different values for the parameter sent to the function.

To summarize:

◆ A function gives the computer a set of instructions that can be used again with different values.

◆ Once the pattern or function is specified, one single statement calls it in a given situation; to apply it three times takes three calls.

HIGHLIGHTS

◆ To use a function to perform a particular task:

1. Write a function which contains the instructions to perform the task.

2. Every time you want to perform the task on actual parameter value(s), call the function with the value(s) specified.

FIGURE 5-2 Using a shopping function

Calls to the shopping function

shopping for _____

shop for **clothing**
shop for **groceries**
shop for **software**

get list
go to the _____ store
buy _____
go home

SELF-CHECK 5-1

1. What is a call to a function? What is a parameter?

2. How many times is the code for a function written? How many times can it be called?

3. What are the two main advantages of using a function?

USING THE LIBRARY FUNCTION sqrt()

We begin our discussion by looking at the library function sqrt( ). Recall from Chapter 2 what a library function is. The pattern or set of instructions for the function is already in the standard library available to the C++ compiler. To use one of these library functions, we must only issue a call.

Assume that we have this main program:

```cpp
// main program which calls the library function sqrt()
#include <iostream>
#include <cmath>
using namespace std;
int main()
{
    double w,y;

    w = 16.0;
    y = sqrt(w);
    cout << y << endl;
    return 0;
}
```

The first assignment statement gives w the value 16.0. In the next line, this value is sent to the function sqrt( ). While sqrt( ) is working, the main program is waiting for an answer to be computed. (It resumes execution after sqrt( ) computes this answer and sends it back.) The function uses some process to find the square root of the number sent to it. In this case, it finds the square root of 16.0, which is 4.0, and then sends the answer back to the main program to be put into the variable y. At that point, the main program resumes execution, prints the value stored in y, and stops.

THE FUNCTION sqrt()

Let's look more carefully at sqrt( ) itself.

EXAMPLE 5-1 This is roughly what the function sqrt( ) looks like:

```cpp
// function to find the square
//   root of the parameter x
double sqrt(double x)                          // function header
{
    compute the square root of x
    return the value computed
}
```

Notice the "scaffolding" surrounding the actual instructions to find the square root. This scaffolding or "shell" is necessary in every function.

WHAT'S OLD?

There are many features of the function that are familiar to us:

◆ The first two lines are comments; every function should have a comment describing what task it is designed to accomplish.

◆ The comment is followed by a line called the **function header**. Among other things, the header gives the identifier (sqrt) that is used to call the function from the main program. Identifier names for functions are lowercase like variable identifier names. The function header, just like the main program header, does not end in a semicolon.

◆ The header starts with a data type which indicates the type of answer returned by the function (the return type); in this case, the answer returned has type **double**. In all of our previous programs, the main program header started with the data type **int**, to indicate that the main program would return an integer value.

◆ Just as in a main program, the function has a pair of braces surrounding the instructions to perform its task.

◆ The final statement of the function, called a **return statement**, returns this value to the program that called the function. In our previous programs, the main program always used a *return 0*; statement, which signals to the operating system that the main program has terminated normally (returning any other value signals an abnormal termination).

WHAT'S NEW?

In addition to these familiar features, there are several new ones.

◆ Instead of the word main, the function header contains the name of the function, sqrt.

◆ This is followed by a set of parentheses, associating a data type with a name: the data type **double** is associated with the name x.

◆ Within the body of the function, a value is computed and that value is returned in the **return** statement at the end of the function.

The value returned should match the data type (**double**) in the function header for the answer. As it is translating the function into C++, the compiler can verify that these things match. This verification of consistency is called **type checking**. (When the compiler is translating the main program's call to the function, it can often perform additional type checking. See the information below on function prototypes.)

FUNCTION TERMINOLOGY

When a function is called, the value of the variable in the parentheses [w in the call y = sqrt(w)] is matched up with the variable in the parentheses in the function header (x in the function header for sqrt). So x actually gets the value of w. The name x in the function is simply a place holder for the value that we want the square root of, in our case, w.

◆ This place holder x is called a **formal** or **dummy parameter** of the function. The word "dummy" is more descriptive of its role as a place holder, but "formal parameter" is the more common term.

FIGURE 5-3 Names for parameters

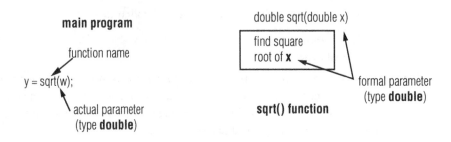

♦ The object that we want to find the square root of (e.g., w or x3 or alpha) is called the **actual** or **real parameter**; sometimes it is called an **argument**.

The names of the formal and actual parameters do not have to match exactly, although, if by chance they do, there is no problem. On the other hand, the data types for both parameters (e.g., **int** or **double**) must match, with a few minor exceptions discussed later. In the main program, we use the actual name of the parameter, but in the function, we use only the formal parameter name. See Figure 5-3.

CAUTION In the function, you should not refer to the name of an *actual* parameter. Similarly, in the main program, you should not refer to the name of a formal parameter. The *scope* of each (where it is known) is limited to the function in which it is declared.

If you wonder why the variable isn't called w inside the function, remember that this particular library function was written quite a while ago. The person writing it didn't know that we wanted to find the square root of a variable called w. What's more, we can use sqrt( ) to find the square root of many different things, such as sqrt(w), sqrt(x3), or sqrt(alpha). There is no possible way for the function's name for the object to always be the same as the one in our program; whatever name we use is replaced by the name in the function. In fact, one of the great virtues of a function is this flexibility in names.

Notice that the value sent to the function (w or alpha) and the one expected by the function (x) both have data type **double**. Also the value computed by the function has the same data type as the variable in the main program that holds the answer (y or beta). In general, the formal and actual parameters should match; in addition, if the function returns a value of a certain type, the main program should store the answer in a variable of that same type.

STYLE WORKSHOP In many cases, an integer value (or a value of type **float**) can be matched to a formal parameter of type **double**. However, this is not considered good style. We recommend that the types of the actual and formal parameters match.

TRACING A CALL TO THE FUNCTION sqrt( )

Let's trace an example to see what happens during execution of the program. Here's the entire main program, including two calls to the function:

```
// main program which calls the library function sqrt()
#include <iostream>
#include <cmath>
```

```
using namespace std;
int main()
{
    double w,y,alpha,beta;

    w = 16.0;
    y = sqrt(w);                        // first call to the function
    cout << y << endl;
    alpha = 2.56;
    beta = sqrt(alpha);                 // second call to the function
    ...
}
```

PROGRAM TRACE

♦ Execution begins in the main program. First, <u>w</u> is assigned the value 16.0.

♦ The value of <u>w</u> is sent to the function <u>sqrt( )</u>. The main program temporarily stops, and the function begins to execute. The first step of every function call is to match the value of the formal and actual parameters.

♦ In the function, the formal parameter <u>x</u> starts out with the value of the actual parameter <u>w</u>. The instructions that find the square root of <u>x</u> find the square root of the value stored in <u>w</u>.

♦ Since <u>w</u> (and thus <u>x</u>) has the value 16.0, the value computed by <u>sqrt( )</u> is 4.0.

♦ When the function executes the **return** statement, it stops execution, returns a value, and control passes to the main program. The function always returns to the point where it was called.

♦ When we get back to the main program, the answer returned by the function is assigned to the variable <u>y</u> and printed.

♦ The main program then assigns 2.56 to <u>alpha</u> and calls the function a second time, with <u>alpha</u> as the parameter.

♦ For this call, the value of <u>alpha</u> is stored in <u>x</u>. The function finds the square root of 2.56, which is 1.6, and returns this value to the main program. Once again, the function returns to the point where it was called.

♦ The main program stores the returned value in <u>beta</u> and continues.

HIGHLIGHTS

The same function, <u>sqrt( )</u>, can be used for two or eight or even two hundred calls, each of which finds the square root of a single value. In every case, the function keeps track of what to work on, what statement to return to, and where to place the answer. The function always returns to the point where it was called.

PARAMETER TRANSMISSION BY VALUE

We should emphasize one other point made previously. During execution of the program, the function is sent the *value* of the actual parameter, and this value is placed in the formal parameter. This method of sending a parameter to a function is called passing a parameter **by value** or **parameter transmission by value**.

CAUTION When a parameter is passed by value, if there is a change in the formal parameter inside the function, the value of the corresponding actual parameter does not change. See Figure 5-4.

FIGURE 5-4 Communication between function and main program

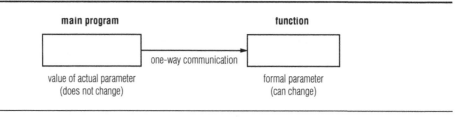

SELF-CHECK 5-2

1. What is an actual parameter in a main program? What is a formal parameter in a function?

2. If a function is called several times, where does it return?

3. In the function call below, which standard function is being called? What is the name of the actual parameter? Where is the answer stored?

```
z = ceil(v);
```

SECTION 2 **PROGRAMMER-DEFINED FUNCTIONS**

In this section, we will learn how to write our own functions instead of relying upon standard functions. Many examples of programmer-defined functions are included, introducing a number of concepts. This is one of the longest sections in the text and one of the most important.

A SIMPLE EXAMPLE OF A PROGRAMMER-DEFINED FUNCTION: THE FUNCTION triple( )

As we have mentioned, there are many other library functions besides sqrt( ). However, there are jobs for which no built-in function is available, such as finding the sum of a number of squares. For this, we have to write our own **programmer-defined function**. To use a library function, all we need do is call it at the appropriate place in a main program. To use a programmer-defined function, we must write the function in addition to calling it.

EXAMPLE 5-2   As our first example of a programmer-defined function, let's write a function called triple( ) that takes an integer and triples it. This is too simple to be a useful function (in fact, the function shell is much larger than the actual instructions), but it is a good first example.

Let's start by giving the function header. The function header must contain the name of the function, the name and type of each formal parameter, and the type of answer to be returned. The function header does not end in a semicolon. Here is a comment describing the job of the function, plus the function header for triple( ):

```
// function to return three
// times the parameter numb
int triple(int numb)                                    // function header
```

After the header, and surrounded by a pair of braces, comes the body of the function, which in this case is a single line.

```
{
    return 3 * numb;
}
```

This statement computes the value of 3 * numb and then returns it to the program that calls the function.

The **return** statement plays two roles in a function. First, it is the logical end of the function, the last statement to be executed. In addition, a **return** statement is usually the last statement before the closing brace of a function. For clarity, some programmers put parentheses around the value to be returned. In that case, the **return** statement looks like this:

```
return (3 * numb);
```

We do not use this form in our programs, but you may want to.

Here is the entire function:

```
// function to return three
// times the parameter numb
int triple(int numb)                              // function header
{
    return 3 * numb;
}
```

The code above for the function is called the **function definition** because it defines to the compiler what this function means. This explains why the function header does not end in a semicolon, since it is just part of the function definition.

PROGRAM TRACE Here is a main program which contains a number of calls to triple( ). Note that all of the variables have data type **int** to be consistent with the formal parameter and the answer returned by the function. In this program, an extra line appears just above the main program header. This line, called the **function prototype**, is discussed next.

```
// main program to test triple
#include <iostream>
using namespace std;
int triple(int);                                  // function prototype
int main()
{
    int a,b,c,numb;

    a = 5;
    b = triple(a);                                // first call
    cout << "original value and its triple: " << a << " " << b << endl;

    numb = 2;
    c = triple(numb);                             // second call
    cout << "original value and its triple: " << numb
        << " " << c << endl;

    numb = triple(a - 1);                         // third call
    cout << "original value and its triple: " << a - 1 << " "
        << numb << endl;
    cout << "the variable is still: " << a << endl;

    c = triple(4);                                // fourth call
    cout << "if the value is the constant 4, triple it is "
        << c << endl;

                                                  // last call
    cout << "if the value is " << a << " triple it is " << triple(a);
    return 0;
}
```

FIGURE 5-5 Call to the function <u>triple( )</u>

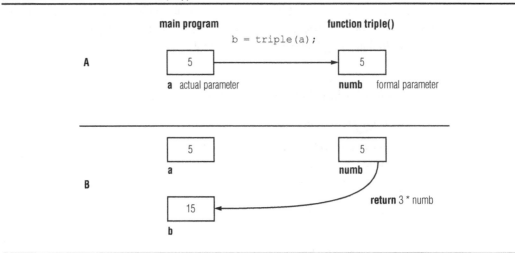

Note that the main program calls the function several times. However, <u>triple( )</u> never gets confused about which call it is executing or where to return the answer.

♦ The main program starts by giving a value to the variable <u>a</u>. For the first call to the function, the main program sends <u>a</u> as the actual parameter. See Figure 5-5A.

♦ In <u>triple( )</u>, the formal parameter <u>numb</u> is given the value of the actual parameter <u>a</u>. The formal parameter is multiplied by 3, giving 3 * 5 = 15.

♦ This is returned to the main program and put into the variable <u>b</u>. See Figure 5-5B. The first line printed is this:

```
original value and its triple: 5 15
```

Notice that the value of the actual parameter <u>a</u> has not changed, but the value of <u>b</u> has changed to reflect the answer returned by the function.

The second call is a little different. The actual parameter is called <u>numb</u>, and the formal parameter is also <u>numb</u>, which is fine. The main program's variable called <u>numb</u> is definitely not the same storage location as <u>numb</u> in the function.

♦ The actual parameter <u>numb</u> in the main program is set to 2, so that value is given to the formal parameter <u>numb</u> inside the function.

♦ This value is tripled to 6, which is returned to the main program and put into the variable <u>c</u>. The second line printed is this:

```
original value and its triple: 2 6
```

It is not significant that the formal and actual parameters have the same name. Whatever the name of the actual parameter, its *value* is sent to the formal parameter in the function.

The third call is trickier. First, note that the actual parameter does not have to be a variable (although things are easier if it is). The actual parameter can be an expression which is evaluated to obtain a value; this value is then sent to the function for the formal parameter.

♦ In this case, we are sending the value of <u>a</u> − 1, which is 5 − 1 = 4, to the function. Inside <u>triple( )</u>, the formal parameter <u>numb</u> has the value 4. This is tripled, giving 12.

♦ Then 12 is sent back to the main program and stored in <u>numb</u>. The printout looks like this:

```
original value and its triple: 4 12
the variable is still 5
```

As can be seen from the printout, the value of <u>a</u> has not changed. Sending <u>a − 1</u> to the function does not change the original value. Note that the identifier <u>numb</u> in the main program is definitely not the same as <u>numb</u> in the function. The <u>numb</u> inside <u>triple( )</u> is the name of the formal parameter every time the function is called. The <u>numb</u> in the main program is the name of a variable whose role can change. For the previous call to <u>triple( )</u>, <u>numb</u> in the main program served as actual parameter; for this call, <u>numb</u> holds the value returned by the function.

For the fourth call, the actual parameter sent to the function is the constant 4. The function expects to receive a parameter of type **int**, and a constant value is perfectly acceptable.

♦ The constant value is sent to the function and matched to the formal parameter. Inside the function, the formal parameter <u>numb</u> has the value 4. This is tripled, giving 12, which is sent back to the main program and stored in <u>c</u>. The printout looks like this:

```
if the value is the constant 4, triple it is 12
```

♦ Finally, the last call shows that the answer returned by a function can be printed directly without being stored.

♦ The value of the actual parameter (5) is sent to the function. This is tripled to give 15.

♦ The value 15 is returned and sent to <u>cout</u>. This call prints the following:

```
if the value is 5, triple it is 15
```

Here is the entire output from this program:

```
original value and its triple: 5 15
original value and its triple: 2 6
original value and its triple: 4 12
the variable is still 5
if the value is the constant 4, triple it is 12
if the value is 5, triple it is 15
```

SELF-CHECK 5-3

1. What type of answer does the function <u>triple( )</u> return?
2. What name are we using for the formal parameter? What is its data type?
3. For each call to <u>triple( )</u>, identify the actual parameter and its data type.

TYPE CHECKING AND THE FUNCTION PROTOTYPE

Earlier, we mentioned that the compiler can do some type checking when it is translating a function from C++ into machine language. In addition, the compiler should check for consistency when it is translating the main program. For example, if the function expects to receive one formal parameter of type **double**, the compiler should make sure that the main program sends a double; if the answer returned by the function has type **double**, the compiler should make sure that the main program expects that.

Inside the function, the compiler can do type checking based on the function header. However, because of the order in which items appear in a program, the compiler may not have seen the function header at the point when the main program calls the function. C++ has a feature, called a **function prototype**, which gives the compiler all the information it needs to perform type checking in the main program. The function prototype contains the type of answer returned by the function, the name of the function, plus the number and type of the parameters.

If we include this function prototype, the compiler knows exactly what to expect when we call triple( ) from the main program:

♦ The function will return an answer of type **int**.

♦ The name of the function is triple( ).

♦ The function will expect to receive one parameter of type **int**.

HEADER FILES AND LOCATION OF FUNCTION PROTOTYPES

In the case of a library function, the function prototype is contained in a header file. Typically, a programmer inserts a header file into a program by using a *#include* directive such as *#include <iostream>*. This directive tells the preprocessor to include the header file iostream.h at this point in the program.

A **header file** contains function prototypes for a series of functions. The header files iostream.h and cmath.h contain function prototypes for the functions in these two portions of the standard library. For example, in the cmath.h header file, the function prototype for sqrt( ) looks like this:

```
double sqrt(double);                              // function prototype
```

Note that we don't have to write this line explicitly. By using the compiler directive *#include <cmath>* , it is as if we have this function prototype, plus many others, in our program. Similarly, the iostream.h header file contains function prototypes for the most important functions related to input/output operations, including cin and cout. By including the compiler directives for these header files, we allow our programs to use the appropriate library functions. The header files for iostream.h and cmath.h are always placed at the beginning, above the main program, so that the prototypes they contain can be accessed from anywhere.

When using a programmer-defined function, it is the programmer's responsibility to include the function prototype explicitly. There is some flexibility, but we recommend that the function prototype should be placed just above the header of the main program. This puts the function prototype directly beneath the lines containing the header files and the line *using namespace std*. With the prototype in this position—the same position as the prototypes for the functions from the C++ library—the function can be accessed correctly by the main program or any other functions in the program.

Here is another main program that calls the function <u>triple( )</u>, highlighting the position of the function prototype:

```
// main program to test triple
#include <iostream>
using namespace std;
int triple(int);                                        // function prototype
int main()
{
    int a,b,c,numb;

    a = 5;
    b = triple(a);
    ...

}
```

HIGHLIGHTS

If the compiler sees the function header before the call to the function, it can do type checking to verify that the function is being called correctly. However, in many cases, it is not possible for the compiler to see the header first. In these cases, the same information is provided by the function prototype.

In general, the information from the function prototype should match the function header.

The function prototype is often called the **function declaration**, to differentiate it from the header and the body of the function, which is called the **function definition**. We will continue to use the term function prototype.

ALTERNATE FORM OF THE FUNCTION PROTOTYPE

The function prototype that we gave above for <u>triple( )</u> can be modified so that it is almost identical to the function header. Here is the modified form:

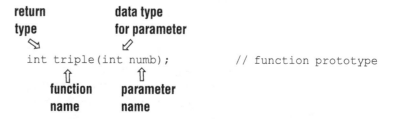

```
int triple(int numb);                                   // function prototype
```

This form gives a name, in addition to a data type, to the function's parameter. In this case, the name in the prototype matches the formal parameter name in the function header, but that is not necessary. Actually, any name can be used (or no name at all). For example, we can use either of these function prototypes:

```
int triple(int y);     or     int triple(int z);
```

The name (either <u>y</u> or <u>z</u>) that appears after the type is a dummy name and is ignored by the compiler. The important point is the type: **int**. Some programmers think it is a good idea to include a dummy name, and the most logical one appears in the function header. If you do this, the function prototype and the function header will be almost identical, except that the function prototype ends in a semicolon because it is a complete C++ statement. (You can think of the prototype as declaring the function, just as a variable is declared.)

STYLE WORKSHOP In the rest of this chapter, we will show how to write function prototypes both with and without dummy names. However, when we give an example of a main program calling a function, we will usually not include dummy names. You can include them in your own programs if you wish.

CAUTION When you are using certain compilers, it may be possible to omit the function prototype, but we strongly recommend that you *always* include it. Some library functions (e.g., sqrt( )) do not work correctly if the header file containing their prototypes is not included. Using a prototype simplifies the compiler's job of type checking. In addition, some programmer-defined functions may not work correctly and/or some mistakes in parameter matching will not be caught if prototypes are omitted.

SELF-CHECK 5-4

1. What is the purpose of a function prototype?

2. What information is contained in the function prototype?

3. How does a function prototype differ from a function header?

THE USE OF LOCAL VARIABLES WITHIN A FUNCTION: THE FUNCTION sign()

Our next example is more realistic and introduces local variables, an important feature of functions.

EXAMPLE 5-3a Let's write a function called sign( ) that does the following: Given a real number x, if x is 0, the function returns 0; if x is positive, it returns 1; if x is negative, it returns −1. This is called the **signum** or **sign function**, since it tells us the sign (but not the value) of the original number.

```
// return the sign of the parameter x: +1, 0, or -1
int sign(double x)
{
    int answer;

    if (x == 0)
        answer = 0;
    if (x > 0)
        answer = 1;
    if (x < 0)
        answer = -1;
    return answer;
}
```

Before we trace any calls to the function, notice that a variable (answer) is declared within the function. Such a variable is called a **local variable** of the function. Each time the function is called, it has a new temporary storage location with this name.

In this function, answer holds the value that is eventually returned. The function can be written without a local variable. We are purposely writing it this way to illustrate the concept. Notice also that even though the formal parameter x has data type **double**, the local variable answer and the value returned by the function both have data type **int**. See Figure 5-6.

FIGURE 5-6   Call to the function sign( )

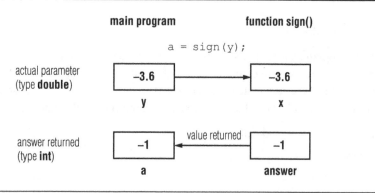

The function prototype for this function can look like either of these:

```
int sign(double);        or        int sign(double x);
```

Here is a main program containing a series of calls to the function sign( ). In each case, the actual parameter sent to sign( ) has data type **double** to match the formal parameter x within the function. However, the answer returned is stored by the main program in a variable of data type **int** to match the type of value returned by the function.

```
// main program to test double
#include <iostream>
using namespace std;
int sign(double);                               // function prototype
int main()
{
    double x,y,z;
    int a,b,c,d;

    x = 5.4;
    a = sign(x);                                // a gets the value 1
    y = 0;
    b = sign(y);                                // b gets the value 0
    z = 7.8976;
    c = sign(z - 9);                            // c gets the value -1
    d = sign(-5);                               // d gets the value -1
    cout << "the answers are " << a << " " << b << " "
        << c << " " << d << endl;
    return 0;
}
```

STYLE WORKSHOP We could eliminate the main program's use of the function sign( ) by replacing each function call by the three **if** statements in the body of the function. That would make the main program longer and more involved.

PROGRAM TRACE Let's see what is printed by this series of calls. In each case, we will list the appropriate part of the main program and discuss what happens on that call.

◆ Let's start with the first call to the function:

```
x = 5.4;
a = sign(x);
```

In the main program, x is set to 5.4. This variable x is the actual parameter for the first call to sign( ). Inside sign( ), the formal parameter x is given the value 5.4. (Note that x in sign( ) is not the same as in the main program, even though for this call they are matched.) The first **if** condition is false, but the second **if** is true, so answer is set to 1; the third **if** is also false. The value of answer is then returned to the main program and stored in the variable a.

◆ Now let's look at the second call:

```
y = 0;
b = sign(y);
```

In the main program, y is assigned the value 0; for this call to sign( ), the formal parameter x is given the value 0. This time, answer gets the value 0, which is returned to the main program where it is stored in b.

◆ For the third call:

```
z = 7.8976;
c = sign(z - 9);
```

In the main program, z – 9 has the value $7.8976 - 9 = -1.1024$; this is the value of the actual parameter that is sent to the function. The function computes a value of –1 for answer and returns this to be stored in c.

◆ Finally, the last call consists of the following line:

```
d = sign(-5);
```

This time the actual parameter is the integer constant –5. This is converted into a value of type **double** and sent to the function. The function computes a value of –1 and returns this to the main program to be stored in d.

The printout is the following:

```
the answers are 1 0 -1 -1
```

🛑 **CAUTION** A function is always allowed to refer to its formal parameters. For example, triple( ) refers to numb, and sign( ) refers to x. In addition, if the function declares one or more local variables, it can refer to them as well. For example, sign( ) refers to answer. However, a function cannot refer to any variables which are declared in the main program.

Similarly, a local variable declared within a function can be used only within that function. It is impossible for the main program to reference a function's local variable. In fact, a local variable can have the same name as a variable within the main program. When the function is executing, a reference to that name means the variable declared in the function; when the main program is operating, a reference to that name means the variable declared in the main program.

STYLE WORKSHOP To avoid confusion, some people like to use names for local variables that differ from those in the main program. In this chapter, we will try to avoid repeating names, but in later chapters, we will use whatever is the best name.

FORMAL PARAMETER AS A LOCAL VARIABLE

It is sometimes useful to view the formal parameter in a function as a local variable. The match-up of actual and formal parameters can then be interpreted as an assignment statement which is executed just before the function starts. For example, consider the function sign( ) from Example 5-3. The formal parameter inside sign( ) is called x. That example has a main program containing several calls to the function. For the last function call, the actual parameter is the constant −5. Therefore, we can view the following assignment as occurring just before the function starts to execute:

```
x = -5;
```

In general, if the actual parameter is the expression expr, and the formal parameter is called param, then the match-up can be interpreted as the following:

```
param = expr;
```

Note that expr gives a starting value to param, but they are in fact separate storage locations. If the formal parameter param changes inside the function, the corresponding actual parameter in the main program does not.

CAUTION Since a formal parameter in a function is a local variable, the function cannot have a local variable and a formal parameter with the same name. However, either of them can repeat a name used in the main program.

USING MULTIPLE return STATEMENTS

There are many other ways to write the body of the function sign( ). As we mentioned earlier, you can avoid the local variable answer. As soon as you determine a value for the function, you can return it. This method is illustrated in the following example.

EXAMPLE 5-3b

```
// return the sign of the parameter x: +1, 0, or -1
int sign(double x)
{
    if (x == 0)
        return 0;
    if (x > 0)
        return 1;
    if (x < 0)
        return -1;
}
```

A function can return only one value. Therefore, this function seems to be illegal because of the three **return** statements. However, the function is valid because only one **return** statement is used on any one call to sign( ). Since only one of the three **if** conditions is true for each x value, only one value is returned by the function. As soon as that particular value is found, the function stops execution and returns to the main program. In other words, the last statement executed in the function will be the **return** statement from one of these three **if** statements, depending upon the particular value stored in x. In fact, if we reach the third **if**, its question must be true. Therefore, the third **if** can be replaced by the following:

```
return -1;
```

SELF-CHECK 5-5

1. What is a local variable? Can a main program refer to a function's local variable?

2. Can a function have more than one **return** statement? Can a function return more than one value on a single call?

3. In the function sign( ), why can only one of the three **if** statements be true on any one call to the function?

STYLE WORKSHOP Many people avoid multiple **return** statements. They think it is better to have one way to enter a function (at the top), and one way to exit (via a single **return** statement at the bottom). On the other hand, some people prefer multiple **return** statements to avoid extra local variables. You should be comfortable with both techniques.

A FUNCTION WITH SEVERAL PARAMETERS: THE FUNCTION max3( )

Our next example of a function has three parameters. Of course, no matter how many parameters are sent by a main program to a function, the function still computes a single answer.

EXAMPLE 5-4   Assume that we have three integers and want to find the largest. We will write a function called max3( ) with three parameters. The header for the function mentions each of these parameters, giving it a name and data type. The code for the function is tricky, so we have included some helpful comments. The first **if** statement determines the larger of the first two formal parameters, a and b. The second **if** statement compares this value to c; the larger must be the largest parameter. If you do not see why this is true, trace a few examples before going on.

```
// function to find the largest
// of three integers a, b, and c
int max3(int a, int b, int c)
{
    int maxsofar;

    // first find the larger of a and b
    if (a >= b)
        maxsofar = a;
    else
        maxsofar = b;

    // now compare the larger of a and b to c
    if (maxsofar < c)
        maxsofar = c;
    return maxsofar;
}
```

Just as the header mentions three parameters, so, too, does the function prototype. We can use either of these forms:

```
int max3(int, int, int);     or     int max3(int a, int b, int c);
```

Now we can analyze some calls to max3( ) from a main program, starting with this one:

```
// main program to test max3()
#include <iostream>
using namespace std;
int max3(int, int, int);                              // function prototype
int main()
{
    int ans,x,y,z;

    x = 3;
    y = 5;
    z = 7;
    ans = max3(x,y,z);
    ...
}
```

FIGURE 5-7 Association of actual and formal parameters for a call to max3( )

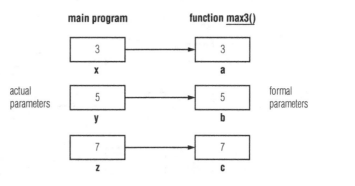

PROGRAM TRACE

◆ For this first call, the formal and actual parameters are matched in the order in which they are specified: x to a, y to b, z to c. Inside the function, a gets the value 3, b gets the value 5, and c gets the value 7. See Figure 5-7.

◆ The first **if** condition is false, so the local variable maxsofar is set to 5 (the value of b). The second **if** condition is false, so the local variable maxsofar is assigned 7 (the value of c).

◆ This value is returned to the main program, the function stops execution, and the main program resumes. Back in the main program, ans is given the value 7, which is the correct answer for the maximum of 3, 5, and 7.

A MORE COMPLICATED FUNCTION CALL

Our next call reiterates several points. First, the answer returned from a function can be part of an expression or printed. Second, the actual parameter can be a constant or even an expression; in fact, as this example shows, it can be an expression whose value depends upon the value returned by a call to another function. Here is another example of how a main program can call the function max3( ):

```
// main program to test max3()
#include <iostream>
using namespace std;
int max3(int, int, int);                        // function prototype
int main()
{
    int p,q;

    p = 10;
    q = -7;
    cout << max3(p + 2, 12, abs(q)) * 3 << endl;
    return 0;
}
```

PROGRAM TRACE Let's show how a complicated expression like this is evaluated. In this case, the function max3( ) is called, and then the answer returned is multiplied by 3. Note that the call to max3( ) has three arguments or parameters. See Figure 5-8.

FIGURE 5-8 Association of actual and formal parameters for a call to max3( )

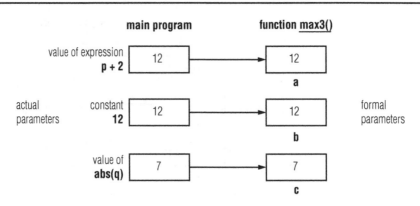

◆ The first actual parameter is the expression p + 2, which has the value 12; this is sent to max3( ) as the value of the first formal parameter a.

◆ The second actual parameter is the constant 12; this becomes the value of the second formal parameter b.

◆ The third argument to max3( ) is actually a call to a library function abs( ). The expression abs(q) computes the absolute value of −7. This is evaluated to 7, then sent to max3( ) as the value for the third formal parameter c.

◆ The function max3( ) finds the largest of 12, 12, and 7, which is 12. The main program multiplies the returned answer by 3 to get 36, then prints this value without storing the result anywhere.

STYLE WORKSHOP Note that to evaluate this one expression in the main program, we executed calls to both abs( ) and max3( ). Even though this is perfectly legal in C++, it is not considered good style. In many cases, it is helpful to break a complicated expression into smaller pieces by adding extra variables to hold the intermediate results.

FUNCTION CALLS AND EFFICIENCY

Calling a function to get an answer is a simple process.   But if you are not careful, you may end up with a program which makes unnecessary function calls. Consider these two methods of calling max3( ) from Example 5-4:

```
int a=10, b=12, c=5;

cout << "the largest of " << a << " " <<  b << " and " << c " is "
     << max3(a,b,c);
if (max3(a,b,c) == a)
     cout << "a is largest";
if (max3(a,b,c) == b)
     cout << "b is largest";
if (max3(a,b,c) == c)
     cout << "c is largest";
```

This set of statements is not efficient because the **if** statements make three identical calls to the function max3( ) to get the same value each time. Each call requires executing the max3( ) function, just to get a value which has already been computed and could have been stored in largest. This could be done more efficiently as follows:

```
int a=10, b=12, c=5, largest;

largest = max3(a,b,c);
if (largest == a)
    cout << "a is largest";
if (largest == b)
    cout << "b is largest";
if (largest == c)
    cout << "c is largest";
```

Avoid extra computation, especially unnecessary function calls. Doing unnecessary work makes your program take longer to run.

A FUNCTION THAT RETURNS A VALUE

The general form of a function that returns a value is as follows:

General Form of a Function that Returns a Value

```
return_type function_name(datatype1 parameter1,datatype2 parameter2,...)
{
    declaration of local variables       // optional

    action statements
    return return_value;
}
```

In this model, **return_type** is the data type of the value returned by the function function_name( ). The parameters to the function follow the function name in parentheses, separated by commas. Each parameter is a variable name preceded by its data type. The ellipses (. . .) indicate that there can be any number of parameters, including none. The item (return_value) following the word **return** is the value returned by the function. It may be a variable or an expression, and it should have the same data type as **return_type**.

SELF-CHECK 5-6

1. Is a function allowed to have more than one parameter? If so, in what order are the formal and actual parameters matched?

2. If a call to function f1( ) contains a call to function f2( ), which call is executed first?

3. What is printed by the following, assuming that x has the value 5?

```
cout << 7 + abs(x - 6) << endl;
```

PROGRAM 5; LOCATION OF FUNCTIONS

In this section, we will use the ideas from the previous section to write a function version of Program 5. This will be the first programmer-defined function to use a **for** loop. We will also discuss where to place a function in relation to the main program.

USING A for LOOP IN A FUNCTION

We have seen a variety of programmer-defined functions, but so far they have accomplished simple tasks. One important reason is that they have not used **for** or **while** loops. Now we are ready to use a loop in a function. In fact, we are ready to write the function to solve Problem 5: to find the sum of a series of squares.

EXAMPLE 5-5

We will write a function called sumofsquares( ) that will receive one parameter n; this parameter represents the number of squares that we want to sum. Inside the function, n will control the **for** loop. The function also has two local variables, i and sum. The function will find the sum of the first n squares; that is, it will compute $1^2 + 2^2 + \cdots + n^2$. This sum will be returned as the value of the function sumofsquares( ).

In the function header, the data type used for both the formal parameter and the answer returned is **int**. The body of the function uses the same instructions as the program at the end of Chapter 4, Section 3, substituting n for numbertosum and returning the answer just before ending the function. Here is the complete function:

```
// find the sum of the first n squares:
//  1*1 + 2*2 + ... + n*n
int sumofsquares(int n)                          // function header
{
    int sum=0;

    for (int item = 1; item <= n; item++)
        sum += item * item;
    return sum;
}
```

USING THE FUNCTION sumofsquares() IN PROGRAM 5

Now let's see how Program 5 uses the function sumofsquares( ). Assume that the main program has already stored a value in numbertosum. The main program that calls the function sumofsquares( ) to sum the first numbertosum squares looks like this:

🖳 **PROGRAM LISTING**

```
// Program prog5.cpp:
// compute the sum of numbertosum squares
// with numbertosum read from a line of data
// using a function to sum the squares
#include <iostream>
using namespace std;
int sumofsquares(int);                           // function prototype
int main()
```

```
    {
        int numbertosum, answer;

        cout << "type in the number of squares to be summed> ";
        cin >> numbertosum;
        answer = sumofsquares(numbertosum);
        cout << answer << " is the sum of the first " << numbertosum
            << " squares" << endl;
        return 0;
    }
```

Notice that the main program's job is simpler when we write the module that does the actual summing as a function. Of course, the original main program in Program 4 was rather elementary, so the difference between the original and the function version is not that dramatic. In a larger program, with many functions, the savings will be significant.

PROGRAM TRACE

◆ Assume that the main program has read in a value of 10 for the variable <u>numbertosum</u>. This is the value of the actual parameter for the call to the function. Inside the function, the formal parameter <u>n</u> also has the value 10.

◆ The body of the function sums the first <u>n</u> (i.e., 10) squares, giving 385.

◆ This value is returned to the main program as the value of the function. It is assigned to the variable <u>answer</u>. Then the program prints this line:

```
    385 is the sum of the first 10 squares
```

◆ If the main program had stored 5 as the value of <u>numbertosum</u>, this same series of instructions would have computed the sum of the first five squares. The output would look like this:

```
    55 is the sum of the first 5 squares
```

LOCATION OF FUNCTIONS

There is one last ingredient in our formula for how to use a function: the placement of the function definition in relation to the main program. For simplicity, we will discuss the case of a main program and one function called <u>func( )</u>. There are a number of ways to arrange them.

One possibility is to place the entire function first, followed by the entire main program. In this case, the definition of the function appears before the main program's call to the function. Therefore, by the time the compiler reaches the call, it knows what to expect. (See Figure 5-9.)

STYLE WORKSHOP In this case, because of the location of the function, the function prototype can be omitted, but we don't recommend it. Almost all C++ programmers recognize that function prototypes add a very valuable feature to the language. It is considered poor style to omit a function prototype, even if it is not technically necessary.

Another possible order is to have the main program first, followed by the function. Even though the function header comes *after* the main program, the function prototype appears *before* the call to the function. As long as the compiler sees the function prototype before the call to the function, it can

FIGURE 5-9   A file <u>method1.cpp</u> containing a function followed by a main program

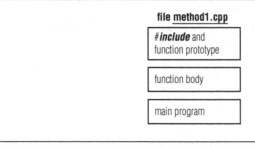

FIGURE 5-10   A file <u>method2.cpp</u> containing a main program followed by a function

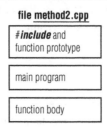

FIGURE 5-11   A file <u>method3m.cpp</u> containing a main program and a separate file <u>method3f.cpp</u> containing a function

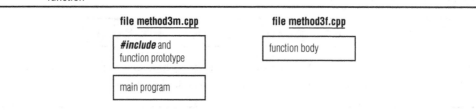

still do type checking. (See Figure 5-10.) In both of these situations, the main program and the function are separate pieces in the same file.

A third possibility (called **separate compilation**) puts the function in one file and the main program in another and compiles them separately. (See Figure 5-11.) This is the way that library functions are used. For example, the C++ standard library contains many functions which have been compiled into machine language. A main program, sitting in its own file, can be compiled so that it accesses these library functions. The main program can also access other user-defined functions that have been separately compiled. This method is extremely common in real-world applications. (However, it is a bit too complicated for a first course.)

Wherever you put the function, the computer knows to start execution in the main program. And in either case, the only way to execute a function is to call it. If a function is included in a file with a main program but never called, it will never be executed. If it is called ten times, it will be executed ten times.

SELF-CHECK 5-7

1.   What are the various options for where a function should be placed in relation to the main program?

2.   In each case, where should the function prototype appear?

3.   Which method is used for library functions?

COMPLETE PROGRAM 5

Here is complete Program 5, including the function prototype, the main program which contains the call to the function, and the function definition:

PROGRAM LISTING

```cpp
// Program prog5.cpp:
// compute the sum of numbertosum squares
// with numbertosum read from a line of data
// using a function to sum the squares
#include <iostream>
using namespace std;
int sumofsquares(int);                                  // function prototype
int main()
{
    int numbertosum,answer;
    cout << "type in the number of squares to be summed> ";
    cin >> numbertosum);
    answer = sumofsquares(numbertosum);
    cout << answer << " is the sum of the first " << numbertosum
        << " squares" << endl;
    return 0;
}

// find the sum of the first n squares:
// 1*1 + 2*2 + ... + n*n
int sumofsquares(int n)                                  // function header
{
    int sum=0;
    for (int item = 1; item <= n; item++)
        sum += item * item;
    return sum;
}
```

TESTING FUNCTIONS

If you go through a detailed trace of this program, you see how many statements are actually executed by a single call to underline{sumofsquares( )}. Notice how much easier this makes tracing the main program. If you are sure the function underline{sumofsquares( )} is working correctly, you can be confident the answer returned is right without analyzing it. Presumably, you have already done many separate tests of the function. This testing can be carried out independent of a particular main program's task. (In this example, there is also a formula to check the sum of the first $\underline{n}$ squares. See Chapter 4, Exercise 16.)

This point will become especially important as your programs get larger. To test a function, you can construct a main program which does nothing except call the function. This main program should consist of declarations and initializations of variables, calls to the function, and printouts of the results. As an example, look at our first programmer-defined function, underline{triple( )}. We gave a number of calls to underline{triple( )} from a main program, testing various cases. In another example, we tested the function underline{sign( )} by giving a series of calls from a main program, including tests of all possible paths (with the parameter positive, negative, or zero) within the function. It is important to be thorough in testing the function.

Such a main program is called a **driver program** since it drives the function. We included a driver program for each function discussed in this section. See the main programs used to test the functions from Examples 5-2, 5-3, and 5-4.

A function can be tested by itself until we believe that it works, and then it can be trusted as a step in a larger process. This is usually much easier than trying to test a large program all at once.

So far, the task of each function we have written has been to compute and return only one value. However, functions in C++ are allowed to be more general than this, and there are examples later in this chapter. For example, in Section 4, we will learn how to write a function which prints a series of output headings; in Chapter 7, we will write a function to read in a series of data values and another to find the average of these values.

SELF-CHECK 5-8

1. How do we test a function?
2. What is a driver program?
3. Is it sufficient to run the function on just one or two sets of values? What must be done to make sure that a function is working correctly?

SECTION 4   VOID AND PARAMETERLESS FUNCTIONS

This section introduces a void function—one which does not return a value. We will also talk about a parameterless function; this type does not receive any parameters when it is called.

A FUNCTION THAT DOES NOT RETURN A VALUE: A VOID FUNCTION

In Section 7, we will discuss how to use a function for the multiplication problem from Chapter 4 (Example 4-2). Before we do that, can a function print a line of output which is a series of numbers (e.g., a row in a multiplication table)? The basic purpose of each function we've seen so far is to compute and return one answer. What answer is returned when a list of numbers is printed? None.

The solution is simple: A function can perform one or more actions (including printing) without returning a particular value. This type of function is called a **void function** and is perfect for the task that we have in mind.

We should emphasize that void functions are real functions. The basic purpose of a function is to perform a well-defined task. Void functions do just that.

VOID FUNCTION HEADER AND RETURN

The first line or header of a void function differs only slightly from the first line of one returning a value. At the beginning of the usual function header is the data type for the answer to be returned; in a void function, the data type is replaced by the keyword **void** because no explicit value is returned. Here is an example of a header for a function func( ) which receives two **int** parameters, x and y:

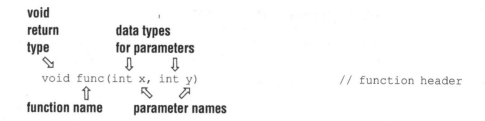

There is one other distinctive feature of a void function. The functions discussed earlier used a **return** statement to return a value. In a void function, no value is returned. To indicate that control should return to the main program, use the keyword **return**, then end the function with the closing brace.

```
        return;
    }
```

STYLE WORKSHOP The word **return** can be omitted in a void function. The closing brace then ends the function. However, it is better style to mark the end of the function with a **return** statement.

A SIMPLE EXAMPLE OF A VOID FUNCTION: printmaxmin( )

Assume that we want to write a function which will find and print both the larger and the smaller of two values, <u>a</u> and <u>b</u>, with identifying labels. In this case, we don't want to return anything, but we do want to print two things: the values of the larger and the smaller.

EXAMPLE 5-6a

Let's use <u>printmaxmin( )</u> as the name of the function. If we start with <u>a</u> = 3 and <u>b</u> = 5, the function should print 5 as the maximum and 3 as the minimum; if <u>a</u> = 7 and <u>b</u> = 2, then <u>printmaxmin( )</u> should print 7 as the larger and 2 as the smaller. If the two values are equal, we don't care which is selected as the larger and the smaller.

In our function, let's call the formal parameters <u>x</u> and <u>y</u> and assume that we are working with integers. In the body of the function, we want to compare <u>x</u> and <u>y</u> to see which is larger. If <u>x</u> is larger, we want to print a message stating this; if not, we want to print a different message. Here is the entire function:

```
// finds and prints both the larger
// and the smaller of x and y
void printmaxmin(int x, int y)
{
    if (x > y)
        cout << x << " is the larger, "
            << y << " is the smaller" << endl;
    else
        cout << y << " is the larger, "
            << x << " is the smaller" << endl;
    return;
}
```

VOID FUNCTION PROTOTYPE AND CALL

The function prototype for a void function can look just like the function header with the addition of a semicolon. Or we can omit the names of the parameters. Here is a version of the function prototype for printmaxmin( ) which does that:

```
void printmaxmin(int, int);                              // function prototype
```

To call a void function, write its name, together with the list of arguments. Since a void function does not return a value, we cannot include its call as part of an expression that appears on the right-hand side of an assignment statement or is sent to cout. The only way to call a void function is to have a statement consisting of the function name, followed by the list of parameters.

In Section 3, we mentioned that a function which returns a value can be tested separately by using a driver program. A void function can also be tested as a separate module. Usually, this will be very easy because there is no answer to be returned.

EXAMPLE 5-6b   Here is an example of a driver program that calls printmaxmin( ):

```
// driver program to test printmaxmin()
#include <iostream>
using namespace std;
void printmaxmin(int, int);
int main()
{
    int a,b;

    a = 5;
    b = 3;
    printmaxmin(a,b);
    ...
}
```

PROGRAM TRACE Now we will trace this call to printmaxmin( ). Execution begins in the main program, with a set to 5 and b to 3. For this call, a and b are the actual parameters which are matched to the formal parameters x and y. Thus, x holds 5 and y holds 3. Inside the function, the **if** condition is true, so we print the following (from the first cout):

```
5 is the larger, 3 is the smaller
```

Then we execute the **return** statement in the function. This returns control to the main program, ending the function. Note that no value is returned to the main program. When the function returns control, the main program resumes execution, as shown by the ... above.

A VOID FUNCTION

The general form of a function that does not return a value is as follows:

General Form of a Void Function

```
void function_name(datatype1 parameter1,  datatype2 parameter2, ...)
{
    declaration of local variables           // optional

    action statements
    return;
}
```

In this model, the return type of the function is **void**, indicating that function function_name( ) does not return a value. The parameters to the function follow the function name in parentheses, separated by commas. Each parameter is a variable name preceded by its data type. The ellipses indicate that there can be any number of parameters, including none. The preferred form is to have **return**; with no value following the word **return**. However, it is also legal to omit the entire **return** statement.

SELF-CHECK 5-9

1. What is a void function?
2. What is omitted in the header of a void function? What is omitted at the end of it?
3. What does the function prototype for a void function look like?

A COMPLETE PROGRAM CONTAINING A VOID FUNCTION

Now that we have written a void function, we have to determine where to place it in a complete program. The rules described in Section 3 also apply here—a void function can be included either before or after the main program.

EXAMPLE 5-6c Here is a sketch of a complete program, including a main program which calls the void function printmaxmin( ):

```
// ...
#include <iostream>
using namespace std;
void printmaxmin(int, int);
int main()
{
    int a,b;

    a = 5;
    b = 3;
    printmaxmin(a,b);
    return 0;
}

// ...
void printmaxmin(int x, int y)
{
    if (x > y)
        cout << x << " is the larger, "
              << y << " is the smaller" << endl;
```

```
        else
            cout << y << " is the larger, "
                 << x << " is the smaller" << endl;

        return;
    }
```

VOID PARAMETERLESS FUNCTIONS

A certain type of void function, called a **void parameterless function**, does not receive any parameters. Such a void function cannot communicate with the main program. Therefore, it has to perform entirely on its own.

The header of a void parameterless function uses the keyword **void** in two places: at the beginning to indicate that there is no answer to return, and inside the parentheses to show that there are no parameters. The header for a function named <u>func</u> looks like this:

```
void           void
return         indicates no
type           parameters
```

```
        void func(void)                    // function header
```

```
        function name
```

The function header can also omit the keyword **void** from the parentheses. Here is a header for <u>func( )</u> with this abbreviated format:

```
    void func()                    // function header
```

STYLE WORKSHOP Although the format which omits the second **void** is shorter, the original format is preferred. In the original format, **void** occurs in two places, signifying that the function does not return an answer and does not expect to receive any parameters. If that format is used for the header and function prototype, the compiler will make sure that each call to the function sends no parameters to the function and does not expect an answer to be returned. But if we omit **void** from within the parentheses in both the header and the prototype, the compiler may not perform this type checking. This could cause all sorts of errors.

EXAMPLE 5-7 As an example of a void parameterless function, assume that we have a program which generates a lot of output in a table. It has four columns, headed Year, Sales, Expenses, and Profits. Each heading should have ten blank columns between it and the next one. There should be a line of output at the top, saying, "Sales Data for the Past 15 Years."

We want to write a function <u>printheadings( )</u> to print these headings. Obviously, <u>printheadings( )</u> should not be written as a function which returns an answer. In addition, <u>printheadings( )</u> does not need any parameters.

Here is one version of <u>printheadings( )</u> (recall the use of \t to tab):

```
// prints headings for a table
void printheadings(void)
{
    cout << endl << "\t\tSales Data for the Past 15 Years"
         << endl << endl;
    cout << "\tYear          Sales          Expenses          Profits"
         << endl;
    return;
}
```

This function prints these lines of output:

```
              Sales Data for the Past 15 Years
   Year           Sales          Expenses          Profits
```

Let's see how a main program uses the void function <u>printheadings( )</u>. Here is a driver program, including the function prototype and the call to the function:

```cpp
// driver program to test printheadings()
#include <iostream>
using namespace std;
void printheadings(void);
int main()
{
    printheadings();
    return 0;
}

// printheadings() goes here
   . . .
```

Note that the driver program does not have to declare any variables or print any results. In fact, the only thing it does is call the void function! For the call, we write the name of the function, followed by a pair of parentheses with nothing inside (do not put the keyword **void** here), followed by a semicolon.

A VOID PARAMETERLESS FUNCTION

The general form of a function that has no parameters and does not return a value is as follows:

General Form of a Void Parameterless Function

```cpp
void function_name( )                    // or void function_name (void)
{
    declaration of local variables    // optional

    action statements
    return;
}
```

In this model, the return type of the function is **void**, indicating that function <u>function_name( )</u> does not return a value. The parentheses that follow the function name are empty or optionally may contain the word **void** to indicate that the function receives no parameters. The preferred form is to have **return**; with no value following the word **return**. However, it is also legal to omit the entire **return** statement.

FUNCTIONS THAT HAVE NO PARAMETERS BUT RETURN AN ANSWER (PARAMETERLESS FUNCTIONS)

It is also possible to write a function that has no parameters but returns an answer. For such a parameterless function, the function call looks like this (where varname is the name of a variable holding the result of the function call, and func( ) is the name of the function):

```
varname = func();
```

As an example, C++ has a parameterless function rand( ) which generates a random number. To assign a random number to the variable x, we call the function like this:

```
x = rand();
```

This function does not receive any parameters, but it does return an answer. (See Exercise 31.)

A PARAMETERLESS FUNCTION THAT RETURNS A VALUE

The general form of a function that has no parameters but that returns a value is as follows:

General Form of a Parameterless Function that Returns a Value

```
return_type function_name( )        // or return_type function_name (void)
{
     declaration of local variables     // optional

     action statements
     return return_value;
}
```

In this model, **return_type** is the data type of the value returned by the function function_name( ). The parentheses that follow the function name are empty or optionally may contain the word **void** to indicate that the function receives no parameters. The item (**return_value**) following the word **return** is the value returned by the function. It may be a variable or an expression, and it should have the same data type as **return_type**.

SELF-CHECK 5-10

1. In the function header, how do we indicate that a function receives no parameters?

2. In the call to the function, how do we indicate that the function receives no parameters?

3. Can a function with no parameters return an answer?

THE MAIN PROGRAM AS A PARAMETERLESS FUNCTION

It may have occurred to you that we have been using a parameterless function already: main( ), the main program. As we have mentioned, a main program is a function, although a special one.

Although we have used this feature, the main program can receive parameters, called **command-line arguments** or **command-line parameters**. However, in all our examples, main( ) has been a parameterless function. We usually omit the keyword **void** from the parentheses in the main program header, so main( ) doesn't look like the parameterless functions in this section.

SUMMARY ON THE USE OF VOID FUNCTIONS

Let's summarize our discussion of void functions versus those that return an answer. Either type of function performs a well-defined task. Either type can receive parameters, declare local variables, and be tested with a driver program. The only difference between them is that a void function does not return an answer.

To determine which type of function to use in a given situation, remember this: Any function is designed for a single task. If that task is to compute an answer and send it back to the program which called the function, write the function to return a value. If the job can be accomplished without returning an answer, use a void function, as we did in the programs using printmaxmin( ) and printheadings( ).

SELF-CHECK 5-11

1. In each of these cases, would you use a void function or one that returns a single answer?

    a. Compute which of the three parameters to the function is the largest.

    b. Print which of the three parameters to the function is the largest.

    c. Print a long series of instructions to the person using the program.

    d. Read in a value n, then print your name n times.

2. For each of the functions in question 1, give a function header.

3. Can the main( ) function receive parameters? If so, what are they called?

<table>
<tr><td>SECTION 5</td><td></td></tr>
</table>

REFERENCE PARAMETERS

FUNCTIONS THAT CHANGE THEIR PARAMETERS

Functions in C++ can do more complicated things than we have shown so far. In fact, all of our examples of programmer-defined functions have ignored a powerful feature. In Sections 1 and 2, we discussed functions which compute and return a single value. In Section 4, we discussed void functions, which do not return any answer. However, sometimes it is convenient to write a function which computes more than one answer. In this section, we introduce reference parameters, which allow a function to change the value of one or more of its formal parameters; each time the function does this, the function changes the value of the corresponding actual parameter. In a sense, reference parameters give the function the ability to return any number of values.

A FUNCTION THAT TRIES TO ADD 1 TO ITS PARAMETER: trytoadd1( )

As our first example, let's write a function that increments or adds 1 to the value of its parameter. The function will not return the new value; instead, it will modify the value of the parameter. Although this function is not the easiest way to add 1 to a variable, it provides a simple illustration of how to change the value of a parameter in C++.

We will call the first version of our function trytoadd1( ) (because our first version doesn't work). It receives one parameter, an integer called x, and does not return an answer. In the body of the function, we simply use x++ to increment x. To make sure everything works, we add extra print statements, one before and one after incrementing.

EXAMPLE 5-8
(incorrect)

Here is the entire function trytoadd1( ):

```
// function that tries to add 1 to its parameter x
void trytoadd1(int x)
{
    cout << "in the function, before adding: " << x << endl;
    x++;
    cout << "in the function, after adding: " << x << endl;
    return;
}
```

The main program will initialize a variable, print its value, call the function, then print again. Here is the entire driver program to test trytoadd1( ):

```
// driver program to test trytoadd1()
#include <iostream>
using namespace std;
int trytoadd1(int);
int main()
{
    int k = 5;
    cout << "in the main program, before the call: " << k << endl;
    trytoadd1(k);
    cout << "in the main program, after the call: " << k << endl;
    return 0;
}
```

Although we expect that this program will correctly add 1 to the parameter, it does not work. If we do actually run the program, we will get the following output:

```
in the main program, before the call: 5
in the function, before adding: 5
in the function, after adding: 6
in the main program, after the call: 5
```

WHAT WENT WRONG?

Everything is perfect until we get back to the main program after the call. At that point, the main program prints the original value for k, not the incremented value printed in the function. To see exactly what went wrong, let's go through the function more carefully.

The formal parameter x in the function is given the *value* of the actual parameter k in the main program. As we saw in Section 2, the formal parameter can be viewed as a local variable inside the function. It starts out with the value of the actual argument (see Figure 5-12A). But if the parameter x changes in the function, as it does here, the main program's k does not change (see Figure 5-12B). The main program does not know about any local variables in a function. The communication between actual and formal parameters is one-way: from the main program to the function.

FIGURE 5-12   Call to the function <u>trytoadd1( )</u>

A, the value of <u>k</u> is transmitted to <u>x</u>; B, the value of <u>x</u> is not transmitted back to <u>k</u>

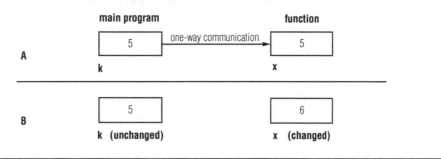

THE USE OF REFERENCE PARAMETERS: add1( ) AS THE CORRECT VERSION OF trytoadd1( )

By using reference parameters, we can make the function work correctly. We have to change both the function header and the function prototype. (We will also change the function's name to <u>add1( )</u>, since this version works.) The new header looks like this (except for this line, the function will not change):

```
void add1(int &x)                       // new function header
```

The only difference is in the data type for <u>x</u>. Originally, it was **int**; now it is **int** &, which is read "reference to integer." This means that the formal parameter is a reference to the actual parameter. In effect, the formal parameter and the corresponding actual parameter are identical; any change to the value of the formal parameter will cause a change in the value of the actual parameter when we return from the function. A parameter of this type is called a **reference parameter**.

The only other change is to make the function prototype match the new function header. The parameter will now be a reference to an integer rather than just an integer. Everything else in the main program will stay the same.

```
void add1(int &);                         // new function prototype
```

THE COMPLETE FUNCTION add1( ) AND THE CALL FROM THE MAIN PROGRAM

The entire function <u>add1( )</u>, together with a driver program to call it, is shown in Example 5-9.

EXAMPLE 5-9   Here is the complete working version of function <u>add1( )</u> and the driver program that calls it.

```
// driver program to test add1()
#include <iostream>
using namespace std;
void add1(int &);
int main()
{
    int k = 5;

    cout << "in the main program, before the call: " << k << endl;
    add1(k);
    cout << "in the main program, after the call: " << k << endl;
    return 0;
}

// ...
```

```
void add1(int &x)
{
     cout << "in the function, before adding: " << x << endl;
     x++;
     cout << "in the function, after adding: " << x << endl;
     return;
}
```

PROGRAM TRACE Let's trace this new program.

♦ The main program prints an initial message with k having the value 5.

♦ We call the function, sending k. According to the function prototype, we are sending a reference to a storage location in the main program which holds the value 5 (see Figure 5-13A).

♦ This is matched to the formal parameter x, which becomes a reference to an integer. In other words, x gives us another name by which we can refer to the storage location k that has the value 5. Whatever happens to x is really happening to k.

♦ In the function, x increments to 6, meaning the storage location that x references changes to 6 (see Figure 5-13B). This new value prints inside the function.

♦ The storage location which x references is the variable k. Back in the main program, the value stored in k changes to 6, and this value is printed.

If we run this program, we get the following output:

```
in the main program, before the call: 5
in the function, before adding: 5
in the function, after adding: 6
in the main program, after the call: 6
```

To sum up, the call to the function has the overall effect of changing the value referenced by the actual parameter.

SELF-CHECK 5-12

1. In the function trytoadd1( ), what is the value of the formal parameter? Inside the body of the function, does the value of the formal parameter change? What is the value of the actual parameter after returning from the function?

FIGURE 5-13 Using a reference parameter [the function add1( )] A, a reference to k is transmitted to x; B, the value in the location x references is changed

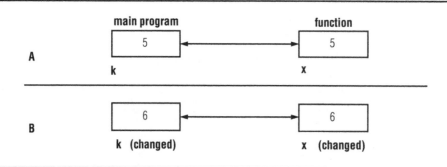

2. Inside the function add1( ), does the value of the formal parameter change? What changes in the main program after the call to the function?

3. What is wrong with each of the following calls from a driver program to the function add1( )?

```
int k = 5;

k = add1(k);
add1(&k);
```

RETURNING MORE THAN ONE VALUE FROM A FUNCTION

Obviously, we could have written add1( ) so that it returns the new value of k, which avoids the entire issue of changing the value of a parameter. However, there are cases where we can't solve the problem by returning a single value. Here is a simple example: Assume we want to modify the function print-maxmin( ) from Example 5-6 in Section 4 so that the main program knows both the larger and smaller of the two values (instead of just printing these values in the function).

EXAMPLE 5-10

Here is a function findmaxmin( ) which finds and returns to the calling function both the larger and smaller of its first two parameters. It returns these values by using the third and fourth parameters. In the function, new values are assigned to max and min, which has the effect of changing two variables in the calling function.

```
// the function stores the larger of x and y
//  in max, and it stores the smaller in min,
//  changing the corresponding locations in the main pgm
void findmaxmin(int x, int y, int &max, int &min)
{
    if (x > y) {
        max = x;
        min = y;
    }
    else   {
        max = y;
        min = x;
    }
    return;
}
```

CALLS TO THE FUNCTION findmaxmin()

We can use the following driver program to test findmaxmin( ):

```
// driver program to test findmaxmin()
#include <iostream>
void findmaxmin(int, int, int &, int &);
int main()
{
    int a = 1,b = 2,larger,smaller;

    findmaxmin(a,b,larger,smaller);
    cout << "the larger is " << larger << " and the smaller is "
        << smaller << endl;
```

```
        findmaxmin(5,a+b,larger,smaller);
        cout << "now the larger is " << larger << " and the smaller is "
            << smaller << endl;
        return 0;
    }
```

According to the function header and prototype, the first two parameters are integers, but the third (called <u>max</u> in the function) and fourth (called <u>min</u>) are references to integers. Therefore, <u>max</u> in the function is a reference to the variable <u>larger</u> from the main program. Similarly, <u>min</u> in the function is a reference to <u>smaller</u>. As the function executes, both <u>max</u> and <u>min</u> are given values, which means that <u>larger</u> and <u>smaller</u> from the main program are given values. Figure 5-14 illustrates the match-up of actual and formal parameters.

Let's give a trace of how this works. In the function, the **if** condition is false, so we set <u>max</u> to 2 and <u>min</u> to 1. Because of the way <u>max</u> and <u>min</u> are specified in the header, anything that happens to these formal parameters will also happen to the corresponding variables in main. The printout, which comes from the main program will be:

```
the larger is 2 and the smaller is 1
```

For the second call to the function, we must be a little more careful. Note that the first two actual parameters (5 and <u>a + b</u>) are a constant and an expression, not two variables. The value of each expression will be assigned to the corresponding formal parameter in the function. The third and fourth parameters (in this case, <u>larger</u> and <u>smaller</u>) are variables, but this time with initial values. However, in the function, the values of the corresponding formal parameters <u>max</u> and <u>min</u> will not be used; instead, <u>max</u> and <u>min</u> will receive values based on the values of <u>x</u> and <u>y</u>. In this case, the **if** condition will be false, <u>max</u> will be set to 5 and <u>min</u> to 3. The printout from the second call will be:

```
the larger is 5 and the smaller is 3
```

It is important to note that the parameters matching <u>max</u> and <u>min</u> must be variables. Since the formal parameters <u>max</u> and <u>min</u> will be assigned values in the function, the corresponding parameters must also be able to accept values—that is, they must be variables, not constants or expressions. Variables have an address or location in memory that can be passed to the function. On the other hand, expressions do not have such an address, and they cannot be matched to reference parameters.

Let's diagram what happens in the function header for <u>findmaxmin( )</u>:

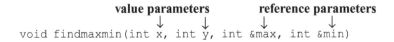

FIGURE 5-14   Using reference parameters to return two values from a function

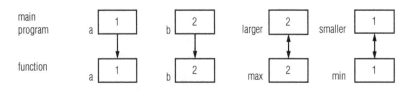

This is paralleled by what happens in the call to the function:

matched to value parameters in the function header

```
findmaxmin(5,a+b,larger,smaller);
```

matched to reference parameters in the function header

Since only the values of the first two actual parameters are needed in the function, they are not preceded by ampersands in the header. However, the third and fourth parameters, which are reference parameters in the function, are preceded by ampersands in the header and function prototype, so that the references to these variables (rather than their values) are sent to the function.

INPUT AND OUTPUT PARAMETERS

A parameter such as <u>max</u> or <u>min</u> in Example 5-10 which is used to hold a value assigned in the function, is sometimes called an **output parameter**. This term signifies that the value it carries on input to the function is not important; the value it holds on output is.

In the same way, an **input parameter** provides some type of input to the function, but it is not used to communicate the results of the function to the outside world. Almost all of the parameters we have used so far have been input parameters.

Finally, a parameter whose value is both used by the function and changed by the function is called an **input-output parameter**. In the function <u>add1( )</u> from Example 5-9, the value of the parameter is incremented by the function. Since we use the value on input and modify it on output, it is an input-output parameter.

A FUNCTION TO INTERCHANGE THE VALUE OF ITS PARAMETERS

As our next example, we will write a function called <u>swap( )</u>. This function is the classic example of why reference parameters are needed. The <u>swap( )</u> function interchanges the values of its two parameters. Assume that you have two variables—call them <u>a</u> and <u>b</u>—and you want the value currently in <u>a</u> to be placed in <u>b</u>, while the value in <u>b</u> is moved to <u>a</u>.

If functions could not change parameters in some way, such a swap function would be impossible. Since a function is restricted to returning at most a single value, we would have to choose between <u>a</u> and <u>b</u>. And even if we could somehow return both <u>a</u> and <u>b</u>, we could never actually interchange their values. Our <u>swap( )</u> function needs a new mechanism to accomplish its task. However, before we can talk about the function, we have to discuss the simpler question of how to interchange the value of two variables.

INTERCHANGING TWO VALUES

The first idea that occurs to most people is simply to move <u>a</u> into <u>b</u> and <u>b</u> into <u>a</u>. That is, we can try something like this:

```
a = b;                                              // incorrect
b = a;
```

This seems easy enough, but it doesn't work.

Let's say, for example, <u>a</u> is 5 and <u>b</u> is 3 to start. We want <u>a</u> to become 3, and <u>b</u> to become 5. But this is not what occurs. The top line sets <u>a</u> to 3, which is fine (see Figure 5-15B); the bottom line sets

FIGURE 5-15   Incorrect way to swap the values of a̲ and b̲
A, the initial values; *B*, the values after *a = b*; *C*, the values after *b = a*

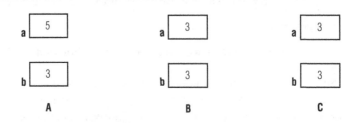

b̲ to the current value of a̲, which is 3, not the old value, which was 5 (see Figure 5-15C). Both a̲ and b̲ are now 3, which isn't what we want.

Changing the order of assignments doesn't help since both locations then end up holding the value 5:

```
b = a;                                                    // also incorrect
a = b;
```

The problem is that we want a̲ and b̲ to change values simultaneously. But in a program, things aren't done simultaneously; one must come first. It seems that whichever statement comes first destroys the other value. How, then, can we swap two numbers?

Here is an analogy: If you have two boxes, one to your left and one to your right, how do you switch their positions? You pick both boxes up at the same time, then move your left hand to the right, and your right hand to the left.

But suppose you can use only one hand to switch the boxes.

◆   You move one box, say the left, temporarily to the middle (see Figure 5-16A).

◆   Then you move the box on the right to the vacant left position (see Figure 5-16B).

◆   Finally, you move the box in the middle to the right (see Figure 5-16C).

It takes three steps and requires an extra place to store the first box temporarily, but the exchange is possible.

The same principle can be used to swap a̲ and b̲. Here is an algorithm to perform this task:

Algorithm to Interchange the Values of a̲ and b̲

◆   *Temporarily move a̲ to some new location, call it* temp̲. *This saves the old value.*

◆   *Move b̲ into a̲, destroying whatever was there.*

◆   *Finally, move* temp̲ *into b̲, which has the effect of moving the original value of a̲ into b̲.*

EXAMPLE 5-11   In C++, the following three assignment statements swap the values of a̲ and b̲:

```
temp = a;
a = b;                       // swapping the values of
b = temp;                    // the variables a and b
```

There is only one way to modify the order of the steps. If we start with ***temp = b***, then the continuation must be ***b = a***, then ***a = temp***.

There is a simple way to remember the correct order of statements. Each of the three variables (a̲, b̲, and temp̲) should appear on the left-hand side of one assignment statement and the

FIGURE 5-16   Correct way to interchange the positions of two boxes *A*, step 1; *B*, step 2; *C*, step 3.

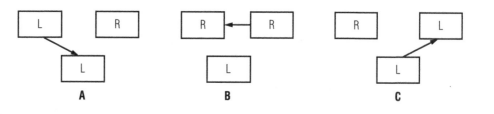

right-hand side of another; the two uses of a and b can be connected by upward arrows as shown below:

```
temp = a;                    temp = b;
   ↗                            ↗
a = b;           or          b = a;
   ↗                            ↗
b = temp;                    a = temp;
```

THE FUNCTION swap()

Now let's see how to do the same thing in a function called swap( ). Our job is to write a function that receives two parameters. The function swaps or interchanges the values of two storage locations in the calling program. In order to work in this way, the function has to receive references, rather than values. If a and b are references to integers, then a and b refer to the underlying values we want the function to swap.

EXAMPLE 5-12a Here is the complete function to swap the values of two variables:

```
// the function will interchange the values
//  in the main pgm referenced by a and b
void swap(int &a, int &b)
{
     int temp;

     temp = a;
     a = b;
     b = temp;
     return;
}
```

CALLING swap() FROM A MAIN PROGRAM

Now let's see how a main program (or any other function) uses the swap( ) function.

EXAMPLE 5-12b Here is a driver program to test swap( ):

```
// driver program to test the function swap()
#include <iostream>
using namespace std;
void swap (int &,int &);
int main()
{
```

```
    int x,y;

    x = 5;
    y = 3;
    cout << "before the call" << endl;
    cout << "x is: " << x << " and y is: " << y << endl;
    swap(x,y);
    cout << "after the call" << endl;
    cout << "x is now: " << x << " and y is now: " << y << endl;
    return 0;
}
```

Note that x is matched to a, and y is matched to b. Inside the function, the values referenced by a and b are exchanged, which means the overall effect of the function call is to swap the values of x and y.

If the driver program is run, the following prints:

```
before the call:
x is: 5, and y is: 3
after the call:
x is now: 3, and y is now: 5
```

SELF-CHECK 5-13

1. Show how to interchange the values of two variables d1 and d2 of type **double**.

2. If we are swapping the values of a and b, and the first step is temp = b, why is there only one possible continuation?

3. What happens if we forget to include an ampersand before the name of a variable in the header of swap( )?

THE FUNCTION setto7()

Let's look at another example of a function that changes more than one variable in the main program. Example 5-13 shows a function that receives three parameters, setting the value pointed to by each of them to 7.

EXAMPLE 5-13

```
// the function sets the values
//  referenced by x, y, and z to 7
void setto7(int &x, int &y, int &z)
{
    x = 7;
    y = 7;
    z = 7;
    return;
}
```

Here is a driver program which will call setto7:

```
// driver program to test setto7
#include <iostream>
using namespace std;
void setto7(int &, int &, int &);
int main()
{
```

```
int a=5, b=1, c=10;

cout << "the original values are: " << a << " "
    << b << " " << c << endl;
setto7(a,b,c);
cout << "the new values are: " << a << " "
    << b << " " << c << endl;
return 0;
}
```

The output from this program is the following:

```
the original values are: 5 1 10
the new values are: 7 7 7
```

SELF-CHECK 5-14

1. Why can't the function findmaxmin( ) return both the larger and smaller values, using either one or two **return** statements?

2. In the function header for findmaxmin( ), why don't the first two parameters have an & between the data type and the name?

3. Give the header for a function settolarger( ), which receives two integer reference parameters, x and y. For example, we can call the function by sending it references to two integer variables a and b.

SUMMARY OF PARAMETER TRANSMISSION

Here is a summary of parameter transmission in C++.

Passing by Value

C++ has two ways of sending parameters to a function. Until this section, we have used only the first method, which is called passing a parameter by value. This means that the value of the actual parameter is assigned to the formal parameter. Before the function starts, the actual parameter is evaluated to a particular value (e.g., 7 or 5). This value is then copied into the corresponding formal parameter inside the function—see Figure 5-12). This has the same effect as this assignment statement:

```
formalparameter = actualparameter
```

The value of such a formal parameter may or may not be changed in the function. However, when we return to the main program, any change to the formal parameter will not be reflected in a change to the corresponding actual parameter. Just as in an assignment statement, even if formalparameter changes, actualparameter will not change. When the function is complete, the actual parameter in the main program will have exactly the same value that it had before the function began, regardless of what happened to the formal parameter. This method of passing parameters is the default method in C++, meaning that it is used unless we explicitly tell the compiler otherwise.

Passing by Reference

However, C++ also allows a parameter to be <u>passed by reference</u>. A parameter passed in this way is called a **reference parameter**. In this case, the formal parameter is really just another way of referencing or referring to the actual parameter. Therefore, a change to the formal parameter will be reflected in a change to the corresponding actual parameter, because they are the same storage location (see Figure 5-13).

WHEN TO USE A REFERENCE PARAMETER

The last topic that we will discuss in this section is the question of which parameters in a function should be reference parameters. Briefly, the answer is those parameters that the main program wants to receive new values in the function should be reference parameters. In other words, we can inspect the body of the function to see which of the formal parameters will get a new value (e.g., appear on the left-hand side of an assignment statement or receive a value in some other way, perhaps from <u>cin</u>). If the main program needs to know the new values for one or more parameters, then these formal parameters will be declared to be reference parameters in the function header. In addition, each reference parameter must be matched to a variable (not a constant or an expression) in the main program. For these parameters, C++ will use **call by reference** to transmit values back and forth between the main program and the function. All other parameters will be sent by the default mechanism, which is **call by value**. In addition, typically a function that computes only one value will return that value using a **return** statement, while a function that computes more than one value will use reference parameters to return those values.

SECTION 6   ENRICHMENT: INPUT-PROCESS-OUTPUT (*I-P-O*) COMMENTS

In this section, we will introduce a more detailed type of comment which helps the programmer work with functions in a systematic way. The comment focuses on three main features of a function: the input, the process to be carried out, and the output.

INPUT-PROCESS-OUTPUT (*I-P-O*) COMMENTS

It is usually quite easy to write simple functions from the English-language description. However, for a more complex function, we should organize our thoughts more systematically.

In analyzing a function, either a main program or any other function, there are three important ideas:

◆ the **input** to the function—the things it receives from the outside world

◆ the **process** taking place in the function—how it accomplishes its task

◆ the **output** from the function—the way it communicates with the outside world

One of the first goals of solving a problem is understanding these three aspects. Then it will be relatively easy for you to write that function. On the other hand, if you are confused about one or more of these points, you will become even more confused as you try to write the function.

Here is a method, called *I-P-O* comments, which emphasizes these three features of a function: *I* (input), *P* (process), and *O* (output). Each function's comment defines what the function's inputs are, outlines how the function processes the data values, and describes what the function's results or output will be. In addition to organizing our thoughts, this is an excellent comment since it emphasizes the task of the function and the way in which it interacts with the outside world.

Let's go through these aspects, then look at a specific example.

♦ *I* stands for the input to the function. For the examples in this chapter, input means the parameters sent to the function from the calling program. However, in more complicated functions, it could mean additional things. For example, a function could ask the user to type in values. In general, *I* is all the information the function needs to do its job.

♦ *P* stands for process, the actual work of the function. This usually entails computing one specific value, which is returned to the calling program. In general, *P* is what is performed by the function.

♦ *O* stands for output. At the simplest level, a function outputs by sending an answer to the calling program. A function can also send output directly to the screen or the printer. In general, *O* is all the ways the function communicates with the rest of the program and the outside world.

Now let's consider a specific example by looking at the function <u>sumofsquares( )</u> that we used in the last version of Program 4. Let's write a function to receive one parameter value (<u>n</u>) and compute the sum of the first <u>n</u> squares. As a first step, start with this analysis:

Input: the parameter value <u>n</u>—the number of squares

Process: compute the sum of the first <u>n</u> squares

Output: return the sum of squares to the calling program

Now translate this into C++. The process step is simply the set of instructions used earlier to compute the sum of the first <u>n</u> squares in the main program. The output step returns this sum to the calling program. The input step is done automatically through the matchup of actual and formal parameters. Thus, we are led almost immediately to the version of the function in Section 3. As we noted, the analysis can be kept as a comment since it concisely summarizes the function's task. Here is the complete function with the new comment:

```
// Function sumofsquares():
// Input:
//   the parameter value n—the number
//    of squares to be summed
// Process:
//    finds the sum of the first n squares:
//   1*1 + 2*2 + ... + n*n
// Output:
//   returns the sum of the first n squares
int sumofsquares(int n)
{
    int sum;

    sum = 0;
    for (int item = 1; item <= n; item++)
        sum += item * item;
    return sum;
}
```

We will continue to use Input-Process-Output (*I-P-O*) comments in our later programs. Try to use them in your own programs as well. By following this format, you will be sure that you can describe these three main features in a function. Note that the comment is spread out over several lines. This draws the reader's attention to it.

SELF-CHECK 5-15

1. In an *I-P-O* comment, what does the *I* stand for? What are the possible forms input to a function can take?

2. What does the *P* stand for?

3. What does the *O* stand for? What are the possible forms output from a function can take?

SECTION 7 ## ENRICHMENT: USING FUNCTIONS TO PRODUCE A MULTIPLICATION TABLE

In this section, we will show how to use functions to construct a multiplication table (see Example 4-2). A void function prints the first ten multiples of a given number. Then another void function produces a set of headings.

PSEUDOCODE FOR PRODUCING A MULTIPLICATION TABLE

Let's go back to an intermediate version of the pseudocode for this problem, which we developed in Chapter 4, Section 4.

> *print the headings at the top of the page*
> *for each multiplicand* m1 *from 1 to 10*
>   *print a line of output showing*
>   m1 *times each multiplier from 1 to 10*

Printing headings is a well-defined task which can be accomplished by a void function without cluttering up the main program. (In fact, one of our examples in Section 4 was a void function to print headings.) We will call this function <u>printheadings( )</u>. Since <u>printheadings( )</u> is a parameterless void function, the main program's call to the function is simply <u>printheadings( )</u>. In top-down fashion, we will give the details of the function later.

Our pseudocode for the main program now looks like this:

> printheadings();
> *for each multiplicand* m1 *from 1 to 10*
>   *print a line of output showing*
>   m1 *times each multiplier from 1 to 10*

In Example 4-2, we refined this pseudocode in the main program. Here we will use a void function to accomplish the task. Let's call this function <u>printrow( )</u>. It needs a parameter <u>m1</u> because it has to know for which number to construct the row of the multiplication table. Therefore, the main program's call to the function is <u>printrow(m1)</u>. The next version of the main program looks like this:

> printheadings();
> *for each multiplicand* m1 *from 1 to 10*
>   printrow(m1);

Of course, the middle line can be implemented as a **for** loop. Here is the complete action portion of the main program:

```
printheadings();
for (int m1 = 1; m1 <= 10; m1++)
    printrow(m1);
```

Notice how simple this main program is. Before we celebrate, we should remember that we also need to include the main program header, comments, declarations, etc. Even more importantly, we must still write the two functions, <u>printheadings( )</u> and <u>printrow( )</u>. To continue our top-down approach, first complete the main program, then write the functions.

THE MAIN PROGRAM

We can copy most of the initial portion of the main program from the original version. The only differences are the modified comment and declaration: the main program declares just one variable (<u>m1</u>) instead of two (what happened to <u>m2</u>?). The action portion is now the call to <u>printheadings( )</u> and the **for** loop containing the call to <u>printrow( )</u>. Here is the entire main program (which we call <u>multfunc.cpp</u>):

```
// Program multfunc.cpp:
// construct a set of multiplication tables,
// showing the multiples of the numbers from 1 to 10
// using two functions: to print headings and tables
#include <iostream>
using namespace std;
int main()
{
    printheadings();
    for (int m1 = 1; m1 <= 10; m1++)
        printrow(m1);
    return 0;
}

// the two functions go here
```

This completes the main program. Next we will write the two functions.

THE FUNCTION printheadings( )

We start with <u>printheadings( )</u>. (You may want to look at the similar function in Example 5-7 in Section 4.) As usual, the function begins with a header and a comment (note that we are using the *I-P-O* comment format from Section 5). The cout statements for the headings are exactly the same as those in our first version of the program.

```
// Function printheadings:
// Input:
//    none
// Process:
//    prints headings to be used at the
//    top of a multiplication chart
// Output:
//    prints several lines of headings
void printheadings(void)
{
    cout << "This is a Multiplication Table, from 1 to 10";
    cout << endl << endl;
```

```
cout << "    X    1    2    3    4    5    6    7    8    9   10";
cout << endl;
return;
}
```

THE FUNCTION printrow()

The function <u>printrow( )</u> is more complicated. For the formal parameter within the function, we can use the same name as the main program, <u>m1</u>. The function's comment and header look like this:

```
// Function printrow():
// Input:
//   the parameter m1 tells which table to produce
// Process:
//   produces a multiplication table for m1
//   this contains the first 10 multiples of m1
// Output:
//   prints the multiplication table
void printrow(int m1)
```

Within the body of the void function, we need all the statements to print a multiplication table, including those to set up the size of the columns. The table consists of the value of <u>m1</u> on the left, followed by its first ten multiples spread out to align under the column headings. To accomplish this, we need a local variable to represent the numbers from 1 to 10 by which <u>m1</u> is multiplied. To be consistent with Example 4-2, <u>m2</u> can be the name of this local variable. We now have the following:

```
{
    cout << endl;
    cout.width(5);
    cout << m1;
    for (int m2 = 1; m2 <= 10; m2++) {
        cout.width(5);
        cout << m1 * m2;
    }
    cout << endl;
    return;
}
```

COMPLETE PROGRAM multfunc.cpp USING TWO FUNCTIONS

Now all we need to do is combine the main program and the two functions. As usual, the functions come after the main program. It does not matter which function comes first, but for clarity, we can put them in their order called: <u>printheadings( )</u> and then <u>printrow( )</u>.

```
// ...
#include <iostream>
using namespace std;
void printheadings(void);
void printrow(int m1);
```

```
int main()
{
    printheadings();
    for (int m1 = 1; m1 <= 10; m1++)
        printrow(m1);
    return 0;
}

// ...
void printheadings(void)
{
    cout << "This is a Multiplication Table, from 1 to 10";
    cout << endl << endl;
    cout << "     X    1    2    3    4    5    6    7    8    9   10";
    cout << endl;
    return;
}

// ...
void printrow(int m1)
{
    cout << endl;
    cout.width(5);
    cout << m1;
    for (int m2 = 1; m2 <= 10; m2++) {
        cout.width(5);
        cout << m1 * m2;
    }
    cout << endl;
    return;
}
```

TRACING PROGRAM multfunc.cpp

A trace of this program is quite similar to the one for the original multiplication table in Chapter 4, Section 4, with only a few extra details because of the function calls.

PROGRAM TRACE As usual, execution begins in the main program.

♦ The first thing the main program does is call the void function <u>printheadings( )</u>.

♦ At this point, the main program suspends execution and control shifts to <u>printheadings( )</u>, which simply prints some headings.

♦ Then the function returns control to the main program, which sets up a **for** loop, with <u>m1</u> going from 1 to 10. For the first pass through this loop, <u>m1</u> has the value 1.

♦ The main program calls the function <u>printrow( )</u>, with <u>m1</u> as the actual parameter.

♦ The main program stops processing, and <u>printrow( )</u> takes over. In <u>printrow( )</u>, the formal parameter is also called <u>m1</u>. The function <u>printrow( )</u> prints a line containing the multiples of <u>m1</u> from <u>m1</u> * 1 to <u>m1</u> * 10. In this case, we get multiples of 1.

♦ When the function finishes, it returns control to the main program, which increments m1 to 2.

♦ The main program calls the function printrow( ) again, with m1 having the value 2, and so on.

♦ Eventually, the main program increments m1 to 10 and sends this value to the function, which prints the multiples of 10 from 10 * 1 to 10 * 10. Then printrow( ) returns control to the main program.

♦ The main program terminates the **for** loop and ends.

The output, some printed in printheadings( ) and some printed in each call to printrow( ), is identical to that shown in Chapter 4.

COMPARISON WITH THE EARLIER VERSION, mult.cpp, FROM CHAPTER 4, SECTION 4

This is a good time to reflect on using functions to solve this problem. On one level, the function version is much longer than the original. However, on a deeper level, once you understand void functions, the new version is easier to follow because the main program has been freed of most of the details. Each individual function is straightforward, and it is clear how both of them interact with the main program. Thus, instead of one complicated main program with a nested loop structure, you have one simple main program and two simple functions. In general, our goal should be to develop a main program which is as simple as possible, with the details supplied in the functions. Someone who is not concerned with the details can concentrate on the main program; someone who needs to know more can study the individual functions.

In a case where the original program is not long or complicated, this approach may not be useful, but for more complex problems, it clearly is. (See Exercise 18 for another way to use functions in this program and a comparison of all three versions.)

EFFICIENCY CONSIDERATIONS

There is one additional consideration: the question of **efficiency**. Both versions include essentially the same arithmetic calculations and print statements. The major difference is the number of function calls, since there is a large amount of overhead every time one is called. In the original version, mult.cpp, all work is done in the main program, so there are no function calls. In the function version, multfunc.cpp, the main program calls printheadings( ) once and printrow( ) 10 times, for a total of 11 function calls. Using this criterion, the second version is much less efficient.

As important as efficiency is, clarity and simplicity are even more vital in a student environment. You must weigh all the factors and decide what to do in each situation.

SELF-CHECK 5-16

1. Why does the function printheadings( ) receive no parameters?
2. Why does the function printrow( ) receive one parameter?
3. What is wrong with the following call to printrow( ) (z is a variable of data type **int**)?

```
z = printrow(m1);
```

SUMMARY

BASIC FUNCTION CONCEPTS

1. A module is a series of instructions that performs a specific task. A module that performs a calculation directly in a main program can be replaced by two things: (1) a general set of instructions describing how to perform that calculation; and (2) the details of which values (called parameters) should be used for a particular calculation. In order to perform a calculation, the program applies the general set of instructions to a specific group of parameter values.

2. The general set of instructions is called a function or a function definition. Each group of parameter values is specified in a call to the function. Once a function has been defined, it can be called any number of times with a new set of parameters each time.

3. Standard or library functions are supplied as part of the C++ standard library. Most of the library functions compute a specific value; for example, sqrt( ) computes a square root, and abs( ) computes an absolute value.

4. Besides using library functions, a person writing a C++ program can include additional functions, called programmer-defined functions. Each programmer-defined function should be designed to perform a single task.

5. Here is the sequence of events in a call to a function. The main program temporarily suspends execution, and the function begins. The main program usually sends some particular value(s) to the function. Each value is called an actual or real parameter (or argument) in the main program; it is matched to a formal or dummy parameter inside the function. In C++, all parameters are passed by value.

6. One type of function uses the parameter value(s) to compute a single answer; this answer is sent back as the value returned by the function. For example, the library function sqrt( ) computes and returns the square root of whatever parameter value it receives. This type of function can have any fixed number (0, 1, 2, ...) of parameters but returns precisely one answer.

FUNCTION HEADER AND DECLARATION OF LOCAL VARIABLES

7. The top line of a function is called the function header. It includes the type of answer returned by the function, the name of the function, plus the name and data type of each formal parameter. Here is an example:

```
double sample(int x, double y)
```

The name of the function is sample; it has two formal parameters. One, x, has data type **int**; the other, y, has data type **double**. The function returns an answer of type **double**.

8. The function header is followed by the declaration of any local variables used in the function. A local variable declared in a function has no relationship to any other variable, even one with the same name, in the main program. Just as in a main program, a pair of braces surrounds the local variable declarations and the actual instructions to perform the function.

9. Here is an example of a complete function definition, including the declaration of a local variable z within it:

```
double sample(int x, double y)
{
     double z;

     z = x + y;
     return z;
}
```

The function sample( ) adds together the values of the two parameters, then returns that sum.

FUNCTION CALL AND RETURN

10. Here is an example of a call from a main program to the function sample( ):

```
#include <iostream>
using namespace std;
double sample(int, double);
int main()
{
     int a;
     double b,c;
     ...
     c = sample(a,b);
     ...
}
```

A call from the main program to the function consists of the name of the function followed by the actual parameter(s) in parentheses. For the call above, the variables a and b in the main program are actual parameters which match the formal parameters x and y inside the function; c holds the answer returned by the function.

11. The function returns an answer through a **return** statement. Back in the calling program, the answer that is returned can be stored directly in another variable, appear as part of an expression, or be sent to cout. In fact, the answer returned by one function can itself be sent to another function as an actual parameter.

12. The function sample( ) returns the value stored in z by the following statement:

```
return z;
```

When the main program calls sample( ), the answer returned is stored in the variable c.

PARAMETER TRANSMISSION AND TYPE CHECKING

13. When the function is called, the value of each actual parameter is copied into the corresponding formal parameter in the function. This is called parameter transmission by value. The actual parameters need not be variables; they can be expressions such as 2 * a + b or constants like −6.

14. The overall task of this type of function is to compute a particular value consistent with the data type mentioned in the function header. The function always returns this value to the point at which it was called.

15. Verification that values have the correct data types is called type checking. The compiler performs this type checking as it translates the function into machine language.

FUNCTION PROTOTYPES

16. When a function is called, the compiler can perform additional type checking. For example, it can verify that the parameters being sent to the function match what is expected. To do this, the compiler needs access to the function declaration or prototype while it is translating the program into machine language.

17. One way to give the compiler access to the function prototype is to place the prototype at the top of a file which contains the main program. This is the way that function prototypes for the standard library functions work. For example, <u>iostream.h</u> contains a number of function prototypes for I/O functions; <u>cmath.h</u> contains a number of function prototypes for mathematical functions.

18. If the function being called is programmer defined, the function prototype should be explicit. The function prototype can look like a function header, or it can omit the names of the parameters. Because it is a complete C++ statement, the function prototype ends in a semicolon. Here is a function prototype for the function <u>sample( )</u>:

```
double sample(int, double);                    // function prototype
```

ADVANTAGES OF FUNCTIONS

19. One major advantage of using functions is the ability to test and debug each one independently. Once a function has been thoroughly debugged, it can be trusted as a module of a larger program. For example, if a main program calls a function, each can be tested and debugged separately until it seems to work, then the pieces can be joined to form a complete program.

VOID FUNCTIONS

20. Certain tasks that a function can be used for (e.g., to print a list of numbers) have no obvious answer to return. A special type of function, called a void function, can be used. A void function does not return an explicit value but performs a task (e.g., printing the results of some calculations).

21. The header of a void function replaces the initial data type for the answer returned by the function with the keyword **void** to indicate that no value is returned. In a void function, the entire **return** statement can be omitted, or the keyword **return** (with no value) can be used. Here is an outline of a void function <u>proc1( )</u> that receives two parameters, <u>a</u> of type **int** and <u>b</u> of type **double**:

```
void proc1(int a, double b)
{
    ...
    return;
}
```

22. The call consists of the name of the void function followed by the name(s) of the actual parameter(s). Here is an example of a call to the void function <u>proc1( )</u>, sending two actual parameters, <u>x</u> and <u>y</u>:

```
int x;
double y;

proc1(x,y);
```

23. Here is the function prototype for the void function <u>proc1( )</u>, showing that it receives one parameter of type **int** and one of type **double**:

```
void proc1(int, double);
```

PARAMETERLESS FUNCTIONS

24. A function that receives no parameters is called a parameterless function. It has to be relatively self-contained since it cannot communicate by way of parameters. A parameterless function can return an answer or can be void.

25. The function header for a void parameterless function called <u>sub( )</u> looks like this:

```
void sub(void)
```

The call to the void parameterless function looks like this:

```
sub();
```

The function prototype looks like this:

```
void sub(void);
```

26. In this example one or more uses of the keyword **void** can be eliminated, but there are slight changes in the meaning. Using the keyword is recommended.

METHODS OF PARAMETER TRANSMISSION

27. C++ has two distinct ways of transmitting a parameter to a function. The first method is called passing a parameter by value. At the time the function is called, the parameter in the main program is evaluated and its value is assigned to the corresponding formal parameter in the function. A change in the value of such a formal parameter in the function will not cause a change in the corresponding actual parameter in the main program. In C++, passing a parameter by value is the default (i.e., this is the method that is used unless other instructions are specified).

28. The second method of parameter transmission is called passing a parameter by reference or address. To use this method, the programmer has to declare the formal parameter to be a reference parameter in the function header (and prototype) and the corresponding parameter in the main program must be a variable, not a constant or an expression. The function receives a reference to the actual storage location (not just the value) of the corresponding parameter. A change in the value of the formal parameter is, in fact, a change in the value of the matching actual parameter.

USING A REFERENCE PARAMETER IN A FUNCTION

29. A function can use a reference parameter to modify one or more corresponding actual parameters in the calling function. Here is a function which has three reference parameters (indicated by the use of & in the function header):

```
void initialize(int &p, int &q, int &r)
{
    p = 0;
    q = 0;
    r = 0;
    return;
}
```

30. Here is a main program that uses the function <u>initialize( )</u>:

```
#include <iostream>
using namespace std;
void initialize(int &,int &,int &);
int main()
{
    int a = 5, b = 3, c = 9;

    cout << "the original values are: "<< a <<", "<< b <<", and" << c << endl;
    initialize(a,b,c);
    cout << "the new values are: "<< a <<", "<< b <<", and" << c << endl;
}
```

The function has the effect of setting the value stored at three locations in the main program (<u>a</u>, <u>b</u>, and <u>c</u>) to 0. The main program prints the following:

```
the original values are: 5, 3, and 9
the new values are: 0, 0, and 0
```

I-P-O COMMENTS

31. Input-Process-Output (*I-P-O*) analysis is a guide to organizing a programmer's thoughts in writing a function. *I* stands for input, the various pieces of information a function needs to do its job. *P* stands for process, the task accomplished by the function. *O* stands for output, the way the function communicates its results. The *I-P-O* analysis can also serve as a comment for the function.

EXERCISES

TRACING EXERCISES

1. Show what is printed by the following program, which calls a function <u>func( )</u> two times.

```
#include <iostream>
using namespace std;
int func(int, int, int);
int main()
{
    int a,b,c,d;

    a = 5; b = 4; c = 2;
    d = func(a,b,c);
    cout << a << " " << b << " " << c << " gives an answer of " << d
        << endl;
    a = func(b,c,d);
    cout << b << " " << c << " " << d << " gives an answer of " << a
        << endl;
    return 0;
}

int func(int x, int y, int z)
{
    int w;

    w = x + y;
```

```
            if (y < z + 1)
                w++;
            return w;
    }
```

2. Show what is printed by the following program, which calls a function <u>powers( )</u>. Describe in words what the function <u>powers( )</u> does. Why is the answer returned by the function given the data type **double** rather than **int**?

```cpp
#include <iostream>
using namespace std;
double powers(int);
int main()
{
    int e;
    double f;

    e = 3;
    f = powers(e);
    cout << e << " terms give a sum of " << f << endl;
    e = 5;
    f = powers(e);
    cout << e << " terms give a sum of " << f << endl;
    e = 7;
    f = powers(e);
    cout << e << " terms give a sum of " << f << endl;
    return 0;
}

double powers(int n)
{
    int i;
    double sum;

    sum = 0;
    for (i = 1; i <= n; i++)
        sum += i*i*i*i;
    return sum;
}
```

3. Show what is printed by the following program, which calls a function <u>eq2( )</u>. Describe in words what the function <u>eq2( )</u> does.

```cpp
#include <iostream>
using namespace std;
int eq2(int, int, int);
int main()
{
    int p = 4, q = 5, r = 7;

    if (eq2(p,q,r) == 1)
        cout << p << " " << q << " "<< r <<" is true\n ";
    else
        cout << p << " " << q << " "<< r <<" is false\n ";
    cout << p+3 << " " << q-1 << " " << r;
```

```
        if (eq2(p+3,q-1,r) == 1)
            cout << " returns true" << endl;
        else
            cout << " returns false" << endl;
        cout << p << " " << 4 << " " << q-1;
        cout << " gives an answer of " << eq2(p,4,q-1) << endl;
        return 0;
    }

    int eq2(int a, int b,int c)
    {
        int ans = 0;

        if (a == b)
            ans = 1;
        if (a == c)
            ans = 1;
        if (b == c)
            ans = 1;
        return ans;
    }
```

4. For each of the functions in exercises 1 to 3, identify the formal parameters and local variables. For each call to a function, identify the actual parameters. Explain the matchup of formal and actual parameters.

5. Describe what is printed by this program.

```
#include <iostream>
using namespace std;
double harmonic(int);
int main()
{
    double sum50,sum100;

    sum50 = harmonic(50);
    sum100 = harmonic(100);
    cout << "sum of 50 terms " << sum50 << endl;
    cout << "sum of 100 terms " << sum100 << endl;
    return 0;
}

double harmonic(int n)
{
    double sum=0;

    for (int i = 1; i <= n; i++)
        sum = sum + 1.0 / i;
    return sum;
}
```

6. Show what is printed by the following program.

```
#include <iostream>
using namespace std;
void printlines(int);
```

```
int main()
{
    int num=5;

    printlines(num);
    num = 3;
    printlines(num);
    return 0;
}

void printlines(int k)
{
    for (int i = 0; i < k; i++)
        cout << "hello" << endl;
    return;
}
```

7. Show what is printed by the following program.

```
#include <iostream>
using namespace std;
void printeach(int,int);
int main()
{
    int a = 4, b = 10;

    printeach(a,b);
    return 0;
}

void printeach(int x, int y)
{
    cout << "here is a list of the numbers in between " << x << " and "
        << y << endl;
    for (int i = x; i <= y; i++)
        cout << i << endl;
    return;
}
```

Show what is printed when a is initialized to 4 and b to 3.

8. Show what is printed by the following program. Assume that the user types in the number 1, then the number 2, and finally, the number 5.

```
#include <iostream>
using namespace std;
void printmenu(void);
int main()
{
    int num;

    printmenu();
    cin >> num;
    if (num == 1)
        cout << "Hello" << endl;
    else
        cout << "Goodbye" << endl;
    return 0;
}
```

```
void printmenu(void)
{
    cout << "type 1 if you want me to say Hello" << endl << endl;
    cout << "type 2 if you want me to say Goodbye" << endl << endl;
    return;
}
```

9. a. Give the function prototype for a function named <u>func1( )</u> that receives one parameter of type **int** and computes an answer of type **int**.
    b. Give the function prototype for a function named <u>func2( )</u> that receives one parameter of type **double** and computes an answer of type <u>char</u>.

MODIFICATIONS OF EARLIER FUNCTIONS AND PROGRAMS

10. The statement below contains a call to the function <u>max3( )</u>:

```
cout << max3(p + 2, 12, abs(q)) * 3 << endl;
```

   Show how to break the expression into smaller pieces before the final value is printed, using extra variables to hold the intermediate results.

11. a. Show how to rewrite the function <u>sign( )</u> using the conditional (?:) operator in Chapter 3, Section 6.
    b. Do the same for the function <u>max3( )</u>.

12. Does it make sense to rewrite Program 1 (the squares of the numbers from 4 to 9) using a function? Explain.

13. Write a void function <u>evalformula( )</u> to evaluate the formula in Program 2. The function is sent the value for <u>gpa</u> and computes the value for <u>result</u>, using the formula in Problem 2. In addition, the function handles all the output associated with printing this value of <u>gpa</u> and <u>result</u>. Show how the main program calls the function.

14. Rewrite the payroll program from Chapter 3, using a function to compute the employee's pay for the week. You must decide exactly what parameter(s) to send to the function.

15. Write a void function <u>printprompts( )</u> to print the prompts in Program 3. The function should print a series of messages asking the user to type in the three pieces of data requested for each employee.

16. Program 5 used a function called <u>sumofsquares( )</u> to compute and return the sum of the squares from 1 to a given number. The main program then printed the sum. Show how to change <u>sumofsquares( )</u> into a void function to compute and print the sum of the squares. What changes have to be made to the main program?

17. a. Write a program to do the following: For each number <u>n</u> from 1 to 15, the main program calls a function to find the sum of the squares of the numbers from 1 to <u>n</u>.
    b. Modify your program so that the function computes the sum of the cubes of the numbers from 1 to <u>n</u>.

18. a. In Section 7, the function printrow( ) prints one row of a multiplication table. Show how to write a function, called multtable( ), which prints an entire multiplication table. (*Suggestion*: This function should contain a nested loop.) Show how the main program has to change to use this function.

    b. Compare this version of the multiplication table program to the original one from Chapter 4 and the one in Section 7.

19. Modify the function printheadings( ) from Section 7 so that it prints the column headings appropriate for a multiplication chart that goes from 1 to 8.

20. Modify the function printheadings( ) from Section 7 so that it prints the column headings appropriate for a multiplication chart that goes from 1 to LIMIT, where LIMIT is a constant defined in the main program. (LIMIT is never more than 10.) For example, if LIMIT is 8, then the function prints the headings from 1 to 8. (*Suggestion*: You may want to use a **for** loop to print the headings instead of mentioning each number.)

PROGRAMMING PROJECTS

21. Many of the programming projects in Chapter 4 can be rewritten to use functions instead of doing the work directly in the main program. Show how to rewrite some of these projects using functions. In each exercise you rewrite, decide exactly what parameter(s) to send to the function and what type of answer the function returns. In some exercises, include more than one function. For example, in Exercise 4-23, one function can do error checking and one can perform calculations.

22. This and the next few exercises explore some ways to determine if one number is divisible by another.

    a. What is the value of 7 % 2? Of 6 % 2? Of 5 % 2? In general, if number has type **int**, what is the value of number % 2 if number holds an even number? What if number holds an odd number?

    b. Write a function, called iseven( ), which receives one parameter x and uses the % operator to determine whether x is divisible by 2.

    c. Rewrite the function from part (b) using truncation on integer division. [*Hint*: Truncation on integer division is illustrated by the difference in the results of these two computations: 2 * (7 / 2) and 2 * (8 / 2). In one case, the result is equal to the original value; in the other case, it is not.]

    d. Write a function isdivisby3( ) to determine whether its parameter x is divisible by 3. Write two versions of your function: one using % and one with truncation on integer division.

23. Write a function isdivisby( ) which receives two parameters: number and divisor. The function determines whether divisor is a divisor of number. For example, the function returns the following values:

    a. If number is 4 and divisor is 3, the function returns 0.
    b. If number is 12 and divisor is 3, the function returns 1.
    c. If number is 12 and divisor is 5, the function returns 0.

    Suggestion: You can use either truncation on integer division or the % operator. See Exercise 22.

24. a. Write a function printalldivisors( ) which receives one parameter, an integer number. The function prints all the divisors of number. For example, if number holds 15, the function prints a line of output that looks like this:

```
Divisors of 15    1 3 5 15
```

    Suggestion: Exercises 22 and 23 discussed several ways to determine whether a given integer divides another. You can set up a loop using one of these methods to test the possible divisors of number (what is the largest possible divisor?).

b. Using the function <u>printalldivisors( )</u>, write a program to print each number from 1 to 40, followed by a list of its divisors.

```
Divisors of 1         1
Divisors of 2         1  2
Divisors of 3         1  3
    . . .
Divisors of 40        1  2  4  5  8  10  20  40
```

25. a. Write a function to find the sum of the proper divisors of a given number <u>n</u>. The proper divisors of <u>n</u> are the numbers less than <u>n</u> that divide it evenly; they do not include <u>n</u> itself. For example, if <u>n</u> is 12, then the sum of the proper divisors is $1 + 2 + 3 + 4 + 6 = 16$. Write a main program that tests the function by reading various values for <u>n</u> and finding the sum of the proper divisors.

   b. A number is called perfect if it is equal to the sum of its proper divisors. For example, 6 is equal to the sum of its divisors $1 + 2 + 3$. A number is deficient if it is greater than the sum of its proper divisors (9 is greater than $1 + 3$). A number is abundant if it is less than the sum of its proper divisors (12 is less than $1 + 2 + 3 + 4 + 6$). Modify your program from part (a) so that it prints the appropriate message (perfect, abundant, or deficient) for each number <u>n</u>.

   c. Modify your program from part (b) so that it computes how many numbers from 1 to 100 are perfect, how many are deficient, and how many are abundant. Print these totals after processing the last number.

26. A number greater than 1 is prime if its only divisors are 1 and itself. For example, the only divisors of 2 are 1 and 2, so 2 is prime. The number 9 has 3 as a divisor, so it is not prime.

   a. Use the program from Exercise 25 (a) to determine whether a number is prime. (Hint: What is the sum of the divisors for a prime number?)

   b. Another way to determine whether a number is prime is to test whether it has any proper divisors greater than 1. If it has none, it is prime. (*Hint*: A simple way to test this is to set a flag or switch to 0 before a **for** loop that processes every possible divisor. Reset the flag to 1 if you find a divisor. If the flag is still 0 at the end of the loop, what does this imply?)

27. The method of testing for divisors in Exercise 26 is extremely inefficient. This exercise discusses several improvements.

   a. Modify the program so that it does not test whether 1 is a divisor of the number (1 must be a divisor—why?).

   b. Modify the program so that it never tests a possible divisor that is greater than the original value of <u>number</u>. Why?

   c. Modify the program so that it never tests a possible divisor that is greater than half the original value of <u>number</u>. What is the only divisor larger than half the value of <u>number</u> that divides it?

   d. Modify the program so that it never tests a possible divisor that is greater than the square root of <u>number</u>. For example, if <u>number</u> is 105, it never tests a possible divisor greater than 10. If you do this, you must print two divisors each time an exact one is found. (Why?) For example, when you find that 3 divides 105, you must also print that 35 divides it.

   e. Compare the original program to the improved versions. Which improvement do you think is the "best?" Why?

28. The factorial of a number <u>n</u>, written <u>n</u>!, is defined as follows:

$$n! = 1 * 2 * ... * (n - 1) * n \qquad (\text{and } 0! = 1)$$

For example, $5! = 1 * 2 * 3 * 4 * 5 = 120$; $3! = 1 * 2 * 3 = 6$.

a. Write a program to do the following: Read in a number n, then use a function to compute n!. (*Suggestion*: Use a **for** loop to compute the product with an appropriate initialization and multiplication step.)

b. Write a program that computes a table of the numbers from 1 to n, together with the factorial of each number. (Do not use a function for this version.) For example, if n is 7, it should print (each pair on a new line):

```
1 1     2 2     3 6     4 24     5 120     6 720     7 5040
```

c. Modify your program from part (a) so that it reads in a series of values for n and computes n! for each value (use a negative value as a trailer).

29. Compare the efficiency of the programs from Exercise 28. (First, you have to specify a way of measuring program efficiency. For example, you can see which program executes fewer instructions.) If you want to compute a large number of consecutive factorial values, which is the more efficient method? If you only want one or two widely spaced factorial values, which is more efficient?

30. Although C++ does not contain an exponentiation operator (e.g., an operator to compute x^y), it does have a standard library function, called pow( ), to compute exponents. Several other computer languages, such as Pascal, do not have any direct way to compute exponents. This exercise explores two possible ways to calculate exponents in these languages.

a. If the exponent y is a positive integer, then exponentiation can be viewed as repeated multiplication. For example, x^3 is x multiplied by itself three times.

   Write a C++ function that accepts two parameters: a real number x and a nonnegative integer y. The function will compute x^y, using a loop for repeated multiplications. In the main program which calls this function, compare the answer to the result from the pow( ) function. (The prototypes for pow( ) and the functions exp( ) and log( ) used below are all in cmath.)

b. In case y is not a positive integer, the method in part (a) cannot be used (why?). However, we can use the following identity:

$$x^y = e^{y \log x} \text{ (assuming } x > 0 \text{)}$$

   Here e is the base of the natural logarithm system and $log\ x$ is the logarithm of x to the base e (the exponent e must be raised to in order to get x). You can use the standard library functions exp( ) and log( ) to evaluate the right-hand side (see Chapter 2).

   Write a C++ function to accept two real parameters, x and y. It computes x^y, using the formula above. Are there any limitations on the parameters to this function?

31. C++ has a library function, rand( ) (the function prototype is located in stdlib.h), which generates random numbers. If n has type **int**, the function call below stores a nonnegative integer value, chosen "at random," in n.

```
n = rand();
```

a. Using rand( ), write a program to generate a list of ten random numbers.

b. Run the program from part (a) a second and third time. What happens?

c. Add the statements below before you generate the first random number (where ... represents some integer value).

```
intval = ...;
srand(intval);
```

This is a call to the parameterless void function <u>srand( )</u>, using <u>intval</u> as a seed to start the process.

Now run the program several times. What happens? Try changing the value assigned to <u>intval</u>. At this point, you might want to read the documentation your compiler has on the <u>rand( )</u> function.

d. How do you generate random numbers in the range from 1 to 6? (*Hint*: You want random values, but you don't want any of them to be 0 or larger than 6.)

e. How do you generate random numbers in the range from 10 to 20? From <u>start</u> to <u>finish</u>?

32. a. Using the ideas in Exercise 31, write a program to simulate tossing a die a hundred times and count how many of the tosses are even numbers. (A die is a cube with the numbers from 1 to 6 written on it.) Then repeat the program using a thousand tosses.

b. Write a program to simulate tossing a pair of dice a hundred times. For example, one toss might give 5 on the first die and 3 on the second; the sum of the dice values for this toss is 8. Count how many of the sums add up to each number from 2 to 12. Then repeat the program using a thousand tosses.

33. Write a complete C++ program to do the following: The main program reads in three bowling scores, <u>score1</u>, <u>score2</u>, and <u>score3</u>. It then calls a series of functions to process these scores.

The main program calls a function <u>validgroup( )</u> to determine if this set of three values forms a valid group. The function <u>validgroup( )</u> receives three parameters. For the group to be valid, each number must be in the range from 0 to 300 (the possible scores in a bowling game). If the group is valid, the function prints a message saying so. If one or more of the numbers is negative or greater than 300, the function prints an overall message that the group is invalid. In addition, for each invalid value, the function prints the score and a message.

If the group is not valid, the main program skips processing and simply goes on to the next group of three values.

If the group is valid, the main program calls a function <u>onegamescore( )</u>, sending it one parameter, the value <u>score1</u>. This value is an integer from 0 to 300 (how can we be sure of this?). The function converts the score into a rating, using the following system: 250 to 300 is a professional game; 200 to 249 is an excellent game; 140 to 199 is a very good game; 100 to 139 is a good game; 50 to 99 is a poor game; below 50 is a horrible game. The function prints a message with the original score and the bowler's rating. Then the main program repeats this process for <u>score2</u> and <u>score3</u>.

Next the main program calls a function <u>avg3scores( )</u>, sending it three parameters: the three scores. The function <u>avg3scores( )</u> finds the average (as an integer) of the three scores and sends it back. The main program prints the average. Finally, the main program calls <u>onegamescore( )</u> again, sending it the resulting average from the function <u>avg3scores( )</u>. The main program then prints three blank lines.

Then the main program goes on to the next group of three values. When the main program runs out of groups (your program must determine this), it prints the final values of three counters it has been keeping track of: the total number of groups processed, the number of valid groups, and the number of invalid groups.

34. Write a complete C++ program to simulate the playing of a game of dice. The program does the following:

a. The main program calls a void function named <u>introduction( )</u> to print out at the top of the first output page a description of what the program does. This function is not sent any parameters and does not return a value.

b. Then the main program asks the user to type in two integer values in the range from 1 to 6. The main program reads the two integers into variables called <u>die1</u> and <u>die2</u> and prints the numbers after they are read in.

c. The main program sends these two integer values to a function named <u>findoutcome( )</u> The function determines the outcome of using these two numbers, according to this scheme:

    i. If the numbers add up to 7 or 11, the player wins, and the function indicates this.

    ii. If the numbers add up to 2 or 12, the player loses, and the function indicates this.

    iii. If the numbers add up to anything else, the player continues, and the function indicates this.

d. When the function returns to the main program, it prints an appropriate message, describing which of the three cases applies in this situation.

e. If the player won or lost, the main program goes back to step (b) to read in two more integers and repeat the process.

    If the player continues, the main program calls a function <u>continueplay( )</u> and sends it the sum of <u>die1</u> + <u>die2</u>. For example, if <u>die1</u> is 4 and <u>die2</u> is 5, then the main program sends the value 9 as a parameter to the function <u>continueplay( )</u>

f. The function <u>continueplay( )</u> asks the player to enter two more integers from 1 to 6. The function determines which of the following applies:

    i. If these two integers add up to 7, the player loses.

    ii. If the two integers add up to the value sent to <u>continueplay( )</u>, the player wins.

    iii. If they add up to anything else, the game continues.

Eventually, the player either wins or loses. Whatever the result, the function should print the two numbers read in each time and the result of this roll of the dice. When the game is over, the function returns to the main program with the outcome (either a loss or a win); the main program continues with the next set of two numbers from step 2.

g. At step (b), if the user types in a special combination (you must determine what this combination is and explain it to the person using the program), the program goes to step (h).

h. At the end, print how many games were won and how many lost.

    Type in a total of about ten games. Have one where the player wins immediately with 7, one where the player wins with 11, a loss with 2, a loss with 12, and have five or six games which continue. If the game continues, make sure that the player wins some and loses some. The output of your program should allow someone to follow the game. Each function should have a good comment explaining two things: what parameter(s) the function will receive and what it will do.

35. Write a complete C++ program to do the following: The main program reads in three values, representing three exam grades.

    The main program calls a function <u>validgroup( )</u> to determine if this set of three values forms a valid group (each value is between 0 and 100). The function sends a signal back to the main program, saying whether this group is valid.

    If the group is not valid, the main program skips processing and simply goes on to the next group of three values.

    If the group is valid, the main program calls a function <u>lettergrade( )</u>, sending it one parameter. This function translates the number into a character, representing the letter grade (90 and above is an A, in the 80s is a B, and so on). The main program prints the result of the function call and repeats this process for all three of the grades.

    Then the main program calls a function <u>avggrades( )</u>, sending it three parameters: the three grades. The function finds the average of the three grades and sends it back. The function returns the average as an integer, ignoring any decimal places (e.g., 87.67 becomes 87).

The main program calls <u>lettergrade( )</u> again, sending it the results of <u>avggrades( )</u>. The main program prints the result of this call to the function with a message saying this is the overall average.

Finally, the main program goes on to the next group of three values until it runs out of groups. At that point, it prints the final values of three counters it has been keeping track of: the total number of groups processed, the number of valid groups, and the number of invalid groups.

EXERCISES USING REFERENCE PARAMETERS—TRACING EXERCISES

36. What is printed by the following program?

```cpp
#include <iostream>
using namespace std;
void whatisit(int &, int &);
int main()
{
    int m=5,n=13,p=7;

    cout << "m is: " << m << " n is: " << n << " p is: " << p << endl;
    whatisit(m,n);
    cout << "m is: " << m << " n is: " << n << " p is: " << p << endl;
    whatisit(p,n);
    cout << "m is: " << m << " n is: " << n << " p is: " << p << endl;
    whatisit(p,m);
    cout << "m is: " << m << " n is: " << n << " p is: " << p << endl;
    return;
}

void whatisit(int &a, int &b)
{
    int temp;

    if (a < b) {
        temp = a;
        a = b;
        b = temp;
    }
    return;
}
```

37. Here are a main program and two functions. Show what is printed as this entire program is executed.

```cpp
#include <iostream>
using namespace std;
int findval(int,int);
void compute(int,int,int,int &);
int main()
{
    int w,y,z;
```

```
        for (int x = 5; x >=1; x—) {
            y = 3;
            z = findval(x,y);
            compute(x,y,z,w);
            cout << x << " " << y << " " << z << " " << w << endl;
        }
        return 0;
}

void compute(int a, int b, int c, int &d)
{
        if (a > b)
            d = a + c;
        else
            d = a + b;
        return;
}

int findval(int a, int b)
{
        int c;

        c = a + b;
        if (c > 4)
            return a;
        return c + a;
}
```

38.   a. Show what is printed by the following program.

```
#include <iostream>
using namespace std;
void changer(int, int &);
int main()
{
        int a = 4, b = 6, c = 2;

        changer(b,a);
        cout << "MAIN " << a << " " << b << " " << c << endl;
        a = 15;   b = 25;   c = 20;
        changer(a,c);
        cout << "MAIN " << a << " " << b << " " << c << endl;
        return 0;
}

void changer(int first, int &second)
{
        int c;

        cout << "TOP " << first << " " << second << endl;
        if (first < second)
            c = -1;
        else
            c = 10;
```

```
        first += c;
        second = second * c;
        cout << "BOTTOM " << first << " " << second << endl;
        return;
    }
```

b. Consider the following calls to the function <u>changer( )</u>; these calls use the variables declared in the main program. Mark each one as valid or invalid. If you mark a call as invalid, explain why.

    i. `b = changer(a,&b)`   ii. `changer(a+1,b)`   iii. `changer(a, b+1)`

39. The person using the program below is ready to type in the integers 1 to 10 in order. However, the program may stop before the user can type in all these values. Show exactly what is printed by the program before it stops.

```cpp
#include <iostream>
using namespace std;
void add(int &);
void subtract(int &);
int main()
{
    int x = 22, y = 1;

    while (y != 5) {
        cin >> y;
        cout << x << " " << y << endl;
        if (y == 1)
            add(x);
        if (y == 2)
            subtract(x);
        if (y == 3)
            x *= 2;
        if (y == 4)
            cout << "illegal input" << endl;
        if (y == 5)
            cout << "no action" << endl;
    }
    cout << "at the end: x = " << x << " and y = " << y << endl;
    return 0;
}

void add(int &w)
{
    w += 5;
    cout << "in add: " << w << endl;
    return;
}

void subtract(int &z)
{
    z -= 10;
    cout << "in subtract: " << z << endl;
    return;
}
```

40. a. Show what is printed by the following program.
    b. Modify the program so that it no longer returns a value; instead, (1) the function becomes a void function; (2) the second parameter to the function is a reference parameter, and the function uses it to return an answer.
    c. Show what the new program prints.

```cpp
#include <iostream>
using namespace std;
int add(int, int);
int main()
{
    int a, sum, ans;

    ans = 0;
    for (a = 1; a <= 5; a++) {
        ans += add(a, sum);
        cout << "in main " << a << " " << ans << endl;
    }
    return 0;
}

int add(int a, int sum)
{
    if (a != 3)
        sum += 10 * a;
    else
        sum = 100;
    cout << "in add: " << a << " " << sum << endl;
    return sum;
}
```

41. Show what is printed by the following program.

```cpp
#include <iostream>
using namespace std;
void flipit(int &, int &, int);
int main()
{
    int a = 2, b = 5, c = 10;

    cout << "first: " << a << " " << b << " " << c << endl;
    flipit(b, a, c);
    cout << "now: " << a << " " << b << " " << c << endl;
    return 0;
}

void flipit(int &p, int &q, int r)
{
    p++;
    q++;
    r = p * q;
    cout << "in flipit: " << p << " " << q << " " << r << endl;
    return;
}
```

42. Show what is printed by the following program.

```cpp
#include <iostream>
using namespace std;
void fancyfunc(int &, int, int &);
int main()
{
    int x = 4, y = 8, z = 12;

    fancyfunc(x,y,z);

    cout << "in main: ";
    cout << x << " " << y << " " << z << endl;

    x = 4; y = 8; z = 10;

    fancyfunc(z,x,y);

    cout << "in main: ";
    cout << x << " " << y << " " << z << endl;

    return 0;
}

void fancyfunc(int & a, int b, int & c)
{
    int d;

    d = a - b;
    a++;

    if (d < 0) {
        c = 50;
        b = 92;
    }
    else {
        c = c + 5;
        b = 43;
    }

    cout << "in fancyfunc: ";
    cout << a << endl << b << " "
        << c << " " << d << endl;
    return;
}
```

43. Show what is printed by the following program.

```cpp
#include <iostream>
using namespace std;
void adder(int, int &);
int main()
{
    int x,z = 7;

    x = 5;
    cout << "first: " << x << " " << z << endl;
    adder(x,z);
```

```
        cout << "second: " << x << " " << z << endl;
        return 0;
}

void adder(int a, int &b)
{
        a++;
        b++;
        cout << " third: " << a << " " << b << endl;
        return;
}
```

44. Show what is printed by the following program.

```
#include <iostream>
using namespace std;
void somechanges(int &, int &, int);
int answer(int,int);
int main()
{
        int a=20, b=7, c=5;
        int result;

        result = answer(a,b);
        cout << result << " " << a << " " << b << " " << c << endl;

        somechanges(a,b,c);
        cout << a << " " << b << " " << c << endl;
        a = 1;
        b = 8;
        c = 6;
        somechanges(a,b,c);
        cout << a << " " << b << " " << c << endl;
        return 0;
}

void somechanges(int &a, int &b, int c)
{
        a += 4;
        c--;
        if (a > b)
            if (b < c)
                 a = 15;
            else
                 b = 100;
        else
            c += 1000;
        cout << "in somechanges " << a << " " << b << " " << c << endl;
        return;
}

int answer(int x,int y)
{
        int c,d;
```

```
                c = x / y + 3;
                d = x % (y + 3);
                cout << "c is " << c << " d is " << d << endl;
                if (c > d)
                        return c;
                else
                        return d;
        }
```

45. Show what is printed by the following program.

```
        #include <iostream>
        using namespace std;
        void modify(int, int &);
        int main()
        {
            int x,z = 7;
            int y;

            x = 5;
            y = z+5;
            cout << "first: " << x << " " << y << " " << z << endl;
            modify(x,z);
            cout << "second: " << x << " " << z << endl;

            modify(x,y);
            cout << "third: " << x << " " << y << " " << z << endl;
            return 0;

        }

        void modify(int a, int &b)
        {
            a++;
            b++;
            cout << a << " " << b << endl;
            return;

        }
```

PROGRAMMING PROJECTS USING REFERENCE PARAMETERS

46. Write a function makefirstmax( ) which receives two integer reference parameters, a and b. When the function is called, values are sent in the parameters a and b. The function stores the larger of the two values in a, and the smaller of the two values in b. (That is, a and b will have one set of values upon entering the function, and another set on leaving it.)

47. Suppose you have a void function called add7( ) that adds a literal 7 to each of its parameters, which are reference parameters. Assume that a program wants to add some value other than 7 to a group of variables.

   a. Is it possible to use add7( ) in its present form?

   b. Show how to modify add7( ) to a new function, addk( ), that does the following: The function addk( ) receives three parameters. The first two (p and q) are the same as the two parameters to add7( ); the third, k, specifies the value to add to p and q.

c. Show how to call <u>addk( )</u> from a main program so that it does each of the following jobs: add 10 to <u>x</u> and <u>z</u>; add –3 to <u>bob</u> and <u>jennifer</u>; add 7 to <u>time</u> and <u>rate</u>; add <u>bonus</u> (a variable) to <u>pay1</u> and <u>pay2</u>.

48. The Euclidean Algorithm is a convenient way to compute the greatest common divisor (*gcd*) of two numbers without doing any division: The *gcd* of two positive integers, x and y, is the largest k that evenly divides both x and y. For example, the *gcd* of 8 and 4 is 4; the *gcd* of 18 and 14 is 2; the *gcd* of 6 and 5 is 1.

   The Euclidean Algorithm works as follows (assume that $x >= y$): subtract y from x, getting a result of z. Then subtract the smaller of y and z from the larger. Repeat this process until 0 is reached. The last non-zero value is the *gcd* of x and y. Here are some examples:

   $$18 - 14 = 4, \ 14 - 4 = 10, \ 10 - 4 = 6, \ 6 - 4 = 2, \ 4 - 2 = 2, \ 2 - 2 = 0.$$

   Therefore, 2 (the last non-zero value) is the *gcd* of 18 and 14.

   $$6 - 5 = 1, \ 5 - 1 = 4, \ 4 - 1 = 3, \ 3 - 1 = 2, \ 2 - 1 = 1, \ 1 - 1 = 0.$$

   Therefore, 1 is the *gcd* of 6 and 5.

   Write a program which uses the Euclidean Algorithm to compute the *gcd*. The program should have at least three functions. One function reads in two data values into variables which are reference parameters. The other two functions divide up the algorithm: one subtracts the smaller value from the larger, and the other subtracts the most recent subtraction result from the previous smaller value.

MORE ON CONTROL STRUCTURES

PROBLEM: Classifying Months and Days

SYNTAX CONCEPTS: do-while loop, nested **if**, **switch**, **break**, **continue**, <u>exit( )</u>, data type **bool**, logical operators

PROGRAMMING CONCEPTS: one function calling another, user-response method for signaling the end of a set of data

CONTROL STRUCTURES: do-while loop, one function calling another, nested **if**, **switch**, **break**, **continue**, <u>exit( )</u>, short-circuit evaluation

PROBLEM-SOLVING TECHNIQUES: defensive programming, error checking, program testing

HOW TO READ CHAPTER 6

OUTLINE:

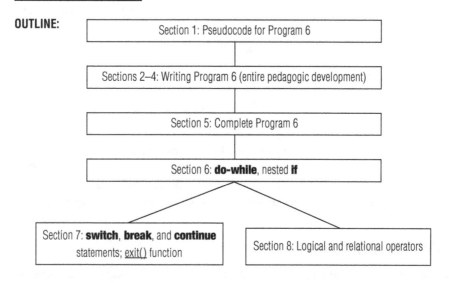

The first five sections completely develop the solution to Problem 6. The remaining three sections discuss additional control structures in C++. It is possible to cover sections 6–8 without first doing sections 1–5.

This chapter solves a simple problem: Given a month and a day within that month (e.g., 6 20, standing for June 20), determine which season of the year (winter, spring, summer, or fall) and which week of the month (1, 2, ..., 5) that date is in. We will continue to use top-down programming and stepwise refinement. A number of important C++ constructions are introduced, including extensive use of nested **if** and **if-else** statements, logical and relational operators, **do-while** loops, and **switch** statements. These new features dramatically increase the complexity of available control structures and allow use of a wide variety of new techniques in our programs.

PROBLEM 6

Write a C++ program that reads in two integer values, standing for a month (from 1 to 12) and a day within the month. The program should classify these two pieces of data into the season the month is in and the week of the month the day is in. The program will print the name of the month, the day, and the results of the classification process. The program should continue to read month-day combinations until the entire set of data has been processed.

Assume that winter consists of three months: 12 (December), 1 (January), and 2 (February); spring consists of three months: 3 (March), 4 (April), and 5 (May); continue for summer and fall. Also assume that all months have exactly 31 days, that the first four weeks in each month have 7 days each, and that week 5 covers days 29, 30, and 31.

The output from the program should look like this (note the format, especially the name of the month):

```
month 5 is May      spring is the season
1 is the week number for day 1

month 6 is June     summer is the season
3 is the week number for day 20

month 11 is November    fall is the season
2 is the week number for day 14
```

The statement of the problem does not discuss what to do if a piece of data is not in the right form (for example, 0 is an illegal value for the day). We will write Program 6 so that it catches many errors of this type, but Exercise 36 discusses other ways to process bad data. In addition, exercises 34 and 35 detail the assumptions about the number of days in each month and months in each season.

SECTION 1 **PSEUDOCODE FOR PROGRAM 6**

In this section, we will develop a pseudocode solution to Problem 6. As usual, we start with rough pseudocode, then refine it into a version that translates more readily into C++.

FIRST PSEUDOCODE SOLUTION TO PROBLEM 6

Here is our rough version of the pseudocode for Program 6:

> *read a month and day*
> *classify the month and day*
> *print the results*
> *repeat the above while there is more data to process*

STYLE WORKSHOP In the last line of the pseudocode, we did not specify how to test whether there is more data to process. Such a test has to be incorporated into the final C++ program. Notice that the test is at the bottom of the loop, not the top.

NEXT REFINEMENT: A FUNCTION TO CLASSIFY THE MONTH AND DAY

Clearly, the next step is to work on the line, "*classify the month and day*." First, we give names to the pieces of data read in; month and day are the obvious choices. It should be clear that each part of the classification process (a month into a season and a day into a week) is fairly involved. As we have learned, it is better not to include all these details in the main program. We will have the main program call a function to perform the classification process, sending month and day as parameters to the function. This function will classify month into one of four seasons and day into one of five weeks and print the results. The name classify( ) is appropriate for the function.

Here is the next version of the pseudocode for the main program:

read month *and* day
call a function classify( ) *to do the classification*
  and print the results
repeat the above while there are more data values to process

PSEUDOCODE FOR THE FUNCTION classify( )

Our next step continues the top-down approach by translating the task of the function classify( ) into detailed pseudocode. Inside the function, we must classify the month into a season and the day into a week. For these two subtasks, we will assume that values are already stored in month and day. Since we have divided the job of classify( ) into two subtasks, it seems better to use a separate function for each one. Since each function will work on one piece of data at a time, each needs just one parameter. In other words, classify( ) calls a function to classify month into one of four seasons and another function to classify day into one of five weeks. Each function will print its own results. Let's use whichseason( ) and whichweek( ) as the names for these two new functions.

We can now give pseudocode for the function classify( ) (which is sent two parameters—month and day):

call a function whichseason( ) *to classify* month *into one of*
    four seasons and print the season
call a function whichweek( ) *to classify* day *into one of*
    five weeks and print the week

Let's look at the format of the output. Earlier, we indicated that a typical line of output looks like this:

```
month 11 is November     fall is the season
2 is the week number for day 14
```

This line of output is constructed by all the functions working together. It contains the original data values (11 and 14), the name of the month (November) corresponding to value 11, and the values computed by the two functions (fall and week 2).

When the functions whichseason( ) and whichweek( ) compute their answers, they should both print them out. The function whichseason( ) prints the season corresponding to the month, and the function whichweek( ) prints a week number from 1 to 5. But how does the month name get printed? Each month is represented by an integer from 1 to 12, but when we print, we want the name of the month rather than the number. Although you might think that the computer knows the names of the months and their order, it doesn't. We'll have to write another function to do the translation from month number to month name. The function classify( ) should call this function, which we can name translate( ). To be precise, we will send translate( ) the number corresponding to a month, and it will print the name of the month without returning anything to <u>classify( )</u>. Below, we add this function call to the pseudocode for <u>classify( )</u>.

> *call a function* translate( ) *to print the month name*
> *call a function* whichseason( ) *to classify* month *into one of*
> *four seasons and print the season*
> *call a function* whichweek( ) *to classify* day *into one of*
> *five weeks and print the week*

PSEUDOCODE FOR THE FUNCTION whichseason( )

Here is a rough version of the pseudocode for <u>whichseason( )</u> (which is sent one parameter—<u>month</u>):

> *classify* month *into one of four seasons*
> *print this answer*
> *return control to the* classify( ) *function*

This can be made more precise. We can classify <u>month</u> into a particular season by comparing its value with the month numbers associated with each season. For example, if we read 12 (December) as the value for <u>month</u>, we can classify it as winter; if we read 4 (April), we can classify it as spring. We could do this classification with 12 separate **if** statements, one for each month. [For example, *if (month == 1)....*] However, it is more efficient to test the months three at a time, combined in each season. We now have the following refinement of the pseudocode for <u>whichseason( )</u>:

> *if* month *is 12, 1, or 2*
>   *the season is winter*
> *if* month *is 3, 4, or 5*
>   *the season is spring*
> *if* month *is 6, 7, or 8*
>   *the season is summer*
> *if* month *is 9, 10, or 11*
>   *the season is fall*
> *print the answer*
> *return control to the* classify( ) *function*

PSEUDOCODE FOR THE FUNCTION whichweek( )

Similarly, we must specify pseudocode for <u>whichweek( )</u> (which is sent one parameter—<u>day</u>). Here is the first rough version:

> *classify* day *into one of five weeks*
> *print the answer*
> *return control to the* classify( ) *function*

Once again, this can be made more precise. We can compare the value of <u>day</u> with the day numbers that correspond to each week. For example, if <u>day</u> has the value 25, then it is between 22 and 28—in week 4; if <u>day</u> has the value 5, we can classify it as week 1. We could use 31 separate

if statements, but that would be ludicrous. Here is a better method (others are discussed in Exercise 39):

> *if* day *is between 1 and 7*
>   *the week is 1*
> *if* day *is between 8 and 14*
>   *the week is 2*
> *if* day *is between 15 and 21*
>   *the week is 3*
> *if* day *is between 22 and 28*
>   *the week is 4*
> *if* day *is 29, 30, or 31*
>   *the week is 5*
> *print the answer*
> *return control to the* classify( ) *function*

ADVANTAGES OF OUR APPROACH

We have now written pseudocode for the functions. In Sections 3 and 4, we will translate each section of pseudocode, writing each one as a function. There are several advantages of dividing up the work. First, it simplifies the main program. As a general rule, as much of the work as possible should be shifted out of the main program and into the functions. In the same way, this division of work simplifies and clarifies the job of <u>classify( )</u>. Each function—including <u>classify( )</u>, <u>whichseason( )</u>, and <u>whichweek( )</u>—has a single well-defined task. This makes testing and debugging easier, as we will discuss in Section 5. Finally, if a function has a single task, it is easier to reuse in another situation.

SELF-CHECK 6-1

1. What is the purpose of the function <u>classify( )</u>?

2. What is the purpose of the function <u>whichseason( )</u>? What is the purpose of the function <u>whichweek( )</u>?

3. Why is it better to use several functions rather than do everything in the main program?

SECTION 2 ## THE MAIN PROGRAM; USING A do-while LOOP AND THE USER-RESPONSE METHOD

In this section, we will evolve the C++ code for the main program from the pseudocode. When we translate the pseudocode into C++, we will introduce two additional features: a new type of loop (a **do-while** loop) and a new way to detect the end of a set of data (the user-response method).

TRANSLATING PSEUDOCODE FOR THE MAIN PROGRAM INTO C++

Here is the main program's pseudocode:

> *read* month *and* day
> *call a function* classify( ) *to do the classification*
>   *and print the results*
> *repeat the above while there are more data values to process*

Following our top-down approach, we begin the C++ program with the main program, then write any needed functions. As usual, the main program starts with a comment and the header:

```
// Program prog6.cpp:
// classify a month-day combination
// in terms of seasons and weeks
#include <iostream>
using namespace std;
int main()
```

Let's assume the main program interactively asks the user to type in the data (first the number of a month, then a day within that month), reads this information, then calls the function classify( ) to perform the classification. We've already decided that classify( ) needs two parameters—the month-day combination. Since the function classify( ) handles the printing through functions that it calls, it does not have to return a value to the main program. Therefore, classify( ) is a void function, and the call to classify( ) from the main program looks like this: *classify(month,day)*.

This is what we have so far for the action portion of the main program:

```
ask the user to enter values for month and day
cin >> month;
cin >> day;
// call a function to classify the month-day
// pair and print the results
classify(month,day);
repeat the above while there are more data values to process
```

DECLARATION OF THE VARIABLES IN THE MAIN PROGRAM

We can flesh this out with declarations for the variables and specific details of the interactive input.

```
{
    int month,day;
    cout << "Type in the number of a month" << endl
        << "from 1 (January) to 12 (December)> ";
    cin >> month;
    cout << "Type in a date within the month, from 1 to 31> ";
    cin >> day;
    // call a function to classify the month-day
    // pair and print the results
    classify(month,day);
```

DETECTING THE END OF THE SET OF DATA: USER-RESPONSE METHOD

Let's continue working on the main program. We must make sure there is a way for the program to end—to detect the end of the set of data. Here is a new method which enables the user to stop the program at any time. After we finish processing a particular month-day pair, we can ask the user the following question: "Do you want to continue?" If the user types in the letter *y* (which is stored as a single character: 'y'), we want to repeat the process by reading in a new month-day pair and calling the classify( ) function; if the user answers 'n', we will stop. This is not quite the same as the trailer-value method, although the two are similar. (See Exercise 37 for a comparison.) To give the user this control, we can issue a prompt, asking whether to continue. Then we can read the user's response into a variable called answer.

The variable <u>answer</u> has type **char**, since the possible values we are interested in are 'y' and 'n'.

```
cout << "Type y to continue; n to stop> ";
cin >> answer;
```

Here is what we have so far; the last two statements are still pseudocode:

```
{
    int month;
    int day;
    char answer;

    cout << "Type in the number of a month" << endl
         << "from 1 (January) to 12 (December)> ";
    cin >> month;
    cout << "Type in a date within the month, from 1 to 31> ";
    cin >> day;
    // call a function to classify the month-day
    // pair and print the results
    classify(month,day);

    cout << "Type y to continue; n to stop> ";
    cin >> answer;

    if answer is 'y' repeat the process given above
    if answer is 'n' stop
}
```

SELF-CHECK 6-2

1. Why is the function <u>classify( )</u> called as a void function?
2. How can we employ the answer typed in by the user to control a program?

WHAT TYPE OF LOOP TO USE IN PROGRAM 6

We have not shown an explicit loop in the pseudocode. While it is clear that a loop is the right way to implement this pseudocode, we do not know in advance how many times the loop should repeat. In fact, we are giving the user the power to end the loop at any time. Therefore, we shouldn't use a **for** loop.

What about a **while** loop? When using a **while** loop, it is sometimes necessary to repeat a statement in two places—once outside the loop, just to get things going, then again at the bottom of the body so that things can continue. This is done because the condition in the **while** loop is tested before the loop is executed for the first time and again before each successive pass. In Program 6, the condition to test involves the user's response (stored in <u>answer</u>) and is something like this: *while (answer == 'y')*. But before the loop is executed the first time, the user has not yet responded to any question, and <u>answer</u> does not have a value. In a case like this, the condition controlling a loop should not be tested the very first time; it makes more sense to test it after the loop has been executed at least once.

As an alternative, we could use a **while** loop in which we set <u>answer</u> to 'y' before the loop is executed for the first time. This can be done either by assigning a value to <u>answer</u> or by the user-response method. However, it is awkward and odd to ask the user "Do you want to continue" before ever processing any values. If you are playing a computer game, you don't expect it to ask "Do you want to play again?" before you've even started to play. The method we are about to introduce is more natural.

A do-while LOOP

Fortunately, C++ has another loop, a **do-while** loop, that is perfect for this situation. The overall structure of the main program says to repeat a series of steps as long as a particular event occurs—the user's typing 'y' in response to the prompt. A **do-while** loop works the way we want because the test is at the bottom of the loop.

The general form of a **do-while** loop looks like this (*cond* is a condition that evaluates to either true or false):

General Form of a do-while Loop

```
do
      body of the loop
while (cond);
```

Let's go through this step by step. First, the body of the loop is executed no matter what the value of *cond* happens to be at this point. When the last line is reached, the condition *cond* is evaluated. If *cond* is true, the loop is executed again, and the condition is retested. (Just as in a **while** loop, the condition in a **do-while** loop usually depends on things that are changing in the body.) If the condition *cond* is false, the body of the loop is not executed again, the loop terminates, and the next statement in the program executes.

The body of a **do-while** loop consists of a single statement. As usual, this restriction can be overcome by using a pair of braces to surround a series of statements.

USING A do-while LOOP IN PROGRAM 6

Let's see how to use a **do-while** loop in Program 6. We want to repeat a series of statements as long as <u>answer</u> has the value 'y'. Note that once the **do-while** loop is finished, we end the main program.

🖳 PROGRAM LISTING

```cpp
// Program prog6.cpp:
// classify a month-day combination
// in terms of seasons and weeks
#include <iostream>
using namespace std;
int main()
{
    int month;
    int day;
    char answer;
    do  {
        cout << "Type in the number of a month" << endl
            << "from 1 (January) to 12 (December)> ";
        cin >> month;
        cout << "Type in a date within the month, from 1 to 31> ";
        cin >> day;
        // call a function to classify the month-day
        // pair and print the results
        classify(month,day);
```

```
         cout << "Type y to continue; n to stop> ";
         cin >> answer;
   } while (answer == 'y');
   return 0;

}
```

PROGRAM TRACE Let's trace a few examples to see how the main program works.

♦ The user enters 5 1 (May 1, the birthday of one of the authors) in response to the first two prompts.

♦ The main program calls the <u>classify()</u> function, which prints that the month is in the spring and the day is in week number 1. Then <u>classify()</u> returns control to the main program.

♦ A prompt then asks whether the user wants to continue. The user enters 'y'. Since the **do-while** condition is true, the program repeats the body of the loop.

♦ The user enters the next <u>month</u>-<u>day</u> pair as 6 20 (June 20, the birthday of the other author).

♦ In the functions, this is classified as summer and week number 3, and control returns to the main program.

♦ Then the user types 'n' in response to the prompt (we have run out of authors). Now the **do-while** condition is false, the loop terminates, and the program continues with the next step.

We have not yet written function prototypes for either <u>classify()</u>, which is called directly by the main program, or for the other functions called by <u>classify()</u>. Once we have written all the functions, the prototypes will be shown in the final version of Program 6.

SELF-CHECK 6-3

1. In a **do-while** loop, when is the test controlling the loop made?
2. How many statements can appear in the body of a **do-while** loop?
3. Is it necessary to enclose the body of the loop in a pair of braces?

SECTION 3   THE FUNCTION <u>classify()</u>

DEFENSIVE PROGRAMMING AND ERROR CHECKING

Before we start the function <u>classify()</u>, there is an important point about the correct way to write a program. The statement of Problem 6 does not say what to do if the user enters an illegal data value (e.g., 15 for <u>month</u>). We could just ignore the issue, saying that the user is at fault in case bad data causes a problem. A more responsible attitude assumes that the user sometimes makes data entry errors and provides a way to catch these errors. In this way, the program protects itself against illegal values. This is called **defensive programming**, by analogy with defensive driving. When we write the function, we will embellish the pseudocode to allow <u>classify()</u> to do error checking by catching bad data values and printing appropriate error messages.

THE FUNCTION classify()

Here is the pseudocode for <u>classify()</u> from Section 1:

call a function translate( ) *to print the month name*
call a function whichseason( ) *to classify* month *into one of four seasons*
and print the season

call a function whichweek( ) *to classify* day *into one of five weeks and print the week*

As we already decided, classify( ) is a void function with two formal parameters. Because day and month are so descriptive, let's continue to use them as the formal parameters in classify( ). Here is the function header, together with an Input-Process-Output comment describing classify( ):

```
// Function classify:
// Input:
//    month—a number specifying a month in the year
//     day—a number specifying a day in the month
// Process:
//    calls a function to print the month name
//    calls a function to determine which season
//    (winter, spring, summer, fall) month is in
//    calls a function to determine which week of
//    the month (1-5) day is in and print result
// Output:
//    none
void classify(int month, int day)
```

According to the process description, classify( ) does three separate things: prints the month name, determines which season month belongs to, and determines which week day belongs to. We already decided to do each in a separate function.

ONE FUNCTION CALLING ANOTHER

A function (such as classify( )) is allowed to call another function (such as whichseason( ) or whichweek( )). This concept is very common in a large program. In Program 6, we will have the main program call classify( ), then have classify( ) call the other functions.

HIGHLIGHTS

♦ In general, the function that issues a call is known as the **calling function**; the one mentioned in the call is the **called function**.

♦ For the first call, the main program is the calling function, and classify( ) is the called function.

♦ Later, when classify( ) calls whichseason( ), classify( ) is the calling function, and whichseason( ) is the called function.

Note that each function returns control to its own calling function.

HANDLING ILLEGAL DATA VALUES

Now let's discuss how to handle bad data. What if the value of month is zero or negative or greater than 12? We will write classify( ) so that if it detects bad data, it will not send the illegal value of month to either translate( ) or whichseason( ). (Later we will handle a bad value for day.) Here is some pseudocode that does what we want:

```
if (month < 1 or month > 12)
    cout << month <<
        " is not a valid value for the month" << endl;
else
    call the functions translate() and whichseason()
```

THE LOGICAL OPERATOR ||

In the pseudocode, we have used the word "or," which corresponds to the **logical operation** "or" in C++. These logical operations are discussed more fully in Section 8. The meaning of the logical operation "or" in C++ is identical to English: one or the other (or both). C++ uses the symbol || for this operation. Using this notation, we have the following **if** statement:

```
if (month < 1 || month > 12)
```

In addition, we have to write the calls to translate( ) and whichseason( ). Since they are both void functions, the calls from classify( ) look like this:

```
translate(month);
whichseason(month);
```

Let's put this together to get the first part of the function classify( ):

```
if (month < 1 || month > 12)
    cout << month <<
        " is not a valid value for the month" << endl;
else  {
    translate(month);
    whichseason(month);
}
```

CALLING THE FUNCTION whichweek()

The call from classify( ) to whichweek( ) is similar. If the value for day is less than 1 or greater than 31, classify( ) will print an error message and not send it to whichweek( ). If the value for day is in the right range, classify( ) will call the function whichweek( ). The call to whichweek( ) is followed by the **return** statement and the closing brace:

```
        if (day < 1 || day > 31)
            cout << day << " is an illegal value for the day";
        else
            whichweek(day);
        return;
}
```

THE ENTIRE FUNCTION classify()

Here is the function classify( ):

```
// ...
void classify(int month, int day)
{
    if (month < 1 || month > 12)
        cout << month <<
            " is not a valid value for the month" << endl;
    else {
        translate(month);
        whichseason(month);
    }
```

```
    if (day < 1 || day > 31)
        cout << day << " is an illegal value for the day" << endl;
    else
        whichweek(day);
    return;
}
```

SELF-CHECK 6-4

1. When function <u>f1</u> calls function <u>f2</u>, which is the calling program? Which is the called program?

2. If function <u>f1</u> calls function <u>f2</u>, and function <u>f2</u> calls function <u>f3</u>, when <u>f3</u> finishes, where does it return control?

3. What symbol is used for the logical operation "or"?

SECTION 4 ## THE REMAINING FUNCTIONS

In this section, we will finish the functions for Program 6. (In Section 6, we discuss several other ways to write them.)

THE FUNCTION translate( )

First, let's write the function <u>translate( )</u>, which receives as a parameter a number representing a month. Recall that <u>translate( )</u> simply changes the number into a name to be printed. We will continue to use <u>month</u> as the name of the parameter. Here are the comment and function header:

```
// Function translate:
// Input:
//    month-a number specifying a month in the year
// Process:
//    translates the number of the month into a
//    name for the month (e.g., 3 into March)
// Output:
//    prints the name associated with month
void translate(int month)
```

The body of translate is straightforward, consisting of a number of **if** statements, one for each month from 1 to 12.

```
{
    cout << endl << "month " << month << " is ";
    if (month == 1)
        cout << "January";
    if (month == 2)
        cout << "February";
    if (month == 3)
        cout << "March";
    if (month == 4)
        cout << "April";
    if (month == 5)
        cout << "May";
```

```
    if (month == 6)
        cout << "June";
    if (month == 7)
        cout << "July";
    if (month == 8)
        cout << "August";
    if (month == 9)
        cout << "September";
    if (month == 10)
        cout << "October";
    if (month == 11)
        cout << "November";
    if (month == 12)
        cout << "December";
    return;
}
```

THE FUNCTION whichseason( )

Next is the function whichseason( ), which receives one parameter called month. Here is the pseudocode from Section 1:

> *classify* month *into one of four seasons*
> *print this answer*
> *return control to the* classify *function*

First comes the comment and header for the function whichseason( ):

```
// Function whichseason:
// Input:
//   month-a number specifying a month in the year
// Process:
//   determines which season month is in
//   (winter, spring, summer, fall)
//   assume winter is December, January, February
//   (make similar assumptions for the other seasons)
// Output:
//   prints the name of the season
void whichseason(int month)
```

In Section 1, we also had a more detailed version of the pseudocode for this particular task:

```
if month is 12, 1, or 2
    the season is winter
if month is 3, 4, or 5
    the season is spring
if month is 6, 7, or 8
    the season is summer
if month is 9, 10, or 11
    the season is fall
print the answer
return control to the classify() function
```

Naturally, it is easier to write the function with this detailed pseudocode. We start by comparing the value of <u>month</u> to the three months classified as winter: 12, 1, and 2 (December, January, and February). If the value of <u>month</u> is equal to any of them, the function <u>whichseason( )</u> should print "winter is the season." Here is an attempt to write the first part:

```
{
    if (month == 12 || 1 || 2)                              // incorrect
        cout << " winter is the season";
```

Unfortunately, as written, this is not correct (the details are discussed in Section 8). In English, we can say "if month is 12 or 1 or 2 …," but this will not work in C++. We have to be more explicit by saying *if (month = = 12 || month = = 1 || month = = 2)*. Here is the correct version of the first **if** statement:

```
    if (month == 12 || month == 1 || month == 2)
        cout <<   " winter is the season";
```

In case the first **if** condition is not true, we must determine whether <u>month</u> is one of the three months in the spring:

```
    if (month == 3 || month == 4 || month == 5)
        cout <<   " spring is the season";
```

Similarly, we check for summer and fall. Then we can end the function. Here is the rest of the code:

```
        if (month == 6 || month == 7 || month == 8)
            cout <<   " summer is the season";
        if (month == 9 || month == 10 || month == 11)
            cout <<   " fall is the season";
    cout << endl;
    return;
}
```

If the value for <u>month</u> is not in the range from 1 to 12, <u>classify( )</u> will not call <u>whichseason( )</u>, so it is not necessary to check for bad values here.

CAUTION You may be tempted to use an **else** statement instead of the last **if**, since it seems clear that if the month is not in the winter, spring, or summer, it must be in the fall. However, doing this in a naive way will not work. We will discuss the correct way to use an **else** in Section 6.

OUTLINE OF THE ENTIRE FUNCTION whichseason( )

Here is an outline of the function <u>whichseason( )</u>:

```
// ...
void whichseason(int month)
{
    if (month == ...)
        cout << "winter is the season";
```

```
    if (month == ...)
        cout << "spring is the season";
    ...
    return;
}
```

THE FUNCTION whichweek( )

Now we can start work on the last function, <u>whichweek( )</u>, which receives one parameter called <u>day</u>. Here is the pseudocode for the function <u>whichweek( )</u> from Section 1:

classify day *into one of five weeks*
print the answer
return control to the classify *function*

The function <u>whichweek( )</u> is simpler than <u>whichseason( )</u> because we are working with consecutive integers. As usual, before we start to translate the pseudocode into C++, we need the function header and introductory comment:

```
// Function whichweek:
// Input:
//    day—a number specifying a day in the month
// Process:
//    determines which week of the month (1-5) day is in
//    assume each week (except the fifth) has 7 days
// Output:
//    prints the week within the month
void whichweek(int day)
```

Once again, recall that we also had a more detailed version of this pseudocode:

if day *is between 1 and 7*
   the week is 1
if day *is between 8 and 14*
   the week is 2
if day *is between 15 and 21*
   the week is 3
if day *is between 22 and 28*
   the week is 4
if day *is 29, 30, or 31*
   the week is 5
print the answer
return control to the classify( ) *function*

THE LOGICAL OPERATOR &&

To determine the number of the week that <u>day</u> is in, we use a method similar to the one in <u>whichseason( )</u>. We ask a series of questions, each of which selects one possible value for the function to return. In English we can say, "if day is between 8 and 14," but C++ must be more specific. For example, if the value in <u>day</u> is more than 7 and also less than or equal to 14, <u>day</u> is in week 2. Here is a pseudocode statement which takes care of this:

```
if (day > 7 and day <= 14)
    cout <<   "2 is the week number for day " << day;
```

This is pseudocode because we still have to translate the word "*and*." As you may guess, it corresponds to the logical operation "and" in C++. The operator for "and" is &&. The C++ statement using the logical **and** operator (&&) is the following:

```
if (day > 7 && day <= 14)
    cout <<   "2 is the week number for day " << day;
```

Here is the entire body of the function:

```
{
  if (day <= 7)
      cout << "1 is the week number for day " << day;
  if (day > 7 && day <= 14)
      cout << "2 is the week number for day " << day;
  if (day > 14 && day <= 21)
      cout << "3 is the week number for day " << day;
  if (day > 21 && day <= 28)
      cout << "4 is the week number for day " < day;
  if (day > 28)
      cout << "5 is the week number for day " << day;
  cout << endl << endl;
  return;
}
```

Because bad data is taken care of in <u>classify( )</u>, we can simplify the first and the last **if** conditions. For the first condition, we do not have to ask whether <u>day</u> is greater than 0; in order for us to reach <u>whichweek( )</u>, that must be true. Similarly, in the last condition, we do not have to ask whether <u>day</u> is less than or equal to 31.

This completes the function <u>whichweek( )</u>, <u>classify( )</u>, and the entire program. The only thing we have to do is put the little pieces together to form Program 6 in the next section.

SELF-CHECK 6-5

1. What symbol is used for the operation "or"?
2. What symbol is used for the operation "and"?
3. What would be bad data for the functions <u>translate( )</u> and <u>whichseason( )</u>? How about for the function <u>whichweek( )</u>?

SECTION 5   ENTIRE PROGRAM 6

In this section, we combine the pieces of C++ code to form Program 6. In addition, we will include the function prototypes and discuss how to test the program.

LOCATION OF FUNCTION PROTOTYPES

The function <u>classify( )</u> is called from the main program. The functions <u>translate( )</u>, <u>whichseason( )</u>, and <u>whichweek( )</u> are called from <u>classify( )</u>. If we include function prototypes in the appropriate place, all four functions can appear before or after the main program.

Here are the function prototypes for all the functions used in Program 6:

```
void classify(int,int);
void translate(int);
void whichseason(int);
void whichweek(int);
```

STYLE WORKSHOP In Chapter 5, we said it is better to put the function prototypes before the beginning of the main program, together with the line containing *#include <iostream>*, which can also be viewed as a collection of function prototypes. If the prototypes appear at the top of the file, any function (main program or other function) which appears later can access them. The function definitions can follow the body of the main program.

OUTLINE OF PROGRAM 6

Now we have the following outline for Program 6. All comments have been eliminated to simplify the format, but some explanations are on the right.

```
#include <iostream>                    compiler directives
using namespace std;
void classify(int, int);               prototypes for the functions
                                          used in Program 6

void translate(int);
void whichseason(int);
void whichweek(int);

int main()                             header for the main program
{

    int month,day;                     main program declarations
    char answer;

    ...                                call to classify( )

}                                      end of the main program

void classify(int month,int day)       header for the function classify( )
{

    ...                                calls to the other functions

}

void translate(int month)              header for the function translate( )
{

    ...

}
```

```
void whichseason(int month)                    header for the function whichseason( )
{
    ...
}
void whichweek(int)                            header for the function whichweek( )
{
    ...
}
```

TESTING THE FUNCTIONS AND THE ENTIRE PROGRAM

Earlier, we traced two examples, 5 1 and 6 20 (May 1 and June 20), to show that the program is working correctly, but we should include representative data values to test all lines of code. This means we need at least one month from each season and one day from each week. It is also important to test the lines of code which catch errors. For example, we need a value of day less than 1 and one greater than 31, and a value of month less than 1 and one greater than 12. We should also test the boundary conditions: day having the values 1 and 31, month being 1 and 12.

In Chapter 5, we discussed how to test a function using a simple driver program. In Program 6, the main program is already so simple that only two things can simplify it: removing the loop and assigning values to day and month instead of reading them in. The function classify( ) is more complicated since it calls the other three functions. We can test those functions by assigning values in classify( ) and calling each function individually.

After running the program on a thorough series of test cases, we can be fairly confident that all the functions are working correctly. At this point, we can start testing the full version of the main program, especially the **do-while** loop; for example, we can test what happens if the user does not answer either 'y' or 'n' to the question about continuing. When we have tested all the pieces, we can be confident the entire program is working correctly.

SELF-CHECK 6-6

1. When a program is being checked, can each function be tested alone?
2. Is it necessary to test a program with bad data or only data that is correct?
3. Can we assume a user always follows directions when typing in data?

PROGRAM 6

Here is the entire program for Problem 6:

🖳 PROGRAM LISTING

```
// Program prog6.cpp:
// classify a month-day combination
// in terms of seasons and weeks
#include <iostream>
using namespace std;
void classify(int, int);
void translate(int);
void whichseason(int);
```

```cpp
void whichweek(int);
int main()
{
    int month,day;
    char answer;
    do   {
        cout <<  "Type in the number of a month" << endl;
        cout <<  " from 1 (January) to 12 (December) > ";
        cin >> month;
        cout <<  "Type in a date within the month, from 1 to 31> ";
        cin >> day;
        // call a function to classify the month-day
        // pair and print the results
        classify(month,day);
        cout <<  "Type y to continue; n to stop> ";
        cin >> answer;
    }  while (answer == 'y');
    return 0;
}

// Function classify:
// Input:
//  month—a number specifying a month in the year
//   day—a number specifying a day in the month
// Process:
//  calls a function to determine the name of
//   the season month is in
//  calls a function to determine which season
//   month is in (winter, spring, summer, fall)
//  calls a function to determine which week
//   of the month (1-5) day is in
//  illegal data values for month or day
//   will be caught
// Output:
//   prints an error message if either
//   month or day has an illegal value
//
void classify(int month, int day)
{
    if (month < 1 || month > 12)
        cout << month <<
            " is not a valid value for the month" << endl;
    else {
        translate(month);
        whichseason(month);
    }
    if (day < 1 || day > 31)
        cout << day << " is an illegal value for the day" << endl;
    else
        whichweek(day);
    return;
}
```

```
// Function translate:
// Input:
//   month—a number specifying a month in the year
// Process:
//   translates the number of the month into a
//    name for the month (e.g., 3 into March)
// Output:
//   prints the name associated with month
void translate(int month)
{
    cout << endl << "month " << month << " is ";
    if (month == 1)
        cout << "January";
    if (month == 2)
        cout << "February";
    if (month == 3)
        cout << "March";
    if (month == 4)
        cout << "April";
    if (month == 5)
        cout << "May";
    if (month == 6)
        cout << "June";
    if (month == 7)
        cout << "July";
    if (month == 8)
        cout << "August";
    if (month == 9)
        cout << "September";
    if (month == 10)
        cout << "October";
    if (month == 11)
        cout << "November";
    if (month == 12)
        cout << "December";
    return;
}
// Function whichseason:
// Input:
//   month—a number specifying a month in the year
// Process:
//   determines which season month is in
//   (winter, spring, summer, fall)
//   assume winter is December, January, February
//   (make similar assumptions for the other seasons)
//    illegal data values for month will be caught
// Output:
//   prints the name of the season
//
```

```
void whichseason(int month)
{
    if (month == 12 || month == 1 || month == 2)
        cout <<   " winter is the season";
    if (month == 3 || month == 4 || month == 5)
        cout <<   " spring is the season";
    if (month == 6 || month == 7 || month == 8)
        cout <<   " summer is the season";
    if (month == 9 || month == 10 || month == 11)
        cout <<   " fall is the season";
    cout << endl;
    return;
}

// Function whichweek:
// Input:
//   day-a number specifying a day in the month
// Process:
//   determines which week of the month (1-5) day is in
//   assume each week (except the fifth) has 7 days
// Output:
//   prints the week within the month
void whichweek(int day)
{
    if (day <= 7)
        cout <<   "1 is the week number for day " << day;
    if (day > 7 && day <= 14)
        cout <<   "2 is the week number for day " << day;
    if (day > 14 && day <= 21)
        cout <<    "3 is the week number for day " << day;
    if (day > 21 && day <= 28)
        cout <<    "4 is the week number for day "<< day;
    if (day > 28)
        cout <<   "5 is the week number for day " << day;
    cout << endl << endl;
    return;
}
```

This completes Program 6.

STYLE WORKSHOP Program 6 is a long program and contains a series of functions which add to its size. If we did all the work in the main program, the overall program would be shorter, but it would probably be much harder to debug and modify. In most cases, it pays to divide the work up into smaller modules, writing each as a function, then combining them to form the complete program.

SECTION 6   MORE ON do-while LOOPS; NESTED if STATEMENT

In the next two sections, we discuss a number of ways that C++ directs the flow of control in a program. We begin by comparing **while** and **do-while** loops. Then we introduce a more generalized version of the **if-else** statement called a nested **if** statement.

COMPARING while AND do-while LOOPS

Let's start by comparing **while** and **do-while** loops. There is really just one important difference. In a **while** loop, the condition controlling the loop is tested at the top in the loop header; therefore, the test is made as soon as the loop begins. In a **do-while** loop, the condition is tested at the bottom; therefore, the test is made after the loop has executed the first time. In a **while** loop, if the condition controlling the loop is false initially, the body is never executed. In a **do-while** loop, even if the condition controlling the loop is false the first time, the body of the loop has already been executed once by that time. As a result, the body of a **do-while** loop is always executed at least once, but the body of a **while** loop may be skipped completely.

Figure 6-1A gives the general form for a **do-while** loop, and Figure 6-1B gives the general form for a **while** loop. Study these pictures until the difference between the two loops is clear. (Actually, anything that can be done with one type of loop can also be done with the other, with appropriate modifications. See Exercise 17.)

General Form for a do-while Loop versus a while Loop

```
do                            while (cond)
     body of the loop              body of the loop
while (cond)
```

SELECTING ONE FROM A SERIES OF ALTERNATIVES

Two other C++ control structures are often useful, especially when a programmer must select from a large series of alternatives, as we did with whichweek( ) and whichseason( ). One of these is called a nested **if** construction; the other is a **switch** statement. Let's begin with the nested **if**. (It may be helpful to review Chapter 3, Section 6, on the basic **if-else** construction.)

Assume that we have a situation with three mutually exclusive outcomes (see Figure 6-2). More precisely, assume that it is impossible for *cond-1* and *cond-2* to be true at the same time. If *cond-1* is true, *st-1* should be executed; if *cond-2* is true, *st-2* should be executed; if neither condition is true, *st-3* should be executed. We can interpret "neither condition is true" as *cond-1* and *cond-2* are false; we will call this *cond-3*. Thus, *cond-1 cond-2*, and *cond-3* are mutually exclusive.

To make things more concrete, here is a specific example with actual conditions. Everything also holds for the general situation of two conditions.

FIGURE 6-1 *A.* General form for a **do-while** loop
            B. General form for a **while** loop

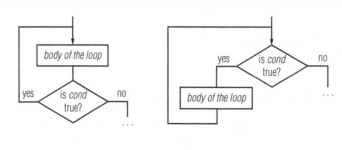

A   B

FIGURE 6-2 Selecting one of the alternatives

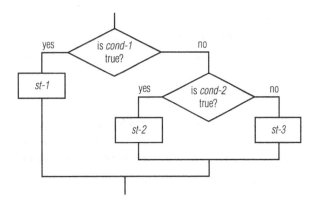

EXAMPLE 6-1

Let's assume that we are testing the value stored in variable x. The three conditions to be tested are $x > 0$, $x == 0$, and $x < 0$.

Given Figure 6-2 to translate into C++, the first idea that occurs to most people is the following C++ code:

```
if (x > 0)
      st-1;
if (x == 0)
      st-2;
if (x < 0)
      st-3;
```

In most cases, this works out. However, there is a special circumstance in which it does not work. (What if the action taken in *st-1* or *st-2* affects a later condition? For example, suppose *st-1* is something like this: $x = x - 1$. See Exercise 19.)

Although this code usually works, let's look at a possible shortcut: Instead of explicitly testing whether or not *cond-3* is true, we will use an **else** statement on the second **if**:

```
if (x > 0)                              // there is a logical error here
      st-1;
if (x == 0)
      st-2;
else
      st-3;
```

Does this shortcut work? Let's trace an example. There are three cases to consider, corresponding to the three possible outcomes. Assume first that x is -7; then the condition $x < 0$ is true (and the other two false). According to the example, we should execute *st-3*. Let's see if the C++ code works. Since the condition $x > 0$ is false, we don't execute *st-1*; the condition $x == 0$ is also false, so we don't execute *st-2*; the **else** statement directs us to execute *st-3*, which is fine.

Now assume that x is 0; then the condition $x == 0$ is true (and the other conditions are false). According to the example, we should execute *st-2*. Let's see if that works. The first **if** condition is false, the second **if** condition is true, so we execute *st-2*; because of the **else** statement, we skip *st-3*.

So far, the C++ code has been right in two cases; now we will check the third. Assume that x is 7; then $x > 0$ is the only condition that is true. According to the example, we should execute *st-1*. When we try it out, unfortunately the program does not stop after testing the first condition. Instead, it goes on to ask the second question: Is $x == 0$ true? Since it is not, we skip *st-2*, but because of the **else** statement, we execute *st-3*. Therefore, the C++ code is not a correct translation of Figure 6-2 because we have executed both *st-1* and *st-3*.

The problem is that in Figure 6-2, if the first alternative is true, we don't even bother to ask about the second and third. But in this C++ code, regardless of the outcome of the first **if**, we ask the second question.

THE NESTED if CONSTRUCTION

To specify that we want to execute *st-1* or test $x == 0$ but not both, we can use a **nested if-else** (sometimes called a **nested if**) construction. (The indentation shown below improves clarity but is not strictly necessary. Another indentation pattern is shown later.) Here is an example:

```
if (x > 0)
    st-1;
else
    if (x == 0)
        st-2;
    else
        st-3;
```

The entire second **if** statement [*if (x == 0) ... st-3*] is now the **else** statement of the first **if**. When the first **if** condition is true, we execute *st-1* and skip the **else** statement; we don't test $x == 0$. But when the first **if** condition is false, we use the second **if** to choose between *st-2* and *st-3*. In this case, if $x > 0$ is false, we do test $x == 0$.

Let's verify that this is a correct C++ translation of Figure 6-2. Table 6-1 summarizes the various cases to consider. The top line reads as follows: If $x > 0$ is true [regardless of the outcome of $x == 0$], we execute *st-1*; the other lines explain the alternatives.

Since Figure 6-2 matches the C++ in every case (would it be enough to match in all but one?), the translation is correct.

NOTE

Some people reserve the term "nested **if**" for a situation in which the second **if** occurs on the true branch of the first **if** and the term "cascaded **if**" for one where the second **if** occurs on the false branch. We will use nested **if** for any structure that contains one **if** inside another.

ADVANTAGES OF THE NESTED if VERSION

The nested **if** method is preferable to the one involving three **if** statements for reasons of correctness as well as efficiency and flexibility. First, as we saw, there are special circumstances in which the three-**if** method will not give the correct answer. In addition, the nested **if** construction is much closer to the spirit of the original diagram, which contains two questions, not three. The three-**if** method assumes that the two conditions *cond-1* and *cond-2* can never be true at the same time, while the nested **if** method does not have to make this assumption.

TABLE 6-1　Cases for Figure 6-2

$x > 0$	$x == 0$	**Figure 6-2**	C++
true	–	st-1	st-1
false	true	st-2	st-2
false	false	st-3	st-3

The nested **if** method is also simpler. When a series of **if** statements is replaced by a nested **if**, the individual conditions to be tested can sometimes be simplified.

EXAMPLE 6-2a
(original indenting style)

For example, a nested **if** version of the <u>whichweek( )</u> function looks like this:

```
if (day <= 7)
    cout << "1 is the week number for day " << day;
else
    if (day <= 14)
        cout << "2 is the week number for day " << day;
    else
        if (day <= 21)
            cout << "3 is the week number for day " << day;
        else
          if (day <= 28)
              cout << "4 is the week number for day " << day;
          else
              cout << "5 is the week number for day " << day;
cout << endl << endl;
```

The **if** conditions have been simplified. For example, the second condition to be tested is now simply *if (day <= 14)*. We don't have to say *if (day > 7 && day <= 14)* because if we reach this point in the nested **if** structure, the condition *(day > 7)* must be true (Exercise 18 has a similar example). In addition, the last possible value to return (in this case, 5) does not need to be preceded by an **if** condition. If we reach this point, 5 must be the correct value.

Finally, the nested **if** version is more efficient. In the three-**if** version, all the conditions must always be tested; in the nested **if** version, when the first condition is true, the second **if** can be skipped completely. When there are more than three choices (four in the <u>whichseason( )</u> function, and five in the <u>whichweek( )</u> function), the savings in time can be substantial when a nested **if** is used.

One other point: The order in which we place the conditions to be tested in a nested **if** is sometimes significant, since the first condition is always tested, whereas some of the others may be skipped (see Exercise 21).

CASCADING if, OTHER INDENTING STYLES IN A NESTED if

Unfortunately, a nested **if** covering more than three cases often has a major disadvantage. The various **if** conditions and **else** statements start shifting to the right, as we can see in Example 6-2a. This is especially serious if the conditions to be tested are complicated. Even if the structure looks good on the screen, when it is printed, the code wraps around from one line to the next, making the overall program listing hard to follow. A nested **if** that continues to have **else if … else if** is called a **cascading if** and often makes the program difficult to read.

There is an alternative which most programmers choose. Instead of continuing to indent each succeeding **if** and **else**, put *else if (…)* on a single line and start each one under the original **if**. Example 6-2b shows how to rewrite Example 6-2b using this format.

EXAMPLE 6-2b
(preferred indenting style)

```
if (day <= 7)
    cout << "1 is the week number for day " << day;
else if (day <= 14)
    cout << "2 is the week number for day " << day;
```

```
else if (day <= 21)
    cout << "3 is the week number for day " << day;
else if (day <= 28)
    cout << "4 is the week number for day " << day;
else
    cout << "5 is the week number for day " << day;
cout << endl << endl;
```

Note that the entire structure fits compactly on the screen (and the printed page), and the various conditions are neatly aligned. Most programmers consider this version significantly easier to read than the other one. When there are three or more **if** statements, we will follow this format.

STYLE WORKSHOP In Example 6-2, we have four **if** statements (with five alternatives), which makes the original version cascade to the right. If there are just two **if** statements (with three alternatives), the cascade is not too pronounced, and the program may be quite readable, as in Example 6-1. If there are only two **if** statements (three alternatives), you may prefer to follow the fully indented style.

OTHER EXAMPLES OF A NESTED if CONSTRUCTION

A nested **if** construction can be used for other situations as well. Figure 6-3 is a slight modification of Figure 6-2. The C++ translation is shown in Example 6-3; we leave it to you to construct a table proving that it works (see Exercise 7).

EXAMPLE 6-3

```
if (cond-1)
    if (cond-2)
        st-1;
    else
        st-2;
else
    st-3;
```

FIGURE 6-3   Example 6-3: another way of selecting one of three alternatives

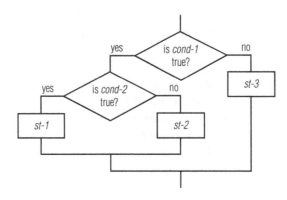

FIGURE 6-4 Example 6-4: a complex example of selecting alternatives

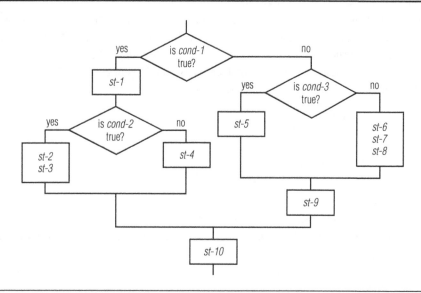

Finally, here is a complicated example that illustrates the use of pairs of braces to execute more than one instruction when the **if** condition is either true or false. See Figure 6-4.

EXAMPLE 6-4   Figure 6-4 translates into C++ as follows:

```
if (cond-1) {
    st-1;
    if (cond-2) {
        st-2;
        st-3;
    }
    else
        st-4;
}
else {
    if (cond-3)
        st-5;
    else {
        st-6;
        st-7;
        st-8;
    }
    st-9;
}
st-10;
```

STYLE WORKSHOP As the complexity of this example suggests, it is easy to go astray in a series of nested **if** statements and pairs of braces. Proper indenting and aligning help avoid this problem. Above all, be sure that every opening brace has a matching closing brace.

RESOLVING THE AMBIGUOUS else

There is one more special case of a nested-**if** to discuss. Let's first look back at Figure 6-3, in which the second condition is tested in case the first condition is true. Note that there are two conditions and two **else** statements, making clear the association of an **if** and its **else**.

Now assume that you are given the two options in Figure 6-5. When trying to translate this figure into C++, your first attempt may be this:

```
if (cond-1)
    if (cond-2)
        st-1;
? ←else→ ?
    st-2;
st-3;
```

We have put two question marks into the C++ code to indicate two possible places to put the keyword **else**. It is not clear whether the **else** is associated with the first **if** or the second **if**. In translating Figure 6-3, where there were two **else** statements, it was clear which **else** went with which **if**. But there are two options in Figure 6-5, and it is unclear which one this code represents.

C++ uses the following rule to resolve this problem: An **else** statement is associated with the closest preceding unmatched **if**. Using this rule, the compiler determines that the **else** statement goes with *if (cond-2)*.

EXAMPLE 6-5 Because of the C++ rule, the code below, with proper indenting and alignment for human readers, translates Figure 6-5A:

```
if (cond-1)
    if (cond-2)
        st-1;
    else
        st-2;
st-3;
```

FIGURE 6-5 Two options for nested **if**

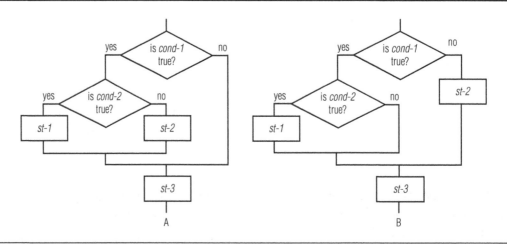

Thus, part (a) of Figure 6-5 is correctly translated by the C++ code. If you want to represent Figure 6-5B, there are several ways to do so. The problem cannot be solved by indenting and alignment (putting the word **else** directly under the first **if**) because the compiler ignores indenting. One solution which does work is using a pair of braces to force the matchup of the **if** and its **else**, as shown below in Example 6-6.

EXAMPLE 6-6

Use braces as follows to translate Figure 6-5B:

```
if (cond-1) {
    if (cond-2)
        st-1;
}
else
    st-2;
st-3;
```

The pair of braces indicates which statements which should be done if cond-1 is true; since the braces end before the **else**, the **else** is forced to be done if cond-1 is false.

EXAMPLE 6-7

We can also use a null **else** to represent Figure 6-5B:

```
if (cond-1)
    if (cond-2)
        st-1;
    else;
else
    st-3;
```

The null **else** (an **else** with no statement following it, but just a semicolon) indicates that nothing should be done if cond-2 is false. You can think of a null **else** as an **else** followed by a **null statement**, which is just a semicolon. In other languages which do not use braces, a null **else** is the only way to translate Figure 6-5B, but this is not the preferred technique in C++.

SELF-CHECK 6-7

1. In a nested-**if**, when both conditions are true, which condition has preference?
2. In order to select one from four alternatives, how many individual **if** statements are needed? In a nested-**if** version, how many conditions have to be tested?
3. How could braces be used to clarify the translation of Figure 6-5A?

SECTION 7 **ADDITIONAL CONTROL STRUCTURES: switch STATEMENT; break AND continue STATEMENTS; exit() FUNCTION**

THE switch STATEMENT

C++ has another method of selecting one from a series of alternatives that is sometimes preferable to the nested **if** construction. It is called a **switch statement** and can be thought of as a question with any number of possible outcomes, not just the two in an **if-else** statement.

General Form of a switch Statement

The basic form of the **switch statement** follows (this form does not include a **default** clause):

```
switch (selector)  {
    case value-1:
        st-1;              // group-1
        st-2;
        ...
        break;

    case value-2:          // group-2
        st-3;
        ...
        break;
    ...

    case value-n:          // group-n
        ...

}
```

The value (*value-1*, *value-2*, ..., *value-n*) of the integer expression <u>selector</u> determines which group of statements to begin executing. Once a group is chosen, statements in that and succeeding groups are executed until the end of the **switch** statement or until execution of a **break statement**. At that point, the **switch** statement is complete, and execution continues with the statement after the closing brace. (In this example, because each group has a **break** statement, we do not automatically fall through into the next group.)

Now let's go through this basic form in more detail.

♦ The various values that *selector* can assume are listed as *value-1*, *value-2*, and so on. These values must be constants, not expressions or variables.

♦ If the value of *selector* is *value-1*, then the group containing *st-1*, *st-2*, ..., **break** is executed.

♦ If the value of *selector* is *value-2*, then the group containing *st-3*, ..., **break** is executed.

♦ In each group, because of the **break**, the rest of the alternatives are skipped.

♦ If *selector* has a value that is not listed, the **switch** statement does nothing, and processing continues after the closing brace. (This assumes there is no **default** clause, which is discussed later.)

♦ If we don't want to take any action when a given alternative occurs, we can use just a **break** statement.

A SIMPLE EXAMPLE OF A switch STATEMENT

Before we talk more about restrictions and special cases, let's look at a specific example.

EXAMPLE 6-8   Assume that we want to determine whether a given number (stored in <u>anynumber</u>) is a multiple of 3, 1 more than a multiple of 3, or 1 less than a multiple of 3. Also assume that <u>anynumber</u> has a value to begin with. In the code shown below, note that <u>remainder</u> has type <u>int</u>; in fact, the only values it can have are 0, 1, and 2 because of the way the modulus or remainder operator % works. Therefore, we can use <u>remainder</u> as the expression to be tested.

```
int anynumber,remainder;
...
remainder = anynumber % 3;
switch (remainder) {
  case 0:
      cout << anynumber << " is a multiple of 3";
      break;
  case 1:
      cout << anynumber << " is 1 more than a multiple of 3";
      break;
  case 2:
      cout << anynumber << " is 1 less than a multiple of 3";
}
```

PROGRAM TRACE Let's trace some examples.

◆ If <u>anynumber</u> has the value 11, <u>remainder</u> is 2, and we print a message that 11 is 1 less than a multiple of 3.

◆ If <u>anynumber</u> is 7, <u>remainder</u> is 1, and we print a message that 7 is 1 more than a multiple of 3.

◆ If <u>anynumber</u> is 24, <u>remainder</u> is 0, and we print a message that 24 is a multiple of 3.

In this example, the **switch** statement provides a convenient way of selecting one of three alternatives.

STYLE WORKSHOP We can eliminate the variable <u>remainder</u> and use *anynumber % 3* directly, as follows:

```
switch (anynumber % 3) {
  ...
}
```

THE break STATEMENT

Now let's discuss the role of the **break** statement, which is often included in each group of statements except the last one. In general, C++ uses the **break** statement to terminate a control structure. As we'll soon see, **break** can terminate execution of a loop. In a **switch** statement, **break** comes at the end of a group of statements to terminate the action. Including **break** is not strictly necessary, but if it is omitted, we "fall through" from one group of statements to another.

For instance, in Example 6-8, assume that <u>anynumber</u> has the value 24. If we remove the **break** statement in *case 0*, after printing the message saying <u>anynumber</u> is a multiple of 3, we fall into the next group of statements. In this case, we also print a message saying <u>anynumber</u> is 1 more than a multiple of 3, which is not true.

There are some rare cases when we purposely want to go from one group of statements to the next, but almost every **switch** statement has **break** statements to separate groups. The last group does not need a **break** statement (why not?), but some people like to put one in anyway so that additional conditions can be easily added.

ANOTHER EXAMPLE OF A switch STATEMENT: THE default CLAUSE

In some cases the selector can have many values which we do not wish to list explicitly in the <u>case</u> statements (there may be many values of this sort). A **default clause** can be used to catch unwanted or illegal values (this is called **error trapping**). Let's consider another example, which shows that several values of the selector can lead to the same action.

EXAMPLE 6-9 We read in an integer value from 2 to 9 and classify it into one of four categories: an even prime number (2), an even number which is not prime (4, 6, or 8), an odd prime number (3, 5, or 7), or an odd number which is not prime (9). In this example, we use a **default clause** to handle values outside the range 2-9.

Here is a **switch** statement that performs the classification and prints the result:

```
int number;

cout << "type in a number from 2 to 9> ";
cin >> number;
switch (number) {
  case 2:
      cout << number << " is an even prime" << endl;
      break;
  case 4:
  case 6:
  case 8:
      cout << number << " is an even non-prime" << endl;
      break;
  case 3:
  case 5:
  case 7:
      cout << number << " is an odd prime" << endl;
      break;
  case 9:
      cout << number << " is an odd non-prime number" << endl;
      break;
  default:
      cout << number << " is not in the range from 2 to 9" << endl;
}
```

Note that it is possible to have more than one value in a particular alternative. For example, 4 and 6 are both classified as even nonprime numbers. Each of the values from 2 to 9 should be mentioned explicitly as possible values for the selector.

Now let's discuss the **default** clause. We have provided actions for values of number from 2 to 9, but it can hold many other possibilities. If, through some error in typing in data, some other value is stored in number, a **switch** statement without a **default** clause does nothing. It is better to catch this mistake and print an error message. The remaining alternatives can be grouped together in a **default** clause; the action of this group is to print an error message.

For example, if number holds 3, a message saying 3 is an odd prime number is printed; if number holds 8, a message saying 8 is an even nonprime number is printed. However, if number holds an inappropriate value (for example, 15, which is value of type **int** but not something we are trying to classify), an error message is printed by the **default** clause.

STYLE WORKSHOP Without a **switch** statement, how could we solve the problem of classifying the numbers? One possibility is a long series of **if** statements, one for each possible value of number; another is a single nested **if** instead of separate **if** statements. By comparison, the **switch** statement is much simpler to write and easier to follow. Notice how close the C++ statements are to the English-language description of the process. The natural correspondence would not be nearly as clear if we used some other method. In general, anything that can be done with a **switch** statement is also possible with a series of **if** statements or a nested **if** construction (see Exercise 24). However, if the problem can be solved with a **switch** statement, that is usually preferable to some type of **if**.

RESTRICTIONS ON THE USE OF A switch STATEMENT

Unfortunately, there are some limitations on the use of the **switch** statement.

◆ The most important one is that the selector must be an expression whose underlying data type is an integer: **int** or **char**. For example, an expression of type **double** or **float** cannot be used. In this case, a programmer has the inconvenience of translating a noninteger type into an appropriate form.

◆ Second, each possible value for the selector must be a constant, not a variable or an expression.

◆ A third major restriction is the need for a **break** statement if we do not want to drop from one group of statements to the next. (Curiously, Example 6-9 can be reorganized to give an equivalent result without a **break** on each path. See Exercise 23.)

C++ LOOP CONTROL FEATURES: break AND continue STATEMENTS

C++ has two statements which are useful for loop control: **break** and **continue**. These statements can be used in all three types of loops (**for** loops, **while** loops, and **do-while** loops).

In a typical situation, the body of a **for** loop is executed a fixed number of times, depending upon the starting value of the **for** loop index and the test condition. In the simplest case, on each iteration through the body of the loop, the control variable increases by 1. For example, consider this **for** loop header:

```
for (int i = 4; i <= 6; i++)
```

We expect this loop to be executed exactly three times, with i having the values 4, 5, and 6. However, there may be situations when the programmer wants to skip a particular iteration of the body of the loop or terminate the execution of the entire loop structure before all values of the **for** loop index have been used. As we will see, the **continue statement** can be used in the first case and the **break** statement in the second.

Let's first consider a situation in which, for certain values of the **for** loop index, we want to skip execution of some or all of the code within the body. To do this, we can use the **continue** statement.

EXAMPLE 6-10 Assume that we have this loop, which is designed to skip part of the processing if i has the value 5 but do all of it if i has the value 4 or 6. In general, the code for *first part of the process* and *second part of the process* can be any combination of C++ statements; in this particular example, each part consists of a single print statement.

```
for (int i = 4; i <= 6; i++) {
    // first part of the process
    cout << "first part with i = " << i << endl;
    if (i == 5)
        continue;
    // second part of the process
    cout << "second part with i = " << i << endl;
}
```

PROGRAM TRACE As usual, the body of this for loop is executed for each value of i from 4 to 6.

◆ When i has the value 4, the program does both parts of the processing, and two lines of output are printed.

◆ When i is 5, the first part of the processing is done, but the **continue** statement causes the second part to be skipped. Only a single line of output is printed.

◆ The program continues with the next iteration through the body of the loop with i = 6. On this pass, both lines of output are printed.

Therefore, execution of the **for** loop generates the following output:

```
first part with i = 4
second part with i = 4
first part with i = 5
first part with i = 6
second part with i = 6
```

Now let's discuss a situation in which we want to terminate the entire execution of the **for** loop. To do this, we can use the **break** statement we've already discussed.

EXAMPLE 6-11 Consider the following version of Example 6-10, in which the **continue** statement is replaced by a **break** statement. This loop terminates when i has the value 5.

```
for (int i = 4; i <= 6; i++) {
    // first part of the process
    cout << "first part with i = " << i << endl;
    if (i == 5)
        break;
    // second part of the process
    cout << "second part with i = " << i << endl;
}
```

PROGRAM TRACE

◆ When i has the value 4, the program does both parts of the processing, and two lines of output are printed.

◆ When i is 5, the first part of the processing is done, but the **break** statement terminates the entire loop. Only a single line of output is printed. Note that i never has the value 6.

Execution of this loop produces the following output:

```
first part with i = 4
second part with i = 4
first part with i = 5
```

After a loop terminates because of a **break** statement, the program resumes execution with the statement after the loop. In a sense, we "break out" of the loop. In contrast, a **continue** statement does not terminate the entire loop; instead the loop "continues."

USING break AND continue WITH A while OR do-while LOOP

As we noted, **break** and **continue** statements can be used with **while** or **do-while** loops as well.

EXAMPLE 6-12

Assume that we want to use a loop to read in a series of data values and process them. If a data value is positive, we want to do both steps of the processing. If the data value is negative, we want to perform step 1 but skip step 2. In either case, we want the loop to keep executing. However, if the data value is 0, we want the loop to terminate after processing steps 1 and 2 with the 0 value.

Here is a piece of code which implements these ideas using a **do-while** loop (for simplicity, we have used pseudocode for the two processing steps):

```
int datavalue;
do {
    cout << "type in a data value; use 0 to terminate> ";
    cin >> datavalue;
    step 1 of the processing
    if (datavalue < 0)
        continue;
    step 2 of the processing
} while (datavalue != 0);
```

Do you see how this works? Can you predict what will happen for the values 15, −3, and 0?

Now let's consider a version of the problem from Example 6-12 in which the value 0 is a termination signal (and everything else stays the same), but the 0 should not be processed at all. In this case, we can use a **while** loop with a peculiar header condition: *while (1 == 1)* or even *while(1)*. Normally, this type of **while** condition would cause an infinite loop (why?). However, because we have added a **break** statement, the loop can terminate when the value of <u>datavalue</u> is 0.

EXAMPLE 6-13

Here is a **while** loop containing both **break** and **continue** statements which implements these ideas:

```
int datavalue;

while (1 == 1) {
    cout << "type in a data value; use 0 to terminate> ";
    cin >> datavalue;
    if (datavalue == 0)
        break;
    step 1 of the processing
    if (datavalue < 0)
        continue;
    step 2 of the processing
}
```

What happens if a positive value is read in? What if a negative value is read in? What if the value of <u>datavalue</u> is 0?

THE exit() FUNCTION

C++ has other ways to control program execution; the most important is the <u>exit()</u> function. If either a function or a main program is executing, a call to the function <u>exit()</u> immediately terminates the entire program, returning control to the operating system. By convention, if the termination is normal, the call to the function looks like this, with 0 sent as a parameter to underline{exit( )}:

```
exit(0);
```

If the termination is considered abnormal, a value other than 0 is sent to the underline{exit( )} function. For example, a call to the function could look like this:

```
exit(1);
```

EXAMPLE 6-14 In the function underline{classify( )}, if the value for underline{month} (or underline{day}) is not valid, underline{classify( )} can stop the program and signal that it has detected bad data by using the following:

```
if (month < 1 || month > 12) {
    cout << month << " is not a valid value for the month" << endl;
    cout << " this program is terminating prematurely" << endl;
    exit(1);
}
else ...
```

This call to underline{exit( )} terminates the entire program.

STYLE WORKSHOP Different codes can signal different error conditions. The return value can be checked by other programs which may use this program's results or by the operating system (this is most common in Unix). Many programmers consider it good style to terminate every main program with underline{exit(0)} for normal completion.

Exercises 28 to 33 contain more material on the features discussed in this section.

THE goto STATEMENT

C++ has an additional control structure, called a **goto statement**, that can also control execution of a loop. In general, the **goto** statement allows a program to transfer control from one point to any other point. (In fact, calls to **break** and **continue** can be thought of as special cases of the **goto** statement.) Unrestricted use of the **goto** leads to programs that are very hard to debug or modify. For this reason, structured programming (see Chapter 4, Section 5) strongly discourages its use. Given all of the control structures available in C++, programmers should never have to use a **goto**. Therefore, we will not use it.

SELF-CHECK 6-8

1. Can a **switch** statement replace a nested **if** in all cases?

2. In Example 6-9, what happens if the **break** statements are removed from each group? For example, what is printed for 2? For 6? For 5? Are any of the answers still correct?

3. If a main program calls function underline{func1( )}, and function underline{func1( )} calls function underline{func2( )}, what happens if underline{func2( )} executes the statement underline{exit(1)}?

SECTION 8   **LOGICAL AND RELATIONAL OPERATORS, SHORT-CIRCUIT EVALUATION, DATA TYPE bool**

Program 6 introduced several new operations that are useful with complex questions. Our last topic in this chapter is to study these operations, which are performed by logical and relational operators. We will also talk briefly about short-circuit evaluation of expressions.

THE RELATIONAL OPERATORS

The six basic **relational operators** were introduced in Chapter 2, Section 2. They are <, <=, >, >=, ==, and !=. Each relational operator takes as operands two expressions and produces an answer which is either true or false. More precisely, false corresponds to the integer value 0, and true corresponds to any other integer value, but we think of it as associated with 1.

THE LOGICAL OPERATORS

There are three **logical operators**: && (conjunction—read as and), || (disjunction—read as or), and ! (negation—read as not). The logical operators act on either one expression (for !) or two expressions (for && and ||) and produce a result which is either true or false.

Often the result of a relational operator is sent as an operand to a logical operator. For example, we could have the expression *! (x > 2)*. Because of the parentheses, we first apply the relational operator (>) to obtain a true or false value for *x > 2*; this value is then negated. The result from a logical operator can also be sent as an operand to another logical operator. For example, consider the expression *!(x > 2) && (y = 3)*. In order to evaluate this expression, we have to discuss the precedence rules for logical and relational operators.

PRECEDENCE RULES FOR LOGICAL AND RELATIONAL OPERATORS

Here are the precedence rules for logical and relational operators (see Table 6.1):

♦ Negation (!) has the same precedence as the other unary operators, including unary minus and the increment and decrement operators; their precedence is higher than any of the other arithmetic operators (see Chapter 2, Section 4).

♦ The relational operators have a lower precedence than any of the arithmetic operators, except for the assignment operators (= or +=, −=, *=, /=, %=).

♦ The logical operator && has a lower precedence than the relational operators.

♦ The logical operator || has a lower precedence than &&.

♦ Both && and || have higher precedence than the assignment operators, which have the lowest precedence.

♦ In a given expression, two or more logical operators with the same precedence are grouped from left to right (except for ! which is grouped from right to left).

♦ Parentheses can be used to override these rules. Anything inside a pair of parentheses is done first; within the parentheses, operations are performed in order of precedence.

STYLE WORKSHOP It is a good idea to include parentheses in certain situations where they are not strictly necessary. Almost everyone knows the C++ precedence rules for arithmetic operations (e.g., multiplication before addition), but many inexperienced programmers are not positive about the ones for the logical and relational operators. (This problem is aggravated by the fact that the rules in C++ are different from those in other computer languages, say, Pascal.) Therefore, extra parentheses are sometimes added for clarity.

Table 6-2 summarizes the precedence rules for all of the operators we have used so far, including logical and relational operators:

TABLE 6-2 Precedence of Arithmetic, Assignment, Logical, and Relational Operators

Precedence	Operation	Associativity
highest precedence (done first)	! − (unary) + (unary) ++ −−	right to left
	* / %	left to right
	+ −	left to right
	< <= > >=	left to right
	== !=	left to right
	&&	left to right
	||	left to right
lowest precedence (done last)	= += −= *= /= %=	right to left

TABLE 6-3 Truth Tables for the Logical Operators

Table for !		*	Tables for		&&	and	||
if *a* is	then !*a* is	*	if *a* is	and if *b* is	then a&&b is		then a||b is
T	F	*	T	T	T		T
F	T	*	T	F	F		T
		*	F	T	F		T
		*	F	F	F		F

TRUTH TABLES FOR THE LOGICAL OPERATORS

In order to evaluate an example involving logical operators, we need a set of standard tables describing how they work. These tables, often called **truth tables**, are given in Table 6-3. In the tables, *a* and *b* are any two boolean expressions. A **boolean expression** is one that evaluates to a boolean value—either true or false. A logical operator is sometimes called a boolean operator since its result is a boolean value. In Table 6-3, we represent true by T and false by F. (Recall that C++ considers 0 to be false and any other value to be true.)

These tables are read in the following way: If *a* is T, then !*a* is F. If *a* is T and *b* is T, then *a* && *b* is T (*a* || *b* is also T in this case), and so on. Note that *a* || *b* is false only when both *a* and *b* are false; *a* && *b* is true only when *a* and *b* are both true. These tables are "known" by the C++ compiler, and a programmer should know them as well.

Table 6-3 describes how the logical operators && and || work. The meaning of && in C++ is identical to "and" in English. Similarly, || in C++ works just like "or" in English. Actually, we use two different kinds of "or" in English: **inclusive or** (one or the other, or both) and **exclusive or** (one or the other, but not both). The operator || corresponds to the use of inclusive or, which is the more common meaning in English. (Exercise 26 discusses modeling the exclusive or operation.)

EVALUATING EXPRESSIONS USING LOGICAL AND RELATIONAL OPERATORS

Now that we know how logical operators work, let's look at a few examples showing how to evaluate boolean expressions.

EXAMPLE 6-15   The first example has two boolean operators: && and ||.

```
int x = 4, y = 0, z = 1;
if (x < y || z >= x && x != 0)
    cout << "it is true" << endl;
else
    cout << "it is false" << endl;
```

Before we go step-by-step through the evaluation, let's note the following: Since && has higher precedence, it will be done before ||. The two boolean expressions that && works on are *z >= x* and *x != 0*. The two boolean expressions that || works on are *x < y* and the result of the &&.

PROGRAM TRACE Now we can trace the example in detail:

♦ First, we substitute numerical values: (4 < 0 || 1 >= 4 && 4 != 0)

♦ Next we evaluate the relational operators: 4 < 0 is F, 1 >= 4 is F, and 4 != 0 is T.

♦ We now have the following:

  (F || F && T)

♦ Now && has precedence over ||. We evaluate F && T which yields F. Then we have the following:

  (F || F)

♦ Since F || F is F, the entire expression is false.

♦ We execute the **else** statement. This prints the following line of output:

  it is false

Now let's trace a more complete example, including parentheses and arithmetic operators.

EXAMPLE 6-16   Assume that we have this **if-else** statement, where *st-1* and *st-2* are any C++ statements:

```
if (a * 2 > b || ! (c == 6) && d - 1 <= e)
    st-1;
else
    st-2;
```

PROGRAM TRACE Assume that <u>a</u> is 2, <u>b</u> is 4, <u>c</u> is 7, <u>d</u> is 4, and <u>e</u> is 3.

♦ As before, we7 start by substituting numerical values:

  (2 * 2 > 4 || ! (7 == 6) && 4 − 1 <= 3)

♦ Then we perform operations which are inside the innermost parentheses. In this case, the condition 7 == 6 is false, so we have the following:

  (2 * 2 > 4 || ! F && 4 − 1 <= 3)

♦ Negation (!) has highest precedence, so we do ! F, which is T. This gives

  (2 * 2 > 4 || T && 4 − 1 <= 3)

♦ Now the multiplication (2 * 2) has highest precedence, so we have

  (4 > 4 || T && 4 − 1 <= 3)

♦ The subtraction now has highest precedence, so we have

  (4 > 4 || T && 3 <= 3)

♦ Next we do the relational operators. Technically, they are done one at a time, from left to right, but we can show both at once since they don't interact with each other: 4 > 4 is false, but 3 <= 3 is true. So we have

F || T && T

♦ Now && has precedence over ||; T && T is T.

F || T

♦ Finally, F || T is T.

♦ Since the entire **if** condition is true, we execute statement *st-1*.

SHORT-CIRCUIT EVALUATION OF BOOLEAN EXPRESSIONS WHICH USE LOGICAL OPERATORS

The rules in C++ to evaluate boolean expressions are slightly different from what we have implied. In giving the rules for evaluating the && of two expressions, we have suggested that C++ evaluates each of them, then sees whether their && is true. Actually, the C++ compiler uses a shortcut method, called **short-circuit evaluation**.

HIGHLIGHTS

The && of two expressions is true only if both the expressions are true. If, for example, the first expression is false, it is impossible for the entire && expression to be true. In such a case, the C++ compiler does not bother to evaluate the second expression. It short-circuits the evaluation process and concludes that the boolean expression using && must be false.

EXAMPLE 6-17

Let's assume that we want to divide one variable y by another variable x, then see whether or not this result is greater than z. We can use y / x for the division, comparing the result to z, but there is a problem if x has the value 0. In languages that do not have short-circuit evaluation, we must use an extra **if** statement to avoid this problem (see Exercise 27). But in C++ we can do something like this:

```
if (x != 0 && y / x > z)
    st-1;
else
    st-2;
```

PROGRAM TRACE Let's trace what happens in this example, assuming first that x has the value 4, y has the value 20, and z has the value 3.

♦ First, we substitute numerical values: 4 != 0 && 20 / 4 > 3.

♦ The first expression, 4 != 0, is true, so the evaluation continues.

♦ The second expression, 20 / 4 > 3, which becomes 5 > 3, is true, so the entire && is true.

♦ Statement *st-1* is executed.

Now let's assume that y and z have the same values, but x has the value 0. We substitute values to get 0 != 0 && 20 / 0 > 3.

♦ The first expression, 0 != 0, is false. Therefore, the entire && must be false, and C++ does not evaluate the second expression. Since the entire && is false, we execute statement *st-2*.

This is exactly what we want to happen in this case, because if 20 / 0 were evaluated, it would cause a division-by-0 error.

Short-circuit evaluation of an || condition can also occur. If the first expression in an || is true, the entire || expression must be true, and the C++ compiler will short-circuit the evaluation of the second expression.

SELF-CHECK 6-9

1. If the && of two expressions is false, what can you say about the two expressions? What if the && is true?

2. If the || of two expressions is false, what can you say about the two expressions? What if the || is true?

DATA TYPE bool

A **boolean expression** is an expression which evaluates to either true or false. In C++, an expression with a value of 0 is interpreted as false, and an expression with any other value is interpreted as true. The ANSI standard for C++ supports the data type **bool** for declaring variables which can hold boolean values; in versions of C++ which do not yet support type **bool**, type **int** must be used instead.

The only values a variable with type **bool** can hold are **true** and **false**. If the variable is assigned an arithmetic expression which has a value of zero, the value is stored as false; if the expression has a non-zero value, the value is stored as true. A **bool** variable can be printed; **false** prints as 0, and **true** prints as 1. Note that the values **true** and **false** are not strings and do not have quotation marks.

EXAMPLE 6-18

```
bool less = false;
int x,y;

cin >> x;
cin >> y;
if (x+y < 100)
    less = true;
```

The variable less is declared to have type **bool**, which means its values can be **true** or **false**. In this example, the variable less is initialized to **false**. If the condition tested is true, less is set to **true**.

USING BOOLEAN VARIABLES

The natural question you might ask is what a boolean variable can be used for. One use is to simplify relatively complicated boolean expressions, as shown in Example 6-19.

EXAMPLE 6-19

```
int x = 4, y = 0, z = 1;
bool cond;

cond = (x < y - 1) || (y + z >= x) && (x != 0);
if (cond == true)
    cout << "yes" << endl;
else
    cout << "no" << endl;
```

The boolean expression on the right side hand side of the assignment statement is evaluated to 0, and the value **false** is assigned to the boolean variable cond. Then the condition tested in the **if** statement (false == true) is false, and the message "no" prints.

USING A VARIABLE AS A CONDITION

An experienced C++ programmer wouldn't use a boolean variable as we did in Example 6-19, because there is a shortcut: The comparison can be omitted from the **if** condition. If <u>cond</u> has the value 1 or **true**, the condition *if (cond = = true)* compares **true** with **true**, and the expression evaluates to **true**. Similarly, if <u>cond</u> has the value 0 or **false**, the condition *if (cond = = true)* compares **false** with **true**, and the expression evaluates to **false**. In each case, the expression evaluates to the value of <u>cond</u>. Therefore, we can simplify the comparison by using the variable directly, as shown in Example 6-20.

EXAMPLE 6-20

```
bool cond;
...
if (cond)
    cout << "yes" << endl;
else
    cout << "no" << endl;
```

This section of code works identically to the same section in Example 6-19. If <u>cond</u> has the value **false**, the condition is false; otherwise, the condition is true.

STYLE WORKSHOP This particular technique is very useful in making code more readable and closer to English. Here are some examples we will use later in the text: *if (swapped)*, *if (!found)*, *if (iseven(x))*.

USING BOOLEAN VARIABLES TO CONTROL LOOPS AND COMMUNICATE BETWEEN FUNCTIONS

There is another use for boolean variables that is important enough to deserve its own subsection. Boolean variables are very often used for control and communication purposes. In this section, we will give one example of each, but many other examples will appear in our later programs. Example 6-21 shows how a boolean variable can be used to control a loop.

EXAMPLE 6-21

In Program 2, we used a **for** loop to create a table showing values of a formula [*result = f(gpa)*] from <u>gpa</u> = 0.00 to 4.00, increasing by 0.50. Let's add one more condition to the problem: If the formula ever has a special value, call it <u>specialval</u>, then we want to stop printing the table, without going all the way to 4.00. If this special value is not found, we want to continue. We will assume that the value of <u>SPECIALVAL</u> is a constant.

C++ allows the condition in the **for** loop header to include multiple tests joined with a logical operator, and we will do that here. The second test will cause the loop to terminate if <u>SPECIALVAL</u> is found. Here is an outline of how this new loop can be implemented:

```
const int SPECIALVAL = ...;

double gpa,result;
bool  found;
...
found = false;
for (gpa = 0; gpa <= 4.00 && !found; gpa += .50){
    result = formula;
    ...
    if (result == SPECIALVAL)
        found = true;
}
```

Initially, <u>found</u> has the value **false**, meaning that <u>SPECIALVAL</u> has not been found. Therefore *!found* has the value **true**; since <u>gpa</u> is 0, which is less than 4, the condition is **true** and the body of the loop is executed. Inside the body of the loop, <u>gpa</u> will be incremented by 0.50, and <u>found</u> may receive a new value—if the value of the formula is equal to <u>SPECIALVAL</u>. The loop will continue until one of two things happens: either the formula is never equal to <u>SPECIALVAL</u>, and <u>gpa</u> is eventually incremented to a value larger than 4.00; or the formula does eventually equal <u>SPECIALVAL</u>, and the boolean variable <u>found</u> is set to **true**, so *!found* has the value **false**. When either part of the condition has the value **false**, we will fall out of the loop.

Finally, a boolean variable can be used to communicate between functions. For example, if a function succeeds in accomplishing some task, it could set a parameter which is a boolean variable to **true** to signal the calling program; if the function is unable to complete the task, it could set the boolean variable to **false**. This is shown in Example 6-22.

EXAMPLE 6-22 Suppose we write a function <u>iseven( )</u> to determine whether or not an integer sent as a parameter is even (meaning evenly divisible by 2). The function will use the remainder operator. If the parameter is even, the remainder is 0 and the function will return **true**; if the parameter is odd, the remainder will be 1 and the function will return **false**. The name of the function has been chosen so that the main program's test will make sense as an expression in English. Notice that the function returns a value of type **bool**.

```
#include <iostream>
using namespace std;
bool iseven(int);
int main()
{
    int x;

    cin >> x;
    if (iseven(x))
        cout << x << " is even" << endl;
    else
        cout << x << "is odd" << endl;
    return 0;
}

bool iseven(int num)
{
    if (num % 2 == 0)
        return true;
    else
        return false;
}
```

We can use a shortcut for the **if** statement in the function. The following **return** statement simply returns the result of the condition:

```
return (num % 2 == 0);
```

If the condition *num % 2 == 0* is true, the function returns **true**, and the condition <u>iseven(x)</u> is **true**; otherwise, <u>iseven(x)</u> is false.

SELF-CHECK 6-10

1. What data type can be used to represent boolean values using a compiler that doesn't support type **bool**?

2. Show how to rewrite this condition without a relational operator.

```
bool islate = false;

if (islate == true)
    cout << "it is late" << endl;
```

3. Change each of the conditions shown below so that it uses the boolean variable directly, without a relational operator.

   a. `bool swapped;`
      `if (swapped == true)`

   b. `bool found;`
      `if (! found == false)`

   c. `bool isodd(int num);  // prototype`
      `if (isodd(val) == true)`

SUMMARY

ONE FUNCTION CALLING ANOTHER

1. One C++ function can call another, which generalizes the idea of a main program calling a function. The function that issues the call is the calling function; the function mentioned in the call is the called function. Each function returns to the function that called it.

do-while LOOPS

2. A **do-while** loop is an alternative to a **while** loop. The general form of a **do-while** loop is shown here. Because a set of braces has been used, the body of the loop can consist of any number of C++ statements; *cond* is a condition that evaluates to true or false.

```
do {
    body of the loop
} while (cond);
```

3. The **do-while** loop is executed as follows: Initially, the body of the loop is executed. When the **while** clause is reached, the condition *cond* is evaluated. If the condition is true, the body of the loop is repeated, and *cond* is evaluated again. If the condition is false, the body of the loop is not repeated, the loop is terminated, and the program continues with the statement after the **while** clause. In general, the body of the loop is repeated as long as the condition evaluates to true.

4. The only major difference between a **while** loop and a **do-while** loop is that the **while** loop tests the condition before entering the body of the loop, whereas the **do-while** loop tests it after executing the body. Therefore, the body of a **do-while** loop is always executed at least one time.

if STATEMENT

5. A single **if-else** statement can be used to select one of two alternatives. A C++ program can choose one of three (or more) alternatives by using a series of **if** statements.

NESTED if STATEMENT

6. A nested **if** construction, in which the first or second clause is another **if-else** statement, can be used to select one of three or more paths.

7. The simplest form of a nested **if** is shown here (*cond-1* and *cond-2* are conditions that evaluate to true or false; *st-1*, *st-2*, etc. are each C++ statements):

```
if (cond-1)
     st-1;
else if (cond-2)
     st-2;
else
     st-3;
st-4;
```

8. This nested **if** is executed in the following way: If condition *cond-1* is true, statement *st-1* is executed; if *cond-1* is false and *cond-2* is true, *st-2* is executed; if *cond-1* is false and *cond-2* is false, *st-3* is executed. The statement *st-4* following the entire nested **if** is always executed.

9. Any statement in a nested **if** can be replaced by a compound statement; a pair of braces is used to execute more than one statement. Here is an example which uses a compound statement in each **else**:

```
if (cond-1)
     st-1;
else  {
     st-2;
     if (cond-2)
          st-3;
     else  {
          st-4;
          st-5;
     }
}
st-6;
```

In case *cond-1* is false, *st-2* is executed, and *cond-2* is tested. If this condition is true, then *st-3* is executed, but if it is false, *st-4* and *st-5* are both executed. In every case, the program continues with *st-6*.

switch STATEMENT

10. The **switch** statement provides another convenient way to select one from a series of alternatives. Here is the general form of a **switch** statement:

```
switch (selector) {
   case value-1:
        group-1 of statements;
   case value-2:
        group-2 of statements;
     . . .
   case value-n:
        group-n of statements;
   default:
        default statements;
}
```

11. In this form, *selector* must be an expression of some integer-valued type (**int** or **char**); each *value-i* is a constant representing a possible value for *selector*; each *group-i* is any number of C++ statements. It is possible to have more than one constant value in a particular alternative; the keyword **case** is followed by a constant value and a colon for each value to be covered by that alternative. The selector in a **switch** statement cannot be of type **float** or **double**.

12. The **switch** statement is executed as follows: The value of *selector* is computed and compared to *value-1*. If they are equal, *group-1 of statements* is selected to be executed. If the values are not equal, the process is repeated for each possible value until a match is found. If a selected groups ends in a **break** statement, the rest of the alternatives are skipped; however, if **break** is not present, execution of one group of statements goes on to execution of the next.

13. A **default** clause, which covers all other possible values, can be used as the last choice. This clause is selected if no match is found. If no match is found and there is no **default** clause, the **switch** statement does nothing.

break AND continue STATEMENTS, exit() FUNCTION

14. The statements **break** and **continue** control execution of a loop, whether it is a **for** loop, a **while** loop, or a **do-while** loop. If the **break** statement is executed inside the body of a loop, the entire loop terminates. If the **continue** statement is executed inside the body, the particular iteration terminates, but the loop continues.

15. For example, consider this **for** loop. The **continue** statement terminates the iteration when i has the value 3, but the **for** loop continues when i is 4, then 5, etc. If the variable x has a value greater than 15, the **break** statement terminates the entire loop.

```
for (int i = 1; i <= 10; i++) {
    . . .
    if (i == 3)
        continue;
    . . .
    if (x > 15)
        break;
    . . .
}
```

16. The exit( ) function also regulates the flow of control by terminating execution of an entire program, whether it is called from a main program or a function. If termination is normal, exit( ) is usually sent 0 as a parameter, as in exit(0). If termination is abnormal, exit( ) is usually sent another value, as in exit(1).

LOGICAL AND RELATIONAL OPERATORS

17. The logical or boolean operators (&&, ||, and !) can be used to formulate complex conditions. For example, using && (and) makes it possible to test if two conditions are both true; using || (or) makes it possible to test if either (or both) of two conditions is true. The operator ! (not) negates a condition.

18. The logical operators receive either one (for !) or two (for && and ||) true-false values and produce an answer that is either true or false. The logical operator ! has the highest precedence (the same as unary minus). The logical operator && has lower precedence than ! but higher precedence than the logical operator ||. Two or more operators in a row with the same precedence are evaluated from left to right.

19. The logical operator ! has higher precedence than any of the relational operators (<, <=, >, >=, ==, and !=). The relational operators have higher precedence than logical operators && and ||. Parentheses override the precedence rules for logical and relational operators.

20. The truth tables for logical operators provide a convenient summary of the rules for evaluating them. In these tables, true and false are represented by T and F. For example, T && F is F; F || T is T; ! F is T.

21. With boolean expressions, C++ uses short-circuit evaluation. In evaluating the && of two expressions, if the first one is false, the overall expression must be false, and C++ does not evaluate the second. Similarly, in evaluating the || of two expressions, if the first is true, the overall expression must be true, and C++ does not evaluate the second.

DATA TYPE **bool**

22. A variable of data type **bool** has two values, **true** and **false**. A variable of this type can be used in a number of situations: to simplify a complicated boolean expression, to control the execution of a loop, or to communicate from one function to another. A **bool** variable can be given an integer value; 0 is interpreted as **false**, and any non-zero value is interpreted as **true**.

EXERCISES

TRACING EXERCISES:

1. Use the following declaration for this problem:

   ```
   int i,j,k,x;
   ```

   For the three sets of values (i) to (iii), show what is stored in the variable x by each of the following program segments. If x is not assigned a value by the code segment, indicate one by ?.

   ```
     i. i = 1;     j = 2;      k = 3;
    ii. i = 7;     j = 10;     k = 4;
   iii. i = 5;     j = 4;      k = 3;
   ```

   a. ```
   if (j > k)
         x = 2;
   if (i > k)
         x = 3;
   ```

   b. ```
   if (i > j)
            x = 1;
      else
            if (j > k)
                  x = 2;
            else
                  x = 3;
   ```

   c. ```
   if (i > j)
         x = 5;
   else if (j > k)
         x = 1;
   else if (i > k)
         x = 3;
   ```

2. Show what is printed by the following C++ statements when the variables a, b, c, d, and e have the values shown in parts (a) to (d) below. In addition, show the intermediate result of each logical and relational operator.

   ```
    i. a = 2;   b = 1;   c = 3;   d = 0;   e = 1;
   ii. a = 3;   b = 3;   c = 3;   d = 3;   e = 3;
   ```
   ```

```
iii.  a = 5;      b = 0;      c = 0;      d = 3;      e = 2;
iv.   a = 3;      b = 5;      c = 7;      d = 4;      e = 2;
      int a,b,c,d,e;

      if (a < b || d > e)
          if (b > c && c > d)
              cout << "win" << endl;
          else if (d < e)
                  cout << "place" << endl;
              else
                  cout << "show" << endl;
      else
          cout << "finish" << endl;
```

3. For each set of initial values for the variables, evaluate the following series of statements according to C++ precedence rules and show what is printed.

```
i.   a = 6;   b = 7;    c = 3;  d = 2;   e = 16;
ii.  a = 1;   b = 18;   c = 6;  d = 42;  e = 8;
     int a,b,c,d,e;
       . . .
     if ( ! (a = b && c * c <= 100 || d != e % 8) )
         cout << "valid " << endl;
     else
         cout << "invalid " << endl;
     if (1000 >> a + b * b * 9 || !(e * d == a / d))
         a += b;
     else
         a -= b;
     cout << a << endl;
```

4. For each set of values for the variables (i) to (iii), show what is printed by code segments (a), (b), and (c). Assume that p, q, and r all have data type **bool**.

```
i.    p = true;        q = true;        r = false;
ii.   p = true;        q = false;       r = true;
iii.  p = false;       q = false;       r = false;
```

```
a. if (p && q || r)                    b. if (p || !(q && r))
       cout << "true" << endl;                cout << "true" << endl;
   else                                   else
       cout << "false" << endl;               cout << "false" << endl;
```

```
c. if ( ! p || (q || r) && !q)
       cout << "true" << endl;
   else
       cout << "false" << endl;
```

5. For these two programs, substitute each of the following specific conditions one at a time for *condition* in the loop control, then trace the loop. Show what is printed in each case. Will any of these cause an infinite loop or some other error? Here are the five conditions:

```
i.   (sum <= 12)
ii.  (num > 4 && sum == num)
```

iii. (sum < 12 || num < 16)

iv. (num <= 32)

v. (sum >= 0)

a.
```cpp
#include <iostream>>
using namespace std;
int main()
{
    int num = 2,sum = 0;
    while (condition) {
        num *= 2;
        sum += num;
        cout << num << " " << sum << endl;
    }
    cout << num << " " << sum << endl;
    return 0;
}
```

b.
```cpp
#include <iostream>
using namespace std;
int main()
{
    int num = 2, sum = 0;

    do {
        num *=2;
        sum += num;
        cout << num << " " << sum << endl;
    } while (condition);
    cout << num << " " << sum << endl;
    return 0;
}
```

6. Show what is printed by each of the following program segments:

a.
```cpp
int a = 2, z = 16;

do {
    z -= a;
    a += z /2;
    cout << a << " " << z << endl;
} while (z >>= a);
```

b.
```cpp
int i = 4, j = 9;

do {
    i += j;
    j--;
    cout << i << " " << j << endl;
} while (i < j);
```

7. a. Construct a table to verify that the nested **if** statement in Example 6-3 correctly translates Figure 6-3.

   b. Do the same for the nested **if** in Example 6-4 that translates Figure 6-4.

8. For each of the sets of values below, determine which statement (*st-1* or *st-2*) is executed by the following **if-else** statement. In addition, show the intermediate result of each logical and relational operator.

   i. x = 7;   y = 3;   z = 1;   r = 3;

   ii. x = -1;   y = -2;   z = -7;   r = 5;

iii.
```
x = 8;     y = 2;    z = 1;    r = -10;
if (x > 2 * y && y - z % 2 < r + 2 * 6 || x == -1)
     st-1;
else
     st-2;
```

9. Translate the following **while** loops into **do-while** loops that do the same thing.

   a.
   ```
   int a = 19,b = 7;

   while (b <= a)
        b += 3;
   ```

   b.
   ```
   int a = 10,b = -6;

   while (a != b || a > 0)
        a += b;
   b += 2;
   ```

10. Show what is printed by each of the following segments. Are (a) and (b) equivalent? What about (c) and (d)?

   a.
   ```
   int a = 1,b = 1,c = 10;

   do {
       cout << a << endl;
       a += b;
       c++;
   } while (a <= c);
   cout << a << " " << b
        << " " << c << endl;
   ```

   b.
   ```
   int a = 1,b = 1,c = 10;

   while (a <= c) {
       cout << a << endl;
       a += b;
       c++;
   }
   cout << a << " " << b
        << " " << c << endl;
   ```

   c.
   ```
   int a = 1,b = 1,c = 10;

   do {
       cout << a << " ";
       a += b;
       b++;
   } while (a <= c);
   cout << a << " " << b
        << " " << c << endl;
   ```

   d.
   ```
   int a = 1,b = 1,c = 10;

   while (a <= c) {
       cout << a << " ";
       a += b;
       b++;
   }
   cout << a << " " << b
        << " " << c << endl;
   ```

11. Show what is printed by the following program. Assume that the set of data consists of these numbers, typed in one at a time in response to the prompt: 12 9 8 6 14 13 10 2.

```cpp
#include <iostream>
using namespace std;
int main()
{
    int i,size;

    for (i = 1; i <= 8; i++) {
        cout << "please enter the size> ";
        cin >> size;
    switch (size) {
        case 9: case 11: case 13: case 15:
            break; // do nothing for larger odd sizes
        case 2: case 4: case 6: case 8:
            cout << "the dress size is " << size;
```

```
                    cout << "--it is small" << endl;
                    break;
                case 10: case 12:
                    cout << "the dress size is " << size;
                    cout << "--it is medium" << endl;
                    break;
                default:
                    cout << "the dress size is " << size;
                    cout << "--it is large" << endl;
            }
        }
        return 0;
    }
```

12. Answer questions (a) to (c) for the following program.

```
#include <iostream>
using namespace std;
int main()
{
    int s1,s2,s3;
    bool code = false;
    do {
        cout << "please enter the 3 sides of a triangle";
        cin >> s1 >> s2 >> s3;
        if ( (s1 == s2 || s1 == s3 || s2 == s3) &&
             (s1 != s2 || s1 != s3 || s2 != s3) ) {
            cout << "isosceles triangle: " << s1
                 << " " << s2 << " " << s3 << endl;
            code = true;
        }
    } while (code != true && s1 != 0);
    return 0;

}
```

a. Show what is printed by the program above. Use this set of data:

   6 3 1   1 6 4   1 3 3   0 1 6

   (assume that each group of three numbers is typed in response to the prompt).

b. What happens if we add 3 9 12 to the end of the set of data? What about 3 9 9? Or 3 3 3? What if these values are added to the beginning of the set of data?

c. What is the purpose of testing whether s1 is equal to zero?

d. Rewrite the entire program using a variable of type **bool** to control the **do-while** loop. (*Suggestion*: Assume that test is a variable of type **bool**, and assume that the last statement in the body of the **do-while** loop assigns a value to test. Then the condition can be changed to the following: *while(test)*. Your task is to determine what assignment statement should be used in order to give test the right value.)

306 ♦ CHAPTER 6 More on Control Structures

13. In the following program segment, the function <u>sums( )</u> calls the function <u>product( )</u>. For each call to a function, identify which is the calling program and which is the called. Indicate where control returns after the call. Show what is printed, assuming that the data values are 5 and 8.

```cpp
#include <iostream>
using namespace std;
int product(int, int);
int sums(int, int);
int main()
{
    int x,y,ans;

    cout << "enter values one at a time for x and y ";
    cin >> x >> y;
    ans = sums(x,y);
    cout << "x = " << x << "  y = " << y " ans = " << ans << endl;
    return 0;
}

int product(int g,int h)
{
    if (g * h >= 40)
        return 3;
    else
        return g - h;
}

int sums(int i,int j)
{
    int a,b;

    a = product(i,j);
    b = product(a,j);
    return a + b;
}
```

14. Here is a main program, together with two functions. Assume that the set of data consists of the integers from 1 to 5 in order. Show what is printed as this program is executed. Note that function <u>sub2( )</u> calls function <u>sub1( )</u>.

```cpp
#include <iostream>
using namespace std;
int sub1(int, int);
int sub2(int, int);
int main()
{
    int d,e,f,g,h,i,j,k;

    cin >> g >> h >> i >> j >> k;
    f = sub1(g,h);
    cout << "first call: " << g << " " << h << " " << f << endl;
    e = sub2(i,j);
    cout << "second call: " << i << " " << j << " " << e << endl;
    d = sub1(g,k);
```

```
        cout << "third call: " << g << " " << k << " " << d << endl;
        return 0;
}

int sub1(int x,int y)
{
        if (x + y == 3)
            return 3;
        else
            return y - x;
}

int sub2(int p,int q)
{
        int r,s;

        r = sub1(p,q);
        s = sub1(q,p);
        return r + s;
}
```

Make up a different set of data and repeat the exercise.

15. Assume that *cond-1* and *cond-2* are conditions or questions which evaluate to either true or false. For parts (a) to (d) below, what statement(s) is executed in each situation:

    i. *cond-1* evaluates to true and *cond-2* to false

    ii. *cond-1* evaluates to false and *cond-2* to true

    iii. both conditions evaluate to true

    iv. both conditions evaluate to false

a. `if (cond-1)`
        `st-1;`
  `if (cond-2)`
        `st-2;`

b. `if (cond-2)`
        `st-2;`
  `if (cond-1)`
        `st-1;`

c. `if (cond-1)`
        `st-1;`
  `else`
        `if (cond-2)`
            `st-2;`

d. `if (cond-2)`
        `st-2;`
  `else`
        `if (cond-1)`
            `st-1;`

ANALYSIS EXERCISES

16. In Exercise 10, parts (a) and (b), how does changing the limiting value inside the **while** or **do-while** loop affect the execution? In parts (c) and (d), how does a change in the increment affect things?

17. Show that anything which can be done with a **do-while** loop can be rewritten to use a **while** loop, and vice versa. Remember that the key difference between the two is that the body of a **do-while** loop always executes at least once. See Figure 6-1.

18. Rewrite the following segment using a **switch** statement instead of the nested **if**. Then rewrite it using a cascading nested **if** with full indentation. Finally, rewrite it using a series of **if** statements instead of a nested **if**. Which version is most efficient? Which is easiest to follow? In the nested **if** versions, why can we use simplified **if** conditions? For example, we can use *if (exam >= 80)* instead of *if (exam >= 80 && exam < 90)*.

```
int exam;

if (exam >= 90)
    cout << "grade = A";
else if (exam >= 80)
    cout << "grade = B";
else if (exam >= 70)
    cout << "grade = C";
else if (exam >= 60)
    cout << "grade = D";
else
    cout << "grade = F";
cout << endl;
```

19. Assume that we have the following problem: The variable x holds some initial value. If the value of x is greater than 99, subtract 25 from it; if the original value is in the range from 80 to 99, add 10 to it; otherwise add 1 to x. For example, if x starts at 120, it ends up as $120 - 25 = 95$; if x is 98, it becomes $98 + 10 = 108$; if x is 37, it is set to $37 + 1 = 38$.

    a. What is wrong with using this series of C++ statements to solve the problem?
    ```
    int x;

        ...
    if (x > 100)
        x -= 25;
    if (x >= 80 && x <= 99)
        x += 10;
    if (x < 80)
        x++;
    ```

    b. Modify the series of **if** statements in part (a) so that it does solve the problem.
    c. Use a nested **if** to solve this problem.
    d. Is it possible to use a **switch** statement to solve this problem? Explain.

20. Assume that we want to process a set of data, with 0 as the trailer value at the end (the 0 value is not processed). At first glance, these two segments seem to be equivalent. However, only the one on the right processes the data correctly. Assume that the set of data consists of 2 31 14 0, typed in one at a time.

i.
```
int num;

num = 1;
while (num != 0) {
      cin >> num;
      process num
}
```

ii.
```
int num;

cin >> num;
while (num != 0) {
      process num
      cin >> num;
}
```

a. Show which values are processed by each segment.
b. What is the purpose of setting <u>num</u> to 1 in segment (i)? What is wrong with that segment?
c. What is the purpose of each use of <u>cin</u> in segment (ii)?
d. Show how to accomplish the same thing as segment (ii) with a **do-while** loop.

21. In a nested **if** which contains a large number of conditions to be tested, it is often more efficient to rearrange the order of the questions, especially if the nested **if** has to be executed a large number of times. For example, consider the nested **if** statement in Exercise 18.

a. In its current form, which condition is tested in every case (i.e., for every possible letter grade)? Which condition is tested in only one case?
b. Assume that this nested **if** statement appears in a loop, where it is executed once for each of 5000 students in a college. Most of the students received a grade of 90 or above on the exam. Is the current form a reasonable way to arrange the nested **if** statement? (*Hint*: If you change the order of the questions, how many conditions have to be tested to assign a grade to the majority of the students?)
c. Assume that most of the students received a grade of 50 or below on the exam. Is the current form reasonable? What is a more efficient way to rearrange the questions in the nested **if**?
d. What if most of the students received a grade in the range from 60 to 69. Is there a more efficient way to rearrange the nested **if** in this case?

22. a. What happens in a **switch** statement if a particular constant value for the selector appears two or more times in the list of alternatives? First, try to predict what happens; then write a program to determine what C++ does in this situation.

b. What happens in a **switch** statement if the value for the selector does not appear in the list of alternatives (and there is no **default** clause)? First, try to predict what happens; then write a program to determine what C++ does in this situation.
c. If you have access to another C++ compiler, try running the programs on that compiler as well.

23. Consider the following version of a **switch** statement in which most of the **break** statements have been eliminated.

```
int number;

cout << "type in a number from 2 to 9> ";
cin >> number;
switch (number) {
    case 2:
        cout << number << " is a prime number" << endl;
    case 4:
    case 6:
    case 8:
        cout << number << " is an even number" << endl;
```

```
            break;
        case 3:
        case 5:
        case 7:
            cout << number << " is a prime number" << endl;
        case 9:
            cout << number << " is an odd number" << endl;
    }
```

a. What is printed if the user types in the following values? 4 7 9 2. Are these correct answers?

b. If the **break** statements are put back in on each path, what does this version print? Are these correct answers?

24. Show that anything possible with a **switch** statement can also be done with a nested **if** construction. (*Suggestion*: Take the general form of a **switch** statement from Section 7 and show how it can be replaced by a nested **if**.)

25. Are there any differences among the code segments below? Explain.

   a. i. `if (!(x == 0)) ...`   ii. `if (x != 0) ...`
      iii. `if ( (x == 0) == 0) ...`   iv. `if ( x == 0 == 0) ...`
   b. i. `if ( !(p || q)) ...`   ii. `if ( !p && !q) ...`
   c. i. `if ( !(p && q)) ...`   ii. `if ( !p || !q) ...`

The equivalences in parts (b) and (c) are called **deMorgan's Laws**.

26. Although C++ does not, some other computer languages (e.g., Turbo Pascal) have an **exclusive-or** operator, which we will denote by *xor*. If p and q are each either true or false, the expression p *xor* q is true if p is true or q is true, but false if they are both true or both false.

a. Construct a truth table for the *xor* operator.

b. Show how to simulate *xor* in C++ using the other three boolean operators.
(*Suggestion*: There are several ways.)

27. In Section 8, we gave an example showing how short-circuit evaluation of boolean operators in C++ can eliminate a possible divide-by-0 error. Show how to solve the problem discussed there (compare the value of y divided by x to z) without taking advantage of short-circuit evaluation.

Hint: Consider the following two nested-**if** statements:

```
    if (cond-1)          compared to      if (cond-1 && cond-2)
        if (cond-2)                           ...
            ...
```

28. a. What is printed by the following program?

```cpp
#include <iostream>
using namespace std;
int main()
{
    int sum = 0;
    for (int i = 1; i <= 5; i++) {
        if (i == 2)
            continue;
        sum += i;
        cout << "the sum is " << sum
            << " and i is  " << i << endl;
    }
```

```
        cout << "after the loop, the total sum is " << sum << endl;
        return 0;
    }
```

b. In the program above, replace the **continue** statement by a **break** statement and show what is printed by the new program.

c. In the program above, replace the **continue** statement by a call to exit( ) and show what is printed by the new program.

29. a. In the program in Exercise 28, replace the entire **if** statement by the following:

```
        if (i % 2 == 0)
            continue;
```

Show what is printed by the new program. Is the output the same as from part (a) of Exercise 28? Explain.

b. Repeat parts (b) and (c) of Exercise 28 using the **if** statement given in part (a) of this exercise. Is the output from each of the new programs the same as from the corresponding original program? Explain.

30. Show what is printed by the following program, assuming that the data values 4 9 23 0 are entered, one at a time, in response to the prompts.

```
#include <iostream>
using namespace std;
int main()
{
    int numb;

    cout << "type in a number; use 0 to stop> ";
    cin >> numb;
    while (numb != 0) {
        if (numb == 6)
            continue;
        cout << numb << " is being processed" << endl;
        statements to process numb
        cout << "type in a number; use 0 to stop> ";
        cin >> numb;
    }
    return 0;
}
```

Repeat the exercise, assuming that the user intends to type in the numbers from 1 to 10, followed by 0. Explain what goes wrong. (*Hint*: What happens when the user types in the value 6?)

31. a. In Example 6-10, a **for** loop contains a **continue** statement. Show how to rewrite the loop without using one. (*Suggestion*: Consider using an **if-else** statement so the program can skip part of the body of the loop.)

b. Repeat part (a) for Example 6-11, in which a **for** loop contains a **break** statement. (*Suggestion*: You may find it helpful to first rewrite the **for** loop with a more complicated condition controlling the loop, then modify the new loop to allow early termination.)

c. Repeat part (a) for the **while** and **do-while** loops which contain **break** and/or **continue** statements (Examples 6-14 and 6-15).

d. Can you replace calls to exit( ) by using other features of C++? Explain.

32. a. Are there any differences between the **while** loop headers in (i) and (ii) below? Explain.

    i. `while (1 == 1)`
    ii. `while (1)`

b. Normally, a **while** loop with a header like this leads to an infinite loop. Why?

c. Below is an example (in pseudocode) of a **while** loop with such a header:

```
while (1) {
    read in a value for x
    if x is negative, terminate the loop
    print x
}
```

    i. Without changing the header of the loop, but using the new C++ statements in this chapter (**break**, **continue**, etc.), show how to translate this into C++ code. Explain how the **while** loop you use terminates.

    ii. By changing the header of the loop and using other features of C++ introduced earlier in the text (but not in this chapter), show how to translate this into C++ code.

33. In Exercise 32, we discussed **while** loops that seem to lead to infinite loops but which do terminate under certain conditions. Show how to do similar things with **do-while** loops.

MODIFYING PROGRAM 6

34. The original version of Program 6 assumes that winter consists of the entire months of December, January, and February (and makes similar assumptions for the other seasons). Rewrite Program 6 so that winter covers the period from December 21 to March 20, and so on for the other seasons.

35. The original version of Program 6 assumes that all months have precisely 31 days. Rewrite Program 6 so that April, June, September, and November have 30 days, February has 28 (we will ignore leap year), and the rest of the months have 31 days. (*Suggestion*: The only time this modification changes the answer computed in the function whichweek( ) is when the month is one of the five listed here and the week is number 5.)

36. a. In Program 6, the allowed values for day are in the range from 1 to 31. Assume that we remove checking for bad data from classify( ). What happens if the user types in an illegal value, say 37, for day?

b. Under the same assumption, what happens if the user types in an illegal value for month?

c. Modify the main program so that if the user types in an illegal value for day, the main program immediately requests another in the correct range. Do the same for an illegal value for month. Compare this method of error checking to the one in Program 6.

37. In Program 3, we introduced the use of a trailer value to end a set of data. Compare the use of a trailer value to the new method in Program 6, where the user has the opportunity to continue or stop after each element is processed. Which method gives the user greater flexibility? Which method limits the values usable as data? Which requires the user to enter more responses?

38. a. In our first attempt to write the function whichseason( ), we included the following line:

    ```
    if (month == 12 || 1 || 2 ) ...
    ```
    According to the C++ precedence rules in Section 8, in what order are the operations performed? Does this cause an error? (Run a test program to check your answer.) How can we modify this statement to correct the order of operations?

    b. Show how to rewrite whichseason( ) with a nested **if** statement rather than a series of **if** statements. Can you use a **switch** statement? Explain why or why not.

39. In the function whichweek( ), we used a series of **if** statements to determine in which week a given date belongs. This exercise offers a number of other ways to accomplish this.

    a. Rewrite whichweek( ) using a separate **if** statement for each possible value of day. (How many **if** statements do you need?)

    b. Rewrite whichweek( ) using a nested **if**.

    c Rewrite whichweek( ) using a **switch** statement.

    d. Rewrite whichweek( ) using integer division to determine the week number.

40. a. Write a nested **if** version of translate( ).

    b. In this version of translate( ), in what order should the months be listed if you know that most people are born in the summer?

    c. What if the fewest people are born in the winter?

    d. Would this special information about the months make any difference in the original version of translate( )?

41. In Program 6, the user is asked to enter either 'y' or 'n', to indicate whether the loop in the main program should continue.

    a. What happens if the user enters a value that is not one of these two responses? For example, what will the program do if the user enters some nonsensical thing like 'H' or '5'? Is what the program does a reasonable way to handle typing in a response of this kind?

    b. What happens if the user enters the value 'N'? Although this response correctly answers the question, will it be handled in a reasonable way?

    c. One possible solution to the problem in part (b) is to test for either 'n' or 'N'. Show how to modify the program to do this.

    d. C++ has a function toupper( ) which can convert a lowercase letter into its uppercase equivalent. For example, toupper('a') returns 'A'. Show how to use this function to solve the problem of alternate responses.

    e. The revision from part (d) does not handle all possible correct responses. What happens if the user enters the value 'f' (for false)? Is this a "reasonable" response? Will it be handled correctly? Is there any method to handle all possible user responses?

    f. What if the user enters a response that is more than one character (for example, if the user enters "Yes", and then a carriage return)?

42. Show how to use one or more boolean variables to communicate between the various functions used in Program 6. For example, you could use a boolean variable in the function whichseason( ) to indicate that the classification process was not successful because of an illegal value for the month.

PROGRAMMING PROJECTS

43. Assume that you are working on a linguistics research project. You want to classify the letters of the alphabet: The letters 'b' and 'd' are type 1; the letters 'c', 'j', and 'q' are type 2; 'a' is type 3; 'h' and

'r' through 'z' are type 4; the rest of the letters are type 5. You want to read in a character (stored in <u>letter</u>) and determine its type (which is stored in <u>lettertype</u>). For this problem, assume that the person typing in data definitely enters one of the 26 lowercase letters.

a. Write a program which performs this classification. Use a series of **if** statements. *Suggestion:* You can handle each value of <u>letter</u> separately or use the logical and relational operators to combine cases like this:

```
if (letter >= 'r' && letter <= 'z') ...
```

b. Use a nested **if** instead of a series of **if** statements.

c. Use a **switch** statement to classify the letters. Note that a variable of type **char** can be the selector in a **switch** statement.

44. In Exercise 43, we assumed that the user enters one of the 26 lowercase letters. But in fact there are actually 256 possible values of type **char** that can be typed in. Show how to use each of the following methods to prohibit the selector's value from falling outside the indicated range.

a. Prompt the user to type in only a lowercase letter and assume he or she follows directions (this is the method used in Exercise 43).

b. Before the **if** or **switch** statement, check that the value typed in is within the allowed range from 'a' to 'z'.

c. As part of the **if** or **switch** statement, list each of the 256 values of type **char** with an appropriate action for each.

d. Can you think of any other ways to limit the legal values which can be entered?

e. Which method is the most reliable? Which method did you refuse to do? Which method depends upon the user's following directions? Which method is the best solution to the problem?

45. Assume that the set of values to be typed in as data for a program consists of a series of positive integers, then a single negative integer, then a second series of positive integers (terminated by 0). For example, the set of data might be 13 2 15 −8 9 87 1 2 1 1 21 0. Write a program that reads the data, then prints two counts at the end: how many positive integers appear before the negative number and how many appear after. (The set of data shown earlier has 3 positive integers in the first set and 7 in the second.) You can use either **while** or **do-while** loops (or one of each).

46. Write a program that does the following: Read a number <u>change</u> from a set of data. The value of <u>change</u> should be in the range from 0 to 99, representing a number of pennies. Your program will find the most economical way (using as few coins as possible) to represent the value <u>change</u>, using quarters, dimes, nickels, and pennies. Assume that this is the most economical way (is it the best?): Always give as many quarters as possible; for whatever amount is left, always give as many dimes as possible, and so on. For example, if <u>change</u> is 87, give three quarters, one dime, no nickels, and two pennies. (*Suggestion:* You can use either a **while** loop, a **do-while** loop, or some other method of integer division to determine how many quarters, dimes, and so on should be given.)

47. Write a complete C++ program to do the following: The main program reads in (and prints) a set of three student exam grades, then calls a function to check whether they are valid. If the function says they are, the main program calls a series of other functions to classify the grades. At the end of the data set, the main program print three counters. Here are the details:

a. The main program reads in three values.

b. The main program calls a function <u>validgroup( )</u> to determine if this set of three values forms a valid group.

The function <u>validgroup( )</u> receives three parameters. For the group to be valid, each number must be in the range from 0 to 100. If the group is valid, the function prints a message saying it. If one or more of the numbers is negative or greater than 100, the function prints out an overall message saying the group is invalid. In addition, for each invalid value, the function prints the invalid grade and a message (for example, if all three are negative, it prints out three values and messages).

If the function says the group is not valid, the main program skips the processing and goes on to the next group of three values.

c . If the function says the group is valid, the main program calls a function <u>trends( )</u>, to determine what trend the grades follow.

The function <u>trends( )</u> receives three parameters: call them *n1*, *n2*, and *n3*. The function classifies these three values in one of four ways: *n1 <= n2 <= n3*; *n1 >= n2 >= n3*; *n1 >= n2* and then *n2 < n3*; or *n1 <= n2* and then *n2 > n3*. The function prints an appropriate message—for example, the numbers increase, the numbers increase and then decrease, etc.

d. Then the main program calls a function <u>comparegrades( )</u>, sending it the three grades as parameters.

The function <u>comparegrades( )</u> determines which of the following cases holds true: all three values are the same, two are the same and the third is larger; two are the same and the third is smaller; all three are different. Either the function or the main program prints an appropriate message.

e. Finally, the main program goes on to the next group of three values. When the main program runs out of groups (you must decide when), it prints the final values of three counters it has been keeping track of: the total number of groups processed, the number of valid groups, and the number of invalid groups.

Be sure to include a complete set of test data, covering all the possible cases. Here are some examples:

If the original group of data values is –2 173 280, the output should be:

```
-2 173 280 is an invalid set
-2 is negative   173 is too big   280 is too big
```

If the original group is 79 84 84, the output should be:

```
79 84 84 is a valid set
the grades go up
two are the same and the third is smaller
```

48. Write a C++ program to do the following: The main program reads in three integers, representing the degree measure of three angles of a triangle, and sends them to a function. If the function says that the three integers form a valid triangle, the main program calls another function to classify the triangle. After repeating this process for the entire set of data, the main program prints how many groups formed valid triangles and how many formed invalid ones.

The first function, which checks for validity, uses the following rule: The three angles form a valid triangle if they add up to 180 and each one is greater than 0. For example, 40 60 80 is a valid set, but –10 40 150 is invalid (the numbers add up to 180, but one is negative), as is 20 40 100.

The classification function calls two additional functions. One of them determines if the triangle is equiangular (all three angles equal), isosceles (exactly two angles equal), or scalene (all three angles different). The other function determines if the triangle is right (has one angle with 90 degrees), obtuse (one angle above 90), or acute (all three below 90). Each function prints an answer giving its part of the classification process.

Include at least 15 groups with at least 5 of them invalid. Be sure to cover all the possible combinations (isosceles right, scalene acute, etc.).

Here are some sample sets of output:

```
20 60 100 is a valid group      40 50 60 is an invalid group
the triangle is scalene
the triangle is obtuse          -10 40 150 is an invalid group
```

49. Repeat Exercise 48 using the sides of a triangle rather than the angles. Three numbers are valid as the sides of a triangle if each one is positive, and the sum of every two numbers is greater than the third. For example, 4 6 7 is valid; 4 −1 3 is not valid; and 4 5 10 is also invalid.

   The sides can be classified in two ways: First, determine if the triangle is equilateral (all three sides equal), isosceles (exactly two sides equal), or scalene (all three sides different). Second, determine whether or not the triangle is a right triangle (the sum of the squares of two sides is equal to the square of the third side). For example, 6 10 8 is a right triangle, but 5 6 7 is not.

50. Write a program which allows the user to perform simple tasks on a calculator. A series of functions allows the user to select an operation to perform and then enter operands.

   The first function displays a menu, giving the user the choice of typing in any one of the following:

+, −, *, /, or %	representing the usual arithmetic operators
A	representing the average of two numbers
X	representing the maximum of two numbers
M	representing the minimum of two numbers
S	representing the square of a number
Q	indicating the user wants to quit the program

   The program reads the user's response into a variable of type **char**. Using a **switch** statement or a series of **if** statements, the program determines what function to call to process the user's request. For example, if the user enters '+', another function asks for two integers. Then it finds the sum of the two integers. If the user enters 'X', a function asks for two integers and finds the larger of the two. If the user enters 'S', a function asks for one value and finds the square of that value. If the user enters 'Q', the program stops.

   For each calculation performed, the program prints the user's original input and the result.

ARRAYS

PROBLEM: Calculating Statistics for a Set of Test Grades

SYNTAX CONCEPTS: arrays, subscript notation, array of **char**, arrays as parameters, casting, two-dimensional arrays

PROGRAMMING CONCEPTS: parameter (or header) value, storing data in an array, using an array in a function, finding the maximum of a list of numbers

CONTROL STRUCTURES: **for** loop to process an array; the parameter method and the end-of-file method for detecting the end of a set of data; is_open( ); file parameters

PROBLEM-SOLVING TECHNIQUES: modular programming, error checking

HOW TO READ CHAPTER 7

OUTLINE:

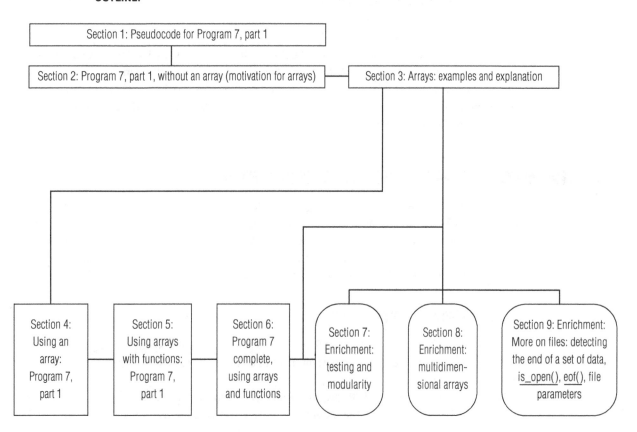

INTRODUCTION

This chapter starts with a problem that comes up often in programming applications: finding the average (sometimes called the mean) of a list of numbers. Even more important is the introduction of a new way to store information, called an array. After discussing arrays, we will use one to solve the rest of Problem 7. One new part of the problem involves comparing all of the values in the array to the average. Arrays, and other data structures based on them, are of central importance to computer science. We will solve the averaging part of the problem without arrays, then with them, so that the advantages are apparent. All of our programs from this point on use the ideas developed here so make sure that you understand this chapter. Problem 7 also introduces a parameter value (sometimes called a header value).

STATEMENT OF THE PROBLEM

PROBLEM 7

An instructor has given an exam in class and wants to find the average mark and the highest mark. Write a complete C++ program to do the following: Read in and print the data, find the average mark in the class and the highest mark, then find how many grades are above, how many are below, and how many are equal to the average. At the end, print the results.

There are no more than 40 students in the class. The data format is as follows: a number $\underline{n}$, called the parameter value, saying how many marks there are for the class, followed by that many marks. For example, the complete set of data might be this:

```
3 91 94 65
```

The 3 is the parameter, promising three marks for the class. They are 91 94 65. Naturally, a real example would be much larger, but the format of the data would remain the same.

In this case, the average of the marks for the class is $(91 + 94 + 65)/3 = 83.33$. The highest mark is 94. The number of grades greater than the average is 2, the number less than the average is 1, and the number equal to the average is 0.

SECTION 1 **HEADER (OR PARAMETER) VALUES; PSEUDOCODE FOR PROGRAM 7**

This section introduces a header value and uses it in developing and refining pseudocode for the first part of Problem 7—finding the average of a set of numbers. Of the two remaining parts of Problem 7, finding the highest mark can be solved with what you know already. However, finding the number of marks greater than, less than, and equal to the average cannot. That part must wait until after Section 3, so we will delay finding the highest mark until then as well.

A HEADER OR PARAMETER VALUE

In one sentence, the first part of Problem 7 can be described as reading in and finding the average of a series of numbers. But there is an important point to be resolved. How will the program know when it has read the last number?

We already have two methods to determine this. One is to use a trailer or sentinel to indicate the end of data. As a second method, the program in Chapter 6 asked the user about being finished, but this makes sense only for a program that uses interactive data entry. Rather than use either, we would like to introduce a third method.

The new method is called the **header value method**. A **parameter or header value** is a number which tells us how many actual pieces of data there are. A program which uses a header value first reads it in, then uses that value to determine how many more data values to read. For example, in the list 5 12 24 56 34 84, the 5 is the header value, telling the program that there are five data values to be read in. The data values are 12 24 56 34 and 84.

Of course, this method also has its flaws and is not always the best choice, but it gives us a third alternative. In a given situation, we can use whichever method seems best. Section 9 introduces a fourth method and compares all four.

CAUTION Notice that the word "parameter" is used in a new way here, different from the meaning it had when we were referring to a value passed to a function. Unfortunately, it is traditional to use the same word for both situations. Try to keep the two meanings separate. It should be clear from the context what the word means.

PSEUDOCODE VERSION OF PROBLEM 7

We will write several versions of Program 7, each time adding new features and taking care of more parts of the original problem. To start, let's just read in the data and find the average for the class. As usual, we begin with a rough pseudocode solution to the problem, then refine it until we reach a level close to C++.

The first thing we must do is read the marks. Each mark should be printed as well so that we can check our computed averages.

read and print the data,
    including the parameter n

STYLE WORKSHOP Printing the data values as they are read in is more important when they are coming from a file than when they are entered interactively. We have written Program 7 as though the data values are being entered interactively. However, by this time, your instructor may have introduced some method that allows the input to come from a data file.

Finding the average for the class is quite easy. We add up the marks (in a variable we'll call sum) and divide by the total number of marks (n in our case) to find the average. We store the average in avgmark and print it. The rest of the pseudocode is as follows:

set sum *to the sum of the marks*
set avgmark *to* sum *divided by* n
print avgmark

REFINING THE PSEUDOCODE: USING THE HEADER VALUE

The next steps to refine are *read and print the data* and *set* sum *to ....* Let's first look at reading the data. Note that the first number of the set (the 3 in the set 3 91 94 65) has to be treated in a different way from the rest since it is not one of the marks to be averaged. Our program must indicate that it is used to decide how many other numbers will be averaged. To make this clear to the computer, we'll read n separately:

read n
print n

After <u>n</u> is read, we want to read <u>n</u> marks and add them up so we can set up a loop to execute <u>n</u> times. In the loop, we will read (one at a time) a series of values into the variable <u>mark</u> and print each <u>mark</u> value. Here is the outline of the loop:

```
for each of n marks {
    read mark
    print mark
    ...
}
```

To determine how many numbers have been read, we use a counter, <u>count</u>; the counter starts at 0, as usual, and increments to <u>n</u>−1. The next version of the pseudocode includes the counting, which occurs in the header of a **for** loop:

```
for (int count = 0; count < n; count++) {
    read mark
    print mark
    ...
}
```

Now let's concentrate on translating *set <u>sum</u> to the sum of the marks*. Computing the sum should be standard by now, with an initialization of <u>sum</u> to 0 and a step that adds a new term to <u>sum</u>. Each value read into <u>mark</u> is added to <u>sum</u>. Finally, when we have added all of the marks, we divide by <u>n</u> to compute the average. Here is the final version of the pseudocode:

```
read n
print n
sum = 0;
for (int count = 0; count < n; count++) {
    read mark
    print mark
    add mark to sum
}
set avgmark to sum divided by n
print avgmark
```

Notice that we start counting from 0 in the header of the **for** loop because that is traditional in C++. (You should be able to convince yourself that counting three things as 0, 1, 2 is just the same as counting 1, 2, 3.) As you will see in Section 3, starting from 0 is necessary in the second version of the program. Meanwhile, there is an added benefit of starting at 0: Each time we reach the top of the loop, the variable <u>count</u> holds the number of marks that have already been processed. (See Exercise 12 and Chapter 3, Exercise 31.)

SELF-CHECK 7-1

1. In the following list, which number is the parameter value? What information does it provide?

   4 27 59 87 98

2. As we read in a series of <u>n</u> numbers, should we count the value we read in for <u>n</u> as one of them?

3. If we start counting from 1, how does the condition in the loop header of the pseudocode have to be changed?

PROGRAM 7, PART 1

This section translates the pseudocode from Section 1 into C++, producing a program that reads in values and finds the average for the class. For reasons which will become clear shortly, we will write the first version of the program without functions and revise it later.

HEADER AND DECLARATIONS

Before we translate the pseudocode, let's write the main program header and declarations. Note that avgmark is declared to have data type **double** because an average usually is not an integer.

```
// Program prog7a.cpp:
// finds the average of the grades for one class,
// reading in data using a parameter value
#include <iostream>
using namespace std;
int main()
{
    int n,sum=0;
    int mark;
    double avgmark;
```

READING THE PARAMETER VALUE

Now we must decide how we intend to read in the data: interactively or from a file (see Chapter 3, Section 7). We will put in prompts and read the data in interactively. However, since this program can handle a large number of students per class, or, with modifications, a large number of classes, some users may want to read the data from a file.

The pseudocode says to read the parameter value into n and print out its value:

```
cout << "Enter the number of marks> ";
cin >> n;
cout << "There are " << n << " marks" << endl;
```

ERROR CHECKING: DOES n HAVE A REASONABLE VALUE?

Actually, this part of Program 7 isn't adequate because it doesn't do enough error checking. Certain integer values of n will cause the program to bomb, for example, 0 or −1. In that case, the rest of the program makes no sense. The program will not read in any data values (which by itself is not a problem), but it will try to compute the average of the data values. This *is* a problem, especially if n is 0. If n is −1, the average is incorrect, but if n is 0, finding the average will crash the program.

A programmer can handle a bad parameter value several ways. One option is to terminate the program; another option is to continue to ask the user to enter a parameter value until it is in the proper range. In this case, we will terminate the program; we leave the other option for Exercise 13. We can revise the section of code to check the value of n and terminate if it is invalid:

```
if (n > 0)
    cout << "There are " << n << " marks" << endl;
```

```
    else {
        cout << "invalid number of marks" << endl;
        exit(1);
    }
```

Remember from Chapter 6, Section 7, that a call to underline{exit( )} terminates the program; sending a nonzero parameter to the function signals an error.

THE LOOP CONDITION

Now we can write the loop to read in the rest of the data. The pseudocode has already translated the header of the **for** loop into C++. Let's check the loop condition. The value of count starts at 0 and increments each time through the loop until the condition count < n is false. What is the final value of count? If you are counting five things starting at 1, you go from 1 to 5. However, if you count starting from 0, you go from 0 to 4, one less than the total. We are counting n things starting from 0, so we go to n −1. When count gets the value n, we fall out of the loop. (As noted above, we could count from 1 to 5 in this loop, but it is traditional in C++ to start at 0; in Section 3, we will see another reason for starting at 0.) We have the following **for** loop header:

```
    for (int count = 0; count < n; count++)
```

READING IN THE DATA AND FINDING THE AVERAGE

Within the loop, we read in a mark, print it, and add it to sum, which was initialized in the declaration. As we translate the loop into C++, we include a comment describing the heart of the program.

```
    // find average of n marks by adding
    // them to sum and dividing by n
    for (int count = 0; count < n; count++) {
        cout << "Enter a mark> ";
        cin >> mark;
        cout << "the next mark is " << mark << endl;
        sum += mark;
    }
```

Since we have added all the marks, we can divide sum by n to obtain the average. We then print the average.

```
    avgmark = sum / n;                                         // incorrect
    cout << "The average is " << avgmark << endl;
```

NUMBER CONVERSIONS

Before we put the program together, there is a problem to fix. The program tries to find the average as follows:

```
    avgmark = sum / n;
```

The program will run, and you will get a value for avgmark, but it isn't the one you expect. If sum has the value 180 and n has the value 3, avgmark has the expected value of 60. However, if sum has the value 182 and n has the value 3, avgmark still has the value 60, not 60.666. In C++, dividing an integer by an integer produces an integer. When we divide sum by n, C++ saves only the integer portion of the quotient; assigning the result to a variable with type **double** is irrelevant because the fractional part of the answer has already been discarded.

There are two ways to solve this problem. One is to assign one of the integer values to a variable of type **double** before dividing:

```
double dsum;

dsum = sum;
avgmark = dsum / n;
```

Because one of the operands (<u>dsum</u>) has type **double**, this forces C++ to do real division, producing a real result. The fractional portion is not lost, and <u>avgmark</u> has the correct value (in this case, 60.67 to two decimal places).

CASTING

The other solution is to use a more general technique called **casting** or **type casting**. Casting is a method for explicitly requesting type conversion. It allows the program to specify the type of result from an operation.

Casting is carried out by placing the desired type in parentheses in front of an operand:

```
avgmark = (double) sum / n;
```

Casting <u>sum</u> to type **double** has the same result as using the variable <u>dsum</u>. It makes a temporary copy of <u>sum</u> with type **double** and uses that value in the division. By casting <u>sum</u>, we guarantee that the C++ compiler performs real division, saves the fractional part of the result, and makes it available when the result is assigned to <u>avgmark</u>. We can obtain the same result by casting <u>n</u> to **double**:

```
avgmark = sum / (double) n;
```

 CAUTION It is important to note that the following cast does not work:

```
avgmark = (double)(sum / n);
```

This cast is done too late to accomplish what we want. The division is done first, producing an integer; the result is cast as **double**, but the fractional part has already been lost.

FINDING THE AVERAGE (FIRST VERSION)

Let's put the program together so we can trace it.

PROGRAM LISTING

```
// Program prog7a.cpp:
// finds the average of the grades for the class,
// reading in data using a parameter value
#include <iostream>
using namespace std;
int main()
{
    int    n,sum=0;
    int    mark;
    double avgmark;
```

```
cout << "Enter the number of marks> ";
cin >> n;
if (n > 0)
    cout << "There are " << n << " marks" << endl;
else {
    cout << "Invalid number of marks" << endl;
    exit(1);
}
// find average of n marks by adding
// them to sum and dividing by n
for (int count = 0; count < n; count++) {
    cout << "Enter a mark> ";
    cin >> mark;
    cout << "the next mark is " << mark << endl;
    sum += mark;
}
avgmark = (double) sum / n;
cout << "The average is " << avgmark << endl;
return 0;
}
```

PROGRAM TRACE Let's trace the program (ignoring printing) with this set of data: 3 91 94 65. Note that n never changes, mark holds the successive numbers to be averaged, count counts the number of mark values read in, and sum holds the sum of the mark values.

0		--		--		--
count		n		mark		sum

♦ Initially, count is 0, indicating that we have not yet read in any mark values.

♦ We first read 3 into n, which tells the program that there are three marks in the set of data; the **for** loop will go from 0 to 2.

♦ Inside the body of the loop, when count is 0, we read 91 into mark and add it to sum, which becomes 91.

♦ At the top of the loop, count becomes 1, indicating that we have read in one mark.

1		3		91		91
count		n		mark		sum

♦ Inside the body of the loop, we read 94 into mark and add it to sum, which becomes 91 + 94 or 185.

♦ At the top of the loop, count becomes 2.

2		3		94		185
count		n		mark		sum

♦ Inside the body of the loop, we read 65 into mark and add mark to sum, which becomes 185 + 65 or 250.

◆ Then <u>count</u> becomes 3, which is too large. We fall out of the **for** loop with the final values for <u>count</u>, <u>mark</u>, and <u>sum</u>.

3   3   65   250
<u>count</u>   <u>n</u>   <u>mark</u>   <u>sum</u>

◆ Outside the loop, we cast <u>sum</u> to type **double**, which makes it 250.00; then we divide this value by <u>n</u>, which is 3, to give <u>avgmark</u> the value 83.33, which is printed.

This completes the first version of Program 7, which finds the average of the marks. This first version simply serves as a base for what we want to do. Before we rewrite the program, we will introduce the new concept that is the focus of this chapter.

SELF-CHECK 7-2

1. Write another version of this program which uses a **while** loop instead of a **for** loop.

2. What is the final value of <u>count</u>?

3. What is the relationship between <u>count</u> and the number of values read in?

SECTION 3   ARRAYS

This section introduces an array, the first data structure in this book. A **data structure** is a method of grouping and organizing information in a way that reflects the relationships among data values.

PROBLEMS WITH THE FIRST VERSION

The program presented in Section 2 works as promised. However, we often find an average as part of a larger problem, as in complete Program 7, and for that reason, the program can be improved. Imagine that we have just completed calculating the average. Can we answer these questions in the main program? Can we write a function to answer them?

1. What was the first grade averaged?

2. The second?

3. The last?

4. Which grade is closest to the average?

5. How many grades are above or below the average?

We can't tell what the first (or second) number was because each was read into <u>mark</u>, then replaced by the next. Questions 4 and 5 are also impossible to answer (and question 5 is part of Problem 7). We can answer question 3 since the last number read in is still in <u>mark</u>, but it's the only one.

Here is a grotesque way to solve some of these problems:

◆ Read the first number into a variable called <u>mark1</u>.

◆ Read the second into a new variable <u>mark2</u>.

◆ Read the third into <u>mark3</u> (and so on).

Each number will be in a distinct variable so if we are asked about one specifically, we will know where to look.

This might be a good idea, but it entails much extra work. Each variable, mark1, mark2, mark3, ..., must be declared. Even worse, we can no longer use a loop to read in the numbers. Each number has to be read, printed, and added to sum separately because they all have their own names. Thus, to add 10 numbers and find their average is burdensome. To add 25 or 30 numbers requires a large (and repetitious) program. It is clear that this is not a clever way to solve the problem.

There is another problem with using many different variables. Suppose we want to read in values in the main program or a function and then call another function to compute the average. How many arguments do we send to the function? The number depends on the value of n, which is not known until the program is running, and we read in a value for n. Given how we currently store the data values, it is impossible to send all of the values to a function at one time. This is why we have written the first version of Program 7 without a function.

THE CONCEPT OF AN ARRAY

Fortunately, C++ (as well as almost every programming language) has a way of assigning unique names to the variables so that one value does not have to be written on top of another, but without the tremendous effort involved in separate variable names. An **array** allows us to use a single variable to store a number of values with the same data type. Each element of the array has its own storage location, which can be referenced like any other variable. The elements of an array are stored in consecutive storage locations in memory and identified by the name of the array followed by a number in brackets; these numbers start at 0. Thus, in an array of numbers called num, we can refer to the first num value, the second num value, and so on. In mathematics, we would identify these values as num_0, num_1, etc. In C++, the parts of a five-element array num are num[0], num[1], num[2], num[3], and num[4] (see Figure 7-1). An array gives us a way to store all the marks for a class and then refer to a specific student's mark.

HIGHLIGHTS

◆ The numbers 0, 1, 2, 3, 4 are called **subscripts**; individual elements of the array are called **subscripted variables**.

◆ The square brackets distinguish array subscripts from other types of parenthesized expressions.

◆ The subscripts of all arrays in C++ are numbered starting with 0 and increase each time by 1.

NAMING THE ELEMENTS OF AN ARRAY

This simple analogy explains the relationship of the individual elements to the entire array. Within the Smith family, the individual members can be referred to by their first names—Joan or Bob or Carol.

FIGURE 7-1   Array num

	num	
0	3	num[0] holds 3
1	15	num[1] holds 15
2	−2	num[2] holds −2
3		num[3] and num[4] do not have values
4		

All of them share a common last name. When we want to distinguish one family from another, we use the last name—the Smith or the Taylor family. When we want to choose a single individual, we use both names—Joan and Smith.

An array is similar. All elements of the <u>val</u> array share the common name <u>val</u>. They are distinguished from each other by their individual subscripts. To refer to an element in the <u>val</u> array, we give the array name and the subscript or location within it—<u>val</u> and 3 designate <u>val[3]</u>. Just as there can be a Joan Smith and a Joan Jacobs, there can be a third element in the <u>val</u> array (called <u>val[2]</u>) and one in the <u>num</u> array (called <u>num[2]</u>).

SELF-CHECK 7-3

1. What is the purpose of an array?
2. Which of the following games use an array in their scoring mechanisms? For each one, identify what a single element of the array represents.

    a. tennis   b. bowling   c. darts   d. baseball
3. How large an array do you need to represent each of the following collections of information?

    a. the days in the week   b. the months in the year

USING ARRAYS

The elements of the array can be treated like simple variables. Each element can be assigned a value, tested, printed, or used in an expression.

EXAMPLE 7-1

Here are some examples using elements of array <u>num</u> instead of simple variables:

```
num[3] = 5;      or      cout << num[4];      or      result = 2 * num[0];
```

A more interesting and powerful feature lets the subscript itself be a variable.

EXAMPLE 7-2

Let's use i as the subscript of array <u>num</u>:

```
i = 4;
num[i] = 7;
```

The variable i is set to 4 by the first line. The reference in the second line to the subscripted variable <u>num[i]</u> really means <u>num[4]</u>, and that storage location is set to 7.

Finally, let's look at the almost perfect marriage between arrays and **for** loops. The array subscript can be changed in the **for** loop header, allowing us to fill consecutive elements efficiently.

EXAMPLE 7-3

What does this loop do?

```
for (int i = 0; i < 5; i++)
    num[i] = i * 3;
```

It assigns each element of array <u>num</u> a value which is 3 times its subscript; that is, <u>num[0]</u> gets the value 0, <u>num[1]</u> gets 3, <u>num[2]</u> gets 6, <u>num[3]</u> gets 9, and <u>num[4]</u> gets 12.

CAUTION Make sure that you know the difference between the value stored in an array element, e.g., 9 in <u>num[3]</u>, and a subscript like 3.

DECLARING AN ARRAY

To use an array, we must declare it. For example, an array called <u>nums</u> that can hold ten integers is declared as follows:

```
int nums[10];
```

♦ The 10 specifies the number of elements in the array (usually referred to as the **size** or **dimension**). Array <u>nums</u> has ten elements, numbered from 0 to 9.

♦ 0 is the **lower bound** or smallest subscript in every array.

♦ 9 is the **upper bound** or largest subscript.

♦ In the program, a subscript which refers to <u>nums</u> should be in the range from 0 to 9.

♦ The type in the array declaration tells what data type applies to each element, from the lower to the upper bound; in the array <u>nums</u>, the data type for each element is **int**.

Keep in mind that the declaration sets aside ten storage locations for the <u>nums</u> array, but the program does not have to use them all.

CAUTION Even though there are ten elements in the array, the highest subscript is 9. An attempt to use subscript 10 references a storage location outside the array, which is usually the location of another variable. If you assign or read a value into that location, you will destroy the value of the other variable. C++ does not send an error message since it does not check for invalid subscripts.

It is possible to initialize all of an array in the declaration, although that usually makes sense only for small arrays. The following declaration initializes all ten elements in the <u>nums</u> array:

```
int nums[10] = {5,11,-1,17,30,6,47,48,21,-32};
```

ARRAYS OF OTHER DATA TYPES

Although the examples so far have all been arrays of type **int**, we can have arrays of other data types, such as **float**, **double**, or **char**.

EXAMPLE 7-4   We want an array <u>sales</u> to hold a company's sales data for three years, 2005 to 2007. The sales data will be values of type **double**. The declaration and initialization for the array <u>sales</u> can be the following:

```
double sales[3] = {123.45, 23456.78};
```

The lower bound for the array is 0; the upper bound is 2, giving a total of three storage locations. Each location can hold a number of type **double**. Note that we have initialized only the first two elements in the array; <u>sales[0]</u> is initialized to hold the sales for 2005, and <u>sales[1]</u> holds the sales for 2006. The third element, <u>sales[2]</u>, will hold the sales for 2007 when that value is entered. Figure 7-2 diagrams what the array <u>sales</u> looks like after it has been initialized.

INTERPRETATION OF SUBSCRIPTS

Since C++ requires that subscripts begin at 0, we can't use subscripts that might otherwise seem logical. For example, the year can't be the subscript in the <u>sales</u> array. Instead, we must interpret the subscripts in the program code, as shown in Example 7-5.

FIGURE 7-2   Array <u>sales</u>

<table>
<tr><td></td><td><u>sales</u></td></tr>
<tr><td>0</td><td>123.45</td></tr>
<tr><td>1</td><td>23456.78</td></tr>
<tr><td>2</td><td></td></tr>
</table>

EXAMPLE 7-5   Suppose we want to read in amounts to update the array <u>sales</u> from Example 7-4. Each transaction consists of two pieces of data: first, the year which is being updated, and then the new amount to add to the total. There may be several transactions for each array element, and the transactions are not necessarily in any order. This means we cannot use the index of the loop to select array elements. The following code updates the appropriate element and then prints the entire array.

```
double sales[3] = {0,0,0};
double amount;
int    year,numtrans;

cout << "Enter the number of transactions> ";
cin >> numtrans;
for (int count = 0; count < numtrans; count++) {
    cin >> year;
    cin >> amount;
    switch (year) {
      case 2005:
            sales[0] += amount;
            break;
      case 2006:
            sales[1] += amount;
            break;
      case 2007:
            sales[2] += amount;
            break;
      default;
    }
}
cout << "sales for 2005 are " << sales[0] << endl;
cout << "sales for 2006 are " << sales[1] << endl;
cout << "sales for 2007 are " << sales[2] << endl;
```

There is a relationship between the years (2005, 2006, and 2007) and the subscripts (0, 1, and 2). We can use this mathematical relationship to replace the <u>switch</u> statement with the following simple statement:

```
sales[year - 2005] += amount;
```

Using the same principle, the three output statements can be replaced by the following loop:

```
for (int i = 0; i < 3; i++)
    cout << "sales for " << (i + 2005) << " are "
         << sales[i] << endl;
```

ARRAY OF VALUES OF TYPE char

As another example, let's look at an array of values of type **char**.

EXAMPLE 7-6

The following declaration sets up an array <u>message</u> that can hold 20 characters:

```
char message[20];
```

We can assign values to each array element, either in the declaration or through assignment statements. Each element can hold a single value of type **char**, including special values like the newline character '\n' and the tab character '\t'.

As usual, an array of **char** can be initialized element by element in the declaration or assignment statements, as shown in Example 7-7.

EXAMPLE 7-7

Here we initialize the first five elements in the declaration and assign values to the next seven; the other elements remain uninitialized:

```
char message[20] = {'w','e','i','r','d'};

message[5] = ' ';                  // assign a blank to message[5]
message[6] = 's';
message[7] = 't';
message[8] = 'u';
message[9] = 'f';
message[10] = 'f';
```

EXAMPLE 7-8

The array <u>message</u> can be printed character by character. Assume that <u>message</u> has been initialized as shown in Example 7-7. In the code below, we stop at the end of the filled elements in the array.

```
char message[20] = {'w','e','i','r','d'};

message[5] = ' ';                  // assign a blank to message[5]
message[6] = 's';
message[7] = 't';
message[8] = 'u';
message[9] = 'f';
message[10] = 'f';

for (int i = 0; i < 11; i++)
    cout << message[i];
cout << endl;
```

The loop prints the individual elements of <u>message</u> one at a time, next to each other, so that the resulting output looks like a string:

```
weird stuff
```

EXAMPLE 7-9

This time we store a newline character in one position of the array.

```
char message[20] = {'w','e','i','r','d'};

message[5] = '\n';                 // assign a newline char to message[5]
message[6] = 's';
message[7] = 't';
message[8] = 'u';
```

```
message[9] = 'f';
message[10] = 'f';

for (int i = 0; i < 11; i++)
    cout << message[i];
cout << endl;
```

This time the characters print on two lines, because printing the newline character in message[5] sent the cursor to a new line.

```
weird
stuff
```

SELF-CHECK 7-4

1. What is the appropriate declaration for each of the following?

    a. an array of 50 numbers with decimal places   b. an array of 26 characters

2. Answer the following questions about this declaration:

    ```
    int amount[25];
    ```

    a. How many elements are in the array?
    b. What are the upper and lower bounds of the array?

EXPRESSIONS AS SUBSCRIPTS

Actually, we have been more restrictive than is necessary. All the subscripts in our examples have been integer constants or variables, but this is not required. A subscript can be an expression as long as it evaluates to an integer.

EXAMPLE 7-10

Here is the declaration for an array item and a variable i. Below the declaration is an assignment using a valid subscript reference.

```
int i=4;
int item[20];

item[2*i + 3] = 76;
```

To which element does the subscript refer? First, the subscript $2*i + 3$ is evaluated to an integer value; call it val. In this case, the subscript val evaluates to $2*4 + 3 = 8 + 3 = 11$, so the value 76 is assigned to item[11].

Although a subscript can be any integer expression, by far the most common choice is an integer variable such as i or a minor modification like $i + 1$. Let's illustrate this with a simple example.

EXAMPLE 7-11

Assume we have read a series of letters into the eight-element array letters. For example, the array might contain 'Y', 'A', 'M', 'L', 'N', 'M', 'M', and 'J'. Figure 7-3 shows the array with these values (the subscripts are along the bottom):

FIGURE 7-3   Letters array

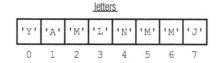

We want to check if any two consecutive entries are equal. Here is a portion of a program to print a message every time there is a match:

```
char letters[8];

for (int i = 0; i < 7; i++)
    if (letters[i] == letters[i + 1])
        cout << letters[i] << " is repeated" << endl;
```

We have declared <u>letters</u> as an array of **char**. Inside the **for** loop, the subscript i refers to an element of the array. The subscript $i + 1$ refers to the next element of the array.

You may wonder why the **for** loop index goes from 0 to 6 ($i < 7$) even though there are eight elements in the array. Remember that the highest subscript in the array is 7; when i is 6, $i + 1$ is 7, so we will be comparing the next-to-last element (<u>letters[6]</u>) with the last (<u>letters[7]</u>). (If we allowed i to go from 0 to 7, the last comparison would use <u>letters[8]</u>, which is out of bounds.)

An alternate way to process the array is to have the subscript i refer to an element and use $i - 1$ as the subscript of the previous element.

PARALLEL ARRAYS

The same subscript can be used for more than one array at the same time. Two arrays which use the same variable as a subscript in a loop are called **parallel arrays**. Consider a situation where we have two arrays, one to store students' ID numbers and another to store the same students' averages. Let's call the two arrays <u>idnum</u> and <u>average</u>. A logical way to store the information is to keep each student's ID number in the same position of the <u>idnum</u> array as that student's average occupies in the <u>average</u> array. Thus <u>average[0]</u> belongs to <u>idnum[0]</u>, <u>average[1]</u> to <u>idnum[1]</u>, and so on (see Figure 7-4).

To print out each student's ID number, followed by that student's average, we can use the same subscript. Example 7-12 shows how to do this.

EXAMPLE 7-12   Assume that both arrays have been initialized:

```
int    idnum[20];
double average[20];

for (int i = 0; i < 20; i++)
    cout << "student " << idnum[i]
        << " has an average of " << average[i] << endl;
```

As i varies from 0 to 19, it allows us to access a new element from both arrays. The element accessed from the <u>idnum</u> array will always have the same subscript as the one from the <u>average</u> array.

FIGURE 7-4   Parallel arrays, <u>idnum</u> and <u>average</u>

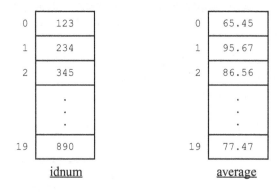

SENDING A SINGLE ELEMENT OF AN ARRAY AS A PARAMETER

A single element of an array is treated like any simple variable of its type. We can send it as a parameter to a function, as we did in Example 7-12, where idnum[i] and average[i] are parameters for cout. Example 7-13 shows how to send an element of an **int** array to a function.

EXAMPLE 7-13   The function add( ) adds two numbers together and returns the result. Here are its prototype and header:

prototype	header
`int add(int,int);`	`int add(int first,int second)`

The calling program can send any integer variable to match parameters first and second. The call below sends the first two elements of the nums array:

```
int result,nums[10];
...
result = add(nums[0],nums[1]);
```

Passing an entire array as a parameter is more complex and will be discussed in Section 5.

SELECTING BOUNDS FOR AN ARRAY

Let's look at some other features of arrays. Suppose an array test is declared to have 40 storage locations. It is certainly legal to fill only three of them since we can leave storage locations unused. However, suppose we provide only two locations by using this declaration:

```
int test[2];
```

Whether this is a problem depends on the size of the set of numbers. The program must provide enough space to hold all the data. If there are only one or two numbers, this array can store all the values. But if the set of data has three numbers, we have a problem: the third value goes into test[2], which is outside the array. Declaring test to have three locations solves the problem for this set of data, but if the data set has four values, the problem arises again.

It is foolish to write a program that is so sensitive to the slightest change in the size of the data set. We should not have to change the declaration and recompile the program every time we change the size of the data set. Declaring arrays with very large bounds is one way to make sure that we won't be caught short, but it is wasteful and inefficient. As a rule, it is best to choose array bounds that are large enough to hold most sets of data comfortably but that are not unwieldy. We usually declare our arrays to hold several more items than we expect. If we expect 120 numbers, we declare 150 locations:

```
int test[150];
```

NOTE   The space is reserved regardless of whether it is filled.

CAUTION A programmer must be careful to reserve enough memory locations for an array and to keep all subscripts within the established bounds. Since C++ does not check to see whether a subscript is out of bounds, using a subscript greater than the upper bound does not generate a warning or error message. C++ uses the subscript to calculate a memory location and uses that location even if it is allocated to another variable.

USING A CONSTANT AS THE ARRAY SIZE

It would be convenient to use the variable <u>num</u> in the declaration, as follows:

```
int num = 10;
int test[num];             // dangerous
```

It would seem that, once <u>num</u> gets a value, we can use it to declare an array of exactly the right size. However, this form is dangerous because the results are unpredictable.

We can, however, use a constant as the size of the array; to modify the array size, we simply change the constant definition.

```
const int NUM = 150;
int test[NUM];
```

The value 150 is substituted for <u>NUM</u> prior to setting up storage for the array, making this a legal declaration.

SELF-CHECK 7-5

1. Given this declaration, answer the following questions.

    ```
    int item[25], amount[25],i;
    ```

    a. If <u>i</u> = 8, what array element is referred to by <u>item[i–3]</u>?

    b. If <u>i</u> is 23, what element is <u>amount[i+1]</u>?

2. Show how to fill all the elements in the <u>item</u> array in question 1 with sequential values, starting from 1.

3. In Example 7-12, why can't the information for arrays <u>idnum</u> and <u>average</u> be stored in one array?

SECTION 4 ## USING AN ARRAY—PROGRAM 7, PART 1

This section illustrates how to use an array by rewriting the part of Program 7 we have done so far.

THE mark ARRAY

Instead of a single variable called <u>mark</u>, we can use an array called <u>mark</u>.

♦ The first number to be averaged goes into <u>mark[0]</u>.

♦ The second number to be averaged goes into <u>mark[1]</u>.

♦ The last number to be averaged goes into <u>mark[n–1]</u>.

This method of naming the elements is close to what we proposed in Section 3 (<u>mark1</u>, <u>mark2</u>, <u>mark3</u> …). Now, because the named elements are part of an array, the notation will help rather than hinder us. When we print and add to <u>sum</u>, we use a particular element of the <u>mark</u> array. Thus, at the end of the averaging process, we still have all the values stored in the <u>mark</u> array.

To instruct the computer to use <u>mark[0]</u> first, then <u>mark[1]</u>, we need a variable for the subscript that can increase from 0 to <u>n–1</u>. Luckily, there already is such a variable, <u>count</u>, the index of the **for** loop, which can be the array subscript. Before the first mark is read in, <u>count</u> has the value 0. Then

<u>count</u> is 1 after the first mark has been processed. The index <u>count</u> continues to increase by 1 as each new <u>mark</u> value is used.

If we use <u>mark[count]</u> as the variable to hold the numbers, the values to be averaged are put successively into <u>mark[0]</u>, <u>mark[1]</u>, ..., <u>mark[num−1]</u>. The only changes we have to make to use an array in Program 7 are to replace <u>mark</u> by <u>mark[count]</u> and change the declaration.

PROGRAM 7: SECOND VERSION, USING AN ARRAY

Now let's rewrite the program. We said that the professor never has more than 40 students in a class. Therefore, we set up the following array declaration (note that we allow for a few extra elements as a precaution):

```
const int SIZE = 50;
int mark[SIZE];
```

Now that we are using an array, we must add an additional check to parameter value <u>n</u>. It is no longer sufficient to check whether <u>n</u> is greater than 0; <u>n</u> must be appropriate for the bounds of the array: in this case, <u>n</u> must be less than <u>SIZE</u>. A program which reads data into an array should always make sure not to exceed the bounds. Here is the complete new version of the program, using an array to hold the marks:

PROGRAM LISTING

```cpp
// Program prog7b.cpp:
// finds the average of the grades for the class
// using a parameter value and an array
#include <iostream>
using namespace std;
const int SIZE = 50;
int main()
{
    int    n,sum;
    int    mark[SIZE];
    double avgmark;

    cout << "Enter the number of marks> ";
    cin >> n;
    if (n > 0 && n <= SIZE)
        cout << "There are " << n << " marks" << endl;
    else {
        cout << "Invalid number of marks";
        exit(1);
    }
    // find average of n marks by adding
    // them to sum and dividing by n
    sum = 0;
    for (int count = 0; count < n; count++) {
        cout << "Enter a mark> ";
        cin >> mark[count];
        cout << mark[count] << endl;
```

```
        sum += markZ[count];
    }
    avgmark = (double) sum / n;
    cout << "The average is " << avgmark << endl;
    return 0;
}
```

The array version is almost identical to the original. To verify this, you should trace it with the same set of values that we used for the first version. Now, however, each value is stored in its own array location; even after the average has been computed, all of the values in <u>mark</u> are still available for other computations.

A MODULAR VERSION OF PROGRAM 7

To illustrate the importance of having all the values available throughout the program, we will rewrite it using two loops rather than one. Each loop performs a separate task. The first loop reads and prints the data, and the second finds the average, using the values which are still in the array. Each loop is thus a self-contained unit, or **module**, which we can use here or somewhere else. Notice that each module performs a separate task, as a function would. This will help us in the next version of this program.

PROGRAM 7: THIRD VERSION, USING AN ARRAY AND TWO LOOPS

Here is the new version of the program so far:

💻 PROGRAM LISTING

```
// Program prog7c.cpp:
// finds the average of the grades for the class
// using a parameter value, an array, and two loops
#include <iostream>
using namespace std;
const int SIZE = 50;
int main()
{
    int    n, sum;
    int    mark[SIZE];
    double avgmark;

    cout << "Enter the number of marks> ":
    cin >> n;
    if (n > 0 && n <= SIZE)
        cout << "There are " << n << " marks" << endl;
    else {
        cout << "Invalid number of marks";
        exit(1);
    }
    // read n marks into the mark array
    // and print each mark as it is read in
    for (int count = 0; count < n; count++) {
        cout << "Enter a mark> ";
```

```
        cin >> mark[count];
        cout << mark[count];
    }
    // find average of n marks by adding
    // them to sum and dividing by n
    sum = 0;
    for (int count = 0; count < n; count++)
        sum += mark[count];
    avgmark = (double) sum / n;
    cout << "The average is " << avgmark;
    return 0;
}
```

SELF-CHECK 7-6

1. a. What is the advantage of the array version of the program?

    b. What changes are necessary to use an array in Program 7?

2. Can we have separate modules to read and to print?

3. If we omit [SIZE] from the declaration of mark, what type of variable will the compiler think mark is?

SECTION 5 USING ARRAYS WITH FUNCTIONS—PROGRAM 7, PART 1

Now that we have seen how to work with arrays, we must learn how to use one in a function. To illustrate this, let's rewrite Program 7, part 1.

SENDING AN ARRAY AS A PARAMETER: PROTOTYPE AND FUNCTION HEADER FOR sumarray()

We want to write a function called sumarray( ) that finds the sum of the elements in the mark array. Of course, we won't sum all the elements in the array, just those filled with useful values. The easiest way to specify this is to use another parameter, say n, to hold the number of values we want to sum (as opposed to the size in the declaration). Inside the function, we call the array num. We want the function to add the array elements from num[0] to num[n−1] and return this value. We call the formal parameter num instead of mark for two reasons: one is so we can distinguish between the formal and actual parameter if necessary; the second is so we can reuse this function for any array of integers and still have a meaningful name.

First, let's look at the prototype of the function sumarray( ), where the array is the first parameter, and n is the second:

```
int sumarray(int [],int);   or   int sumarray(int num[],int n);
```

In the left version of the prototype, we do not give names to the formal parameters, while in the version on the right, we do give them names. Some people prefer a name when the parameter is an array, even if they just write ***int array[]***, using array as the name of the parameter.

The header of the function follows logically from the prototype, although, of course, a name must be given to the formal parameter. Once again, we use [], with no size, to indicate the array parameter:

```
int sumarray(int num[], int n)      // function header
```

In C++, an array is always passed as a reference parameter; for this reason, it is not necessary to use & in the function header or prototype.

CAUTION In a function prototype or header, to indicate that a parameter is an array, insert brackets following the data type (or name, if supplied) of the parameter.

◆ Do not omit the array brackets. If you do, the compiler will expect the parameter to be a simple integer variable rather than an array.

◆ It is not necessary to put a size into the array brackets. (If you supply one, it will be ignored.)

In a function that receives an array as a parameter, the formal parameter can be matched up with an array of any size. However, the actual and formal parameters must have the same underlying type (e.g., array of **int** or array of **double**). This means that we can use sumarray( ) to sum integer arrays of different sizes.

THE FUNCTION sumarray( )

The rest of the function is very straightforward. Assume that a separate function, readdata( ) (to appear shortly), has already read values into the array before this function is called. All sumarray( ) has to do is add up the elements in the array (which is what we did earlier in the main program) and return the result. Here is the entire function:

PROGRAM LISTING

```
// Function sumarray:
// Input:
//    num: an array of integers
//    n: the number of elements in the array
// Process:
//    finds the sum of the first n elements
//    in the num array
// Output:
//    returns the sum to the calling function
int sumarray(int num[], int n)
{
    int sum = 0;

    for (int count = 0; count < n; count++)
        sum += num[count];
    return sum;
}
```

THE FUNCTION avgarray( )

Now that we have a simple example of an array as a parameter to a function, we are ready to write the function for Program 7. To do this, we need a function to find an average, not a sum. We can call the function avgarray( ). Let's again call the parameters to this function num and n; in fact, we can use num and n in all the functions. Note the type of answer the function returns.

```
double avgarray(int num[], int n)
```

To find an average, we add up a series of numbers (in this case, n of them) and divide by the total number of values (again n). One way to do this is to write a **for** loop to sum the num array, then have a last step which divides this sum by n. This isn't hard to do, but we want to limit the burdensome work we must do as programmers by having the computer do it for us. There is an easy way to sum the num array by using the function sumarray( ). In other words, the function avgarray( ) calls the function sumarray( ). The answer from sumarray( ) is put into a local variable total.

```
total = sumarray(num,n);
```

The answer stored in total is cast to **double**, divided by n, and then returned:

```
return (double) total / n;
```

Actually, the local variable total can be eliminated. In the version of avgarray( ) below, we get rid of total. Here is the entire function:

```
// Function avgarray:
// Input:
//   num: an array of integers
//   n: the number of elements in the array
// Process:
//   calls sumarray to find the sum of the first n elements
//   in the num array; divides sum by n to obtain the average
// Output:
//   returns the average to the calling function
double avgarray(int num[], int n)
{
    return (double) sumarray(num,n) / n;
}
```

In this version, the value returned from the function sumarray( ) is used directly in the computation; this value is cast as **double** and then divided by n without first being stored in total.

THE FUNCTION readdata( )

In order to write a complete version of Program 7, we also need a function readdata( ) to read in and print the data. The readdata( ) function performs the same task as the first loop of the modular version of the program. It does not, however, print a heading on the output since the main program prints headings. The function readdata( ) reads in the values from the set of data; first it reads n, and then it reads n values into an array num, which holds the numbers we have read in.

Clearly, readdata( ) should receive as a parameter the array which we want to fill. You may recall from Chapter 5 that a variable whose value will change in a function must be sent to the function by reference. That is, for most variables, we must use the & operator in the function prototype (and the function header) when we want to send a reference to the variable to the function. However, an & is not used with the name of an array parameter, because an array parameter is always sent by reference.

The mark array will receive values in readdata( ), and so will n, which will carry back to main the number of values read into the array. While the function could change the parameter num and return the value of <u>n</u>, it is better style to pick one way of having a function communicate with the program that called it. In this case, it will change two parameters. Here are the prototype and the header for the function <u>readdata</u>:

prototype	header
`void readdata(int [], int &);`	`void readdata(int num[], int &n)`

You may ask why <u>readdata( )</u> can't return the array. Remember that a function can only return a single value. Which value of the array would it return? The first? The last? None of these makes sense. The array cannot be returned but must have its values changed instead.

Here is the complete function <u>readdata( )</u>:

 PROGRAM LISTING

```
// Function readdata:
// Input:
//    num: the array to fill
//    parameter is uninitialized upon entry
// Process:
//    reads n and reads n values
//    into the num array; prints n and num
// Output:
//    fills array num
//    prints num array
//    returns n
void readdata(int num[],int &n)
{
    cout << "Enter the number of marks> ";
    cin >> n;
    if (n > 0 && n <= SIZE)
        cout << "There are " << n << " marks" << endl;
    else {
        cout << "Invalid number of marks" << endl;
        exit(1);
    }
    for (int count = 0; count < n; count++) {
        cout << "Enter a mark> ";
        cin >> num[count];
        cout << num[count];
    }
    return;
}
```

When we send the <u>mark</u> array to <u>readdata( )</u>, the array contains no values; it receives its values in <u>readdata( )</u>. After the function returns to the main program, the array <u>mark</u> that was matched with the formal parameter <u>num</u> holds the information read in by the function <u>readdata( )</u> (see Figure 7-5). Of course, if the value entered for <u>n</u> is invalid, the program terminates, and the function does not return to the main program. (In Section 9, we explore other ways of handling invalid data.)

FIGURE 7-5   Sample values of <u>num</u> and <u>n</u> as changed by <u>readdata()</u>

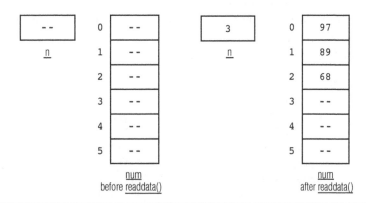

REVISING THE MAIN PROGRAM: SENDING AN ARRAY AS A PARAMETER

We have written the functions; now we must write the main program. The main program has to establish the prototypes, call the functions, and print out the results.

To send an array as a parameter to a function, we include its name in the parameter list of the function call, just as we would any other variable name. Here are the two function calls:

```
readdata(mark,n);
avgmark = avgarray(mark,n);
```

Here is the complete main program, including the calls:

PROGRAM LISTING

```
// Program prog7d.cpp:
// finds the average of the grades for the class using
// functions readdata, sumarray, and avgarray
#include <iostream>
using namespace std;
const int SIZE = 50;
void readdata(int [],int &);
int sumarray(int [], int);
double avgarray(int [], int);
int main()
{
    int    n;
    int    mark[SIZE];
    double avgmark;

    // call functions to read and process the marks
    readdata(mark,n);
    avgmark = avgarray(mark,n);
    cout << "The average is " << avgmark;
    return 0;
}
```

FOURTH VERSION OF PROGRAM 7

Now we are ready to combine the functions with the (revised) main program.

 PROGRAM LISTING

```cpp
// Program prog7d.cpp:
#include <iostream>
using namespace std;
const int SIZE = 50;
void readdata(int [], int &);
int sumarray(int [], int);
double avgarray(int [], int);
int main()
{
    int    n;
    int    mark[SIZE];
    double avgmark;

    // call functions to read and process the marks
    readdata(mark,n);
    avgmark = avgarray(mark,n);
    cout << "The average is " << avgmark;
}
// ...
void readdata(int num[], int &n)
{
    cout << "Enter the number of marks> ";
    cin >> n;
    if (n > 0 && n <= SIZE)
        cout << "There are " << n << " marks" << endl;
    else {
        cout << "Invalid number of marks" << endl;
        exit(1);
    }
    for (int count = 0; count < n; count++) {
        cout << "Enter a mark> ");
        cin >> num[count];
        cout << num[count] << endl;
    }
    return;
}
// ...
int sumarray(int num[], int n)
{
    int sum = 0;

    for (int count = 0; count < n; count++)
        sum += num[count];
    return sum;
}
```

```
// ...
double avgarray(int num[], int n)
{
      return (double) sumarray(num,n) / n;
}
```

SELF-CHECK 7-7

1.   a. Why is it necessary for <u>avgarray( )</u> to have a return value of type **double**?

     b. Why doesn't the main program have to call <u>sumarray( )</u>?

2.   How is a parameter identified as an array in the prototype?

3.   What is the reason for omitting the size of an array in the prototype and function header?

4.   Upon its return from <u>readdata( )</u>, the <u>mark</u> array has values in it, even though we didn't use the & operator. How?

SECTION 6   THE REST OF PROGRAM 7

This section shows how to find the maximum of a list of numbers, which we incorporate into Program 7. We write a function for Program 7 to find the number of marks less than and greater than the average. Then we complete Program 7.

FINDING THE MAXIMUM

We have two more sections of Program 7 to write. First, the professor wants to know the highest grade in the class. We already have the grades stored in an array where we can look at each one. To find which grade is the highest, we could say, "Look through the grades for a 100—if it is there, it must be the highest; if not, look for a 99, and so on." However, this method is incredibly inefficient, especially if the highest grade is something like 73 or, even worse, 54. We need to devise an algorithm for finding the largest number.

AN ALGORITHM FOR FINDING THE LARGEST ELEMENT IN AN ARRAY

Let's take a look at a possible algorithm for finding the largest element in an array.

Algorithm for Finding the Largest Element in an Array

♦   *Initially, pick the first number in the array to be the largest so far.*

♦   *Compare this number to the next one in the array. If the next is larger, then it is the largest so far; otherwise do nothing.*

♦   *Repeat this process until every number in the array has been compared to the largest so far.*

♦   *Whichever number is the larger after the last comparison (the largest so far at the end) is the largest in the entire array.*

Before we refine this, let's make sure that the algorithm is correct. It's impossible that an earlier number could be larger than the value of the largest at the end, this algorithm works. Now we can use it to find the largest value in an array.

Here is a pseudocode version of this algorithm, applied to the first n elements of the num array:

largest so far = first number in the num *array*
for *each of the remaining* n−1 *numbers in the array*
compare largest so far with this number
if *this number > largest so far*
  largest so far = this number

This is easy to translate into C++. Let's use largestsofar for the variable that holds the largest number seen so far in the array. We can initialize largestsofar to an actual candidate for the largest number, num[0]:

```
largestsofar = num[0];
for (int count = 1; count < n; count++)
    if (largestsofar < num[count])
        largestsofar = num[count];
```

PROGRAM TRACE Let's trace this code before writing the function, using the set of data shown earlier (grades 91, 94, 65 in the num array, and n equal to 3).

♦ We initialize largestsofar to the value of num[0], which is 91.

♦ Then we enter the loop, where we compare largestsofar with num[1], which is 94.

♦ Since largestsofar is smaller, we assign the new value of 94 to largestsofar.

♦ The second time through the loop, we compare largestsofar with num[2], which is 65. Since largestsofar is larger, we do nothing.

♦ When we fall out of the loop, largestsofar has the value of the highest grade in the array, which is 94.

CAUTION Do not initialize largestsofar to a small number like 0, rather than the first element in the array. This does not work. For example, suppose that all the elements in the array are negative. Then no element will be greater than largestsofar, and the program will not find the largest value in the array.

THE FUNCTION findmax( )

Now we modify the C++ code to fit our particular situation. Let's call our function findmax( ). It has to return only one value, the highest grade. The parameters this function needs are the array and the number of array elements that have to be searched for the highest grade. Here is the prototype:

```
int findmax(int [], int);
```

In the main program, the parameters are called mark and n; in the function, they are called num and n. Here is the call from the main program:

```
higrade = findmax(mark,n);
```

The array mark is matched with num in findmax( ), and n is matched with n. The body of findmax( ) is what we just traced. Here is the entire function:

PROGRAM LISTING

```
// Function findmax:
// Input:
//    num: an array of integers
```

```
//     n: the number of elements in the array
// Process:
//     finds the highest value in the first
//     n elements of the num array
// Output:
//     returns the maximum of the elements
int findmax(int num[], int n)
{
      int largestsofar = num[0];

      for (int count = 1; count < n; count++)
          if (largestsofar < num[count])
                largestsofar = num[count];
      return largestsofar;
}
```

STYLE WORKSHOP It is not necessary to use an array to find the largest of a list of numbers. The same algorithm can be applied to numbers as they are being read in and processed.

```
// finding the largest in a list of numbers
// without using an array
#include <iostream>
using namespace std;
int main()
{
      int num,largest;

      cin >> num;
      largest = num;
      while(cin) {
            cout << num << endl;
            if(num > largest)
                  largest = num;
            cin >> num;
      }
      cout << "the largest value entered was " << largest;
      return 0;
}
```

Similarly, in Section 2 of this chapter, we found the average without using an array by processing numbers as they were read in. In this chapter, we have used an array because this way we can perform each task as an independent module through a function.

FINDING THE NUMBER OF MARKS ABOVE, BELOW, AND EQUAL TO THE AVERAGE

Now let's turn to the last task of Program 7: finding and printing the number of grades above, below, and equal to the average. This is the only part which really requires an array because the comparison with avgmark cannot be performed until avgmark has been computed. Without an array, the individual marks won't be available once avgmark has been computed.

PSEUDOCODE

As usual, we will start by writing pseudocode. This is at heart a comparison and counting problem. We must compare each mark with the average; if the mark is less, we increment one counter; if it is greater, we increment a different counter; if it is equal, we increment a third counter. Here is the pseudocode:

> *for each mark*
>   *compare it with* avgmark
>   *if the mark is less than* avgmark, *increment* numless
>   *if the mark is greater than* avgmark, *increment* numgreater
>   *if the mark is equal to* avgmark, *increment* numequal

THE FUNCTION countmarks()

The function—we'll call it countmarks( )—is simple to write from the pseudocode. We need to send the function three parameters: the array of marks; n, the number of elements in the array; and avgmark, the average of the marks in the array. In addition, we will send the three counters to countmarks( ) as reference parameters. We'll send them as reference parameters, since a function can return only a single value, yet countmarks( ) computes three separate values. Here is the prototype:

```
void countmarks(int [], int, double, int &, int &, int &);
```

Here is the complete function countmarks( ):

💻 PROGRAM LISTING

```
// Function countmarks:
// Input:
//    num: an array of integers
//    n: the number of elements in the array
//    avgnum: the average of the elements in the array
// Process:
//   find how many grades in the array num are greater than avgnum
//   find how many grades in the array num are less than avgnum
//   find how many grades in the array num are equal to avgnum
// Output:
//    change the values of numless, numgreater, and numequal
void countmarks(int num[], int n, double avgnum, int &numless,
                int &numgreater, int &numequal)
{
    numless=0;
    numgreater=0;
    numequal=0;

    for (int count = 0; count < n; count++)
        if (num[count] < avgnum)
            numless++;
        else if (num[count] > avgnum)
            numgreater++;
        else
            numequal++;
    return;
}
```

That's all there is to this function; we can put it into the final version of Program 7. The only remaining question is where the main program calls <u>countmarks( )</u>. It must be called sometime after the main program calls <u>avgarray( )</u>.

FIFTH VERSION OF PROGRAM 7: MAIN PROGRAM, findmax(), AND countmarks()

Here is the the main program for the complete version of Program 7, including the functions for finding the maximum mark and the number of marks above and below the average, with simplified comments:

PROGRAM LISTING

```cpp
// Program prog7e.cpp
#include <iostream>
using namespace std;
const int SIZE = 50;
void readdata(int [], int &);
int sumarray(int [], int);
double avgarray(int [], int);
int findmax(int [], int);
void countmarks(int [], int, double, int &, int &, int &);
int main()
{
    int    n;
    int    mark[SIZE];
    double avgmark;
    int    numless,numgreater,numequal,higrade;

    // call functions to read and process the marks
    readdata(mark,n);
    avgmark = avgarray(mark,n);
    cout << "The average is " << avgmark << endl;
    higrade = findmax(mark,n);
    cout << "The highest mark is " << higrade << endl;
    countmarks(mark,n,avgmark,numless,numgreater,numequal);
    cout << "the number of marks less than the average is "
        << numless << endl;
    cout << "the number of marks greater than the average is "
        << numgreater << endl;
    cout << "the number of marks equal to the average is "
        << numequal << endl;
    return 0;
}

// ...
void readdata(int num[], int &n)
{
    cout << "Enter the number of marks> ";
    cin >> n;
    if (n > 0 && n <= SIZE)
        cout << "There are " << n << " marks" << endl;
    else {
        cout << "Invalid number of marks" << endl;
        exit(1);
```

```cpp
    }
    for (int count = 0; count < n; count++) {
        cout << "Enter a mark> ";
        cin >> num[count];
        cout << num[count] << endl;
    }
    return;
}
// ...
int sumarray(int num[], int n)
{
    int sum = 0;

    for (int count = 0; count < n; count++)
        sum = sum + num[count];
    return sum;
}

// ...
double avgarray(int num[], int n)
{
    int sum = 0;

    for (int count = 0; count < n; count++)
        sum += num[count];

    return (double) sum / n;
}

// ...
int findmax(int num[], int n)
{
    int largestsofar = num[0];

    for (int count = 0; count < n; count++)
        if (largestsofar < num[count])
            largestsofar = num[count];
    return largestsofar;
}

// ...
void countmarks(int num[], int n, double avgnum, int &numless,
                int &numgreater, int &numequal)
{
    numless=0;
    numgreater=0;
    numequal=0;

    for (int count = 0; count < n; count++)
        if (num[count] < avgnum)
            numless++;
        else if (num[count] > avgnum)
            numgreater++;
```

```
        else
            numequal++;
    return;
}
```

In this version, the main program prints a heading and calls <u>readdata( )</u> to read in and print the data. The function <u>readdata( )</u> gets the value for <u>n</u>, and fills the array with values. Both <u>n</u> and the array are changed when we return to the main program. Then the main program calls <u>avgarray( )</u> to compute the average for the class. The function <u>avgarray( )</u> calls the function <u>sumarray( )</u> to find the sum of the marks in the class and return the sum to <u>avgarray( )</u>. Then <u>avgarray( )</u> divides the sum by the number of students to get the average, which it returns to the main program. Next the main program calls <u>findmax( )</u> to find the highest grade in the class. Finally, the main program calls <u>countmarks( )</u>, which computes the number of marks above, below, and equal to the average. The main program prints these counters.

ORDER OF PARAMETERS

Once a program calls many functions, the programmer can get confused as to the order of the parameters in the prototype, call, and function header. It is helpful to keep all the parameters for all functions in the same order. For example, each of the functions in this program receives the array <u>num</u> and the integer <u>n</u>. In each case, the array is the first parameter and <u>n</u> is the second.

STYLE WORKSHOP In writing Program 7, we have made extensive use of stepwise refinement. We started with a simple version of the program and gradually refined it to handle more and more details of the task. This is an important skill to master.

SELF-CHECK 7-8

1. What is the difference between the way a person finds the maximum of a list of numbers and the way a computer does it?

2. What happens if we pick -1 as <u>largestsofar</u> and the elements in the array are -100, -34, -76, -92, and -3?

3. What is an algorithm for finding the smallest element in a list of numbers? The second largest? What if there are ties?

SECTION 7   ## ENRICHMENT: ANALYSIS OF PROGRAM 7: TESTING AND MODULARITY

This section discusses testing and error checking in Program 7. In addition, it analyzes the contribution of arrays to programming modularity.

TESTING PROGRAM 7

Now that we have written the entire program, we must test it. Of course, we could have tested each function as we incorporated it into the program. For example, we could have tested <u>sumarray( )</u> before writing <u>avgarray( )</u>. In this particular case, we can trust <u>sumarray( )</u> because it basically repeats a module which we know works from a previous program.

You may think that we don't need to test readdata( ) since it prints the data that it reads in; you are wrong. You must make sure that it does what it should. The simplest way to test readdata( ) is to print out n and the mark array after returning to the main program. Since readdata( ) already prints, you will have two lists of values to compare. If there is any discrepancy, something is wrong. To test the error checking, try entering different parameter values, including a positive number, a negative number, and 0.

To test avgarray( ) and sumarray( ), we can send as parameters arrays containing varying numbers of elements; within each array, the elements should have simple values whose average we can easily compute by hand. Within sumarray( ), we can print the sum of the array and n. Upon our return to avgarray( ), we can again print the sum and n, as well as the computed average. Finally, upon our return to the main program, we can print the returned average as a comparison. If any computed values do not match, or if the results do not jibe with computations done by hand, we have an error.

For findmax( ) and countmarks( ), we can send in a few arrays, one at a time. For findmax( ), if we already know the largest value in each array, we can compare our hand-computed results with the value returned. For countmarks( ), if we already know the average of the array, we can count by hand the number of values greater than, less than, and equal to the average and compare the results with those printed in main.

SELECTING TEST DATA

In testing findmax( ), we should be careful to use all possible sets of values. We should test a case where the highest grade is in the first position of the array, one where it is in the middle, and one where it is last. In addition, we should add a set of test data where the highest grade occurs twice or three times, or all the grades are the same. Frequently, a program is written so that it works for the expected set of data but not for unexpected combinations; often, first and last elements in an array or list are treated differently, and a good set of test data uncovers any errors in processing these anomalous cases.

In our test data for the calls to readdata( ) and avgarray( ), we should also use a range of possible cases; in particular, we should include a set of data where n is 0, one where n is negative, and one where n does not actually match the number of grades. If we include test data of this sort, we have a better chance of discovering flaws in our program.

Program 7 should work for all sets of data. (See Section 9 for further discussion of error checking and Exercise 12 for one remaining problem.) Actually, thinking through the possible values that may occur in a set of data is a good way to discover errors like dividing by 0 if there are no students in the class.

ADVANTAGES AND DISADVANTAGES OF ARRAYS

This is a good point to evaluate the use of an array in solving Problem 7. The first version of the program could average any size of a set of marks, but the array versions must have some prior knowledge of the amount of data. In that sense, the first version is superior; there are problems which are solvable only without an array. (For example, suppose you are asked to average a list of numbers, but you do not know how many numbers are in the list; no matter how many numbers there are, the problem can be solved without an array. However, an array solution needs an upper bound.)

On the other hand, there are some clear advantages to the array versions. An important one has already been mentioned. After computing the average, every piece of data is still available for further processing. For example, we were able to find the average and the maximum, and also the number of elements above and below the average. We could also have found the grade closest to the average. In order to find the average and maximum grades, we need to go through the array entries only once; however, if we want to find the grade closest to the average, we must go through them more than once. This can be done only if we have saved all the array entries. Later programs exploit the flexibility of being able to use the same data for different calculations.

MODULAR VERSION OF PROGRAM 7

There is another important advantage to the array method. In the first version of the program, we read in a <u>mark</u> value, printed it and added it to <u>sum</u>, then read in another <u>mark</u>, and so on. In other words, we processed each <u>mark</u> value completely before going on to the next. With arrays, we were able to use a more modular method in the third version of the program: First, read in all the data, then print all the data (we decided to combine the reading and printing), finally add all the data together. This method of solving the problem is possible only with arrays because all the values of <u>mark</u> must be saved.

A diagram illustrating this idea is shown in Figure 7-6. Such a diagram is called a **functional flowchart** since it illustrates the main functions or jobs to be performed and the flow of control through them.

In a further step toward modularity, arrays allowed us to write Program 7 using functions. We were able to write a function to add up the marks for each class because we did not have to know in advance how many marks there were. Without arrays, we would need a function with three parameters for this class, perhaps another one with eight parameters for a different class, and maybe another one with four parameters for a third class (and each class would have to be exactly this size). However, we

FIGURE 7-6 Functional flowchart for Problem 7

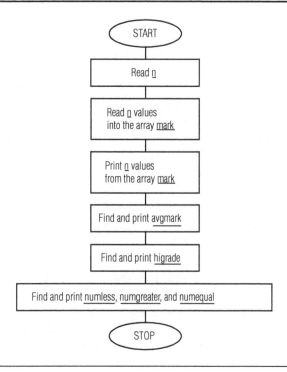

were able to write one function that accepted an array (of any size) as its principal parameter. This array could contain a variable number of marks, thus increasing the flexibility of the function.

Using an array is helpful for the following reasons:

◆ It gives us the ability to store and retrieve large amounts of data without declaring many separate variable names.

◆ It allows us to break a program down into modules or functions which can then be programmed one at a time in a straightforward way.

Modules provide reusable code to perform tasks that we do frequently. They can be used as building blocks in later, more complex programs.

SELF-CHECK 7-9

1. What happens in Program 7 if the parameter value n is given the value 0?
2. Why is it important to select test data carefully?
3. What are some advantages of modular programming?

SECTION 8 ENRICHMENT: TWO-DIMENSIONAL ARRAYS

This section introduces two-dimensional arrays. We also briefly mention arrays with more than two dimensions.

STORING FOUR GRADES FOR EACH STUDENT IN A CLASS

Let's imagine a slight modification of Problem 7. Assume that each student in the class has four grades, rather than one, representing marks on four exams. The instructor still wants to do things like find the average mark or the highest or lowest mark in the entire class. In addition, the instructor wants to be able to find each student's average and the class average on each of the four exams.

This is a large amount of information. There are potentially 50 students in the class, and each student has four marks. It is necessary to deal with each mark several times—for example, we need to use the same mark to find a student's average and the class average on a particular exam. Therefore, after we process a mark once, we still need to have it available.

The need to keep many values available suggests an array. However, some major questions have to be resolved about how to organize the data.

How can we store the grades using arrays? Each student has four grades, and there are up to 50 students. One possibility is to have a separate array for each student, with four entries. If this is our choice, finding a particular student's average is easy: just add up the elements of that student's array and divide by 4. But the class average on the first exam is much harder to compute. We have to jump from array to array, adding all the first elements. Also each of these 50 arrays has to be given a distinct name and declared.

This method obviously has problems, so let's try to think of another way to store the data. Another possibility is to set up one array for each exam. In this case, we have to declare each of the four arrays. To find the class average on an exam, we can sum the appropriate array and divide by the number of students. But using this method to find individual student averages is more complicated. Overall, this method is much better than the first but still not very good.

TWO-DIMENSIONAL ARRAYS

A better way to store the data is to use a new data structure called a **two-dimensional array**. (We can call the arrays so far one-dimensional arrays.) A two-dimensional array is useful when we need to keep track of two coordinates of data—for example, a company may have sales data for three stores for the 12 months of the year. A scientist may have data from ten experiments performed on five subjects. A two-dimensional array can be visualized as a rectangle, as shown in Figure 7-7.

To locate a particular point in the array, we must specify two positions or subscripts: one to describe how far down the point is, one to say how far across. The subscript governing how far down we go is called the **row subscript**; the one determining how far across is the **column subscript**. To describe any entry in the array accurately, we need the row and column subscripts.

EXAMPLE 7-14

In Figure 7-7, the rows are numbered from 0 to 2; the columns are numbered from 0 to 5. The number 10 is in the first row, third column. The number 98 is in the third row, fifth column.

In our program, we want a two-dimensional array with 50 rows, one for each student, and 4 columns, one for each exam. To locate a particular mark, we specify which student got it (the row) and on which exam (the column). Figure 7-8 provides an illustration of such an array with some entries filled in.

We can call this array grade. Each element in grade is selected by specifying first a row and then a column.

EXAMPLE 7-15

In Figure 7-8, *grade[0][0]* holds 95. The 91 is in *grade[0][3]*, the first row and the fourth column; *grade[49][3]* is 8; 97 is in *grade[2][1]*. In all, the grade array has room for $50 \times 4 = 200$ marks.

FIGURE 7-7 A two-dimensional array with 3 rows and 6 columns

FIGURE 7-8 A two-dimensional array with 50 rows and 4 columns

ANALYSIS OF THE DATA STRUCTURE

Let's see how a two-dimensional array helps solve this problem. To find a student's average, we average a row of the two-dimensional array; for example, we use row 2 for the third student's average. To find the class average on an exam, we average a column of the two-dimensional array; for example, we use column 0 for the class average on the first exam. The other parts of the problem are also easy because of the way we have decided to store the marks.

STYLE WORKSHOP Note that we decided which major data structure to use even before we started to talk about writing the program in C++. A programmer must often think as much about how to store data as process it. A clever choice of how to organize data—a useful data structure—makes the rest of the program much easier, while a poor choice leads to all sorts of programming problems.

DECLARING A TWO-DIMENSIONAL ARRAY

Of course, we must declare the two-dimensional array <u>grade</u> before we can use it in the program. The declaration is similar to the one for a one-dimensional array; we must provide the number of rows, followed by the number of columns. Here is a possible declaration:

```
int grade[50][4];
```

This says that <u>grade</u> has 50 rows, numbered from 0 to 49; each row has 4 column entries, numbered 0 to 3.

Assuming that we have defined the constant <u>MAXSIZE</u>, we can use the following declaration for the array:

```
const int MAXSIZE = 50;

int grade[MAXSIZE][4];
```

Similarly, we can use a constant to define the number of columns. For clarity in the first part of this section, however, we will use a constant for the number of rows but 4 for the number of columns.

SELF-CHECK 7-10

1. In the declaration for this array, how many rows are there? How many columns?

    ```
    int grade[25][5];
    ```

2. Give the declaration for a two-dimensional array <u>labdata</u> which can hold data collected from ten experiments performed on five subjects. Assume that each piece of lab data is a value of type **double**.

3. Show how to locate the items in the <u>labdata</u> array from question 2 which represent the data collected from the first experiment on the second subject and the fourth experiment on the third subject.

PROCESSING A TWO-DIMENSIONAL ARRAY IN A MAIN PROGRAM

Let's see how to use a two-dimensional array to extend Program 7. We can process a two-dimensional array directly in a main program or pass it as a parameter to a function. To illustrate both methods, we read values into the array in a main program, then show how to find each student's average in a function.

Assume that the variable class_size holds the number of students in the class. The maximum value for class_size is 50, but it may very well be less. A moment's thought suggests that we employ a **for** loop to read in the grades. We will call the control variable for this **for** loop stnum (short for student number) since it runs through all the students. Here is a main program that reads in a value for class_size, then reads in four grades for each student:

🖥️ PROGRAM LISTING

```cpp
// program to read data into
// a two-dimensional array
#include <iostream>
using namespace std;
const int MAXSIZE = 50;

int main()
{
    int grade[MAXSIZE][4];
    int class_size;

    cout << "how many students in the class?> ";
    cin >> class_size;
    for (int stnum = 0; stnum < class_size; stnum++) {
        cout << "type in four grades for this student> ";
        cin >> grade[stnum][0] >> grade[stdnum][1]
            >> grade[stnum][2] >> grade[stdnum][2];
        cout << "the test grades typed in were: "
            << grade[stnum][0] << grade[stnum][1]
            << grade[stnum][2] << grade[stnum][3]
            << endl;
    }
    return 0;
}
```

PROGRAM TRACE Let's see how this works on a simple set of data.

♦ The program starts by asking how many students are in the class. If the user types in 3, the stnum loop will run from 0 to 2.

♦ In the body of the loop, the program asks the user to type in 4 values. The first time through the loop, these four values are read into columns 0 to 3 in the first row of grade. For example, the user could type 5, 6, 7, and 98. Then 5 goes into *grade[0][0]*, 6 into *grade[0][1]*, 7 into *grade[0][2]*, and 98 into *grade[0][3]*.

♦ Then the user types in four more grades into the second row of grade, and so on for the third row.

Figure 7-9 shows the grade array after reading in values for three students.

PASSING A TWO-DIMENSIONAL ARRAY AS A PARAMETER TO A FUNCTION

To illustrate how to pass a two-dimensional array as a parameter, we can write a function, findstudentavg( ), to find and print the average for each student in the class. Let's begin by writing the

FIGURE 7-9   grade array after reading in the data for three students

	0	1	2	3
0	5	6	7	98
1	93	71	53	38
2	95	97	93	96
3				
. . .		. . .		
49				

prototype. Since the function prints every student's average without returning any value to the main program, it is a void function. The array grade must be a parameter to the function, and looks like this in the prototype:

```
void findstudentavg(int grade[][4], ...
```

The parameter includes the data type for the elements of the array (optionally followed by the name of the array), followed by two sets of brackets, one for each subscript. The set of brackets for the rows can be empty, but the other set must give the number of columns in the array. Any value placed in the brackets for the number of rows is ignored, but the number of columns is needed to identify where a new row begins.

We can define constants for the number of tests as well as the number of students (remember that these constants will be defined above main, so that they can be used everywhere in the program), and the constant NUMTESTS should be used to specify the second parameter:

```
const int MAXSIZE = 50;
const int NUMTESTS = 4;

void findstudentavg(int grade[][NUMTESTS], ...
```

Since the function needs to know the number of students in the class, class_size is also a parameter to the function. Here are three equivalent function prototypes:

```
void findstudentavg(int grade[][NUMTESTS], int);

void findstudentavg(int grade[MAXSIZE][NUMTESTS], int); // MAXSIZE is ignored

void findstudentavg(int [][NUMTESTS], int);            // omits the array name
```

The main program reads in the data, then calls the function. Here is the call to the function:

```
findstudentavg(grade,class_size);
```

THE FUNCTION findstudentavg()

Finally, we can write the function. Let's use the same names, grade and class_size, for the formal parameters in the function. Here are the comment and function header:

💻 PROGRAM LISTING

```
// Function findstudentavg:
// Input:
//    two-dimensional array grade holds
//    NUMTESTS grades for each of class_size students
// Process:
//    finds each student's average
// Output:
//    prints each student's average
void findstudentavg(int grade[][NUMTESTS], int class_size)
```

Note once again that, in the function header, we must specify the number of columns (NUMTESTS), but the number of rows is indicated by an empty set of brackets ([]). A two-dimensional array is stored as a collection of rows; the number of columns tells how many elements are in each row. The function is sent the name of the array (grade) plus the number of columns (NUMTESTS). In this way, the function knows when one row ends and the next one begins.

Inside the function, we must find each student's average. Here is a pseudocode version of the body of the function:

```
for (int stnum = 0; stnum < class_size; stnum++) {
    find the average for student number stnum
    print the average
}
```

To find the average for each student, average that student's row. Finding the average for student number stnum is similar to what we did in Program 7. First, initialize sum to 0; then add to sum each grade in the row for student number stnum; at the end, divide by NUMTESTS. To add the grades, we will not mention each column explicitly, since the number of exams is now defined as a constant.

Instead, there is a better method to add up the marks in row number stnum. We can use a second **for** loop; the first loop is for the rows, and the second for the columns. We put one **for** loop inside another, forming a nested **for** loop (see Chapter 4, Section 4). Here is the code for the function (including the declaration of local variables):

💻 PROGRAM LISTING

```
// ...
void findstudentavg(int grade[][NUMTESTS], int class_size)
{
    int     sum;
    double avg;

    for (int stnum = 0; stnum < class_size; stnum++) {
        sum = 0;
        for (int test = 0; test < NUMTESTS; test++)
            sum += grade[stnum][test];
        avg = (double) sum / NUMTESTS;
        cout << "student number " << stnum
             << " had an average of " << avg << endl;
    }
    return;
}
```

We have used <u>stnum</u> as the control variable for the rows and <u>test</u> as the control variable for the columns, running from 0 to <u>NUMTESTS</u> - 1, or 3. Inside both **for** loops, <u>grade[stnum][test]</u> refers to the particular mark we are interested in.

PROGRAM TRACE We trace this function on the data shown in Figure 7-9. Assume that we are working with a class of three students.

◆ The outer **for** loop processes each of the students; the inner loop processes each grade of each student.

◆ The outer loop starts with <u>stnum</u> equal to 0. In the inner loop, row 0 of <u>grade</u>, from *grade[0][0]* to *grade[0][3]*, is summed to obtain 116. After the inner loop ends, the average is computed to be 29.00, and this is printed as the average of student number 0.

◆ Then <u>stnum</u> is incremented to 1, and <u>sum</u> is reset to 0 for the second student (otherwise <u>sum</u> for this student would start with 116). Row 1 of <u>grade</u>, from *grade[1][0]* to *grade[1][3]*, is summed to obtain 255, so the average is 255/4, which is 63.75. This is printed as the average of the second student.

◆ Then <u>stnum</u> is increased again to 2, we set <u>sum</u> back to 0 and sum the third row, which totals 381; the average here is 381/4 = 95.25, and this is printed.

Finally, we exit from the outer loop. The entire output from this function looks like this:

```
student number 0 had an average of   29
student number 1 had an average of   63.75
student number 2 had an average of   95.25
```

PROCESSING DOWN A COLUMN OF A TWO-DIMENSIONAL ARRAY

Once the data values have been stored, we can use a nested loop to process a two-dimensional array in other ways. In general, one **for** loop controls the row subscript, and the other controls the column subscript. For example, by interchanging the row and column loops, we can process down a column.

EXAMPLE 7-1 We can write a function <u>findexamavg( )</u> to find the class's average on each test. The function has to find the average value in each column:

```
// ...
void findexamavg(int grade[][NUMTESTS], int class_size)
{
    int     sum;
    double avg;

    for (int test = 0; test < NUMTESTS; test++) {
        sum = 0;
        for (int stnum = 0; stnum < class_size; stnum++)
            sum += grade[stnum][test];
        avg = (double) sum / class_size;
        cout << "test number " << test
            << " had an average of " << avg << endl;
    }
    return;
}
```

Here are the function prototype and the call to the function:

```
void findexamavg(int grade[][NUMTESTS], int);

findexamavg(grade,class_size);
```

We leave it to the reader to trace this function for the grades shown earlier.

Finally, a single row of a two-dimensional array can be sent as a parameter to a function. In this case, we specify only the row subscript. For example, we can use the function underline{sumarray( )} from Section 5 to sum the elements in row 1 of the two-dimensional array. Here is the call to underline{sumarray( )}:

```
sum = sumarray(grade[1],NUMTESTS);
```

MULTIDIMENSIONAL ARRAYS

It is also possible to have an array with more than two dimensions. As an example, we might want to extend the two-dimensional array underline{grade} to include information about five classes. To do this, we could form a new array by adding a third dimension.

EXAMPLE 7-17   Consider a three-dimensional array called underline{marks}; three subscripts are required to locate a particular entry.

♦ the first subscript of underline{marks} selects one of five classes;

♦ the second subscript picks one of 50 students;

♦ the third subscript chooses one of four exams.

For example, the assignment statement *marks[3][1][2] = 5* means that in the fourth class, for the second student, the third mark is set to *5*. Similarly, *marks[1][6][0]* is a reference to the second class, seventh student, first mark.

The declaration for underline{marks} must specify bounds for all three dimensions. We can use something like this:

```
int marks[5][50][4];
```

Actually, almost all C++ compilers allow more than three dimensions in an array. You can use four, five, six, or more subscripts. In general, any array with more than one dimension is called a **multidimensional array**. However, past the second or third dimension, it becomes harder and harder for most people to visualize a multidimensional array. The basic data structure in such a program is probably too complex and should be simplified. In addition, the amount of space occupied by, for example, a five-dimensional array can become astronomical. Let's assume that each of the five dimensions has bounds 0 to 9, which is not that large. Then the total number of storage locations is 10^5 or 100,000. Quite possibly, this number exceeds the space allocated to your program, causing an error. Therefore, except in rare circumstances, three-dimensional arrays are the largest used.

STYLE WORKSHOP In most cases, a one-dimensional array is sufficient to represent the information in a program. In a few situations, a two-dimensional array is more useful. It is very rare that a program needs more than two dimensions.

SELF-CHECK 7-11

1. When passing a two-dimensional array to a function, which dimension must be stated explicitly in the function header and prototype?

2. Give a declaration for a three-dimensional array <u>sales</u> which holds sales data for five stores, for 12 months, for three years.

SECTION 9   **ENRICHMENT: MORE ON FILES: DETECTING THE END OF A SET OF DATA: THE END-OF-FILE METHOD; FUNCTION is_open(); FILE PARAMETERS**

This section discusses various ways of detecting the end of a set of data, in the process introducing the end-of-file method. It also introduces the file stream function is_open( ).

METHODS OF DETECTING THE END OF A SET OF DATA

When reading in values, it is often necessary to determine when the set of data has ended, whether the set of data is entered interactively or from a file. A **file** is a collection of data values on a disk (see Chapter 3, Section 7). So far, we have discussed three methods of finding the end of a set of data, which we summarize below; then we introduce a fourth method, called the end-of-file method (or technique). Each method has advantages and disadvantages, and sometimes a program uses more than one (see Exercise 9).

The **trailer** or **sentinel method** requires that the program specify a single value as a signal that the set of data is complete. The last item should be this value. (We used this method in Program 3 with the phony negative ID value.) Each data value that is read in is compared to the trailer value to determine if it is a real piece of data. There are two basic advantages to this method: It is not necessary to know in advance how many items are in a set of data (compare with the parameter or header method), and it is possible to have separate groups of data, each with its own trailer value.

The **user-response method** asks the user to answer a question. Usually it is something like "Do you want to continue (y/n)?" This method works best with interactive programming. The user enters the character *y* to continue and *n* to stop. (We used this method in Program 6.) One disadvantage of this method is that it requires a response from the user each time, which is time consuming and can be annoying.

The **parameter** or **header method** uses a signal at the beginning of each group of data. The first item read is a number indicating how many pieces of data follow. (We used this method in Program 7.) The major disadvantage of this method is the need to know this number in advance, since an incorrect value often leads to an execution error. The advantages of the parameter method are that it does not require the use of a phony value, and it allows more than one group of data, each with its own parameter value. It can be used with interactive data entry as well as data from a file. Almost all of our later programs use the parameter method to detect the end of a set of data, sometimes together with the end-of-file method.

There are problems with all these methods of indicating the end of a set of data. The trailer or sentinel method requires that you devise a phony value which cannot exist in the set of data, but sometimes it is impossible to find a phony value. The user-response method requires that the program be run interactively so that the user can answer (unless you put responses in the data file, which is highly inappropriate); in addition, the user must be asked an additional question each time a data value is entered. The parameter method requires that you know in advance how many values are in the data set.

READING TO INPUT FAILURE (THE END-OF-FILE METHOD)

The fourth method, called the **end-of-file method** (also called "reading to input failure") has the computer test for the actual end of the set of data. When the program tries to read past the last value in the file, the end-of-file condition is true.

One advantage of the end-of-file method is that the computer, rather than the programmer, handles the details of detecting the end of the set of data. No phony values are needed, and the person entering the data does not have to know in advance how many values there are. The method can be used when reading from an input stream or a file stream, and whether the program is reading individual numbers, strings, or characters (see its use with getline( ) and get( ) in Chapter 8).

When you read from a stream or a file stream, the stream variable gets a value indicating the success or failure of the attempt to read. The attempt to read can fail either because you have come to the end of the input or because the data value read in cannot be appropriately converted to the type needed by the variable into which it is to be stored. The value of the stream variable can be used in a standard structured read loop so that the program will fall out of the loop at input failure.

READING FROM AN INPUT FILE STREAM

Example 7-18 shows how to read from an input file stream until input failure.

EXAMPLE 7-18   This example reads data into num from the file stream in7 (associated with an input file called "in7.dat") and writes it to file stream out7. This process continues until the attempt to read from the file fails; at that point, the program falls out of the loop.

```
ifstream in7("in7.dat");
ofstream out7("out7.out");
in7 >> num;
while (in7) {                   // while a value was successfully read
    out7 << num;                // process it
    in7 >> num;                 // try to get another value
}
in7.close();
out7.close();
```

The stream variable in7 reports failure when the program tries to read past the last data value in the input stream (that is, when the program tries to read a value and there is no value present in the file). If there is a data value, the program enters the loop, reads and processes the value. If there is no value left in the file, the program falls out of the loop.

READING GROUPS OF VALUES IN A DATA SET

Some programs read and process groups of data (for example reading three temperatures and comparing them, or reading three grades and averaging them). There might be 15 to 20 groups of data in the file.

Reading groups of values from a file can be accomplished simply by using one statement that reads the entire group of values. This is not considered good style when reading data interactively, because of the need to use prompts, but it is fine when reading from a file.

EXAMPLE 7-19

```
int num1, num2, num3, result;
ifstream infile("ftest.dat");

infile >> num1 >> num2 >> num3;
while (infile) {
    ...                                    // process values here
    infile >> num1 >> num2 >> num3;
}
```

The program reads three values at a time from infile; if the read is successful, the program enters the loop, processes those three values, and goes to get three more. If the read is not successful, infile gets a value indicating failure and the loop terminates. The problem with this method is that it does not tell which value caused input failure; as long as that doesn't matter to the programmer, this is acceptable.

Example 7-20 shows how to use the end-of-file method in the readdata( ) function from Program 7, reading from an input file stream into an array.

EXAMPLE 7-20

This version of readdata( ) reads data into array num from the file stream in7 (associated with an input file called "in7.dat") until the attempt to read from the file fails; at that point, the program falls out of the loop. This version does not ask the user to enter the number of values in advance, but instead counts the number of values as they are read in. When the program reaches the end of file, n contains the number of values read in.

```
// Function readdata: reads from a data file until end-of-file
// array num gets gets values from the file;
// parameter n carries back to main the number of values read in
void readdata(int num[], int &n)
{
    ifstream in7("in7.dat");

    n = 0;

    in7 >> num[n];
    while (in7) {                     // while a value was successfully read
        n++;                          // process it
        in7 >> num[n];                // try to get another value
    }
    in7.close();
    return;
}
```

The stream variable in7 reports failure when the program tries to read past the last data value in the input stream (that is, when the program tries to read a value and there is no value present in the file). If there is a data value, the program enters the loop, reads and processes the value. If there is no value left in the file, the program falls out of the loop.

If the data file contains the values 6, 25, the first read statement gives num[0] the value 6 and sets in7 to report success. The program enters the loop, increments n to 1 and reads 25 into num[1]. Since the read is successful, in7 again reports success, the program again enters the loop and increments n to 2. When the program tries to read another value, the attempt to read will fail, in7 will get a value indicating failure, and the program will fall out of the loop without giving a value to num[2]. There will be values in num[0] and num[1], and n will be 2.

USING THE END-OF-FILE METHOD WITH cin; SIGNALING END-OF-FILE

When reading from <u>cin</u>, the user must enter a special value, called the end-of-file character, to signal that there are no more data values. When the program reads this special value, the program inteprets the value to mean that there are no more values to read in.

The end-of-file character is entered by pressing <Ctrl>-z in Windows or DOS or <Ctrl>-d in Unix. The user must enter the end-of-file character when the program requests a data value. When the program reads this character, it stops looking for data values.

NOTE

The user does not need to do anything special to mark the end of an actual input file, since the computer can determine by itself that it has reached the end.

READING FROM cin UNTIL INPUT FAILURE

Example 7-21 shows a simple loop that reads from the stream variable <u>cin</u> until input failure.

EXAMPLE 7-21

This program reads values from <u>cin</u> and writes them to <u>cout</u> until the attempt to read fails; at that point, the program falls out of the loop. In the loop, the program counts the number of values as they are read in. When the user has run out of data, he or she enters the end-of-file character, signaling end-of-file and terminating the loop. When the loop terminates, <u>n</u> contains the number of values read in.

```
int n = 0,num;
cout << "Enter a number> ";
cin >> num;
while (cin) {                    // while a value was successfully read
    cout << num << endl;        // process it
    n++;

    cout << "Enter a number> ";
    cin >> num;                 // try to get another value
}
cout << n << " values were entered" << endl;
```

Suppose the user enters 5 and then 12. First <u>num</u> gets the value 5, and <u>cin</u> has a value indicating success; the program enters the loop, prints 5, counts it, and goes to read another value. The next value entered into <u>num</u> is 12. At the top of the loop, <u>cin</u> again reports success, and the program enters the loop, prints 12, and counts it. The next time the program asks for a value, the user presses <Ctrl>-z in Windows (or <Ctrl>-d in Unix). The program interprets this to mean that there are no more data values; as a result, <u>cin</u> reports failure, and the program falls out of the loop and prints "2 values were entered."

LIMITATIONS ON THE END-OF-FILE METHOD

One disadvantage of the end-of-file method is that it cannot be used in every situation. For example, some programs read several sets of data in separate loops. Such a program might want to read in the following set of data, where the first set of values is to be read into an arrray, and the second set is a list of values to search for in the array:

```
45 67 89 93
45 -2
```

Reading to input failure (end-of-file) will work only once. The program must use some other method (like a header value—shown as the first value below) to determine the end of the earlier set of data (see Self-Check 7-12 for more on this):

```
4
45 67 89 93
45 -2
```

The idea of reading several sets of data in a program is explored further in Exercise 15.

Another limitation on the end-of-file method is that it will not distinguish between reaching the end of the file and reading a bad data value. Reading a bad data value will cause the program to fall out of the input loop, and so will reaching the end of the file.

THE eof( ) MEMBER FUNCTION

We should note that there is a file stream member function eof( ) that returns **true** when it reaches the end of a stream and **false** if it is not at the end. Unfortunately, implementation of this function varies by compiler, which makes using it tricky if you plan to move your code from compiler to compiler or if students in the class are using different compilers.

THE is_open( ) MEMBER FUNCTION

There is another file stream member function that is quite useful. When writing a program, the programmer must name, open and close files. If the user types the name of a file incorrectly, or gives the wrong path for the file, the file can't be opened. No error message is produced; the program just stops. Since the program can't continue if a file is not opened correctly, the programmer should check whether the attempt to open a file has been successful or not. The file stream member function is_open( ) does this checking.

This function returns **true** if the file was successfully opened. If there was an error in opening the file (the file name is incorrect, the file does not exist, or the output file cannot be created), the function returns **false**. If is_open( ) returns **false**, the program can print a message and terminate. Since is_open( ) is a file stream member function, its name is preceded by the name of the stream we are trying to open, as shown in this example which calls is_open( ) for file stream fin:

```
fin.is_open() . . .
```

Example 7-22 revises the function from Example 7-20 to check for an error in opening the file.

EXAMPLE 7-22

```
// Function readdata: reads from a data file
// checks for success in opening the file
void readdata(int num[], int &n)
{
    ifstream in7("in7.dat");

    if (!in7.is_open()) {
        cout << "error opening file in7.dat" << endl;
        exit(1);
    }

    n = 0;

    in7 >> num[n];
```

```
        while (in7) {          // while a value was successfully read
            n++;               // process it
            in7 >> num[n];     // try to get another value
        }
        in7.close();
        return;
    }
```

It is a good idea to do this kind of checking in every program that uses files.

SELF-CHECK 7-12

1. What does it mean to read to end of input?
2. How does an interactive user signal the end of the set of data using the end-of-file method?
3. Explain how to interpret the following set of data, according to the discussion on page 364:

    ```
    4
    45 67 89 93
    45 -2
    ```

SENDING A FILE AS A PARAMETER TO A FUNCTION

A file stream or a standard I/O stream may be sent as a parameter to a function. The data type can be **ifstream** or **istream** (for input) or **ofstream** or **ostream** (for output). The parameter must be passed as a reference, even if the file is not going to be changed in the function. If you use **ifstream** or **ofstream,** you can send only an actual file name as a parameter. If you use **istream** or **ostream,** you can send either a file or a standard input stream (cin or cout) as a parameter. By changing only the call, you can send a standard I/O stream, instead of a file, to the function. This makes it very easy to switch from using cin and cout while debugging to using files for the final version. If you are sending a file using type **istream** or **ostream**, the file must be opened before being sent to the function; types **istream** and **ostream** do not have open( ) member functions associated with them. Example 7-23 shows how to send both an input file and an output file to a function.

EXAMPLE 7-23   The function readdata( ) receives four parameters; the first two are stream parameters, the last two are the array and the number of filled positions (the last two get values in the function). The calling program can send either the standard input stream (cin) or an input file as the first parameter; it can send either the standard output stream (cout) or an output file as the second parameter.

Here is the prototype for readdata( ); note that the file parameters are reference parameters:

```
void readdata(istream &, ostream &, int [], int &);
```

Here is a call from the main program that sends two files as the first two parameters. Note that the calling program must open and close any files sent as parameters:

```
ifstream infile("in7.dat");
ofstream outfile("out7.out");

readdata(infile,outfile,mark,n);

infile.close();
outfile.close();
```

The name of the input (or output) file can be replaced by <u>cin</u> (or <u>cout</u>); in that case, the function will read from standard input (<u>cin</u>) instead of from the input file, or write to standard output (<u>cout</u>) instead of to the output file.

```
readdata(cin,cout,mark,n);
```

Here is the <u>readdata( )</u> function:

```
// readdata reads values into the first n elements of array num
//  and outputs those values
// the first two parameters can be I/O streams or files
void readdata(istream &in, ostream &out, int num[], int &n)
{
    n = 0;
    in >> num[n];
    while (in) {
        out << num[n] << endl;
        n++;
        in >> num[n];
    }
    return;
}
```

Depending on the call, <u>in</u> will mean either <u>infile</u> or <u>cin</u> (or a different file, if one is sent) and <u>out</u> will mean either <u>outfile</u> or <u>cout</u> (or a different file).

SUMMARY

PARAMETER (OR HEADER) VALUES

1. A parameter or header value is a number entered prior to a set of data values which tells how many data values are in the set. Using a header value has several advantages, including the ability to read several different sets of data, one after another.

2. A program can read the parameter value <u>n</u>, then read <u>n</u> groups of values from the set of data. The value read for the parameter must be treated differently from the rest of the data.

COMPUTING THE AVERAGE OF A LIST OF NUMBERS

3. The average or mean of a list of numbers can be computed in the following way: Initialize a sum to 0. Each time through a loop, add another number to the sum. After adding the entire list, divide by the number of values to obtain the average.

CASTING

4. Casting refers to changing the data type of a variable or expression in the middle of an evaluation.

5. When dividing integer operands, casting is necessary to obtain a result of type **float** or **double**. To cast a variable or expression as another type, place the desired type in parentheses in front of the variable or expression. Here is an example that casts the value of <u>num</u> as a **double** before the division (which means the division will be a real division):

```
double ans;
int    num,n;

ans = (double) num / n;
```

Without casting, the result of the division (<u>num</u> / <u>n</u>) is an integer, which is stored in a variable of type **double**.

ARRAYS

6. If a program reads a series of numbers into a variable called <u>x</u>, at the end of the process, only the last value of <u>x</u> is available for further use. All previous values stored in <u>x</u> are lost since a storage location can hold just one value at a time.

7. However, using an array for <u>x</u> solves this problem. The array provides a separate storage location for each value. Each location within the array is referenced by giving the name of the array and the subscript or position (<u>i</u>), where <u>i</u> may be a constant or a variable. The subscripted variable <u>x[i]</u> can be treated like any variable, appearing on either side of an assignment statement or in a <u>cin</u> or <u>cout</u> statement, for example.

8. In addition to the usual data type such as **int** or **double**, the declaration must also specify the size of an array. For example, we can use this declaration:

   ```
   int x[25];
   ```

   This says that <u>x</u> is an array of integers which can hold 25 values; it has a lower bound of 0 and an upper bound of 24. All subscripts referring to elements of the array must be between 0 and 24.

9. A **for** loop is useful to access the elements of an array. In most common situations, the **for** loop index acts as the array subscript. As the index ranges from the lower to the upper bound, the array elements can be processed one by one.

10. One major advantage of an array is that it gives us the ability to divide a large program into smaller, relatively self-contained units called modules. These modules can transform a large, unwieldy program into a series of easy-to-follow functions.

11. One disadvantage of an array is the need to specify a size, which limits a program. However, this size can be adjusted by modifying the declaration for the array, although the adjustment requires the program to be recompiled. In most programs, the benefits of using arrays far outweigh the disadvantages.

ARRAYS AS PARAMETERS

12. To send an array as a parameter to a function, the formal parameter in the prototype and the function header must be declared as an array.

13. To send array <u>x</u> from paragraph 8 to a function <u>func</u>, we can use the following prototype:

    ```
    int func(int []);   or   int func(int array[]);
    ```

    In the prototype on the right, <u>array</u> is a dummy name, used so the brackets aren't standing alone.

14. To send an array to a function <u>func</u>, we can use the following function header:

    ```
    int func(int x[])
    ```

15. The declaration in a function prototype or header omits the size of the array. This allows the function to receive an array of any size. Of course, the data type of each array sent as an actual parameter must match that of the formal parameter.

16. It is not necessary to use the & operator to send an array as a reference parameter, since an array is automatically passed by reference.

17. An array cannot be the return value of a function. It also cannot be treated as a single unit, so it is not possible to read an entire array at once, print it, or copy it to another array in a single assignment statement.

FINDING THE LARGEST NUMBER IN A LIST

18. Here is an algorithm for finding the largest in a list of numbers: Pick the first number as the largest seen so far. Compare this to each number in turn. If the new number is larger, make it the largest value seen so far. At the end of the process, the largest value seen so far is the largest in the entire group.

TWO-DIMENSIONAL ARRAYS

19. A data structure is a framework for organizing and storing information. A one-dimensional array is a simple data structure. A two-dimensional array is a generalization of a one-dimensional array.

20. Every element or storage location in a two-dimensional array is specified by two subscripts. If you picture the array as a grid, the row subscript indicates how far down the element is, and the column subscript indicates how far across. Each element is uniquely determined by the combination of row and column. The declaration for the two-dimensional array gives the number of rows followed by the number of columns. For example, the following declaration specifies that <u>sales</u> is a two-dimensional array of real numbers, with rows numbered from 0 to 5, and columns from 0 to 9.

```
double sales[6][10];
```

21. A **for** loop can appear within the body of another **for** loop, producing a nested **for** loop construction which is extremely useful with a two-dimensional array. Typically, one **for** loop controls the row subscript, and the other controls the column subscript. By changing the relative positions of the row and column loops and/or using a specific value for one subscript, a programmer can process the entire two-dimensional array, process across a row, or process down a column.

22. Here is a **for** loop that processes across the rows of a two-dimensional array. It prints the entire two-dimensional array, with the entries for each row printed on a new line:

```
int num[10][5];
...
for (int i = 0; i < 10; i++) {
    for (int j = 0; j < 5; j++)
        cout << num[i][j] << "   ";
    cout << endl;
}
```

23. Here is a **for** loop that processes down the columns of the two-dimensional array declared in paragraph 22. It finds the sum of the entries in each column.

```
for (int j = 0; j < 5; j++) {
    sum = 0;
    for (int i = 0; i < 10; i++)
        sum += num[i][j];
    cout << "the sum for column " << j << " is "
        << sum << endl;
}
```

24. Here is a loop that prints every element in a particular row (in this case, the third row) of the same two-dimensional array:

```
for (int j = 0; j < 5; j++)
    cout << num[2][j] << " ";
cout << endl;
```

25. Arrays can be generalized to three or even more dimensions. For example, in a three-dimensional array, three subscripts are necessary to reference a particular location. However, very few problems require the use of an array with more than two or at most three dimensions. In fact, one-dimensional arrays are by far the most common.

THE END-OF-FILE METHOD

26. When you read from a stream or a file stream, the stream variable gets a value indicating the success (true) or failure (false) of the attempt to read. The return value can be used in a standard structured read loop to read until input failure (also called end of file).

    The following loops read in and print a series of numbers, terminating when there are no more values.

reading from <u>cin</u>	**reading from an input stream**
`int num;`	`int num;`

`cin >> num;`
`while (cin) {`
    `cin >> num;`
    `cout << num;`
`}`
	`infile >> num;`
	`while (infile) {`
	    `infile >> num;`
	    `cout << num;`
	`}`

27. When using the input stream <u>cin</u>, a user can signal the end of a set of data by pressing <Ctrl>-z in Windows or DOS or <Ctrl>-d in Unix.

FILE STREAM FUNCTION is_open()

28. File stream function is_open( ) should be used to test the success of opening a file. If the file was successfully opened, the function returns **true**; otherwise it returns **false**. Here is how to use the function in a program:

```
ifstream infile("sum7-28.dat");

if (!infile.is_open())
    cout << "unable to open file stream infile" << endl;
    exit(1);
}
```

If the file has been successfully opened, the program will continue; if not, the program will print an error message and then stop.

FILE PARAMETERS

29. A file stream or a standard I/O stream can be sent as a parameter to a function. The data type can be **ifstream** or **istream** (for input) or **ofstream** or **ostream** (for output). The parameter must be passed as a reference, even if the file is not going to be changed in the function. If you use

ifstream or **ofstream,** you can send only an actual file name as a parameter. If you use **istream** or **ostream,** you can send either a file name or a standard input stream (<u>cin</u> or <u>cout</u>) as a parameter. With a change only to the call, you can send a standard I/O stream to the function instead of a file. Here is a sample function prototype and two calls to that function:

Prototype:

```
void readdata(istream &, ostream &, int [], int &);
```

Calls: the first sends file names; the second sends standard streams.

```
readdata(infile,outfile,mark,n);
readdata(cin,cout,mark,n);
```

EXERCISES

TRACING EXERCISES

1. For each part of this exercise, assume that the array a starts with the values in Figure 7-10. For each of the program segments, show what values are stored in a after executing the segment. Use this declaration for each part:

```
int a[6];
int i,j,q;
```

a.
```
a[4] = a[2] + a[2 + 1];
a[0] = a[6 - 1] + a[6 - 2];
```

b.
```
j = 4;
a[3] = a[j] + a[j - 1];
a[2] = a[j + 1];
```

c.
```
i = 1;
j = i + 2;
a[i] = a[j] + a[j + 1];
```

d.
```
for (int i=0; i < 5; i++)
        a[i] = a[i + 1];
```

FIGURE 7-10 Array a for Exercise 1

FIGURE 7-11   Arrays x and y for Exercise 2

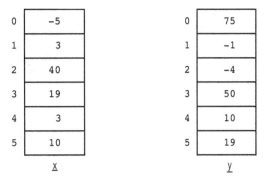

2. Show what is stored in the x and y arrays after the following program segment is executed. Also show what is printed. Assume that the arrays have the initial values in Figure 7-11.

```
int x[6],y[6];
...
x[3] = x[3] + x[5];
y[1] = y[2] + y[3];
x[5] = x[0] + x[2];
x[1] = x[4] + x[x[1]];
for (int i = 0; i <= 5; i++) {
    if (x[i] > 10)
        cout << x[i] << endl;
    if (x[i] < 50)
        cout << y[i] << endl;
}
```

3. Show what values are stored in the x array after executing this program segment. Also show what is printed.

```
int x[5] = {2,2,1,3,1};
int y;

y = x[1] + 1;
cout << y << endl;
x[4] = 1;
cout << x[x[4]] << endl;      // be careful of the subscript here
y--;
cout << y << " " << x[y] << endl;
```

4. Show what is printed by each of these programs. If the program reads in data, the values are shown after it:

a.
```
#include <iostream>
using namespace std;
int main()
{
    int i,k,m;
    int a[9];
```

```
        for (int p = 0; p <= 8; p++)
            a[p] = 0;
        m = 1;
        k = 1;
        for (i = 2; i <= 6; i++) {
            a[i + k] = 20 * i;
            k += m;
            m = -m;
            cout << "k = " << k << " m = " << m << endl;
        }
        cout << "i = " << i << " k = " << k
            << " m = " << m << endl;
        for (int j = 0; j <= 8; j++)
            cout << j << "    " << a[j] << endl;
        return 0;
    }
```

b.
```
#include <iostream>
using namespace std;
int main()
{
    double a[20],b[20],large[20];
    int     num;

    cin >> num;
    for (int i = 0; i < num; i++) {
        cin >> a[i];
        cin >> b[i];
        if (a[i] > b[i])
            large[i] = a[i];
          else
                large[i] = b[i];
    }
    for (int i = 0; i < num; i++)
        cout << "large[" << i << "]= " << large[i] << endl;
    return 0;
}
```

Here are the input data values:

```
6
-4.2 1.56 0 8 1.0 6.75 20.3 -1 -54.2 -33.7 -41.3 -41.3
```

c.
```
#include <iostream>
using namespace std;
int main()
{
    int f[21];

    for (int x = 8; x <= 14; x++)
        f[x] = 3 * x - 5;
    cout << "for the function f(x) = 3x - 5" << endl;
```

```
        for (int x = 8; x <= 14; x++)
            cout << "f(" << x << ")= " << f[x] << endl;
        return 0;
    }
```

d.
```
    #include <iostream>
    using namespace std;
    void calc_tax(double [], double []);
    int main()
    {
        double sales[4], tax[4];

        for (int season = 0; season < 4; season++)
            cin >> sales[season];
        calc_tax(sales,tax);

        cout << "\tsales\ttax" << endl;
        for (int season = 0; season < 4; season++)
            cout << '\t' << sales[season] << '\t'
                << tax[season] << endl;
        return 0;
    }

    void calc_tax(double sales[], double tax[])
    {
        for (int season = 0; season < 4; season++)
            tax[season] = sales[season] * 0.20;
        return;
    }
```

Here are the input data values:

```
12000 24000 21000 46000
```

5. a. Draw a picture of the a and b arrays after executing this program segment. Assume that the set of data consists of 23 100 231 245 9.

```
    #include <iostream>
    using namespace std;
    int main()
    {
        int a[5],b[5];
        int j=0;

        for (int i = 0; i <= 4; i++) {
            cin >> a[i];
            if (a[i] > 100) {
                b[j] = a[i];
                j++;
            }
        }
        return 0;
    }
```

b. Describe what happens if the initialization *j* = *0* is removed from this program. Is there any set of data for which this does not lead to an error?

6. In Exercise 5a, assume that the following statement is added after the **for** loop:

```
cout << b[1] << " is the second value greater than 100" << endl;
```

   a. What does this new statement do? Will it work correctly on this set of data?

   b. Is there any case where it will not work correctly? Explain.

   c. Give a method that works in all cases. Your method should print the second value greater than 100, if there is such a value, and an appropriate message if there isn't.

7. Assume that we want a set of data to contain a parameter value of 5 and then five numeric values. Which of the following show the correct form for the data? Which work but do not read all the data shown? Which run out of data?

   a. 6 12 3 4 5 19   b. 5 5 5 5 5
   c. 5 12 3 4 5 19   d. 5 12 3 4 5 19 87
   e. 5 3 5 4 3 t

8. What is the result of each of the following, using the declarations shown below?

```
int    first = 26, second = 4;
double ans, dval = 4.52;
```

```
a. ans = first / second;
b. ans = (double) (first / second);
c. ans = (double) first / second;
d. ans = first / (double) second;
e. ans = first;
f. first = dval;
g. ans = dval / second;
h. first = dval / second;
```

ANALYSIS EXERCISES

9. This exercise compares the various methods for detecting the end of a set of data.

   a. You want to find the average of a series of real numbers (allowing all possible values, positive, negative, or zero). Can you use a trailer value? If you do not know in advance how many values there are, is it possible to use a parameter value? Explain. What method works best?

   b. You want to find the average of a series of numbers with this extra information: No two consecutive values can be the same. Describe a way to use the trailer method to detect the end of the set of data. What if two, but never three, consecutive values can be equal?

   c. You want to find the averages of two series of numbers from two different groups of data, one following the other. What method(s) can you use?

MODIFICATIONS OF PROGRAM 7

10. a. Rewrite prog7a.cpp so that it reports an error in reading in the value for n and gives the user a chance to correct the error before continuing.

    b. Why do we use exit(1) if n <= 0? What happens as a result of calling exit( )? How is a normal exit indicated? In this case, what happens to the rest of the program?

c. If you type in a bad response when you are using the cash machine at your bank, does the program terminate? What happens?

d. While the way errors are handled in prog7a.cpp may be adequate in a student program, would it work in a commercial environment?

11. In Program 7, we wrote functions sumarray( ) and avgarray( ) to do much of the processing as modules in a large program.

a. Write a driver program that tests these two functions separately. Which one should be tested first?

b. Instead of having avgarray( ) call sumarray( ), it is possible to have avgarray( ) compute the array average directly. Show how to do this. What are the advantages and disadvantages of this approach?

12. In Program 7, we checked for the possibility that n was less than 1. Can we catch the error where n is less than the number of values in the data? For example, what happens if the parameter n is 2, but there are three grades?

13. Even though we decided to allow function readdata( ) to use a reference value to change the value of n, there are other methods of handling this problem.

a. One method is to let the main program read a value into n before calling readdata( ). (*Note*: this method isn't true to the idea that all the data in this program is read in the function readdata( ).) Rewrite Program 7 using this method of getting a value into n.

b. Another method is to let readdata( ) read n and return the value of n as the return value of the function. Rewrite Program 7 using this method of getting a value into n.

14. In the functions for Program 7, instead of calling the array mark or grade, we used the generic name num. We did this so that we could reuse the functions in other programs, without having to rename the arrays. However, several functions, primarily readdata( ) and countmarks( ), have features which make them inappropriate in a different program. What are they? Fix these features so that these functions are reusable.

15. a. Rewrite Program 7 so that it performs the same tasks for three classes rather than just one. This requires the program to read in three sets of data. Consider carefully which method of detecting the end of the set of data works in this case. If you use the header method, how many header values do you need? If you use the end-of-file method, how many times do you need to check for end-of-file? If you redirect the data to come from a file, can you use the end-of-file technique?

b. Rewrite Program 7 so that it performs the same tasks for three classes, rather than just one. In addition, have the program calculate the overall average for the three classes, the highest and lowest marks overall, and the total number of marks above, below, and equal to the overall average. This version requires at least three arrays (one for each class).

TWO-DIMENSIONAL ARRAY EXERCISES

16. a. Give the declaration for a two-dimensional array sales which can hold sales data for three stores for each of 12 months. Assume that each piece of sales data is a value of type **double**.

b. Show how to locate the items in the sales array which represent the sales of the first store in May, the second store in June, and the third store in January.

FIGURE 7-12   Array y for Exercise 17

	0	1	2	3
0	5	11	6	0
1	91	3	-12	2
2	14	1	219	7

17. Assume that a two-dimensional array of integers, called y, initially has the values in Figure 7-12. Show what values are stored in the array after executing each of these program segments. Each part uses this declaration and starts from these values:

```
int y[3] [4];
int i,j;
```

a.
```
y[1][2] = y[0][3] + y[1][1];
y[0][3] = y[2][0] + y[2][1];
y[1][3] = y[0][1] + y[1][3];
```

b.
```
i = 0;
y[i+1][0] = y[i+1][i+3];
i = 1;
y[0][3] = y[2][i-1]
```

c.
```
i = 1;     j = 2;
y[2][1] = y[2][0] + y[1][2];
y[i][j] = i + j + y[2][3]
```

18. a. Draw a picture showing the values stored in arr2 after executing this program segment. Assume that the user types in the integers from 1 to 24 in order.

```
int array2[6][4];
int num;

for (int i = 5; i >= 0; i--)
    for (int j = 0; j < 4; j++) {
        cin >> num;
        if (j > i)
            num++;
        array2[i][j] = num;
    }
```

b. Rewrite the program using a third (outermost) loop. This loop supplies the values (integers from 1 to 24) to use for num.

19. For each of the following program segments, show exactly what is printed. Also draw a picture showing the final values stored in the array arr. If a storage location does not have a value, indicate its value with ?. Use this declaration for each part:

```
int arr[5][6];
```

a.
```
for (int i = 0; i < 5; i++)
    for (int j = 0; j < 6; j++) {
        arr[i][j] = 10 * i + j;
```

```
                    cout << "i = " << i << " j = " << j
                        << " and the array is " << arr[i][j] << endl;
            }
    b. for (int i = 5; i < 10; i++)
            for (int j = 6; j > 2; j--)
                if (i > j)
                    arr[i-5][j-1] = i + j;
                else
                    arr[j-i+1][j-1] = 19;
        for (int i = 0; i < 5; i++)
            for (int j = 0; j < 6; j++)
                cout << "i = " << i << " j = " << j
                    << " and the array is " << arr[i][j] << endl;
```

PROGRAMMING PROJECTS

20. Write a program to do the following: Read a series of numbers into an array numb (there are never more than 50 numbers). Then multiply each number by 3, storing the new values in an array prod. Write the program using a parameter value to govern the amount of data read in.

21. Write a program that reads a series of numbers into an array numb (there are no more than 100 numbers). Go through the elements of the numb array one by one, moving the positive (or zero) elements to an array pos and the negative elements to an array neg. For example, if numb holds 5 −9 2 −7 −4 0 2, then array pos gets 5 2 0 2, and array neg has −9 −7 −4. Print the three arrays.

22. a. Write a program that reads in a number ans of type **double** and a parameter value n, then reads n numbers of type **double** into an array results (assume there are no more than 500 numbers). Determine which of these numbers is closest in absolute value to ans. Find the average of the results values and the number closest to it.

    b. Can this exercise be solved without using an array? Explain. Do you need an array if the set of data contains the value for ans after the values for results?

23. Write a program that reads in a parameter value n, then reads n numbers into the x array. It then reads in another parameter value m, and reads m values into the y array. It finds the average of the n values in the x array and the m values in the y array. Then it reads both arrays into a single large array z (which consists of the elements of x followed by those from y). Finally, it finds the average of the $n + m$ values in the z array.

24. Write a program that reads a series of integer values into an array, then finds the mode of the array, which is the number that occurs most often. (*Suggestion*: One possible method is to count how many times each value occurs, then find which of these counts is the largest.)

25. A company manufactures two items, each with a price that can vary. The company receives orders which contain two numbers for each item; the first represents the number of units ordered, and the second number represents the price of that item. A program has been written to find the total cost of the order by reading the amounts ordered, then multiplying the price of the first item (stored in price1) by the amount ordered (read into amt1) and adding this to the total cost for item two, which is computed in the same way.

    The company expands its product line to include ten items instead of two. One way to handle this is to introduce variables for each of the new prices and amounts, then multiply the appropriate values and add the total costs for the ten items. Another method is to store the ten prices in an array, read the ten amounts ordered into another array, then multiply the corresponding elements of the two arrays. Write a program that uses the first method, then another program that uses the second method. Compare the two programs.

26. Write a program that counts the number of votes received by each of 20 candidates in an election. Each piece of data is a number from 0 to 20, with 0 representing a vote for candidate 0, 1 for candidate 1, and so on. The program reads in an arbitrary number of votes. At the end of the set of data, it prints the number of votes received by each candidate. Determine which candidate receives the most votes. (*Suggestion*: Store the vote totals in an array, using the piece of data as the subscript.)

27. The well-known Fibonacci series consists of the numbers 1, 1, 2, 3, 5, 8, 13, ... The first two terms are both 1; thereafter, each term is the sum of the two previous ones (e.g., $8 = 3 + 5$, $13 = 5 + 8$).

    a. Write a program (without an array) to read in a value n, then compute and print the values of the first n terms of the Fibonacci series. (*Suggestion*: You have to keep track of the last term and the next-to-last term and update them at the appropriate time.)

    b. Solve the same problem using an array to hold the terms of the series. (This is significantly easier than part (a) but is limited by the bounds of the array.)

28. a. Write a function smallarr( ) that returns the smallest element in an array. The function receives two parameters: an array x of numbers of type **double** and an integer n, representing the number of values in the array x.

    b. Write a main program that tests the smallarr( ) function. The main program calls the function with several different arrays, containing varying numbers of elements.

    c. Write a function avg_large_and_small( ) that returns the average of the largest and smallest elements in an array. (*Suggestion*: The function can use smallarr( ) and a version of findmax( ) from Program 7, revised to operate on numbers of type **double**.)

    d. Write a function findlimits( ) that finds and returns (using reference parameters), the largest value in the array and the smallest value in the array.

29. Write a program that calls a function poslarg( ) that returns the position of the largest element in an array. The function receives as parameters an array of integers val and an integer n, representing the number of elements in the array. (*Note*: This function finds the subscript or position of the largest value, not the value itself.) For example, if the array holds 5 7 3 2 6, then the function returns 1 since the largest element (7) is in position 1. If the largest value occurs several times, return the first occurrence.

30. a. Write a function zerotest( ) that searches for an array element with a value of 0. The function receives as parameters an array of integers s and an integer r, representing the number of values to be tested in the array. The function returns **true** if 0 occurs one or more times in the first r positions of s; it returns **false** if no 0 is present. Here is the function prototype:

    ```
    bool zerotest(int [],int);
    ```

    b. Write a driver program that tests the function zerotest( ). The driver program should use several arrays and sizes. For example, if the x array holds 7 4 3 2 0 −1 0 5, zerotest( ) can be called with the first four elements of x, the first six, and so on.

31. a. Write a function zeroposit( ) which modifies the function zerotest( ) from Exercise 30. Instead of returning **true** or **false**, zeroposit( ) returns the position of 0 within the first r elements of the s array. If 0 occurs several times, the function returns the position of the first 0; if it does not occur at all, the function returns −1, indicating failure.

b. Write a driver program to test zeroposit( ). On the array x in Exercise 30(b), zeroposit(x,6) is 4; zeroposit(x,8) is also 4; zeroposit(x,3) is −1.

32. Write a function search( ) to generalize the function zeroposit( ) from Exercise 31. Instead of always searching for the position of 0, search( ) receives the number to be located as one of its parameters. The function receives an array of integers numb, a size m, and a particular integer p. It returns the position of the first value of p within the first m elements of the numb array; it returns −1 if p does not occur. (The problem of searching for a particular value is extremely common in business and commercial situations. It is discussed in Chapter 9.)

33. You have been hired as a programmer by a major bank. Your first project is a small banking transaction system. Each account consists of a number and a balance. The user of the program (the teller) can create a new account, as well as perform deposits, withdrawals, and balance inquiries. Initially, the account information of existing customers is to be read into a pair of parallel arrays—one for account numbers, the other for balances. Use the following function to read in the data values:

```
int read_accts(int acctnum_array, double balance_array, int max_elems);
```

This function fills up the account number and balance arrays (up to max_elems) and returns the actual number of accounts read in (later referred to as num_elems).

The program then allows the user to select from the following menu of transactions:

Select one of the following:

W - Withdrawal

D - Deposit

N - New account

B - Balance

Q - Quit

Use the following function to produce the menu:

```
char menu(void);
```

This function displays the menu and reads in the user's choice. You should verify that the user has typed in a valid selection (otherwise print out an error message and repeat the prompt). The user's selection is returned by the function.

Once the user has entered a selection, one of the following functions should be called to perform the specific transaction. At the end, before the user quits, the program prints the contents of the account arrays.

```
int findacct(int acctnum_array, int num_elems, int account);
```

This function returns the index of account in account_array if the account exists, and −1 if it doesn't. It is called by all the remaining functions.

```
void withdrawal(int acctnum_array, double balance_array, int num_elems);
```

This function prompts the user for the account number. If the account does not exist, it prints an error message. Otherwise, it asks the user for the amount of the withdrawal. If the account does not contain sufficient funds, it prints an error message and does not perform the transaction.

```
void deposit(int acctnum_array, double balance_array, int num_elems);
```

This function prompts the user for the account number. If the account does not exist, it prints an error message. Otherwise, it asks the user for the amount of the deposit.

```
int new_acct(int acctnum_array, double balance_array, int num_elems);
```

This function prompts the user for a new account number. If the account already exists, it prints an error message. Otherwise, it adds the account to the account array with an initial balance of 0. It returns the new number of accounts.

```
void balance(int acctnum_array, double balance_array, int num_elems);
```

This function prompts the user for an account number. If the account does not exist, the function prints an error message. Otherwise, it prints the account balance.

```
void print_accts(int acctnum_array, double balance_array,
    int num_elems);
```

This function prints all customer information—account number and balance.

PROGRAMMING PROJECTS FOR TWO-DIMENSIONAL ARRAYS

34. The arrays x and y both have five rows and three columns. Write two functions, one to do each of the following:

    a. Determine if each storage location in x holds the same value as the corresponding location in y.

    b. Determine if each storage location in y holds the same value as any location in x.

    Print an appropriate message for each case. Write a main program that tests these functions. Test your program with various sets of data.

35. Assume that values have been read into the array a, which has four rows and nine columns.

    a. Write a function that adds 10 to each negative value stored in the array (e.g., if *a[2][3]* is −19, it should be changed to −9).

    b. Modify your function from part (a) so that, instead of adding 10 just once, it adds 10 repeatedly until the value is no longer negative (−19 becomes −9 and then +1; −7 becomes +3; −30 becomes 0).

36. A square two-dimensional array has equal numbers of rows and columns (e.g., five of each). Given such an array called x, the locations with equal row and column subscripts (*x[1][1]*, *x[2][2]*, etc.) form the main diagonal of the array. These entries go from upper left to lower right. The antidiagonal consists of the entries from lower left to upper right.

    Write a function to sum the entries on the main diagonal of an array. Write a function to sum the entries on the main diagonal and the antidiagonal. Write a main program that tests these functions.

37. Write a complete program to do the following: A function interactively reads in nine values, each of which is the character X or O, corresponding to moves on a tic-tac-toe board. (Assume that the first row is read in, then the second row, then the third row.) Another function prints the board in the form of a three-by-three array, with an X or an O in the appropriate location. Another function determines the winner of the game (whichever player has three marks in a row: horizontally, vertically, or on either diagonal). The function determines if X won, if O won, if the game is a draw, or if the result is impossible. (Many results are impossible—for example, if there are two winners. What are some other impossible results?)

38. Write a program that plays tic-tac-toe. Instead of simply reading in the moves, it decides which move to make in a given situation, based on rules that you provide. For example, if the opponent has two marks in the same column, the machine should select the third position in that same column. Write two versions of the program: one in which the machine plays interactively with a human opponent and one in which the machine makes the moves for both sides.

39. a. Assume that a two-dimensional array <u>letter</u> with four rows and four columns holds a single character in each storage location (***letter[2][1]*** might hold 'y'). Write a function that determines whether any row or column or either diagonal of the array consists of the characters 'h', 'e', 'l', 'p', either forward or backward.

   b. Modify your function from part (a) so that the array <u>letter</u> has six rows and six columns. See if any four consecutive row (or column or diagonal) entries contain the sequence of characters 'h', 'e', 'l', 'p', either forward or backward.

40. Write a program that does grade analysis using the two-dimensional <u>grade</u> array from Section 8. Each row contains the grades for one student; each column reflects the grades on a given exam. There should be four exams. The set of data starts with a parameter value indicating the number of students. Then the program reads in and prints four grades for each student. The program does the following tasks, each in its own function.

   a. Find and print the class average on each exam.

   b. Find and print the highest mark on each exam.

   c. For each exam, find and print how many grades are above, below, and equal to the average.

   d. Find and print each student's average. Use the <u>grade</u> array subscript to identify each student.

   e. Find the overall class average. There are three ways to do this: averaging the individual student averages, averaging the four class exams, and averaging all the separate grades.

      i. Try to estimate the number of arithmetic operations needed for each method.

      ii. Which method requires the fewest arithmetic operations?

      iii. Of the three methods, which is the most reliable? That is, which does not depend upon previous calculations?

41. Expand the program from Exercise 40 by adding functions for each of the following parts:

   a. Determine each student's high and low grades, the exam on which they were obtained, and the difference between the high and low grades.

   b. In the entire class (and for each student separately), find the number of grades that are 90 or more, 80 to 89, and so on.

   c. Print the number of every student who receives at least one grade of 90 or more. If a student has two or more grades in this range, print the number only once. Use the <u>grade</u> array subscript to identify each student.

   d. Go through the array and make sure that every mark is valid (in the range from 0 to 100). If any mark is invalid, print an error message and the position of the invalid mark.

   e. Convert invalid grades to valid ones in the following way: If the grade is negative, make it positive (if necessary, apply the next step as well). If the grade is over 100, keep only the last two digits of the number. For example, 687 becomes 87; 135 becomes 35; −200 becomes 200 and then 0.

   f. Before computing each student's average, drop the lowest grade. For example, if a student's grades are 90 45 89 91, drop the 45, and the other three grades average to 90.00.

g. Assume that the last test is optional. If student number i took the test, then (in row i) the fourth column of the <u>grade</u> array holds the grade, but if the student didn't, the fourth column of <u>grade</u> holds −1. Modify the function which computes student averages to handle this feature. (Do any other functions have to be modified to make this change?)

h. In the original version of the program, each exam had equal weight. Assume that the weight of each exam is not the same. Instead, each exam has associated with it an integer (you determine how these integers receive values) such that the sum of the four is 100. Each integer is the relative weight of that exam. For example, to give the exams equal weight, each integer would be 25. But if the weights are 20 20 20 40, then the last exam counts twice as heavily as the others. Modify the function which computes student averages to handle this feature. (Do any other functions have to be modified to make this change?)

42. A company has records for the hours worked by each employee per week. Each employee's record consists of the employee's hourly rate of pay and seven numbers, representing the hours worked by the employee on the seven days of the week. For example, a typical entry could be the following:

```
13.25   1.3   7   8   0   4.7   0   0
```

The first piece of data entered (not shown) is a parameter value, specifying the number of employees (there are no more than 20).

Write a program that reads in the specified data and then does the following:

a. For each employee, finds the total number of hours worked for the week.

b. For each employee, finds the weekly pay by multiplying the hours worked by the rate per hour.

c. Finds the number of employees absent on each day of the week. An employee is considered absent on a given day if the hours worked are less than 1.

d. Finds which day has the most absentees.

43. The game of Life was developed by a mathematician named John Conway. It is intended to provide a model of life, death, and survival among simple organisms that inhabit an n by m board. The current population of the board comprises one generation. There are only four rules that govern the birth or death of cells from one generation to the next:

a. Every empty cell with three living neighbors comes to life in the next generation.

b. Any cell with one or zero neighbors dies of loneliness.

c. Any cell with four or more neighbors dies from overcrowding.

d. Any cell with two or three neighbors lives into the next generation.

All births and deaths occur simultaneously.

A cell's neighbors are the eight cells surrounding it, as shown in Figure 7-13.

FIGURE 7-13   Cell x and its eight neighboring cells

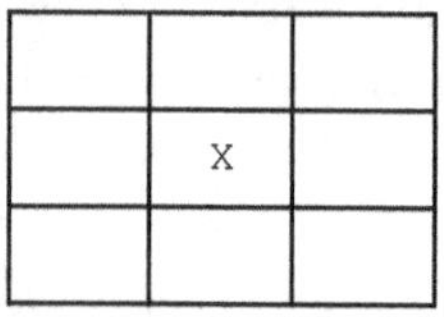

Why is Life a game? It turns out that some starting populations die out quickly, while others form interesting patterns that repeat, grow, or move across the board as they go from generation to generation.

a. Write a program that plays Life on the screen. Let the user specify the locations of the starting population as well as the number of generations that should be shown as output. Use a two-dimensional array to represent the board. In order for the board to fill the screen, use an array with rows from 0 to 24 and columns from 0 to 79. Use a letter, like *x*, to represent each living cell.

b. Write a function that pauses between generations so that the screen image can be printed.

EXERCISES USING REFERENCE PARAMETERS

44. Show what is printed by the following program.

```cpp
#include <iostream>
using namespace std;
int flipagain(int &, int &, int &);
int main()
{
    int a = 2, b = 5, c = 7, f[3];

    f[0] = 10;
    f[1] = 100;
    f[2] = -10;
    cout << "first: " << a << " " << b << " " << c
        << " " << f[0] << " " << f[1] << " " << f[2] << endl;

    c = flipagain(a,b,f[0]);
    cout << "second: " << a << " "<< b << " " << c
        << " " << f[0] << " " << f[1] << " " << f[2] << endl;
    c = flipagain(f[0],f[1],f[2]);
    cout << "second: " << c << " " << f[0] << " " << f[1] << " "
        << f[2] << endl;
    return 0;
}
int flipagain(int &q, int &p, int &r)
{
    int s;

    q++;
    r += 5;
    p -= 3;
    s = p * r;
    cout << " in flipagain: " << r << " " << p << " " << q << endl;
    cout << " still here: " << s << endl;
    return s;
}
```

45. a. Write a function underline(findsum( )) which finds the sum of the values in an array and returns the sum using a reference parameter. The parameters to the function are an array of type **double,** an integer representing the size of the array, and a reference parameter to hold the sum.

b. Show how to call the function <u>findsum( )</u> from a main program. The main program sends <u>findsum( )</u> an array <u>numbers</u>, the size of the array <u>n</u>, and the reference parameter <u>sum</u>. The array contains ten elements.

c. In the main program, give the function prototype and the declaration for each variable mentioned in the call to the function.

46. a. Write a void function <u>changetoavg( )</u> which has three parameters:

<u>numbs</u>—an array of values of type **double**

<u>n</u>—an integer from 1 to 100, representing the number of values in the <u>numbs</u> array

<u>avg</u>—a value of type **double**

The function determines the average of the first <u>n</u> elements in the <u>numbs</u> array. It prints this average and stores the result in <u>avg</u>, a reference parameter. Then the function sets each of the first <u>n</u> elements in the array to the value computed for the average.

For example, assume that <u>n</u> is 4 and the array holds 5.0 −7.0 3.0 6.0. The function prints a message saying the average is 1.75, stores the average, and changes each of first four elements of the array to this value. The new array holds these values: 1.75 1.75 1.75 1.75.

b. Write a main program that uses the function <u>changetoavg( )</u> to modify the first 20 elements in an array called <u>xyz</u>, storing the average in a variable called <u>xyzavg</u>. When the function returns, the main program prints the average and the new values in the array. Assume that the array <u>xyz</u> will hold no more than 100 values of type **double**.

47. Write a complete program to do the following:

a. Write a function called <u>readdata( )</u> which receives two parameters, an integer <u>n</u> and an array of integers called <u>vals</u>, both of which are changed in the function. The function reads a value into <u>n</u> and reads in <u>n</u> integers, storing the data values in the array <u>vals</u>. Print the data values as they are read in.

b. Write a function called <u>countzeros( )</u> which receives two parameters, an integer <u>n</u> and an array <u>vals</u>. The function counts how many of the first <u>n</u> elements of the <u>vals</u> array are 0. Print the number of 0 values (in either the main program or the function).

For example, if the array holds 66 0 −4 0 4 31 with <u>n</u> = 6, it has two 0 values.

c. Write a function called <u>append( )</u> which reads in several new values into the array, putting them at the end. As a result, it must change both the array and the value of <u>n</u>. The function receives the same two parameters as <u>readdata( )</u>. Assume the array initially holds 66 0 −4 0 4 31 with <u>n</u> = 6; after the function call, the array might hold 66 0 −4 0 4 31 22 0 49 with <u>n</u> = 9.

d. Write a main program which calls these functions. First the main program reads an integer which it calls <u>size</u>. Then the main program calls <u>readdata( )</u> to read a set of data containing <u>size</u> elements into an array called <u>numbers</u>, which contains no more than 100 integers. Then the main program calls the function <u>countzeros( )</u> to find how many of the <u>size</u> array elements are 0. Next the main program calls <u>append( )</u> to modify the <u>numbers</u> array and <u>n</u>. The <u>append( )</u> function reads in new values until input failure, adding the new values to the array and incrementing <u>n</u>. The new values in the array are printed (in either the main program or the function). Finally, the main program calls the function <u>countzeros( )</u> again to determine how many elements in the new array are 0.

48. Write a function <u>countem( )</u> which does the following. Sent an array of <u>n</u> integers, the function counts how many of the array elements are positive, how many are negative, and how many are zero. Using reference parameters, the function returns these three counters.

49. Write a complete program to do the following: The main program calls a function <u>readdata( )</u> to read in a set of integers representing IQ scores. Then the main program calls another function <u>aboveandbelow( )</u> which determines how many of the scores are above 100 and how many are 100 or below. Using reference parameters, the function sends these two counters back to the main program where they are printed.

STRINGS

PROBLEM: Editing a Text

SYNTAX CONCEPTS: **string** class, **string** operations: assignment, concatenation, comparison; **string** member functions: <u>length( )</u>, <u>clear( )</u>, <u>size( )</u>, <u>find( )</u>, <u>substr( )</u>, <u>insert( )</u>, <u>erase( )</u>, <u>replace( )</u>; I/O functions for strings: <u>get-line( )</u>; file I/O with strings; strings as parameters; data type **char,** <u>get( )</u>, <u>put( )</u>, and functions from <u>cctype.h</u>; arrays of strings

PROGRAMMING CONCEPTS: replacing one string by another, editing a text

HOW TO READ CHAPTER 8

OUTLINE:

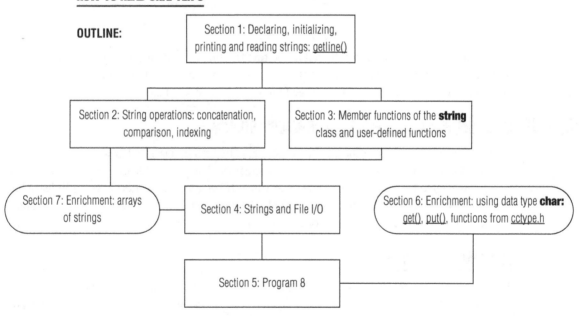

Section 1 is required for all but Section 6. Section 2 is not required for Section 3. Section 5, however, depends on Sections 1 through 4 and uses two items from Section 6. Section 6 is otherwise independent of the rest of the chapter and can be covered at any time after functions. Section 7 requires only Sections 1 and 2, but one example uses reading from a file, covered in Section 4.

INTRODUCTION AND STATEMENT OF THE PROBLEM

C++ has a **string** class, which allows us to declare variables with data type **string**. This class also provides functions of a special type, called *member functions*, for manipulating strings. This chapter will discuss how string handling is implemented in C++.

In this chapter, you will learn how to assign a value to a string, how to read string values, and how to compare two strings. What other types of things can be done with strings? Just to give a preview of what you will be learning, here are some examples:

♦ Add an 's' to the end of a word

♦ Count the number of times the letter 'e' occurs in a string

♦ Change the third letter of a string to some new value

♦ Replace all occurrences of 'his' by 'her'

Notice that each of these examples is concerned with accessing some part of a string, rather than the string as a whole.

PROBLEM 8   We want to write a simple editing program which reads a text line by line from a file, presents it to the user, and allows the user to do one or more of these tasks: remove text, add text, or replace some text by other text. For example, if the original line of text is "My bog is not funny, but your bog is funny", a user might want to remove "not", add the word "very" before "funny", and change "bog" to "blog" (either once or every time it occurs).

Here is a sample text file to edit:

```
My bog is not funny, but your bog is funny.
I must fixx it.
LOL, your Facebook entry looks dump.
```

Write a C++ program that will read in the text file line by line, displaying each line as it is read in, and ask the user to make any number of changes (insertions, deletions, and replacements), then display the revised line of text. The changed lines will be written to a new file.

SECTION 1   DECLARING, INITIALIZING, PRINTING AND READING STRINGS

We've already worked with a special type of string, called a literal string. However, the only thing we did with literal strings was send them to output streams. Now you will learn how to declare a string, how to give it a value, and how to change that value. In addition, in Section 2, you will learn how to compare one string with another, how to find whether or not one part of a string is contained in another, and many other useful string operations.

USING HEADER FILE string

To use C++ strings, we should include the string.h header file in our program. The #include directive for this header file, shown below, is placed together with *#include <iostream>* and the #include directives for any other header files. These headers can appear in any order.

```
#include <string>
```

The file string.h includes the prototypes for the string manipulation functions, just as cmath.h contains the prototypes for mathematical functions, and just as iostream.h contains the prototypes for I/O functions. Here are the header files we will use for this program:

```
#include <iostream>
#include <string>
```

DECLARING A STRING

In C++, **string** is an example of a class: the **string** class. We use the class **string** to declare a string object (or variable).

NOTE

Technically, **string** is a class in C++, but for now we can think of it as a data type, just as **double** and **int** are data types. Just as we use a data type to declare variables, we use a class to declare objects of that class. We will have much more to say about classes in Chapter 10. For simplicity, in this chapter we will use the terms variable (of type **string**) and object (of the **string** class) interchangeably if there is no confusion. Also, **string** is not a keyword, but since it is used as a data type, like **int** and **double**, we will put it in boldface type in this text.

Here is an example declaring two variables, str1 and str2, and then using them to send a message to cout.

```
string str1 = "Hello";
string str2 = "computer science students";

cout << str1 <<  ", " <<  str2 << endl;
```

This will print "Hello, computer science students" and go to a new line.

ASSIGNING A VALUE TO A STRING

A string can be given a value using the assignment operator. This can be done in the declaration, as shown above, or at any point later in the program. The string can be assigned a literal string value or the value of another string variable.

```
str1 = "Today is Monday";
str2 = str1;
```

At this point, str1 and str2 have the same value, "Today is Monday".

READING IN A STRING FROM cin; SENDING A STRING TO cout

You can read in a string from cin using the extraction operator, >>.

Reading a single-word string from cin using >> is done just like reading a value of type **int** or type **double** or type **char**.

```
string str;

cin >> str;
cout << str;
```

Whatever value is typed at the keyboard (up to the first whitespace character) will be read into str. In this example, if we type in "cobwebs" (without the quotation marks), str will get the value "cobwebs" and that will be sent to cout.

A problem with the >> operator is that it stops reading when it encounters a whitespace character (that is, a space, tab, or a newline character). This is quite limiting if you want to read in someone's name (e.g., John Doe), the names of some states (New York), or a sentence, like "This is the first line of input." In the example above, if you type in "cob webs", str will get just the value "cob".

READING IN A STRING USING getline()

Fortunately, C++ has another way to read a value into a string, using the function getline( ). This function takes two or three parameters: the first is the name of the input stream (cin in this example), the second is the variable into which to read a value (<u>name</u> in this example), and the last is optional (see below). Here is a call with just two parameters:

```
string name;

getline(cin,name);
cout << name << endl;
```

As shown above, when the third parameter is omitted, <u>getline( )</u> reads until the newline character is encountered (that is, until the user presses "Enter").

Alternatively, the third parameter can be any one character used as a delimiter to mark the separation between two items on a line. In the code below, the first <u>getline( )</u> reads until it encounters a question mark, and the second reads until it encounters a 'w'. The delimiter is not read into the string.

```
string first, second;

getline(cin,first,'?');
getline(cin,second,'w');
```

Thus, if the line typed in was "Have you heard? The lights went out!" followed by a newline character, the string <u>first</u> would get the value "Have you heard" and <u>second</u> would get the value " The lights ", including the space before 'T' and the space after 's'. Neither string would include the question mark or the 'w', because those were the delimiters.

Note that in almost all cases the version of <u>getline( )</u> with two parameters is used.

SELF-CHECK 8-1

1. Show how to declare and initialize a string to hold the value "potato chips".

2. Show how to read a value from <u>cin</u> into a variable called <u>str,</u> and show how to send that same string to <u>cout</u>.

3. Show how to read a complete sentence (for example, "I am happy.") from <u>cin</u> into the string <u>sentence</u>.

SECTION 2   STRING OPERATIONS: CONCATENATION, COMPARISON, INDEXING

String operations in C++ are performed using some of the same operators that are used for arithmetic operations. The symbols are interpreted slightly differently in some cases. We've already seen the use of the = operator for assignment. This section will discuss a few more.

CONCATENATION

It is possible to join two or more strings together using the + operator. The operation, called **concatenation**, joins one string to the end of another.

```
string str1, str2, str3;

str1 = "yesterday";
str2 = "morning";
str3 = str1+ " " + str2;

cout << str3 << endl;
```

String str3 has the value "yesterday morning", and that value is sent to cout. Note that we concatenated a space between the two words to produce a space in the resulting string; the space could have been included in either str1 or str2.

The use of an operator (like +) for some action other than its original use is called **operator overloading**.

EXAMPLE 8-1

Adding an 's' to the end of a string can be done by concatenation.

```
string str = "empty train";
str = str + 's';              // or str = str + "s";
```

The result of this operation is that str has the value "empty trains". Note that it is also possible to use the += operator to perform concatenation:

```
str += 's';                   // or str += "s";
```

Starting from the original value in str, this produces "empty trains", the same result as in the example above.

COMPARING STRINGS

You can compare two strings using the standard relational operators (<, <=, >, >=, ==, and !=). Two strings are the same (equal to each other) if they have the same number of characters and if each corresponding character matches: e.g., "cat" is the same as "cat" but not the same as "act", "Cat" or even "cat " (with a space at the end).

```
string str1 = "cat";
string str2 = "dog";

if (str1 == str2)
     cout << "alike" << endl;
else
     cout << "different" << endl;
```

This will, of course, print "different" because "cat" is not the same string as "dog".

Beyond looking for equal or not equal, you can compare strings to determine whether one is greater than or less than the other.

What does it mean to compare strings? String comparison is simply an extension of character comparison. In Chapter 3, Section 2, we saw that each element of data type **char** has a numeric equivalent. Because values of type **char** are assigned numbers in consecutive order, characters can be put in order or alphabetized. The number for 'a' is less than the number for 'b' which is less than the number for 'c', etc. The capital letters are assigned numbers in a different series, which are smaller than all the lowercase letters. Thus 'A' < 'Z' < 'a' < 'z'. A blank has a numeric value which is less than any printable character. Some sample characters and their numeric equivalents (called ASCII codes) are shown in Table 8-1. A complete list is in the Appendix.

When strings are compared, the computer uses an algorithm similar to what people use: it compares pairs of characters, one from each string, until it finds a pair of characters that are not the same. That is, if the first characters are alike, the computer looks at the next character in each string, etc., until it gets to the end of one of the strings, or until it finds a pair of characters that are not alike. Thus when comparing "car" with "cat", the first two characters are alike; but 'r' is less than 't', which means that "car" is less than "cat" (see Figure 8-1).

TABLE 8-1 Selected Characters and Their Numeric Equivalents

Character	' '	'A'	'B'	'Z'	'a'	'b'	'c'	'z'
Numeric equivalent	32	65	66	90	97	98	99	122

FIGURE 8-1 Comparison of two strings

Similarly, both "car" and "cat" are less than "cloth" (because 'a' is less than 'l').

Normally, the length of the strings will not be a factor, because the character by character comparison starts at the left end of the string. However, there is a special case where two strings have different lengths and are identical in all positions up to the length of the shorter string. In this case, the shorter string is called a **prefix** of the other string. The prefix is considered less than the other string: thus, "cat" is less than "catalog".

Notice, too, that "cat" and "Cat" are different strings, since uppercase and lowercase letters have different numeric values. "Cat" is less than "cat", because the uppercase letters have smaller numeric values than the lowercase letters.

THE POSITION OR INDEX OF A CHARACTER IN A STRING

The characters in a string have numbered positions, starting at 0, just like the values in an array. We can refer to the position (or **index**) of a character or a group of characters in a string. For example, Figure 8-2 shows the string "hello" together with the position (or index) of each character.

MODIFYING THE VALUE AT A SPECIFIC POSITION IN A STRING

Since each position in a string has a number associated with it, we can use that number to access the value stored at that location.

EXAMPLE 8-2

```
string str = "lone";

cout << str << " ";
str[2] = 'v';
cout << str << endl;
```

First, this prints "lone" and a space. Then it changes the third character of str to 'v', which changes str to "love". Note that the third character is numbered 2 since we start counting at 0. The output is:

```
lone love
```

FIGURE 8-2   The positions of the characters in a string

character	h	e	1	1	o
position	0	1	2	3	4

ITERATING THROUGH POSITIONS IN A STRING

It is possible to iterate through a string character by character, for example to print each character of the string on a new line. We must stop at the end of the string, which we've done in Example 8-3 by specifying the number of positions in the string (4) as a literal. In the next section, we'll show how to determine the length of a string using a string member function.

EXAMPLE 8-3

```
string str = "lone";

for (int i = 0; i < 4; i++)
    cout << str[i] << endl;
```

We start i at 0, since that is the position of the first character. As the subscript i increments from 0 to 3, it specifies the position of the character to print.

SELF-CHECK 8-2

1. Suppose you have these two strings:

```
string weather = "storm";
string noise = "thunder";
```

a. Show how to join these two strings together to produce the string "thunderstorm" (with no spaces) in string variable weather. Show how to join them to produce "thunder storm" (with one space between the words).

b. Show how to join these two strings together to send "thunderstorm" to cout without changing any variables.

2. What character is stored in weather[2] (from question 1)? In what position of noise is the character 'n' found?

3. Which of the following comparisons are true?

a. "storm" > "thunder"   d. "cat" < "Cat"
b. "water" >= "waste"   e. " stone" <= "stone"
c. "heat" != "HEAT"   f. "banana" > "bananas"

SECTION 3   MEMBER FUNCTIONS OF THE STRING CLASS AND USER-DEFINED FUNCTIONS

The **string** class is a pre-defined class. Classes in C++ can have functions associated with them, called **member functions** of the class. Member functions define the operations that can be performed on objects of the class. The member functions that are included in the **string** class permit some fairly complex operations to be performed on strings.

We've already used several member functions of other classes: in Chapter 3, we introduced the iostream member functions cout.precision( ) and cout.width( ). These member functions work on cout, which—like cin—is an object of the iostream class. We also introduced the fstream member functions open( ) and close( ) which work on files, objects of the fstream class.

A string variable is, in fact, an object of the **string** class. There are more than 30 member functions defined for the **string** class; each member function works on an object of that class. A few are discussed here. Among the most useful are length( ), substr( ), find( ), insert( ), and erase( ).

To use a member function, you first specify the name of the object, followed by a period, followed by the name of the member function, followed by a pair of parentheses (with no spaces in between the parts). For example,

```
object     period     member function     ( )
  ↓          ↓               ↓               ↓
cout         .          precision          ()        or    cout.precision()
cout         .            width            ()        or    cout.width()
```

Note that when we use a member function with a string object, we place the name of the string in front of the name of the member function. Here is an example using the member function length( ), applied to city:

```
string city;

object     period     member function     ( )
  ↓          ↓               ↓               ↓
city         .           length            ()        or    city.length()
```

FINDING THE LENGTH OF A STRING

A string has a length (or size). The length of a string is the number of characters currently in the string. There are two string member functions in C++ that will return this value: length( ) and size( ). (The two functions do the same thing.)

```
string state = "New York";
string city = "Cincinnati";
int len,numchars;

len = state.length();
numchars = city.size();
```

Note that we are using the names of the strings—state and city—in front of the name of the member function to indicate what string the member function should act upon. The length of state is 8 (the space is counted); that value will be returned and assigned to len. The size of city is 10, and that value will be assigned to numchars.

DATA TYPE string::size_type

Actually, this last example was a bit sloppy because many C++ string member functions return a numeric value which is not, technically, of type **int**. For example, the string member functions size( ) and length( ) return a value which has type *string::size_type*. This is an unsigned integer type. (An unsigned integer can never be negative.) A more precise version of the code above would declare len and numchars to have data type *string::size_type*, as shown below. Note that to use this data type, the identifier size_type must be preceded by the word **string** and two colons, the scope resolution operator.

```
string state = "New York";
string city = "Cincinnati";
```

```
string::size_type len, numchars;

len = state.length();
numchars = city.size();
```

In this particular case, using **int** instead of **size_type** will not hurt, but there are some occasions when using type **int** instead of type size_type will cause problems (for example, an infinite loop), because of the difference in interpretation of the signed vs. unsigned value (see Example 8-6). Therefore, it is safest to use size_type when referring to string sizes or to positions within a string.

THE EMPTY STRING OR CLEARING A STRING: clear( )

A string with no characters in it is called the empty string or null string. A string in C++ is by default empty of characters until you give it a value. However, there are times when you need to return the string to its empty state (see Exercise 8-27). The string member function clear( ) removes all characters from the specified string. Example 8-4 illustrates its use.

EXAMPLE 8-4
```
string name = "Lenny";

name += " Lyman";
cout << name << endl;
name.clear();
```

String name is given the value "Lenny Lyman" and sent to cout; then the clear( ) function changes the value to the empty string, one with no characters. The empty string can also be produced in the following manner:

```
name = "";
```

This method assigns a string of length 0 to name, by using two quotation marks with nothing between them.

FINDING THE POSITION OF A CHARACTER OR A STRING WITHIN ANOTHER STRING: find( )

When working with strings, it is often useful to find whether one string is contained in another (for example, "count" is found in "discount," and "chest" is found in "orchestra"). C++ has a string member function called find( ) which tries to find one string in another. If the string is present, find( ) returns the position of the first occurrence.

The member function find( ) has a number of variants, most of which we omit. The simplest form is illustrated below. In this version, the member function takes two parameters: the first parameter is the string to find, and the second is the starting position for the search. The search continues to the end of the string. The member function returns the position of the first occurrence of the item within the source string. If the item is not found, the function returns a special value called npos (see the next subsection).

General Form of a Call to find( )
The general form of a call to find( ) for the string named source is as follows:

found_position = source.find(string_to_find, start_position);

The string <u>source</u> is searched for string <u>string_to_find</u> starting in position <u>start_position</u>. The function returns the position of the first occurrence of <u>string_to_find</u> from <u>start_position</u> to the end of <u>source</u>.

Let's go through a series of examples to illustrate some of the options. For the first set of examples, the string we are searching for will always be found. In addition, we will start with examples in which the search begins at the start of the string.

EXAMPLE 8-5

In this first example, we search the string <u>source</u> for the value stored in string <u>findit</u>, and the value is found.

```
string source = "this orchestra is fabulous";
string::size_type pos;
string findit = "orchestra";

pos = source.find(findit,0);
```

This example searches for "orchestra" within string <u>source</u>, starting at the beginning (position 0). Since the string "orchestra" is found starting at position 5 of <u>source</u>, the function <u>find( )</u> returns 5.

In the next example, the string to be found occurs more than once in the original string, at positions 3 and 6, but <u>find( )</u> returns the position of the first occurrence, since a function can return only one value.

EXAMPLE 8-6

```
string source = "My blog is read more than your blog"
string::size_type pos;
string findit = "blog";

pos = source.find(findit,0);
```

In this case, <u>find( )</u> will find "blog" in position 3; <u>find( )</u> will not go further to see the second occurrence of "blog" at position 6 of string <u>source</u>. The function will return 3,

The parameters to <u>find( )</u> can be literals or constants

EXAMPLE 8-7

Using the variables from Example 8-5:

```
pos = source.find("is",0);
```

This call will return 2, since the string "is" is found in position 2 of <u>source</u>.

You can also look for a single character in a string, starting at any position.

EXAMPLE 8-8

Again, using the variables from Example 8-5, you can find the letter 'c':

```
pos = source.find('c',0);
```

The character 'c' is found in position 7.

A useful feature of <u>find( )</u> is that you can start the search in any position after the first position of the string. Very often this option is used to skip over an earlier occurrence which has already been found.

FIGURE 8-3   The position of the characters in a string <u>str</u>

character	t	o	d	a	y
position	0	1	2	3	4

EXAMPLE 8-9

You can look for "is" in string <u>source</u> starting from position 5:

```
string source = "this orchestra is fabulous";
pos = source.find("is",5);
```

Note that the position returned will be 15. The function finds the first occurrence of "is" beginning in or after position 5, but returns the position of "is" within the entire string, not the distance from position 5.

SEARCHES THAT ARE NOT SUCCESSFUL: THE CONSTANT string::npos

What should <u>find( )</u> return if the search is unsuccessful? It can't return 0, since that is a position in the string. It could return a negative number like -1, but it doesn't. Instead it returns a special value called <u>npos</u>, which is a constant defined in the **string** class.

Suppose that you have the string <u>str</u> holding the value "today", shown in Figure 8-3. If you used the function <u>find( )</u> to find the position of the letter 'd' in this string, it would return 2. If you were to use <u>find( )</u> to find the position of the string "day", it would return 2, since "day" is found in position 2 of this string. However, if you used <u>find( )</u> to find the letter 'x', 'x' would not be found. In this case, <u>find( )</u> would return a value that signifies the string has not been found. This value is the constant *string::npos*.

The constant <u>npos</u> is what is called an **unsigned integer**—an integer data type that can never be negative. The value of <u>npos</u> is too large to be stored in a variable of type <u>int</u>. Instead, it has type *string::size_type*, defined earlier. In general, when you use the function <u>find( )</u>, the variable used to hold the return value should have data type *string::size_type* to be able to hold the value of <u>npos</u>. The exact value of <u>npos</u> is machine dependent and irrelevant; what matters is that it represents a value which cannot be an index into the string. In fact, because of the difference between signed and unsigned integers, the value of <u>npos</u> is too large to be stored in a variable of type **int**. If you do assign it to a variable with type **int,** it will have the value -1, which will cause some of the code below not to work correctly. Writing code that interprets <u>npos</u> as -1 is not appropriate in C++, though it will sometimes appear to work correctly.

The item <u>npos</u> is a data member of the string class (which is why we wrote *string::npos* in the header of this section). Because of this, when using <u>npos</u> in a program, you must precede the word <u>npos</u> by the word **string** followed by two colons.

Let's revisit the example from Example 8-5, this time searching for a string that is not found.

EXAMPLE 8-10

Suppose you search string <u>source</u> to find "band" (which is not contained in the string). Before using the result of a call to <u>find( )</u>, you should check whether the string was actually found.

```
string source = "this orchestra is fabulous";
string::size_type pos;
string findit = "band";
```

```
pos = source.find(findit,0);
if (pos != string::npos)
    cout << findit << " was found in position " << pos << endl;
else
    cout << findit << " was not found" << endl;
```

Since "band" is not contained in <u>source</u>, <u>find( )</u> will return ***string::npos***, which will become the value of <u>pos</u>, and the code will print this:

```
band was not found
```

AN EXAMPLE: FINDING THE NUMBER OF 'E'S IN A STRING

Finding the number of times a specific character occurs in a string can be done using calls to <u>find( )</u> in a loop and counting the results.

EXAMPLE 8-11

```
string str = "The elephant was easily tired";
int count=0;
string::size_type pos;

pos = str.find('e',0);
while(pos != string::npos) {
    count++;
    pos = str.find('e',pos+1);
}
cout << "e is found " << count << " times" << endl;
```

In this example, we find the first occurrence of 'e' outside the loop. As long as <u>pos</u> is not equal to <u>npos</u>, 'e' is found in the string, so we enter the loop, count the occurrence, and look for the next occurrence. Note that each subsequent search starts at index <u>pos</u>+1, so that we do not repeatedly find the same occurrence. When <u>find( )</u> returns <u>npos</u>, there are no more 'e's in the string. At that point, we fall out of the loop and print the result, which is 5, since the letter 'e' appears 5 times. Note that <u>pos</u> should have type ***string::size_type*** and not type **int** since it will at some point get the value <u>npos</u>.

FINDING REPEATED OCCURRENCES OF A STRING WITHIN ANOTHER STRING

Suppose that we want to find how many times a string (not just a single character) occurs inside another string? This requires a modification of the code from Example 8-11. Instead of starting each search one position past where the letter was found, we should start past the end of the entire found string. For example, if we are searching for "top" in "stop top hat topping", we'll find "top" starting in position 1; but why start looking for it again in position 2? We should start looking past the end of the occurrence of "top", starting in position 4. Example 8-12 shows how to do this by adding the length of the found string to <u>pos</u>.

EXAMPLE 8-12

```
string str = "stop top hat topping", lookfor = "top";
int count=0;
string::size_type pos;
```

```
pos = str.find(lookfor,0);
while(pos != string::npos) {
        count++;
        pos = str.find(lookfor,pos+lookfor.length());
}
cout << "e is found " << count << " times" << endl;
```

Keep in mind that if you want to find the word "top" only when it stands alone, rather than when it is contained in other words, you will have to supply spaces before and after the letters, as in " top ". There are other issues which we leave for the exercises.

REPLACING PART OF A STRING BY ANOTHER STRING: replace( )

The member function replace( ) permits replacing part of a string by another string. The function has a number of variants, most of which we omit. One simple variant of replace( ) has three parameters: the first is the position in which to start replacing characters, the second is the number of characters to replace, and the third is the string from which to get the new characters.

General Form of a Call to replace( )

The general form of a call to replace( ) for the string named source is as follows:

> source.replace(starting_pos,numchars,newstr);

The string to modify is source; starting_pos is the position from which to remove numchars characters, and they will be replaced by newstr. The string source is changed.

Using replace( ) in this simplest fashion is illustrated in Example 8-13.

EXAMPLE 8-13

```
string message = "my inkjet printer";
string str = "laser";
```

The word "inkjet" starts in position 3 of message, and we can replace it with "laser" as follows:

```
    message.replace(3,6,str);
or  message.replace(3,6,"laser");
```

Either version changes string message to "my laser printer".

It doesn't matter whether the new string is longer or shorter than the string it replaces; the second parameter specifies the number of characters to remove from the source string, and the third parameter specifies the new value to insert.

DELETING PART OF THE VALUE OF A STRING: erase( )

Removing characters from a string can be done using erase( ). This member function takes two parameters, the starting position and the number of characters to remove. The erase( ) function removes the characters and closes up the string. If the second parameter is omitted, the function erases characters from the starting position to the end of the string.

THE GENERAL FORM OF A CALL TO erase( )

The general form of a call to erase( ) for the string named source is as follows:

General Form of a Call to erase( )

> source.erase(starting_pos, numchars);

The string source is changed by removing numchars characters starting at position starting_pos. The parameter numchars can be omitted.

EXAMPLE 8-14

We can delete letters from message in one of two ways (the letter 'i' is in position 11):

```
string message = "George Washington";

message.erase(11,3);
or message.erase(11);
```

The first line removes the three characters starting with the 'i' of "ing", leaving message as "George Washton". The second line removes all characters from the 'i' to the end, leaving message as "George Wash".

EXAMPLE 8-15

Either parameter to erase( ) can be a variable or an expression. Here we use find( ) to look for the first occurrence of string old in message, putting its location in pos. (We assume the string old will be found.) Once we've found old, we erase it from message, using length( ) to specify the number of characters to erase.

```
string message = "George Washington";
string old = "ing";
string::size_type pos;

pos = message.find(old,0);
message.erase(pos,old.length());
```

This removes the three characters starting with the 'i' of "ing", leaving message as "George Washton".

INSERTING A STRING INTO ANOTHER STRING: insert()

It is often also useful to insert a string (or part of a string) into another string. For example, we might want to insert a middle name into string message above. The function insert( ) is used for this purpose. The simplest form of the member function insert( ) takes two parameters: here is the general form.

General Form of a Call to insert( )

The general form of a call to insert( ) for the string named source is as follows:

> source.insert(starting_pos,string_to_insert);

The string source is changed by inserting the string string_to_insert at position starting_pos.

EXAMPLE 8-16

Suppose message has this value:

```
string message = "I have a melon";
```

We'd like to insert "water" in position 9. We can insert it as follows:

```
message.insert(9,"water");
```

This inserts "water" into <u>message</u> at position 9, changing message to "I have a watermelon".

EXAMPLE 8-17   Either parameter to the member function <u>insert( )</u> can be a variable or an expression:

```
string newstr = "water";
int pos = 9;

message.insert(pos,newstr);
```

This also inserts "water" into <u>message</u> at position 9, changing message to "I have a watermelon".

EXAMPLE 8-18   In the next section of code, we use <u>find( )</u> to look for the first occurrence of string <u>old</u> in <u>message</u>, putting its location in <u>pos</u>. (We assume string <u>old</u> will be found.) Once we've found <u>old</u>, we erase it from <u>message</u>, using <u>length( )</u> to specify how many characters to erase. Then we insert <u>newstr</u> in the place where <u>old</u> once was. (Of course, we could also use <u>replace( )</u> to do this task.)

```
string message = "what a nice day!";
string old = "nice";
string newstr = "rotten";
string::size_type pos;

pos = message.find(old,0);

message.erase(pos,old.length());

message.insert(pos,newstr);
```

This changes <u>message</u> to "what a rotten day!"

EXAMPLE 8-19   Suppose we want to find and replace all occurrences of <u>old</u> by <u>newstr</u> (in this example, replacing all occurrences of "cause" by "because"). This employs ideas from Examples 8-18 and 8-11. Each search after the first must start after the end of the inserted string.

```
string line = "cause, cause, cause";
string old = "cause";
string newstr = "because";
string::size_type pos;

pos = line.find(old,0);
while(pos != string::npos) {
    line.erase(pos,old.length());
    line.insert(pos,newstr);
    pos = line.find(old,pos+newstr.length());
}
cout << line << endl;
```

Finding the first occurrence is easy; "cause" starts in position 0, and we replace it with "because". However, if we start again from position 0 (or even from position 1, which would be <u>pos</u> + 1, as in Example 8-18), we will find "cause" in position 3, part of the first word "because" that we just inserted. Replacing the occurrence at position 3 would lead to an infinite loop producing the string "bebebebebebe ... cause". To avoid this problem, the new starting position should be past the end of the inserted string; setting it to *pos + newstr.length( )* does the job.

EXAMPLE 8-20

Note that using <u>replace( )</u> instead of <u>erase( )</u> and <u>insert( )</u> will require the same change in starting position.

```
pos = line.find(old,0);
while(pos != string::npos) {
      line.replace(pos, old.length(),newstr);
      pos = line.find(old,pos+newstr.length());
}
cout << line << endl;
```

EXTRACTING A SUBSTRING FROM A STRING: substr( )

When working with strings, it is sometimes useful to extract part of a string, either to copy it to another string, concatenate it with other strings, or send it to <u>cout</u>. For example, we might want to extract "count" from "discount", or "York" from "New York". The string member function <u>substr( )</u> extracts part of a string, leaving the original string unchanged.

The <u>substr( )</u> member function takes either one or two parameters of type *string::size_type*: the first is the position to start extracting, and the second (if it is present) is the number of characters to extract. The member function <u>substr( )</u> returns a substring consisting of the extracted characters. If you omit the second parameter, <u>substr( )</u> will extract characters from the starting position continuing to the end of the string.

General Form of a Call to substr( )
The general form of a call to <u>substr( )</u> for the string named <u>source</u> is as follows:

> **result_string = source.substr(starting_pos,numchars);**

The string <u>result_string</u> gets the result of copying <u>numchars</u> characters from position <u>starting_pos</u> of string <u>source</u>. String <u>source</u> is unchanged. The parameter <u>numchars</u> may be omitted.

Here is an example which uses both forms of the call to <u>substr( )</u>:

EXAMPLE 8-21

```
string str = "the movie was awesome";
string sub1,sub2;

sub1 = str.substr(4,5);
cout << "str is: " << str << endl;
cout << "sub1 is: " << sub1 << endl;

sub2 = str.substr(4);
cout << "sub2 is: " << sub2 << endl;
```

Here is the output resulting from the code above:

```
str is: the movie was awesome
sub1 is: movie
sub2 is: movie was awesome
```

The first call to <u>substr( )</u> said to copy 5 characters starting at position 4 of <u>str</u>; this gave <u>sub1</u> the value "movie". The second call to <u>substr( )</u> copied the substring starting at position 4. Because we didn't specify how many characters to copy, the <u>substr( )</u> function copied all the characters from 'm' to the end of the string, giving <u>sub2</u> the value "movie was awesome".

USER-DEFINED STRING FUNCTIONS: REFERENCE PARAMETERS AND RETURN VALUES

Now that we've seen the member functions of the **string** class, it is time to write some user-defined functions. Sending a string to a function works the same way as sending an item of any other type to a function. The type of the formal parameter must be **string**. If the string is to be changed inside the function, it must be sent as a reference parameter, using the & symbol. It is also possible to use **string** as the return type of a function. Example 8-22 shows an example of sending a string to the programmer-defined function append( ) to be changed. In the header of the append( ) function, the formal parameter st is a reference parameter.

EXAMPLE 8-22

```
        string str = "cat";
        append(str);
. . .

// add an 's' to the parameter st
void append(string &st)
{
    st += 's';              // or  st = st + 's';
    return;
}
```

Here is the prototype for the function:

```
void append(string &);
```

After the call to the function, str has been changed to "cats".

Example 8-23 shows a function which returns a value of type **string**.

EXAMPLE 8-23

Here is another way to do the same thing, by using a function dontchange( ) which returns a value of type **string** instead of changing the original string:

```
string result, str  = "cat";

result = dontchange(str);
```

Here is the function dontchange( ):

```
// construct a new string by adding an 's' and then
// returning the new string, without changing the original
string dontchange(string st)
{
    string newstr;

    newstr = st + 's';
    return newstr;

}
```

After the call to the function, result has the value "cats" but str is still "cat".

In this program, using the local variable newstr is not necessary. We can just use this **return** statement in place of the last two lines.

```
return st + 's';
```

In fact, if <u>st</u> is not a reference parameter, we can even write this:

```
st += 's';
return st;
```

Here is the prototype for the <u>dontchange( )</u> function:

```
string dontchange(string);
```

SELF-CHECK 8-3

1. What task does each of these functions perform? Write an example using each one.

    a. find( )   d. insert( )
    b. substr( )   e. erase( )
    c. replace( )   f. clear( )

2. Which function would you use to locate the position of "tree" in "street"? Show how to do it.

3. Which function would you use to remove "fur" from "furniture"? Show how to do it.

SECTION 4   STRINGS AND FILE I/O

When processing strings, it is often necessary to work with large chunks of text. Because it is tedious to enter a large amount of text from the keyboard, the text is often stored in a file. The standard method of reading and processing text using files is to read a line from a file, process the line, and write the line out to a file, repeating this until the entire file has been processed.

READING STRINGS FROM A FILE AND WRITING STRINGS TO A FILE

To read a string from a file, we use <u>getline( )</u>, just as when reading a string from <u>cin</u>. The file must be declared, and the file's name (instead of <u>cin</u>) is the first parameter to <u>getline( )</u>. To write a string to a file, first declare the file. Then send the string to the file using the name of the file instead of <u>cout</u>. Example 8-24 reads a series of strings from input file <u>fin</u> and then writes each string to the output file stream <u>fout</u>.

We'll use the reading to input failure method to find the end of the input stream, as we did at the end of Chapter 7. That is, if <u>getline( )</u> tries to read from the file <u>fin</u> and there are no more lines to read, <u>fin</u> will get a value indicating failure. (This technique can also be used when reading strings from <u>cin</u>.)

EXAMPLE 8-24

```
ifstream fin("ex824.in");
ofstream fout("ex24.out");

getline(fin,line);
while(fin){
    fout << line << endl;
    getline(fin,line);
}
```

The loop above is set up to continue to read from the file <u>fin</u> and write to file <u>fout</u> as long as there are more lines to read from the file <u>fin</u>. When there are no more lines to read, <u>fin</u> gets a value indicating failure.

EXAMPLE 8-25   Many C++ programmers would handle the input loop in a slightly different way, shown below.

```
ifstream fin("ex825.in");
ofstream fout("ex25.out");

while(getline(fin,line))
    fout << line << endl;
```

The function <u>getline( )</u> continues to read as long as there are lines to read from the file, and when it gets to the end of the file, the loop condition becomes false. This loop structure is more compact than the one shown above, and we will continue to use this form.

EXAMPLE 8-26   In this complete program example, we read a line from an input file, use a function to change the line read in, and write the line out to an output file, continuing until there are no more lines to be read in.

```
// reads a line at a time from an input file, until there are no more
// changes each line, and writes each line to an output file
#include <iostream>
#include <string>
#include <fstream>
using namespace std;
void change(string &);
int main()
{
    string line;
    ifstream fin("data9.in");
    ofstream fout("data9.out");

    while(getline(fin,line)) {
        change(line);
        fout << line << endl;
    }
    fin.close();
    fout.close();
    return 0;
}
// add an 's' to line
void change(string &line)
{
    line += 's';
    return;
}
```

SECTION 5   **PROGRAM 8**

Now that we have seen a number of functions which use strings, we are ready to solve the chapter problem.

PSEUDOCODE FOR THE MAIN PROGRAM

As usual, we will begin Program 8 by writing some pseudocode.

> *while there is a line of the text to read*
> > *read in a line from the file*
> > *print the original line*
> > *repeatedly ask the user what changes to make in the line*
> > > *and make those changes*
> >
> > *print the new line*
> > *write the new line to an output file*

We can get started from this pseudocode pretty quickly. As you can see, we've chosen to process the text line by line; that's a standard way of processing large amounts of data, especially when the data values are being read in from a file. The changes themselves will come from the user entering data from the keyboard. Therefore, this program uses both interactive I/O and reading from a file.

DIVIDING UP THE TASKS

How shall we divide up the processing? We need to read the lines of the text from the input file; we'll let main do that. Now let's think a little about the I/O. Since the data consists of lines of text containing whitespace characters, we can't read the data with the >> operator, but instead we must use get-line( ). What about the output? The statement of the problem says that we will send each line of output to a file, and main will also take care of that.

The rest of the processing is represented in the pseudocode by these lines:

> *print the original line*
> *repeatedly ask the user what changes to make in the line*
> > *and make those changes*

We'll let main call a function to do the processing. Let's call this function change( ). It should receive one line of text as a parameter and call functions to do all the processing of that line of text. With those decisions made, we can go ahead and write the main program.

THE MAIN PROGRAM

The main program will read the original text from the file one line at a time until there are no more lines, using the reading-to-input-failure method. The variable line will hold each line of data as it is read in. After reading the line, we'll send it to the function change( ) as a reference parameter, since it will be changed by the action of the function, and we will send the changed string to outfile.

The main program will look like this:

🖥 PROGRAM LISTING

```cpp
// prog8.cpp reads in lines of text from a file
// asks the user what changes to make in each line
//    until the user wants to stop making changes
// writes the changed line to a new file
#include <iostream>
#include <fstream>
#include <string>
```

```
using namespace std;
void change(string &);
. . .                               // other prototypes will go here
int main()
{
    string line;
    ifstream infile("ch8dat.dat");
    ofstream outfile("ch8.out");

    getline(infile, line);
    while(infile)
    {
        change(line);
        outfile << line << endl;
        getline(infile, line);
    }
    infile.close();
    outfile.close();
    return 0;
}
```

In keeping with the technique of top-down programming, we will now leave the main program and start to discuss the functions.

PLANNING THE FUNCTION change()

What will the function change( ) have to do? The change( ) function will accept one parameter: the line to change. Since it will be in charge of making all changes in a line, change( ) should ask the user what changes to make and, in modular fashion, call other functions to read in the values and make the actual changes. The action of the change( ) function will be to make all changes in the old line of text.

PSEUDOCODE FOR change()

Let's start by developing a rough version of the pseudocode for change( ). The function change( ) has to show the user the line of text, present the user with a set of choices, and ask what the user wants to do. Since we've said the program will repeatedly ask the user to make changes, this function should use a loop, displaying the line each time. We'll assume that the user wants to make at least one change; this suggests using a **do-while** loop:

> *display line*
> *do*
> > *ask user what change to make*
> > *call functions to make the changes*
> > *display line*
> *while (user wants to make changes in this line)*

THE FUNCTION change()

The line *ask user what change to make* can easily be translated by presenting the user with a list of choices and reading in the user's answer. One of the choices on the list will be the choice to quit editing the current line and move on to the next. For each choice, we should tell the user what character to enter to select that choice and what each choice means.

```
char choice;

cout << "Enter the letter of your choice" << endl;
cout << " e: erase text" << endl;
cout << "i: insert text" << endl;
cout << "r: replace text" << endl;
cout << "n: edit next line" << endl;
cin >> choice;
```

To translate *call functions to make the changes*, <u>change( )</u> will simply look at the user's response in <u>choice</u> ('i', 'e', 'r' or 'q') and call a function to perform the appropriate action. This is the perfect setup for a **switch** statement (see Chapter 6, Section 7). We'll let the choices 'e', 'i', and 'r' call functions to erase, insert, or replace text. The choice 'n' will simply cause the program to stop processing the current line. Any other choice is an error.

```
switch(choice) {
    case 'e': erasetext(line);
            break;
    case 'i': inserttext(line);
            break;
    case 'r': replacetext(line);
            break;
    case 'n': break;
    default:  cout << "error, invalid choice; try again" << endl;
}
```

This code will all go into a **do-while** loop that continues until the user enters 'n'. If the user does not enter 'n', the loop will present the now-changed line and continue at the top, asking if the user wants to make another change. If the user wants to continue editing, the loop will again present the list of choices, but if the user is finished editing this line, the function will return to main to read the next line of text.

```
cout << endl << "the line is now: " << line << endl;
do {
    cout << "Enter the letter of your choice" << endl;
    cout << " e: erase text" << endl;
    cout << "i: insert text" << endl;
    cout << "r: replace text" << endl;
    cout << "n: edit next line" << endl;
    cin >> choice;
    switch(choice) {
        case 'e': erasetext(line);
                break;
        case 'i': inserttext(line);
                break;
        case 'r': replacetext(line);
                break;
        case 'n': break;
        default:  cout << "error, invalid choice; try again" << endl;
    }
    cout << endl << "the line is now: " << line << endl;
} while(choice != 'n');
```

HOUSEKEEPING

There is one last item to take care of in change( ). It's an annoyance, but one that we must deal with. This function uses the >> operator, while later functions will use getline( ), though we haven't seen that yet. Reading a single character with the >> operator leaves a character in the input buffer; that character is the <Enter> pressed so that the user's response can be read into choice. We need to get rid of that <Enter> character or it will prevent the next line from being read. We'll get rid of the character by using cin.get( ) after cin >> choice (see Example 8-29).

THE change( ) FUNCTION

Now we can write change( ) before going on to the functions it calls.

```
// function change() receives line as a parameter, prints it, and
// asks the user what kind of change to make: erase, insert or replace
void change(string &line)
{
    char choice;

    cout << endl << "the line is now: " << line << endl;
    do {
        cout << "Enter the letter of your choice" << endl;
        cout << " e: erase text" << endl;
        cout << "i: insert text" << endl;
        cout << "r: replace text" << endl;
        cout << "n: edit next line" << endl;
        cin >> choice;
        cin.get();
        switch(choice) {
            case 'e': erasetext(line);
                    break;
            case 'i': inserttext(line);
                    break;
            case 'r': replacetext(line);
                    break;
            case 'n': break;
            default:  cout << "error, invalid choice; try again" << endl;
        }
        cout << endl << "the line is now: " << line << endl;
    } while(choice != 'n');
    return;
}
```

THE FUNCTION erasetext( )

The task for the erasetext( ) function is simple. In pseudocode,

> *ask the user to enter the text to erase*
> *read the text*
> *find the text in the line*
> *if found*
> > *call erase( ) to erase it*

      else

          print "not found"

For this program, we will assume that the user wants to erase only the first occurrence of the text in the line, but Exercise 8-30 asks you to expand this to erasing all occurrences of the text in the line.

    The function underlined change( ) will use <u>getline( )</u> to read in the text (which we'll call <u>text_to_erase</u>); <u>change( )</u> will then call <u>find( )</u> and then call <u>erase( )</u>, if <u>text_to_erase</u> is found, or print an error message if <u>text_to_erase</u> is not found.

```
cout << "Enter the text you would like to erase" << endl;
getline(cin,text_to_erase);
pos = line.find(text_to_erase,0);
if (pos != string::npos)
    line.erase(pos,text_to_erase.length());
else
    cout << text_to_erase << " is not found in the line" << endl;
```

The rest of the function is code is quite straightforward, and the entire function follows:

```
// function erasetext() receives line as a parameter;
// asks user what text to erase and erases that text
void erasetext(string &line) {
    string::size_type pos;
    string text_to_erase;

    cout << "Enter the text you would like to erase" << endl;
    getline(cin,text_to_erase);
    pos = line.find(text_to_erase,0);
    if (pos != string::npos)
        line.erase(pos,text_to_erase.length());
    else
        cout << text_to_erase << " is not found in the line" << endl;
    return;
}
```

THE FUNCTION inserttext( )

The <u>inserttext( )</u> function is only a little more complex than <u>erasetext( )</u>. It must ask the user what text to insert, and it must also ask where the text is to be inserted. It is silly to ask the user to count the number of positions to the insertion point, so we'll ask the user to pick the word after which the new text should be inserted. If the word occurs more than once, we'll insert the text after the first occurrence of the word.

    ask the user to enter the text to insert
    read the text
    ask the user what word the new text should follow
    read the word to follow
    find the word to follow in the line
    if found
        call insert( ) to insert the new text in the proper position
    else
        print "not found"

Again, we'll use <u>getline( )</u> to allow entry of more than one word either for the text to insert (which we call <u>text_to_insert</u>) or for the text to follow (which we call <u>text_to_follow</u>).

```
cout << "Enter the text you would like to insert" << endl;
getline(cin,text_to_insert);
cout << "Enter the word it should follow" << endl;
getline(cin,text_to_follow);
```

After we read in <u>text_to_follow</u> , we find it in <u>line</u>.

```
pos = line.find(text_to_follow,0);
```

If <u>text_to_follow</u> is found, we want to insert <u>text_to_insert</u> after <u>text_to_follow</u> . To do that, we must find the insertion point, which is after the position of the last letter of <u>text_to_follow</u> in the line. For example, suppose our string is "My blog is certainly short", and we want to insert "too" after "certainly". We will find "certainly" starting in position 11, but we don't want to insert "too" in position 11. We want to insert the word "too" after the end of "certainly," in position 20 (11 plus the length of "certainly", which is 9).

```
line.insert(pos+text_to_follow.length(),text_to_insert);
```

In addition, in order to make it easier to insert complete words, we'll insert the new text preceded and followed by a space. We use concatenation to add a space to the end of <u>text_to_insert</u> , and we'll add 1 to our insertion position to leave a space after <u>text_to_follow</u> in the line.

```
if (pos != string::npos) {
    text_to_insert += ' ';
    line.insert(pos+text_to_follow.length()+1,text_to_insert);
}
else
    cout << text_to_follow << " is not found in the line" << endl;
```

The entire function follows:

```
// function inserttext() receives line as a parameter;
// asks user what text to insert and where to insert that text
void inserttext(string &line)
{
    string::size_type pos;
    string text_to_insert,text_to_follow;

    cout << "Enter the text you would like to insert" << endl;
    getline(cin,text_to_insert);
    cout << "Enter the word it should follow" << endl;
    getline(cin,text_to_follow);
    pos = line.find(text_to_follow,0);
    if (pos != string::npos) {
        text_to_insert += ' ';
        line.insert(pos+text_to_follow.length()+1,text_to_insert);
    }
    else
        cout << text_to_follow << " is not found in the line" << endl;
    return;
}
```

THE FUNCTION replacetext( )

The replacetext( ) function is similar to the others, in that it asks the user for input (a string to erase, and a string to put in its place) and uses that input to call a string member function, in this case, replace( ). This time, however, we will give the user the additional option of replacing either the first or all the occurrences of the old text by the new text.

> *ask the user to enter the text to remove*
> *read the text to remove*
> *ask the user to enter the text to insert in its place*
> *read the text to insert*
>
> *ask the user how many changes to make (one or all)*
> *read the response*
>
> *find the text to remove in the line*
>   *if response is "one change"*
>   *if text is found*
>   *call replace( ) to replace the old text by the new text*
>   *else print "not found"*
>   *else if response is "all changes"*
>   *if text is not found*
>   *print "not found"*
>   *else while the old text is found in the line*
>   *call replace( ) to replace the old text by the new text*
>   *look for the next occurrence of the old text*

The user response part of the code is very similar to the code for erasetext( ) and inserttext( ). The number of times to replace the text can be one or all, so we will read in '1' or 'a' into a **char** variable.

```
cout << "Enter the text you would like to remove" << endl;
getline(cin,text_to_remove);
cout << "Enter the text you would like to put in its place" << endl;
getline(cin,text_to_insert);
cout << "Do you want to replace the first occurrence, or all?"
     << " (press 1 or a)" << endl;
cin >> ans;
```

The rest of the code is based on whether the user enters '1' or 'a'. If the user enters '1', the program will make one replacement; otherwise, it will make replacements until text_to_remove is not found. In either case, the actual replacement starts by calling find( ) to see whether text_to_remove occurs in line.

```
if (ans == '1') {
    pos = line.find(text_to_remove,0);
```

If ans is '1' and text_to_remove is found, we will call replace( ) to replace text_to_remove by text_to_insert; if text_to_remove isn't found, we'll print an error message.

```
// see if text_to_remove occurs, and replace it if it does
if (pos != string::npos)
    line.replace(pos,text_to_remove.length(),text_to_insert);
else
    cout << text_to_remove << " is not found in the line" << endl;
```

In contrast, if <u>ans</u> is 'a', we'll start by checking whether <u>text_to_remove</u> is not found, and print-ing an error message. We'll print an error message only if the text is not found before we begin replacements.

```
else if (ans == 'a') {
    // see if text_to_remove occurs, and replace it each time it does
    pos = line.find(text_to_remove,0);
    if (pos == string::npos)
        cout << text_to_remove << " is not found in the line" << endl;
```

If <u>text_to_remove</u> is found, we'll call <u>replace( )</u> and <u>find( )</u> repeatedly until the search fails. This will require a loop that replaces one occurrence of <u>text_to_remove</u> and then looks for the next. As long as the text is found at least once, we'll enter a loop to replace all occurrences of that text.

```
else
    while (pos != string::npos) {
        line.replace(pos,text_to_remove.length(),text_to_insert);
        pos = line.find(text_to_remove,
              pos+text_to_insert.length());
    }
```

Putting it all together gives us the final function of Program 8:

```
// function replacetext() receives line as a parameter;
// asks user what text to replace and what text to insert in its place
void replacetext(string &line)
{
    string::size_type pos;
    string text_to_remove,text_to_insert;
    char ans;

    cout << "Enter the text you would like to remove" << endl;
    getline(cin,text_to_remove);
    cout << "Enter the text you would like to put in its place" << endl;
    getline(cin,text_to_insert);
    cout << "Do you want to replace the first occurrence, or all?"
        << " (press 1 or a)" << endl;
    cin >> ans;
    if (ans == '1') {
        pos = line.find(text_to_remove,0);
        // see if text_to_remove occurs, and replace it if it does
        if (pos != string::npos)
            line.replace(pos,text_to_remove.length(),text_to_insert);
        else
            cout << text_to_remove << " is not found in the line" << endl;
    }
    else if (ans == 'a') {
        // see if text_to_remove occurs, and replace it each time it does
        pos = line.find(text_to_remove,0);
        if (pos == string::npos)
            cout << text_to_remove << " is not found in the line" << endl;
        else
            while (pos != string::npos) {
                line.replace(pos,text_to_remove.length(),text_to_insert);
```

```
                                 pos = line.find(text_to_remove,
                                      pos+text_to_insert.length());
                        }
                }
                return;
        }
```

Now we have written the entire Program 8, and it is shown below.

COMPLETE PROGRAM 8

Here is the complete version of Program 8.

PROGRAM LISTING

```
// prog8.cpp reads in lines of text from a file
// asks the user what changes to make in each line
//     until the user wants to stop making changes
// writes the changed line to a new file
#include <iostream>
#include <fstream>
#include <string>
ifstream infile;
ofstream outfile;
using namespace std;
void change(string&);
void erasetext(string &);
void inserttext(string &);
void replacetext(string &);
int main()
{
        string line;

        infile.open("ch8.dat");
        outfile.open("out8.out");
        while (getline(infile,line)) {
                change(line);
                outfile << line << endl;
        }
        infile.close();
        outfile.close();
        system("pause");
        return 0;
}

// function change() receives line as a parameter;
// asks the user what kind of change to make: erase, replace, or insert
void change(string &line)
{
        char choice;
```

```
        cout << endl << "The line is now: " << line << endl << endl;
    do {
            cout << "Enter the letter of your choice" << endl;
            cout << " e: erase text" << endl;
            cout << "i: insert text" << endl;
            cout << "r: replace text" << endl;
            cout << "n: edit next line" << endl;
            cin >> choice;
            cin.get();
            switch(choice) {
                case 'e': erasetext(line);
                        break;
                case 'i': inserttext(line);
                        break;
                case 'r': replacetext(line);
                        break;
                case 'n': break;
                default:  cout << "error, invalid choice; try again" << endl;
            }
            cout << endl << "The line is now: " << line << endl;
        } while(choice != 'n');
        return;
}

// function erasetext() receives line as a parameter;
// asks user what text to erase and erases that text
void erasetext(string &line)
{
    string::size_type pos;
    string text_to_erase;

    cout << "Enter the text you would like to erase" << endl;
    getline(cin,text_to_erase);
    pos = line.find(text_to_erase,0);
    if (pos != string::npos)
        line.erase(pos,text_to_erase.length());
    else
        cout << text_to_erase << " is not found in the line" << endl;
    return;
}

// function inserttext() receives line as a parameter;
// asks user what text to insert and where to insert that text
void inserttext(string &line)
{
    string::size_type pos;
    string text_to_insert,text_to_follow;

    cout << "Enter the text you would like to insert" << endl;
    getline(cin,text_to_insert);
    cout << "Enter the word it should follow" << endl;
    getline(cin,text_to_follow);
```

```
        pos = line.find(text_to_follow,0);
        if (pos != string::npos) {
            text_to_insert += ' ';
            line.insert(pos+text_to_follow.length()+1,text_to_insert);
        }
        else
            cout << text_to_follow << " is not found in the line" << endl;
        return;
    }

// function replacetext() receives line as a parameter;
// asks user what text to replace and what text to insert in its place
void replacetext(string &line)
{
    string::size_type pos;
    string text_to_remove,text_to_insert;
    char ans;

    cout << "Enter the text you would like to remove" << endl;
    getline(cin,text_to_remove);
    cout << "Enter the text you would like to put in its place" << endl;
    getline(cin,text_to_insert);
    cout << "Do you want to replace the first occurrence, or all?"
         << " (press 1 or a)" << endl;
    cin >> ans;
    if (ans == '1') {
        pos = line.find(text_to_remove,0);
        // see if text_to_remove occurs, and replace it if it does
        if (pos != string::npos)
            line.replace(pos,text_to_remove.length(),text_to_insert);
        else
            cout << text_to_remove << " is not found in the line" << endl;
    }
    else if (ans == 'a') {
        // see if text_to_remove occurs, and replace it each time it does
        pos = line.find(text_to_remove,0);
        if (pos == string::npos)
            cout << text_to_remove << " is not found in the line" << endl;
        else
            while (pos != string::npos) {
                line.replace(pos,text_to_remove.length(),text_to_insert);
                pos = line.find(text_to_remove,pos+text_to_insert.length());
            }
    }
    return;
}
```

ENRICHMENT: USING DATA TYPE char: get(), put(); FUNCTIONS FROM cctype.h

In this section, we discuss using data type **char**. We introduce character I/O functions get() and put(), whose headers are in iostream.h. In addition, we explain functions which allow us to check and change the values of variables of type **char** (or individual characters in a string). The headers for these functions are located in the file cctype.h.

CHARACTER-ORIENTED I/O

So far, we have discussed token-oriented input, performed when the operator >> is used on an input stream. Token-oriented input reads a **token**, which is an item (generally) separated from the next token by whitespace characters. We have also discussed line-oriented input, performed by getline( ), which reads an entire line of input. C++ has a third kind of I/O, **character-oriented I/O**, which reads in or prints out one character at a time. Character-oriented I/O is performed by the functions get( ) and put( ).

Here is an example showing the difference between token-oriented, line-oriented, and character-oriented input. Suppose we have this line of data:

```
45 years
```

Token-oriented input would read this as two tokens—45 and "years"—separated by whitespace.
Line-oriented input would read this as one line—"45 years".
Character-oriented input would read this as 8 characters: '4', '5', ' ', 'y', 'e', 'a', 'r', and 's'.

THE get( ) FUNCTION

The function specifically designed for input of a single character value is get( ). In its most common form, this function reads a single character from the keyboard and returns that character. The get( ) function will read whitespace characters (spaces, tabs and newline characters). Typically, the value returned is assigned to a variable of type **char**.

General Form of a Call to get( )
The general form of a call to get( ) to read from an input stream into a variable ch is as follows; the statement on the left reads from a file, infile, while the statement on the right reads from cin.

ch = infile.get ();	or	ch = cin.get();

In this form, the function get( ) typically doesn't receive parameters. It returns a single value, which is the character just read in from cin or from a file stream. If get( ) attempts to read past the end of input, the stream variable gets a value indicating failure.

WHY DO WE NEED get( )?

You might ask why we need the get( ) function, since the extraction operator >> is capable of reading a character from a stream. The answer is that the extraction operator will not read whitespace characters. Suppose you want to read all the characters in this line and count them:

```
This is the string.
```

If you were to read this string character by character with the >> operator and count the characters, you would read in 16 characters. If you were to read it character by character with get( ), you would read in 19 characters, counting the spaces (actually, it reads 20, counting <Enter>—see Example 8-27 for more). By comparison, if you were to read it with getline( ), you'd read the whitespace characters, but you'd read the whole string at once; and you couldn't count the characters as they are being read in.

Example 8-27 shows a simple way to use the get( ) function.

EXAMPLE 8-27

Here is an example which uses a loop to read characters from cin until the user signals the end of data input (<Ctrl>-z in Windows, <Ctrl>-d in Unix) and to count the number of characters read in. If the user enters "this one" (without quotation marks), count will get the value 8. (See Chapter 7, Section 9, for more details on reading to the end of input.)

```
char let;
    int count = 0;

let = cin.get();
while (cin) {
    count++;
    let = cin.get();
}
cout << "the number of characters entered is " << count-1 << endl;
```

Notice that we must subtract one from count to get the proper value, since get( ) reads in the <Enter> key and this loop counts it.

USING get( ) WITH THE USER-RESPONSE METHOD

We can also use get( ) to implement the user-response method, as shown in Example 8-28, but there are problems with this. The problems are solved in Example 8-29.

**EXAMPLE 8-28
(Incomplete)**

Suppose we want to continue processing in a program if the user enters 'y', but terminate if the user enters 'n'. (This is an example of the user-response method introduced in Chapter 6.) The code below reads in a single character, assigns it to the variable answer, and continues processing as long as answer equals 'y':

```
char answer;

do {
    action of the loop goes here
    cout << "Do you want to continue?> (y/n)" ;
    answer = cin.get();
} while (answer == 'y');
```

Here is what you might expect to happen:

♦ If the person using the program types in 'y' (and then <Enter>), answer gets the value 'y'. The **while** condition is true, and the loop repeats.

♦ If the person using the program types in the letter 'n' (and then <Enter>), answer gets the value 'n'. The **while** condition is false, and the loop terminates.

♦ If the user enters a response like 'M' or '?' or even 'Y', the loop also terminates.

Unfortunately, this loop does not work correctly. The loop behavior will be erratic, sometimes terminating when the user wants to continue, sometimes continuing without allowing the user to enter another response. The next subsection explains the problem.

BUFFERING OF INPUT

The function get( ) may appear not to work properly in some circumstances, as in Example 8-28. This happens because pressing <Enter> causes the entire line to be stored in an input area called a **buffer**. An input function like get( ) first tries to retrieve data values from the input buffer. If the user enters 'y', the buffer contains two characters: 'y' and the newline character ('\n') caused by pressing <Enter>. First, get( ) reads the 'y', causing the loop to repeat. However, on the next call, get( ) doesn't wait for the user to enter a new value; instead, get( ) reads '\n' from the input buffer. Since '\n' is not 'y', the loop stops.

You may think that changing the loop condition will make the loop wait for an 'n' to stop:

```
while (answer != 'n');
```

However, this also won't work. Each user response of 'y' causes the loop to execute twice, once for 'y' and once for the newline character. Example 8-29 shows a simple solution to this problem.

EXAMPLE 8-29

To eliminate the newline character, place an extra get( ) in the loop (to read the newline character) and ignore the value read by this extra call:

```
char answer,trash;

do {
    action of the loop goes here
    printf("Do you want to continue? (y/n)> ");
    answer = cin.get();
    trash = cin.get();
}  while (answer == 'y');
```

The response is read into answer, and the newline character is read into trash, which is ignored. (Because of this, the line trash = cin.get( ) can be simplified to cin.get( ), which doesn't even bother to store the value returned by the call to get( ).)

THE put( ) FUNCTION

Hand in hand with reading in characters goes printing. The function put( ) has the task of sending **char** values to an output stream or file stream. Because put( ) works just like the << operator, it isn't strictly necessary.

General Form of a Call to put( )
The general form of a call to put( ) to send a character ch to an output stream is as follows; the first sends the character to a file, outfile, while the second sends the character to cout.

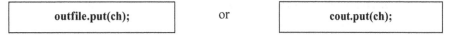

| **outfile.put(ch);** | or | **cout.put(ch);** |

The put( ) function takes one parameter—the **char** value to print (in this example, ch)—and sends it to the specified stream, in this case cout or outfile.

Example 8-30 modifies Example 8-27 to display each character as it is read in.

EXAMPLE 8-30   This loop will read characters from <u>cin</u> until the user signals the end of data input (<Ctrl>-z in Windows, <Ctrl>-d in Unix) and count the number of characters read in. The code also sends a copy of each character to <u>cout</u>.

```
char let;
int count = 0;

let = cin.get();
while (cin) {
    count++;
    cout.put(let);
    let = cin.get();
}
cout << "the number of characters entered is " << count-1 << endl;
```

Suppose you type in these characters, terminated by pressing <Ctrl>-z. (You'll have to press <Enter> before or after <Ctrl>-z, and it will be counted, but our code subtracts one to compensate for that.)

```
abc def
```

The screen display will show this:

```
abc def
abc def
the number of characters entered is 7
```

Notice that characters don't appear in the order that you might expect. You might think you'd see the echo of the character typed into <u>cin</u> followed by the character sent to <u>cout</u> (aabbcc ddeeff). However, the echo of all the characters typed into <u>cin</u> shows up as the first line on the screen, followed by a line consisting of all the characters sent to <u>cout</u>.

SELF-CHECK 8-4

1. What is the purpose of the <u>get( )</u> function?

2. Suppose a program contains the following lines of code:

    ```
    char let;

    let = cin.get();
    cout.put(let);
    ```

    If the call to <u>get( )</u> reads in the newline character, what is the effect of the subsequent call to <u>put( )</u>?

3. What is the difference between these two input methods?

    a. `cin >> let;`   b. `let = cin.get();`

    Give an example of a value that will be read differently using the two different methods.

TESTING A VALUE OF DATA TYPE char

Often it is useful to know what kind of value is stored in a variable of type **char** (or in one position in a string). For example, you may want to know whether the character is a letter, a digit, a space, or a piece of punctuation, or whether an alphabetic character is uppercase or lowercase (so that you can change its case).

It is possible to test the value of a specific character by comparing it with others in a specific range. For example, we can write a function to detect a lowercase alphabetic character, as shown in Example 8-31 (although, as we'll see shortly, such a function already exists in C++).

EXAMPLE 8-31 Here is a possible definition for a function islower( ), which receives a character ch as a parameter and returns **true** if ch is a lowercase alphabetic character or **false** if it is not:

```
// returns true if ch is lowercase letter, false if anything else
bool islower(char ch)
{
    if (ch >= 'a' && ch <= 'z')
        return true;
    else
        return false;
}
```

We can write similar functions for the other tasks described above, but some of them are rather complicated (the **char** values representing punctuation, for example, have ASCII codes which are not consecutive). To make the task simpler, C++ has a series of functions to perform these checks. Some of these functions are isalpha( ), isdigit( ), isalnum( ), isspace( ), ispunct( ), islower( ), and isupper( ). Each function takes a single character as its sole parameter and returns **true** or **false**. The prototypes for these functions are in cctype.h, and a program which uses them should insert the following line with the other #include directives:

```
#include <cctype>
```

Table 8-2 shows the task of each of the functions.

Example 8-32 shows how to use these functions to count the number of each type of character received as input.

EXAMPLE 8-32 The following section of code uses four function calls to determine the type (alphabetic, digit, space, or punctuation) of each character read in and count how many there are of each type.

```
char ch;
int alpha=0,digit=0,space=0,punct=0;

ch = cin.get();
while (cin) {
    if (isalpha(ch))
        alpha++;
    else if (isdigit(ch))
        digit++;
    else if (isspace(ch))
        space++;
    else if (ispunct(ch))
        punct++;
    ch = cin.get();
}
cout << "The number of alphabetic characters is " << alpha << endl;
cout << "The number of digits 0-9 is " << digit << endl;
cout << "The number of spaces entered is " << space << endl;
cout << "The number of pieces of punctuation " << punct << endl;
```

TABLE 8-2 Selected Functions from cctype.h

Function	Checks
isalpha()	is the parameter alphabetic ('A'..'Z' or 'a'..'z')
isdigit()	is the parameter a digit (0..9)
isalnum()	is the parameter alphabetic or a digit
isspace()	is the parameter a space (' ')
ispunct()	is the parameter a piece of punctuation (punctuation includes @, $, ., {, etc. —anything on the keyboard that is not a letter, a digit, or a control character)
islower()	is the parameter a lowercase alphabetic character ('a'..'z')
isupper()	is the parameter an uppercase alphabetic character ('A'..'Z')

UPPERCASE AND LOWERCASE: THE toupper() AND tolower() FUNCTIONS

Often it is useful to change the case of a character, possibly for testing purposes. For example, we can ask a user to enter a response ('y' for "yes" or 'n' for "no"). The user may assume that 'Y' and 'N' are equally good responses, and our program must be prepared for that. We can use the toupper( ) or the tolower( ) function in a case like this.

♦ The toupper( ) function takes a character as a parameter and returns the corresponding uppercase character.

♦ The tolower( ) function takes a character as a parameter and returns the corresponding lowercase character.

If sent anything else as a parameter, either function returns the value unchanged. (For example, toupper('g') returns 'G', but toupper('T') returns 'T', and toupper('6') returns '6'.) Example 8-33 gives two examples of a user-response loop, first without toupper( ) and then with it.

EXAMPLE 8-33a Without using toupper( ) or tolower( ), here is one thing we can do to allow the user to enter either 'n' or 'N' to stop executing the loop:

```
char ans;

do {
    ...
    cout << "Do you want to continue? (y/n)> ";
    ans = cin.get();
    cin.get();
} while (ans == 'y' || ans == 'Y');
```

Actually, any character but 'y' or 'Y' will cause the loop to terminate. This is also true in Example 8-33b.

EXAMPLE 8-33b With toupper( ), the same test is simpler:

```
char ans;

do {
    ...
```

```
        cout << "Do you want to continue? (y/n)> ";
        ans = cin.get();
        cin.get();
} while (toupper(ans) == 'Y');
```

In this case, if the user enters 'y', 'y' is sent to toupper( ), which returns 'Y' for the comparison, and the result is true. If the user enters 'Y', then 'Y' is returned and the result is also true. If the user enters anything else, the result of the comparison is false.

The call to toupper( ) in Example 8-33b doesn't change the value of ch. If you want to change the value of the character sent to toupper( ) or tolower( ), you must assign the return value to a variable (this can be the same variable as the parameter). Example 8-34 shows how to use tolower( ) in this way.

EXAMPLE 8-34

```
string str;

str = "3 BlinD MICe";
for (int i = 0; i < str.length(); i++)
    str[i] = tolower(str[i]);
```

Each call to tolower( ) sends the function one character from string str as a parameter. It also assigns the return value (the corresponding lowercase character, if there is one) to the same position in the string, as shown in Figure 8-4.

As an example, let's look at one particular call:

str[2] = tolower(str[2]);

The 'B' originally stored in str[2] is sent to the function tolower( ), which returns 'b'; this value is then assigned to str[2], replacing 'B'.

FIGURE 8-4A   str before calls to tolower()

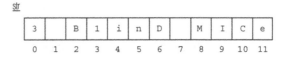

FIGURE 8-4B   str after calls to tolower()

SELF-CHECK 8-5

1.   What value is returned by each of the following calls?

   a. isdigit('a');   **b.** ispunct('?');
   c. isupper('t');   **d.** islower('k');
   e. toupper('P');   **f.** toupper('j');
   g. tolower('M');   **h.** isalpha('c');

2. In Example 8-33b, could we use the following test? What would the user have to enter to continue the loop? To terminate the loop?

```
while (tolower(ans) == 'y');
```

SECTION 7 ENRICHMENT: ARRAYS OF STRINGS

This section shows how to declare and use arrays of strings, including reading and printing them, sending their elements as parameters, and referencing their individual characters.

DECLARING AN ARRAY OF STRINGS

The declaration for an array of strings looks like other array declarations, and most of what we can do with an array of strings is also similar to what we do with other arrays.

EXAMPLE 8-35 Suppose we want to declare an array to hold the names of the 12 months of the year. We can call the array <u>months</u>. There should be 12 elements in array <u>months</u>, and each element should have type **string.** Here is a declaration for <u>months</u>:

```
string months[12];
```

INITIALIZING AND PRINTING AN ARRAY OF STRINGS

Examples 8-36 and 8-37 do input/output on arrays of strings.

EXAMPLE 8-36 The following section of code initializes and then prints the elements of the <u>months</u> array:

```
string months[12] = {"January","February","March","April","May","June",
             "July","August","September","October","November","December"};

for (int i = 0; i < 12; i++)
     cout << months[i] << endl;
```

The positions won't correspond to our usual numbering of the months, since "January" will be in position 0.

READING IN AN ARRAY OF STRINGS

Now let's look at a loop that reads values into an array of strings. Example 8-37 reads in a set of strings until there are no more data values, storing each string in a position in the array.

EXAMPLE 8-37 In this example, we use <u>getline( )</u> to read the strings, in case the values read in contain whitespace characters.

```
string lines[20];
int i = 0;

getline(cin,lines[i]);
while(cin) {
    i++;
    getline(cin,lines[i]);
```

```
        }
        cout << i << " lines were entered" << endl;
```

This loop reads data into the <u>lines</u> array, which can hold up to 20 strings. Each call to <u>getline( )</u> reads a string into an element of the <u>lines</u> array. When we are finished, <u>i</u> holds the number of filled positions in the array.

USING A STRING MEMBER FUNCTION WITH AN ELEMENT OF AN ARRAY OF STRINGS

Let's look at how we send an element of an array as a parameter to a string member function. Example 8-38 sends each string from a string array to the function <u>length( )</u>:

EXAMPLE 8-38

```
string animal[3] = {"cat", "tiger", "hound dog"};

for (int i = 0; i < 3; i++)
    cout << "the length of " << animal[i] << " is "
            << animal[i].length() << endl;
```

In this example, we initialize the <u>animal</u> array of strings. Then we print the length of each string in the array. The code shown above prints:

```
the length of cat is 3
the length of tiger is 5
the length of hound dog is 9
```

SENDING AN ARRAY OF STRINGS TO A FUNCTION

Like any array, an array of strings is always a reference parameter when sent to a function. You must use [ ] in the function header and prototype to indicate that the parameter is an array. Example 8-39 shows how to send an array of strings as a parameter to a function which will change the array.

EXAMPLE 8-39

The function <u>readin( )</u> reads lines of data from a file into the array <u>lines,</u> sent as a parameter. It reads till the end of the file and counts the lines read in (see Section 4 on reading strings from a file). The main program calls the function and prints out the lines read in. Here is the function prototype:

```
void readin(string [],int &);            // prototype
```

Here is part of the main program:

```
string lines[10];
int n;

readin(lines,n);                         // function call
for (int i = 0; i < n; i++)
    cout << lines[i] << endl;
```

Here is the function:

```
// read lines of text into an array of strings until input failure
// count the lines and store the count in reference parameter n
void readin(string lines[], int &n)
{
    ifstream textin("e825.dat");
```

```
        n = 0;
        getline(textin,lines[n]);
        while(textin) {
            n++;
            getline(textin,lines[n]);
        }
        textin.close();
        return;
    }
```

REFERENCING A SINGLE CHARACTER IN AN ELEMENT OF A STRING ARRAY

To refer to a single character in a string which is an element of a string array requires two subscripts:

```
    months[3][1]
```

This refers to position 1 in the string months[3]. (You might wish to look at Chapter 7, Section 8, on two-dimensional arrays.) If the months array is initialized to the months of the year, months[3] has the value "April", and position 1 of that string is the character 'p'. Example 8-40 illustrates how to change and print a single character in a string which is an element of the pets array.

EXAMPLE 8-40

```
    string pets[4] ={"dog","cat","fish","gorilla"};

    pets[0][1] = 'i';
    cout << pets[0] << endl;
    cout << pets[2][3] << endl;
```

The assignment statement changes pets[0] from "dog" to "dig". The second line prints the changed pets[0] value, and the last line prints position 3 from "fish" which is the character 'h'.

SELF-CHECK 8-6

1. Give a declaration for each of the following:

    a. courses: an array of 20 strings   b. lines: an array of 50 strings

2. How can we refer to the second element in the array lines?

3. If the second element in the array lines has the value "fields of grain", what character does lines[1] [8] refer to?

SUMMARY

STRING BASICS

1. C++ has a **string** data type, which is more precisely called a **string** class.

2. The declaration of a string specifies the name of an object of class **string**; the name of the object in this example is str.

    ```
        string str;
    ```

3. A string can be given a value in the declaration or in an assignment statement, as shown below:

```
string fruit, dessert = "pie";

fruit = "apple";
dessert = fruit;
```

INPUT AND OUTPUT

4. A string can be sent to <u>cout</u> or to a file stream using the insertion operator (<<). Here is an example that prints the two strings from paragraph 3.

```
cout << fruit << " " << dessert << endl;
```

The output from this line will be

```
apple apple
```

5. A value can be read from <u>cin</u> or from a file stream into a string variable using the extraction operator (>>). However, since the extraction operator (>>) stops when it finds a whitespace character, this does not permit reading in strings that contain blanks or tabs:

```
cin >> fruit;
```

This can read in "apple", but not "apple pie".

6. C++ has a stream input function, <u>getline( )</u>, which allows a program to read a line of input from <u>cin</u> or from a file stream. This function reads past whitespace characters, which allows it to read in a string like "New York". The function <u>getline( )</u> generally takes two parameters, the name of a stream and the name of the string into which to read the input value. It reads until it encounters a newline character (or until it reads a specific character which may be specified as a third parameter).

```
string str, line;

getline(cin,str);
getline(infile,line);
```

The first call reads a line of text into <u>str</u> from <u>cin</u>, and the second reads a line into <u>line</u> from the input stream file <u>infile</u>.

CONCATENATION, COMPARISON, AND INDEXING

7. A string can be concatenated (joined to) the end of another string by using the + or += operator.

```
string first = "beach";
string second,third;

second = first + " towel";
third = "wet " + second;
first += "ball";
```

At the end of these lines of code, <u>second</u> has the value "beach towel", <u>third</u> has the value "wet beach towel", and <u>first</u> has the value "beachball".

8. A string variable can be compared with another string variable or with a literal string using the standard relational operators. Strings are compared character by character using their ASCII codes, which are assigned in increasing alphabetic order, with all capitals less than all lowercase letters. (See the Appendix for a complete list of ASCII codes, and see Chapter 2, Section 5, for more

discussion of data type **char.**) If the first characters in the two strings are the same, the next characters are compared, and so on, until a difference is found. At that point, the string whose character is closest to the beginning of the alphabet is considered "less" than the other string. A string which is a prefix of the other string is also considered "less". Here are some examples:

```
string first = "laugh";
string second = "laughing";
string third = "lasting";

if (first  == "laugh")      // true (same values)
if (first > third)          // true ('u' > 's')
if (first > second)         // false (first is a prefix of second)
```

9. Each position in a string has a number, starting at position 0. Individual positions in a string can be accessed or changed using those numbers, just like the positions in an array. Here is an example:

```
string str = "pixels";

str[3] = 'i';
str[4] = 'e';
cout << str[2] << endl;
cout << str << endl;
```

The two assignment statements change str to "pixies", and the last two lines print 'x' (the character at position 2 of str) and "pixies", the new value of str.

STRING MEMBER FUNCTIONS

10. Most other operations on strings are performed through member functions of the **string** class. The string member functions have their headers in file string.h. A program which uses strings should have the following #include statement at the beginning:

```
#include <string>
```

11. String member functions are called by appending the name of the function to the name of the string. If the string is named str and the string member function is called func( ), this would be the format for a call to the function (assuming the function does not return a value and has no parameters).

```
str.func();
```

12. Two member functions, length( ) and size( ), do the same thing. Each returns an unsigned integer representing the number of characters in the string; this is known as the size or length of the string. There is a better data type to use for the variable len (see paragraph 14).

```
int len,numchars;
string str = "computer services";

len = str.length();        // len and numchars both get the value 17
numchars = str.size();
```

13. A string of length 0 is called an empty or null string. It can be produced by using the string member function <u>clear( )</u>. Here is an example:

```
string name = "Warren";

cout << name << endl;
name.clear();
```

After the call to <u>clear( )</u>, there will be nothing in <u>name</u> and its length will be 0. An empty string can also be produced by assigning a value that consists of two quotation marks placed side by side (""), as shown below:

```
name = "";
```

14. The string class includes a data type: ***string::size_type***. This is an unsigned integer type. The string member functions <u>size( )</u> and <u>length( )</u> return a value which has type ***string::size_type***. (An unsigned integer can never be negative and can hold a value larger than what can be stored as an **int**.) A more precise version of the code in paragraph 12 would declare <u>len</u> and <u>numchars</u> to have data type ***string::size_type***, as shown below. Note that to use this data type, the identifier <u>size_type</u> must be preceded by the word **string** and two colons, the scope resolution operator, as shown below:

```
string city = "Chicago";
string::size_type len;
len = city.length();
```

15. The string class has a member constant, ***string::npos***, which is the value returned by the function <u>find( )</u> in order to signify that the item searched for is not found. The value of <u>npos</u> is a value that cannot be a possible character position in a string; it is a number larger than type **int** can hold. Since the value of ***string::npos*** is too large to be stored in an integer variable, it has data type ***string::size_type***.

16. The **string** member function <u>find( )</u> tries to find one string in another. In its simplest form, <u>find( )</u> takes two parameters: the first parameter is the string to find, and the second is the position in which to start the search. The search continues to the end of the string. The member function returns the position in which the item is found within the source string. Here are three examples; the first tries to find "chest" in "orchestra", starting at position 0. The next call tries to find the letter 'r' starting at position 5, and the last tries to find the letter 'r' starting at position 10.

```
string music = "orchestra";
string::size_type pos1,pos2,pos3;

pos1 = music.find("chest",0);
pos2 = music.find("r",5);
pos3 = music.find("r",8);
```

The variable <u>pos1</u> gets the value 2, which is the position of "chest" in string <u>music</u>; <u>pos2</u> gets the value 7, which is the position of the second 'r' in <u>music</u>. This 'r' is the first one found when we start looking in position 5. Finally, <u>pos3</u> gets the value <u>npos</u>, since 'r' is not found starting in position 8 of string <u>music</u>.

17. The function <u>replace( )</u> allows replacing part of a string by another string. One simple variant of <u>replace( )</u> has three parameters: the first is the position in which to start replacing characters, the

second is the number of characters to replace, and the third is the string from which to get the new characters. Here is an example:

```
string sciencefiction = "space warp";

science.replace(6,4,"invaders");
```

This removes 4 characters from string <u>sciencefiction</u>, starting at position 6, and replaces them with the 8-character string "invaders", leaving <u>sciencefiction</u> with the value "space invaders". Note that the inserted string may have a different length than the string it replaces.

18. The function <u>erase( )</u> allows removing characters from a string. This function generally takes two parameters, the starting position and the number of characters to remove. The <u>erase( )</u> function removes the characters and closes up the string. Here is an example:

```
string review = "abcdefgh12345";

review.erase(4,5);
```

This call erases the 5 characters starting in position 4 of <u>review</u>, leaving <u>review</u> with the value "abcd2345 ". If the second parameter is omitted, the function erases characters from the starting position to the end of the string.

19. The function <u>insert( )</u> permits inserting one string (or part of a string) into another string. The simplest form of the member function <u>insert( )</u> takes two parameters: the first is the position into which to insert characters, the second is the string to insert. Here is an example:

```
string ad = "eat1234";

ad.insert(3,"lunch");
```

This inserts the string "lunch" into position 3 of <u>ad</u>, leaving <u>ad</u> with the value "eatlunch1234".

20. The <u>substr( )</u> function extracts part of a string, leaving the original string unchanged. The most common form of the function takes two parameters: the first is the position from which to start extracting, and the second is the number of characters to extract. The function returns a substring consisting of the extracted characters. If you omit the second parameter, <u>substr( )</u> will extract characters from the starting position and continuing to the end of the string. Here is an example:

```
string review = "not a great movie";
string word,phrase;

word = review.substr(6,5);
phrase = review.substr(6);
```

The string <u>word</u> will get the value "great" (5 characters starting at position 6), while the string <u>phrase</u> will get the value "great movie" (everything from position 6 to the end of the string). The string <u>review</u> remains unchanged as "not a great movie".

USING STRINGS WITH FUNCTIONS

21. When you send a string as a parameter to a function, the type of the formal parameter must be **string**. If the string is to be changed inside the function, it must be sent as a reference parameter, using the & symbol. Here is an example that sends a string to a function to be changed.

```
void makecapital(string &);                          // prototype

string supplies = "pencils";
```

```
makecapital(str);                              // call

    . . .

// capitalize first letter of the string       // function
void makecapital(string &st)
{
    st[0] = toupper(st[0]);
    return;
}
```

The function <u>makecapital( )</u> receives the string <u>supplies</u> as a parameter. It changes "pencils" to "Pencils". The function above also uses the function <u>toupper( )</u> discussed in paragraph 32.

22. It is also possible to use **string** as the return type of a function. Here is an example of a function which receives a string as a parameter and returns a string:

```
string func(string str)
{
    if (str == "Yes")
        return "wow";
    else
        return "sorry";
}
```

Here is are the prototype for <u>func( )</u> and the call to the function from the main program:

```
string func(string);         // prototype

string answer;
cin >> answer;
cout << func(answer);        // call
```

STRINGS AND FILE I/O

23. Typically, processing strings involves working with large chunks of text. The text is stored in a file. The standard method of reading and processing text from a file is to read a line from the input file, process the line, and write the line to an output file, repeating this until the entire file has been processed.

THE **char** DATA TYPE, CHARACTER I/O FUNCTIONS, AND FUNCTIONS FROM <u>cctype.h</u>

24. The **char** data type has 256 possible values, including all the letters, digits, and symbols on the keyboard. Each character of a string is a member of the **char** data type. The **char** data type is a subset of type **int**, and each character has a numerical equivalent—called its ASCII code—in the range from 0 to 255.

25. C++ has two stream functions dedicated to character I/O; the functions allow input or output to be done one character at a time. The functions for character-oriented I/O are <u>get( )</u> and <u>put( )</u>.

26. The <u>get( )</u> function is useful because the extraction operator (>>) skips over whitespace characters (tab, space, and newline) when reading from a stream. The <u>get( )</u> function reads any character, including whitespace characters.

27. The <u>get( )</u> function reads in one character at a time. A call to <u>get( )</u> returns the next character in the input stream. A call to <u>get( )</u> to read from <u>cin</u> looks like this:

```
char ch;
ch = cin.get();
```

28. The <u>put( )</u> function displays a character to a stream; it does the same thing as printing a character with the insertion operator (<<). Here is a call to <u>put( )</u> to send a character to <u>cout</u>:

```
char let = 'B';

cout.put(let);
```

The call to <u>put( )</u> displays 'B'.

29. You can use the <u>get( )</u> function to read in one or more lines of text, perhaps counting the number of characters read in. Here is an example which reads and prints characters in a loop, reading to input failure to detect the end of the set of data:

```
char ch;
int numstrings = 0;

ch = cin.get();
while (cin) {
    cout.put(ch);
    numstrings++;
    ch = cin.get();
}
cout << numstrings-1 << " characters were read in" << endl;
```

30. The header file <u>cctype.h</u> contains the prototypes for a number of functions dedicated to testing and manipulating characters. A program which uses these functions should contain the following line:

```
#include <cctype>
```

31. Among the functions in <u>cctype.h</u> are <u>isalpha( )</u>, <u>isdigit( )</u>, <u>isspace( )</u>, <u>ispunct( )</u>, <u>islower( )</u>, <u>isupper( )</u>, and <u>isalnum( )</u>. These functions accept a character as a parameter and classify the character as, respectively, an alphabetic character, a digit, a space, punctuation, lowercase, uppercase, or an alphanumeric character (a letter or a digit). Each function returns **true** to indicate success or **false** if not. The form of a call to one of these functions is illustrated by this call to <u>ispunct( )</u>:

```
char ch;

ch = cin.get();
if (ispunct(ch))
    cout << "the character " << ch << " is punctuation" << endl;
```

32. Two other useful functions from <u>cctype.h</u> are <u>toupper( )</u> and <u>tolower( )</u>. These allow conversion of a letter from lowercase to uppercase and vice versa. Conversions of this sort allow the programmer to simplify conditions which test a user's response. Rather than checking whether the user has entered 'y' or 'Y', the program can use the following call to <u>toupper( )</u> [or a similar call to <u>tolower( )</u>]. Recall that <u>cin.get( )</u> is used to delete the <Enter> character from the input buffer.

```
char answer;

do {
    ...
    answer = cin.get();
    cin.get();
} while (toupper(answer) == 'Y');
```

ARRAYS OF STRINGS

33. It is possible to use an array of strings in a C++ program. Here is a declaration that sets up an array of ten strings and initializes the first five:

```
string names[10] = {"Susan", "Shlomo", "Ming", "Christopher", "Ahmed"};
```

34. You can use an element of a string array with a string member function. Here is an example that uses the member function <u>length( )</u> with each of the first five strings from the <u>names</u> array (from paragraph 33):

```
for (int i = 0; i < 5; i++)
    cout << names[i] << "has length " << names[i].length();
```

35. As usual, if the string is to be changed in the function, it must be sent as a reference parameter. Here is an example which sends an element of the <u>pets</u> array to the function <u>makecapital( )</u> from paragraph 21:

```
makecapital(string &);                          // prototype

string pets[5] = {"kitty", "rover"};

makecapital(pets[1]);                           // call
```

This call will change "rover" to "Rover".

36. A string array can be sent as a parameter to be changed in a function. A parameter which is a string array is always a reference parameter and does not need the & symbol but does need the symbols [ ] in both the function header and prototype. Here is an example that changes each movie title by adding II to the end:

```
void stickon(string [],int);        // prototype

string titles[3] = {"Harry Potter","Spiderman","Batman"};

stickon(titles,3);                  // call

void stickon(string titles[], int n)    // function
{
    for (int i = 0; i < n; i++)
        titles[i] += " II";
    return;
}
```

This function call changes the array <u>titles</u> to hold "Harry Potter II", "Spiderman II", and "Batman II".

37. To access any single string in an array of strings requires one subscript; to access a character in that string requires two subscripts. An element of a string array can be used in the same way as a single string. Here are some examples:

```
string names[3];

names[0] = "Julie";
names[1] = "Janice";

if (names[0] > names[1])
    cout << names[0] << " is greater than " << names[1] << endl;
```

```
    else
        cout << names[1] << " is greater than " << names[0]
            << " or they are equal" << endl;

    cout << names[0][1] << "is the second character in " << names[0]
        << endl;
```

These lines print the following:

```
Julie is greater than Janice
u is the second character in Julie
```

EXERCISES

TRACING EXERCISES

1. Suppose you have the following declaration.

   ```
   string str;
   ```

   Which of the following values can be assigned to the variable str? If any value cannot be assigned, explain why not.

   a. "dog"   b. "4315"   c. 43   d. 4.5   e. 'h'

2. What value will this string get after each of the following?

   ```
   string day;
   ```

   a. cin >> day;   and user enters "Tuesday"
   b. cin >> day;   and user enters "next Tuesday"
   c. getline(cin,day);   and user enters "Tuesday the 24th"
   d. getline(cin,day);   and user enters "last Wednesday"

3. Show how to represent each of the following (assume that all variables have been declared to have type **string**):

   a. the character in position 5 of arr   b. the character in the first position of hold
   c. the character in position 3 of str   d. the character in position 1 of line
   e. the last character in hope (*Hint*: this one is harder than the others—why?)

4. What is the result of each of the following operations? (Start in each case from the initial values shown.)

   ```
   string big = "a sunny day";
   string little = "was";
   string middle = "in the park";
   ```

   a. middle = little + middle;   b. big += middle;   c. middle += big;

5. For (a), (b), and (c), show what each variable contains after the series of statements is executed. Use these declarations for each part:

   ```
   string str, str1, str2, str3;
   int  i,j;
   ```

   a. str1 = "fantastic";   b. str = "123456";
      str3 = " weekend";   str2 = "hi";
      str = str1;   str += str2;
      str += str3;
```
```

```
  c. str3 = "waterfall";
     j = str3.length();
     i = str3.size();
```

6. Show the result of each of the following comparisons:

   a.
   ```
   string flower = "tulips";
   string plant = "tulip";
   if (flower >> plant)
        cout << "case 1";
   else
        cout << "case 2";
   ```

   b.
   ```
   string wood = "live oak";
   string table = "oak";
   if (wood >> table)
        cout << "case 3";
   else
        cout << "case 4";
   ```

   c.
   ```
   string color = "blue";
   string feeling = "blues";
   if (feeling == color + "s")
        cout << "case 5";
   else
        cout << "case 6";
   if (feeling == color + 's')
        cout << "case 7";
   else
        cout << "case 8";
   ```

7. What is the result of each of the following comparisons (**true** or **false**)? Use these declarations for each part:

   ```
   string str = "water";
   string str2 = "waterfall";
   string str3 = "what";
   ```

   a. `if (str == "water")...`   b. `if (str3 < str)...`
   c. `if (str < str3)...`   d. `if (str > str2)...`
   e. `if (str2 > str)...`   f. `if (str3 > "where")...`

8. Using the string member function <u>length( )</u>, show how to find the number of characters in each of the following strings. In each case, give the actual length.

   a. `string name = "Winnie";`   b. `string starting = "";`
   c. `string msg = "Happy birthday";`   d. `string newone; // no initial value`

9. Show what is printed by the following section of code:

   ```
   string p = "another value";

   p.erase(3,4);
   cout << "p is: " << p << endl;
   p.insert(4,"done");
   cout << "p is: " << p << endl;
   p[2] = 'X';
   p[1] = 'Y';
   cout << "p is: " << p << endl;
   ```

10. Show what is printed by the following section of code:

    ```
    string p, q, t = "long string";

    q = t.substr(2,3);
    p = t.substr(5,3);
    cout << "p is: " << p << endl;
    cout << "q is: " << q << endl;
    ```

11. Show what is printed by the following section of code:

    ```
    string t = "cannon ball news";
    int     m,k,j;

    k = t.find("all",0);
    m = t.find("all",10);
    j = t.find("call",0);
    cout << "m ,k, and j: " << m << " " << k
         << " "   << j << endl;
    ```

12. Repeat Exercise 11 using *string::size_type* instead of **int** as the data type for m, k, and j.

13. For each of the following, show what values are assigned to the variables. For each part, start from the following declaration and initial values:

    ```
    string str = "good morning";
    string str1 = "evening news";
    string str2 = "bad";
    ```

    a. str1 = str.substr(5);   b. str2 = str1.substr(5);
    c. str1 = str.substr(5,4);   d. str2 = str1.substr(5,4);

14. Assuming the following declarations, show how to assign values to these strings as indicated in (a)–(c).

    ```
    string start = "input the catalog", str1, str2;
    ```

    a. copy "catalog" to str1   b. copy "input" to str2   c. copy "log" from str1 to str2, after (a) and (b) have been done

15. Using only the values in the variables big, little, and middle (and the string member function sub-str( )), write code to put each of the following values into the variable dest. (*Hint:* There may be more than one way to do some of these.)

    ```
    string big = "sun in the daytime";
    string little = "sunshine";
    string middle = "a sunny day";
    string dest;
    ```

    a. "day"   b. "sun"   c. "time"   d. "shine"

16. For each of the following, show the result of the function call. For each part, start from the following declaration and initial values:

    ```
    string str = "it is too hot";
    string str1 = "the ice is hardly frozen";
    string str2 = "my soup is just right";
    ```

    a. str.erase(5,4);   b. str1.erase(15);
    c. str2.erase(0,7);   d. str1.erase(11,7);

17. For each of the following, show the result of the function call. For each part, start from the following declaration and initial values:

    ```
    string str = "July is the month";
    string str1 = "the asphalt is melting";
    string str2 = "no rain for a week";
    ```

    a. str.insert(11," cruelest");   b. str1.insert(4,"street's ");
    c. str2.insert(13," whole");   d. str.insert(4," of 2006");

18. For each of the following, show the result of the function call. For each part, start from the following declaration and initial values:

    ```
    string str = "your hamster is full of fur";
    string str1 = "lunchtime aggravation";
    string str2 = "half of the apple";
    ```

    a. str.replace(5,7,"dog");   b. str.replace(20,3,"food");
    c. str1.replace(5,4,"room");   d. str2.replace(12,5,"orange");

19. For each of the following, show what is printed. For each part, start from the following declaration and initial values:

    ```
    string str = "happy home appliances";
    string str1 = "living room refrigerator";
    string str2 = "microwave telephone";
    string str3;
    ```

    a. str.replace(6,4,"workplace");   b. str1.replace(0,11,"office");
       cout << str << endl;   cout << str1 << endl;
    c. str2.erase(5,4);   d. str1.replace(14,12,"treat");
       str3 = str2.substr(10,5); //careful   cout << str1 << endl;
       str2.insert(5,str3);
       str2.replace(15,5,"vision");
       cout << str2 << endl;

20. Show what is printed by each of the following programs:
    a.
    ```
    #include <iostream>
    #include <string>
    using namespace std;
    int main()
    {
        string str1;
        string str2;
        string str3;
        int len;

        str1 = "first";
        str2 = "alexander";
        str3 = str2;
        len = str3.length();
        str3 = str3+str1;
        cout << str1 << " " << str2 << " " << str3 << endl;
        cout << len << endl;
        return 0;
    }
    ```

b.
```cpp
#include <iostream>
#include <string>
using namespace std;
int main()
{
    string str;
    string str1;
    int k, m, n;

    str = "jacksonville fl";
    m = str.length();
    str1 = "here is ";
    str1 += str;
    k = str1.size();
    n = str1.length();
    cout << str << " " << str1 << endl;
    cout << k << " " << m << " " << n << endl;
    return 0;
}
```

21. Show what is printed by the following program:

```cpp
#include <iostream>
#include <string>
using namespace std;
int main()
{
    string str,temp;
    int i,k;

    str = "large array of stuff";
    k = str.length();
    for (i = 0; i <= k; i += 5) {
        temp += str[i];
        cout << temp << " " << str << endl;
    }
    return 0;
}
```

22. a. Show what is printed by the following program as it executes. Assume that the set of data read in is the following: Smith Brown Jones.

```cpp
#include <iostream>
#include <string>
using namespace std;
void makename(string, string, string &);
int main()
{
    string part[3],title[3];
    string name;

    part[0] = "Linda";
    part[1] = "Mary";
    part[2] = "Bill";
```

```
            title[0] = "Mr.";
            title[1] = "Ms.";
            title[2] = "Mrs.";

            for (int i = 0; i < 3; i++) {
                makename(part[i],title[i],name);
                cout << name << endl;
            }
            return 0;
    }
    void makename(string first, string title, string &whole)
    {
            string last;

            cout << "Enter the last name>> ";
            cin >> last;
            whole.clear();
            whole += title;
            whole += " ";
            whole += first;
            whole += " ";
            whole += last;
            return;

    }
```

b. Explain why the formal parameters <u>first</u> and <u>title</u> are not arrays of strings even though <u>part</u> and <u>title</u> in the main program are.

23. Show what is printed by the following program.

```
#include <iostream>
#include <string>
using namespace std;
int main()
{
    string msg = "the students who ";
    char grade;
    string name1;
    string passed[10];
    string failed[10];
    string heading;
    int i=0,j=0;

    cin >> name1;
    while (cin) {
        cin >> grade;
        if ((grade=='A') || (grade=='B')
            || (grade=='C') || (grade=='D')) {
            passed[j] = name1;
            j++;
        }
        if (grade=='F') {
            failed[i] = name1;
```

```
                    i++;
            }
          cin >> name1;
      }
    heading = msg;
    heading += "passed";
    cout << heading << endl;
    for (int k = 0; k <= j; k++)
        cout << passed[k] << endl;

    heading = msg;
    heading += "failed";
    cout << heading << endl;
    for (int m = 0; m <= i; m++)
        cout << failed[m] << endl;
    return 0;
}
```

Enter the following data values, each on a new line:

```
Yaroslav
F
Jose
C
Wai
F
Kwazi
A
Boris
B
Ali
C
```

24. What is the output from the following program?

```cpp
#include <iostream>
#include <string>
using namespace std;
int main()
{
    string str = "artist";
    string arraystr, str1, str2;

    arraystr[0]='x';
    arraystr[1]='y';
    arraystr[2]='z';
    arraystr[3]='a';
    arraystr[4]='b';
    arraystr[5]='c';

    for (int i = 0; i < 6; i++)
        cout << "Element number " << i << " is " << arraystr[i]
            << endl;

    str1 = "hunger";
```

```
        arraystr = str;
        for (int i = 0; i < 6; i++)
            cout << arraystr[i];
        cout << endl;

        str2 = str1;
        str2 += arraystr;
        cout << "The new string is " << str2 << endl;

        arraystr = "widget";
        cout << "arraystr is now " << arraystr << endl;
        return 0;
    }
```

25. Show what is printed by the following program.

```
#include <iostream>
#include <string>
int main( )
{
        string t = "Help is on the way";
        string p = "abcdef", q = "PQRSTU";
        int i;

        q = q + p;
        p = "done";
        cout << p << endl;
        cout << q << endl;

        cout << "now: " << t.size() << endl;
        if (t > q)
            cout << t.size() << endl;
        else

        cout << p.size() << endl;
        cout << "the original string: "
            << t << endl;
        cout << "plus that: " << t[3] << endl;

        t = "new values";
        t[4] = 'F';
        t[2] = '\n';
        t[3] = 'S' + 1;
        t[6] = 'X';

        cout << "the new string: "
            << t << endl;

        for (i = 0; i <= 7; i++)
            cout << " " << t[i];

        return 0;
    }
```

26. Show what is printed by the following program.

```cpp
#include <iostream>
#include <string>
using namespace std;
int main ( )
{
        string t = "cannon ball news";
        string p = "RSTU", q = "rstu";
        int    m,k;

        if (p == q)
            cout <<"equal to start" << endl;
        else
            cout <<"not equal" << endl;
        cout << endl;

        p = p + q;
        q = t.substr(2,3);
        cout << "p is: " << p << endl;
        cout << "q is: " << q << endl << endl;

        m = t.size();
        k = t.find("all",0);
        cout << "m and k: " << m << " "
            << k << endl << endl;

        p = "a new value";
        p.erase(3,4);
        cout << "p is: " << p << endl;
        p.insert(4,"done");
        cout << "p is: " << p << endl;
        p[2] = 'X';
        p[1] = 'Y';
        cout << "p is: " << p << endl;

        return 0;
}
```

MODIFICATIONS TO PROGRAMS, EXAMPLES, AND EXERCISES

27. Program 3 read in an employee ID number, then hours and rate for each employee. Modify the program so that it reads in each employee's name rather than an ID number. First write it with last names only; then write it with two-word names. Notice the problems involved in combining getline( ) with the >> operator. Try reading the two words one by one with the >> operator, contcatenating them to form the name.

28. Make two modifications to Exercise 22.
    a. Show how to modify makename( ) so that in three calls it fills an array names instead of producing a single string name.
    b. Show how to modify makename( ) so that in one call it fills an array names with three names. Show how to modify the call to makename( ) from the main program. (*Hint:* You need to use arrays of strings as formal parameters.)

29. Make two modifications to Exercise 23.

    a. Modify this program to allow grades of A-, B+, C+, etc.

    b. Modify this program to allow names of more than one word.

30.   a. Modify Program 8 so that <u>erasetext( )</u> gives the option of erasing the same text multiple times. For example, if the line of text is "my dog has a dog to dog", it would give the option of removing all three occurrences of "dog".

    b. The function <u>inserttext( )</u> in Program 8 is word-oriented. That is, it puts spaces before and after the text that is inserted. Change the code for this function so that it does not supply spaces, but simply inserts the entered text without adding additional spaces.

    c. The functions in Program 8 do not print error messages if <u>find( )</u> returns <u>npos</u> and no changes can be made. Modify the program to print error messages.

    d. The functions in Program 8 are case sensitive. If you search for "blog", it will not find "Blog". Fix the functions so that they will work for lowercase or capitals in any position.

    e. The <u>inserttext( )</u> function in Program 8 allows inserting new text only after a word. Modify it to allow inserting text after a specified character.

    f. The <u>inserttext( )</u> function in Program 8 asks after which word you'd like to insert text, and inserts the new text after the first occurrence of that word. Modify it so that it allows inserting the new text after all occurrences of the specified word. For example, if the line is "he he he", insert "is" after each "he" to produce "he is he is he is".

    g. The <u>replacetext( )</u> function in Program 8 will replace text wherever it occurs. If we want to replace "her" by "him", it will change "here" to "hime". Suggest several ways to fix this.

    h. Add options to Program 8's list of user choices, and write functions to perform those tasks. Here are some examples: make the line of text all capitals, make the line of text all lowercase, reverse the characters in the line of text (so that "my name" would become "enan ym"), eliminate all blanks in the line.

    i. Modify Program 8 to allow the user to enter either a lowercase or a capital letter as the value of <u>choice</u>.

31. The program in Chapter 6 read in a number for the month and did all its processing using a month number. Rewrite the program so that it reads in a month name, like "January", and does string comparison to determine the season.

    a. Use an array of months in the function <u>classify( )</u>.

    b. Have <u>classify( )</u> return the name of a season, and print the season in <u>main( )</u>. If the month value entered is an error (like "Rectober") have <u>classify( )</u> return the string "error".

    c. Modify the program so that entering a value like "january" (with a lowercase 'j') will not be an error.

32. There are many possible ways of organizing Program 8. Try some of them.

    a. Write the program so that the main program does all the work, without dividing the task into functions.

    b. Write the program so that the main program calls <u>change( )</u> to present a menu, and <u>change( )</u> calls another function <u>choose( )</u> to read in the choice and call the functions.

    c. Write the program so that the main program calls a function to read the lines from an input file. You will need to devise a signal for the function to return to let main know that the function has read to the end of the input file.

PROGRAMMING PROJECTS

33. a. Write a programmer-defined function, like the one in Example 8-31, that performs the same task as isdigit( ).
    b. Do the same for isupper( ), isalpha( ), isalnum( ), and isspace( ).

34. a. Write a function removeblanks( ) to delete blanks from a string. The function receives a string variable as a parameter and returns the string with all blanks removed. For example, if the value sent to removeblanks( ) is " I am sad ", the function returns "Iamsad".
    b. Modify the function so that only trailing blanks are deleted. Call the new function trailing( ). It receives a variable str of type **string** as a parameter and returns the string with all trailing blanks removed. For example, if the value sent to trailing( ) is "I me you   ", the function returns "I me you".
    c. Write parts (a) and (b) using a void function. Each function modifies a string sent as a parameter.

35. Write a function rev_position( ) that receives two string parameters, str1 and str2. It returns the position where str2 in reverse order starts in str1. For example, if str1 is "melon" and str2 is "nol", then rev_position returns 2 (since the reverse of str2 is "lon" and "lon" starts in position 2). If str1 is "melon" and str2 is "lon", the function returns -1.

36. Write a function right_position( ) that receives two string parameters, str1 and str2. It returns the start of the last occurrence of str2 in str1. For example, if str1 is "misses" and str2 is 's', the function returns 5. If the string is not found, it returns npos.

37. a. Write a function reverse( ) that receives a string str as a parameter and returns the characters in str in reverse order. For example, if the value sent to reverse( ) is "I me ", the function returns " em I".
    b. Write a void function version of reverse( ) that receives two parameters. One parameter holds the original string. The second is an output parameter to hold the reversed string produced by the function.

38. a. Write a function countblanks( ) that receives a string str as a parameter and returns the number of blanks in str. For example, if the value sent to countblanks( ) is " help me ", the function returns 4. The function should not change the value of the parameter.
    b. If you use the function removeblanks( ) from Exercise 34, there is a very simple version of countblanks( ). What is it?
    c. Write a function count( ) that receives a string str and a character ch as parameters. It returns the number of times that ch occurs in str1. Do not change either parameter.
    d. Modify count( ) from part (c) so that it takes two strings str1 and str2 as parameters and counts the number of times that str2 occurs in str1. However, each character in str1 can be counted only once. For example, "eve" occurs just once in "eveve".

39. a. Write a function non_alpha( ) that receives a string str as parameter and returns the position of the first nonalphabetic character in str. For example, if str has the value "stev7n", the function returns 4. If none is found, the function returns npos.
    b. Write a function alpha( ) that receives a string str and returns the position of the first alphabetic character in str. For example, if str has the value "3315 Main St.", the function returns 5. If none is found, the function returns npos.
    c. Write a function after( ) that receives a string str and returns the position of the first alphabetic character that occurs after a nonalphabetic character. For example, if str has the value "stev9n",

the function returns 5; if <u>str</u> has the value "stev9 n", the function returns 6. If none is found, the function returns <u>npos</u>.

40. Assume you have two strings, <u>s1</u> and <u>s2</u>, and you want to determine if the characters in one are a rearrangement of the ones in the other. Write a function <u>order( )</u> to solve this problem.

41. a. Write a function <u>common( )</u> that receives two parameters, strings <u>s1</u> and <u>s2</u>. The function returns a string consisting of the characters which appear at least once in both strings. For example, if <u>s1</u> has the value "johnson" and <u>s2</u> has the value "honor", then the function returns "hon" (or these characters in some other order). The function <u>common( )</u> returns a string containing the common letters.

    b. Write a function <u>split( )</u> to break up a two-word string into its two components, <u>first</u> and <u>last</u>, at the first space.

    c. Write a program that reads in a series of names (first name, last name). Call <u>split( )</u> to break up the name into <u>first</u> and <u>last</u>. Next, call <u>common( )</u> to determine if there are any letters in common in the first and the last name. You can make the letters all capitals, all lowercase, or ignore case. For example, if the name is "JOHN JONES", then the two parts are "JOHN" and "JONES". The letters in common are "JON".

    d. Write a version of <u>common( )</u> that does the same thing as the original version of <u>common( )</u> but leaves no repeated letters in the returned string. For example, if the name is "BOB BOKO", the returned string is "BO".

    Test the functions with the following strings:

    ```
    JOHN JONES
    april fresh
    madonna
    SANDY E. LANDY
    WILSON ACTS
    anna anna
    ```

For Exercises 42–43, assume that all words are composed of only lowercase letters.

42. Write a function <u>code( )</u> that receives two parameters, a string <u>words</u> and an integer <u>m</u>. The function encodes each letter in <u>words</u> into a new letter <u>m</u> positions down in the alphabet. For example, if <u>m</u> is 3, then 'a' is encoded as 'd', 'k' as 'n','y' as 'b', and so on. (Assume that the alphabet is circular, so that 'z' is followed by 'a'.) All nonalphabetic symbols in <u>words</u> are unchanged. You can write <u>code( )</u> as a function that returns a value or as a void function. Write a driver program to test <u>code( )</u>.

43. Write a complete program that calls the functions described below first to encode and then to decode a series of strings. The main program tests <u>encode( )</u> and <u>decode( )</u>. It reads a 26-letter alphabet string indicating what code is to be used. Then it reads a series of strings. Each string is encoded by <u>encode( )</u>. The new string is then decoded by <u>decode( )</u>. (What happens if we call them in reverse order?)

    a. Write a function <u>encode( )</u> that receives two string parameters, <u>str</u> and <u>alpha</u>. The first parameter is a word to be encoded; the second is a permutation of the 26 letters of the alphabet. Each letter in <u>str</u> is encoded according to this scheme: If a letter in <u>str</u> is the <u>k</u>th letter of the alphabet in the usual order, then its encoding is the letter in <u>alpha</u> that is in position <u>k</u>. For example, if <u>alpha</u> starts with "eps...", then each 'a' in <u>str</u> becomes 'e', each 'b' becomes 'p', and so on.

    b. Write a function <u>decode( )</u> that receives the same parameters as <u>encode( )</u>. This function decodes <u>str</u> letter by letter. If a particular letter of <u>str</u> occurs in position <u>k</u> of <u>alpha</u>, it is decoded into the letter at position <u>k</u> in the alphabet. For example, if <u>alpha</u> starts with "txe...", each 't' in <u>str</u> becomes 'a', each 'x' becomes 'b', and so on.

c. Modify the main program to do error checking. For example, the alphabet string must contain each letter exactly once. Are there any restrictions on the individual strings?

44. a. Write a program that reads in a series of strings, then determines whether or not each string is a valid "mini-C++" identifier. Here is a brief summary of the rules: The name may be up to 30 characters long; the first character must be a letter; every remaining character must be a letter, a digit (0 to 9), or an underbar symbol.

In your program, use the following functions:

<u>sizeOK( )</u>: to determine if the size of the identifier name is within the allowed range;

<u>first( )</u>: to determine if the name starts with an allowed symbol; and

<u>others( )</u>: to determine if all other characters are allowed symbols.

You should decide exactly what parameter(s) are required by these functions and whether to write them as void functions or as functions that return values.

If an identifier name is valid, print "ok". If it is invalid, print at least one thing that is wrong with it (e.g., "it does not begin with a letter").

b. Modify the program to reject keywords as well. Use a function <u>iskey( )</u> to determine if the string is a keyword. Assume that there are only five keywords: **if, for, while, do**, and **else**.

c. Modify the program to reject an identifier name that has appeared previously. Use a function <u>isrepeated( )</u> to determine if the string repeats an earlier valid name. (*Hint:* Use an array to hold the valid names.)

d. Modify the program to convert an invalid identifier name to a valid one. If the first character is not a letter, add 'x' at the front of the string. If there are illegal symbols in the string, delete them.

45. Write a complete program that calls <u>convert( )</u>, described below, to convert dates from one format to another. Test the program with the following dates, among others:

```
11/17/08
01/01/10
12/31/09
```

a. Write a function <u>convert( )</u> that receives as a parameter a string <u>date</u> of the form "mm/dd/yy". For example, <u>date</u> can be "11/17/09". The function converts this value to the form "month day, year". For example, "11/17/09" becomes November 17, 2009 (all years are in the twenty-first century).

b. Modify the function to allow one or two digits for the month and/or day. For example, "5/17/09" becomes May 17, 2009.

c. Modify the function to reject an invalid string. What constitutes an invalid string?

46. Write a function to break a sentence into individual words and produce a new sentence made up of the words in reverse order. Thus, if the original is "I am eating eggs", the result is "eggs eating am I".

47. Write a program to read in a word and send it to a function <u>finddouble( )</u> to determine whether it contains any double letters, and if so, how many sets. Test <u>finddouble( )</u> on the following words, among others: "spelling" (double 'l'), "bookkeeper" (three sets of double letters), "helper" (no double letters, even though the 'e' is repeated). If there are three letters in a row, such as "ddd", this should be counted as two doubles.

48. Write a program to read in a string and send it to a function IsPal( ) to determine whether it is a palindrome. A string is a palindrome if it reads the same backward and forward, like "Madam, I'm Adam". You can make the letters all capitals, all lowercase, or ignore case.

49. Write a program to read in a string that is a sentence and send it to a function lettercount( ). The function counts how many times each letter in the sentence occurs. The program produces a printed list of each letter and the number of times the letter appears. Write the program in two different forms:

   a. Produce a list containing counts for only those letters which actually occur in the string.

   b. Produce a list containing counts for all the letters in the alphabet. If a letter does not occur in the string, it appears on the list with a count of 0.

   Do these alternatives suggest two very different ways of counting the letters? Before you start, think carefully about the various ways you can count.

50. Write a program that reads in and prints a text, line by line, and calls a series of functions. The main program calls a function diffwords( ) to count the number of different words in the entire text (ignoring case). It also calls a function wordcount( ) to count the number of times each word appears in the text. Then it calls a function printcount( ) to print a list of all the words in the text, together with the count of the number of times they appear. For example, if a word occurs twice in the text, it appears only once on the list, with a count of 2. Print the list of words in alphabetical order. Use other functions wherever appropriate.

   For example, suppose the text is this:

   ```
   The elephant ate the banana and the giraffe ate the banana.
   ```

   The function diffwords( ) produces a count of 6 ("the", "elephant", "ate", "banana", and "giraffe"); wordcount( ) produces this list:

   ```
   and        1
   ate        2
   banana     2
   elephant   1
   giraffe    1
   the        4
   ```

51. Write a program that reads in a string and calls a function uplow( ) to convert each letter to the opposite case: if the letter is lowercase, uplow( ) converts it to a capital; if it's a capital, it becomes lowercase. If a character in the string is not a letter, uplow( ) leaves it the same. The program prints the original string and the converted string. For example, if the string is "IBM is in New York, USA", uplow( ) produces the string "ibm IS IN nEW yORK, usa". *Hint:* can you call functions from cctype.h to help solve this problem?

52. Write a program that reads in a string and translates it into Pig Latin. Pig Latin is a secret language that converts words in the following way:

   a. If the word starts with a consonant, the consonant moves to the end of the string and is followed by an "ay": the words "pig latin" become "igpay atinlay".

   b. If the word begins with a vowel, the letters "ay" are added to the end of the word: the words "is any" become "isay anyay".

   Write a function to split the string into words. Write another function to convert each word to Pig Latin. Print the original string and the converted string.

53. Write a program that reads in a string and translates it into Algebra. Algebra is a secret language that converts words in the following way:

   a. If the word starts with a consonant or a group of consonants, the letters "iaz" are added after the consonant or group of consonants: the words "crazy cat" become "criazazy ciazat".

   b. If the word begins with a vowel, the letters "iaz" are added to the beginning of the word: the words "is any" become "iazis iazany".

   Write a function to split the string into words. Write another function to convert each word to Algebra. Print the original string and the converted string.

54. Write a program that reads in a series of strings, stopping when there are no more strings. For each string, the program should call each of the following functions and print the results:

   cat( ): Takes two strings, s1 and s2 as parameters. Concatenates s2 to the end of s1, changing s1.

   remove( ): Takes a string, s, and a character, c, as its parameters. Removes all occurrences of c from s, changing s.

55. Write a program that plays a simplified form of Hangman. Your program prints out the length of a word (using underscores), and the player tries to guess what the word is by filling in letters. Each time the player guesses a letter, the program checks to see if the word contains that letter. If it does, the program fills in the letter wherever it occurs. If it does not, the program adds the letter to a list of unsuccessful letters. A player wins by replacing all the underscores with letters in seven or fewer guesses (seven guesses correspond to drawing the head, neck, two arms, body, and two legs in Hangman).

   After the game is over, the user should be given the option of playing again. Your program should have an array of words, so that the player is given a different word each time. Include both long and short words, easy ones and hard ones. Include some words that have a lot of repeated letters and some that have none.

MIX AND MATCH

PROBLEM: Sorting And Searching An Array

PROGRAMMING CONCEPTS: sorting, linear sort, bubble sort, interchanging two values, searching, linear search, binary search

PROBLEM-SOLVING TECHNIQUES: analysis of algorithms, bottom-up approach

HOW TO READ CHAPTER 9

OUTLINE:

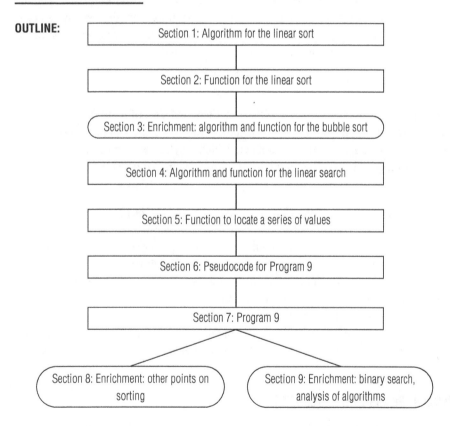

Section 1: Algorithm for the linear sort

Section 2: Function for the linear sort

Section 3: Enrichment: algorithm and function for the bubble sort

Section 4: Algorithm and function for the linear search

Section 5: Function to locate a series of values

Section 6: Pseudocode for Program 9

Section 7: Program 9

Section 8: Enrichment: other points on sorting

Section 9: Enrichment: binary search, analysis of algorithms

It is possible to cover Sections 4 and 9 before sorting. It is also possible to use the bubble sort instead of the linear sort in Program 9.

INTRODUCTION AND STATEMENT OF THE PROBLEM

INTRODUCTION

This chapter starts by introducing **sorting**—one of the most common applications of computers today. For example, a bank's files of its customers and their transactions, a college registrar's student records, and the names in a telephone book are all sorted to make access easier. Simply stated, sorting means to put objects into order (numerical for numbers or alphabetical for characters), either ascending or descending.

We discuss two sorting methods: a linear or selection sort and a bubble sort. Neither is particularly efficient or used very often in the business or scientific world. We study them because for most small cases (fewer than 100 numbers), they are adequate. A more practical reason is that these two methods are closest to the way a person sorts. Thus they are probably easiest to describe in an algorithm and use in a program. The sorting methods used for actual commercial or scientific applications (e.g., to sort 100,000 numbers) are much too complicated for our current programming ability. Any further discussion has to be postponed until a higher-level course in data structures. [For examples, see *Data Structures Using C and C++, Second Edition,* by Y. Langsam, M. Augenstein, and A. Tenenbaum (Upper Saddle River, N.J.: Prentice-Hall, Inc., 1996).]

In addition to sorting, the chapter introduces **searching**—another widely used computer function. Searching means finding a value in a list. We discuss several types of searches; the decision of which to use is largely based on whether the list has been sorted.

Let's start with the statement of the problem:

PROBLEM 9

Read a parameter value, which we will call n, then read a set of n numbers. Print the numbers in their original order. Sort the numbers into ascending order. Print the numbers in sorted order. Then read in a second set of data, consisting of numbers which may or may not occur in the original list. For each such number, print its position in the list if it does occur; if it doesn't, print a message saying this.

We use a bottom-up approach to solve the problem. We start by writing a function to sort an array. (In fact, we will write two functions which sort in different ways.) Next we add the searching component. Then we combine these pieces with other functions to read in and print a set of data. Finally, we tie everything together with a main program that calls the functions.

We also write this program in a modular way. We present two sorting methods, either of which can be used to sort the list of numbers. We also present two searching methods. Once again, either can be used to search the sorted list. The decision on which sort or search to use is somewhat arbitrary, although the chapter does analyze and compare the various sorting and searching methods. These functions are like books or tools in a library. A programmer can decide which one to use in a given situation.

SECTION 1   USING A LINEAR OR SELECTION SORT

Much of Problem 9 consists of things that we have done before (reading in and printing a set of numbers) so we concentrate first on the new portions: sort the numbers into ascending order and then search through the list. The next few sections are devoted to sorting. After that, we discuss searching.

In this section, we develop an algorithm for sorting, using what is called a linear or selection sort. We trace the algorithm on a few examples and then translate it into pseudocode.

SORTING INTO ASCENDING ORDER

It seems clear that the numbers to be sorted should be stored in an array. Therefore, we need an algorithm describing how to sort an array into ascending order. Ascending order means that the numbers are increasing. For the moment, we assume that no two numbers are equal so that we do not have any repeated elements.

Let's store the numbers to be sorted in an array called <u>numb</u>. Rather than specifying a particular size (e.g., 50 or 100) for the array, assume that it has <u>n</u> values to be sorted; these values are stored in positions 0 to <u>n</u> − 1 within the array. The problem boils down to this: Given the <u>numb</u> array, rearrange the first <u>n</u> elements so that they are in increasing order. Figure 9-1 provides an example of the <u>numb</u> array before and after sorting (with <u>n</u> equal to 5).

AN INFORMAL ALGORITHM FOR SORTING

Now we must construct an algorithm for sorting the <u>numb</u> array. We can't be vague and say "put the numbers in order." We need a step-by-step process that can be written as a program.

Here is a possible way to approach the problem:

◆ Start by finding the smallest number in the array and putting it in the first position since in the final sorted array, the smallest element comes first.

◆ Look through the rest of the numbers for the smallest one left, which goes into the next position of the array.

◆ Do the same to find the next smallest and so on until all the positions have been filled.

CAUTION Once we have determined the proper item for a position, we cannot consider that item in determining the proper item for other positions because we already know it is smaller than the remaining values.

This is not quite precise enough to be an algorithm, but we can continue to improve this method until it becomes an algorithm. The first step is to find the smallest number in the array and put it in the first position. We did something similar when we found the largest of a set of marks in Program 7. Finding the smallest is exactly the same idea.

ALGORITHM TO FIND THE SMALLEST ELEMENT IN AN ARRAY

◆ *Pick one of the numbers (usually, the first element) in the array as the smallest so far.*

◆ *Compare it to each of the other numbers.*

FIGURE 9-1   <u>numb</u> array before and after sorting

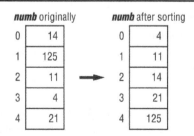

♦ *If one of them is smaller, this new value becomes the smallest so far.*

♦ *Continue to compare the smallest so far to the rest until all the numbers have been compared.*

The method for finding the smallest can be combined with the informal sorting algorithm to create a more precise one. This sorting algorithm is called a **linear** or **selection sort** since we compare the elements in linear order (first, second, third, etc.) as we select the correct one for each position in the array.

A FORMAL ALGORITHM FOR SORTING

Now we modify this algorithm so that it can be used to sort the elements of the numb array. We pick numb[0] to be the initial value for smallest so far since position 0 is where we want the smallest value to end up. To find the smallest, compare each element in the array with numb[0]. If the new value is less than numb[0], we swap their positions within the array (this allows us to save the old value of numb[0]); if the new value is greater than or equal to numb[0], we do nothing. (This also takes care of the question of repeated elements—do you see how?) Then we do the same thing for the other positions in the array.

Here is a complete algorithm for sorting the first n elements of the numb array:

ALGORITHM FOR THE LINEAR OR SELECTION SORT

♦ *Find the smallest element in the array and put it in* numb[0], *as follows:* compare each array element to numb[0]. *If it is smaller, swap it with* numb[0] *(if not, do nothing).*

♦ *Ignore the element in position 0 and repeat the process for the rest of the elements to find which one belongs in position 1—*numb[1].

♦ *Repeat the process for the other positions in the array down to the next to last.*

We stop at the next-to-last position because filling it leaves only one number, which automatically goes in the last position.

PSEUDOCODE TRANSLATION OF THE ALGORITHM

Now let's translate the algorithm into pseudocode in preparation for writing a function to sort. Looking at the algorithm, we see a nested loop structure. One loop takes care of the various positions within the array, and the other determines which of the candidates for a particular position should go there. Here is the algorithm rewritten in pseudocode:

PSEUDOCODE FOR THE LINEAR SORT

for each position in the array (except the last)
  for each candidate for that position
    compare the candidate to the element currently in that position
    if the candidate is smaller
      swap them

What do we mean by the phrase *for each candidate for that position*? At any point in the process, the only candidates for a given position are those elements whose subscript is greater than that of the given position. For example, the candidates for position 3 have subscripts of 4 or higher.

TRACING THE PSEUDOCODE FOR THE LINEAR SORT ALGORITHM

Let's trace an example to verify that our pseudocode translation of the linear sort algorithm works.

EXAMPLE 9-1   Assume that the underline{numb} array holds 14 125 11 4 21 (with $\underline{n} = 5$). We simplify our trace by showing only the numbers, not the subscripts from the underline{numb} array. We also use) to stand for a comparison between any two elements. If the two are swapped, then we rewrite the entire revised array immediately to the right.

PROGRAM TRACE   Figure 9-2 shows a trace of the first pass through the algorithm to find the smallest number and put it into underline{numb[0]}. First 14 is compared to 125. Since it is less, we do nothing. Then 14 and 11 are compared, and these two items must be swapped. We move to the second column in the figure. Now 11 (the smallest so far) and 4 are compared; once again, these two items must be swapped. We move to the third column in the figure. Finally, 4 is compared to 21, and there is no change. Note that 4, the smallest number, is now correctly placed in underline{numb[0]}.

Once the first pass is complete, we start a second pass to fill the second position. (In Figure 9-3, we use a vertical line to separate passes from each other.) For the second pass, we ignore underline{numb[0]}. We want to determine the second smallest in the entire array, the smallest in the remaining group. We start by comparing 125 to 14, and these two values swap places. Then we compare 14 and 11, resulting in another swap. Finally, 11 and 21 are compared, but they do not swap.

The second pass is followed by a third pass to determine the third smallest, and a fourth one, to determine the fourth (and also fifth) position. On the third pass, 125 and 14 swap, but 14 and 21 do not. On the fourth pass, 125 and 21 swap. The complete trace of the pseudocode for the algorithm is shown in Figure 9-3.

SELF-CHECK 9-1

1. In the linear sort algorithm, why is the element chosen for a position not considered for any other position?

2. If we sort 5 elements, how many passes are needed? If we sort 56, how many are needed? If we sort $\underline{n}$ elements, how many do we need? On each pass, how many items are put in their correct position?

3. If we want to sort a group of two or three numbers, is it necessary to store them in an array? What if we have four or five numbers? What if we have an arbitrary number (that is, $\underline{n}$ values)?

FIGURE 9-2   Trace of the First Pass of the Pseudocode for the Linear Sort Algorithm: Example 9-1 ($\underline{n} = 5$)

first pass

```
14 )   11 )    4
125    125    125 )
11     14     14
4      4      11
21     21     21
```

FIGURE 9-3   Complete Trace of the Pseudocode for the Linear Sort Algorithm: Example 9-1 ($\underline{n} = 5$)

```
   first pass        second pass        third pass    fourth pass
 14 )  11 )   4    | 4    4    4    | 4    4    | 4     4
125   125   125 )  |125 ) 14   11 ) |11   11   |11    11
 11    14    14    | 14 ) 125   125 |125 ) 14   |14    14
  4     4    11    | 11   11    14  | 14 ) 125 )|125 ) 21
 21    21    21    | 21   21    21  | 21   21   | 21   125
```

FUNCTION FOR THE LINEAR SORT

In this section, we translate the pseudocode into a function to perform a linear sort. This function is then used in Program 9. (Concentrating on the functions before the main program is called a bottom-up approach to solving a problem; see Section 6.)

A FUNCTION TO SORT

We've traced a few examples to prove that the algorithm and pseudocode are correct; now it is time to write a function. There is no single answer to return so we use a void function. Instead of returning an answer, the function changes the values stored in the entire array.

We write a function called _linearsort( )_ to sort or rearrange the _numb_ array, assuming that values have already been stored in positions 0 to $n - 1$. Later we show how to call this function from a main program.

Here is the comment, followed by the function header:

```
// Function linearsort:
// Input:
//    numb: the array to sort
//    n: the number of elements to sort in the array
// Process:
//    linear sorts into ascending order
//    the first n values of the numb array
// Output:
//    function modifies array numb
//
void linearsort(int numb[], int n)
```

Notice once again that _numb_ is changed in the function. This is crucial because we must have the changed order of the array available in the main program once we return from the function.

Let's look at the pseudocode again:

> _for each position in the array (except the last)_
> > _for each candidate for that position_
> > > _compare the candidate to the element currently in that position_
> > _if the candidate is smaller_
> > > _swap them_

The outer loop takes care of positions in the array. When $n = 5$, it takes 4 passes through the body of the outer loop to sort the array; when $n = 6$, there are 5; if $n = 100$, there will be 99 passes. In general, it takes _n − 1_ passes to sort n values since each pass except the last fills one position, and the last pass fills two. Following normal C++ practice, we start counting at 0 so we number these passes 0, 1, 2, ..., _n − 2_. For example, if n is 5, the passes are 0, 1, 2, 3.

On each pass, we want to do the same job—find the smallest value of the elements of the array still left and put it into the correct position in _numb_. Thus we can use a **for** loop, with index _pass_, to take care of the $n − 1$ passes. Notice that we've modified the pseudocode to refer to the identifier _pass_.

```
for (int pass = 0; pass < n - 1; pass++)
        for each candidate for position pass
            compare the candidate to the element in position pass
        if the candidate is smaller
            swap it with the element in position pass
```

Inside the <u>pass</u> loop, we want to compare each of the remaining numbers to the value that is in position <u>pass</u> of <u>numb</u>. However, as we noted earlier, we don't want to consider any number that has already been chosen. Using our example, note that once 4 is chosen to go in <u>numb[0]</u>, it is not a candidate for <u>numb[1]</u>; once 11 is fixed in <u>numb[1]</u>, neither 4 nor 11 should can go in <u>numb[2]</u>, and so on.

Let's use <u>cand</u> as the control variable of the **for** loop to run through the candidates. The candidates for position <u>pass</u> are the values in <u>numb[pass + 1]</u>, <u>numb[pass + 2]</u>, ... , <u>numb[n − 1]</u>. Each candidate should be compared to <u>numb[pass]</u>. If it is smaller, it is swapped with <u>numb[pass]</u>. Therefore, we have this nested **for** loop construction (and an additional declaration for <u>cand</u>):

```
for (int pass = 0; pass < n - 1; pass++)
    for (int cand = pass + 1; cand < n; cand++)
        if (numb[pass] > numb[cand])
            swap them
```

Note that the outer or <u>pass</u> loop only goes up to <u>n − 2</u> because the last pass determines the position of two elements. The inner or <u>cand</u> loop goes up to <u>n − 1</u> because each element in the array must be considered. In the last comparison of the entire nested loop, <u>pass</u> equals <u>n − 2</u> and <u>cand</u> equals <u>n − 1</u>, so <u>numb[n − 2]</u> is compared to <u>numb[n − 1]</u>. For example, if <u>n</u> is 5, the last comparison is <u>numb[3]</u> to <u>numb[4]</u>.

DISSECTING THE LINEAR SORT FUNCTION

Before going on, let's check that this portion of the pseudocode has been translated correctly.

PROGRAM TRACE We return to our example: <u>n</u> = 5, <u>numb</u> holding 14 125 11 4 21. Let's analyze the overall setup. Note that *n − 1* is 4, and *n − 2* is 3.

♦ The outer loop has <u>pass</u> going from 0 to 3 since we want to fix the values for <u>numb[0]</u> to <u>numb[3]</u> (<u>numb[4]</u> is the value which is left).

♦ The inner loop has <u>cand</u> going from <u>pass + 1</u> to 4.

♦ For position 0, the candidates are <u>numb[1]</u> to <u>numb[4]</u>, competing with <u>numb[0]</u>.

♦ For position 1, the candidates are <u>numb[2]</u> through <u>numb[4]</u>, competing with <u>numb[1]</u>.

♦ For position 2, they are <u>numb[3]</u> and <u>numb[4]</u>, competing with <u>numb[2]</u>.

♦ For position 3, just <u>numb[4]</u> and <u>numb[3]</u> compete.

♦ Finally, <u>numb[4]</u> must be the largest.

Note once again that <u>numb[4]</u> can be a candidate for the other passes, but no separate pass determines position 4.

The trace matches the step-by-step analysis of the algorithm and pseudocode in Figure 9-3. We urge you to do a detailed trace on an example with five or six elements to prove the code works.

INTERCHANGING TWO VALUES

We must still interchange the two values, <u>numb[pass]</u> and <u>numb[cand]</u>, in case there is a swap. Recall from Chapter 5, Section 5 the method to interchange two values. (In Section 8 of this chapter, we show

how to use the function swap( ) from Chapter 5, Section 5.) The following three statements inter-change the two array elements:

```
temp = numb[pass];               // swapping the values of
numb[pass] = numb[cand];         // numb[pass] and numb[cand]
numb[cand] = temp;
```

In the sorting function, we want to interchange the two values only if they are out of order—if numb[pass] is greater than numb[cand]. Therefore, we use the following **if** statement:

```
if (numb[pass] > numb[cand]) {
    temp = numb[pass];               // swapping the values of
    numb[pass] = numb[cand];         // numb[pass] and numb[cand]
    numb[cand] = temp;
}
```

THE linearsort( ) FUNCTION

Here is the entire linearsort( ) function:

```
// ...
void linearsort(int numb[], int n)
{
    int temp;
    for (int pass = 0; pass < n - 1; pass++)
        for (int cand = pass + 1; cand < n; cand++)
            if (numb[pass] > numb[cand]) {
                temp = numb[pass];
                numb[pass] = numb[cand];
                numb[cand] = temp;
            }
    return;
}
```

PROGRAM TRACE To make sure the function works, let's trace a simple example with four elements: 8 23 6 5 (n = 4).

♦ The outer **for** loop sets pass to 0, which is less than n-1.

♦ The inner **for** loop sets cand to pass + 1, which is 0 + 1 or 1. This value is less than or equal to n.

♦ The first comparison is numb[0], which is 8, to numb[1], which is 23. They are in order so we do nothing.

♦ Then cand increments to 2, and we compare position 0 (which holds 8) and position 2 (which holds 6). Since 8 > 6 is true, we interchange these two values.

♦ Next cand increments to 3 (which is still less than n). We compare position 0 (which now holds 6) and position 3 (which holds 5), and these values are swapped.

♦ Then cand increments to 4, which terminates the inner loop. The first pass is complete, and the smallest value (5) is now in position 0. The array holds the following values: 5 23 8 6.

♦ Next pass increments to 1. A new cand loop starts with cand initialized to 1 + 1, which is 2.

♦ We compare position 1 (which holds 23) and position 2 (which holds 8). They swap places.

♦ Then cand increments to 3, and we compare position 1 (which now holds 8) with position 3 (which holds 6). They swap places.

◆ Then <u>cand</u> increments to 4, which terminates the inner loop. The second pass is complete, and the second smallest value (6) is now in position 1. The array holds the following values: 5 6 23 8.

◆ Next <u>pass</u> increments to 2. A new <u>cand</u> loop starts with <u>cand</u> initialized to $2 + 1 = 3$.

◆ We compare position 2 (which holds 23) with position 3 (which holds 8). They swap places.

◆ Then <u>cand</u> increments to 4, which terminates the inner loop. The third pass is complete, and the third smallest value (8) is now in position 2; in addition, the largest value (23) is in the last position. The array holds the following values: 5 6 8 23.

SELF-CHECK 9-2

1. Trace the <u>linearsort( )</u> function on this set of numbers: 20 100 −12 5 (<u>n</u> = 4)

2. If we are sorting 5 elements, how many passes are needed? With 75 elements, how many passes are there? How about <u>n</u> elements? On each pass, how many items are put into their correct position?

SECTION 3   **ENRICHMENT: USING A BUBBLE SORT**

This section shows a second way to sort an array, called a bubble sort, and briefly compares the two methods.

PROBLEMS WITH THE LINEAR SORT

Why do we need another sorting method? Imagine the following situation: The <u>numb</u> array holds the numbers from 1 to 78, followed by 80 and then 79, so it is in ascending order except for the last two items, which are swapped.

A person would quickly notice that the numbers from 1 to 78 are in order, then swap 80 and 79, but it takes the linear sort function a long time to sort this array. The program does not (why not?) notice that the items are almost all in their correct positions. Instead, it first determines the smallest number and puts it in <u>numb[0]</u>. This takes 79 comparisons. Then it ignores that number and determines the second smallest by comparing the second number to each of the others. This process goes on for a total of 79 passes and slightly over 3000 comparisons. (See Exercise 9 for a way to calculate the precise number.)

This is not even the worst possible case. What if the entire array is in order to begin with? The same number of passes and comparisons are used. Thus, we have an incredible situation where it takes more than 3000 comparisons to "sort" a sorted array. No matter what the original order, the linear sort algorithm uses the same comparisons to sort an array with 80 elements (see Exercise 7). Of course, in an array that is almost sorted, there are relatively few swaps, and this saves time.

A NEW APPROACH USING ADJACENT POSITIONS

The problem is that the linear sort does not take advantage of any information that it has already obtained about the array. A "smarter" sorting algorithm could use the results of earlier comparisons to decide what to do next. For example, if <u>numb[3]</u> < <u>numb[4]</u> and <u>numb[4]</u> < <u>numb[5]</u>, it is stupid to compare numb[3] and numb[5]. Shortcuts like this are used by a person to speed up the sorting process. Let's build a smarter algorithm that uses some of these shortcuts.

Assume that we find the following:

♦ numb[0] < numb[1]

♦ numb[1] < numb[2]

♦ numb[2] < numb[3]

   . . .

♦ numb[n - 2] < numb[n - 1]

The numb array must be in order. If each number is in the correct position relative to the one after it (and, therefore, the one before it), the array is sorted.

This means that we can use only neighboring positions in our comparisons. Instead of comparing numb[0] to numb[1], numb[2], ..., numb[n − 1], we need only compare numb[0] to numb[1]. If it is less than (or equal to—do you see why?) numb[1], we compare numb[1] to numb[2]. If a number is larger than the one after it, we swap the two of them and continue. But we must be a little more careful. If, for example, numb[1] and numb[2] are swapped, perhaps the old value of numb[2], now in numb[1], is also smaller than numb[0]. For example, if numb holds 14 125 11 4 21, 125 and 11 should swap, but 11 is also less than 14. If we stop after one pass, the array holds 14 11 4 21 125, which is not in sorted order (although 125, the largest element, is in the correct position).

Therefore, when we finish going through the array, we must go back to the beginning and start over. The numbers are gradually put into their correct positions starting from the end of the list. If we ever have one pass through the entire array without a swap, we are done. In that case, numb[0] < numb[1], numb[1] < numb[2], ..., numb[n − 2] < numb[n − 1]. We know this means the array is sorted.

ALGORITHM AND PSEUDOCODE FOR THE BUBBLE SORT

This new method is called a **bubble sort** for reasons that become clear when we trace a few examples. Here is the bubble sort algorithm to sort the first n elements of the numb array:

Algorithm for the Bubble Sort
Repeat the following process until an entire pass has no swaps:

♦ *Compare adjacent elements of the array (numb[0] with numb[1], numb[1] with numb[2], ..., numb[n − 2] with numb[n − 1]).*

♦ *If they are out of order, swap them.*

Here is a pseudocode version of this algorithm:

Pseudocode for the Bubble Sort

> *do the following as long as there has been a swap on the last pass*
>   *for each element of the array*
>   *compare the element to its neighbor*
>   *if they are out of order*
>   *swap them*

TRACING THE BUBBLE SORT ALGORITHM

Let's trace an example before going on.

EXAMPLE 9-2 Assume that <u>numb</u> holds 14 125 11 4 21 (<u>n</u> = 5). We use the earlier conventions in the trace, which is illustrated in Figure 9-4.

PROGRAM TRACE

- In the first pass, we compare 14 and 125, and they are in correct order.
- In the linear sort, we would compare 14 and 11, but in the bubble sort, we compare 125 and 11. They swap positions.
- Then we compare 125 and 4, which also get swapped, as do 125 and 21. This ends the first pass.
- Because there has been at least one swap in the first pass, we must have a second.
- In the second pass, 14 and 11 (and then 14 and 4) swap places so we need a third pass.
- The third pass swaps 11 and 4, requiring a fourth. There are no swaps; we are done.

There are several ways to speed up the bubble sort algorithm; a few are explored in exercises 12 through 14.

EXAMPLE 9-3 Let's try another example: <u>numb</u> = 4 7 11 15 20 13 (<u>n</u> = 6). On this example, which is almost in order to start, the bubble sort is significantly better than the linear sort (see Figure 9-5).

CAUTION While a bubble sort is usually better than a linear sort, there are cases where it is worse, for example, on an array that starts in descending order.

EXAMPLE 9-4 As an example where the bubble sort does very poorly, let <u>numb</u> = 7 6 5 4 (<u>n</u> = 4). Trace this one on your own.

FIGURE 9-4 Trace of the Pseudocode for the Bubble Sort Algorithm: Example 9-2 (<u>n</u> = 5)

first pass				second pass			third pass		fourth pass
14	14	14	14	14	11	11	11	4	4
125	11	11	11	11	14	4	4	11	11
11	125	4	4	4	4	14	14	14	14
4	4	125	21	21	21	21	21	21	21
21	21	21	125	125	125	125	125	125	125

FIGURE 9-5 Trace of the Pseudocode for the Bubble Sort Algorithm: Example 9-3 (<u>n</u> = 6)

first pass		second pass		third pass
4	4	4	4	4
7	7	7	7	7
11	11	11	11	11
15	15	15	13	13
20	13	13	15	15
13	20	20	20	20

In general, the bubble sort works best if the original array is almost sorted. For a random array, this is quite rare, but it is fairly common in practice. For example, if you have a sorted array and want to add two new elements, you can place them in the front (why is this better than the rear?) and do a relatively fast bubble sort.

A trace of the bubble sort shows elements moving to their correct locations like bubbles in water. In Figure 9-4, watch a large number like 125 descending and a small number like 4 rising. Figure 9-5 shows 13 rising while 15 and 20 descend.

COMPARISON OF THE TWO ALGORITHMS

In many cases, the bubble sort is not much better than the linear sort. However, if the array is fairly close to sorted order, the bubble sort is a significant improvement. Thus, for relatively small applications ($n < 100$), where an extremely efficient sort is not necessary, the bubble sort is preferred. Another advantage of the bubble sort is that the numbers to be compared are always adjacent in the array, whereas the linear sort often compares numbers that are widely spread. In certain circumstances, this takes longer.

One curious feature about the bubble sort algorithm is that there is no way to predict exactly how many passes are necessary to sort n numbers. The number of passes ranges from a low of one (if the array is in order) to a high of n (if the array is completely reversed). The linear sort always takes $n - 1$ passes. (See Exercise 9 for an analysis of the sorting algorithms.)

Neither sort is useful in real business or scientific applications where the amount of data is in the thousands or larger.

FUNCTION FOR THE BUBBLE SORT

Now let's translate the pseudocode for the algorithm into a function. The bubble sort algorithm says to repeat something as long as an event, *a swap on the last pass*, occurs. In addition, we must go through the process at least once. As we saw in Chapter 6, the best way to implement such a structure is with a **do-while** loop.

We want to repeat the body of the loop as long as a swap occurs on each pass. In fact, we use that as our condition controlling the **do-while** loop:

```
do {
   . . .
} while (there has been a swap on the last pass);
```

Inside the **do-while** loop, we want to have a complete pass through the array, comparing each position to the one after it; for this, we use a **for** loop. If we use pos as the **for** loop index, the two items to be compared are numb[pos] and numb[pos + 1]. The **for** loop index pos goes from 0 to $n - 2$ (we use $n - 2$ so that we don't compare the last item in the array to the one after it). Here is the first version of the function for the bubble sort:

```
// Function bubblesort:
// Input:
//    numb: the array to sort
//    n: the number of elements to sort in the array
// Process:
//    bubble sorts into ascending order
```

```
//   the first n values of the numb array
// Output:
//   function modifies array numb
//
void bubblesort(int numb[], int n)
{
    do {
            for (int pos = 0; pos < n - 1; pos++)
                if (numb[pos] > numb[pos + 1])
                        swap them
          } while (there has been a swap on the last pass)
        return;
}
```

Let's check this. The body of the **do-while** loop continues to be executed as long as a swap was made on the last pass. This means that at least one more pass is needed to check for further swaps. If we ever escape from the loop, it is because an entire pass of the **for** loop did not cause a swap. This means that numb[0] and numb[1], numb[1] and numb[2], ... , numb[n − 2] and numb[n − 1] are all correctly positioned relative to each other so the entire array is sorted.

CAUTION a common mistake is to use the following **if** condition:

```
if (numb[pos] > numb[pos] + 1) ...
```

This is wrong because the + 1 has been moved outside the array brackets. Inside the brackets, + 1 means add 1 to the subscript; outside the brackets, it means add 1 to the value of numb[pos]. We are asking if the value of numb[pos] is greater than itself plus one, and this can never be true.

DETERMINING WHETHER A SWAP HAS BEEN MADE

We still have to define the **while** condition of the loop. To tell if a swap was made on the last pass, we can use a signal or flag: we'll use a **bool** variable called swapped. A value of **false** indicates that no swap was made, while **true** means a swap was made. The condition to be tested is this: *while (swapped == true)*. This can be abbreviated to *while (swapped)*. This leads to the following format for the outer loop structure:

```
do {
    ...
} while (swapped);
```

There are still a few loose ends. One fundamental problem is where to give swapped a value to indicate whether a swap has been made. Since swapped equal to **true** indicates a swap, the natural time to set swapped to 1 is when we interchange the two values. This means we should insert the statement *swapped = true* inside the compound statement that swaps numb[pos] and numb[pos + 1]. This time, we also include the actual statements to do the swap:

```
do {
    for (int pos = 0; pos < n - 1; pos++)
        if (numb[pos] > numb[pos + 1]) {
```

```
            // swap the values
            temp = numb[pos];
            numb[pos] = numb[pos + 1];
            numb[pos + 1] = temp;
            swapped = true;
        }
} while (swapped);                         // incomplete
```

Unfortunately, this leads to the following situation: we have set swapped to **true** at one point, and we have checked to see if swapped is **true**, but we have never given swapped the value **false**. If the array is initially unsorted, the **do-while** loop will continue forever because the condition *while(swapped)* is always true.

CAUTION An infinite loop, caused by forgetting to initialize (or reinitialize) a variable, is a common error with a **do-while** loop.

The problem can be solved by giving swapped an initial value of **false** somewhere. One possibility is to set it to 0 in an **else** statement:

```
if (numb[pos] >> numb[pos + 1]) {
    // swap the values
    temp = numb[pos];
    numb[pos] = numb[pos + 1];
    numb[pos + 1] = temp;
    swapped = 1;
}
else
    swapped = 0;                           // incorrect
```

However, this is not the correct spot. For example, if numb[1] and numb[2] swap, but numb[2] and numb[3] don't, swapped should remain at **true** to indicate the swap on this pass. We want swapped to be **false** only if an entire pass through the inner loop does not produce a swap. This suggests setting swapped to **false** between the two loops.

THE bubblesort() FUNCTION

Here is the complete version of the bubblesort( ) function:

```
// ...
void bubblesort(int numb[], int n)
{
    int temp;
    bool swapped;

    do {
        swapped = false;
        for (int pos = 0; pos < n - 1; pos++)
            if (numb[pos] > numb[pos + 1]) {
                // swap the values
                temp = numb[pos];
                numb[pos] = numb[pos + 1];
```

```
                    numb[pos + 1] = temp;
                    swapped = true;
                }
        } while (swapped);
        return;
    }
```

PROGRAM TRACE Let's trace the function on the set of values we used in Example 9-3: <u>numb</u> = 4 7 11 15 20 13 (<u>n</u> = 6).

♦ The **do-while** loop starts, and <u>swapped</u> is set to **false**.

♦ The **for** loop starts, and <u>pos</u> is initialized to 0, which is less than the limiting value of <u>n − 1</u>.

♦ The first comparison is <u>numb[0]</u> to <u>numb[1]</u>. Since 4 > 7 is false, we do nothing.

♦ Then <u>pos</u> increments to 1, and we compare position 1 (which holds 7) to position 2 (which holds 11). Once again they are in order already.

♦ We compare positions 2 and 3, and then positions 3 and 4, without change.

♦ Then <u>pos</u> increments to 4, and we compare position 4 (which holds 20) and position 5 (which holds 13). They swap places, and we also set <u>swapped</u> to **true**, indicating a swap was made.

♦ Next <u>pos</u> increments to 5, but now the condition (<u>pos</u> < <u>n − 1</u>) is false, and we fall out of the **for** loop.

♦ Then we test the **while** condition. Since <u>swapped</u> is **true**, the condition is true, and the body of the **while** loop is executed again. The array now holds the following values: 4 7 11 15 13 20.

♦ On the second pass, <u>swapped</u> is set to **false**, and the **for** loop starts again with <u>pos</u> set to 0.

♦ We compare positions 0 and 1, 1 and 2, 2 and 3, all without a swap taking place.

♦ We compare position 3 (which holds 15) to position 4 (which holds 13). They swap places, and <u>swapped</u> is set to **true**.

♦ Then we compare position 4 (which holds 15) to position 5 (which holds 20). They do not swap.

♦ Next <u>pos</u> increments to 5, and we fall out of the **for** loop.

♦ When we test the condition at the bottom of the **do-while** loop, it is true since there was a swap on the last pass. The array now holds the following values: 4 7 11 13 15 20. This happens to be in sorted order, but we must have another pass through the **do-while** loop to verify that.

♦ In the new pass, <u>swapped</u> is set to **false**, and the **for** loop starts with <u>pos</u> set to 0.

♦ We compare positions 0 and 1, 1 and 2, 2 and 3, 3 and 4, 4 and 5 without any swaps taking place. Eventually, <u>pos</u> increments to 5, and we fall out of the **for** loop.

♦ The condition at the bottom of the **do-while** loop is now false since <u>swapped</u> is still **false**. Therefore, the **do-while** loop ends, and the sort is complete.

✋ **CAUTION** In both the linear and the bubble sort, we do not swap two elements if they are equal, but only if the first is greater than the second. In the linear sort, this is done for efficiency. However, in the bubble sort, it is crucial not to swap adjacent elements that are equal. (See Exercise 8 for details.)

DISSECTING THE bubblesort() FUNCTION

This function contains two loops, which serve very different purposes. The outer or **do-while** loop forces us to repeat the **for** loop as long as swaps of adjacent elements are made. The inner or **for** loop lets us compare all pairs of adjacent elements in the <u>numb</u> array. The body of the **for** loop is done exactly <u>n − 1</u> times for each execution of the outer loop. The outer loop is repeated an unknown number of times [see Exercise 9(b)] until <u>swapped</u> is 0. When this occurs, it means that an entire pass through the array has not found two adjacent elements out of order so the array must be sorted.

SELF-CHECK 9-3

1. Trace the pseudocode for the bubble sort algorithm on the following set of numbers: 20 0 −2 15 (<u>n</u> = 4).

2. Is it possible to initialize <u>swapped</u> to 0 as part of the **for** loop header? If yes, show how to do it. If no, explain why it is not possible.

3. Why must the **while** condition controlling the outer loop eventually become **false**? That is, why must there be a pass where no swap takes place?

SECTION 4   SEARCH TECHNIQUES: LINEAR SEARCH

One of the most common ways to take advantage of the speed and power of a computer is to search through a list. This section examines the most basic technique to do this, called a linear or sequential search.

A SIMPLE SEARCHING PROBLEM

Assume we are given an initial list of <u>n</u> numbers. Then we receive a series of new numbers, which are read in one at a time. We want to see if each number in the new series occurs in the original list. If it does, we want to print its position. If it doesn't, we want to print a message saying it was not found. For example, the original list contains five numbers: 4 99 2 90 16. The first new number is 90, and the second is 7. The number 90 is found in position 3 of the original list; the number 7 is not found.

    The first simplification we make is to concentrate on searching for a single item at a time instead of worrying about the entire set of new values. We write a function to search a list of numbers and determine the location of a single new value. (Later we use this function as part of Program 9.)

    We start by talking about a searching method that does not require a sorted list. In Section 9, we present an algorithm which takes advantage of searching a list that is already sorted. However, it is not always more efficient to sort the list before starting to search. For example, if we are searching for only one or two items, it is not worthwhile to sort the list.

    On the other hand, if we are searching hundreds, thousands, or even millions of times, it is more efficient if the list is sorted before the search. Consider how often people look up numbers in the phone book.

ALGORITHM FOR THE LINEAR OR SELECTION SORT

Our first searching technique uses an algorithm called the **linear** or **sequential search**. We start with an array of numbers called <u>numb</u>, a new integer to locate in the array, called <u>newnumber</u>, and the number of elements to search in the array, called <u>n</u>. The algorithm determines the position of <u>newnumber</u> within the array <u>numb</u>.

    The algorithm simply compares <u>newnumber</u> to each element of the array. If they are equal, it returns the position of the element. If it does not find <u>newnumber</u>, it signals that fact.

Here is a more formal version of the algorithm with these variable names:

Algorithm for the Linear Search

♦ *Compare* newnumber *to each element in the* numb *array.*

♦ *If a particular element is equal to* newnumber, *return the position of that element.*

♦ *If a particular element is not equal to* newnumber, *try the next element.*

♦ *If no element is equal to* newnumber, *return a failure signal.*

As usual, we translate the algorithm into pseudocode before writing a function to do the search. Looking at the algorithm, we see an obvious loop to go through all positions in the array. In this loop, we compare <u>newnumber</u> to the element in the array at that position. Here is the algorithm rewritten in pseudocode:

Pseudocode for the Linear Search

> *for each position in the* numb *array*
> > *compare the element in that position to* newnumber
> > *if they are equal*
> > > *return the position in the array*
> > *if no element is equal to* newnumber,
> > > *return a failure signal*

THE FUNCTION linearsearch( )

Now we are ready to write a function, called <u>linearsearch( )</u>, which translates the algorithm into C++. The function receives the following parameters: <u>numb</u>, <u>n</u>, and <u>newnumber</u>. There is an obvious answer to return—the position of <u>newnumber</u> in the array—so we write <u>linearsearch( )</u> as a function that returns an integer value. Consider the five numbers at the start of this section: 4 99 2 90 16. If <u>linearsearch( )</u> is asked to locate 90, it returns 3. If it is asked to locate 7, it returns a signal that 7 does not occur. Any number which can't be an array position is a good signal; we can use −1.

Here are the function comment and header:

```
// Function linearsearch:
// Input:
//   numb: the array to search
//   n: the number of elements to search in the array
//   newnumber: the value to search for
// Process:
//   using a linear search, determines the position of
//   newnumber within the first n elements of numb
// Output:
//   returns the position of newnumber in the array;
//   returns -1 if newnumber is not found

int linearsearch(int numb[], int n, int newnumber)
```

The pseudocode translates naturally into a **for** loop, with each position from 0 to <u>n − 1</u> being tested for <u>newnumber</u>. If the value in the array at a particular position matches <u>newnumber</u>, we return that position, terminating the **for** loop and the function. If the **for** loop does not terminate prematurely, the new value has not been found, and the function returns −1 to signal failure. Because the entries are checked one after another, this method is called a linear or sequential search.

Assume that <u>newnumber</u> is somewhere in the array. Regardless of whether it is found in the first or last position, or somewhere in between, the ***return position*** statement terminates the function, sending back the position of <u>newnumber</u>. However, if <u>newnumber</u> is not found in the array, then ***return −1*** terminates the function. Here is the body of the function:

```
{
    for (int position = 0; position < n; position++)
        if (numb[position] == newnumber)
            return position;
    return -1;
}
```

We are assuming that each value occurs just once in the array <u>numb</u> (or if it occurs several times, we are interested only in the first one). This means that once a match has been found, it is not necessary to search any further. It is possible to modify the search so that it finds all occurrences.

PROGRAM TRACE Let's trace the two examples from earlier in this section. Here are the parameters to the function: the array <u>numb</u> holds 4 99 2 90 16, <u>n</u> is 5, and we are searching for 90 as <u>newnumber</u>.

♦ Inside the function, the **for** loop compares 90 to each element in the array, for <u>position</u> equal to 0, 1, …

♦ A match is found at the fourth element in the array with <u>position</u> equal to 3.

♦ This value is returned to the calling program, and the function terminates.

Assume now that <u>newnumber</u> is 7.

♦ In the function, the entire **for** loop, from 0 to $n-1$, is processed without finding a match.

♦ After the loop ends, the function returns −1 to the calling program. If the loop ends without executing the ***return position*** statement, it must be because <u>newnumber</u> has not been found.

STYLE WORKSHOP Note that the **return** statement in the middle of the loop terminates both the loop and the function. As an alternative, we can use a **break** statement (see Chapter 6, Section 8) to get out of the loop, then modify the single **return** statement at the end of the loop to return the appropriate value (see Exercise 40).

ANALYZING THE LINEAR SEARCH ALGORITHM

The algorithm for the linear search seems efficient since each entry in the array of numbers is checked at most one time per new number. If nothing is known about the original array (the array is not sorted, and all elements are equally likely to be selected), this search method is as good as any other. However, in many situations, we know that the array is in sorted order. In that case, the linear search is extremely inefficient. To determine why, we must analyze the behavior of the linear search algorithm.

Average Behavior of the Linear Search Algorithm

Assume we have 100 elements in an array of integers and all elements are equally likely to be selected.

◆ On the average, it takes approximately 50 comparisons to find the position of a new number if it is already in the array. It actually takes anywhere from 1 to 100 comparisons, depending on the position of the number.

◆ If the new number is not in the array, we have to search all 100 elements to find out.

Now assume we have 1000 entries in the array (of course, the constant definition has to change to accommodate an array this size).

◆ An average of 500 comparisons is required to find an entry if it is present.

◆ A thousand comparisons are necessary to verify that an entry is not present.

Finally, assume we have an array of n numbers.

◆ On the average, to find the position of a given number takes $n / 2$ comparisons.

◆ n comparisons are needed to show that a number is not there.

These results are tabulated in Table 9-1.

HIGHLIGHTS

The key observation about the linear search is that the average number of comparisons required remains the same, regardless of how the values are ordered in the array.

ACCELERATED REJECTION IN A SORTED LIST

As we have already noted, it is usually not more efficient to sort a list before a search; but, if the list has already been sorted, this extra information can increase the efficiency of the search. If the array is sorted, one improvement is to accelerate the rejection process. As soon as the number being checked is larger than the new number, we can exit the search loop and return a signal that the new number is not in the list without checking the rest of the array. (A more detailed discussion of this method, called the **accelerated rejection** method, is found in exercises 26 and 33.)

SELF-CHECK 9-4

1. Why doesn't the linearsearch( ) function return 0 if an item is not found in the array?

2. Why must the linearsearch( ) function return an integer if an item is not found, rather than some other type of answer?

3. Trace the linear search algorithm and function on the following lists and new values to be located:

    a. list: 7 2 4 −2 0 8 15 34 6   new values: 4 and then 1

    b. list: 10 20 30 ... 100   new values: 5 and then 20

TABLE 9-1   Analysis of the Linear Search Algorithm

Average number of tries using linear search to:

n	Locate	Reject
7	4	7
100	50	100
1,000	500	1,000
1,000,000	500,000	1,000,000

A FUNCTION TO LOCATE A SERIES OF VALUES

LOCATING A SERIES OF NEW VALUES

In the original statement of Problem 9, we specified a series of items whose location in the array should be determined. However, to simplify our discussion in Section 4, we wrote a function, linearsearch( ), to find the position of a single item in the array. Now we show how to use that function together with a new one to locate the position in an array of each item in a series.

CAUTION In Program 9, the array is sorted by the time we start to locate new values. However, we do not take advantage of that fact in writing this new function.

The new function, which we call locatevalues( ), is given two parameters, the array numb and n, the size of the array. It asks the user to type in a new number whose position in the array is to be found. Then it calls linearsearch( ), sending it the three required parameters: the array, its size, and the new number to be located. When linearsearch( ) returns with an answer, the locatevalues( ) function prints an appropriate message. Then it asks the user whether to continue.

In Chapter 6, we had a similar problem when we classified month/day combinations. In that chapter, we decided to use a loop with a question at the bottom asking the user whether to continue. We use a similar structure in the locatevalues( ) function. Here is a pseudocode version of the function:

repeat the following as long as the user wants to continue:
    ask the user to type in a value for newnumber
    call linearsearch( ) *to find the position of* newnumber *in the array*
    print the position
    ask whether the user wants to continue

Recall that we translated this structure into a **do-while** loop. Here is the next version of the pseudocode, showing this loop structure and making the input more specific:

```
do {
    cout << "Please enter a number to locate in the array";
    cin >> newnumber;
    call linearsearch() to locate newnumber in the numb array
    print the answer returned by linearsearch
    cout << "do you want to continue (y/n)?";
    cin >> answer;
} while (answer != 'n');
```

Although this is not quite C++ code, it is close. At this point, we can write the function.

THE FUNCTION locatevalues( )

First, we give the function header and comment for locatevalues( ). Unlike linearsearch( ), this function does not return a value.

```
// Function locatevalues:
// Input:
//    two input parameters
//       numb: an array of integers
//       n: the size of the array
//    also reads in a series of new values one by one
```

```
// Process:
//    for each new value, calls the function linearsearch()
//    to find the location of each new value in the numb array
// Output:
//    prints a message giving the location of each new value
void locatevalues(int numb[], int n)
```

Now we translate the remaining pseudocode into C++. The function linearsearch( ) returns an integer value, which we store in a local variable called location. Therefore, the call from locatevalues( ) to the function linearsearch( ) looks like this:

```
location = linearsearch(numb,n,newnumber);
```

We shouldn't simply print the value stored in location. If the linearsearch( ) function does not find newnumber, it returns −1. What happens if we use the following statements?

```
location = linearsearch(numb,n,newnumber);
cout << newnumber << " is located in position " << location << endl;
```

If we print the value returned directly and newnumber is not found, it will certainly look awkward to have a message saying newnumber is located in position −1. To fix this problem, we ask a question to determine the correct way to phrase the message describing the position of newnumber. This question appears in the final version.

In addition, to make the program easier to use, we allow the user to type either *N* or *n* in response to the prompt at the end of the loop. This is taken care of by the call to the function toupper( ) (see Chapter 8, Section 6). Once the **do-while** loop ends, nothing else is necessary so the function also ends. Here is the entire locatevalues( ) function:

```
// ...
int locatevalues(int numb[], int n)
{
    int newnumber;
    int location;
    char answer;
    do {
        cout << "Please enter a number to locate in the array";
        cin >> newnumber;
        location = linearsearch(numb,n,newnumber);
        if (location >= 0)
            cout << newnumber << " is located in position "
                << location << endl;
        else
            cout << newnumber << " does not occur" << endl;
        cout << "do you want to continue (y/n)?";
        cin >> answer;
    }  while (toupper(answer) != 'N');
    return;
}
```

Since we have already traced the linearsearch( ) function, it is easy to trace locatevalues( ). Let's assume that the array holds the same values (4 99 2 90 16), and the series of values to be located consists of 90 and 7.

PROGRAM TRACE

♦ The underlined locatevalues( ) function asks the user to type in a value for newnumber. The user enters 90.

♦ This value is sent to linearsearch( ), together with the array numb and the value of n.

♦ In this case, linearsearch( ) returns the value 3 to the function locatevalues( ), and this is stored in location.

♦ The **if** statement determines that this is an actual position, and the following message is printed:

```
90 occurs at position 3
```

♦ The user is asked whether to continue, and the user types in y (or Y). The **while** condition is true, and the **do-while** loop repeats the series of instructions.

♦ The user is asked for a new value to locate, and the user types in 7 as the value for newnumber.

♦ This value is sent to linearsearch( ) (together with the same values for numb and n).

♦ The linearsearch( ) function sends back −1 to indicate that 7 does not occur in the array.

♦ The **if** statement determines that this is not an actual position so the following message is printed:

```
7 does not occur in the array
```

♦ The user is asked whether to continue and types in n (or N). The **do-while** loop terminates since the **while** condition is false.

♦ The locatevalues( ) function returns to the program which called it.

SELF-CHECK 9-5

1. What is the smallest number of new values that can be searched for in Program 9? What is the largest number?

2. Trace the locatevalues( ) function on the following lists and new values to be located:

   a. list: 7 2 4 −2 0 8 15 34 6   new values: 4 1 7 15 6 7 5
   b. list: 10 20 30 ... 100   new values: 5 20 0 60 −11

SECTION 6 **PSEUDOCODE FOR PROGRAM 9: BOTTOM-UP APPROACH**

In this brief section, we give a pseudocode solution to Problem 9, using a bottom-up approach. In the next section, we translate this pseudocode into a complete program.

PSEUDOCODE FOR THE MAIN PROGRAM

From the statement of the problem, it is easy to give a first version of the pseudocode for Program 9. As usual, we write the program so that each task is handled by a function: one to read in the data, one to print the data, one to sort, etc. The main program continues to use the variable names n and numb.
Here is the pseudocode:

call a function readdata( ) *to read* n, *then read* n *numbers into an array* numb
call a function printarray( ) *to print the array in the original order*
call a function linearsort( ) *to sort the array into ascending order*
call a function printarray( ) *to print the array in sorted order*
call a function locatevalues( ) *to locate the position of a series of new values in array* numb

The first two tasks of the main program are handled by functions which read in the set of data and print an array. Then we call the linearsort( ) function from Section 2 to sort the array. This is followed by another call to printarray( ) to print the newly sorted array. Finally, we call the function locatevalues( ) from Section 5 (which calls linearsearch( ) from Section 4). In the pseudocode, the linearsort( ) function is called to perform the sort. We could instead use the bubblesort( ) function from Section 3.

Notice that the same function, printarray( ), prints both the original and the sorted array. The main program differentiates between these two by printing a message before it calls the function to print the numbers stored in the array. Also notice that the function readarray( ) performs a task identical to the one in Program 7. Therefore, we can reuse this function when we put everything together for Program 9.

DIVISION INTO MODULES; BOTTOM-UP APPROACH

Problem 9 divides up easily into a series of steps. However, the approach we use in attacking this problem differs from the top-down design. We consider each of the steps to be a separate subproblem for which we create a function. After writing the functions, we devise a main program to call them. This method of attacking a problem is called a **bottom-up approach**.

COMPARISON TO TOP-DOWN DESIGN

This approach is not the same as the top-down method we introduced in Chapter 4 and have used since then. With the top-down approach, we would start by planning the main program. As we developed the main program, we would recognize distinct tasks to be performed by functions. Once the plan for the main program was complete, we would write the individual modules to perform these tasks. The bottom-up method starts with the modules (functions), then writes a main program to put the pieces together. Usually, this approach is followed when it is clear in advance that the overall task divides up into a series of well-defined subtasks which can become functions. However, the top-down approach is more flexible and minimizes the possibility of confusion in communication between the main program and the functions (e.g., in parameter transmission).

Most programmers use a combination of the two techniques. For example, a programmer may start by dividing the job into a series of tasks, then work on some simple modules, then link them together. In any case, the bottom-up method offers another way of attacking a problem.

SELF-CHECK 9-6

1. Is it possible to use two separate print functions, one to print the original and one to print the sorted array? Does it make sense to do this?
2. Why doesn't the main program call linearsearch( )?
3. In a bottom-up design, what is the last step worked on? In a top-down approach, what is the last step?

 SECTION 7   **PROGRAM 9**

In this section, we combine the pseudocode from Section 6 with the individual functions from earlier sections to write a complete C++ program to solve Problem 9.

THE MAIN PROGRAM

Let's start with the initial portion of the main program, up to the declaration of variables.

```
// Program prog9.cpp:
// sorting using the linear sort algorithm
// searching using the linear search algorithm
#include <iostream>
using namespace std;
int main()
{
    const int SIZE = 50;
    int numb[SIZE];
    int n;
```

In the first sections of this chapter, we examined the sorting phase of Problem 9. In the last two sections, we handled the searching phase. As a last step, we write the easy parts of the program: the calls to the functions which read in the original data, sort and search the array, and print both the original and the sorted array.

The function linearsort( ) was given in Section 2, the function locatevalues( ) appeared in Section 6, and linearsearch( ) was in Section 5. Another function we need is readdata( ), to read a set of data into an array and return its size. This function was used in Chapter 7, and we will adapt it for Program 9. (The original version printed the data read in; the new version will not since we now have a separate function to print.) The call from the main program to readdata( ) is similar to the one used earlier. It looks like this:

```
readdata(numb,n);
```

Then we need a function printarray( ) to print a set of data stored in an array. The call to printarray( ) is preceded by a message printed by the main program. This message displays a heading above the printed array. By varying the message, we can print appropriate headings for both the original data and the sorted array. Here is the first call to printarray( ), which prints the original set of data:

```
cout << "original data" << endl << endl;
printarray(numb,n);
```

For the call to linearsort( ), we use the following:

```
linearsort(numb,n);
```

The second call to printarray( ), after the array has been sorted, looks like this:

```
cout << endl << "sorted array" << endl << endl;
printarray(numb,n);
```

Then the main program calls locatevalues( ) to read in the new set of values to locate within the array.

```
locatevalues(numb,n);
```

This completes the body of the main program. The only things left to include are the prototypes and definitions for all the functions. These are given below with the entire program.

COMPLETE PROGRAM 9

PROGRAM LISTING

```cpp
// Program prog9.cpp:
// sorting using the linear sort algorithm
// searching using the linear search algorithm
#include <iostream>
using namespace std;
void linearsort(int [], int);
void readdata(int [],int &);
void printarray(int [], int);
int linearsearch(int [], int, int);
void locatevalues(int [], int);

int main()
{
    const int SIZE = 50;
    int numb[SIZE];
    int n;

    readdata(numb,n);                          // read in the data

    cout << "original data" << endl << endl;
    printarray(numb,n);                        // print the original array

    linearsort(numb,n);                        // sort the array

    cout << endl << endl << "sorted array" << endl << endl;
    printarray(numb,n);                        // print the sorted array

    locatevalues(numb,n);
    return 0;
}


// Function readdata:
// Input:
//    numb: the array to fill
// Process:
//    reads parameter value into n and reads
//    that many elements into the numb array
// Output:
//    returns n and stores values in array numb
void readdata(int numb[], int &n)
{
    cout << "enter the number of elements in the array";
    cin >> n;
    for (int i = 0; i < n; i++) {
        cout << "enter a number to be put into the array";
        cin >> numb[i];
    }
    return;
}
```

```
// Function printarray:
// Input:
//     numb: the array to print
//     n: the number of elements to print
// Process:
//     prints out the n elements in the numb array
// Output:
//     prints array numb
void printarray(int numb[], int n)
{
    for (int i = 0; i < n; i++)
        cout << numb[i] << endl;
    return;
}

// Function linearsort:
// Input:
//     numb: the array to sort
//     n: the number of elements to sort in the array
// Process:
//     linear sorts into ascending order
//     the first n values of the numb array
// Output:
//     function modifies array numb
void linearsort(int numb[], int n)
{
    int temp;

    for (int pass = 0; pass < n - 1; pass++)
        for (int cand = pass + 1; cand < n; cand++)
            if (numb[pass] > numb[cand]) {
                temp = numb[pass];
                numb[pass] = numb[cand];
                numb[cand] = temp;
            }
    return;
}

// Function locatevalues:
// Input:
//     two input parameters
//        numb: an array of integers
//        n: the size of the array
//     also reads in a series of new values one by one
// Process:
//     for each new value, calls the function linearsearch
//     to find the location of each new value in the numb array
// Output:
//     prints a message giving the location of each new value
void locatevalues(int numb[], int n)
{
```

```
    int  newnumber;
    int  location;
    char answer;

    do  {
        cout << "Please enter a number to locate in the array";
        cin >> newnumber;
        location = linearsearch(numb,n,newnumber);
        if (location >= 0)
            cout << newnumber << " occurs at position "
                << location;
      else
            cout << newnumber << " does not occur";
        cout << "do you want to continue (y/n)?";
        cin >> answer;
    } while (toupper(answer) != 'N');
  return;
}

// Function linearsearch:
// Input:
//    numb: the array to search
//    n: the number of elements to search in the array
//    newnumber: the value to search for
// Process:
//    using a linear search, determines the position of
//    newnumber within the first n elements of numb
// Output:
//    returns the position of newnumber in the array;
//    returns -1 if newnumber is not found
int linearsearch(int numb[], int n, int newnumber)
{
    for (int position = 0; position < n; position++)
        if (numb[position] == newnumber)
            return position;
    return -1;
}
```

This completes Program 9.

We have written Program 9 to read in the original set of data interactively and send output to the screen. You can easily revise the program to read some of the data from an external file or through redirection (see Chapter 3), and send the output to the screen, the printer, or an external file (see Exercise 24).

SELF-CHECK 9-7

1. Make up a set of data with five values (n is 5), plus some new values to be located, and trace Program 9.

2. Show how to use the function bubblesort( ) in Program 9.

ENRICHMENT: OTHER POINTS ON SORTING

In this section, we discuss more on sorting, including a function to interchange two array elements.

SORTING INTO DESCENDING ORDER; ALLOWING REPEATED ELEMENTS

First, let's learn how to sort numbers into descending instead of ascending order. We simply replace the condition on the left (or the corresponding line in a bubble sort) by the opposite condition on the right:

replace   **by**

```
if (numb[pass] > numb[cand])         if (numb[pass] < numb[cand])
        . . .                                   . . .
```

That's it! Try an example to see that this works.

We have mentioned that two equal numbers in a list do not cause a problem; for example, the values 14 125 11 4 14 21 are sorted into 4 11 14 14 21 125. This is true because when the repeated elements are compared, they do not swap places, but they eventually end up in adjacent positions.

SORTING NONINTEGER VALUES; ASCII CODES

Both sorting programs assume that the <u>numb</u> array holds integers. To sort real numbers, the only change is a trivial one. The declarations for <u>numb</u> and <u>temp</u>(why is <u>temp</u> important?) have to be modified, but nothing else in the body of the function is altered.

For example, in the <u>bubblesort( )</u> function, to sort values of type **double**, we use the following header and declaration of local variables (the array is still called <u>numb</u>):

```
void bubblesort(double numb[], int n)
{
    bool swapped;
    double temp;
```

In the rest of the program, only the function prototype and the main program's declaration of the array change. Here is the new function prototype:

```
void bubblesort(double [], int n);
```

Finally, here is the new declaration for the array in the main program:

```
double numb[SIZE];
```

Of course, the other functions, including <u>readdata( )</u>, <u>printarray( )</u>, etc., also have to be modified.

What about sorting variables of type **char**, for example, putting letters into alphabetical order? Even this is quite simple. As we note in Chapter 8, Section 2, each individual character (including digits, letters, punctuation, etc.) is represented in a computer by a number, called its **ASCII code** (see the Appendix). The numbers are selected so that the one for a is less than the one for b, and so on. (This should be clear if you understand how types **char** and **int** are related; see Chapter 2, Section 5.) If <u>c1</u> and <u>c2</u> are two characters, when we ask, "Is <u>c1</u> > <u>c2</u>?", the computer interprets this as "Is the number for <u>c1</u> greater than the one for <u>c2</u>?" It is not necessary to explain that a < b because this is automatically built into the system. Therefore, our two sorting methods work on any type of data.

SORTING AN ARRAY OF STRINGS

And what about sorting an array of strings, for example, putting names into alphabetical order? (If you have not yet learned about strings, read Chapter 8 before reading this subsection.) To mention just one problem: In numerical order, any three-digit number (112) is larger than a two-digit number (98), but in alphabetical order some three-letter words (like "and") come before two-letter ones (like "me"). Fortunately, we don't have to explain this to the computer.

Modifying our original function to sort strings just consists of changing the declarations. To clarify things, let's change the name of the array we are sorting from underline numb to underline name. The array underline name is an array of strings. In a function header, the parameter for this array is represented by the following:

```
string name[]                          // name is an array of strings
```

Recall the local variable underline temp, used to hold a value as we swap two array elements. It must also have type **string**.

Once we have changed the declarations, we can give the function header and declaration of local variables for a function to sort strings. (We use the underline linearsort( ) function, rather than the underline bubblesort( ) function, but this is not crucial.)

```
void linearsort(string name[], int n)
{
    string temp;
```

Here is the body of the function underline linearsort( ) to sort strings; except for the declarations, it is the same as sorting integers or doubles:

```
if (name[pass] > name[cand]) {
    // statements to interchange the two strings
    temp = name[pass];
    name[pass] = name[cand];
    name[cand] = temp;
}
```

FUNCTION linearsort( ) TO SORT AN ARRAY OF STRINGS

Now we rewrite the entire function to sort an array of strings using a linear sort.

```
// ...
void linearsort(string name[], int n)
{
    string temp;

    for (int pass = 0; pass < n - 1; pass++)
        for (int cand = pass + 1; cand < n; cand++)
            if (name[pass] > name[cand]) {
                // statements to interchange the two strings
                temp = name[pass];
                name[pass] = name[cand];
                name[cand] = temp;
            }
    return;
}
```

This sort function will sort whatever strings it receives in the array underline name. Note, however, that the main program uses underline cin and, unless modified, will read in only strings without spaces. To read in strings that include spaces, you will have to modify not only the variables in the main program, but also the function that reads in the data, so that it uses underline getline( ).

ALPHABETIZING STRINGS

When two strings are compared, they are matched character by character, starting at the left, using their ASCII codes (as explained above). For example, the string "and" starts with the character 'a', and "me" starts with 'm'. Since 'a' is before 'm' in the alphabet, it is also numerically less than 'm'; therefore, "and" is alphabetized before "me". However, if we compare "and" with "aid", 'a' has the same value as 'a', and the computer moves to the next character; 'i' is numerically less than 'n', so "aid" is less than "and".

Here are some things to remember about alphabetizing strings:

◆ The ASCII code for 'a' is less than that for 'b' which is less than 'c'... up to 'z'. This pattern is also true for capitals: 'A' < 'B' < 'C' ... < 'Z'.

◆ However, the values for capitals are all less than those for lowercase letters, so 'A' through 'Z' are all less than 'a'.

◆ A blank is assigned a value which is less than any printable character.

◆ If two strings are the same up to the end of one string, but the other string has more characters or blanks at the end (for example, "sunny" or "sun" compared to "sun"), the longer string is greater, because any character is greater than nothing.

EXAMPLE 9-5 Here are some examples of comparing strings and characters:

Case	Reason
'a' < 'b' is true	'a' < 'b'
'Z' < 'a' is true	'Z' < 'a'
"bob" > "Bob"	'b' > 'B'
"ccc" > "cc"	"ccc" **is longer than** "cc"
"an" > "an"	"an" **is longer than** "an"
"an" > " Bob"	' ' (before 'B') < 'a'
"an" == "an"	**the strings are identical**

A FUNCTION TO INTERCHANGE TWO ARRAY ELEMENTS

In Section 2, when we wrote the linearsort( ) function, we interchanged the values of two array elements by writing three assignment statements. To do this, we used a technique from Chapter 5, Section 5. But in Chapter 5, we also gave a function called swap( ) to perform a swap of two values. Now we'll see how to use the swap( ) function in Program 9.

Here is the swap( ) function from Chapter 5:

```
// Function swap
// Input:
//   a and b: references to two integer values
// Process:
//   interchange a and b
// Output:
//   values have been interchanged
void swap(int &a, int &b)
```

```
{
    int temp;

    temp = a;
    a = b;
    b = temp;
    return;
}
```

USING swap( ) IN linearsort( )

Instead of three assignment statements to interchange the values of the two array elements, the linearsort( ) function uses the following call to swap( ):

```
swap(numb[pass],numb[cand]);
```

Let's rewrite the linearsort( ) function, showing the call to swap( ) in context:

```
//...
void linearsort(int numb[], int n)
{
    int pass,cand;
    for (pass = 0; pass < n - 1; pass++)
        for (cand = pass + 1; cand < n; cand++)
            if (numb[pass] > numb[cand])
                swap(numb[pass],numb[cand]);
    return;
}
```

Note that we can drop the declaration of the local variable temp, and we no longer need a compound statement after the **if** condition. The swap( ) function also works with the bubblesort( ) function. If you wish, you can use an appropriate version of linearsort( ) or bubblesort( ) with the function swap( ) in Program 9.

CAUTION This version of swap( ) works only if we want to exchange integers, not values of a different type. A separate version of swap( ) is needed to exchange characters or doubles.

In Chapter 10, we discuss a using a class to store related items which do not have the same data type—for example, the name, age, and occupation of a person. To sort an array of these structures based on the name, it is necessary to exchange the additional information on age and occupation. Exercises 45 and 46 discuss this idea, together with a suggestion on using a version of swap( ) to interchange the names.

SELF-CHECK 9-8

1. Trace the linear sort (either algorithm or function) on the following set of data: 50.1 6.3 4.4 50.1 6.3 4.4 ($\underline{n} = 6$).

2. In the version of linearsort( ) which uses the function swap( ), why isn't it necessary to declare a local variable temp?

3. Show how the bubblesort( ) function can use swap( ). (Don't forget the variable swapped.)

SECTION 9   ENRICHMENT: BINARY SEARCH

In this section, we provide a searching algorithm which is much better than the sequential search. However, it can be used only if the array is already sorted. The new algorithm is called a binary search.

THE BINARY SEARCH METHOD

The original linear search algorithm and its accelerated rejection version from Section 4 are hopelessly inefficient for searching a long list. For example, if you used either method to look up a name in the telephone directory of a large city with perhaps 1,000,000 names, it would take an incredibly long time. Without even realizing it, most people probably use a variant of the **binary search** method. The basic idea is not to do an element-by-element linear search but make better and better "guesses" as to where the new element must be.

Assume that we have a sorted array called <u>numb</u>; the variable <u>n</u> holds the number of elements in the array; we are looking for the position of <u>newnumber</u>. At the beginning, the entire array from the lowest position (0) to the highest (<u>n – 1</u>) must be searched. We start by "guessing" that <u>newnumber</u> occurs halfway between the low and high elements; we test whether <u>newnumber</u> is equal to the array element at this position. For example, in Figure 9-6, we first guess that <u>newnumber</u> occurs at position 3, which is halfway between 0 and 6 (assume that <u>newnumber</u> is 50).

Note the following facts for developing the binary search algorithm:

♦ If the array element in the tested position is equal to <u>newnumber</u>, the search is over since <u>newnumber</u> has been found.

♦ If the array element in the tested position is larger than <u>newnumber</u>, all elements after it must also be larger and can be ignored. Thus, if <u>newnumber</u> is in the array, it must lie in the portion between the first element and the tested one, and this is the section we should search further.

♦ Similarly, if the array element in the tested position is smaller than <u>newnumber</u>, all elements before it can be ignored; the array should be searched from the element after it to the end.

The binary search then repeats the same process: Make guesses and test the value at the position halfway between the low and high elements until <u>newnumber</u> is located. This idea of halving explains the name of the method: binary search.

Before we write this formally as an algorithm, let's look at some examples.

FIGURE 9-6   First Step of the Binary Search Algorithm to Locate a New Value

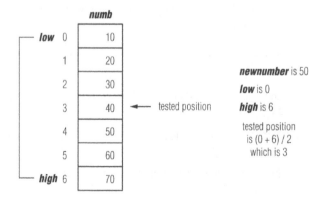

FIGURE 9-7   Using the Binary Search Algorithm to Locate a New Value

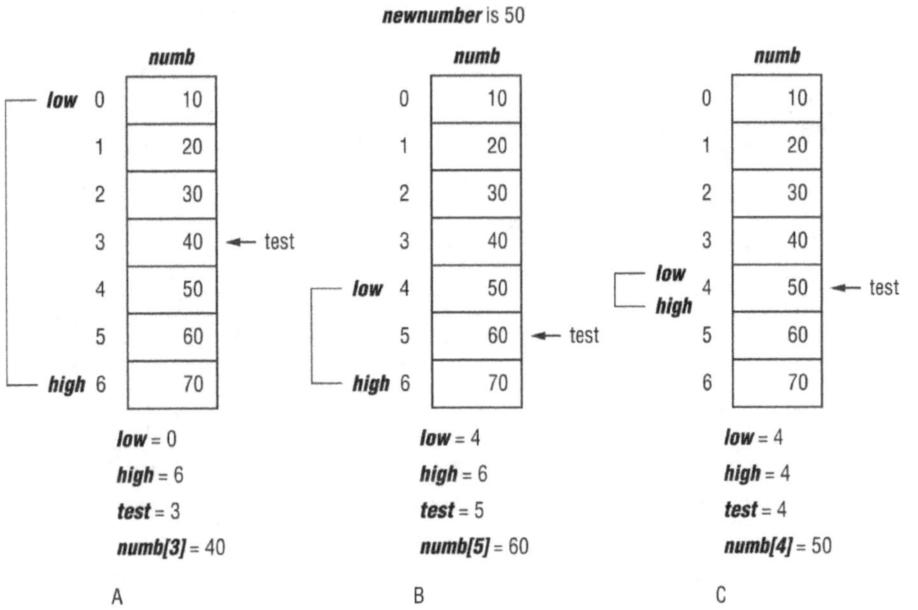

EXAMPLE 9-6

Consider the array in Figure 9-7. Assume that the new number we are seeking is 50.

Figure 9-7A shows that initially the entire array, from a low of 0 to a high of 6, must be searched.

◆   The first position tested is 3. The element in position 3 is smaller than <u>newnumber</u> so the next pass of the algorithm is restricted to positions 4 to 6 of the array.

◆   The next test is position 5 (see Figure 9-7B). The number in position 5 is too large so the next pass is restricted to the range 4 to 4, which is just position 4.

◆   The third test is position 4 (see Figure 9-7C), and the item is found there.

Of course, it is possible that <u>newnumber</u> is not in the original array. The algorithm determines this when the range that must still be searched is empty. This occurs if we just had a pass where the high and low values to be searched are equal and <u>newnumber</u> is not there.

EXAMPLE 9-7

Consider the same array as Example 9-6, but assume that 15 is the value of <u>newnumber</u>.

Figure 9-8A shows that initially the entire array, from a low of 0 to a high of 6, must be searched.

◆   The first position tested is 3. The element in position 3 is larger than <u>newnumber</u> so the next pass of the algorithm is restricted to positions 0 to 2 of the array.

◆   The next test is position 1 (see Figure 9-8B). The number in position 1 is too large, so the next pass is restricted to the range 0 to 0, which is just position 0.

◆   The third test is position 0 (see Figure 9-8C), which has a value that is too small. Now the low value of the range shifts to 1, while the high value remains at 0.

◆   The low value is larger than the high value, which means that the range to be searched is empty, and 15 has not been located (see Figure 9-8D).

FIGURE 9-8   Using the Binary Search Algorithm to Determine
That a New Value Is Not in the Array

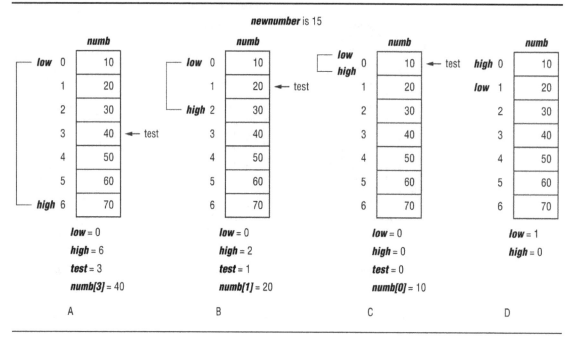

ALGORITHM FOR THE BINARY SEARCH

Let's formalize the binary search algorithm. Assume again that we have a sorted array called <u>numb</u> which has <u>n</u> elements; we are looking for the position of <u>newnumber</u>. Initially, the entire array, from <u>low</u> = 0 to <u>high</u> = <u>n</u> − 1, is to be searched. Here is the algorithm:

Algorithm for the Binary Search

♦   *Initialize* low *to 0 and* high *to* n − 1

♦   *Continue the following process as long as* newnumber *has not been found and* low *is less than or equal to* high.

♦   *Test whether the array element halfway between positions* low *and* high *is equal to* newnumber.

♦   *If the element is equal to* newnumber, *the search is successful.*

♦   *If the array element at the position tested is too large, change the value of* high *to one less than the tested position.*

♦   *If the array element at the position tested is too small, change the value of* low *to one more than the tested position.*

Now we translate the algorithm into pseudocode and write a function to do the binary search. The algorithm has a process which continues as long as <u>low</u> is less than or equal to <u>high</u>. For the pseudocode, we translate this into a loop. In this loop, we determine our next guess as to where <u>newnumber</u> occurs, then compare <u>newnumber</u> to the element in the array at that position. Depending upon the outcome, we either stop searching because we have found <u>newnumber</u> or adjust our search range by changing <u>low</u> or <u>high</u>. Here is the algorithm rewritten in pseudocode:

Pseudocode for the Binary Search

```
low = 0;
high = n – 1;
while (low <= high)
        look at the element halfway between positions  low and high
        if (the element in the tested position equals newnumber)
                return the position of newnumber
        else if (the element is larger than newnumber)
                high = the tested position – 1
        else
                low = the tested position + 1
```

FUNCTION FOR THE BINARY SEARCH

The function for the binary search method is a straightforward translation of the pseudocode. We continue to call the formal parameters numb, newnumber, and n to correspond with the names in linearsearch( ).

```
// Function binarysearch:
// Input:
//    numb: the array to search—the array must be sorted
//    n: the number of elements to search in the array
//    newnumber: the value to search for
// Process:
//    using a binary search, determines the position of
//    newnumber within the first n elements of numb
// Output:
//    returns the position (test) of newnumber in the array numb;
//    returns -1 if newnumber is not found
int binarysearch(int numb[], int n, int newnumber)
```

The function needs local variables to hold the low and high points for the searching range, and these are initialized to 0 and $n - 1$. In addition, the function needs another local variable to hold the guess as to where to look next for newnumber. We call this variable test. The declaration for these variables looks like this:

```
{
    int low,high,test;
```

This is followed by a loop. In this case, a **while** loop seems most appropriate. The **while** loop is controlled by the relative values of high and low. Here is the loop header:

```
low = 0;
high = n - 1;
while (low <= high)
```

Inside the body of the **while** loop, test holds the current guess as to where to look within the array. Initially, it is the midpoint of the entire array, but later test is the midpoint of the section of the array which must still be searched. To assign test a value that is midway between high and low, use integer division on the sum of high and low:

```
while (low <= high) {
        test = (low + high) / 2;
```

This gives <u>test</u> an integer value, appropriate for a subscript of the <u>numb</u> array. Once we have calculated the midpoint of the section of the array being searched, a nested **if** statement compares the value in position <u>test</u> with <u>newnumber</u>.

```
while (low <= high) {
    test = (low + high) / 2;
    if (numb[test] == newnumber)
        return test;                    // newnumber found at test
    else if (numb[test] > newnumber)
        high = test - 1;                // adjust range
    else
        low = test + 1;
}
```

When we terminate the **while** loop, we return −1 (a failure signal), then end the function.

```
    return -1;
}
```

THE FUNCTION BINARYSEARCH( )

Let's put the whole thing together:

```
// ...
int binarysearch(int numb[], int n, int newnumber)
{
    int low,high,test;

    low = 0;
    high = n - 1;
    while (low <= high) {
        test = (low + high) / 2;
        if (numb[test] == newnumber)
            return test;                    // newnumber found at test
        else if (numb[test] > newnumber)
            high = test - 1;                // adjust range
        else
            low = test + 1;
    }
    return -1;                               // newnumber not found
}
```

USING A BINARY SEARCH IN PROGRAM 9

Once we have the <u>binarysearch( )</u> function, we can use it in Program 9 since the array is sorted by the time we search. In fact, the call to <u>binarysearch( )</u> is exactly the same as the call to lnearsearch in Program <u>prog9.cpp</u> [called by the function <u>locatevalues( )</u>]. Here is the relevant portion of the function <u>locatevalues( )</u> (note once again that the search function is called by <u>locatevalues( )</u> rather than the main program):

```
location = binarysearch(numb,n,newnumber);
if (location >= 0)
    cout << newnumber << " occurs at position "
        << location;
else
    cout << newnumber << " does not occur";
```

EXAMPLE 9-8 Let's trace the binarysearch( ) and locatevalues( ) functions on the two earlier examples, one where newnumber is present and another in where it isn't. Assume that the set of data stored in the array contains the values 10 20 30 40 50 60 70 (n is 7). Note that these values are in sorted order, which is crucial to the operation of the binary search algorithm.

PROGRAM TRACE Let's assume that, inside the function locatevalues( ), the user asks to find the position of 50 in the array, so newnumber is 50.

♦ The function locatevalues( ) calls binarysearch( ), sending it the relevant parameters (see Figure 9-7).

♦ Inside binarysearch( ), low is set to 0 and high to 6. In the body of the **while** loop, test is set to (0 + 6) / 2, which is 3; numb[3] contains 40. Since numb[3] is not equal to or greater than newnumber, low is set to 3 + 1, which is 4.

♦ We reenter the body of the loop, and test is set to 5. Since numb[5] contains 60, which is greater than newnumber, high is set to 5 − 1, which is 4.

♦ We reenter the body of the loop, where test is set to 4. Now numb[4] contains 50, which is equal to newnumber. The value of test, which is 4 in this case, is returned to the locatevalues( ) function.

♦ The locatevalues( ) function tests the answer returned, then prints the following output:

```
50 is in position 4
```

Now the user asks to locate 15 (newnumber). The function locatevalues( ) calls binarysearch( ) (see Figure 9-8).

♦ The first few steps inside the binarysearch( ) function are exactly the same: low is set to 0 and high to 6, the **while** loop condition is true, and test is set to 3.

♦ Since numb[3] contains 40, high is set to 2.

♦ We reenter the body of the loop; test is set to 1; since numb[1] contains 20, high is set to 0.

♦ This time through the body of the **while** loop, test is set to 0. Now numb[0] contains 10, and low is set to 1. Note that low is now greater than high.

♦ Since the **while** condition (1 <= 0) is false, we continue after the end of the loop. The function returns −1 because newnumber does not occur in the array.

♦ The locatevalues( ) function tests the answer returned, then prints the following:

```
15 is not in the array
```

✋ **CAUTION** It is imperative that the original array be in order. In practice, this is often true, but in some situations, it may not be. In that case, the binary search method cannot be applied.

ANALYSIS OF THE BINARY SEARCH ALGORITHM

Here is a brief analysis of the efficiency of the binary search algorithm. In our two examples of the binary search, n was equal to 7. It took three guesses to locate 50 and three to determine that 15 was not in the array.

Three guesses were needed because the number 8 (which is one more than the number of elements in the array) must be divided in half three times before 1 is reached. In general, if the number of array elements plus 1 (n + 1) must be divided in half k times before 1 is reached, no more than k guesses are needed to find an element in the array (or reject it).

How does the binary search algorithm do on larger values of n? Table 9-2 compares the efficiency of the linear and binary searches for various values of n. The accelerated version of the linear search

TABLE 9-2 Analysis of the Linear Search and the Binary Search

	Average number of tries using linear search to:		Maximum number of tries using binary search to:	
n	**Locate**	**Reject**	**Locate**	**Reject**
7	4	7	3	3
100	50	100	7	7
1,000	500	1,000	10	10
1,000,000	500,000	1,000,000	20	20

discussed in exercises 26 and 33 is not much better than the original. It is clear that the binary search is significantly more efficient than the linear search, both in locating and rejecting, for values of n as small as 100. The advantage becomes even greater as the value of n increases.

SELF-CHECK 9-9

1. Exactly why is it crucial for the array to be in order before a binary search is performed?

2. Trace the binary search algorithm and the locatevalues( ) function on the following lists and new values to be located:

   a. list: −2 0 2 4 6 7 8 15 34   new values: 4 1 7 25
   b. list: 10 20 30 ... 100   new values: 20 5 −11

3. If a sorted list of items contains 4,000,000 values, how many guesses does it take the binary search algorithm to locate the position of an item?

SUMMARY

BOTTOM-UP VERSUS TOP-DOWN DESIGN

1. A large program often divides into a series of relatively simple parts. Each part can be solved in an individual module; those modules are combined to form a program for the entire problem. A top-down approach starts with a main program, refines it into modules, and then works on each module. A programmer using a bottom-up design starts by working on the individual modules, then writes the main program which calls them. Many programmers use a combination of the two techniques.

SORTING

2. Sorting, which means putting a list of objects into order (either ascending or descending), is an extremely common and important application of computers.

3. There are many possible sorting methods. Unfortunately, the most efficient ones are rather difficult to program. The two discussed in this chapter are easy to program but not very efficient. However, for small cases (under 100 items), they are adequate. Understanding these simple methods is useful before learning more complex techniques.

LINEAR SORT

4. An algorithm for the linear sort of an array into ascending order consists of these steps:
   Find the smallest element in the array and place it in the first position. Do this by comparing each element of the array to the one in the first position. If the new element is smaller, swap it with the

element in the first position. Repeat this process for the other positions in the array, at each stage ignoring all elements whose positions have already been filled.

5. The function for the linear sort implements this algorithm by using a nested **for** loop construction. The outer loop corresponds to the various positions to be filled; the inner loop considers all possible candidates for that position. A total of $n - 1$ passes through the outer loop are needed to sort n elements. Each pass determines one position except for the last, which determines two.

BUBBLE SORT

6. The bubble sort improves on the linear sort algorithm by comparing only adjacent elements of the array. The key to the bubble sort is this observation: If each element is in order relative to its two neighbors, the entire array is in sorted order. Here is the bubble sort algorithm:

   Repeat the following process as long as each entire pass through the array has a swap: Compare each element of the array to the one after it; if they are out of order, swap them; continue processing until the end of the array.

7. The module for the bubble sort implements this algorithm using a **do-while** loop that contains a **for** loop. The outer loop repeats the inner loop as long as an entire pass has at least one swap of adjacent elements. The inner loop compares each element to the one after it, swapping them if they are out of order and noting that a swap has been made.

ANALYSIS OF THE TWO SORTING ALGORITHMS

8. Although the linear sort is easy to program, it is incredibly inefficient since it makes the same number of comparisons in every case. One of the exercises shows that a total of $n^2 / 2$ comparisons are needed to sort n elements, regardless of what order they are in. This includes an array that is already in order. A "smarter" algorithm takes advantage of previous information to decrease the number of comparisons.

9. In the worst case, the bubble sort is about as poor as the linear sort is in every case. But if the elements are almost in sorted order, the bubble sort is significantly faster. Although this is unlikely to happen randomly, in practice it is fairly common to have an array where most of the elements are in order except for a few misplaced values. Nevertheless, neither sort is useful in real-world applications.

SORTING VARIATIONS

10. Sorting into descending order is a trivial modification of the one into ascending order: Replace the test for "greater than" by "less than." The sorting algorithms work for integers or real numbers as well as other data types. The only changes necessary are in the declaration for the array and the temporary storage location used for the swap. In fact, characters can be sorted into alphabetical order by the same method since the computer assigns each character a numerical value, called its ASCII code, and these values are used in the comparisons.

SEARCHING

11. There are also several searching techniques discussed in the chapter, all having the following goal: Given a list of items, determine if a new item is an element of the list. If it is, return the position of the new item; if it is not, return some indication of failure (typically −1). If an item occurs several times, report only the first occurrence.

LINEAR OR SEQUENTIAL SEARCH

12. The linear search (also called a sequential search) algorithm is the simplest searching method. Each element in the array is compared sequentially to the new item. If the two match, the subscript of the array element is the position of the new item. After searching the entire array, if a match has not been found, the item is not in the array.

BINARY SEARCH

13. If the array is in sorted order, another searching method, called the binary search, can be used. Instead of searching the array sequentially, the binary search method guesses that the new item is the middle element among the remaining elements. At each step of the algorithm, the number of elements to be searched is cut in half, from n to $n/2$ to $n/4$, ... Either the new item is found on one of these guesses, or eventually there are no more items to be searched, which means that the new item is not in the array.

14. Here is an outline of the binary search algorithm:

    Initially, set low = 0 *and* high = n − 1. *The first guess for the new item sets position* test *halfway between* low *and* high. *If the new item equals the element at position* test, *the search is successful. If the element in position* test *is too large, then* high *is set to one less than* test. *If the element in position* test *is too small, then* low *is set to one more than* test. *This process of averaging* low *and* high *is then repeated to test another position. Eventually either the new item is found (success), or* low *is greater than* high *(failure).*

ANALYSIS OF THE SEARCHING ALGORITHMS

15. If no special information is known about the elements in the array, the linear search method is as good as any other. However, if the array is in sorted order, the linear search algorithm is extremely inefficient. Given an array with n elements, on the average it takes $n/2$ comparisons to locate the position of a new item, but it always takes n comparisons to determine that a new item is not present. These values are independent of the order of the elements in the array. As a minor improvement, in a sorted array, the average number of comparisons needed to determine that an item is not in the array can be reduced to $n/2$ by using an accelerated rejection process.

16. The maximum number of tests required by the binary search algorithm to locate or reject an item is $\log_2 (n+1)$, where $\log_2 (n+1)$ is the smallest integer k such that 2^k is at least $n+1$. For example, if n is 100, no more than seven tests are needed (since $2^7 = 128$); if $n = 1000$, no more than ten tests are required ($2^{10} = 1024$). On the average, if the number of elements to be searched is doubled, only one more test is needed.

EXERCISES

Note: The exercises for sorting and searching are grouped separately. In addition, the programming exercises which assume a knowledge of strings are grouped together at the end.

TRACING EXERCISES

1. Trace the linear sort algorithm on each of the following lists of items. Then do the same for the bubble sort algorithm.

    a. n =   6   45   32   17   6   1   0
    b. n =   5   3   −8   129   2   3

```
c. n =  7   -1   -76   508   -87   -34   124   -54
d. n =  4   2   1   18   5
e. n =  8   's'   'x'   'q'   'u'   'b'   'a'   'V'   'T'
f. n =  5   12.3   154.56   97.5   3.37   -5.32
g. n =  6   9   9   6   1   -3   2
h. n =  13   "WenEng"   "Ayshea"   "Hong"   "Alex"   "Dmitry"   "Ari"   "Yukie"
        "Malky"   "Henry"   "Vitaly"   "Ezhar"   "Boris"   "Yuriy"
```

2. Given the following set of strings, sort them in ascending alphabetical order. Does it matter whether we use a linear or a bubble sort?

   ```
   "a"    "b"    "an"   "a "  "a "    " a"
   " an" "and" "Bob" "bob" " Bob" "an "
   ```

3. a. Modify the function for the linear sort so that it can be used to sort the types of values in Exercise 1(e). Then trace the function on the values shown. Do the same for the bubble sort function.
   b. Repeat part (a) for the data in Exercise 1, parts (f) and (h).
   c. Make up your own set of data with n = 8. Trace the linear sort and the bubble sort on it.

4. In translating the linear sort algorithm into pseudocode, is it possible to eliminate either loop from the nested loop structure?

5. In the linearsort( ) function, the inner **for** loop header looks like this:

   ```
   for (int cand = pass + 1; cand < n; cand++)
   ```

   What happens if this is changed to each of the following?
   a. `for (int cand = pass + 1; cand <= n; cand++)`
   b. `for (int cand = pass; cand < n; cand++)`
   c. `for (int cand = pass + 1; cand < n - 1; cand++)`
   d. `for (int pass = pass + 1; pass < n; pass++)`

   If you are unsure of an answer, try running a program using each header on a set of data.

6. a. Assume that you want to sort the values stored in the three variables n1, n2, and n3 into order so that n1 holds the smallest and n3 holds the largest value. Show how to do this using a nested **if** or a series of **if** statements.
   b. Repeat part (a) for four variables, n1 to n4. [*Hint*: This is much harder than part (a).] If you are successful, try the same thing for five variables.
   c. Assume that you have values in six variables, n1 to n6, and you want to sort them. Show how to use an array to accomplish this task.
   d. In order to sort a group of numbers, is it necessary to store them in an array? Is it helpful?

ANALYSIS OF THE SORTING ALGORITHMS

7. Show that the linear sort algorithm uses precisely the same set of comparisons to sort an array of n elements regardless of the order of the values. (*Suggestion*: You can list the exact set of comparisons that the algorithm uses.)

8. In both the linear and the bubble sort, we do not swap two elements if they are equal but only if the first is greater than the second.

a. In the linear sort function, what happens if we replace the test

```
if (numb[pass] > numb[cand])          by
if (numb[pass] >= numb[cand]) ?
```

b. In the bubble sort function, what happens if we replace the test

```
if (numb[pos] > numb[pos + 1])        by
if (numb[pos] >= numb[pos + 1]) ?
```

Run a program for each part on a simple example with a repeated value (e.g., 5 7 3 5). The results may surprise you.

9. a. Given an array with n elements, how many passes does the linear sort algorithm require to sort it? On each pass, how many comparisons are necessary? What is the total number of comparisons required to sort n elements using the linear sort algorithm? (*Hint*: The sum of the first n numbers is roughly $n^2 / 2$. See Chapter 4, Exercise 19.)

   b. Given an array with n elements, what is the maximum number of passes required by the bubble sort algorithm to sort it? (This is called the **worst case behavior** of the algorithm.) What is the minimum number? (This is called the **best case behavior**.)

   c. On each pass, how many comparisons are necessary? In the worst case, what is the total number of comparisons required to sort n elements using the bubble sort algorithm?

10. a. Evaluate your answers from Exercise 9 assuming that $n = 10$, $n = 100$, $n = 1000$.

    b. In the worst case, the best sorting algorithms require about 1.5 n log n comparisons. Using this fact, verify the following: For the values of n from part (a), the worst case behavior of the best sorting algorithms requires roughly 50, 1000, and 15,000 comparisons, respectively.

    c. What can you conclude about using the linear or the bubble sort for large ($n > 500$) examples?

MODIFICATIONS TO THE SORTING ALGORITHMS

11. The linear sort algorithm in the text can be improved so that it does not make as many switches of array elements. (However, it still makes the same number of array comparisons.) It is not necessary to interchange two array elements every time the first one is not smaller. Instead, on each pass through the array, the program can keep track of the position of the smallest element seen on that pass. At the end of each pass, the smallest element can be interchanged with the one currently in that array position.

    Show how to use this idea in the linear sort function. Trace a few examples to compare this new version to the original function. Compare the number of comparisons and the number of switches.

12. The bubble sort algorithm in the text can be improved in several ways. The next few exercises discuss a few improvements.

    The maximum number of passes through the outer or **do-while** loop can be predicted in advance. Since each pass determines the position of at least one element, the maximum number of passes is $n - 1$, where n is the number of values to be sorted. One simple way to take advantage of this is to count, within the outer loop, the number of passes that have been made. Then change the condition tested in the **while** clause so that it also checks the count of the number of passes. The loop continues as long as both of the following are true: count is less than $n - 1$ (fewer than $n - 1$ passes have been completed) and swapped is **true** (each pass has had a swap).

Show how to use this idea in the bubble sort function. Trace a few examples to compare this new version to the original function.

13. Once the suggestion from Exercise 12 has been followed, there is another improvement that can also be made. The first pass through the outer loop determines the largest element; the next pass determines the second largest, and so on. We can use a variable count to count how many positions have already been determined. The inner **for** loop [*for (pos = 0; ...)*] need not go from position 0 to position $n - 2$ each time. For example, on pass 2 (when count = 1), pos need only go from 1 to $n - 3$; on pass 3 (when count = 3), pos need only go from 1 to $n - 4$, and so on. To convince yourself, review the traces from Section 3.

Show how to use this idea in the bubble sort function by modifying the **for** loop header. Trace a few examples to compare this latest version to the function from Exercise 12 and the original bubble sort function.

14. Here is another possible improvement to the bubble sort algorithm: If two adjacent array elements (say numb[4] and numb[5]) are out of order, swap them. However, instead of comparing the new numb[5] to numb[6], determine the correct location of numb[4] by allowing it to "bubble up" in the array. For example, compare the new numb[4] to numb[3]. If numb[3] is greater, swap them and compare numb[3] to numb[2] until an equal or smaller value is encountered or you reach numb[1]. In this way, the value originally in numb[5] moves into numb[4], numb[3], ..., as it seeks its ultimate location.

Show how to use this idea in the bubble sort function [what other change(s) should be made?]. Trace a few examples.

PROGRAMMING PROJECTS INVOLVING SORTING

15. In order to interchange the values of two variables, a and b, it is necessary to use three statements and one temporary storage location.

a. Show how to interchange the values of three variables, a, b, and c (a to b, b to c, c to a). How many statements must be used? How many temporary locations?

b. Show how to interchange the values of four variables, a, b, c, and d (a to b, b to c, c to d, and d to a).

c. Show how to interchange the values of n variables stored in array x (x[0] to x[1], ..., x[n − 1] to x[0]).

16. Assume that the first n elements of the numb array have been sorted into ascending order.

a. Show how to print the values in descending order.
b. Show how to sort the array into descending order.

17. Give an algorithm for the following: Given an array with n elements, sort the elements into ascending order and discard all duplicates; if necessary, modify n. For example, if the original array holds 3 7 2 3 7 3 (n = 6), the final array is 2 3 7 (n = 3).

18. a. Write a function findsecond( ) that finds the second-smallest element in an array. The function receives the array x and the number of elements as parameters. The function can use the function bubblesort( ); however, the program that calls findsecond( ) does not expect the array to be sorted. Therefore, findsecond( ) should make a copy of the array parameter and ask bubblesort( ) to sort the copy.

b. Write a function median( ) that finds the median of an array. The median is the array element such that half the elements are greater and half are less (if n is even, it is the average of the middle two elements). The function receives the array x and the number of elements as parameters. As in part (a), ask bubblesort( ) to sort a copy of the array.

c. Write a function sortmedian( ) that does two things: sort an array that is sent as a parameter, and find the median of the array. Should sortmedian( ) be written as a void function or as one that returns a value?

d. Write a function mode( ) that finds the mode of an array. The mode is the value that occurs most frequently. The function receives the same parameters as median( ) in part (b). It also has the same restriction on sorting the original array.

e. Write a function sortmode( ) to sort an array and find the mode.

f. Is it possible to solve parts (a), (b), or (d) without first sorting the array?

19. Give an algorithm for the following: Insert a new number x into its proper location within a sorted array (assume that there is room in the array to add another element). For example, if numb holds 2 7 11 12 13, and x is 10, then x is inserted into position 2, and the values after are shifted.

　　Is it better to start x at the front of the list or the back? Is it easier if the list is in ascending or descending order? Explain.

20. a. Write a function elimdups( ) that eliminates the duplicate elements in an array. The function receives as parameters an array of integers numb and an integer n representing the number of elements in numb that are to be processed. The function removes duplicate elements from the array, shifting the other elements down and modifying n if necessary. For example, if n = 5 and an array holds 3 7 3 7 2, then after the call to elimdups( ), the array holds 3 7 2 and n is 3. Write elimdups( ) without sorting the numb array since the remaining elements should be in their original order.

b. Assume that you can use the function bubblesort( ) and elimdups( ) can change the order of the elements in the numb array. Show how to use bubblesort( ) to simplify elimdups( ).

21. Write a function sortpart( ) that sorts part of an array. The function receives as parameters the name of the array to be sorted (y), and the first (first) and last position (last) to be sorted. The function sorts the elements of the y array from positions first to last inclusive. For example, if y holds 14 7 5 6 2, first = 1, and last = 3, the y array holds 14 5 6 7 2 after the partial sort is complete.

22. Write a function sorteither( ) that receives an extra parameter called order. This parameter indicates whether the array is to be sorted into ascending (+1) or descending (−1) order. Try to do this without two separate sets of sorting instructions. (*Hint*: If $a > b$, then $-1 * a < -1 * b$.)

23. a. Write a function sorthigh( ) (with two parameters numb and n) that does two things: sorts the first n elements of the numb array and returns the largest element in the array. For example, if an array with four elements holds 5 3 7 6, the function changes the array to hold 3 5 6 7 and also returns 7.

b. Rewrite sorthigh( ) as a void function (with the obvious modifications).

c. Is it better to write sorthigh( ) as a void function or one that returns a value?

24. a. Rewrite Problem 9 so that it reads the original data from a file rather than interactively from the keyboard.

b. Which version (interactive or reading from a file) is more useful for a set of 10 numbers? 1,000 numbers? 10,000 numbers? Which sort would you use in each case?

c. Rewrite Problem 9 so that it sends the output to a file rather than the screen. Then (if your system allows it) rewrite it again so that it sends the output to a printer.

d. Which version (printer, screen, or file) would be more useful for a set of 10 numbers? 1000 numbers? 10,000 numbers?

25. Write a complete program to do the following:

    The main program calls a function to read in a set of people's three-digit ID numbers and their donations to a charity. The main program calls a function to sort the ID numbers into numerical order, being sure to carry along the corresponding donations. (See Exercise 45.) The main program calls a function to print the sorted lists, giving both ID numbers and donations. The main program also calls a function to sort the donation amounts into ascending order, carrying along the corresponding ID numbers. Print the sorted lists, giving both ID numbers and donations.

    Here are the details:

    a. The main program calls a function to read in the data. The data set consists of a parameter value which the main program calls n and n groups of data, each of which contains a person's three-digit ID number and an integer (e.g., 456 20000 or 123 30234).

       The main program calls these arrays <u>idnumbers</u> and <u>donations</u>. A separate printing function prints the original set of data in the form of a neat table. When the arrays print, there should be an overall heading, plus headings for the columns of ID numbers and donations.

    b. Then the main program sends the array of ID numbers, the array of donations, and the size n to a sorting function. This function sorts the ID numbers into numerical order. Be sure to maintain the matchup of ID numbers and donations. For example, 456 should always be associated with 20000, no matter where 456 moves in numerical order; similarly, 123 should stay with 30234.

       When the sorting function finishes and returns control to the main program, it calls the printing function to print the two arrays.

    c. Next the main program sends the same three parameters to the sorting function, which sorts the donations into numerical order, being sure to maintain the linkup of ID numbers and donations.

       When the sorting function finishes and returns control to the main program, it calls the printing function to print the two arrays with appropriate headings.

       Your arrays should have room for up to 50 entries. To test the program, have a set of data with at least 15 to 20 values in each array. Make sure that your original order is not close to numerical order for either array and that the two numerical orders are not close to each other.

ANALYSIS OF THE SEARCHING ALGORITHMS

26. This exercise discusses the accelerated rejection searching algorithm from Section 4. Here is a more precise version:

    Assume that <u>numb</u> is an array of n integers in ascending order; <u>newnumber</u> is the integer whose position in <u>numb</u> is to be determined. The algorithm works as follows: *Compare* <u>newnumber</u> *to the elements of* <u>numb</u> *in order. If the current element is less than* <u>newnumber</u>, *compare* <u>newnumber</u> *to the next element. If* <u>newnumber</u> *is equal to the current element, the search is over (success). If* <u>newnumber</u> *is less than the current element, the search has failed since every later element in* numb *must also be greater than* <u>newnumber</u>.

    a. Write pseudocode for the accelerated rejection version of the linear search.

    b. Write a function <u>fastreject( )</u> that receives as parameters <u>numb</u>, an array of integers in ascending order; an integer n, the size of the array; and an integer <u>newnumber</u>. Use the accelerated rejection algorithm to return the location of <u>newnumber</u> within the first n elements of <u>numb</u> (return −1 if it is not found).

27. Assume that an array <u>vals</u> of integers holds the following numbers: 3 7 12 14 16 35 123. Here is the list of values whose positions (if any) in <u>vals</u> are to be located: 8 16 12 26 112 35 6 7 14 13.

    a. Trace the linear search algorithm in processing this set of data. Find the average number of comparisons required to locate an integer in the array and the number needed to show that a new value is not present.

    b. Repeat part (a) using the binary search algorithm.

    c. Compare your answers from parts (a) and (b). Is this a good test of the two algorithms? Explain.

28. Select a page at random from a telephone directory. Make up 15 to 20 names that are in the range covered by this page, including some that are in the directory and some that are not. Then repeat Exercise 27 using the page of the directory as the array <u>vals</u> and the names you made up as the items to be located.

29. Repeat Exercise 28 using 20 pages from the directory. What trend do you see as the size of the original list increases?

30. In order to use the binary search algorithm to look up a name in the telephone directory, we must assume that the list is in alphabetical order. Since the directory has an immense number of names (100,000 or more), it is quite time consuming to arrange the list in alphabetical order. Explain why this is not as great a problem as it seems. You may want to consider the following in your answer: the use of clever sorting methods that are much faster than the linear or the bubble sort; the number of times the directory is used compared to the number of times the entries must be sorted; the ease of updating (inserting or deleting names from) an already sorted list (see exercises 43 and 44).

31. The binary search algorithm assumes that the original array is in increasing (or alphabetical) order. Show how to modify it to work on an array that is in decreasing order.

32. This exercise analyzes the linear search algorithm from Section 4.

    Assume that <u>numb</u> is an array of <u>n</u> integers in ascending order; <u>newnumber</u> is the integer whose position in <u>numb</u> is to be determined. If <u>newnumber</u> is in <u>numb</u>, it requires a minimum of one and a maximum of <u>n</u> steps to determine this fact, where each step consists of a comparison of <u>newnumber</u> to an element in the array.

    a. Give an example that requires one step and an example that requires <u>n</u> steps.

    b. On the average, how many steps are required?

    c. In every case, it require <u>n</u> steps to show that <u>newnumber</u> is not in <u>numb</u>. Why?

    d. Show that these results are true regardless of the order of the elements in <u>numb</u>.

33. This exercise analyzes the accelerated rejection method from Section 4 and Exercise 26.

    a. If <u>newnumber</u> is in <u>numb</u>, the accelerated rejection algorithm still requires an average of <u>n</u>/2 steps to locate its position. Explain why.

    b. If <u>newnumber</u> is not in <u>numb</u>, it takes a minimum of one and a maximum of <u>n</u> steps to determine this fact. Give an example that requires one step and an example that requires <u>n</u> steps.

    c. On the average, how many steps are required to reject a new value?

    d. Compare these results to the linear search algorithm. If you expect to find almost every new value somewhere in the original array, is the accelerated rejection process worthwhile? What if most new values are not found?

34. a. Actually, the accelerated rejection algorithm is worse than we have implied since two comparisons are required for each step, as opposed to one for the linear search algorithm. Explain why this is true.

b. In addition, in order to use the accelerated rejection algorithm, the array <u>numb</u> must be in sorted order. Explain why this is true.

Therefore, the accelerated rejection algorithm is very rarely used.

35. This exercise analyzes the binary search algorithm from Section 9.

   a. The minimum number of steps needed to locate a new value is one and the maximum is $\log_2 (n + 1)$. Give examples for both.

   b. The number of steps required to show that a new value is not in the <u>numb</u> array is always $\log_2 (n + 1)$. Justify this statement.

   c. Explain why it is relatively unimportant if each step consists of one or two comparisons.

36. Assume that the number of elements in the original array is doubled (for example, <u>n</u> is increased from 100 to 200). Analyze the effect this has on the performance of the linear search, accelerated rejection, and binary search algorithms. (*Hint*: One of them requires just a single extra step. Which one?)

37. Assume that the array <u>numb</u> contains a particular number twice. Assume that this value is equal to the new number we are seeking.

   a. In the linear search algorithm, which of the two occurrences of the number is selected? Explain.

   b. In the binary search algorithm, which of the two occurrences of this value is selected? Explain. Does this cause any problems?

MODIFICATIONS TO THE SEARCHING ALGORITHMS

38. Modify the functions <u>linearsearch( )</u> and <u>binarysearch( )</u> so that they work on an array of real numbers (or an array of characters) rather than integers. Are any changes needed in the basic algorithms?

39. a. Modify the function <u>linearsearch( )</u> so that rather than returning the position where it finds the new number, it simply indicates whether the search has been successful. (Depending on the application, you may want <u>linearsearch( )</u> to do this or to indicate the position in the array where the element is found.)

   b. How does the main program's call to <u>linearsearch( )</u> have to be modified to accommodate this change?

   c. How does the main program's processing after the return from <u>linearsearch( )</u> have to be changed?

40. In the function <u>linearsearch( )</u>, we used two **return** statements: one in the middle of the loop and one after the end of the loop. Rewrite the function so that it uses a single **return** statement at the end of the loop.

   a. To do this, use a **break** statement to exit the loop in case <u>newnumber</u> has been found. In addition, modify the **return** statement at the end of the loop so that it returns the appropriate value (either the position of <u>newnumber</u> or −1). (*Hint*: At the end of the loop, how can you tell which value should be returned?)

   b. As a second method, do it by adding a **bool** variable <u>found</u> which is tested as part of the loop header.

PROGRAMMING PROJECTS INVOLVING SEARCHING

41. a. Write a function <u>shift( )</u> that receives as parameters an array of integers <u>arr</u>, an integer <u>n</u> representing the number of elements in the array, and two integers, <u>first</u> and <u>last</u>, representing the first and last positions in the array to be moved. The function shifts each element in the array from position <u>first</u> to <u>last</u> forward one place, and adds 1 to <u>n</u>. Thus, <u>arr[first]</u> ends up in <u>arr[first+ 1]</u>, <u>arr[first + 1]</u> in <u>arr[first + 2]</u>, ..., <u>arr[last]</u> in <u>arr[last + 1]</u>. (Assume that the array has a position <u>last + 1</u>.) Can you move the elements in this order?

b. Write a function shiftsome( ) that receives one extra parameter, a positive integer k representing the number of positions to be shifted. (Assume that there is room in the array to shift as far as k positions.) For example, if k is 3, shiftsome( ) shifts each element three positions. Do not use shift( ) in writing shiftsome( ).

c. Rewrite shiftsome( ) by calling shift( ) a total of k times. Compare the efficiency of the two versions.

42. Write a function shiftback( ) with the same parameters as shift( ) that shifts backward each array element from position last to position first. Thus, arr[last] ends up in arr[last − 1], ..., arr[first] in arr[first − 1]. Assume that first is not 0. Why must we make this assumption?

43. a. Write a function insert( ) that receives as parameters numbers, a sorted array of integers, an integer n representing the size of the array, and an integer newnumber. The function inserts newnumber into its correct position in ascending order within the array. (*Note*: In addition to changing certain positions in numbers, the function must modify n as well. Why?)

b. Rewrite the function insert( ) using the function shift( ) from Exercise 41.

c. Rewrite the function insert( ) to handle the case where the array is full, and it is impossible to insert a new element. What should the function do?

44. Write a function delete( ) that receives the same parameters as the function insert( ) (see Exercise 43). It deletes newnumber from the array numbers. This involves shifting certain elements of the array and modifying n. Assume that newnumber does occur in the numbers array. You can use a function from an earlier exercise (which one?) if it is helpful.

EXERCISES INVOLVING STRINGS (TO BE DONE IF YOU'VE ALREADY COVERED CHAPTER 8)

45. In most applications of sorting, there is usually other information along with the array. For example, consider the following problem: Read in a parameter value n, then read in n groups of data, each consisting of a name and a number. Typical groups might be: "Rocky" 5, "Space" 1999, or "Indy" 500. Sort the numbers into alphabetical order. Print the values after sorting.

If a programmer solves this problem in a naive way, the final printout may be some mishmash like this:

```
Indy        5
Rocky     1999
Space      500
```

When sorting, we must maintain the association of name and number. Every time two names swap places, the corresponding numbers must also swap.

Write a program that solves this problem by carrying along extra information. You may want to use a version of the swap( ) function from Section 8 to interchange the names while maintaining the association with numbers.

46. (*Note*: If you have already covered Chapter 10, store the data for this exercise using a class. If you have not yet covered Chapter 10, use a series of arrays. In either case, try to use a version of the swap( ) function.)

A set of data consists of groups of information, consisting of people's names, ages, and social security numbers. Sort the list of ages into ascending order, being sure to carry along the names and social security numbers. Then sort the names into alphabetical order, carrying along the other data. Finally, sort the social security numbers. Print each sorted list, together with the associated information, with appropriate headings.

(*Warning*: A social security number, with nine digits, may be larger than the largest integer value in your system, and thus it cannot be represented using data type **int**. Think of another representation. *Suggestion*: A social security number is never used in mathematical computations but is simply a string of digits.)

47. A set of data consists of a series of names and numbers. Sort the numbers into ascending order. If two or more numbers are equal, sort their corresponding names into alphabetical order. For example, 5 "Pieces" comes before 5 "Rocky."

48. A set of data consists of a series of names and numbers. Sort the names into alphabetical order. If a name occurs more than once, remove the extra one(s) but modify the number to the sum of the numbers for the separate occurrences. For example, if you find "Rocky" 5 and "Rocky" 11, the final list shows only "Rocky" 16.

49. In a commercial or scientific application, the amount of information carried along as an array is sorted may be very large (e.g., 70 to 80 pieces of data per person). Therefore, it is helpful to minimize the number of times this extra information must be swapped. Devise an algorithm that does not require every piece of extra information to be swapped each time the actual values are. [*Suggestion*: Swap only the values but keep track of their original positions within the array. Once a given value is permanently placed, move its extra information. (Is it even necessary to swap the actual values?)]

50. Suppose that you have two arrays, name and grade. The name array contains students' names, and grade contains their grades on a test. Write a program that finds all the students who have a grade of 90 to 100 and prints their names and their grades in numerical order.

SIMPLE CLASSES (WITHOUT MEMBER FUNCTIONS)

PROBLEM: Creating a Database of Contestants for a Quiz Show

SYNTAX CONCEPTS: classes and objects, accessing members of a class, dot operator

PROGRAMMING CONCEPTS: setting up a menu

PROBLEM-SOLVING TECHNIQUES: creating and accessing a database

HOW TO READ CHAPTER 10

OUTLINE:

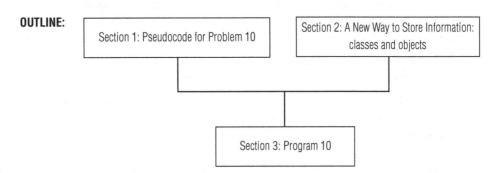

Section 1: Pseudocode for Problem 10

Section 2: A New Way to Store Information: classes and objects

Section 3: Program 10

Section 2, which introduces basic concepts about classes and objects, is the most important part of the chapter and can be covered before Section 1. Section 3 requires both earlier sections.

INTRODUCTION AND STATEMENT OF THE PROBLEM

In this chapter, we introduce an important C++ concept: using a class to define an object which can hold data of mixed types. This new concept provides the focus for the entire chapter and Problem 10. (In fact, it ultimately provides the basis for object-oriented programming, which is the main difference between C and C++.) In Program 10, we read in data about a series of contestants for a quiz show, followed by some questions about the data. Using fancier terminology, we can say that Program 10 creates a database and responds to a series of questions or queries about it. (A **database** is a collection of related information organized in a way that permits easy access.) Before we write code for Program 10, we will discuss classes and objects in Section 2.

PROBLEM 10   A television quiz show has information about a number of people who want to become contestants. The name of each potential contestant and some personal characteristics are on file. The quiz show producer wants to get an answer to a question such as: "Which contestants have blonde hair?" or "Which contestants are 21 years old?"

Write a complete C++ program to do the following: Read in a header value $\underline{n}$ and then read in information for a group of $\underline{n}$ contestants. The information about each contestant consists of

> name (last name, then first name)
> sex (F or M)
> hair color (red, black, brown, blond, gray, or bald)
> age
> title of job
> annual salary (with two decimal places)

Here is a typical entry for a contestant:

> Smith Mary F brown 27 lawyer 85456.78

Mary Smith is a female with brown hair, 27 years old, a lawyer, and earns $85,456.78 per year.

Once the information on the entire group of contestants has been read in, print it in tabular form under a set of column headings (e.g., Name, Sex, etc.). The contestant's name should appear in normal order (first name, last name) with a single space between the two parts. The salary should be printed with a dollar sign and decimal point. For example, the line in the table for Mary Smith should look like this:

```
Mary Smith F brown 27 lawyer $85456.78
```

Then print a menu on the screen, allowing the user to select a particular trait which is desired in a contestant. The menu contains the names of all possible traits: age, hair color, salary, sex, and title. In addition, the menu offers the option of quitting the program.

After identifying the trait that is desired, prompt the user to enter a value that corresponds to that trait (e.g., 17 for age, or M representing male, or 40000 for salary). The program prints a list of all contestants who have the selected value for the chosen trait (for salary, we want all contestants whose salary is above the number requested). The program prints their names in as they appear in the table. There should also be a heading indicating what question is being answered. For example,

```
Contestants whose age is 27

Mary Smith
Paul Cooper
```

Then the program presents the menu again to allow the user to make another selection. The program continues to process requests until the user selects "Quit" from the menu.

<hr>

SECTION 1   PSEUDOCODE FOR PROBLEM 10

This section develops pseudocode for Problem 10 in top-down fashion, beginning with the main program. Before actually solving the problem in Section 3, we introduce classes in Section 2.

PSEUDOCODE FOR THE MAIN PROGRAM

Let's begin our top-down analysis of Program 10 by deciding upon the overall organization. Suppose we divide up the work as follows: The main program calls a function—<u>readdata( )</u>—to read in from a data file information about the contestants. This information is stored to form a database. Then the main program calls a function, prettyprint( ), to print the entire collection of data in a nice format with column headings.

Here's the pseudocode for this section of the main program:

```
// first part
call readdata() to read in data about the contestants
     and store it in a database
call prettyprint() to print the contestant database
```

This section of the program needs to be executed only once. After the data values have been read in and stored, they can be used many times until the program terminates.

Next, the main program calls a function, printmenu( ), to produce a menu of choices on the screen for the user. The user's choices are *sex, age, hair color, title,* and *salary.* Another function, selecttrait( ), reads in the user's choice and asks for the specific value desired.

For example, the user may select *age* from the menu, and then enter 27, meaning, "List all contestants whose age is 27." Another possible selection could be *salary* and a value like 40000, meaning, "List all contestants whose salary is greater than $40,000." The selecttrait( ) function calls other functions to do the processing necessary to produce the list of contestants meeting the criteria.

Before we write the rest of the pseudocode, one question remains. Should we write the program so that the user can process only one request? It seems more efficient to let the program continue until the user is finished asking questions. In fact, we will make quit one of the options in the menu. If the user selects *quit,* the program terminates. Here is the pseudocode for the second part of the main program:

```
// second part
do {
     call printmenu() to print a menu of choices on the screen
     call selecttrait() to respond to a particular choice
} while user wishes to continue
```

In the display below, we've combined the two parts. As usual, there are many other ways to organize the program, some of which are discussed in the exercises.

```
// first part of main
call readdata() to read in data about the contestants
     and store it in a database
call prettyprint() to print the contestant database

// second part of main
do {
     call printmenu() to print a menu of choices on the screen
     call selecttrait() to respond to a particular choice
} while user wishes to continue
```

Since all the actual work of Program 10 is done in the functions, let's write pseudocode for each.

PSEUDOCODE FOR THE FUNCTION readdata( )

The function readdata( ) sets up the database. The function reads in a header value num and then num sets of data values; it changes the value of parameter num. Here is the pseudocode for readdata( ):

```
// readdata()
read num;
for num sets of values
     read in data for each contestant
```

PSEUDOCODE FOR THE FUNCTION prettyprint()

The function <u>prettyprint()</u> accomplishes a simple task: printing the database in a nice format. Since we are still writing pseudocode, we won't worry about the details. Here is the pseudocode for <u>prettyprint()</u>:

```
// prettyprint()
print headings
for each of the num contestants
     print database information in a neat format
```

SETTING UP A MENU—PSEUDOCODE FOR THE FUNCTION printmenu()

To set up a menu, all the program has to do is print the words that we want on the screen. The <u>printmenu()</u> function simply prints messages on the screen in an attractive format; the <u>selecttrait()</u> function does the rest of the work by reading in the user's selection. Here is pseudocode for <u>printmenu()</u>:

```
// printmenu()
print instructions to the user
print a heading
print choices for the user
ask the user to make a selection
```

PSEUDOCODE FOR THE FUNCTION selecttrait()

The <u>selecttrait()</u> function is actually the heart of Program 10. Once <u>printmenu()</u> has presented the user's list of choices and asked for a selection, <u>selecttrait()</u> takes over. The <u>selecttrait()</u> function determines the user's choice; if the user chooses to quit, the function returns a value signalling the main program to terminate; otherwise, the function calls another function appropriate to the choice. For example, if the user selects age, <u>selecttrait()</u> calls a function <u>findage()</u>; if the user selects hair color, <u>selecttrait()</u> calls a function <u>findhair()</u>, and so on. Here is the pseudocode for <u>selecttrait()</u>:

```
// selecttrait()
read in the user's choice
if user selects "quit"
     terminate
else
     call the appropriate function to search the database
```

Of course, we can not complete the pseudocode for <u>selecttrait()</u> until we see what goes on in each of the functions it calls. Since each function does essentially the same thing, we can use <u>findage()</u> as an example.

THE findage() FUNCTION

The function that is selected asks the user for a value for the trait and then searches the database for all contestants satisfying the request. The function <u>findage()</u> asks the user for an age; if the user enters 27, <u>findage()</u> creates a list of all those contestants whose age is 27. Similarly, the <u>findhair()</u> function asks the user for a hair color; if the user chooses *red*, <u>findhair()</u> creates a list of all contestants whose hair is red.

The function prints the query and a list of all contestants satisfying it. If there are no contestants who do, it prints a message to that effect. Here is the pseudocode for <u>findage()</u>:

```
// findage()
ask user for the desired age value
```

> *search the database for contestants matching the requested age value*
> *print a list of contestants with the requested age*
> *if there are none, print a message*

Each function performs a task which is quite straightforward. The only remaining problem is how to store the data. Section 2 introduces a new data structure suitable for this task, and we use it in Section 3 to write Program 10.

SELF-CHECK 10-1

1. Can you think of a way to store the data for Program 10? What is the problem with using an array? How about a collection of parallel arrays?

2. Suggest some other ways to organize the solution to Problem 10 by dividing the tasks into different modules.

SECTION 2 — A NEW WAY TO STORE INFORMATION: CLASSES AND OBJECTS

A class allows you to group data items that can have different data types; these items are called data members of the class. In addition, a class can specify behavior for these data items using member functions of the class. This section introduces how to define a class, how to create an object of a class, and how to use the object in a program.

NOTE

There are various kinds of classes. In this chapter, we are going to define and use only a limited kind of class, one that contains only data items. A class of this type (that is, a class without member functions) is sometimes called a class without behavior or a behavior-less class.

All of our previous programs have used classes and objects of one type or another. For example, cin and cout are objects of class fstream; in Chapter 8, we discussed the **string** class and objects of that class. In this chapter, we will talk about programmer-defined classes.

ORGANIZING THE DATA FOR THIS PROGRAM

You already know enough to write Program 10. The data can be stored in a collection of arrays, one for the first name of each contestant, one for the last, one for the sex, and so on. Although you may consider using a two-dimensional array, with all of the data about one contestant constituting a row, we cannot do this because all elements of an array, regardless of the number of dimensions, must be of the same type.

Using separate arrays to store the data is possible but awkward. It forces us to jump back and forth from array to array as we process each contestant. This method also scatters information about one contestant in many different places instead of concentrating it in a single data structure. Because the pieces of data are clearly related to each other, there should be a way of storing them that indicates this connection. In fact, we will solve Program 10 by using a new concept—the class—rather than by using arrays.

HIGHLIGHTS

A programmer must often think as much about how to store as how to process the data. A clever principle of organization—that is, a useful data structure—often makes the rest of the program much easier, while a poor choice can lead to all sorts of problems.

TWO RESTRICTIONS ON ARRAYS

Before discussing classes, let's point out two restrictions imposed by arrays. One has already been noted: All elements of an array must have the same data type—for example, **int** or **double** or **string**. In other words, an array must consist of homogeneous data.

The second restriction is more subtle: All elements of the array must be at the same level of organization; there is no hierarchy or structure among elements. For example, in an array called x, x[0] is not more important, more complex, or in any way more basic than x[1], x[2], or any other array element. This may not seem like much of a restriction, but when we present the alternative, you will see that it is.

C++ does provide an alternative to an array. A **class** allows grouping of data values which are heterogeneous (of mixed type); it also imposes on the various parts of the data a hierarchy or structure which reflects the relationships among these parts. The best way to convey the idea of a class is with a picture. Figure 10-1 is a picture of a class called address, which consists of a house number and a street name. In a moment, we will show how to define address so that it has this organization.

A PROGRAMMER-DEFINED CLASS

A **class** is a composite data type which contains declarations for several items called **members**. The members of a class can have any data type allowable in C++, including another class.

A class definition does not set up any storage; it defines a template (or pattern) for variables. In a sense, a class definition defines a new data type. Example 10-1 shows how to define a class and use it to declare variables.

EXAMPLE 10-1   Assume that we want to define the class address, illustrated in Figure 10-1. The class consists of a house number (an integer) and a street name (a string). We can define this class as follows:

```
class address {
    public:
        int housenumb;
        string streetname;

};
```

In this case, the new type is class address. Once the class has been defined, we can declare **objects** of that class. (Technically, they are called objects of the class, or instances of the class; but in most cases they act just like variables.)

```
address home_address, work_address;
```

ACCESSING MEMBERS OF A CLASS: THE DOT (.) OPERATOR

In Example 10-1, we declared two objects, home_address and work_address, each of which has the same two members: streetname and housenumb.

FIGURE 10-1   Class address

Several questions come to mind. First, how does the program distinguish between the <u>housenumb</u> which is part of <u>home_address</u> and the <u>housenumb</u> which is part of <u>work_address</u>? Second, is it legal to have a simple variable in the program also named <u>housenumb</u>, and, if it is, how does the program distinguish this variable from the member <u>housenumb</u>?

A third, related question is how to address the various members of a class. The answers to all these questions are interdependent.

An object of a class is identified and accessed using the . operator, called the **dot operator**. The dot operator connects the object to the member name:

```
object_name.membername
```

EXAMPLE 10-2

The data members of the objects <u>home_address</u> and <u>work_address</u> can be identified and distinguished from each other by using the . (dot) operator. The four members are accessed this way:

```
home_address.housenumb            work_address.housenumb
home_address.streetname           work_address.streetname
```

In fact, it is legal (though perhaps not the best style) to have a simple variable with the same name as a member of a class since the way members must be addressed guarantees that there is no ambiguity. A program which contains objects <u>home_address</u> and <u>work_address</u> may also contain a (scalar or simple) variable named <u>housenumb</u>, and the compiler will always be able to distinguish between this simple variable and <u>home_address.housenumb</u> or <u>work_address.housenumb</u>.

Example 10-3 gives values to the members of the objects <u>home_address</u> and <u>work_address</u>. Note that we can use members just like simple variables: we can assign values to them, read, print, or compare these values, etc.

EXAMPLE 10-3

Here are some examples of C++ statements using the objects <u>home_address</u> and <u>work_address</u> of class <u>address</u>:

```
home_address.housenumb = 123;
home_address.streetname = "Main";
cin >> work_address.streetname;
cout << work_address.housenumb;
```

General Form of the Definition for a Class

```
class class_name {
   public:
      type_1 var_1;
      type_2 var_2;
      ...
      type_n var_n;
};
class_name object1, object2;
```

♦   The word **class** is a keyword in C++ (as is **public**).

♦   The item identified as <u>class_name</u> is the name of the class. As shown on the line following the closing brace, the name of the class can be used to instantiate (declare) objects of that class.

♦   The word **public** allows the data members to be accessed outside the class.

♦   Each *type_1 ... type_n* can be any data type in C++, including another class.

♦ The items *var_1*, *var_2*, … *var_n* are the members of the class.

♦ The items <u>object1</u> and <u>object2</u> are objects; objects are instances of the class <u>class_name</u> and have the members specified by <u>class_name</u> .

ASSIGNING ONE OBJECT TO ANOTHER

It is legal to copy one entire object to another object of the same class, by using a single assignment statement, as shown in Example 10-4:

EXAMPLE 10-4   Once object <u>new_address</u> has values, those values can be copied or assigned to object <u>home_address</u> in one assignment statement:

```
class address {
    public:
        int housenumb;
        string streetname;
};
address home_address, new_address;

new_address.housenumb = 123;
new_address.streetname = "Main";
home_address = new_address;
```

At this point, both data members of the two objects will hold the same values.

MORE EXAMPLES OF CLASSES AND OBJECTS

Let's look at a few more simple examples of classes and objects. Figure 10-2 shows a class called <u>student</u>.

As you can see, <u>student</u> has three component parts: <u>name</u>, <u>average</u>, and <u>lettergrade</u>. In Example 10-5, we define a class, <u>student</u>, and then declare two objects of the class, each matching Figure 10-2.

EXAMPLE 10-5
```
class student {
    public:
        string name;
        double average;
        char lettergrade;
};
student freshman, beststudent;
```

FIGURE 10-2   Class <u>student</u>

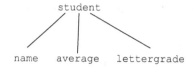

Notice that we have declared two objects (what are their names?). The two objects have the same type—they are both objects of class <u>student</u>.

Example 10-6 shows sample statements using the members of the objects <u>freshman</u> and <u>beststudent</u>.

EXAMPLE 10-6 Assume that the members of the objects <u>freshman</u> and <u>beststudent</u> have been given values. Using dot notation, we can use a member of either object like any simple variable. Here are some examples:

```
if (freshman.average > 3.5)
    freshman.lettergrade = 'A';

if (freshman.average > beststudent.average) {
    beststudent.name = freshman.name;
    beststudent.average = freshman.average;
    beststudent.lettergrade = freshman.lettergrade;
}
```

Because an object can be copied as a unit, this last statement can be written more easily:

```
if (freshman.average > beststudent.average)
    beststudent = freshman;
```

As another example, suppose a used car dealer needs to store information about each vehicle in the showroom. The dealer may use the class <u>vehicle</u>, which is shown in Figure 10-3.

Example 10-7 shows a possible definition for this class and a declaration of objects <u>v1</u> and <u>v2</u> of that class.

EXAMPLE 10-7 Here is a possible definition for class <u>vehicle</u>, based on Figure 10-3, followed by the declaration of two objects, <u>v1</u> and <u>v2</u>:

```
class vehicle {
  public:
      string make;
      string model;
      string year;
      int doors;
      double price;
      int mileage;
      string car_id;
};
vehicle v1,v2;
```

FIGURE 10-3 Class <u>vehicle</u>

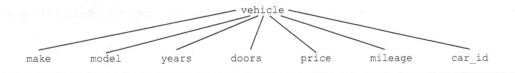

The dealer can use a statement like this to compare the cars and their mileage:

```
if (v2.year < v1.year && v2.mileage < v1.mileage) {
    cout << "This is a great buy!" << endl;
    cout << v2.year << " " << v2.make << " " << v2.model << endl;
}
```

SELF-CHECK 10-2

1. What is the advantage of a class over an array?

2. Write a definition for a class <u>bus</u>, which contains all the information about a specific bus route, including the name of the route (a code like *B34* or *63*), the number of times that buses run that route each day, the starting and ending points for the route (street names), and the cost of the fare (a number like 1.50 or 1.75).

3. Complete the analogy: _____ is to a class, as a variable is to a data type.

A CLASS VERSUS AN ARRAY

Let's look at another example of a class, one that a banker might use to store the information about a loan. Example 10-8 declares the class <u>loan</u>.

EXAMPLE 10-8

```
class loan {
  public:
      double years;
      double rate;
      double apr;
      double amount;
      double month_interest;
      double month_principal;
      double month_payment;
};
loan mortgage;
```

Alternative definition, showing factoring:

```
class loan {
  public:
      double years, rate, apr, amount, month_interest,
              month_principal, month_payment;
};
loan mortgage;
```

This class is unusual because its data members all have the same type. An array of **double** could be used to store the same information. However, a class allows the programmer to use names rather than subscripts; this makes the program easier to write and debug.

Example 10-9 shows the difference between using an array and a class containing the same information.

EXAMPLE 10-9 Using the object <u>mortgage</u> of class <u>loan</u> from Example 10-8, the following statements will calculate interest and monthly payments:

```
mortgage.years = 30;
mortgage.rate = 8.5;
mortgage.apr = mortgage.rate / 100;
mortgage.amount = 150000;
mortgage.month_interest = mortgage.amount * mortgage.apr / 12;
```

In contrast, suppose we declare <u>mortgage</u> as an array:

```
double mortgage[7];

mortgage[0] = 30;                                                    // years
mortgage[1] = 8.5;                                          // interest rate
mortgage[2] = mortgage[1] / 100;               // annual percentage rate
mortgage[3] = 150000;                                   // amount borrowed
mortgage[4] = mortgage[3] * mortgage[2] / 12;
                                               // interest = amount * apr / 12
```

Notice that the code needs numerous comments to clarify how the variables are used, while this clarity is built into the solution using a class and an object.

Another reason for using a class rather than an array is that items in an array usually have more in common than their data type. For example, you may have an array of test scores, but the test average is usually not stored in the same array; instead, it is stored in a separate variable. On the other hand, it would make sense to store the average together with the individual values in a class.

MORE COMPLICATED CLASS DEFINITIONS

As mentioned, the members of a class may have any type. That includes simple variables, arrays, and even other classes. Let's first look at a class that has a string and an array as members. The class <u>triangle</u>, shown in Figure 10-4 and defined in Example 10-10, includes an integer array (<u>angle</u>) to hold the angles and a string (<u>type</u>) to hold the type of the triangle: equilateral, isosceles, or scalene.

EXAMPLE 10-10 Here is the definition of class <u>triangle</u> from Figure 10-4:

```
class triangle {
    public:
        string type;
        int angle[3];
};
triangle t1;
```

FIGURE 10-4 Class <u>triangle</u>

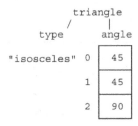

Since <u>angle</u> is an array, its elements are identified by subscripts. The three elements of the <u>angle</u> array for object <u>t1</u> are identified as follows:

```
t1.angle[0]        t1.angle[1]        t1.angle[2]
```

EXAMPLE 10-11   The following code classifies triangle <u>t1</u> as equilateral, scalene or isosceles.

```
if (t1.angle[0] == t1.angle[1] && t1.angle[1] == t1.angle[2])
    t1.type = "equilateral";
else if (t1.angle[0] == t1.angle[1] || t1.angle[1] == t1.angle[2]
        || t1.angle[0] == t1.angle[2])
    t1.type = "isosceles";
else
    t1.type = "scalene";
```

SUB-CLASS DEFINITIONS

A class can be a member of another class. This allows the creation of a **sub-class**.

Suppose a library wants to store information about its books. There is a lot of information for each book: the author's name (first and last), the title, the publication details (publisher name, city, and state), and the year the book was published, as well as information such as the call number and the number of copies. Figure 10-5 shows one possible hierarchy for this information:

EXAMPLE 10-12   Here is a definition for the class from Figure 10-5:

```
class book {
  public:
      string lastname;
      string firstname;
      string title;
      string pubname;
      string pubcity;
      string pubstate;
      int yearpub;
      string call_number;
      int numcopies;
};
```

The problem with this class is that it is too flat; that is, the hierarchy has only one level. That's like having a company where all the employees report to the same person. The hierarchy doesn't reflect the actual relationships among the data values represented in the class. Let's see how to break this up and then rearrange the pieces in a way that shows the relationship hierarchy.

FIGURE 10-5   Class <u>book</u>

FIGURE 10-6   Class <u>name_info</u>

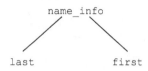

FIGURE 10-7   Class <u>publisher_info</u>

EXAMPLE 10-13a

The class in Figure 10-6 can be represented by this definition:

```
class name_info {
  public:
     string last;
     string first;
};
```

Similarly, several items are all related to the publisher of the book: the publisher name, city, and state. Figure 10-7 shows this relationship.

EXAMPLE 10-13b

The class in Figure 10-7 can be represented by this definition.

```
class publisher_info {
  public:
     string name;
     string city;
     string state;
};
```

Once the classes <u>name_info</u> and <u>publisher_info</u> have been defined, we can use them in the book class, as shown in Example 10-13c.

EXAMPLE 10-13c

This class definition uses the classes <u>name_info</u> and <u>publisher_info</u> from Examples 10-13a and 10-13b to revise the <u>book</u> class defined in Example 10-12. We then declare an object <u>onebook</u>.

```
class book {
  public:
     name_info author;
     string title;
     publisher_info publisher;
     int yearpub;
     string call_number;
     int numcopies;
};
book onebook;
```

FIGURE 10-8 Class <u>book</u>, with sub-classes

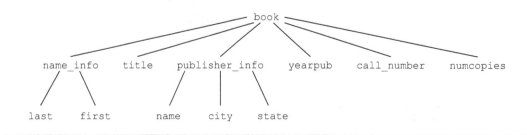

The class <u>book</u> contains a member—<u>author</u>—which is an object of class <u>name_info</u>. The class <u>book</u> also contains a member—<u>publisher</u>—which is an object of class <u>publisher_info</u>.

The class <u>book</u> from Example 10-13c now more accurately reflects the relationship between its members, as shown in Figure 10-8.

ACCESSING MEMBERS OF A SUB-CLASS

Using a class that contains a sub-class is only slightly more complex than using a one-level class. To use a particular data item, we must identify the item by its full name, which uses the dot operator to connect all its levels. As an example, in the object <u>onebook</u>, which is an object of class <u>book</u>, the publisher's name can be accessed as follows:

```
onebook.publisher.name
```

The author's last name can be accessed like this:

```
onebook.author.last
```

Notice that the names in the full identification of a member are always the variable names, not the names of the classes. We use the identifier <u>author</u>, not the class <u>name_info</u>, and the identifier <u>publisher</u>, not the class <u>publisher_info</u>.

REUSABILITY OF CLASS DEFINITIONS

One advantage of defining small classes which can be used as sub-classes is that the definitions are reusable. For example, we can modify the class <u>student</u> from Example 10-5 so that it separates the name into two parts for easy alphabetization; in addition, we may want to separate the name information from the grade information to reflect the hierarchy more accurately. Here is the original definition:

```
class student {
  public:
      string name;
      double average;
      char lettergrade;
};
student freshman;
```

Example 10-14a shows the revised definition (which we call <u>student_info</u> for clarity).

FIGURE 10-9   Class student_info

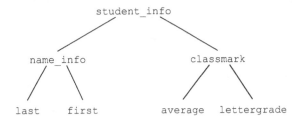

EXAMPLE 10-14a   To define student_info, we use the class name_info, from Example 10-13a (originally defined for the book class), as well as a new class, classmark.

```cpp
class name_info {
  public:
      string last;
      string first;
};
class classmark {
  public:
      double average;
      char lettergrade;
};
class student_info {
  public:
      name_info sname;
      classmark grade;
};
student_info freshman;
```

Figure 10-9 shows a picture of the revised student_info class.
Example 10-14b shows how to access the members of object freshman.

EXAMPLE 10-14b   Here are some examples using dot notation to access the various levels of object freshman of class student_info:

```cpp
freshman.sname.last = "Bueller";
freshman.grade.lettergrade = 'F';
cin >> freshman.sname.first;
cout << freshman.grade.average;
```

ANOTHER EXAMPLE USING A SUB-CLASS

Let's look at another example that uses a sub-class. Suppose that we want to store the following information about employees of a company: the name, social security number, and address.

Figure 10-10 presents a picture of a class named employee. It can hold varied pieces of information about the employee: the name (first and last); the social security number; the address, made up of street address (which in turn consists of house number and street), city, state, and zip code.

FIGURE 10-10   Class <u>employee</u>

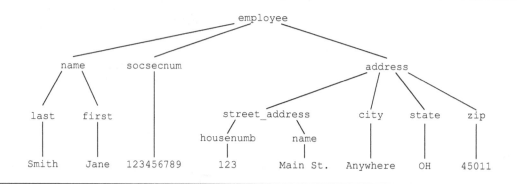

STYLE WORKSHOP Although social security numbers and zip codes are composed of integers, both are normally treated as strings (see Exercise 19).

Example 10-15 shows how to break this class up into several smaller ones. Then it combines the sub-class definitions to create a definition for class employee.

EXAMPLE 10-15 Since it is clear from the figure that <u>name</u> and <u>address</u> are further subdivided, each can be defined as a separate class. We've already defined the class <u>name_info</u> in Example 10-13a, and we can reuse it here.

Defining <u>address</u> is more complex, because it contains <u>street_address</u>, which itself is further divided. The simplest way is to work from the lowest level up, so let's define <u>street_address</u> next. We define a class named <u>street_address</u>, which is close to the definition of the class <u>address</u> from the beginning of this section:

```
class street_address {
  public:
     int housenumb;
     string name;
};
```

Once <u>street_address</u> has been defined, we can use it for the member <u>street</u>, within the class <u>address</u>:

```
class address {
  public:
     street_address street;
     string city;
     string state;
     string zip;
};
```

Finally, once we have defined <u>address</u>, we can define the entire class <u>employee</u>, as well as an object <u>emp</u> of that class:

```
class employee {
  public:
     name_info empname;
```

```
        string socsecnum;
        address home_address;
};
employee emp;
```

Here is the final set of definitions for class <u>employee</u> and object <u>emp</u>. Note that each sub-class must be defined before it is used.

```
class name_info {
  public:
      string last;
      string first;
};
class street_address {
  public:
      int housenumb;
      string name;
};
class address {
  public:
      street_address street;
      string city;
      string state;
      string zip;
};
class employee {
  public:
      name_info empname;
      string socsecnum;
      address home_address;
};
employee emp;
```

CAUTION When smaller classes are incorporated into larger ones, the order of their definitions matters. A class must be defined before it is used, either to declare objects or as part of another class definition.

Example 10-16 illustrates reading in values for the object <u>emp</u> used in Example 10-15.

EXAMPLE 10-16

```
cin >> emp.empname.last;
cin >> emp.empname.first;
cin >> emp.socsecnum;
cin >> emp.home_address.street.housenumb;
cin >> emp.home_address.street.name;
cin >> emp.home_address.city;
cin >> emp.home_address.state;
cin >> emp.home_address.zip;
```

Notice that we entered the data in the order of the declaration. This is, of course, not the only possible order to enter data.

SELF-CHECK 10-3

1. For Example 10-8, explain why we prefer to use a class rather than an array.

2. Write statements to initialize all the members of the object myclass, either by using assignment statements or by reading from cin.

```
class courseinfo {
  public:
      int coursenumber;
      double num_credits;
      int class_size;
};
class classinfo {
  public:
      string department;
      courseinfo course;
};
classinfo myclass;
```

3. What is the purpose of defining a sub-class?

AN ARRAY OF OBJECTS

As you may imagine, we can use an array with classes and objects. Example 10-17 shows a declaration for an array emp, with room for 100 objects of class employee, defined in Example 10-15.

EXAMPLE 10-17   Each element of the emp array is an object of class employee.

```
class employee {
  public:
      name_info empname;
      string socsecnum;
      address home_address;
};
employee emp[100];
```

Each element of the array (that is, each object) is referenced using normal subscript notation, with the subscript right after the name of the array variable. To print the zip code of emp[0], we write the following:

```
cout << emp[0].home_address.zip;
```

Example 10-18 illustrates how to access the objects in a **for** loop.

EXAMPLE 10-18   Let's print the first ten names (in the order of first name, then last name) from the emp array.

```
for (int i = 0; i < 10; i++)
    cout << emp[i].empname.first << " " << emp[i].empname.last << endl;
```

As another example, suppose we want to print a list of the names of all the employees who live in New Jersey (represented by "NJ"). Example 10-19 shows how to do this.

EXAMPLE 10-19

```
cout << "All employees who live in New Jersey:" << endl << endl;
for (int i = 0; i < 100; i++)
      if (emp[i].home_address.state == "NJ")
            cout << emp[i].empname.last << " "
                  << emp[i].empname.first << endl;
```

USING AN ARRAY AT A MIDDLE LEVEL

So far, we have seen an example where a class contains an array as a member—at the lowest level (the class <u>triangle</u> from Example 10-11a). We also have seen an example of an array of objects—that is, an array at the highest level (the array <u>emp[100]</u> from Example 10-17). It is possible to have an array at a middle level and to have arrays at more than one level. In every case, the appropriate subscript is always used right after the name of the array variable.

To illustrate this concept, suppose we create a new <u>studentrecord</u> class.

♦ It should hold the student's name (one string, for simplicity) and information about the student's grades for three courses.

♦ For each course, it should contain the average and letter grade, plus an array of the student's test grades which were used to compute the average.

EXAMPLE 10-20

Here is the class <u>studentrecord</u>, which contains an array of objects of class <u>classmark</u>.

```
class classmark {
  public:
      int test[2];                    // array of 2 tests for each course
      double avg;
      char letgrade;
};
class studentrecord {
  public:
      string name;
      classmark course[3];           // new array, one for each course
};
studentrecord stu;
```

Figure 10-11 illustrates the structure for object <u>stu</u>, showing the array <u>course</u>, which reserves space for information on three courses.

FIGURE 10-11 Object <u>stu</u> showing <u>course</u> array

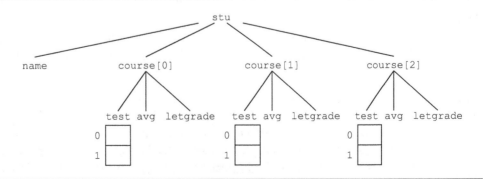

When accessing an element from an array at any level, the subscript is attached to the level to which it refers. Example 10-21 shows how to do this using stu.

EXAMPLE 10-21   To refer to student stu's grade on test number 1 in course number 2, we write the following:

```
stu.course[2].test[1]
```

The student's average in course[0] is the following:

```
stu.course[0].avg
```

Example 10-22 illustrates the use of subscripts when working with object stu.

EXAMPLE 10-22   Let's find student stu's average in each course and print the student's name and all three averages.

```
int sum;
cout << stu.name << " got these averages: "
for (int i = 0; i <= 2; i++) {
    sum = stu.course[i].test[0] + stu.course[i].test[1];
    stu.course[i].avg = sum / 2.;
    cout << stu.course[i].avg << endl;
}
```

USING AN OBJECT IN A FUNCTION

An object can be sent as a parameter to a function, it can be the value returned by a function, and it can be changed in a function. To send an object as a parameter (or to return an object), we use the name of the class as the type of the formal parameter (or the return value) in the function header. Unlike an array (which is sent as a reference parameter), an object by default is sent to a function as a value parameter.

CAUTION The position of definitions is important when you use a class in both the main program and the function. You must place the class definition where it can be seen by both of them. The class cannot be defined inside the main program. Instead, it must be defined above the main program so that the function can use the class definition. (Any objects should be declared within the individual functions.) This is the same rule that we have already followed for #include directives and for function prototypes.

ANSI C++ under Unix is even more exacting: it requires that the class definition come before any prototypes that use it. Although some C++ compilers do not require this order, we will use it so that our programs work on all systems.

Let's first look at an example which sends a single object to a function to be printed. We'll outline a program that calls a function to print the values in an object worker of class employee.

EXAMPLE 10-23a   This complete program defines class employee before all functions, so that the definition for class employee can be accessed by the main function as well as printemp( ). The main function declares the object worker, reads values into it, and then sends the object to printemp( ) to be printed. Both the main function and the function printemp( ) use worker as the name of the object of class employee.

```cpp
// prints components from the worker object of class employee
#include <iostream>
using namespace std;
class name_info {
  public:
      string last;
      string first;
};
class street_address {
  public:
      int housenumb;
      string name;
};
class address {
  public:
      street_address street;
      string city;
      string state;
      string zip;
};
class employee {
  public:
      name_info empname;
      string socsecnum;
      address home_address;
};

void printemp(employee);

int main()
{
    employee worker;

    // read in data
    ...
    printemp(worker);
    return 0;
}

// Function printemp():
// ...
void printemp(employee worker)
{
    cout << worker.empname.last << " " << worker.empname.first << endl;
    cout << worker.socsecnum << endl;
    cout << worker.home_address.street.housenumb << " "
         << worker.home_address.street.name << endl;
    cout << worker.home_address.city << " "
         << worker.home_address.state << " "
         << worker.home_address.zip << endl;
    return;
}
```

The next example will show how to send a part of an object to a function.

EXAMPLE 10-23b   In this extension to Example 10-23a, we send one part (a string representing the state) of the object <u>worker</u> to a function. Note that when a data member which is part of an object is sent as a parameter to a function, the corresponding formal parameter should have the same type as the individual data member.

Here is the prototype for the new function:

```
void matchNYstate(string);
```

Here is the call from the main program, sending a part of object <u>worker</u>:

```
matchNYstate(worker.home_address.state);
```

Finally, here is the new function.

```
// Function matchNYstate:
// find whether this employee lives in New York state
void matchNYstate(string emstate)
{
    if (emstate == "NY")
        cout << "the employee lives in New York State" << endl;
    else
        cout << "the employee does not live in New York State"
            << endl;
    return;
}
```

HIGHLIGHTS   Example 10-23a illustrates one of the most important features of classes: they group logically related data values. Without the structure provided by a class, we would have to send nine parameters to <u>printemp( )</u>; with an object of the appropriate class, we send only one.

CHANGING AN OBJECT IN A FUNCTION

Changing an object in a function is just a bit more complex. Remember that a single object is passed like an ordinary variable, as a value parameter; it is *not* passed like an array. In order for a function to change values in an object, we must send the object as a reference parameter.

Let's review the notation to send a reference parameter to a function. To illustrate, we'll give the call, prototype, and header for a function <u>reademp( )</u>, which receives an object of class <u>employee</u> as a parameter. The function reads values into that object.

To change a parameter in a function, we put the & operator in front of the parameter's name in the function header and the prototype. For this call to <u>reademp( )</u>, the prototype and header are the following:

```
void reademp(employee &);                                    // prototype

void reademp(employee &worker)                               // function header
```

The call is the same as for any variable. For the function <u>reademp( )</u> to read values into the <u>worker</u> object, we use the following call:

```
reademp(worker);                                             // call
```

Example 10-24 shows a main program that calls a function <u>reademp( )</u> to read values into a single object (for simplicity, we use <u>cin</u> and assume that no values will be longer than one word—that is "Main" but not "Main St."). This example extends Example 10-23.

EXAMPLE 10-24

```
// calls reademp()to fill worker object of class employee
// calls printemp() to print worker
#include <iostream>
using namespace std;
class employee {
    ...
};
void reademp(employee &);
void printemp(employee);

int main()
{
    employee worker;

    reademp(worker);
    printemp(worker);
    return 0;
}

// Function printemp():
    ...

// Function reademp():
// reads values into the object worker references
void reademp(employee &worker)
{
    cin >> worker.empname.last;
    cin >> worker.empname.first;
    cin >> worker.socsecnum;
    cin >> worker.home_address.street.housenumb;
    cin >> worker.home_address.street.name;
    cin >> worker.home_address.city;
    cin >> worker.home_address.state;
    cin >> worker.home_address.zip;
    return;
}
```

SENDING AN ARRAY OF OBJECTS AS A PARAMETER

To send an array of objects as a parameter to a function requires no special operators since the name of an array is already a reference. Example 10-25 shows a main program that calls a function <u>readvotes( )</u> to read in and print out an array of objects of class <u>votes</u>.

EXAMPLE 10-25

This program sets up an array of objects of class <u>votes</u>. The class members are the name of a candidate and the number of votes that candidate received. The main program declares an array of up to 100 candidates, and the function <u>readvotes( )</u> fills as many elements of the array as there are candidates.

```
// establishes a database of candidates and their votes
#include <iostream>
#include <string>
using namespace std;
class votes {
  public:
      string name;
      int numvotes;
};

void readvotes(votes [], int &);

int main()
{
    votes candidates[100];
    int numcands;

    readvotes(candidates,numcands);
    return 0;
}

// Function readvotes:
// reads in and prints the cand array of objects
void readvotes(votes cand[], int &numcands)
{
    cin >> numcands;
    for (int i = 0; i < numcands; i++) {
        cin >> cand[i].name;
        cin >> cand[i].numvotes;
        cout << cand[i].name << endl;
        cout << cand[i].numvotes << endl;
    }
    return;
}
```

FUNCTION WHICH RETURNS AN OBJECT

A function can also return an object by using the class name as the return type. Example 10-26 illustrates returning an object from a function.

EXAMPLE 10-26 This program calls a function whowon( ), sending it as a parameter an array of objects of class votes. Assume that this array has been declared and filled by function readvotes( ) from Example 10-25. The function whowon( ) determines which candidate has the highest number of votes and returns an object containing that candidate's name and number of votes. (It does not allow for ties.) Notice the use of object assignment.

```
// calls whowon() to determine who has highest number of votes
// whowon() returns an object of class votes
#include <iostream>
#include <string>
using namespace std;
class votes {
```

```
    public:
        string name;
        int numvotes;
};
votes whowon(votes [],int);
void readvotes(votes[],int &);

int main()
{
    votes candidates[100],winner;
    int numcands;

    readvotes(candidates,numcands);   // from Example 10-25

    winner = whowon(candidates,numcands);
    cout << winner.name << " won with " << winner.numvotes
        << " votes" << endl;
    return 0;
}

// Function whowon:
// returns an object which contains name and number of votes of
// candidate with highest number of votes
votes whowon(votes v[],int numcands)
{
    votes highest;

    highest = v[0];
    for (int i = 1; i < numcands; i++)
        if (v[i].numvotes > highest.numvotes)
            highest = v[i];
    return highest;
}
```

There are three viewpoints to keep in mind to understand classes. One is the picture of the class in our minds or on paper; this picture has a tree structure and shows the hierarchy and relationships among the elements.

HIGHLIGHTS

The second is the way to define a class (and then declare an object). Start by defining any classes used as components. Once a class is defined, it can be used to declare an object—either a simple one or a component of another class.

The third is the way elements of the object are accessed, using the . operator. To identify a member of the object, specify each level; use the names of the objects, not the names of the classes. If any level is an array, place the subscript next to the array name.

SELF-CHECK 10-4

1. Write the header for a void function <u>fillstudent( )</u> which receives as a parameter an object <u>student</u> and fills it with values.

2. Write the header for a function <u>findtop( )</u> which receives as parameters an array of objects of class <u>course</u> and an integer <u>numcourses</u>. The function returns an object of that class.

3. Give the prototypes for the functions from questions 1 and 2.

PROGRAM 10

This section solves Problem 10 using the pseudocode from Section 1; the program uses an array of objects to store the data.

PSEUDOCODE FOR THE MAIN PROGRAM

Let's take another look at the pseudocode for the main program before we translate it into C++:

```
call readdata() to read in data about the contestants
    and store the data values in a database
call prettyprint() to print the contestant database
do {
      call printmenu() to print a menu of traits on the screen
      call selecttrait() to respond to a particular query
} while user wishes to continue
```

STORING THE DATA IN AN ARRAY OF OBJECTS

The first line of the pseudocode says *call* readdata( ) *to read in data ... and store the data values in a database*. Before we can read in the data, we must decide how to store the values—that is, the internal form of the database. After Section 2, you should realize that an array of objects is the most logical data structure to use. We call this array of objects contestants.

Before we give the declaration for contestants, let's look at a typical element of the array, say contestants[5]. An obvious way to divide contestants is into person_name, which consists of last and first; and person_info, which holds the personal traits—sex, age, job, and so on. One of these, job_info, is itself divided into title and salary. A single array cannot hold this information (unless we consider each piece of information to be a string—see Exercise 19). Supplying data for the fifth contestant, we can draw a picture that looks like Figure 10-12.

THE DECLARATION FOR contestants

Once the picture is clear, the declaration for contestants is straightforward. We define several simpler classes, then combine them into a class con. We use that class to declare an array in the main program, assuming a maximum of 50 contestants. Here is the definition for the class:

```
const int NUMCONS = 50;
class person_name {
  public:
      string last;
      string first;
};
class job_info {
  public:
      string title;
      double salary;
};
```

FIGURE 10-12   Object <u>contestants[5]</u>, showing values stored in the data members

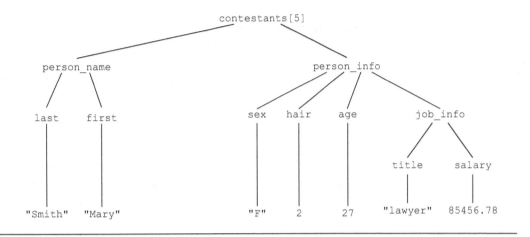

```
class person_info {
  public:
     char sex;
     string haircolor;
     int age;
     job_info job;
};
class con {
  public:
     person_name name;
     pers_info personal;
};
```

In the main program, we include this declaration to establish the <u>contestants</u> array of objects:

```
con contestants[NUMCONS];
int num;
```

We will use the names <u>contestants</u> and <u>num</u> in each function in Program 10.

THE MAIN PROGRAM

Now that we have decided on the structure of the database, we can continue to translate the pseudocode. The main program is divided into two parts: Part I consists of reading in the original database and printing it in a nice format, and Part II processes the queries about the database.

To start Part I, the main program calls a function <u>readdata( )</u>, which reads in information for all contestants, returning the number of contestants in <u>num</u>. Then the main program calls the function <u>prettyprint( )</u> to print the entire database in a nice format. The <u>prettyprint( )</u> function needs the same parameters as <u>readdata( )</u>. Here are the calls from Part I of the main program:

```
// Program prob10.cpp:
// Part I: calls readdata() to read the original database
// then calls prettyprint() to print it
```

```
readdata(contestants,num);
prettyprint(contestants,num);
```

Next the main program calls functions to handle Part II—answering queries about the database. The pseudocode says that the main program calls a function printmenu( ) to display a menu of the possible traits. This function does not need any parameters since it only prints some information on the screen. After printmenu( ) sets up the menu, the main program calls the function selecttrait( ) to allow the user to choose from the menu. Like prettyprint( ), selecttrait( ) needs contestants and num as parameters.

As the pseudocode shows, the calls to printmenu( ) and selecttrait( ) are repeated until the user is finished. Since the user selects *quit* from the menu and this selection is handled within selecttrait( ), the **do_while** loop can continue until selecttrait( ) returns a value meaning quit. We put the call to selecttrait( ) in the loop condition; when the return value is 0, the loop terminates.

```
// Part II—calls functions to read and process the requests
do
     printmenu();
while (selecttrait(contestants,num) != 0);
```

Let's add the #include directives and the function prototypes before writing the functions. Here is an outline of whole program so far:

```
// Program prob10.cpp:
// creates a database about quiz show contestants,
// then answers questions about the database
#include <iostream>
#include <fstream>
#include <string>
using namespace std;
const int NUMCONS = 50;

// class definitions go here

void readdata(con [],int &);
void prettyprint(con [],int);
void printmenu(void);
int selecttrait(con [],int);
```

THE FUNCTIONS FOR PART I: CREATING AND PRINTING THE DATABASE

Part I of the program sets up the database by calling the function readdata( ); then the main program calls prettyprint( ) to print the data. Let's write the functions one at a time from the pseudocode.

THE FUNCTION readdata( )

The function readdata( ) sets up the database. Here is its pseudocode:

> *read* num
> *for* num *sets of values*
>   *read in data for each contestant*

The function reads in data from a file, which we have called "p10.dat". (If necessary, review the material from Chapter 3 on reading from a file.) From the file, readdata( ) reads a header value <u>num</u> and then reads <u>num</u> sets of data into the <u>contestants</u> array.

Here are the data values for one contestant:

```
Smith Mary F brown 27 lawyer 85456.78
```

The data file contains seven items of data for each contestant. The items must be separated by white-space characters: tabs, spaces, or newline characters. A sample data file (with two contestants) might look like this:

```
White  William
M red 52 analyst 100635.12
Smith
Mary
F brown
27 lawyer 85456.78
```

We can expand the pseudocode for <u>readdata( )</u> into the following:

```
read num
for each of num contestants
    read data into the contestants array:
        read name (first, last)
        read personal data (sex, haircolor, age, title, salary)
```

MEMBER FUNCTION is_open( )

Now let's write the <u>readdata( )</u> function from the pseudocode. The function opens and closes the data file. Since it makes no sense to continue the program if the file is not opened correctly, the function calls file stream member function <u>is_open( )</u>. As you may recall from Chapter 7, this function returns **true** if the file was successfully opened. If the function returns **false**, there was an error opening the file (it may not exist), and in this case our code terminates the entire program.

```
// Function readdata:
// Input:
//   values are read from the file cfile
//   contestants: the array to fill
//   both parameters are uninitialized upon entry
// Process:
//   reads num and num data values from file cfile
//   into the contestant array of objects
// Output:
//   gives values to parameters contestants and num
// Called by: main         Calls: none
void readdata(con contestants[], int &num)
{
    ifstream cfile("p10.dat");

    if (!cfile.is_open()) {
        cout << "Error opening input file" << endl;
        exit(1);
    }
```

```
        cfile >> num;
        for (int count = 0; count < num; count++)
            cfile >> contestants[count].name.last;
            cfile >> contestants[count].name.first;
            cfile >> contestants[count].personal.sex;
            cfile >> contestants[count].personal.haircolor;
            cfile >> contestants[count].personal.age;
            cfile >> contestants[count].personal.job.title;
            cfile >> contestants[count].personal.job.salary;
            cfile >> contestants[count].name.last
        }
        cfile.close();
        return;
    }
```

NEW FEATURE OF COMMENTS: FUNCTION DEPENDENCIES

There is one unusual feature in this function. We have added a line to each function's primary comment. The last line indicates what function(s) each function is called by and what functions (other than standard library functions) it calls. In a large program, this information is very useful in debugging.

STYLE WORKSHOP   You may wish to print the data in rough format in readdata( ) as a check against the neatly printed output from the prettyprint( ) function. After using this kind of "debug printout," programmers comment out the extra print statements once the program works correctly. (If you are using an interactive debugger, you may not need debug printout.)

THE FUNCTION prettyprint( )

To complete Part I, we write the function prettyprint( ). It accomplishes a simple task, printing the database in a nice format. Here is the pseudocode for prettyprint( ):

```
print headings
for each of the num contestants
    print database information in a neat format
```

DESTINATION OF THE OUTPUT

Let's consider where prettyprint( ) should direct its output. Certainly, prettyprint( ) could send the nicely formatted database to the screen, but the output may be too long to fit; besides, we need a permanent copy of the formatted database. Since we want prettyprint( ) to produce a printed listing of the database, the function should direct its output to a file, which we can later print. The prettyprint( ) function opens and closes the file; if there is an error, prettyprint( ) terminates the program after printing a message.

PLANNING THE APPEARANCE OF THE OUTPUT

It is helpful to decide what we would like the report to look like. Then we can figure out how to format it. Since we have to print seven different values for any number of contestants, it makes sense to print

FIGURE 10-13   Output from <u>prettyprint()</u>

```
                   Contestants in the Database

      Name              Sex     Hair    Age    Title    Salary

      William White     M       red     52     analyst  $100635.12
      Mary Smith        F       brown   27     lawyer   $ 85456.78
      John Smith        M       gray    67     retired  $     0.00
```

the output in columns with headings. Figure 10-13 shows the output as we intend to print it using
<u>prettyprint()</u> (of course, this is only one possible format):

We use tabs to space the output and align the data under headings, as we did in Chapter 3. You
may find that you need to adjust the number of tabs based on the size of your data values.

To make the output attractive, we will use the method introduced in Chapter 3 to format the salary
with exactly two decimal places. This time, the method will be applied to the output file (<u>dbfile</u>) rather
than to <u>cout</u>, as it was in Chapter 3.

CAUTION   It is difficult to produce neatly formatted output in C++. Tabs do not always produce neat columns. To
be honest, we were careful to select data values that do not cause a problem. Since tab positions are eight
characters apart, the effect of a tab depends on the length of the preceding value. A name or title which goes past
the next tab position destroys the appearance of the table. In an introductory course, the exact appearance of the
output should not be your primary concern.

```cpp
// Function prettyprint:
// Input:
//    contestants: the array to print
//    num: the number of contestants
// Process:
//    sends the database in a nice format to the file dbfile
// Output:
//    nicely displayed listing of array of objects in file dbfile
// Called by: main       Calls: none
void prettyprint(con contestants[], int num)
{
    ofstream dbfile("p10.out");

    dbfile.setf(ios::fixed,ios::floatfield);
    dbfile.precision(2);

    if (!dbfile.is_open()) {
        cout << "error opening output file" << endl;
        exit(1);
    }
    dbfile << "\t\tContestants in the Database" << endl << endl;
    dbfile << "Name \t\tSex \tHair \tAge \tTitle \tSalary"
           << endl << endl;
    for (int count = 0; count < num; count++) {
```

```
            dbfile << contestants[count].name.first;
            dbfile << ' ' << contestants[count].name.last;
            dbfile << '\t' << contestants[count].personal.sex;
            dbfile << '\t' << contestants[count].personal.haircolor;
            dbfile << '\t' << contestants[count].personal.age;
            dbfile << '\t' << contestants[count].personal.job.title;
            dbfile << "\t$" << contestants[count].personal.job.salary
                    << endl;
        }
        dbfile.close();
        return;
    }
```

THE FUNCTIONS FOR PART II: INTERROGATING THE DATABASE

We now write the functions for Part II of the program—answering queries about the database. The function <u>printmenu( )</u> sets up a menu from which the user can select a trait or choose to quit; then <u>selecttrait( )</u> reads in the user's request and either terminates the program (if the user asks to quit) or calls the appropriate function to process the query. The functions <u>printmenu( )</u> and <u>selecttrait( )</u> are called over and over until the user asks to quit. Let's take another quick look at Part II of the main program:

```
// Part II: calls functions to read and process the requests
do
    printmenu();
while (selecttrait(contestants,num) != 0);
```

SETTING UP A MENU: THE FUNCTION printmenu( )

To set up a menu, we have to print a series of choices on the screen, along with an indication of how the user can select them. Here is the pseudocode for <u>printmenu( )</u>:

```
print instructions to the user
print a heading
print choices for the user
ask the user to make a selection
```

This part of the program is interactive, letting the user enter requests from the keyboard and receive responses on the screen. Here is the entire function:

```
// Function printmenu:
// Input:
//   none
// Process:
//   sets up a menu of from which the user
//   may choose a trait or choose to quit
// Output:
//   displays a menu on the screen
// Called by: main   Calls: none
void printmenu(void)
{
    cout << endl << endl << endl;
    cout << "To obtain a list of contestants with a given trait,"
        << endl;
```

```
        cout << "select a trait from the list and type in the number"
            << endl;
        cout << "corresponding to that trait." << endl << endl;
        cout << "To quit, select 0." << endl << endl;
        cout << "\t*****************************" << endl;
        cout << "\t   List of Choices      " << endl;
        cout << "\t*****************************" << endl;
        cout << "\t 0 -- quit" << endl;
        cout << "\t 1 -- age" << endl;
        cout << "\t 2 -- sex" << endl;
        cout << "\t 3 -- hair color" << endl;
        cout << "\t 4 -- title" << endl;
        cout << "\t 5 -- salary" << endl;
        cout << endl << endl << "\tEnter your selection, 0 through 5 > ";
        return;
}
```

You should make sure that the number of lines in a menu does not exceed the number of lines on the screen (25 for most monitors, but it may be determined by the size of your output window); this ensures that the entire menu is displayed on the screen.

Notice that we have printed some blank lines to clear part of the screen before producing the menu. If your compiler has a function to clear the screen, you may want to call it from printmenu().

THE FUNCTION selecttrait()

Once printmenu() has presented the user's list of choices, the main program calls selecttrait(). This function reads in the user's choice and then either terminates the program or calls the appropriate function to search the database. Here is the pseudocode for selecttrait():

```
read in the user's choice
if user selects "quit"
    terminate
else
    call the appropriate function to search the database
```

Since the main program expects a return value of 0 from selecttrait() if the user wants to quit, selecttrait() returns an integer. The header and comment for selecttrait() are the following:

```
// Function selecttrait:
// Input:
//   reads a value typed from the keyboard
// Process:
//   based on the value typed in, either terminates
//   the program or calls a function to search the database
// Output:
//   returns user's choice to main
int selecttrait(con contestant[], int num)
```

Since printmenu() has already asked the user to enter the selection, selecttrait() simply reads in the choice and calls the appropriate function to continue the search. For example, if the user enters 2, selecttrait( ) calls findsex( ), which prompts the user to enter the value M or F and then finds all the contestants who meet the criterion (all the males, or all the females).

The setup here is perfect for a **switch** statement (if necessary, review the material from Chapter 6, Section 7). Using choice as a selector, the **switch** statement calls findage( ), findsex( ), findhair( ), findtitle( ), or findsalary( ). Each of the five search functions is sent two parameters: contestants and num. A curious point: Notice that selecttrait( ) doesn't use contestants or num, but it has to receive both parameters so that it can send them on to the functions it calls.

If the user chooses to quit, selecttrait( ) returns 0; a simple way to handle this is to let selecttrait( ) return the user's choice. Here is the heart of the selecttrait( ) function:

```
cin >> choice;
switch(choice) {
    case 0: break;
    case 1: findage(contestants,num);
            break;
    case 2: findsex(contestants,num);
            break;
    case 3: findhair(contestants,num);
            break;
    case 4: findtitle(contestants,num);
            break;
    case 5: findsalary(contestants,num);
            break;
    default: cout << "Incorrect value; try again" << endl << endl;
             cout << "\tEnter your selection, 0 through 5 > ";
}
...
return choice;
```

One issue remains for selecttrait( ). Since the program is run interactively, what should selecttrait( ) do if the user enters an incorrect choice, for example, 6 or 9? The best thing is to give the user another chance to enter a correct value; therefore, we incorporate the **switch** statement into a loop that continues as long as the user enters an incorrect value. On error, the **default** clause prints a message and prompts the user to enter another choice.

THE ENTIRE FUNCTION selecttrait( )

Here is the complete function selecttrait( ):

```
// Function selecttrait:
// Input:
//    reads a value typed from the keyboard
// Process:
//    based on the value typed in, either terminates
//    the program or calls a function to search the database
// Output:
//    returns user's choice to main
//    error message, if necessary
// Called by: main
// Calls: findage(),findsex(),findhair(),findtitle(),findsalary()
int selecttrait (con contestants[], int num)
```

```
{
    int choice;

    do {
        cin >> choice;
        switch(choice) {
            case 0: break;
            case 1: findage(contestants,num);
                    break;
            case 2: findsex(contestants,num);
                    break;
            case 3: findhair(contestants,num);
                    break;
            case 4: findtitle(contestants,num);
                    break;
            case 5: findsalary(contestants,num);
                    break;
            default: cout << "Incorrect value; try again" << endl;
                     cout << endl <<
                         "\tEnter your selection, 0 through 5 > ";
        }
    } while (choice < 0 || choice > 5);
    return choice;
}
```

The function selecttrait( ) calls one of the five functions to answer a particular question. The function that is called asks for the desired trait and prints the list of matching contestants.

STYLE WORKSHOP The functions printmenu( ) and selecttrait( ) are called from inside a loop in the main program. If the **default** clause and the loop in selecttrait( ) are omitted, the program works much the same way: the menu is presented, and the user is asked to make a selection. The difference is that there is no error message printed, and the user has no way of knowing why the last request remains unfulfilled. Printing the error message and giving the user a second chance to respond are both parts of making a program user friendly.

ACCESSING THE DATABASE: THE SEARCH FUNCTIONS

Now we are ready for the most interesting part: finding all contestants who have the requested trait. We have to write five functions to process the queries. Each function should ask the user for a value and then print the query as a heading. The query may be something like "Contestants whose age is 27," "Contestants whose hair is red," or "Contestants whose salary is above $40,000." The function then searches the database for all contestants satisfying the criterion. Below the heading, the function prints the first and last names of the contestants who have that trait; if no contestants do, the function prints "No matching contestants."

THE findage( ) FUNCTION

We will write the function findage( ), which is typical. It asks the user for an age value; if the user enters 27, it creates a list of all contestants whose age is 27.

Here is the pseudocode for findage( ):

ask user for the desired age value
search the database for contestants matching the requested age value

print a list of contestants with the requested age
if there are none, print a message

In <u>findage( )</u>, we call the value we are looking for <u>agewanted</u>; the function continues to use <u>contestants</u> and <u>num</u> for the array and the number of contestants. Here are the comment and header for the function:

```
// Function findage:
// Input:
//     reads requested value from the keyboard into agewanted
//     contestants: array of objects
//     num: number of elements in the contestant array
// Process:
//     finds all contestants in array contestant
//     with age equal to agewanted
// Output:
//     prints the first and last name of all contestants
//        with age equal to agewanted
//     otherwise prints a message that none were found
// Called by: selecttrait()   Calls: none

void findage(con contestants[], int num)
```

The first thing the function does is ask the user for the desired age and print the query:

```
cout << "\tEnter the age that you want > ";
cin >> agewanted;
cout << "Contestants whose age is " << agewanted << endl << endl;
```

Then the function must find all contestants with that age. As we saw in Chapter 9, Section 4, if the set of data is not sorted, the simplest way of finding all contestants with a given value is a sequential search. That is, the function goes through the entire list of contestants one by one, comparing each one's age to what we want. Each time it finds a contestant of the right age, it prints the name:

```
for (int count = 0; count < num; count++)
    if (contestants[count].personal.age == agewanted) {
        cout << contestants[count].name.first << " ";
        cout << contestants[count].name.last << endl;
```

However, what if no contestant is that age? If we leave the page blank or print a heading with no names under it, the output looks incomplete. To avoid this problem, it is customary to print a message when there is no list—in this case, saying that no contestants are that age.

To know when to print this message, we can use a boolean variable, <u>found</u>, to indicate whether the search was successful. This variable keeps track of whether any matching contestants have been found. Initializing <u>found</u> to **false** at the beginning of the function indicates that initially we have found no contestants of the right age. If we find such a contestant, we change <u>found</u> to **true**. After the **for** loop ends, if <u>found</u> still has the value **false**, there are no contestants of the appropriate age, and we print a message saying this; otherwise, we say the list is ended. Here is the complete function <u>find-age( )</u> revised to print a message if no contestants match the query:

```
// Function findage:
void findage(con contestants[], int num)
{
    int agewanted;
    bool found = false;
```

```
        cout << "\tEnter the age that you want > ";
        cin >> agewanted;
        cout << "Contestants whose age is " << agewanted << endl << endl;
        for (int count = 0; count < num; count++)
            if (contestants[count].personal.age == agewanted) {
                cout << contestants[count].name.first << " ";
                cout << contestants[count].name.last << endl;
                found = true;
            }

        if (!found)
            cout << "No contestants of this age" << endl << endl;
        else
            cout << "end of list" << endl;
        return;
}
```

PAUSING A PROGRAM

The findage( ) function (and each of the other search functions) has one more task to perform that is not obvious until you actually run the complete program. At that point, the output printed by the findage( ) function may disappear off the screen, pushed off by the action of the printmenu( ) function, which is called from main( ) as soon as findage( ) completes its task.

An interactive program needs to display its output on the screen until the user has a chance to look at it. We can write a function that stops the program until the user presses a key. (The Bloodshed Dev-C++ compiler has such a function built-in. The call *system("pause")* can be used wherever you need to pause to view output.) For those of you who are not using Dev-C++, we'll write the function, pause( ), which is called at the end of findage( ) and all the other search functions.

THE FUNCTION pause( )

The function pause( ) is simple. It prints a message on the screen: "Press any key and then <Enter> to continue." Then it reads from cin to get the key pressed (but it needs to read <Enter> to know that it is done). Because the sole purpose of pause( ) is to wait until the user presses a key, the actual value of the key pressed is discarded. Note that because the >> operator skips whitespace characters, you can't press the spacebar for "any key." Here is the complete function pause( ):

```
// Function pause:
// Input:
//    key pressed from stdin
// Process:
//    delays program by waiting for key to be pressed
// Output:
//    displays "Press any key and then <Enter> to continue"
// Called by: findage(),findhair(),findsex(),findtitle(),findsalary()
//    Calls: none

void pause(void)
{
    char trash;
```

```
        cout << endl << endl
            << "Press any key and then <Enter> to continue";
        cin >> trash;
        return;
    }
```

The pause( ) function is called at the very end of findage( ), after findage( ) has displayed all its output, but before it returns:

```
    if (!found)
        cout << "No contestants of this age" << endl << endl;
    else
        cout << "end of list" << endl;
    pause();
    return;
```

The complete version of findage( ) appears at the end of this section.

THE OTHER FOUR FUNCTIONS

The other four functions are similar, requiring only trivial modifications. In findsalary( ), our comparison is somewhat different since we want to find all contestants with a salary greater than the salary requested, rather than matching it exactly. (Writing the rest of the four functions is left as an exercise.)

COMPLETE PROGRAM 10

We are finally finished with Program 10. Here is the final version, showing the entire main program plus all the functions and prototypes (except the four left as an exercise):

 PROGRAM LISTING

```cpp
// Program prob10.cpp:
// creates a database about quiz show contestants,
// then answers questions about the database
#include <iostream>
#include <fstream>
#include <string>
using namespace std;
const int NUMCONS = 50;
class person_name {
  public:
    string last;
    string first;
};
class job_info {
  public:
    string title;
    double salary;
};
```

```cpp
class person_info {
  public:
      char sex;
      string haircolor;
      int age;
      job_info job;
};
class con {
  public:
      person_name name;
      person_info personal;
};
void readdata(con [],int &);
void prettyprint(con [],int);
void printmenu(void);
int selecttrait(con [],int);
void findage(con [], int);
void findsex(con [], int);
void findhair(con [], int);
void findtitle(con [], int);
void findsalary(con [], int);
void pause(void);
int main()
{
      con contestants[NUMCONS];
      int num;

      // Part I: calls readdata() to read the original database
      // then calls prettyprint() to print it
      readdata(contestants,num);
      prettyprint(contestants,num);

      // Part II: calls functions to read and process the requests

      do
            printmenu();
      while (selecttrait(contestants,num) != 0);
      return 0;
}

// Function readdata:

void readdata(con contestants[], int &num)
{
      ifstream cfile("p10.dat");

      if (!cfile.is_open()) {
            cout << "Error opening input file" << endl;
            exit(1);
      }
```

```
        cfile >> num;
        for (int count = 0; count < num; count++) {
            cfile >> contestants[count].name.last;
            cfile >> contestants[count].name.first;
            cfile >> contestants[count].personal.sex;
            cfile >> contestants[count].personal.haircolor;
            cfile >> contestants[count].personal.age;
            cfile >> contestants[count].personal.job.title;
            cfile >> contestants[count].personal.job.salary;
            cfile >> contestants[count].name.last
        }
        cfile.close();
        return;
}


// Function prettyprint:
void prettyprint(con contestants[], int num)
{
        ofstream dbfile("p10.out");

        dbfile.setf(ios::fixed,ios::floatfield);
        dbfile.precision(2);

        if (!dbfile.is_open()) {
            cout << "error opening output file" << endl;
            exit(1);
        }
        dbfile << "\t\tContestants in the Database" << endl << endl;
        dbfile << "Name \t\tSex \tHair \tAge \tTitle \tSalary"
               << endl << endl;
        for (int count = 0; count < num; count++) {
            dbfile << contestants[count].name.first;
            dbfile << ' ' << contestants[count].name.last;
            dbfile << '\t' << contestants[count].personal.sex;
            dbfile << '\t' << contestants[count].personal.haircolor;
            dbfile << '\t' << contestants[count].personal.age;
            dbfile << '\t' << contestants[count].personal.job.title;
            dbfile << "\t$" << contestants[count].personal.job.salary
                   << endl;
        }
        dbfile.close();
        return;
}

// Function printmenu:
void printmenu(void)
{
        cout << endl << endl << endl;
        cout << "To obtain a list of contestants with a given trait,"
             << endl;
        cout << "select a trait from the list and type in the number"
             << endl;
```

```
        cout << "corresponding to that trait." << endl << endl;
        cout << "To quit, select 0." << endl << endl;
        cout << "\t****************************" << endl;
        cout << "\t        List of Choices       " << endl;
        cout << "\t****************************" << endl;
        cout << "\t  0 -- quit" << endl;
        cout << "\t  1 -- age" << endl;
        cout << "\t  2 -- sex" << endl;
        cout << "\t  3 -- hair color" << endl;
        cout << "\t  4 -- title" << endl;
        cout << "\t  5 -- salary" << endl;
        cout << endl << endl << "\tEnter your selection, 0 through 5 > ";
        return;
}

// Function selecttrait:
int selecttrait (con contestants[], int num)
{
        int choice;

        do {
            cin >> choice;

            switch(choice) {
                case 0: break;
                case 1: findage(contestants,num);
                        break;
                case 2: findsex(contestants,num);
                        break;
                case 3: findhair(contestants,num);
                        break;
                case 4: findtitle(contestants,num);
                        break;
                case 5: findsalary(contestants,num);
                        break;
                default: cout << "Incorrect value; try again" << endl;
                         cout << endl <<
                               "\tEnter your selection, 0 through 5 > ";
            }
        } while (choice < 0 || choice > 5);
        return choice;
}

// Function findage:
void findage(con contestants[], int num)
{
        int agewanted;
        bool found = false;

        cout << "\tEnter the age that you want > ";
        cin >> agewanted;
        cout << "Contestants whose age is " << agewanted << endl << endl;
        for (int count = 0; count < num; count++)
```

```
            if (contestants[count].personal.age == agewanted) {
                cout << contestants[count].name.first << " ";
                cout << contestants[count].name.last << endl;
                found = true;
        }
        if (!found)
            cout << "No contestants of this age" << endl << endl;
        else
            cout << "end of list" << endl;
        pause();
        return;
    }

// Function pause:
void pause(void)
{
    char trash;

    cout << endl << endl
        << "Press any key and then <Enter> to continue";
    cin >> trash;
    return;
}

// other functions--findsex(), findhair(), findtitle(), findsalary()
//    -- go here
```

This completes Program 10.

SELF-CHECK 10-6

1. If we use arrays instead of a class in Program 10, how many arrays are needed?

2. If we use arrays instead of a class in Program 10, how many parameters have to be sent to each function?

SUMMARY

CLASSES VS. ARRAYS

1. There are two major restrictions imposed by arrays. First, all elements must be homogeneous; that is, they must share a single data type. The second restriction is that all elements of the array must be at the same level of organization; no structure or hierarchy is possible.

2. C++ provides another method of storing information, called a **class,** that eliminates these two restrictions. The data members in a class need not be homogeneous, and the class structure establishes a hierarchy or relationship between the parts.

ORGANIZATION AND DEFINITION OF CLASSES

3. A class with data members (but without member functions) can be viewed as an inverted tree, with one element at the top, and branches or subdivisions leading to further elements. The subdivisions impose a hierarchical structure on the data. Figure 10-14 shows an example.

FIGURE 10-14   Class <u>bookinfo</u>

4. The general form of a definition for a class is as follows:

```
class class_name {
   public:
       type_1 var_1;
       type_2 var_2;
       . . .
       type_n var_n;
};
class_name classvar1, classvar2;
```

Following the keyword **class** is the name of the class being defined. The keyword **public** allows the data members to be accessed outside the class. Each *type_1 .. var_1* pair is a member of the class, representing a data item. The items <u>classvar1</u> and <u>classvar2</u> are objects of the class <u>class_name</u>. Only the members of an object of the class can hold data values.

5. Here is a definition for the class in Figure 10-14. First, we define the class <u>bookinfo</u>. Then we use the class to declare objects in two ways:

```
class bookinfo {
   public:
       string callnumber;
       string author;
       string title;
       int pages;
};
bookinfo book, novel;
```

The object variables (or just objects) <u>book</u> and <u>novel</u> have identical organization: each consists of three strings (<u>callnumber</u>, <u>author</u>, and <u>title</u>) and one integer (<u>pages</u>).

IDENTIFYING MEMBERS OF A CLASS OR OBJECT

6. A member of a class or object is referenced by specifying all the parts on a path from the name of the object down to the member, with the dot operator used to separate the names of the levels. For example, <u>novel.author</u> is the <u>author</u> part of the object <u>novel</u>.

7. One advantage of using a class is that it allows grouping related data while giving each item a label. This makes a class useful even if the grouped items all have the same data type and could be stored in an array. Notice the difference in clarity in the following declarations:

```
class info {                 vs.          int personal[3];
   public:
       int age;
       int height;
       int weight;
};
info personal;
```

The class definition allows the program to refer to <u>personal.age</u> instead of <u>personal[0]</u>, or <u>personal.weight</u> instead of <u>personal[2]</u>.

MORE COMPLEX CLASSES

8. A class can be extended in several ways. A member of a class can be an array or another class. A class that is contained within another class is called a sub-class. It is also possible to declare an array of objects.

9. Figure 10-15 shows another, more complex example of a class. The class <u>student</u> contains an integer <u>id</u>, an array <u>grade</u>, as well as classes <u>name_info</u> and <u>course</u>. The class <u>course</u> contains array <u>tests</u> as one of its members.

10. Here is a definition for the class in Figure 10-15. In this example, we define sub-classes for the component parts of class <u>student</u>; then we use these sub-class definitions to build the complete class definition for <u>student</u>. (C++ requires that you define a sub-class before using it.) Finally, we declare an object <u>freshman</u> of this class.

```cpp
class name_info {
   public:
        string first;
        string last;
};
class course {
   public:
        string name;
        int tests[4];
        double average;
};
class student {
   public:
        name_info name;
        int id;
        course onecourse;
        string grade;
};
student freshman;
```

USING MEMBERS OF A CLASS OR OBJECT

11. In a program, a data member of an object can be used wherever a single variable can be used—for example, on either side of an assignment statement or in a function call.

FIGURE 10-15   class student

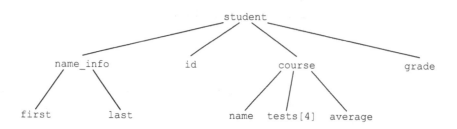

12. To refer to a data member in a sub-class, we must include all names on the path from the top of the tree to the member. Two of the members of the object <u>freshman</u> are <u>freshman.name.first</u> and <u>freshman.id</u>.

13. Because a member of a class is identified only by its complete name, including all levels, names can be reused without ambiguity. A name can be used in different places in a class, in different classes, or in a class and as a single variable; however, the same name cannot be used twice at the same level in the same class. In paragraph 10, the identifier <u>name</u> is used twice: <u>freshman.name.first</u> and <u>freshman.onecourse.name</u>.

14. When an array element which is part of a class is referenced, the array subscript must appear next to the level to which it applies. For example, using the object <u>freshman</u>, we can refer to <u>freshman.onecourse.tests[0]</u>.

15. In a class definition, an array can appear at any level—including the top—so that there is an array of objects. We can modify paragraph 10 so that we declare <u>seniors</u> to be an array of 100 objects of class <u>students</u>, as follows:

```
class student {
    public:
        name_info name;
        int id;
        course onecourse;
        string grade;
};
student seniors[100];
```

To print information about <u>seniors[8]</u> from this example, we can use the following:

```
cout << "student " << seniors[8].name.last << " got a grade of "
     << seniors[8].onecourse.tests[0] << " on the first test " << endl;
cout << "the final grade is " << seniors[8].grade << endl;
```

16. When a data member which is part of an object is sent as a parameter to a function, the corresponding formal parameter should have the same type as the data member. Here is an example which sends the <u>id</u> member (an integer) of object <u>freshman</u> of class <u>students</u> to a function <u>matchid( )</u>; the corresponding formal parameter is also an integer.

```
found = matchid(freshman.id,275);
```

Here is the function <u>matchid( )</u> which returns **true** for a match, **false** otherwise:

```
// function matchid
bool matchid(int id, int value)
{
    return id == value;
}
```

USING COMPLETE OBJECTS

17. All values in an object can be copied to another object of the same class by using a single assignment statement. If <u>first</u> and <u>second</u> are objects of the same class, it is possible to write the following:

```
first = second;
```

18. It is possible to initialize an entire object, or part of one, in the declaration. Here is an example which initializes the first three members of object <u>part</u>:

```
class partinfo {
    public:
        string item;
        string partnum;
        int quantity;
        double cost;
};
partinfo part = {"screwdriver","S34A",26};
```

USING CLASSES AND OBJECTS WITH FUNCTIONS

19. An entire object can be sent as a parameter to a function. The data type of the formal parameter must be the class used for the actual parameter. An object is sent as a value parameter. Here is the call to send the object <u>part</u> to the function <u>list( )</u>:

```
list(part);
```

Here is the function <u>list( )</u>:

```
// function list
void list(partinfo part)
{
    cout << part.partnum << " " << part.item << " "
        << part.quantity << " " << part.cost << endl;
    return;
}
```

20. If a class definition is used both in the main program and in a function, the class definition must be placed in a position where it is accessible to all functions that use it. This can be accomplished by placing the definition outside the main program, above the function prototypes.

21. To change an object in a function, the function must use a reference parameter (in both the header and the function prototype). Here is the call to send the object <u>part</u> (from paragraph 18) to the function <u>change( )</u>:

```
change(part);
```

Here is the function <u>change( )</u>:

```
void change(partinfo &p)
{
    int amtbought;

    cin >> amtbought;
    p.quantity += amtbought;
    return;
}
```

Here is the corresponding function prototype:

```
void change(partinfo &);
```

22. An advantage of using a class is that a single parameter, rather than many, can be passed to a function. For example, the function list() in paragraph 19 receives one parameter. Without a class, the program would have to send four parameters.

23. An array of objects can also be sent to a function. Since an array of objects is an array, it is always a reference parameter. Here is an example which declares an array of objects of class partinfo (from paragraph 18) and sends it to a function addup():

```
partinfo part[25];
double totalvalue;
int n;

totalvalue = addup(part,n);
```

Here is the function addup():

```
// function addup
double addup(partinfo part[ ], int n)
{
    double total = 0;

    for (int i = 0; i < n; i++)
        total += part[i].quantity * part[i].cost;
    return total;
}
```

Here is the corresponding function prototype:

```
double addup(partinfo [ ], int n);
```

24. An object can be returned from a function. Below is a function findbest() which finds the object in the part array with the largest quantity and returns its name and quantity in an object of class limits:

```
// class definitions
class partinfo {
  public:
      string item;
      string partnum;
      int quantity;
      double cost;
};
class limits {
  public:
      string name;
      int amt;
};

// declarations and call from main
partinfo part[25];
limits highest;
int n;

highest = findbest(part,n);
```

Here is the function <u>findbest( )</u>:

```
// function findbest
limits findbest(partinfo part[], int n)
{
    int most, largest = 0;
    limits best;

    most = part[0].quantity;
    for (int i = 1; i < n; i++)
        if (most < part[i].quantity) {
            most = part[i].quantity;
            largest = i;
        }
    best.name = part[largest].item;
    best.amt = part[largest].quantity;
    return best;
}
```

Here is the corresponding function prototype:

```
limits findbest(partinfo [], int n);
```

MISCELLANEOUS TOPICS

25. A database is a collection of related groups of information organized in a way which permits easy access. In C++, the most natural way to implement a database is through an array of objects.

26. A menu is presented to a user by using <u>cout</u> to print each of the desired messages. The user can be offered a selection of items and asked to choose one.

27. In interactive programming where output is sent to the screen, it is sometimes necessary to pause the program so that the output can be read. A function to do this is shown in the text.

EXERCISES

DECLARATION AND TRACING EXERCISES

1. Each of the pictures in Figure 10-16 describes a class. Assume that all variables have type **int**.

   a. Give a definition for each class.

   b. Describe each picture in English (e.g., <u>a</u> is divided into ...).

   c. How many data items can be stored in each class?

2. Given the tree structure in Figure 10-17, write a definition for class <u>orderinfo</u> as requested:

   a. Write a class definition for <u>addressinfo</u> and one for <u>iteminfo</u>, and use them in the definition of <u>orderinfo</u>. Write a declaration for an object called <u>order</u> using these class definitions.

   b. Write a declaration for an array <u>orders</u>, which consists of 300 objects of class <u>orderinfo</u>.

3. For each of the following descriptions, draw a picture of the class described. Then give a definition for the class. How many data items can be stored in each?

   a. A small library has fiction and nonfiction books with up to ten of each. Each book has a title, an author, a classification number (e.g., QA237), a publication date (e.g., 1992), and the number of pages.

FIGURE 10-16   Classes for Exercise 1

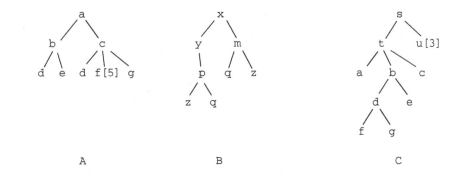

FIGURE 10-17   Tree structure of <u>orderinfo</u>

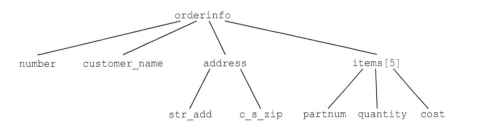

b. A club has 30 members. Each member has a name (divided into first and last), a member number (e.g., 27) and up to five interests. Each interest consists of a name (e.g., chess or video games) and an integer from 1 to 10 representing the level of interest.

4. We want to use a class to store the following information about a digital camera for sale: the name of the digital camera, the resolution in megapixels, and the price.

  The name is divided into two parts: the manufacturer and the model number (for example, the two parts could be Kodak and Pro 850). The resolution is an integer (for example, 5 or 6). The price is divided into two parts: the list price for the digital camera and the sales price (each is a number like 345.67 or 276.54).

a. Draw a picture for the class described above.

b. Give the definition for a class called <u>cameraData</u> that can hold this information. Then use this definition to declare an object <u>newCamera</u> which can hold this information for one digital camera.

c. Use the object <u>newCamera</u> declared above to do the following:

  i. Read in values for the manufacturer and the resolution. Print the values read in.
  ii. If the selling price is greater than the list price, print a message saying the digital camera is selling above cost; otherwise add 10 to the selling price.
  iii. Compare the manufacturer of the digital camera to "Canon". If the two strings are identical, print a message saying this is the camera we want; otherwise, print a message saying this is not the camera we want.

5. We want to use a class to store the following information about a house for sale: the address of the house, the number of rooms, the color, and the price.

The address is divided into two parts: the city and the state (for example, the pieces could be Long Beach, NY). The number of rooms in the house is an integer. The color is a single word (for example, brown or yellow). The price is divided into two parts: the asking price for the house and the bid price (each is a number like 212345.67 or 329876.54).

a. Draw a picture for the class described above.

b. Give the definition for a class called <u>houseData</u> that can hold this information. Then use this definition to declare an object of that class called <u>newHouse</u> which can hold this information for one house.

c. Use the object <u>newHouse</u> declared above to do the following:

   i. Read in values for the state and the number of rooms. Print the values read in.

   ii. If the asking price is less than or equal to the bid price, print a message saying the house is sold; otherwise print a message saying the offer is too low.

   iii. If the number of rooms is over 10, add 5000 to the bid price; otherwise, add 1 to the number of rooms.

6. We want to use a class to store the following information about a television show: the name of the show, the running time of the show, and the rating for the show.

   The name of the show is something like the following: "24 Desperate Lost Idol Survivors". The running time is divided into two parts, each of which is an integer: the length in minutes of the original version without commercials and the length in minutes of the show with commercials (for example, the two lengths could be 23 and 49). The rating is a value like 19.50.

a. Draw a picture for the class described above.

b. Give the definition for a class called <u>show</u> that can store the information described above. Then use this definition to declare an object <u>newShow</u> which can hold this information for one television show.

c. Use the object <u>newShow</u> declared above to do the following. In each part, if you need to use any additional variables, give the declaration for each one used.

   i. Read in values for the show's name and the running time of the show with commercials. Print both values read in.

   ii. Compute the sum of the rating for the show and the running time of the original version of the show (without commercials).

   If the sum is greater than or equal to 50, print a message saying we can run the show without commercials; otherwise print a message saying we will need to include commercials.

7. We want to use a class to store the following information about a movie: the name of the movie, the running time of the movie, and the average ticket price.

   The name of the movie is something like the following: "Prada Pirates III". The running time is divided into two parts, each of which is an integer: the length in minutes of the original version and the length in minutes of the director's cut version (for example, the lengths could be 93 and 112). The average ticket price is a value like 9.50.

a. Draw a picture for the class described above.

b. Give the definition for a class called <u>movie</u> that can store the information described above. Then use this definition to declare an object <u>newMovie</u> which can hold this information for one movie.

c. Use the object <u>newMovie</u> declared above to do the following. In each part, if you need to use any additional variables, give the declaration for each one used.

i. Read in values for the movie name and the average ticket price. Print both values read in.

ii. Compute the sum of the length of the director's cut version of the movie and the length of the original version. If the result is less than or equal to 250, print a message saying both versions can fit on a single DVD; otherwise print a message saying they will not fit on one DVD.

8. a. Here is a definition for a class <u>subinfo</u> and a declaration for an object of that class, called <u>subscriber</u>. Draw a picture for this class. Describe it in English as well.

```cpp
class nameinfo {
    public:
        string title;
        char firstinit;
        string last;
};
class addressinfo {
    public:
        string first_line;
        string second_line;
};
class subinfo {
    public:
        nameinfo mailing_name;
        addressinfo address;
        string date_end;
};
subinfo subscriber;
```

b. Assume that a set of data contains the following:

Mrs.
R.
Kuhn
1900 CherryBlossom Lane
Cincinnati OH 45231
05/02/98

Write one or more C++ statements to read these pieces of data into the object declared in part (a).

c. Note that the subscriber's address consists of two strings rather than a house number, street, city, and zip code in separate variables. Compare the two methods of storing the addresses. For example, how easy is it to read the data in the two formats? How easy is it to access the zip code?

d. Modify the declaration to allow up to 50 elements in an array of objects called <u>subscribers</u>.

9. Show what is printed by the following program segment. Assume that the set of data consists of the following:

```cpp
25 Sue Juan 35

#include <iostream>
using namespace std;
int main()
```

```
{
        class stuff {
           public:
                int id;
                string name;
        };
        stuff person;
        cin >> person.id;
        cin >> person.name;
        cout << person.id << " " << person.name << endl;
        cin >> person.name;
        cin >> person.id;
        cout << person.id << " " << person.name << endl;
        return 0;
}
```

10. Show what is printed by the following program segment. Assume that the set of data consists of the following:

```
5 Jack 3 Peggy 21 105 16 abc 91
```

```cpp
#include <iostream>
#include <string>
using namespace std;
int main()
{
        class btype {
           public:
                int c;
                string d;
        };
        class gtype {
           public:
                int h;
                int i;
        };
        class atype {
           public:
                btype b;
                int e;
                string f;
                gtype g;
        };
        atype a;

        cin >> a.b.c;
        cin >> a.b.d;
        cin >> a.e;
        cin >> a.f;
        cin >> a.g.h;
        cin >> a.g.i;
        cout << "This is the first output:" << endl;
        cout << a.b.c << " " << a.b.d << " " << a.e << " "
             << a.f << " " << a.g.h << " " << a.g.i << endl;
```

```
                cin >> a.g.h;
                cin >> a.f;
                cin >> a.b.c;
                cout << "This is the second output:" << endl;
                cout << a.b.c << " " << a.b.d << " " << a.e << " "
                    << a.f << " " << a.g.h << " " << a.g.i << endl;
                return 0;
            }
```

11. Show what is printed by each of the following program segments. Assume that this portion of code is used for each part:

```
        class ctype {
            public:
                int d;
                int e;
        };
        class atype {
            public:
                double b;
                ctype c;
                int f[4];
        };
        atype a;

        a.c.d = 1;
        a.c.e = 0;
```

   a.
```
        a.f[2] = a.c.d;
        a.f[a.c.e] = a.c.e;
        a.f[a.c.d] = a.c.d + a.c.e;
        a.b = (double) (a.f[0] + a.f[1] + a.f[2]) / 3;
        cout << a.b << " " << a.f[0] << " " << a.f[1]
            << " " << a.f[2] << endl;
```

   b.
```
        for (int sub = 0; sub < 3; sub++)
            a.f[sub] = a.c.d + a.c.e;
        a.c.d = 4;
        a.c.e = 4;
        cout << a.b << " " << a.f[0] << " " << a.f[1]
            << " " << a.f[2] << endl;

        a.f[1] = a.c.d;
        a.f[2] = a.c.e;
        cout << a.c.d << " " << a.c.e << endl;
        cout << a.f[0] << " " << a.f[1] << " " << a.f[2] << endl;
```

12. Show what is printed by the following program segments. Use this set of code for each part.

```
        class btype {
            public:
                int c;
                int d;
        };
```

```
class atype {
   public:
       btype b;
       int e;
};
class btype2{
   public:
       int e;
       int c;
};
class gtype {
   public:
       btype2 b;
       int d;
};
class utype {
   public:
       string v;
       string w;
};
class stype {
   public:
       int t;
       utype u;
};
atype a;
gtype g;
stype s;
string str;
```

a.
```
a.e = 1;
g.d = 0;
a.b.d = 5;
g.b.e = 10;
g.b.c = 2;
a.b.c = a.e + g.b.e;
cout << a.b.c << " " << a.b.d << " " << a.e << " "
     << g.b.e << " " << g.b.c << " " g.d << endl;
```

b.
```
s.u.v = "my";
s.u.w = "age";
cout << "This is the length of the string: " << s.u.v.length() << endl;
str = s.u.v;
str = str + " ";
str = str + s.u.w;
s.t = s.u.w.length();
cout << s.t << " " << s.u.v << " " << s.u.w << " " << str << endl;
```

13. Show what is printed by the following program. (The set of data appears after it.)

```
#include <iostream>
using namespace std;
```

```
class studtype {
   public:
      string name;
      int grade[2];
      double avg;
};
void mark(studtype &);
int main()
{
     studtype student;
     int num;

     cin >> num;
     for (int j = 0; j < num; j++) {
         cin >> student.name;
         for (int i = 0; i < 2; i++)
             cin >> student.grade[i];
         mark(student);
         cout << student.name << " " << student.grade[0] << " "
             << student.grade[1] << " " << student.avg << endl;
     }
     return 0;
}

void mark(studtype &stud)
{
     stud.avg = (double)(stud.grade[0] + stud.grade[1])/2;
     return;
}
```

Use the following data:

```
3
Smart    96 94
Stupid   48 54
SoSo     71 68
```

14. Show what is printed by the following program.

```
#include <iostream>
#include <string>
using namespace std;
class studtype {
   public:
      string name;
      double index;
      string major;
};
void sub1(studtype &);
int main()
{
     studtype student;
```

```
        student.name = "Joe College";
        student.index = 1.78;
        student.major = "football";
        sub1(student);
        cout << student.name << " " << student.index << " "
            << student.major << endl;
        return 0;
    }


    void sub1(studtype &stud)
    {
        string temp;

        cout << stud.name << " " << stud.index << " "
            << stud.major << endl;
        stud.index += 0.25;
        temp = "Mr";
        temp += " ";
        temp + = stud.name;
        stud.name = temp;
        return;
    }
```

15. Show what is printed by this program. Assume that the set of data contains the following:

```
Armstrong machinist 4 7 6.3 8.2 9.4 10.1 0

#include <iostream>
#include <string>
using namespace std;
class workertype {
   public:
       string name;
       string title;
       double hours[7];
};

int most(workertype, int);
int main()
{
    workertype worker;
    int j,k;

    cin >> worker.name;
    cin >> worker.title;
    for (int i = 0; i < 7; i++)
        cin >> worker.hours[i];
    cout << worker.name << " " << worker.title << endl;

    for (int i = 0; i < 7; i++)
        cout << worker.hours[i] << " ";
    cout << endl << endl;
```

```
        k = most(worker,5);
        j = most(worker,7);
        cout << "Day " << k << " had the most hrs in the first 5" << endl;
        cout << "Day " << j << " had the most hrs in the week" << endl;
        return 0;
}

int most(workertype worker, int day)
{
        int top = 0;

        for (int i = 1; i < day; i++)
                if (worker.hours[top] < worker.hours[i])
                        top = i;
        return top;
}
```

16. For each of the following situations, would you use an array, a class, or one or more single variables to hold the information? Give a one or two sentence justification for each answer.

    a. Find the average of an arbitrary (maybe 10, maybe 500, maybe 10,000 or more) number of integers.

    b. In a list of 50 names, see if one occurs twice.

    c. Store payroll data (including name, address, annual salary, dependents, etc.) for an employee of a company.

    d. Store a student's marks on five exams.

    e. Store a student's grade point average.

    f. Store a student's name, marks, and grade point average.

    g. Store 50 students' names, marks, and grade point averages.

17. Answer these questions based on the following class definitions, used to hold information on two car-rental companies.

```
class descrip {
   public:
      string model;
      int year;
      string color;
};
class mileinfo {
   public:
      int starting, ending;
};
class carinfo {
   public:
      descrip description;
      mileinfor mileage;
};
carinfo rentacar[10], carforhire[10];
```

For each of the following, write one or more C++ statements that will

a. Read data to fill both arrays

b. Compute the distance traveled (ending minus starting mileage) for each car owned by rentacar.

c. Print the model of each car (of either company) whose color is red.

d. Count how many elements of carforhire have a value for year in the range between 2004 and 2006 (inclusive).

e. Copy the information for the third rentacar to the fifth carforhire.

18. Add more information to the class carinfo from Exercise 17. If the car is currently rented, the class should contain the name and address of the person renting the car, as well as the rental date. If the car is in the shop for repair, the class should contain the date when the car was taken out of service and the reason for the repair.

19. When storing elements such as zip codes, house numbers, or social security numbers, it is preferable to use strings, not integers.

a. Explain why **string** is a better data type for zip code than **int**. (*Hint:* How does a zip code of 07632 print if stored as an integer? What if it is stored as a string?)

b. Why is **string** better for a social security number than **int**? This time, also consider size. Is there any C++ integer data type which could store the largest social security number? Suppose you have used that data type to store a social security number; how does the number 000 00 0004 print? What about dashes in the middle of the value? Give a declaration for socsecnum which allows these numbers to be printed with hyphenation (e.g., 123-45-6789).

c. Some people have a house number which can be stored using type **int**. For each of the following, say whether the house number can be stored as an integer.

i. $21^1/_2$ Merwin Ave.   ii. 432a Catalina Ave.

iii. 1239 Windham Ave.   iv. 110-34 68th Ave.

MODIFICATIONS TO PROGRAM 10 AND TO THE EXAMPLES

20. Show how to solve Problem 10 without using a class (more precisely, an array of objects). Compare your program to the one using a class. What is your conclusion?

21. In Program 10, suppose that the data items in the contestants array of objects have been put into alphabetical order based on the last name. If you know this information, is there any way to speed up the search to answer the requests?

22. In the text, only the findage() function from Part II is written out explicitly. To complete Program 10, write the other four query-answering functions: findsex(), findhair(), findtitle(), and findsalary().

23. Discuss other ways to structure Program 10. For example, printmenu() could call selecttrait(), or selecttrait() could call printmenu(), or printmenu() could contain the loop that controls the number of queries entered. Give a brief outline of three or four alternate ways to allocate the work between the main program and the various functions. Compare the alternatives.

24. Write a function sortname() that receives two parameters, an array of objects contestants and an integer num, representing the number of elements in the array. The function sortname() sorts the elements of the contestants array into alphabetical order, based on the values stored in last, being sure to carry along the rest of the information stored in the object (see Chapter 9, Exercises 45–50).

25. Modify the function <u>prettyprint( )</u> from Program 10 so that it prints the contestants in the database in alphabetical order by last name. You can use the <u>sortname( )</u> function from Exercise 24.

26. Modify the function <u>selecttrait( )</u> so that it calls functions that set up a menu from which the user can choose a value for a trait. For example, the menu for <u>sex</u> asks the user to select *M* for male or *F* for female. Which menus are easy to write? Which cannot list all possible choices? What can you do instead?

27. Look back at several of our earlier programs and exercises. For each, determine if an object or array of objects is an appropriate way to store the information required.

PROGRAMMING PROJECTS

28. Using the array of objects <u>subscribers</u> from Exercise 8(d), write a program to do the following:

    a. Read and print a list of subscribers.

    b. Determine which subscriptions end in May, 2008.

    c. Determine which subscribers use Miss as their title.

29. This exercise (and the next two) will continue to use the array of objects <u>subscribers</u> from Exercise 28. Determine which subscribers satisfy both of these criteria from parts (b) and (c).

30. Assume we want to determine which subscribers live in zip code 10036. Because of the way the address is stored, it will require string manipulation to find each subscriber's zip code. Describe how to do this.

31. What is a better way to store the information, which will alleviate the problem referred to in Exercise 30? (*Hint:* What if you store the individual parts of an address, rather than storing the entire address in a single string?)

32. Write a program to compute the course grades for a group of students. Use a class definition to organize the data.

    The input for each student consists of the name, three quiz grades, and a final exam grade. For example,

    ```
    John Brown 73 57 94 82
    ```

    The program finds the average of the three quiz grades and stores it in the variable <u>avg</u>. Then it finds the average of the final exam grade and <u>avg</u>, storing this in <u>numerical</u>. Based on the numerical average, it determines the student's letter grade (90 to 100 is an A, in the 80s is a B, etc.). Print the results. Use functions to accomplish each task; all the main program should do is call functions.

33. A college housing office is attempting to match prospective roommates. Each student has listed his or her name, student number (a seven-digit code), major, sports interests, and hobbies. These last three are all three-digit numbers. A typical set of data might be this:

    ```
    Jill James 1234567 327 964 135
    ```

    First, read in a series of ten students, storing the data in the form shown below. Initialize <u>roommate</u> to -1 for all students.

    ```
    class sname {
      public:
          string first;
          string last;
    };
    ```

```
class interestinfo {
  public:
      int major;
      int sports;
      int hobbies;
};
class studinfo {
  public:
      sname name;
      string studentnum;
      interestinfo interests;
      int roommate;
};
studinfo student[10];
```

Starting with the first student, find the best possible roommate by matching as many interests as possible. (If there is a tie, resolve it by selecting the first.) That is, go through the remaining students to find someone whose interests match the first student's as closely as possible. Once a match is found, enter the student number for the original student and the matching person in each other's <u>roommate</u> field. Then select the next unmatched student (one whose <u>roommate</u> field is still -1) and repeat the process. After matching everyone, print the five pairs of roommates. Use functions in your program for modularity.

34. The method described in Exercise 33 won't necessarily produce the best matchups in all cases. A problem arises if the first person takes as a roommate a mediocre match that would be better for someone else. Try to design a better algorithm.

35. Once parents heard of the scheme used in Exercise 33 to match roommates, they immediately protested since it did not take anyone's sex into account. Modify the program to read in a student's sex (male or female), then try to match as roommates only students of the same sex. At the end, print a list of any unmatched students. Why can there be unmatched students now?

36. The students in turn protested the scheme used in Exercise 35. The final compromise had each student specify his or her sex and the sex desired for a roommate. Modify the program to handle this new situation.

37. Write a program that maintains a database for a car dealership. The information stored for each car includes the make and model (like a Ford Mustang), the year, mileage, color, number of doors, the price, and any other information you think is relevant. Store the information in an array of objects (you must decide what class definition to use for the objects).

    First, your program should read in and print out the information about each car in the database. Then it should present a menu to the user (the prospective car buyer), who queries the database. The user may want to see a listing for all red cars, all cars with mileage under 25,000, all cars with four doors, etc. When the user has selected the feature of interest, your program should search the database and print a listing of all cars that satisfy the user's request. Print all the information in the database for each car that matches. If no car meets the requirements, print a message saying so.

    Write a function to read in the data, one to print the data, one to present a menu, one to read in requests, and functions to search the database.

38. Write a program to read in a series of names. The main program calls a function to read in a set of data. The set of data (which can be read from a file or interactively) consists of a parameter value <u>n</u> and then <u>n</u> strings. Each string represents a person's name—for example, William

Chang or Diana Lewis. Each name has exactly one blank separating the first name and the last name. The program should read the data into an object (you must decide what class definition to use for that object), storing the entire name in a single field. As each name is read in, it is printed.

The main program then calls a function to break the name into two pieces—a first name (everything up to the blank) and a last name (everything after the blank). The function stores these two pieces in the appropriate parts of the object. As each name is broken up, the function prints the original name and the new first and last names.

The main program calls a function to find the lengths of the original name, the first name, and the last name. These values are printed and stored in the appropriate parts of the object.

The main program calls a function to rearrange the first and last names. For example, if the first name is Diana and the last name is Lewis, then the rearrangement would be Lewis, Diana, including the comma. The rearranged name is printed and stored in the object.

The main program calls a function which is sent one element of the array of objects. The function neatly prints, with headings or messages, all of the values stored in that object. Since this function is sent one object at a time, it is called for each element of the array.

The main program then calls a function that determines which entire name in the array is the longest, which first name is the longest, and which last name is the longest. These three things are printed, together with identifying messages. Send this function the entire array of objects as a parameter. If you wish, this function may call other functions to perform the subtasks.

NOTE

The array of objects should be able to store everything read in and computed (except for the longest names). In particular, for each person, the object must be able to hold the original name and its size, the first name and its size, the last name and its size, and the rearranged name. The class definition for the object must be available to both the main program and the functions.

Have at least ten names in the data set. You can assume some reasonable size for the maximum length of the whole name and the first and last names. Some of the names should be short and others long. Be sure that different people have the longest entire name, the longest first name, and the longest last name.

39. Write a program which reads in data from files <u>master</u> and <u>trans</u>. Each related group of data in a file is called a record; a record should be stored in an object. Each record in <u>master</u> consists of two values separated by a blank. The first value in the file is the part number of an item, while the second value is the quantity of that item on hand. Here are two examples:

```
12345        4
23456       12
```

Each record in <u>trans</u> contains three items. The first is a letter, *s* or *p*, indicating whether the transaction is a sale or a purchase. The second is a part number, and the third is a quantity. Here are two examples:

```
s    12345    2
p    12345    6
```

An *s* means that the company has sold some of the item and the quantity should be subtracted from the inventory. A *p* means that the company has purchased more of the item, and the quantity should be added to the inventory.

Both files are in order by item number, but there may be more than one transaction record for any record in the master file.

The program reads in a record from file <u>master</u>. Then it reads in records from file <u>trans</u> as long as the item number is the same. It performs the appropriate update for each transaction record, and writes a new record out to file <u>newmastr</u>. It continues to do this until there are no records in file <u>master</u> or file <u>trans</u>.

The program checks for one error condition: the part number in <u>trans</u> is not found in <u>master</u>. If this error occurs, the program writes an appropriate message to file <u>errors</u>, including all the information in the record that is in error.

40. The Big Bank maintains two files on its depositors (each related group of data in a file is called a record; a record should be stored in an object of the appropriate class).

     <u>master</u> is the master file, containing records consisting of a 5-digit account number and yesterday's balance (a real number)

     <u>trans</u> is the transaction file, containing records consisting of a 5-digit account number and either a deposit (positive) or withdrawal (negative); a deposit or withdrawal is a real number. There may be many transaction records per account number.

     PART 1: Read each file into an array of objects (you must decide what class definition to use for the objects), printing each record as it is read in. Sort each array in increasing order by account number. Send the sorted version of the master file to a new file called <u>smaster</u> and the sorted version of the transaction file to a new file called <u>strans</u>, printing each record as it is written out to the file.

     PART 2: Read in the two sorted files, <u>smaster</u> and <u>strans</u> and create two new files, <u>newbal</u> and <u>negbal</u>. The file <u>newbal</u> contains a list of account numbers and new balances at the end of the day, and <u>negbal</u> contains a list of all customers whose balance was negative at any time during the day; list both account number and balance. Close <u>smaster</u>, <u>strans</u>, <u>newbal</u>, and <u>negbal</u>.

     PART 3: Open <u>newbal</u> and <u>negbal</u>. Read records in from <u>newbal</u> and <u>negbal</u> and print the records from each file on separate pages with headings. Close <u>newbal</u> and <u>negbal</u>.

     Your program must detect the following error conditions and send a message about each to a file <u>errors</u>:

     a. duplicate records in <u>smaster</u>

     b. records in <u>strans</u> which do not appear in <u>smaster</u>

     c. any record with improper format

     Your program must also create a file <u>report</u>, which consists of the following:

     a. a log listing all rejected transactions, with reasons for rejection

     b. the number of records in the original master file

     c. the number of records in the original transaction file

     d. the number of records in the updated master file

     e. the number of transactions applied

     f. the number of transactions rejected

     Print files <u>errors</u> and <u>report</u>.

41. The Happily Hardware Company has hired you to program its Accounts Receivable department. (Accounts Receivable are accounts that owe money to the company for purchases from the company.) Each related group of data in a file is called a record; a record should be stored in an object of the appropriate class.

INPUT: The program reads from these two files:

master is the master file, in ascending order by customer number, containing a five-digit customer number, a 20-character customer name, and a balance due (a real number). If the balance due is negative, the customer has a credit balance.

trans is the transaction file, containing records of each transaction by each customer. This file is in ascending order by customer number. There may be more than one transaction record per master record.

Each record starts with a character, O for order or P for payment. Each also contains a 5-digit customer number, a 5-digit transaction number, plus up to three more values:

♦ If the code is O, the record contains the name of the item ordered, the quantity ordered (an integer), plus the cost of the item (a real number).

♦ If the code is P, the record contains the amount of the payment (a real number).

PROCESSING: Read in records one at a time from the two files and use the transaction records to update the master file. Process all transaction records for each master record before going on the the next master record. If the transaction record contains an O in column 1, calculated the order amount and add it to the balance due. If the record contains a P in column 1, subtract the payment amount from the balance due.

Keep a running total of the accounts receivable balance of Happily Hardware Company (that is, the sum of the balances due for each customer).

Your program must detect the following error conditions:

1. duplicate records in the master file

2. records in the transaction file with a customer number which does not appear in the master file

3. any record with improper format; look for characters in numeric fields, missing field values, extra field values, improper code, etc.

OUTPUT: After you have processed a master record and all its transaction records, prepare and print an invoice for the customer, in the following format:

```
                              Customer name
                              Customer number

                                       Previous balance    $XXXXXXXX.XX
  transaction number           item ordered                order amount
  transaction number           item ordered                order amount
  transaction number           payment                     payment amount
                                       Balance due          $XXXXXXXX.XX
```

The transactions should appear in the order in which they are processed. In the example above, the words in italics indicate the information that should be listed in each location. The words that are not in italics should be printed as is. Indicate a negative previous balance or a negative balance due by printing CR to the right of the amount. Print all dollar amounts with a decimal point. Put a dollar sign on only the first and last amounts in the column, as shown above.

In addition to printing the invoices, your program must produce three reports on disk:

a. File <u>error</u> is a listing of all rejected master records and rejected transaction records. For each record that is rejected, include all the information in the record, plus a message indicating why the record was rejected.

b. File <u>log</u> keeps track of all records processed. Include the following in this file:

    i. the total number of records in the master file
    ii. the number of rejected records in the master file
    iii. the number of correct records in the master file
    iv. the total number of records in the transaction file
    v. the number of rejected transaction records
    vi. the number of correct transaction records

c. File <u>receive</u> lists the accounts receivable. In this file, include the customer name, the customer number, and the balance due for each customer. Use one line per customer. At the bottom of the list, include the total accounts receivable balance.

At the end, print all files. Print a heading at the beginning of the output for each printed file.

ASCII CODES

Symbolic characters can be represented by numbers, called ASCII codes; these numbers range from 0 through 255. ASCII codes 32 through 126 have been assigned to the printable character set; 128 through 255 represent the extended character set. Members of the extended character set can be displayed on the screen, but they may not be printable, or they may be interpreted in different ways by different printers. Among these characters are some Greek letters, specialized typographical characters, box drawing characters, and other graphics symbols. The ASCII codes from 0 through 31, together with 127, correspond to control characters (like line feed, carriage return, etc.), and most are interpreted in different ways by different devices.

Here are the printable ASCII characters, together with their codes:

ASCII	char	ASCII	char	ASCII	char	ASCII	char	ASCII	char
32	blank	52	4	72	H	92	\	112	p
33	!	53	5	73	I	93	]	113	q
34	"	54	6	74	J	94	^	114	r
35	#	55	7	75	K	95	_	115	s
36	$	56	8	76	L	96	`	116	t
37	%	57	9	77	M	97	a	117	u
38	&	58	:	78	N	98	b	118	v
39	'	59	;	79	O	99	c	119	w
40	(	60	<	80	P	100	d	120	x
41	)	61	=	81	Q	101	e	121	y
42	*	62	>	82	R	102	f	122	z
43	+	63	?	83	S	103	g	123	{
44	,	64	@	84	T	104	h	124	|
45	–	65	A	85	U	105	i	125	}
46	.	66	B	86	V	106	j	126	~
47	/	67	C	87	W	107	k		
48	0	68	D	88	X	108	l		
49	1	69	E	89	Y	109	m		
50	2	70	F	90	Z	110	n		
51	3	71	G	91	[	111	o		

INDEX

Bold typeface indicates most important reference.

{}, *See* braces
;, *See* semicolon
<>, *See* angle brackets
(), *See* parentheses
=, *See* assignment operator
==, *See* relational operators, logical equals operator
<, *See* relational operators
>, *See* relational operators
<=, *See* relational operators
>=, *See* relational operators
!= , *See* relational operators, not equal operator
!, *See* logical operator, not
||, *See* logical operator, or
&&, *See* logical operator, and
/* and */, *See* comment delimiters
//, *See* comment delimiters
/, *See* division operator
/=, *See* compound assignment operators
+, *See* addition operator, concatenation operator
++, *See* increment operator
+=, *See* compound assignment operators, concatenation operator
–, *See* subtraction operator
--, *See* decrement operator
-=, *See* compound assignment operators
*, *See* multiplication operator
*=, *See* compound assignment operators
%, *See* remainder operator
%=, *See* compound assignment operators
., *See* class, access using dot operator
::, *See* scope resolution operator
?:, *See* conditional operator
[and], *See* array, brackets
\, *See* escape character
'\n', *See* newline character
'\t', *See* tab character
<<, *See* insertion operator
>>, *See* extraction operator
#, *See* compiler directive
#include, xvi, 5, 7, 23

#include <cmath>, 69
    containing prototypes, 74, 194
#include <fstream>, 115
#include <iostream>, xvi, 5, 115
    containing prototypes, 194
#include <string>, 388, 428

abs() function, 68, 74
accelerated rejection algorithm for searching, analysis, 485–86, 488, 493–95
action portion of the program, 5, 35
addition operator +, 27, 28, 35
algorithm, 3, 34
    best case behavior, 490
    for accelerated rejection in a sorted list, 467
        analysis, 485–86, 488, 493–95
    for binary search, 482–83, 488
        analysis, 485–86, 488, 494–95
    for bubble sort, 458
        analysis, 487, 489–90
    for counting, 96–97
    for finding largest element in an array, 343–44, 368
    for finding the largest element (without using an array), 345
    for linear search, 464–65, 488
        analysis, 466–67, 486, 488, 494
    for linear sort, 451–52, 454, 486–87
        analysis, 487, 489–90
    for finding smallest element in an array, 451–52
    for summing a series of terms, 152–53, 173
    worst case behavior, 490
alignment, xvii, 5, 18, 34
    in **if-else,** 108, 110
    left, 102, 129
    output, 59–60, 102, 124, 129
    right, 102, 129
analysis of
    accelerated rejection algorithm for searching, 493–95
    binary search algorithm, 485–86, 488, 494–95
    bubble sort algorithm, 487, 489–90
    linear search algorithm, 466–67, 486, 488, 494
    linear sort algorithm, 487, 489–90